A Practical Guide to Video and Audio Compression

This book is dedicated to my
friend Bernard Fisk.

A Practical Guide to Video and Audio Compression

From Sprockets and Rasters to Macroblocks

Cliff Wootton

ELSEVIER

AMSTERDAM • BOSTON • HEIDELBERG • LONDON
NEW YORK • OXFORD • PARIS • SAN DIEGO
SAN FRANCISCO • SINGAPORE • SYDNEY • TOKYO
Focal Press is an imprint of Elsevier

Acquisition Editor: Joanne Tracy/Angelina Ward
Project Manager: Brandy Lilly
Editorial Assistant: Becky Golden-Harrell
Marketing Manager: Christine Degon
Cover Design: Eric DeCicco

Focal Press is an imprint of Elsevier
30 Corporate Drive, Suite 400, Burlington, MA 01803, USA
Linacre House, Jordan Hill, Oxford OX2 8DP, UK

Library of Congress Cataloging-in-Publication Data
Application submitted.

British Library Cataloguing-in-Publication Data
A catalogue record for this book is available from the British Library.

ISBN: 0-240-80630-1

For information on all Focal Press publications
visit our website at www.books.elsevier.com

05 06 07 08 09 10   10 9 8 7 6 5 4 3 2 1
Printed in the United States of America

Working together to grow
libraries in developing countries

www.elsevier.com | www.bookaid.org | www.sabre.org

ELSEVIER   BOOK AID International   Sabre Foundation

Table of Contents

Preface

The last few years have been an extraordinary time for the digital video industry. Not long before the turn of the millennium, digital video editing systems were expensive capital items of equipment that only major broadcasters and production companies could afford. To think that now the same capability is available in a laptop that you can buy off the shelf and it comes with the software for something in the region of $1200 is amazing. This is a capability we have dreamed about having on our desktops for 15 years. The price of the hardware and software needed to run an entire TV broadcast service is now within the reach of any organization or individual who cares to get involved.

Recall the boom in publishing that happened when the Apple LaserWriter was launched with Adobe PostScript contained inside and those early page composition programs enhanced what we were able to do with Word version 1 or MacWrite. We are now at that place with digital media and while some people will create an unattractive mess with these powerful tools, they will also enjoy themselves immensely and learn a lot at the same time. Eventually, a few skilled people will emerge from the pack and this is where the next generation of new talent will come from to drive the TV and film industry forward over the next couple of decades.

When Joanne Tracey asked me to prepare a proposal for this book I realized (as had most authors I have spoken to) that I didn't know as much about the topic I was about to write on as I thought I did. So this book has been a journey of exploration and discovery for me, just as I hope it will be for you. And yet, we also don't realize how much we do already know, and I hope you will find yourself nodding and making a mental comment to yourself saying "Yes—I knew that" as you read on.

We excel through the efforts of those around us in our day-to-day interactions with them. I have been particularly lucky to enjoy a few truly inspirational years with a group of like-minded people at the BBC. We all shared the same inquisitive approach into how interactive TV news could work. Now that we have all gone our separate ways I miss those "water cooler moments" when we came up with amazingly ambitious ideas. Some of those ideas live on in the things we engineered and rolled out. Others are yet to develop into a tangible form. But they will, as we adopt and implement the new MPEG-4, 7, and 21 technologies.

We are still at a very exciting time in the digital video industry. The H.264 codec is achieving enormous potential and there is much yet to do in order to make it as successful as it could be. Looking beyond that is the possibility of creating HDTV services and interactive multimedia experiences that we could only dream about until now.

Video compression can be a heavy topic at the best of times and we cover a lot of ground here. I thought the idea of illustrating the concept with a cartoon (see the first illustration in Chapter 1) would be helpful, because this subject can be quite daunting and I have purposely tried not to take it all too seriously. The cartoon is in order to disarm the subject and make it as accessible as possible to readers who haven't had the benefit of much experience with compression.

In some chapters you'll find a gray box with an icon on the left and a briefly encapsulated hot tip. These have been placed so that they are relevant to the topic areas being discussed but also to help you flick through the book and glean some useful knowledge very quickly. They have come out of some of those brainstorming times when I discussed digital video with colleagues in the various places I work and in online discussions. It's a bit of homespun wisdom based on the experiences of many people and intended to lighten the tone of the book a little.

If you are wondering about the face on the cover, it is my daughter Lydia. But if you look more closely at the cover, it tells a story. In fact, it is an attempt to show what the book is all about in one snapshot.

On the left you'll see the sprocket holes from film. Then in the background some faint raster lines should be evident. As you traverse to the right, the detail in the face becomes compressed. This illustrates how an image becomes degraded and finally degenerates into small macroblock particles that waft away in the breeze. Coming up with these illustrative ideas is one of the most enjoyable parts of writing a book.

So there you have it. I've enjoyed working on this project more than any other book that I can recall being involved with. I hope you enjoy the book too and find it helpful, as you become a more experienced compressionist.

In closing I'd like to say that the finer points of this publication are due to the extremely hard work by the team at Focal Press and any shortcomings you find are entirely my fault.

Cliff Wootton
Crowborough, South East England

Acknowledgments

When you write a book a book like this, it is the sum of so many people's efforts and good-will. I would like to especially thank "J and Lo" (Joanne Tracey and Lothlórien Homet) of Focal Press for guiding me through the process of writing this book. Thanks to Gina Marzilli, who guided us down the right path on the administrative side. The manuscript was skill-fully progressed through the production process by Becky Golden-Harrell—thanks, Becky. Let's do it again. Copyediting was ably managed by Cara Salvatore, Sheryl Avruch, and their team of experts. Thanks guys; you really turned this into a silk purse for me.

Of course, without the products in the marketplace, we'd have very little success with our endeavors. I'd like to send warm thanks to the team at Popwire in Sweden. Anders Norström and Kay Johansson have been immensely helpful. Over the last couple of years I've enjoyed getting to know members of the QuickTime team at Apple Computer. Thanks to Dave Singer, Rhondda Stratton, Tim Schaaf, Vince Uttley, and Greg Wallace for their help and inspiration. Guys, you are doing wonderful stuff. Just keep on doing that thing that you do. Also at Apple, I'd like to thank Sal Soghoian for pointing out some really cool stuff that AppleScript does. Thanks go to Envivio for some very thought-provoking and inspiring conversations, especially the time I've spent with Rudi Polednik, Frank Patterson, and Sami Asfour. Greetings also to Diana Johnson, Dave Kizerian, and Matt Cupal of Sorenson and Annie Normandin of Discreet. Thanks for being there when I needed your help. In the latter stages of completeing the book, Janet Swift and Barbara Dehart at Telestream came through with some coolness that enabled me to make Windows Media files effortlessly on a Mac.

To the people who work so hard at the MPEGIF (formerly known as the M4IF), Rob Koenen, Sebastian Möritz, and your team, I thank you for your time and patience explain-ing things to me. I hope this is a journey we can travel together for many years yet as we see the new MPEG standards being widely adopted.

I have so many friends from my time at the BBC who unselfishly shared their expert-ise and knowledge. Foremost of these must be Russell Merryman, who produced the ele-phant cartoon and was also responsible—with Asha Oberoi, Robert Freeman, Saz Vora, and John Nicholas—for the MPEG-4 packaged multimedia concept studies way back in 2002. Thanks also to Julie Lamm, John Angeli, and everyone in the News Interactive department.

Thanks are due also to those individuals, companies, and organizations who gra-ciously permitted me to use their images in this project or spent time talking to me about their work: Christopher Barnatt from the University of Nottingham; Simon Speight and Mark Sherwood from Gerry Anderson Productions; Guan at Etiumsoft; Jim Cooper at MOTU; David Carew-Jones, Anna Davidson, and Paul Dubery at Tektronix; Diogo Salari at DPI Productions; the folks at M-Audio; the Sales Web team at Apple Computer; Grant Petty and Simon Hollingworth at Black Magic Design; Julie Aguilar of ADC Telecommunications; Victoria Battison of AJA Video Systems; and Amanda Duffield of Pace Micro Technology.

I'd also like to thank Ben Waggoner for his unselfish sharing of many Master Compressionist's secrets at conferences. Ben, I've learned many new things from you whenever I've been at your presentations. Thank you so much for encouraging people the way you do.

Introduction to Video Compression

1.1 Starting Our Journey

We (that is, you and I) are going to explore video compression together. It is a journey of discovery and surprise. Compression might seem daunting at this point, but like the old Chinese proverb says, "Even the longest journey starts with a single step." Let's head into that unknown territory together, taking it carefully, one step at a time until we reach our destination.

1.2 Video Compression Is Like . . .

It really is like trying to get a grand piano through a mailbox slot or an elephant through the eye of a needle. In fact, we thought the elephant was such an appropriate description, my friend Russell Merryman created a cartoon to illustrate the concept:

Video compression is all about trade-offs. Ask yourself what constitutes the best video experience for your customers. That is what determines where you are going to compromise. Which of these are the dominant factors for you?

- Image quality
- Sound quality
- Frame rate
- Saving disk space
- Moving content around our network more quickly
- Saving bandwidth
- Reducing the playback overhead for older processors
- Portability across platforms
- Portability across players
- Open standards
- Licensing costs for the tools
- Licensing costs for use of content

Figure 1-1 How hard can it be?

- Revenue streams from customers to you
- Access control and rights management
- Reduced labor costs in production

You will need to weigh these factors against each other. Some of them are mutually exclusive. You cannot deliver high quality from a cheap system that is fed with low-quality source material that was recorded on a secondhand VHS tape. Software algorithms are getting very sophisticated, but the old adage, "Garbage in, garbage out" was never truer than it is for video compression.

1.3 It's Not Just About Compressing the Video

The practicalities of video compression are not just about how to set the switches in the encoder but also involve consideration of the context—the context in which the video is arriving as well as the context where it is going to be deployed once it has been processed.

Together, we will explore a lot of background and supporting knowledge that you need to have in order to make the best decisions about how to compress the video. The actual compression process itself is almost trivial in comparison to the contextual setting and the preprocessing activity.

1.4   What Is a Video Compressor?

All video compressors share common characteristics. I will outline them here and by the end of the book you should understand what all of these terms mean. In fact, these terms describe the step-by-step process of compressing video:

- Frame difference
- Motion estimation
- Discrete cosine transformation
- Entropy coding

Wow! Right now you may be thinking that this is probably going to be too hard. Refrain from putting the book back on the shelf just yet though. Compression is less complicated than you think. If we take it apart piece by piece and work through it one item at a time, you will see how easy it is. Soon, you will be saying things like, "I am going to entropy code the rest of my day," when what you actually mean is you are going home early because there is nothing to do this afternoon. You can have a secret guffaw at your colleagues' expense because you know all about video compression and they don't.

1.5   The Informed Choice Is Yours

Despite all the arguments about the best technology to use, in the end your decisions may be forced by your marketing department arguing about reaching larger audiences. Those decisions should be backed up by solid research and statistics. On the other hand, they might be based just on hearsay. The consequences of those decisions will restrict your choice of codecs to only those that your selected platform supports. However, you will still have some freedom to innovate in building the production system.

Video compression is only a small part of the end-to-end process. That process starts with deciding what to shoot, continues through the editing and composition of the footage, and usually ends with delivery on some kind of removable media or broadcast system. In a domestic setting, the end-to-end process might be the capture of analogue video directly off the air followed by digitization and efficient storage inside a home video server. This is what a TiVo Personal Video Recorder (PVR) does, and compression is an essential part of how that product works.

There is usually a lot of setting up involved before you ever compress anything. Preparing the content first so the compressor produces the best-quality output is very important. A rule of thumb is that about 90% of the work happens before the compression actually begins. The content of this book reflects that rule of thumb: about 90% of the coverage is about things you need to know in order to utilize that 10% of the time you will actually spend compressing video in the most effective way possible.

1.6 Parlez-Vous Compressionese?

A few readers may be unfamiliar with the jargon we use. Words such as *codec* might not mean a lot to you at this stage. No need to worry—jargon will be explained as we go along. The important buzzwords are described in a glossary at the end of the book. Glossary entries are italicized the first time they are used.

The word codec is derived from coder–decoder and is used to refer to both ends of the process—squeezing video down and expanding it to a viewable format again on playback. Compatible coders and decoders must be used, so they tend to be paired up when they are delivered in a system like QuickTime or Windows Media. Sometimes the coder is provided for no charge and is included with the decoder. Other times you will have to buy the coder separately. By the way, the terms coder and encoder in general refer to the same thing.

1.7 Tied Up With Your Cabling?

Because there are so many different kinds of connectors, where it is helpful, there are diagrams showing how things connect up. In Appendix M, there are pictures of the most common connectors you will encounter and what they are for. Even on a modest, semi-professional system, there could be 10 different kinds of connectors, each requiring a special cable. FireWire and USB each have multiple kinds of connectors depending on the device being used. It is easy to get confused. The whole point of different types of connectors is to ensure that you only plug in compatible types of equipment. Most of the time it is safe to plug things in when the cable in your left hand fits into a socket in the piece of hardware in your right (okay, if you are left-handed it might be the other way around). Knowing whether these connections are "hot pluggable" is helpful, too.

Hot-pluggable connections are those that are safe to connect while your equipment is turned on. This is, in general, true of a signal connection but not a power connection. Some hardware, such as SCSI drives, must never be connected or unconnected while powered on. On the other hand, Firewire interfaces for disk drives are designed to be hot pluggable.

1.8 So You Already Know Some Stuff

Chapters 2 to 7 may be covering territory you already know about. The later chapters discuss the more complex aspects of the encoding process and will assume that you already know what is in the earlier chapters or have read them.

1.9 Video Compression Is Not Exactly New

Video compression has been a specialist topic for many years. Broadband connections to the Internet are becoming commonplace, and consumers are acquiring digital video cameras. Those consumers all have a need for video compression software.

The trick is to get the maximum possible compression with the minimum loss of quality. We will examine compression from a practical point of view, based on where your source material originated. You will need to know how film and TV recreate images and the fundamental differences between the two media. Then you will make optimal choices when you set up a compression job on your system.

You don't have to fully understand the mathematics of the encoding process. This knowledge is only vital if you are building video compression products for sale or if you are studying the theory of compression. Some background knowledge of how an encoder works is helpful though. In a few rare instances, some math formulas will be presented but only when it is unavoidable.

Our main focus will be on the practical aspects of encoding video content. Once you've read this book, you should be able to buy off-the-shelf products and get them working together. However, this book is not a tutorial on how to use any particular product. We discuss compression in a generic way so you can apply the knowledge to whatever tools you like to use.

1.10 This Is Not About Choosing a Particular Platform

We will discuss a variety of codecs and tools, and it is important to get beyond the marketing hyperbole and see these products independently of any personal likes, dislikes, and platform preferences.

My personal preference is for Apple-based technologies because they allow me to concentrate on my work instead of administering the system. I've used a lot of different systems, and something in the design of Apple products maps intuitively to the way I think when I'm doing creative work. You may prefer to work on Windows- or Linux-based systems, each of which may be appropriate for particular tasks. Compression tools are available for all of the popular operating systems.

This book is about the philosophy and process of compression. The platform is irrelevant other than to facilitate your choosing a particular codec or workflow that is not supported elsewhere, although even that problem is becoming obsolete as we move forward with portability tools and wider use of open standards.

Sometimes, lesser-known technology solutions are overlooked by the industry and are worth considering, and I've tried to include examples. But space is limited, so please don't take offense if I have omitted a personal favorite of yours. Do contact us if you find a particularly useful new or existing tool that you think we should include in a later edition.

1.11 Putting the Salesmen in a Corner

You need to be armed with sufficient knowledge to cut through the sales pitch and ask penetrating questions about the products being offered to you. Always check the specifications thoroughly before buying. If you can, check out reference installations and read reviews before committing to a product. If this book helps you do that and saves you from an expensive mistake, then it has accomplished an important goal: to arm you with enough knowledge to ask the right questions and understand the answers you get.

1.12 Testing, Testing, Testing

Test your own content on all the systems you are considering for purchase and prove to yourself which one is best. Demonstrations are often given to potential customers under idealized and well-rehearsed circumstances with footage that may have been optimally selected to highlight the strengths of a product. I've been present at demonstrations like this, and then when customer provided footage is tried, the system fails utterly to deliver the same performance. Of course, sometimes the products do perform to specification and well beyond, which is good for everyone concerned. There is no substitute for diligence during the selection process.

1.13 Defining the Territory

If you are presented with a large meal, it is a good idea to start with small bites. Video compression is a bit indigestible if you try and get it all in one go.

We need to start with an understanding of moving image systems and how they originated. Early in the book, we look at film formats since they have been around the longest. It is also helpful to understand how analogue TV works. Much of the complexity in compression systems is necessary because we are compressing what started out as an analog TV signal.

We will use the metaphor of going on a journey as we look at what is coming up in the various chapters of the book.

1.14 Deciding to Travel

In Chapter 2, we will examine the content we want to compress and why we want to compress it. This includes the platforms and systems you will use to view the compressed video when it is being played back. If you just want an overview of why compression is important, then Chapter 2 is a good place to start.

1.15 Choosing Your Destination

In Chapters 3, 4, 5, and 6, we look at the physical formats for storing moving images. We will examine frame rates, image sizes, and various aspects of film and the different ways that video is moved around and presented to our video compression system. It is important to know whether we are working with high-definition or standard-definition content. Moving images shot on film are quite different from TV pictures due to the way that TV transmission interlaces alternate lines of a picture. Don't worry if the concept of interlacing is unfamiliar to you at this stage. It is fully explained in Chapter 5.

Interlacing separates the odd and even lines and transmits them separately. It allows the overall frame rate to be half what it would need to be if the whole display were delivered progressively. Thus, it reduces the bandwidth required to 50% and is therefore a form of compression.

Interlacing is actually a pretty harsh kind of compression given the artifacts that it introduces and the amount of processing complexity involved when trying to eliminate the unwanted effects.

Harsh compression is a common result of squashing the video as much as possible, which often leads to some compromises on the viewing quality. The artifacts you can see are the visible signs of that compression.

1.16 Got Your Ears On?

It's been a long time since audiences were prepared to put up with silent movies. Chapter 7 looks at how to encode the audio we are going to use with our video. Because the sampling and compression of audio and video are essentially the same, artifacts that affect one will affect the other. They just present themselves differently to your ears and eyes.

1.17 Checking the Map

In Chapters 8 to 14, we investigate how a video encoder actually works. If you drive a car, you may not know how the right fuel and air mixture is achieved by adjusting the carburetor. But everyone who drives a car will know that you press the accelerator pedal to go and the brake pedal to stop. Likewise, it is not necessary to use mathematical theory to understand compression. Pictures are helpful; trying it out for yourself is better still.

1.18 Working Out the Best Route

Chapter 15 is about live encoding. This is content that is delivered to you as a continuous series of pictures and your system has to keep up. There is little opportunity to pause or buffer things to be dealt with later. Your system has to process the video as it arrives. It is often a critical part of a much larger streaming service that is delivering the encoded video to many thousands or even millions of subscribers. It has to work reliably all the time, every time. That ability will be compromised if you make suboptimum choices early on. Changing your mind about foundational systems you have already deployed can be difficult or impossible.

1.19   Packing Your Bags for the Trip

Chapter 16 looks at how we store video in files. Some applications require particular kinds of containers and will not work if you present your video in the wrong kind of file. It is a bit like taking a flight with a commercial airline. Your suitcase may be the wrong size or shape or may weigh too much. You have to do something about it before you will be allowed to take it on the plane. It is the same with video. You may need to run some conversions on the video files before presenting the contents for compression. Chapter 17 examines tape formats.

1.20   Immigration, Visa, and Passport

When you travel to another country, you must make sure your paperwork is all in order. In the context of video encoding, we have to make sure the right licenses are in place. We need rights control because the content we are encoding may not always be our own. Playback clients make decisions of their own based on the metadata in the content, or they can interact with the server to determine when, where, and how the content may be played.

Your playback client is the hardware apparatus, software application, movie player, or web page plug-in that you use to view the content. Chapter 18 examines digital rights management (DRM) and commercial issues.

1.21   Boarding Pass

Where do you want to put your finished compressed video output? Are you doing this so you can archive some content? Is there a public-facing service that you are going to provide? This is often called deployment. It is a process of delivering your content to the right place and it is covered in Chapter 19.

1.22   On the Taxiway

Chapter 20 is about how your compressed video is streamed to your customers. Streaming comes in a variety of formats. Sometimes we are just delivering one program, but even then we are delivering several streams of content at the same time. Audio and video are processed and delivered to the viewer independently, even though they appear to be delivered together. That is actually an illusion because they are carefully synchronized. It is quite obvious when they are not in sync, however, and it could be your responsibility to fix the problem.

1.23   Rotate and Wheels-Up

In Chapters 21 to 25, we look at how those codec design principles have been applied in the real world. This is where we discuss the generally available tools and what they offer you as their individual specialty. Some of them are proprietary and others are based on open standards. All of these are important things to consider when selecting a codec for your project.

1.24 Landing Safely

In the context of your video arriving at some destination, Chapters 26 to 28 talk about the client players for which you are creating your content. Using open standards helps to reach a wider audience. Beware of situations where a specific player is mandated. This is either because you have chosen a proprietary codec or because the open standard is not supported correctly. That may be accidental or purposeful. Companies that manufacture encoders and players will sometimes advertise that they support an open standard but then deliver it inside a proprietary container. We will look at some of the pros and cons of the available players.

1.25 Learning to Fly on Your Own

By now, you may be eager to start experimenting with your own encoding. Maybe you just took a job that involves building a compression system and that seems a bit daunting. Or maybe you have some experience of using these systems and want to try out some alternatives. Either way, Chapter 29 will help you set up your own encoding system. Along the way, we examine the implications for small systems and how they scale up to commercial enterprises. This should be valuable whether you're setting up large- or small-scale encoding systems.

1.26 Circuits and Bumps

We built the hardware in Chapter 29. In Chapter 30, we add the software to it. This is a lot easier to do, now that open standards provide applications with interoperability. Whilst you can still purchase all your support from a single manufacturer, it is wise to choose the best product for each part of the process, even if different manufacturers make them. Standards provide a compliance checkpoint that allows you to give evidence that some corrective work needs to be done to an application. If you have some problematic content, then standards-compliance tools can help you to isolate the problem so that you can feed some informative comments back to the codec manufacturer. An integration problem can be due to noncompliant export from a tool, or import mechanisms in the next workflow stage that are incorrectly implemented.

1.27 Hitting Some Turbulence on the Way

In Chapter 31, we begin to discuss how to cope with the difficult areas in video compression. You are likely to hit a few bumps along the way as you try your hand at video compression. These will manifest themselves in a particularly difficult-to-encode video sequence. You will no doubt have a limited bit rate budget and the complexity of the content may require more data than you can afford to send. So you will have to trade off some complexity to reduce the bandwidth requirements. Degrading the picture quality is one option, or you can reduce the frame rate. The opportunities to improve your encoded video quality begin when you plan what to shoot.

1.28 Going Solo

In Chapters 32 to 38, you will have a chance to practice using the encoding system we just built. We will discuss all those complex little details such as scaling and cropping, frame rate reduction, and the effects of video noise on the encoding process. Don't worry that there are a lot of factors to consider. If we are systematic in the way we experiment with them, we will not get into too much trouble.

1.29 Planning Future Trips

Chapter 39 draws some conclusions and looks at where you might go next. It also looks at what the future of video compression systems might be as the world adopts and adapts to a wholly digital video scenario. The appendices follow the final chapter, and they contain some useful reference material. The scope of the book allows for only a limited amount of this kind of reference material, but it should be sufficient to enable you to search for more information on the World Wide Web. Of particular note is the problem solver in Appendix A. It is designed to help you diagnose quality issues with your encoded video.

Likewise, due to space constraints, we do not delve into the more esoteric aspects of audio and video. Many interesting technologies for surround sound and video production can only be mentioned here, so that we can remain focused on the compression process. You should spend some time looking for manufacturers' Web sites and downloading technical documents from them. There is no substitute for the time you spend researching and learning more about this technology on your own.

1.30 Conventions

Film size is always specified in metric values measured in millimeters (mm). Sometimes scanning is described as dots per inch or lines per inch. TV screen sizes are always described in inches measured diagonally. Most of the time, this won't matter to us, since we are describing digital imagery measured in pixels. The imaging area of film is measured in mm, and therefore a film-scanning resolution in dots per mm seems a sensible compromise.

TV pictures generally scan with interlaced lines, and computers use a progressive scanning layout. The difference between them is the delivery order of the lines in the picture. Frame rates are also different.

The convention for describing a scanning format is to indicate the number of physical lines, the scanning model, and the field rate. For interlaced displays, the field rate is

Table 1-1 Units of Measure

Quantity	Unit of measure	Abbreviation
Data transfer	Bits per second	bps
	Thousands of bits per second (Kilo)	Kbps
	Millions of bits per second (Mega)	Mbps
	Thousands of millions of bits per second (Giga)	Gbps
Data storage	Bytes	B
	Thousands of bytes (Kilo)	KB
	Millions of bytes (Mega)	MB
	Thousands of millions of bytes (Giga)	GB
	Millions of millions of bytes (Tera)	TB
	Thousands of Terabytes (Peta)	PB
Audio levels	Tenths of Bels (deci)	dB
Frames	Frames per second	fps
Tape transport	Inches per second	ips
Screen resolution	Dots per inch	dpi
Film resolution	Dots per mm	dpmm

twice the frame rate, while for progressive displays, they are the same. For example, 525i60 and 625i50 describe the American and European display formats, respectively.

It is very easy to confuse bits and bytes when talking about video coding. Table 1-1 summarizes the basic quantities we will be using.

In the abbreviations we use, note that uppercase B refers to bytes, and lowercase b is bits. So GB is gigabytes (not gazillions of bytes). When we multiply bits or bytes by each increment, the value 1000 is actually replaced by the nearest equivalent base-2 number. So we multiply memory size by 1024 instead of 1000 to get kilobytes. As you learn the numbers represented by powers of 2, you will start to see patterns appearing in computer science, and it will help you guess at the correct value to choose when setting parameters.

Already this is becoming complex, and we have scarcely begun, but don't worry, we will get to the bottom of it all in due course. Everything will become clear as we persevere and work our way steadily through the various topics chapter by chapter.

1.31 What Did You Call That Codec?

Video compression terminology is already confusing enough without having to worry about codecs having several names for the same thing. There are lots of unfamiliar terms and concepts to understand. It makes it even more difficult for the beginner when new codecs are launched with several names. The latest codecs are described elsewhere in the book, but one in particular leads to much confusion even amongst experienced professionals. The MPEG-4 part 10, otherwise known as H.264 codec, is part of a family of video encoders that is listed in Table 1-2.

Table 1-2 MPEG Codec Names

Convention	Description
MPEG-1	The "grandfather" of the MPEG codecs. This is where it all began.
MPEG-2	Probably the most popular video codec to date when measured in numbers of shipped implementations.
MPEG-4	A large collection of audio/visual coding standards that describe video, audio, and multimedia content. This is a suite of approximately 20 separate component standards that are designed to interoperate with one another to build very rich, interactive, mixed-media experiences. You must be careful to specify a part of the MPEG-4 standard and not just refer to the whole. Beware of ambiguity when describing video as MPEG-4.
MPEG-4 part 2	Specifically, the video coding component originally standardized within MPEG-4. The compression algorithms in part 10 are improved but the way that part 2 can be alpha-channel coded is more flexible. If people refer to MPEG-4 video without specifying part 2 or part 10, they probably mean part 2, but that may change as part 10 becomes dominant by virtue of the H.264 codec being more widely adopted.
MPEG-4 part 10	A more recent and superior video coding scheme developed jointly by ISO MPEG and the ITU. This codec is a significant milestone in video-coding technology, and its importance to the delivery of video over the next few years will be profound. It is expected to have at least as much impact as MPEG-2 did when it was launched. It is likely that MPEG-4 part-2 video coding will become outmoded in time and people will use the term MPEG-4 when they really mean part10 video coding.
JVT	The Joint Video Team that worked on the MPEG-4 part 10, H.264 standard. The standard is sometimes referred to as the JVT video codec.
AVC	Advanced Video Coding is the name given to the MPEG-4 part-10 codec in the standard. Whilst the term AVC is popular amongst marketing departments, H.264 seems to be used more often by manufacturers in technical documents.
H.26L	An early trial version of the H.264 codec.
H.264	The present champion of all codecs governed by the MPEG standards group. This is the most thoroughly scrutinized and carefully developed video-coding system to date.

To be buzzword compliant, I will use the term H.264 to refer to the latest codec throughout this book unless I am talking specifically about the codec in the MPEG-4 or

Table 1-3 SMPTE VC-1 Codec Names and Aliases

Convention	Description
Windows Media Series 9	The original terminology used when Microsoft was the only party with "ownership" of the codec name.
WM9	An often-used abbreviation. We will use this when specifically referring to Windows Media Series 9 and not the SMPTE standardized version.
WM8	An older version of Windows Media.
WM7	An even older version.
WM6.5	The oldest version currently mentioned in product specs.
VC-9	One of the proposed names for the SMPTE standardized version of WM9 that emerged during 2004.
VC-1	Apparently, the codec will be officially known as VC-1.
VC1	Note that this codec might also be shown in some literature as VC1 without the dash. This might be important when searching text-based archives.
WM10	The newest version of the Windows Media series codecs. This is currently on beta release for the Windows operating system platform.

AVC context. Having observed the usage amongst the video-compression community over some time, I have found that engineering people use the term H.264 and commercial or marketing people prefer AVC.

Further confusion arises during discussion of the Windows Media codecs, since they have been lodged with SMPTE for ratification as an open standard. All of the naming conventions in Table 1-3 have been used in documents about video compression and codecs:

Unless it is necessary to refer to the Windows Media codec by a different alias, the term VC-1 will be used in this book as far as possible.

1.32 Where to Next?

So, let's go on a voyage of discovery together throughout the rest of this book. By the end of it, you should discover that although video compression is sometimes complex, the complexity comes from a large number of small subsystems. Individually, they are quite simple to understand, so don't be frightened by the complexity. It is challenging at first, but after a little experimentation and a look at the practical encoding chapter, it should all fall into place. By the end of the book, you should have a good idea of how to build a small, medium, or large compression system from the available hardware components and software applications.

No doubt you will be tempted to start playing with your video-compression tools right away. If so, the early chapters of this book will be important because they describe why the results you are getting are not what you expected. If you are approaching compression for the first time, it is especially important that you read the early chapters in order to understand fundamental topics. I have tried to arrange the chapters in a logical way that introduces you to more complex ideas as we go along, and those early chapters lay the groundwork for the later ones.

Why Video Compression Is Needed

2.1 Every Journey Begins with a Single Step

So you are thinking about compressing some video. It might seem like a daunting subject, but it isn't really. If you begin with small steps, soon you'll be taking the whole thing in stride. In this chapter, we will examine the history and significance of video compression, along with its practical uses—some of the reasons you are on this journey today. There are quite a few products and services available today that just wouldn't be possible without compression. Many more are being developed. Let's see what's out there.

2.2 Compression Is Necessary Because . . .

Delivering digital video and audio through the available networks is simply impossible without compressing the content first.

To give you some history, there has been a desire to deliver TV services through telephone networks for many years. Trials were carried out during the 1980s. Ultimately, they were all unsuccessful because they couldn't get the information down the wire quickly enough.

Now we are on the threshold of being able to compress TV services enough that they can fit into the *bandwidth* being made available to broadband users. The crossing point of those two technologies is a very important threshold. Beyond it, even more sophisticated services become available as the broadcast on-air TV service comes to occupy a smaller percentage of the available bandwidth.

So, as bandwidth increases and compressors get better, all kinds of new ways to enjoy TV and Internet services come online. For example, a weather forecasting service could be packaged as an interactive presentation and downloaded in the background. If this is cached on a local hard disk, it will always be available on demand, at an instant's notice. An updated copy can be delivered in the background as often as needed. Similar services can be developed around airline flight details, traffic conditions, and sports results.

2.3   Compression Is About Trade-Offs

Compressing video is all about making the best compromises possible without giving up too much quality. To that end, anything that reduces the amount of video to be encoded will help reduce the overall size of the finished output file or *stream*.

Compression is not only about keeping overall file size small. It also deals with optimizing data throughput—the amount of data that will steadily move through your playback pipeline and get onto the screen. If you don't compress the video properly, it will not fit the pipe and therefore cannot be streamed in real time.

Reducing the number of frames to be delivered helps reduce the capacity required, but the motion becomes jerky and unrealistic. Keeping the *frame* count up may mean you have to compromise on the amount of data per frame. That leads to loss of quality and a blocky appearance. Judging the right setting is difficult, because certain content compresses more easily, while other material creates a spike in the *bit rate* required. That spike can be allowed to momentarily absorb a higher bit rate, in which case the quality will stay the same. Alternatively, you can cap the bit rate that is available. If you cap the bit rate, the quality will momentarily decline and then recover after the spike has passed. A good example of this is a dissolve between two scenes when compressed using *MPEG-2* for broadcast TV services operating within a fixed and capped bit rate.

2.4   First We Have to Digitize

Although some compression can take place while video is still in an analog form, we only get the large compression ratios by first converting the data to a digital representation and then reducing the redundancy. Converting from analog to digital form is popularly called digitizing. We now have techniques for digitally representing virtually every thing that we might consume. The whole world is being digitized, but we aren't yet living in the world of *The Matrix*.

Digitizing processes are normally only concerned with creating a representation of a view. Video structure allows us to isolate a view at a particular time, but unless we apply a lot more processing, we cannot easily isolate *objects* within a scene or reconstruct the 3D spatial model of a scene.

Software exists that can do that kind of analysis, but it is very difficult. It does lead to very efficient compression, though. So standards like *MPEG-4* allow for 3D models of real-world objects to be used. That content would have the necessary structure to exploit this kind of compression because it was preserved during the creation process.

Movie special effects use 3D-model and 2D-view digitizing to combine artificially created scene components and characters with real-world pictures. Even so, many measurements must still be taken when the plates (footage) are shot.

2.5   Spatial Compression

Spatial compression squashes a single image. The encoder only considers that data, which is self-contained within a single picture and bears no relationship to other frames in a sequence. This process should already be familiar to you. We use it all the time when we take pictures with digital still cameras and upload them as a *JPEG* file. GIF and TIFF images are also examples of spatial compression. Simple video codecs just create a sequence of still frames that are coded in this way. *Motion JPEG* is an example in which every frame is discrete from the others.

The process starts with uncompressed data that describes a color value at a Cartesian (or X–Y) point in the image. Figure 2-1 shows a basic image *pixel* map.

The next stage is to apply some run-length encoding, which is a way of describing a range of pixels whose value is the same. Descriptions of the image, such as "pixels 0,0 to 100,100 are all black," are recorded in the file. A much more compact description is shown in Figure 2-2.

This coding mechanism assumes that the coding operates on scan lines. Otherwise it would just describe a diagonal line.

The run-length encoding technique eliminates much redundant data without losing quality. A lossless compressor such as this reduces the data to about 50% of the original size, depending on the image complexity. This is particularly good for cell-animated footage.

The TIFF image format uses this technique and is sometimes called LZW compression after its inventors, Lempel, Ziv, and Welch. Use of LZW coding is subject to some royalty fees if you want to implement it, because the concepts embodied in it are patented. This should be included in the purchase price of any tools you buy.

The next level of spatial compression in terms of complexity is the JPEG technique, which breaks the image into *macroblocks* and applies the discrete cosine transform (*DCT*). This kind of compression starts to become lossy. Minimal losses are undetectable by the human eye, but as the compression ratio increases, the image visibly degrades.

Compression using the JPEG technique reduces the data to about 10% of the original size.

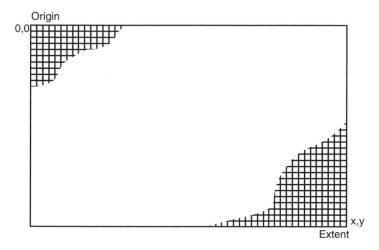

Figure 2-1 Uncompressed image pixel map.

0,0

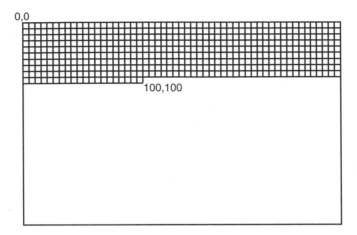

100,100

Figure 2-2 Run-length encoding.

2.6 Temporal Compression

Video presentation is concerned with time and the presentation of the images at regular intervals. The time axis gives us extra opportunities to save space by looking for redundancy across multiple images.

This kind of compression is always lossy. It is founded on the concept of looking for differences between successive images and describing those differences, without having to repeat the description of any part of the image that is unchanged.

Spatial compression is used to define a starting point or key frame. After that, only the differences are described. Reasonably good quality is achieved at a data rate of one tenth of the original data size of the original uncompressed format.

Research efforts are underway to investigate ever more complex ways to encode the video without requiring the decoder to work much harder. The innovation in encoders leads to significantly improved compression factors during the player deployment lifetime without needing to replace the player.

A shortcut to temporal compression is to lose some frames, however it is not recommended. In any case, it is not a suitable option for TV transmission that must maintain the frame rate.

2.7 Why Do I Need Video Compression?

Service providers and content owners are constantly looking for new avenues of profit from the material they own the rights to. For this reason, technology that provides a means to facilitate the delivery of that content to new markets is very attractive to them. Content owners require an efficient way to deliver content to their centralized repositories. Cheap and effective ways to provide that content to end users are needed, too. Video compres-

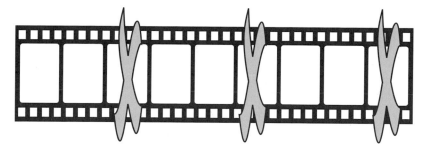

Figure 2-3 Removing frames for temporal compression.

sion can be used at the point where video is imported into your workflow at the beginning of the content chain as well as at the delivery end. If you are using video compression at the input, you must be very careful not to introduce undesirable artifacts. For archival and transcoding reasons, you should store only uncompressed source video if you can afford sufficient storage capacity.

2.8 Some Real-World Scenarios

Let's examine some of the possible scenarios where video compression can provide assistance. In some of these examples, video compression enables an entire commercial activity that simply would not be possible otherwise. We'll take a look at some areas of business to see how compression helps them.

2.8.1 Mobile Journalism

News-gathering operations used to involve a team of people going out into the field to operate bulky and very expensive equipment. As technology has progressed, cameras have gotten smaller and easier to use. A film crew used to typically include a sound engineer, cameraperson, and producer, as well as the journalist being filmed. These days, the camera is very likely carried by the journalist and is set up to operate automatically. Broadcast news coverage is being originated on videophones, mini-cams, and video-enabled mobile-phone devices. The quality of these cameras is rapidly improving. To maintain a comfortable size and weight for portable use, the storage capacity in terms of hardware has very strict limits. Video compression increases the capacity and thus the recording time available by condensing the data before recording takes place.

Current practice is to shoot on a small *DV* camera, edit the footage on a laptop, and then send it back to base via a videophone or satellite transceiver. The quality will clearly not be the same as that from a studio camera, but it is surprisingly good even though a high compression ratio is used.

Trials are underway to determine whether useful results can be obtained with a *PDA* device fitted with a video camera and integral mobile phone to send the material back to

Figure 2-4 PDA video player prototype. Source: courtesy of Christopher Barnatt.

a field headquarters. The problem is mainly one of picture size and available bandwidth for delivery. Figure 2-4 shows an example design provided by Christopher Barnatt.

2.8.2 Online Interactive Multi-Player Games

Multi-player online gaming systems have become very popular in recent years. The realism of the visuals increases all the time. So, too, does the requirement to hurl an ever-growing quantity of bits down a very narrow pipe. The difficulty increases as the games become more popular, with more streams having to be delivered simultaneously.

Online games differ significantly from normal video, because for a game to be compelling, some aspects of what you see must be computed as a consequence of your actions. Otherwise, the experience is not interactive enough. There are some useful techniques to apply that will reduce the bit rate required. For example, portions of the image can be static. Static images don't require any particular bit rate from one frame to the next since they are unchanged. Only pixels containing a moving object need to be delivered.

More sophisticated games are evolving, and interactivity becomes more interesting if you cache the different visual components of the scene in the local player hardware and then composite them as needed. This allows some virtual-reality (*VR*) techniques to be employed to animate the backdrop from a large static image.

Nevertheless, compression is still required in order to shrink these component assets down to a reasonable size, even if they are served from a local cache or *CD-ROM*.

New standards-based codecs will facilitate much more sophisticated game play. Codecs such as *H.264* are very efficient. Fully exploiting the capabilities of the MPEG-4 standard will allow you to create non-rectangular, alpha-blended areas of moving video. You could map that video onto a 3D mesh that represents some terrain or even a face. The MPEG-4 standard also provides scene construction mechanisms so that video assets can be projected into a 3D environment at the player. This allows the user to control the point of view. It also reduces the bit rate required for delivery, because only the flat, 2D versions of the content need to be delivered as component objects. Figure 2-5 shows an example of a high-quality interactive snooker game developed by Etiumsoft. As the scene becomes more realistic, video compression helps keep games like this small enough to deploy online or on some kind of sell-through, removable-disk format.

2.8.3 Online Betting

Betting systems are sometimes grouped together with online gaming, and that may be appropriate in some cases. But online gaming is more about the interaction between groups of users and may involve the transfer of large amounts of data on a peer-to-peer basis.

Betting systems can be an extension of the real-world betting shop where you place your wager and watch the outcome of the horse race or sports event on a wall of monitor screens. The transfer of that monitor wall to your domestic PC or TV screen is facilitated by efficient and cheap video compression. Real-time compression comes to the fore here because you cannot introduce more than fractions of a second of delay—the end users have wagered their own money and they expect the results to arrive in a timely manner.

Another scenario could involve a virtual poker game. These are often based around VR simulations of a scene, but with suitable compression a live game could be streamed

Figure 2-5 Live snooker? Source: courtesy of Etiumsoft.

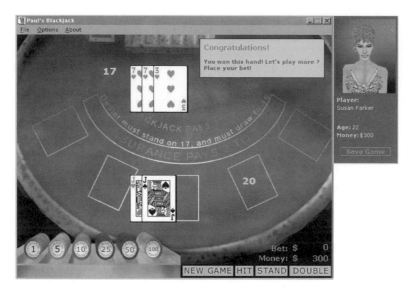

Figure 2-6 Online casino example. Source: copyright © Diogo Salari.

to anyone who wants to dial in and watch. Virtualizing a pack of cards is possible by simulating the cards on the screen, and a video-conferencing system could be used to enable observation of facial expressions of the other players in the game.

2.8.4 Sports and News coverage

Of all the different genres of content that broadcasters provide to end users, news and sports have some particularly important criteria that directly affect the way that video is compressed for presentation. Figure 2-7 shows an example of the BBC News Online video console that presents news video clips for broadband use in the United Kingdom.

News and sports are both very information-rich genres. Archiving systems tend to be large in both cases because there is a lot of material available. The metadata associated with the content assists the searching process and also facilitates the digital rights management (DRM) process. The content is easily accessible and widely available, but the playback can be controlled. Video may need to be encrypted as well as encoded. Other technologies such as watermarking are used, and these present additional technical problems. This is all addressed in more detail in Chapter 18, where DRM is covered extensively. In general, the rights protection techniques that are available impose further loads on an already hardworking compression system.

The nature of news content is that the material must be encoded quickly and presented as soon after the event as possible. The same is true of sports coverage, and services

---

BBC News Online: http://www.bbc.co.uk/news/

Figure 2-7 BBC News' broadband video console. Source: courtesy of BBC News Interactive.

that present the highlights of a sporting event need to be able to select and encode fragments of content easily, quickly, and reliably.

These demands lead to the implementation of very large infrastructure projects such as the BBC Colledia-based Jupiter system deployed in its news division. This facilitates the sharing of media assets as soon as they start to arrive. Editing by multiple teams at the same time is possible, and the finished *packages* are then routed to transmission servers in a form that is ready to deploy to the national TV broadcast service as well as to the Internet.

2.8.5 Advertising

Advertising on the Internet is beginning use video to present more compelling content. The newer codecs such as H.264 allow the macroblocks to be presented in quite sophisticated geometrical arrangements. It is now feasible to fit video into the traditional banner advertising rectangles that have a very different *aspect ratio* from normal video. Creating the content may need to be done using video editing tools that allow non-standard *raster* sizes to be used.

More information about these standard sizes is available at the Interactive Advertising Bureau Web site.

Interactive Advertising Bureau (IAB): http://www.iab.com/standards/index.asp

2.8.6 Video Conferencing

Large corporations have used video conferencing for many years. As far back as the 1980s, multinational corporations were prepared to permanently lease lines from the telecommunications companies in order to link headquarters offices in the United States with European offices. This generally required a dedicated room to be set aside and was sufficiently expensive that only one video-conferencing station would be built per site. Only one group of people could participate at a time, and the use of the technology was reserved for important meetings.

Video conferencing can now be deployed to a desktop or mobile phone. This is only possible because video compression reduces the data-transfer rate to a trickle compared with the systems in use just a few years ago.

Video conferencing applications currently lack the levels of interoperability between competing systems that telephone users enjoy for speech. That will come in time. For now, the systems being introduced are breaking new ground in making this available to the general public and establishing the fundamental principles of how the infrastructure should support it.

Figure 2-8 shows an example of an advanced video-conferencing user interface that supports multiple simultaneous users. This is available in the MacOS X version 10.4 operating system and is called iChat AV.

2.8.7 Remote Medicine

The use of remote apparatus and VR techniques for medicine is starting to facilitate so-called "telemedicine," where an expert in some aspect of the medical condition participates in a surgical operation being performed on the other side of the world. Clearly there are issues here regarding the need for force feedback when medical instruments are being oper-

Figure 2-8 Apple iChat AV user interface.

ated remotely. Otherwise, how can the operating surgeon "feel" what the instrument is doing on the remote servo-operated system? Game players have used force-feedback systems for some time. The challenge is to adapt this for other situations and maintain a totally synchronized remote experience. Video compression is a critical technology that allows multiple simultaneous camera views to be delivered over long distances. This will also work well for MRI, ultrasound, and X-ray-imaging systems that could all have their output fed in real time to a remote surgeon. The requirements here are for very high resolution. X-ray images need to be digitized in grayscale to increased bit depths and at a much higher resolution than TV. This obviously increases the amount of data to be transferred.

2.8.8 Remote Education

Young people often have an immediate grasp of technology and readily participate in interactive games and educational uses of video and computing systems. The education community has fully embraced computer simulation, games, and interactive software. Some of the most advanced CD-ROM products were designed for educational purposes. With equal enthusiasm, the education community has embraced the Internet, mainly by way of Web sites. Video compression provides opportunities to deploy an even richer kind of media for use in educational systems. This enhances the enjoyment of consumers when they participate. Indeed, it may be the only way to enfranchise some special-needs children who already have learning difficulties.

2.8.9 Online Support and Customer Services

Online help systems may be implemented with video-led tuition. When designing and implementing such a system, it is important to avoid alienating the user. Presenting users with an experience that feels like talking to a machine would be counterproductive. Automated answering systems already bother some users due to the sterile nature of the interchange. An avatar-based help system might fare no better and present an unsatisfying experience unless it is backed up by well-designed artificial intelligence.

2.8.10 Entertainment

Online gaming and betting could be categorized as entertainment. Uses of video compression with other forms of entertainment are also possible. *DVD* sales have taken off faster than anyone could ever have predicted. They are cheap to manufacture and provide added-value features that can enhance the viewer's enjoyment.

The MPEG-4 standard offers packaging for interactive material in a way that the current DVD specification cannot match. Hybrid DVD disks with MPEG-4 interactive content and players with MPEG-4 support could herald a renaissance in content authoring similar to what took place in the mid-1990s with CD-ROMs.

The more video can be compressed into smaller packages without losing quality, the better the experience for the viewer within the same delivery form factor (disk) or capacity (bit rate).

The H.264 codec is being adopted widely as the natural format for delivering high-definition TV (HDTV) content on DVD and allows us to store even longer definition programs on the existing 5-GB and 9-GB disks.

2.8.11 Religion

All of the major religions have a presence on the Internet. There are Web sites that describe their philosophy, theology, and origins. Video compression provides a way to involve members of the community who may not be physically able to attend ceremonies. They may even be able to participate through a streamed-video broadcast. This may well be within the financial reach of medium to large churches, and as costs are reduced, even small communities may be able to deploy this kind of service. There are great social benefits to be gained from community-based use of video-compression systems. Such applications could be built around video-conferencing technologies quite inexpensively.

2.8.12 Commerce

Quite unexpectedly, the shopping channel has become one of the more popular television formats. This seems to provide an oddly compelling kind of viewing. Production values are very low cost, and yet people tune in regularly to watch. Broadcasting these channels at 4.5 megabits per second (*Mbps*) on a satellite link may ultimately prove to be too expensive. As *broadband* technology improves its reach to consumers, these channels could be delivered at much lower bit rates through a networked infrastructure.

A variation of this that can be combined with a video-conferencing system is the business-to-business application. Sales pitches; demos; and all manner of commercial meetings, seminars, and presentations could take place courtesy of fast and efficient video compression.

2.8.13 Security and Surveillance

Modern society requires that a great deal of our travel and day-to-day activity take place under surveillance. A commuter traveling from home to a railway station by car, then by train, and then on an inner-city rapid-transit system may well be captured by as many as 200 cameras between home and the office desk. That is a lot of video, which until recently has been recorded on *VHS* tapes, sometimes at very low resolution, at reduced frame rates, and presented four at once in quarter-frame panes in order to save tape.

Newer systems are being introduced that use video compression to preserve video quality, increase frame rates, and automate the storage of the video on centralized repositories. By using digital video, the searching and facial-recognition systems can be connected to the repository. Suspects can be followed from one camera to another by synchronizing the streams and playing them back together.

This is a good thing if it helps to trace and then arrest a felon. Our legislators have to draw a very careful line between using this technology for the good of society as a whole and infringing on our rights to go about our daily lives without intervention by the state.

You may disagree with or feel uncomfortable about this level of surveillance, but it will likely continue to take place.

2.8.14 Compliance Recording

Broadcasters are required to record their output and store it for 90 days, so that if someone wants to complain about something that was said or a rights issue needs to be resolved, the evidence is there to support or deny the claim. This is called compliance recording, and historically it was accomplished through a manually operated bank of VHS recorders running in LP mode and storing 8 hours of video per tape, requiring three cassettes per day per channel. The BBC outputs at least six full-frame TV services that need to be monitored in this way. The archive for 90 days of recording is some 1620 tapes. These all have to be labeled, cataloged, and stored for easy access in case of a retrieval request.

The TX-2 compliance recorder was built on a Windows platform and was designed according to the requirements of the regulatory organizations so that UK broadcasters could store 90 days' worth of content in an automated system. The compliance recorder is based on a master node with attached slaves, which can handle up to 16 channels in a fly-configured system. Access to the archived footage is achieved via a Web-based interface, and the video is then streamed back to the requesting client.

This recorder could not have been built without video compression, and it is a good example of the kind of product that can be built on top of a platform such as Windows Media running on a Windows operating system, or other manufacturer's technology.

Because this is a software-based system, the compression ratio and hence the capacity and quality of the video storage can be configured. Less video but at a higher quality can be stored, or maximal time at low quality. The choice is yours.

2.8.15 Conference Proceedings

Using large-screen displays at conferences is becoming very popular. These are being driven by a video feed shot by professional camerapeople, and the video is often captured and made available to delegates after the conference. Siggraph conference proceedings, for example, make significant use of compression to create the DVD proceedings disk, and the Apple developer conference proceedings have for some years been a showcase of Apple's prowess with video workflow and production processes as well as its engineering work on codecs.

2.8.16 Broadband Video on Demand

During 2004, the BBC tested a system called the Internet Media Player (BBC iMP). This system presents an electronic program guide (EPG) over a 14-day window. The user browses the EPG listings and is able to call up something that was missed during the previous week. Alternatively, a recording can be scheduled during the next few days. In order to adequately protect the content, the BBC iMP trials are run on a Windows-based platform that supports the Windows Media DRM functionality. If the iMP player were used on a laptop connected to a fixed broadband service, the downloaded material could be taken on the road and viewed remotely. This enables video to be as mobile as music carried around on Walkman and iPod devices.

Future experiments in the area of broadband-delivered TV will explore some interesting peer-to-peer file techniques, which are designed to alleviate the bandwidth burden on service providers. For this to work, we must have reliable and robust DRM solutions, or the super-distribution model will fail to get acceptance from the content providers.

2.8.17 Home Theatre Systems

Hollywood movies are designed to be viewed on a large screen in a darkened room with a surround-sound system. There is now a growing market for equipment to be deployed at home to give you the same experience. The media is still mostly available in standard definition but some high-definition content is being broadcast already. More high-definition services will be launched during the next few years. Plasma, *LCD,* or *LED* flat screens are available in sizes up to 60 inches diagonal. If you want to go larger than that, you will need to consider a projection system.

At large screen sizes, it helps to increase the resolution of the image that is being projected, and that may require some special hardware to scale it up and interpolate the additional pixels. At these increased screen sizes, any artifacts that result from the compression will be very obvious. Higher bit rates will be necessary to allow a lower compression ratio. Some DVD products are shipped in special editions that give up all the special features in order to increase the bit rate. The gradual advancement of codec technology works in your favor. New designs yield better performance for the same bit rate as technology improves.

The bottom line is that compressing video to use on a standard-definition TV set may not be good enough for home-cinema purists.

2.8.18 Digital Cinema

Interestingly, the high-definition TV standards that are emerging seem to be appropriate for use in digital-cinema (D-cinema) situations. The same content will play in the domestic environment just as easily. As high-definition TV becomes more popular and more people install *home theatre systems,* commercial cinema complexes will need to develop their business in new ways. They will have to do this in order to differentiate their product and give people a reason to visit the cinema instead of watching the movie at home.

2.9 Platforms

With the increasing trends toward technological convergence, devices that were inconceivable as potential targets for video content are now becoming viable. Science fiction writers have been extolling the virtues of portable handheld video devices for years, and now the technology is here to realize that capability. In fact, modern third-generation mobile phones are more functional and more compact than science fiction writers had envisaged being available hundreds of years into the future. Handheld video, and touch-screen, flat-screen, and large-screen video, are all available here and now. They are being rolled out in a front room near you right this minute. What we take for granted and routinely use every day is already way beyond the futuristic technologies of the *Star Trek* crew.

2.9.1 Portable Video Shoot and Edit

Portable cameras have been around for a long time. Amateur film formats were made available to the consumer as 8-mm home movie products; they replaced earlier and more unwieldy film gauges. The 8-mm formats became increasingly popular in the 1950s and '60s. The major shortcomings of these were that they held only enough footage to shoot 4 minutes, and most models required that the film be turned over halfway through, so your maximum shot length was only 2 minutes. At the time, battery technology was less sophisticated than what we take for granted now, and many cameras were driven by clockwork mechanisms.

These devices were displaced quite rapidly with the introduction of VHS home-video systems in the late 1970s. Several formats were introduced to try and encourage mass appeal. But editing the content was cumbersome and required several expensive four-head video recorders.

Just after the start of the new millennium, digital cameras reached a price point that was affordable for the home-movie enthusiast. Now that the cameras can be fitted with *Firewire* interfaces (also called *iLink* and *IEEE* 1394), their connection to a computer has revolutionized the video workflow. These cameras use the digital video (DV) format that is virtually identical to the *DVCAM* format used by professional videographers and TV companies. The DV format was originally conceived by Sony as digital 8-mm tape for use in Sony Handycam® recorders.

Figure 2-9 illustrates the current state of the art that is represented by a system such as an Apple Macintosh G4 12-inch laptop with a FireWire connection to a Sony DCR PC 105 camera. The camera and laptop fit in a small briefcase. This combination is amazingly capable for a very reasonable total purchase price of less than $3000. The Apple laptop comes already installed with the iMovie video-editing software that is sufficient to edit and then burn a DVD (with the iDVD application). You can walk out of the store with it and start working on your movie project right away.

Of course, there are alternative software offerings, and other manufacturers' laptops support the same functionality. Sony VAIO computers are very video capable because they are designed to complement Sony's range of cameras, and the Adobe Premier and Avid DV editing systems are comparable to the Apple Final Cut Pro software if you want to use Windows-based machines.

This is all done more effectively on desktop machines with greater processing power. The laptop solution is part of an end-to-end process of workflow that allows a lot of work to be done in the field before content is shipped back to base.

Figure 2-9 Portable laptop and video camera.

2.9.2 Video Playback on Handheld Devices

Handheld video playback is becoming quite commonplace. There are several classes of device available depending on what you need. Obviously, the more sophisticated they are, the more expensive the hardware. There is a natural convergence here, so that ultimately all of these capabilities may be found in a single generic device. These fall into a family of mobile video devices that include

- Portable TV sets supporting terrestrial digital-TV reception
- Portable DVD viewers
- Diskless portable movie players
- PDA viewers

2.9.3 Video Phones

The new generation of mobile-phone devices is converging with the role of the handheld personal digital assistant (PDA). These mobile phones are widely available and have cameras and video playback built in. They also have address books and other PDA-like applications, although these may be less sophisticated than those found in a genuine PDA. Some services were being developed for so-called 2.5G mobile phones, but now that the genuine *3G phones* are shipping, they will likely replace the 2.5G offerings.

2.9.4 H.264 on Mobile Devices

H.264 is designed to be useful for mobile devices and consumer playback of video. Rolling this standard out for some applications must take account of the installed base of players, and that will take some time. So it is likely that, initially, H.264 will be used primarily as a mobile format.

2.9.5 The Ultimate Handheld Device

Taking the capabilities of a portable TV, DVD player, PDA, and mobile phone and integrating them into a single device gets very close to the ultimate handheld portable media device. Well it might, if the capabilities of a sub-notebook computer are included.

A fair use policy is now required for consumer digital video that allows us to transfer our legitimately purchased DVD to a "memory card" or other local-storage medium. These memory cards are useful gadgets to take on a long journey to occupy us as we travel, but the content owners are not comfortable with us being able to make such copies.

There are still issues with the form factor for a handheld device like this. To create a viewing experience that is convenient for long journeys, we might end up with a device that is a little bulkier than a phone should be. Maybe a hands-free kit addresses that issue or possibly a Bluetooth headset. Usable keypads increase the size of these devices. Currently, it is quite expensive to provide sufficient storage capacity without resorting to an embedded hard disk. That tends to reduce the battery life, so we might look to the new storage technologies that are being developed. Terabyte memory chips based on holographic techniques may yield the power–size–weight combination that is required. Newer display technologies such as organic LED devices may offer brighter images with less power consumed. Cameras are already reduced to a tiny charged cathode device (*CCD*) assembled on a chip, which is smaller than a cubic centimeter.

The key to this will be standardization. Common screen sizes, players, video codecs, and connection protocols could enable an entire industry to be built around these devices. Open standards facilitate this sort of thing, and there are high hopes that H.264 (*AVC*) and the other parts of the MPEG-4 standard will play an important role here.

3GPP home page: http://www.3gpp.org/

2.9.6 Personal Video Recorders

Personal video recorders (*PVRs*) are often generically referred to as *TiVo*, although they are manufactured by a variety of different companies. Some of them do indeed license the TiVo software, but others do not. Another popular brand is DirecTV.

2.9.7 Analog Off-Air PVR Devices

A classic TiVo device works very hard to compress incoming analog video to store it effectively and provide trick-play features. The compression quality level can be set in the preferences. The compromise is space versus visible artifacts. At the lowest quality, the video is fairly noisy if the picture contains a lot of movement. This is okay if you are just recording a program that you don't want to keep forever—for example, just a time shift to view the program at a different time. If you want to record a movie, you will probably choose a higher-quality recording format than you would for a news program.

The functionality is broadly divided into trick-play capabilities and a mechanism to ensure that you record all the programs you want to, even if you do not know when they were going to be aired.

In the longer term, these devices scale from a single-box solution up to a *home media server* with several connected clients. This would be attractive to schools for streaming TV services directly to the classroom. University campus TV, hospital TV services, and corporate video-distribution services are candidates. Standards-based solutions offer good economies of scale, low thresholds of lock-in to one supplier, and good commercial opportunities for independent content developers.

2.9.8 Digital Off-Air PVR Devices

When digital PVR devices are deployed, recording television programs off-air becomes far more efficient. In the digital domain, the incoming *transport stream* must be de-multiplexed, and packets belonging to the *program stream* we are interested in are stored on a hard disk. The broadcaster already optimally compresses these streams. Some storage benefits could be gained by transcoding them. Note that we certainly cannot add any data back to the video that has already been removed at source.

Future development work on PVR devices will focus on storing and managing content that has been delivered digitally. This is within the reach of software-based product designs and does not require massive amounts of expensive hardware.

There are complex rights issues attached to home digital-recording technology, and it is in constant evolution.

TiVo: http://www.tivo.com/
DirecTV: http://www.directv.com/

Figure 2-10 Pace PVR2GO. Source: courtesy of Pace Micro Technology.

2.9.9 Mobile PVR Solutions

Another interesting product was demonstrated by Pace at the International Broadcasting Convention (IBC) in 2004. It was a handheld PVR designed to record material being broadcast using the *DVB-H* mobile-TV standard. Coupling this with the H.264 codec and a working DRM solution brings us very close to a system that could be rolled out very soon. Provided rights issues and the content-delivery technology can be developed at the front end, products such as the PVR2GO shown in Figure 2-10 could be very successful.

2.10   The Future

The technology that enables PVR devices is getting cheaper, and the coding techniques are pushing the storage capacity (measured in hours) ever upward. Nevertheless, not every household will want to own a PVR. In addition, the higher end of the functionality spectrum may only ever be available to users with a lot of disposable income. Some of the basic functionality may just be built into a TV set. As TV receivers are gradually replaced with the new technology, they ship with video compression and local storage already built in.

Pause and rewind of live video, for instance, is very likely to be built into TV sets, and for it to be manufactured cheaply enough, the functionality will be implemented in just a few integrated circuits and will then be as ubiquitous as the Teletext decoders found in European TV sets.

Broadband connectivity is penetrating the marketplace very rapidly—perhaps not quite as fast as DVD players did, but in quite large numbers all the same.

A critical threshold is reached when video codecs are good enough to deliver satisfactory video at a bit rate that is equal to or less than what is available on a Broadband connection. Indeed, H.264 encoding packed into MPEG-4 multimedia containers coupled with a PVR storage facility and a fast, low-*contention* broadband link is a potential fourth TV platform that offers solutions to many of the problems that cannot be easily solved on the satellite-, terrestrial- and cable-based digital-TV platforms. MPEG-4 interactive multimedia packages could be delivered alongside the existing digital-TV content in an MPEG-2 transport stream. Indeed, the standards body has made special provision to allow this delivery mechanism, and MPEG-4 itself does not need to standardize a transport stream because there is already one available.

2.11 On with the Journey

So we have some ideas now about the kind of platform the video we compress might be played on. This helps us to assess the best way to encode it. We also know something about the target size and the delivery mechanism. That will help us choose players and codecs.

Now we can consider the scenario from the other end. The material we use will be sourced in a range of formats, and we need to know something about how each one works.

What Are We Trying to Compress? 3

3.1 Where Do You Want to Go Today?

That was a very good advertising line dreamed up by Microsoft. It is full of adventure and potential excitement and is based on you, the consumer, making a choice. So now we have to make a choice about what kind of moving-image content we are going to compress. Will it be film, video, or computer-generated digital imagery? They are all different. Let's find out why in the next few chapters.

3.2 What Is a Moving Image?

Think about moving pictures. How are they captured? They are two-dimensional recordings of an array of pixels at an instant in time. Film and TV cameras both capture motion, but the resulting images have very little in common when they are examined from a technical standpoint.

3.3 What Sort of Compression Do You Need?

There are two basic kinds of compression. The first is utterly lossless, while the other sacrifices some fidelity in order to improve the compression ratio. Lossless compression is a format-conversion process that compresses the physical manifestation of the video. Lossy compression actually compresses the informational content of the video. This is a subtle and very important distinction. Lossy compression ranges from high quality with undetectable artifacts down to massively degraded viewing experiences. The developers of video-compression technology continually strive to improve the ratio of quality to bit rate or compression.

3.4 What Sort of User Are You?

Video compression is of interest to a variety of users. Professionals see it as a full-time occupation and may have significant funding to support building large and complex systems. At the other end of the scale is the enthusiastic amateur videographer who wants to create a DVD to record some family history. Compression systems are available for both extremes as well as for those whose needs are somewhere in between.

We will consider the larger scale first. Then we will work our way down to something suitable for single users running a small operation.

3.4.1 Broadcasters

There are relatively few large broadcasters in the world compared with the number of small- to medium-sized potential compressionists. By large broadcasters, we mean organizations that are broadcasting multiple channels of content simultaneously. Examples might be the BBC; MTV; or News Corporation, which is the parent company of all the Sky brands and others such as Fox Television.

The BBC broadcasts more than 26 hours of content for every hour of the day. This includes multiple national and international TV services and many audio services that are going out in the form of AM, FM, and digital radio. Some of this content is also streamed on the Internet to augment a large-scale Web site operation.

The production processes for that content are now almost completely digital, from inputting the source material and passing it through the editing process, to putting it on the air. Some content still arrives in analog form, and the U.K. still has some analog broadcasting for the domestic user. That analog service is actually delivered using digital systems almost to the very last point in the chain before the transmitter.

Video compression is fundamental to the broadcasting workflow. Storing everything in a totally uncompressed form is unrealistic for both technical and financial reasons. The compression chosen must allow the footage to be edited and reused without a generational loss being introduced. High-quality master copies of content might be preserved using a 50-Mbps storage format and routine content would use 25 Mbps. Other intermediate formats are used that have lower bit rates.

Archives require a lossless or nearly lossless storage format. By the time the video reaches the TV set in your living room, it has been compressed by a factor of 10 to 1 and is no longer anything like archival quality.

Long-term archival storage will almost certainly be in a variety of different formats. Some of them are lower quality than current production and broadcast standards allow because the older legacy systems could not achieve the quality levels that are now commonplace.

You cannot put back what is not there. Repurposing old archival content presents some special problems, and finding ways to get the very best quality out of old material is an ongoing challenge. The BBC Research Centre develops technology solutions to this sort of problem from time to time. A recent innovation was a digital processing tool that samples the *PAL* recorded color sub-carrier more accurately in order to restore old PAL footage, eliminating a lot of analog noise and cross-color artifacts. This sort of research requires considerable resources and it benefits the entire industry.

3.4.2 Production Company

Independent production companies now produce a lot of their own programs. They don't have the money available to invest in massive technical infrastructures that the broadcasters use, but they do use similar equipment to shoot and edit.

Programs are typically delivered on Sony Digital betacam-based systems or on a format called DVCAM and its derivatives such as DVCPRO. These correspond to the 50-Mbps and 25-Mbps formats that broadcasters prefer. HDTV variants of these are also beginning to be used. These formats are slightly compressed. All formats in use sacrifice some small portion of the picture information, even if it is just recording color data at a lower resolution than brightness.

The original material might have been shot on film or on video. Today's material is delivered to broadcasters in a digital format. New technologies such as Material eXchange Format (MXF) allow media to be delivered in files rather than on tapes, and this allows transfers to be networked through an information technology (IT) infrastructure.

Any long-term storage of programs must be in a form that is ready to be reprocessed for new platforms and markets. A production company that has been in business for a while is likely to have some format-conversion and storage problems similar to those experienced by the broadcaster due to the continued change in video formats.

3.4.3 Pro-Consumer

This is a category of consumer that buys high-end equipment that is near professional quality and is almost good enough for production companies and broadcasters to use. The gap is narrowing, and the difference between pro-consumer and professional equipment is likely to be in the quality of the imaging optics and the storage capacity. Many of the physical components in the camera are common to consumer and professional equipment—especially in the case of DV-format cameras.

The imaging chip in professional broadcast-standard equipment produces a higher resolution and has a greater dynamic range from black to white, resulting in high-quality images. Sometimes a professional system will use multiple *CCD* chips rather than a single chip to get even better quality.

Broadcasters will require lenses with good depth-of-field control and little or no distortion of the image. The storage capacity of the videotape in a professional system will be higher than a consumer model in terms of bit rate. A professional format is also likely to record for less time because the amount of data recorded is larger. The consequence is that tape-based systems must transport the tape faster to record sufficient data. The same applies to solid-state storage because the bulk of the stored data is larger.

3.4.4 Amateur

The pricing of digital handycams is reducing to the point where this market is opening up now. Analog video recorders can still be purchased, but most manufacturers are also shipping a range of digital camcorders. Sony, for instance, manufactures the DCR PC105E model, which will play back DVCAM tapes recorded in low-end studio digital VCRs such as the DSR 11. DVCAM is widely used in news-gathering operations, and the video is often manipulated using the 25-Mbps *DV25* format. A range of video formats is discussed in Chapter 5 and tabulated in Appendix E.

3.5 Problems You May Encounter

If the video you are trying to compress is of particularly poor quality, you will find the results of compressing it to be disappointing. The encoder interprets any significant noise in the original as frame-to-frame changes. Even non-moving background content will compress badly if there is significant noise present. Either your compressor will be unable to reach the target bit rate, or if you cap the bit rate, quality of the video when played back will be very bad indeed.

Motion artifacts are particularly hard to deal with when your source is interlaced video. Removing the interlacing is a significant challenge.

Digitizing home movie film may be subject to unstable positioning of the film within the gate of the projector or telecine unit unless you are using a professional system. This is called gate weave, and it leads to tracking errors and unintended frame-to-frame differences that must be motion compensated. Since the camera introduced some gate weave as well, you have two film-weave artifacts to cope with.

Tools that track the frames and stabilize the video before compression are worth investing in. Stabilization is not vital to the compression process, of course, but the output quality will be improved. The bit rate is consumed by compressing movement within the frame and not by the movement of the frame.

This last point is very subtle, isn't it? This is very typical of the sort of complexity you will encounter in the compression process.

3.5.1 Dealing With Difficult Content

Preprocessing your video through a noise filter will help the compression process. At the outset, you are unlikely to purchase products such as Final Cut Pro or Premier as a priority. Their superior color-correction and noise-reduction plug-ins will rescue footage that was unusable, and you can add them to your system when you can afford to.

Tracking errors due to gate movement could be corrected by using the motion-tracking capabilities of Adobe After Effects to gently coerce the frames back to their optimum position with respect to one another. A slight loss of resolution will happen because you must frame a portion of the screen that always encloses a picture. If the film shifts significantly in the gate, you will lose some of the picture around the edges. A neatly cropped final output will remedy this, and as long as you only crop the over-scanned part of the picture, it is unlikely to seriously affect your viewing enjoyment. There is always the option to scale or composite into a frame of some kind if the movement is significant and the necessary cropping becomes extreme.

3.5.2 Data Loss During Digital Transcoding

Compression is simply a data-reduction process. No compression is genuinely lossless except perhaps for some of the production techniques used at the high end. In order to compress video to usable sizes for DVD or domestic-video archiving, some considerable data loss has to take place. This data simply cannot be put back once it has been discarded.

Figure 3-1 shows the output of a video analyzer that is comparing the image before and after coding and then scaling the residual error so it is visible.

More recent codecs provide additional compression tools to alleviate these effects, which will help a great deal. The H.264 codec, for example, offers some very sophisticated compression features, but the penalty is increased CPU power and time required to compress the content.

You have to decide for yourself what the acceptable level of data loss is going to be. For film, there is no point in trying to preserve detail that is finer than the film grain, because all you are doing is preserving noise in the original photographed image. Mathematicians are bound to argue about this, and it is similar to the situation regarding audio sample rates. But that is a topic for later on. For now, note the name Harry *Nyquist*, who conceived the idea of digital sampling 60 years before the technology was available to realize his invention.

Trading off horizontal resolution for video is preferable to losing vertical resolution due to the artifacts that vertical interpolations will introduce. If there is significant fine detail such as text, that will become illegible after severe compression.

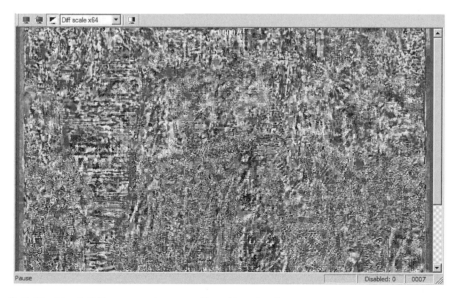

Figure 3-1 Residual differences after encoding (data loss).

Variable-bit-rate compression is much preferred for content that is not intended to be broadcast within a fixed-bit-rate budget. If the bit-rate budget is constrained in some way, a cooperative compression process on several channels will deliver some benefits. Two or more channels can make room for each other and be transmitted using less bandwidth than they would require if they were compressed independently of each other. This technique is called statistical multiplexing, and it is covered in some detail in Chapter 14.

3.6   Downsides to Video Compression

There are times when video compression causes more problems than it solves. Trying to deploy it in unsuitable circumstances leads to difficulty later in the production and consumption cycle.

3.6.1   Origination Stage

Video compression should be avoided at the origination stage. Some cameras compress the video as it is written to tape or disk inside the camera. These devices never yield an uncompressed output. The consequence is that any content you shoot with such a camera will probably turn out to be totally useless for anything other than home movies.

For example, suppose you are shooting some training video and you want to color key the background. Regardless of whether you use blue or green screens or even the newer retro-reflective materials to get a good hard edge for your matte, any compression that loses detail will immediately compromise your ability to pull a matte off that video. The jaggies and edge-coded artifacts are so severe that your footage is rendered useless. The solution is to get a better camera and shoot the footage at the best-quality camera settings available, and then write it to tape with a high-bit-rate storage format with a near-lossless compression method.

3.6.2   Not for Archiving Master-Quality Material

For much the same reasons that you would a) shoot footage using the best available quality of equipment, film stock, or video recording format and b) use lossless compression techniques (the intent is to preserve the maximum information), the archives must be maintained at the highest possible quality. A completely lossless coding format is desirable but expensive in terms of storage space. Experience shows that if content is compressed with poorly chosen coding techniques, the archives become unusable very quickly. Putting the tracking systems in place and logging the rushes as soon as they arrive from the field must be seen as a benefit and not a cost. In the long term it will save money.

I will describe a very painful episode based on a true story. Only the names and places have been changed to protect the innocent.

Let's say it is 2 years after you've launched a major multimedia-based Web site, and through cost-reduction exercises, you gave up logging the incoming material and just encoded it for delivery via *modem*, and then discarded the originals.

When your marketing people strike the deal with a broadband portal to deliver your site as a major broadband experience, just how are you going to re-encode all that content? That is when you say, "If only we had kept the originals and built ourselves a media database to track and manage it all." But the situation gets worse than that. Much worse.

You have important and very complicated rights issues with media. Maybe your rights to use some of the clips have expired and they ought not to be visible on your site. Rights are sometimes granted only for modem delivery and either specifically exclude broadband or omit it. That gives the legal experts an opportunity to argue for additional payment. Some rights are clear and the media can be repurposed immediately. But how would you know which is which? In the words of the Ghostbusters, "Who you gonna call?"

Effectively, the only archives you have are that rather scratchy looking, modem-quality, postage stamp-sized, frame-dropped, pixelated mess on your *streaming server*, and because your finance people talked you into saving money at the outset, you are going to reap the results of a very bad business decision.

Maybe your business will recover from that. But in all likelihood it won't, not without spending an awful lot of time and money reworking some content over again. And that assumes you are still able to find original master tapes—and get the rights to use them again.

The moral of this story is to think ahead to what you might be doing in the future—not just next year but 5 and 10 years from now.

3.7 Getting Out of the Mire

The solution is to institute a media audit and try to trace where the originals of some of that footage are. The avoidance strategy in the first place would have been to build a media database even if it was manually operated. Keeping track of the location of every master copy of a clip and any compressed instances of it requires a reliable record-keeping system. Diligence is the only way to track the provenance of your media. Given that the originals are stored online somewhere, it is possible to set up some automation to load and transcode them one at a time without any human intervention. You have to plan way ahead, anticipate future needs of your content, and maintain archive-quality copies reliably. If they are compressed at all, they should be stored using a lossless compression format so that a transcoder is able to down sample to any format that is required. You cannot transcode up to a higher-quality format and not see some artifacts as a result. At best you can blur them to hide the worst effects.

3.8   Scoping the Problem

To be able to compare the various picture sizes and frame rates, the size of the data sets we are operating on must be taken into consideration. Then the capacity planning for a new compression workflow system can take place. The calculations are fairly simple, although finding the initial values to use is not easy. Some helpful tables are provided in the appendices.

Planning the capacity of a system to provide sufficient disk space for the projects being developed on it is vital. If the cost of storage is the limiting factor, then the equation is reversed. The decision then becomes how much video and at what picture size is going to be stored in the available disk space.

3.9   Moving-Image Formats

Now that we understand the basic requirements of a compression system, we can look at what kind of material is going to be processed. Film, TV, and computer data are all different. The next few chapters look at each of them in detail and close with an examination of audio, which is an important component of the viewing experience.

4 Film

4.1 The Traditional Route

On our journey through the complexities of video compression, we now look at movie film. Film has been around for a while. It was the first kind of moving image to be recorded, so we could think of film as a classic or traditional format.

TV has been with us for many years, too, but film has been around much longer. Most major studios have been in existence for 80 years or more, and the technology existed for some time even before Hollywood became properly established.

So for this part of our trip, we'll look at how film technology creates those images flickering on the movie screen, which will help us understand the other formats better when we get to them.

4.2 Back in the Old Days

Film stock and camera manufacturers have made some significant improvements in what can be accomplished with movie film. The most problematic aspect of film is that because a chemical reaction imprinted the images, the film ages; that is, the images will degrade with time. They will lose contrast and the color will shift because each emulsion on the film substrate ages differently. This applies equally to films made by Hollywood movie companies and to those home movies shot in the 1950s and `60s on *8 mm* film.

Recovering and restoring some of our older footage and archiving it in a digital form are vitally important. If we neglect to do this over the next few years, it will be gone forever.

In this chapter the important aspects of film are examined. Knowing about the nature of film will help you get the most out of the compression process if this is where your source material is coming from.

4.3 How Film Projectors Work

Projectors and cameras transport the film in the same way. The camera simply uses a slightly larger shutter aperture than the projector. Many alternative mechanisms were tried and discarded before the sprocket-driven serial frame design became dominant. A visit to the National Museum of Film and Television in Bradford, UK or the Science Museum in London will reward you with some insights into the way that film technology has evolved. Both of these are worth visiting if you have the time. There are similar museums in the United States (such as the California Museum of Photography) and in other countries where there is any history of filmmaking. Some URLs for Web sites of other museums are listed at the bottom of the page. Museums featuring scientific or engineering subjects may also have sections devoted to filmmaking.

4.3.1 Gate and Film Transport Mechanism

The film is pulled through the gate of the camera and projector by a claw mechanism that is driven by a cam or eccentric motion of some kind. This is easier to understand if it is shown visually. Figure 4-1 demonstrates how this mechanism works.

As the motor drives the eccentric cam around, the claw is moved up and down and in and out. This is a vastly simplified example and the actual mechanism is a bit more complicated than this, but the principle is the same. The claw moves up, the teeth come out through an aperture in the gate, and they penetrate the film via the sprocket holes and

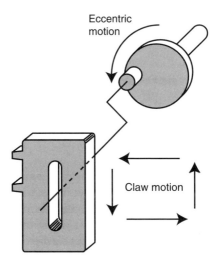

Figure 4-1 Film gate claw mechanism.

National Museum of Film & Photography: http://www.nmpft.org.uk/

George Eastman House: http://www.eastmanhouse.org/

American Widescreen Museum: http://www.widescreenmuseum.com/

California Museum of Photography: http://www.cmp.ucr.edu/

American Museum of Photography: http://www.photographymuseum.com/guide.html

International Centre of Photography: http://www.icp.org/

The Big Camera: http://www.thebigcamera.com.au/

pull the film down through the gate. This movement has to be very precise. The film must be moved by exactly one frame distance. The sprockets must be aligned perfectly each time or the film will be torn by the claw mechanism.

4.3.2 *The Shutter*

The shutter allows the light through in order to expose the film in the camera or project it onto a screen when viewing. The shutter is mounted on a spindle and rotates once per frame. The projector contrives to flash the image on the screen twice. This effectively presents the image at 48 fps (frames per second), although the film is only moving at 24 fps through the gate. Figure 4-2 shows shutter designs for a camera and projector.

Some projectors allow the shutter timing synchronization to be adjusted so as to open or close the aperture with respect to the gate movement. Even more sophisticated projectors allow adjustments to how much time the aperture stays open.

4.4 Picture Formats and Sizes

Probably the most important parameters that you have to know are the physical characteristics of your source material.

These include the following:

- Width in pixels
- Height in pixels
- Color depth
- Frames per second
- Scanning method (interlaced or progressive)

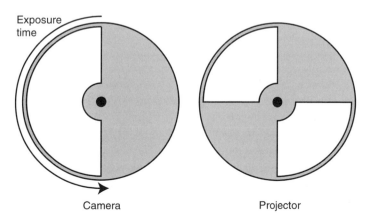

Figure 4-2 Camera and projector shutter designs.

The width, height, and color depth dictate how much information you have to deal with per frame. Some of your pre-compression processing, such as cropping and scaling, is going to be based on what you know about these values.

The frames per second (fps) value tells you whether any time-based correction or pulldown is necessary to introduce additional frames for your target output platform.

The scanning method indicates the complexity of any motion-based processing. Raw film can be converted to interlaced or *progressive scanning* quite easily. Video originates in an interlaced format, and that does not conveniently convert to progressive scanning without some complex interpolation. This interpolation is difficult because it takes place in space (X and Y) and on the time axis (between successive fields). The interpolation is much easier if the video was created from a film format with a telecine process. This will become apparent after the discussion of how pulldown works.

Film formats have picture information at the highest resolution. Frame rates are generally stable across all sizes at 24 fps. Some older home-movie footage may have been shot at 18 fps to economize on film stock. This text will work down from the highest quality to the lowest, making some simple calculations about potential digitized image sizes on the way.

4.5 Film Grain and Scanning Resolution

During the research for this book, a number of conflicting dimensions for film formats were discovered. Film grain is such a variable attribute that scanning resolutions will vary widely.

You may choose to scan at a higher or lower resolution in your own projects. Simply recalculate the storage density equations, which are straightforward. Here is an example:

Given:
W = Imaged area width in mm.
H = Imaged area height in mm.
D = Dots-per-millimeter (dpmm) resolution selected.
F = Frame rate in fps.
T = Duration of the movie in minutes.
Z = Bytes per pixel (RGB 8 bit = 3).
GigaBytes per movie:
Disk space required = $W * H * Z * F * T * 60 * D^2 / 2^{30}$

Having decided on a scanning resolution, the frame size in pixels is then computed. The storage sizes for our capacity planning are derived from those values.

A resolution of approximately 115 dots per millimeter (dpmm) is considered a reasonable compromise for a maximum scanning density for the purposes of calculating image sizes. This is why:

An IMAX movie was produced by the Massachusetts Institute of Technology in 1996 and worked on at a resolution of 4K in the horizontal axis. This was considered to be an adequate resolution for IMAX at the time. It would result in a raster size of approximately 4096 × 2854. Taking film grain size into account, the theoretical maximum for this format is approximately 8192 × 5944. The picture size of the image on the *70 mm* film stock is approximately 69.6 mm by 48.5 mm. Taking that size and the pixel dimensions into account, a scanning resolution of 115 pixels per mm or 2920 pixels per inch is derived. At an 8K resolution, each pixel would be about 25 mm square on the screen surface of a 215-meter wide screen.

Scanner manufacturers have standardized some popular resolutions regardless of the technology they use. They are based on the number of pixels scanned across the image area, regardless of its size, and they tend not to discuss dots per millimeter.

- 2K (2048 pixels across)
- 3K (3072 pixels across)
- 4K (4096 pixels across)
- 6K (6144 pixels across)

The normal working resolution for digital film projects is 2048 × 1536. It's commonly referred to as "2K," but of course that doesn't describe any aspect ratio or anamorphic scaling. It is an industry standard, however. At 2K, the results look a little soft and fine detail gets lost. To compensate for this, some companies work at 4K resolution, with its attendant increase in storage and file sizes. The 6K resolution is considered to be as high as the industry is prepared to go for normal projects; due to the massive increase in data sizes, it's only used for the largest projects.

At a 2K working resolution, fine detail in hair is resolved quite poorly. The 4K resolution solves this, and even if the final output is reduced to 2K, the difference is still apparent. This high-resolution scanning and subsequent "down-rezzing" was developed by Cinesite as part of the digital intermediate process and is known as Super 2K.

The 6K scanning resolution is sometimes used to pull a single still frame image off of the film so that it can be used in book projects. These tend to be photoset at very high resolutions, and they therefore can benefit from the denser scanning.

Table 4-1 suggests some alternative scanning densities based on conversations with manufacturers of telecine systems and film scanners.

Choosing the right scanning density is crucial to achieving the best possible quality. The resolution depends on the grain size of the stock and the image size being scanned.

Table 4-1 Some Examples of Scanning Resolutions

Description	Resolution
IMAX on a 4K scanner	58 dpmm
IMAX on a 8K scanner	115 dpmm
VistaVision on 4K scanner	109 dpmm
16 mm frame on 2K scanner	212 dpmm
16 mm film full width including sound track on 2K scanner	128 dpmm

Film stocks all exhibit different grain sizes, and the processing of the stock to force exposures will also affect grain size because it's a chemical reaction based on crystals. One way this could happen would be if the chemical reaction were caused to happen more slowly by use of a more diluted solution. Some care is necessary with the formulation of chemicals for film processing, because you only get one chance at it. It is best left to a competent laboratory.

4.5.1   Real-World Scanning Resolutions

Examining some manufacturer literature provided by FilmLight Ltd. reveals some recommended scanning resolutions for different film sizes on their Northlight scanner. Bear in mind that film stock, age, and desired output resolution all affect the final choice of scanning resolution. Table 4-2 summarizes some alternatives.

   The quoted resolutions are approximate and based on nominal film sizes divided into the maximum scanning resolution. This assumes the entire camera gate area is being imaged and that may not necessarily be the case.

   Scanning times are quoted as 4.7 seconds per frame when scanning 4 perf *35mm* film at 4K resolution. This needs to be taken into account when calculating how long a job will take to complete. A roll of film that is 2000 feet long might contain 28,000 frames, and this could take a couple of days to scan completely at the higher resolutions. Scanning is much slower than simply projecting the film by a factor of more than 100:1. A similar roll of *16mm* film might take even longer, although the scanning time per frame would be shorter so the duration might be compensated accordingly.

   Cintel uses flying spot CRT technology that seems to offer a slight increase in scanning speed, but the output quality may be somewhat compromised in return.

Table 4-2 Northlight Scanner Resolutions Versus Film Sizes

Stock	Imaging size		Resolution
	Width	*Height*	
16 mm	3.0k	1.5k	290 dpmm
4 perf 35mm	6.0k	4.5k	280 dpmm
Super 16mm	3.0k	1.5k	240 dpmm
4 perf 35mm (4.7 seconds per frame scan)	4.0k	3.0k	190 dpmm
16 mm	2.0k	1.0k	180 dpmm
Super 16mm	2.0k	1.0k	140 dpmm
4 perf 35mm	3.0k	2.0k	140 dpmm
4 perf 35mm (2.6 seconds per frame scan)	2.0k	5.0k	96 dpmm

Filmlight Ltd.: http://www.filmlight.ltd.uk/
Cintel International Ltd.: http://www.cintel.co.uk/

4.5.2 Nyquist and Grain Size

The concepts developed by Harry Nyquist regarding sample rates needing to be twice the resolvable detail in order to preserve information apply to film as much as they do to sound and video. In this case the sampling needs to be twice the grain size or better. To arrive at a suitable scanning resolution for your footage, you need to know the film stock characteristics and how the processing will affect the grain. Then, given the picture size, you can work out how big the grain particles are. Double that and you have the target resolution that you need to scan with. Figure 4-3 shows the relationship between the grain size and the scanning grid.

The vertical pixel dimension is governed by the aspect ratio of the frame and is set up to deliver square pixels.

4.6 Cinema Formats

These formats have been around for a very long time. Most footage exists on 35mm, although there are variants such as Todd AO, 70mm, Vista Vision, Cinerama, CinemaScope, TechniScope, and others.

Hollywood movies shown in cinemas are usually presented on 35mm film projected with an 1.85:1 aspect ratio or stretched to 2.39:1 with an anamorphic lens (CinemaScope). Most cinemas will use those two formats, but a few will also support 1.37:1 Academy Aperture 35mm format as well.

Note that for some formats, the negative master films have sprocket holes that are a different shape or size. You must be careful to ensure that they are not conveyed through a film transport designed for a different sprocket format. Mismatching the transport and film formats will permanently damage the film the first time it is used. If this is the master negative, the damage may not be repairable.

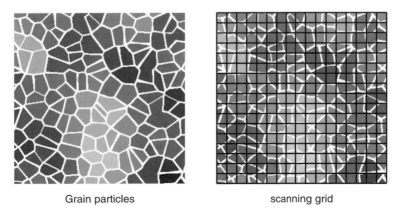

Grain particles   scanning grid

Figure 4-3 Film grain and nyquist scanning limits.

4.6.1 Aspect ratios

Original material could have been shot on larger stock and then reduction-printed down to 35mm for distribution. Aspect ratios broadly fall into three categories:

- Normal aspect ratio that roughly corresponds to 4:3 on a TV set
- Wide screen, which is somewhat equivalent to 16:9 on TV
- Ultra-wide screen, which has to be cropped or letterboxed to fit a TV

Figure 4-4 shows the difference between these aspect ratios. A lot more of the scenery is visible with the wider aspect ratios. In fact, on extremely wide screen presentations, the human peripheral vision is included within the viewing angle. This creates an impression of being immersed in the movie. TV does not adequately convey this impression, and it is one reason why we still enjoy going to the cinema to see those big blockbuster movies.

Figure 4-4 Cinema aspect ratios.

The physical imaging area of 35mm is conveniently mapped to 2048 × 1536 for production work. Anamorphic compression (squeeze prints) allows a wider aspect ratio to be worked on. The final raster is computed digitally or squeezed optically during printing.

The normal aspect ratio fits reasonably well on a TV monitor and many TV programs are shot on 35mm or 16mm normal aspect-ratio film stock.

Wide screen is accomplished either by shooting on wider film stock and maintaining roughly the same height, or by applying an optical distortion to squeeze a wider image in the horizontal axis into normal aspect-ratio film stock. This is called anamorphic distortion, and the same effect happens electronically when normal aspect-ratio video is stretched from 4:3 to fit a 16:9 wide-screen monitor.

4.6.2 Anamorphic Printing

Anamorphic lenses were available in the 1960s as a retrofit accessory so that you could attach them to a 16mm movie camera. The same anamorphic lens is designed be attached to the projector. This leads to some distortion if the axis of the lens is not precisely perpendicular, and the image will appear skewed if it is not fitted correctly. The effect is shown in Figure 4-5. Professional anamorphic lenses are integral to the camera optics and are factory aligned.

4.6.3 IMAX

The largest cinema format in current use is the IMAX theatre presentation. This is projected onto a screen that is 215 meters wide by 156 meters high. The audience sits abnormally close to this screen, therefore artifacts in the rendering process will be more visible than usual. For this reason the film must be rendered at quite a high resolution.

The film is presented on 70mm stock with the picture oriented sideways, and it passes horizontally through the projector. The frames occupy an area that is roughly three times the size of a normal 70mm frame, with a corresponding increase in resolution.

Figure 4-6 illustrates a single frame of IMAX film. Note the placement of the small circular holes. This ensures that the operator loads the film the correct side up.

Correctly adjusted   Off axis by 15 degrees

Figure 4-5 Incorrect anamorphic stretch.

IMAX 70 mm format

Imaging area
69.6 mm x 48.5 mm

Figure 4-6 IMAX film dimensions.

IMAX programs tend to be quite short. Due to the nature of the projection equipment and the way the film is spooled, older installations were limited to a maximum time of 120 minutes. Upgrades to the projector extend this to 150 minutes. IMAX movies are also projected at 48 frames per second. This will reduce the available run time to 75 minutes.

Some IMAX programs are shot in 3D, giving a separate image to the left and right eye. Compression work to display this content on normal TV sets begins with a 50% reduction right off the bat, simply by choosing one or the other image. The 48 fps frame rate is used in IMAX presentations to produce a pair of images for 3D, interleaved, with left and right on alternate frames, effectively presenting a 24 fps frame rate.

4.6.4   VistaVision

One format of note is VistaVision. This is shot on 70mm film stock running horizontally, which is the same way IMAX film travels through the projector gate. In this case the format is an ultra-wide aspect ratio. In fact, VistaVision uses one of the largest possible imaging areas of any film format (the Todd-AO format is a similar size). While it was used by production companies in the 1960s, all the available cameras were later acquired by Lucasfilm during the production of the early Star Wars movies because they found it to be ideal for use in special effects work. They adapted and modified the format throughout their work on these films. Figure 4-7 shows an example of the VistaVision film format.

Working digitally makes most of these formats obsolete, so optical film is usually just 35 or 70mm for projection.

The imaging area on 70mm film stock is approximately 48.5mm by 22.1mm. If this were scanned at the maximum 115 pixels per mm, resolution would yield a picture that is 5577×2541.

The corresponding imaging area on 35mm film is of course much smaller at 21.0×15.2mm (2415×1748).

VistaVision
35 mm format

Imaging area
37.72 mm x 20.4 mm

Note action safe area

Figure 4-7 VistaVision film dimensions.

Refer to Appendix D for a summary of the image sizes and nominal bit rates for uncompressed digitized footage.

4.7   Semi-Professional and News-gathering Formats

Before portable video cameras were available at a size, cost, and performance that was suitable for news-gathering, reportage took place with 16mm cameras and the film stock had to be physically taken to a lab and then converted with a telecine system. This introduced enormous delays in getting the content to air.

A lot of this original footage has probably been lost over the years, but with more restoration work being done and the gradual opening of archives, some of this material may still come to light and require processing through a video-compression system.

All the issues covered already with cinematic film apply here with the additional consideration that the imaging rectangle of 16mm film is smaller. The consequence is that the pixel size of the images is smaller and the relative grain size is effectively twice that of 35mm film. The results you get from 35mm will therefore be much better than 16mm.

Figure 4-8 shows the 16mm film format. Note the optical audio track. There is a variety of audio formats for 16- and 35mm film, and extracting the audio is quite a different challenge from dealing with the image frames. This audio track is run continuously through the projector while the images are pulled through the gate one frame at a time.

The audio is offset by some distance from the frame to which it should be synchronized. This is necessary because the sound pickup cannot be mounted adjacent to the film gate. If it were, the sound would suffer from the non-linear way that the film is pulled through the gate. The solution is to offset the audio and allow a loop of film in the projector

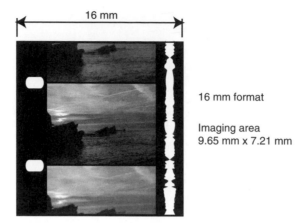

16 mm format

Imaging area
9.65 mm x 7.21 mm

Figure 4-8 16mm film dimensions.

mechanism to smooth out the motion so that the film can be passed over the sound pickup at a constant speed. The audio bandwidth is limited by the speed of the film and the grain size of the emulsion.

The image size for standard 16mm film is 9.65mm × 7.21mm, and using the reference point of 115 pixels per mm as the highest resolvable scanning quality, a maximum image size of 1110 × 829 is possible. This is coincidentally similar to emerging HDTV standards, making the 16mm material suitable for transfer to HDTV. The perceived viewing quality will be slightly less than video that is shot at HDTV resolution due to the grain size.

4.8 Home Movie Formats

There were mainly three movie film formats used by amateur photographers before the introduction of portable VHS equipment in the 1970s:

- Pathé baby 9.5mm, used until around 1950
- Standard 8mm, popular during the 1950s and 60s
- Super 8mm, popular during the 1970s until video replaced it in the 1980s

4.8.1 Pathé Baby 9.5mm

During the early to middle part of the 20th century, the 9.5mm format was widely used. The archives are likely to contain quite a lot of interesting material shot by enthusiastic amateurs in this format. The *9.5mm* format was unusual in that it had a single center-located sprocket, where all the other formats either have sprocket holes at both sides of the film for professional use or down one side only for amateur/semi-professional use. This is shown clearly in Figure 4-9.

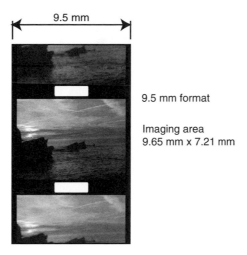

9.5 mm format

Imaging area
9.65 mm x 7.21 mm

Figure 4-9 9.5mm film dimensions.

The imaging rectangle for this format would be approximately 978 × 736, which is quite good for an amateur film format. The only material I have ever seen in this format is black and white, and any color footage would be very rare indeed. Very little of this material has a sound track associated with it, although it was possible to add a magnetic stripe to the edge of the film and use the projector with an auxiliary sound unit.

Scanning this material is somewhat problematic because 9.5mm telecine units are quite rare. There are specialists who will scan this material for you, or you could build a telecine unit of your own. The center sprocket hole is also the source of a lot of film damage and ghosting artifacts when watching this format. If the shutter and film movement are not perfectly synchronized in the projector, you will see the sprocket hole projected on the screen. Figure 4-10 illustrates the effect.

Most formats place the sprocket holes so they are offset from the horizontal position of the picture.

A 2K scanner has more than sufficient resolving power for film sizes of 16mm and below. For example, scanning 8mm film with a 4K scanner just wastes time because the detail isn't there to begin with.

4.8.2 Standard 8mm

In the 1950s, home movie enthusiasts embraced the standard 8mm format and it became very popular. The image rectangle on this film stock is the smallest of all the commonly used formats. Scanning the projected area at 115 pixels per millimeter will yield an image size of approximately 529 × 391. This is somewhat smaller than TV resolution even at standard definition. Grain size is going to be a significant problem with scanned material from this format. Figure 4-11 shows the layout of standard 8mm film.

Figure 4-10 9.5mm Sprocket hole ghosting.

Note that the sprocket holes interfere with the picture. The cameras would often overscan the image area, and the aperture in the projector gate was made somewhat smaller than the camera gate aperture so as to crop the projected image. This also helped to hide the gate weave in the camera. The actual size of images on 8mm film is quite variable, and a casual search of the Web reveals a variety of different sizes and specifications. The values quoted here are approximate. The make and model of the camera the film was exposed in will determine the actual image dimensions on the emulsion.

If you are digitally scanning the film, it is a good idea to extract a slightly larger image area than if you project the movie and film the result with a video camera. You will also get a better-quality image that will be more stable.

4.8.3 Super 8mm

Super 8mm superseded the standard 8mm format in the 1970s and provided a larger image size. It also had the advantage that the unexposed film was delivered in a single 50-foot reel of 8mm stock and was mounted inside a cartridge. This made loading the camera much easier and less prone to fogging the already exposed film.

Figure 4-12 illustrates how this format is different from the standard 8mm layout. Note, for example, that the sprocket holes are oriented so the long axis is aligned with the film. This allows a little extra room for an enlarged picture area. The frame sizes are bigger and the film would run to a slightly shorter playback time when projected.

Digitally scanned image sizes for this format would yield a raster that is almost the same as a standard-definition TV picture in the USA at 633 × 460 pixels. Grain size is still

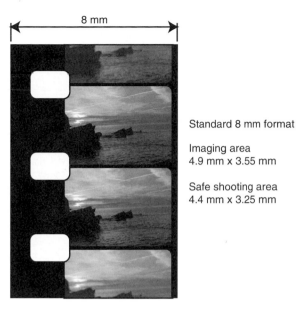

Standard 8 mm format

Imaging area
4.9 mm x 3.55 mm

Safe shooting area
4.4 mm x 3.25 mm

Figure 4-11 Standard 8mm film dimensions.

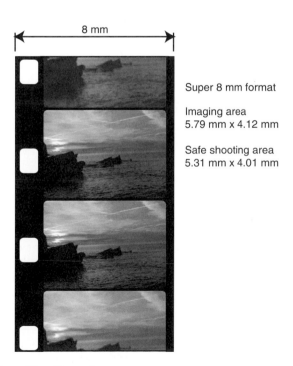

Super 8 mm format

Imaging area
5.79 mm x 4.12 mm

Safe shooting area
5.31 mm x 4.01 mm

Figure 4-12 Super 8mm film dimensions.

an issue with this format, but slightly less so than for standard 8mm. This is somewhat smaller than European TV picture sizes, though.

The camera gate is still larger than the projector gate, so there is some variability of image size according to how you scan it in.

4.9 Audio Synchronization

Be aware that the audio track is running at the same speed as the film being transported through the projector but is not placed adjacent to the frame to which it should be synchronized. The 8mm home movie film format has a de-facto standard 56-frame offset. This distance is different for all formats, and there is no guarantee that the films you are converting have the same offset even though they are shot on the same size stock.

Digitizing the picture and sound separately is a good idea. Modern nonlinear editing systems allow the audio and video to be processed independently of each other and then merged back together on the desktop. The timing of the audio may need to be adjusted so it is the same as the video. The start and end of both media must coincide, and any lip sync might need to be fixed. Resampling the audio within your editing system will correct the sample rate, although you may want to perform that in an external audio-processing application to achieve the best-possible quality.

If you are doing a lot of this work, investing in some good audio-processing tools would be worthwhile. Final Cut Pro on the Macintosh is supplemented by adding a copy of the Apple/E-Magic Logic application.

Apart from Logic, MacOS supports other tools such as Bias Deck, Peak or Cubase, and Pro Tools. PC-based systems can deploy tools that work well with Avid editors or Adobe Premier. Pro Tools is a good example. There are many other alternatives for Windows users and far fewer for Linux.

Bear in mind that for some formats, the speed of the film through the projector will seriously affect the available audio bandwidth. For 8mm movie film, the frequency range is between 35 Hz and 9 KHz, which results in a lot of top-end loss, and audio resolution is therefore somewhat limited. This plays into your hands, though, when compressing the audio, as the reduced detail yields some slight bit-rate benefits.

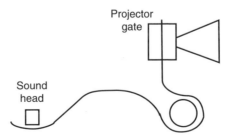

Figure 4-13 Audio track offset on film.

When working with 16mm film, the audio bandwidth will be higher. The audio bandwidth of 35mm film should go well beyond the audible range of a human ear, depending on whether it uses a magnetic stripe or an optical track on the edge of the film.

4.10 Magnetic Stripe for Sound Recording

There is certain to be some interesting archival material in people's attics, and during the 1960s a small UK-based company called SuperSound developed a method of adding a stripe of magnetic tape down the sprocketed edge of the film so that a sound track could be added. Figure 4-14 shows where the stripe was placed.

Wider-gauge film required a balancing stripe so that the film could be spooled evenly. Adding the stripe reduced the amount of film that could be carried on the spools because it was thicker and couldn't therefore wind as tightly. Note also that the stripe is on the emulsion side. Be aware of this when scanning because it offsets the emulsion away from the focal plane of the scanner, and this might slightly blur the scanned image.

The development of this striping technology spawned a successful business that either added the stripe to customers' films or sold them the equipment and materials to do it themselves. Figure 4-15 shows a photograph of the striper unit that you could buy and use at home. These were marketed all over the world during the 1960s, which means there may be significant quantities of archival 8mm material out there that also has an interesting sound track.

Film stock was available in monochrome and color and was based on a 16mm stock that was turned over after the first pass through the camera. The film was then slit down the middle during processing and spliced together before sending back to the photographer. Typical film roll sizes were 25, 50, 100, and 200 feet long. A roll of 16mm stock was supplied on 25-foot spools and played for about 4 minutes when slit and returned from processing as a 50-foot reel. The exact time depended on the shooting frame rate, which could be between 18 and 24 fps. This short duration somewhat limited the creative possibilities, although some enthusiasts edited together programs of several hours at what must have been an extraordinarily high cost.

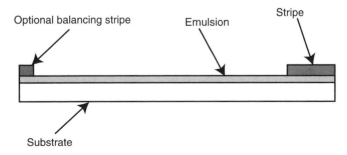

Figure 4-14 Placement of the magnetic sound stripe on the film.

Figure 4-15 Supersound super stripe unit.

The same technique for adding sound stripe down the sprocketed edge of the film was provided by Supersound for all the major film gauges that were in common use at the time.

4.11 Telecine

Film is scanned using a telecine unit when converting to video, or a film scanner when making a digital version for computer manipulation. Professional systems are very expensive and way beyond the means of the amateur user with a collection of home movies to process.

4.11.1 How Telecine Works

Film-to-TV transfer has been around for some time. There are fundamentally two technical solutions. One is to present a moving point source of light that scans the film surface using the same technique as a TV set; the other is to use a charge coupled device (CCD) sensor. The older technique is to place a cathode ray tube (CRT) at one end of the machine and fly a spot across it. The film is then positioned between that flying spot and the light sensor. Optical components collimate (or make parallel) the light transmitted through the film, and the analog waveform is recorded. This design works well because it mimics exactly the way a TV picture is produced but in reverse. Figure 4-16 shows how this works.

The resolution of the output of a flying spot scanner is fixed at 2K or 4K or whatever the manufacturer provides. The film is positioned and optical components introduced so that the scanning area completely covers the frame. Resolution is inferred from the fixed 2K/4K sizes and the physical size of the film substrate.

Flatbed scanners that have backlight hoods for scanning film have a fixed resolution and yield a varying-sized pixel image according to the area of the film being scanned. A flying spot telecine always yields the same-sized image. This is another subtle point that you need to understand to ensure you get what you want out of the scanner.

Modern scanners are more precise and have a CCD device lit by a projected image of the film, and the electronics are very similar to those of a digital camera. This design is technically superior since the imaging component creates a much better-quality result. The recorded image is crisper and less prone to analog noise artifacts. This arrangement is shown in figure 4-17.

The downside of the flying spot scanner is that the beam intensity is not 100% stable all the time. The linearity and convergence of the telecine must be carefully adjusted and

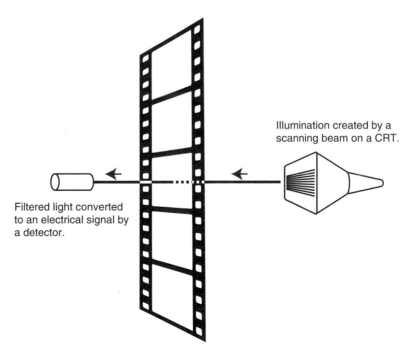

Illumination created by a scanning beam on a CRT.

Filtered light converted to an electrical signal by a detector.

Figure 4-16 Flying spot scanner.

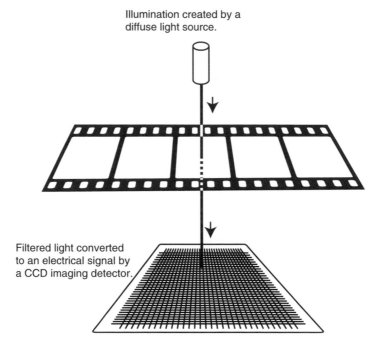

Illumination created by a
diffuse light source.

Filtered light converted
to an electrical signal by
a CCD imaging detector.

Figure 4-17 Modern CCD scanner.

calibrated regularly. The beam has a halo that reduces the focus and some blurring is evident if this is not correctly calibrated. This defocusing effect or softening of the beam edges is an artifact of CRT tubes and is called the Kell effect. Spot shape is adjustable in some TV receivers, and making the beam oval prevents some twittering artifacts when the beam shape is vertically oriented in an interlaced system. This allows the beam edges to overlap slightly on successive lines. Flattening the beam horizontally sacrifices resolution across the screen.

4.11.2 Pulldown—60 Hz Frame Rate

In the United States, the frame rate of the film must be altered from 24 to 30 fps. Running the film at a faster frame rate is not a viable solution. The change in motion is too extreme and everything will appear to be *over-cranked*.

The trick is to introduce an extra frame every now and then. By keeping an occasional frame in the gate slightly longer, the time base is stretched.

To attain a smooth pulldown and an integer relationship between the frame rate of the film and video, the film is run a little slower than normal (at 23.97 fps instead of 24 fps). The first frame is transferred to the first 2 fields and the second frame to the next 3 fields. At this point, the film is out of synchronization with the interlaced field structure of the video. If this is repeated for the next 2 frames as well, the fields and frames will come back into sync. Over the course of 4 frames of film, 5 frames of video are created (or 10 fields of video). Figure 4-18 shows how these frames are mapped between the two kinds of media.

This is called 3-2 pulldown but is more accurately described as 2-3 pulldown because it better describes the input-to-output transformation.

The *QuickTime* software developed by Apple has tools built in to remove or add this pulldown conversion. In fact, most compression tools on all platforms provide support for this as well. Uniquely, the QuickTime platform provides it in a way that you can exploit from within your own applications.

Because the pulldown is distributed evenly throughout the time base, the effect is imperceptible until you push the pause button on a video recorder and you often see frames on the TV screen that appear to contain a double image. This is only obvious when there is some movement.

You also occasionally see this artifact when running video input cards in preview mode or when you monitor an incoming DV stream via FireWire. That is just an artifact of the monitoring stream, and when you play the ingested video back it looks fine.

Because the movie is running a little slower, the overall run time is a little longer. Since the change is only 3%, it makes hardly any difference.

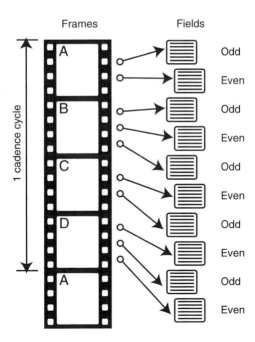

Figure 4-18 Film-to-video pulldown.

Editing of the video must be sensitive to these transfers. For example, editing anywhere other than at 5-frame intervals changes the cadence of the starting frame of a 5-frame sequence. The viewer may not notice the change in cadence, but it does make subsequent processing of that footage very difficult. If you are editing interlaced video, then after an inverse telecine process the *field dominance* could be compromised and fields after the edit may exhibit a twittering effect. As long as the edit point is an integer multiple of 5 frames, then this problem will not occur. That constraint is a very large burden to place on a film editor. It is much better to compress from the unedited original material.

4.11.3 Pulldown—50 Hz Frame Rate

The techniques that work for transferring film to 30 fps video will not work for transfer to 25 fps video in Europe. The European TV frame rate is much closer to the correct frame rate for film. To use a pulldown effect requires that we introduce just one additional frame per second. This produces a noticeable flicker in the movement, so it is not used as a solution.

Transfers to 30 fps video run the film a little slower, and that does not materially alter the sound quality. Running 24 fps film at 25 fps looks okay visually because the motion is only slightly faster. The pitch of the sound is increased noticeably and must be corrected. Pitch correction is tricky because you must preserve synchronization or the lip sync gets off track.

You are also freed from the cadence and field dominance issues because there are no pulldown frame cadences to consider.

4.11.4 Line-Based Telecine Transfer

A more sophisticated approach is to index the film at 24 fps and scan the appropriate lines of the raster. This results in a frame of video containing portions of two frames of film. There is no obvious pulldown happening. Determining which part of a composite frame belongs to one or the other of the original 24 FPS source is very hard indeed unless there are some obvious clues. This would require some sophisticated image processing software to compare one frame of video with another and see which lines have changed between successive frames or corresponding odd or even fields.

4.12 Building Your Own Telecine System

It might be feasible (and fun, perhaps) to construct your own film scanner using some components that are cannibalized from other sources.

4.12.1 Choosing a Film Scanner

The most expensive part of building your own system will be the film scanner. You will require one that has a straight path through the unit, and you will also have to manufac-

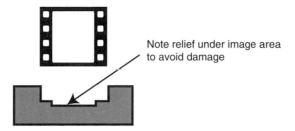

Figure 4-19 Film guide cross-section.

ture a gate to hold the film steady as it passes through. This need not be anything more complex than a film guide, but you must be careful to protect the imaging area of the film to avoid scratching it, as you see in Figure 4-19.

Rather than use a slide scanner, consider carefully dismantling a video camera and using the imaging system in that. Some high-end Telecine manufacturers such as CTM Debrie Cinematography use Sony *HDCAM* components on an OEM basis to build their systems.

4.12.2 Film Transport

Next you have to construct a framework to create a film path through the scanner. You will need a couple of film pulleys. Most important for driving the film through, you will require a suitable sprocket for the film gauge you are using. But there is no need to manufacture a proper film gate with a claw mechanism. Dismantling a broken film projector will yield the parts you need.

If you place a friction pulley on one side of the gate and a motorized sprocket to pull it through the gate from the other side, this will provide sufficient control. The film must remain taut. There are other tensioning devices available, and perhaps the cannibalized projector will yield up a sprung double-pulley tensioner.

A projector synchronizes the movements of the film and the shutter by a complex mechanism of gears and cams as discussed at the beginning of this chapter. That is

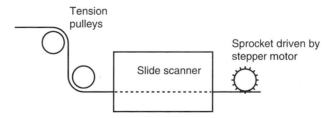

Figure 4-20 Film path through scanner.

CTM Debrie Cinematography: http://www.ctmsolutions.com/

unnecessary here because our exposure time happens under software control. The film must be moved through the gate, advancing by one frame's worth of distance each time.

Attach a stepper motor to the sprocket drive to provide the motive force. Stepper motors are obtained by dismantling old floppy-disk drives to remove the head-positioning motor. An interface is required to contrive some kind of electrical connection to the computer, and one of the servo control interfaces used by amateur robotics enthusiasts would do. Some of these I/O controllers are now available as USB connected devices. Controlling this machinery should not involve any particularly complex driver writing.

4.12.3 Software Support

Once the whole machine is assembled, two sets of utility code must be provided.

The first one will control the stepper motor. This must be moved one step forward at a time. The code is called a number of times depending on the distance from one frame to the next, measured in steps. Hopefully the step distance will be small enough that there is an integer relationship between the two.

The second part of the utility software is designed to drive the film scanner in order to capture a frame. Scanning the whole 35mm film surface area is not necessary, as the device was likely a 35mm slide scanner to start with. The *API* support in the TWAIN interface will provide the support necessary to frame the scanning area so it just covers the imaged part of the film. This is known to be feasible here because it is done all the time with paper scanners during a preview and crop. They use the same TWAIN driver code.

4.12.4 Running the Process

Scanning the full 8mm width will include the sprocket holes. That provides a reference that will reduce the software-process tracking errors later on.

An application uses these utilities to drive the stepper motor and take a snapshot. That application could just capture the frames as a series of still images or make a movie file one frame at a time.

After a successful run, the application will have created a file containing a digitized version of the film at probably as good a resolution as it is possible to achieve (depending on the quality of the film scanner you start with). Some remedial work to stabilize any camera gate weave and crop the output will be necessary.

Some variants on this theme are possible if the scanner is driven one line of pixels at a time. In that case alternating steps of the film transport and the scanning head will yield a continuous series of scan lines that will then need to be sliced into frames. This will deliver a slightly more stable scanned result. The quality of the whole project is dependent on your mechanical skills and how well you conceive the software to process the results. This design will eliminate the gate weave you normally get with a projector because the film is being moved far more gently through the gate. None of the scanners can eliminate the gate weave from the camera because that is an integral part of the film once it has been exposed. We stabilize the footage in software to remove that problem.

4.13   Ingest and Restoration

Any currently existing movie film from the 8mm era is likely to have faded. After scanning this material in, at least some color correction is going to be necessary to get the best result. Modern compression software provides this. Software like Final Cut Pro or Premier will work from the raw, uncorrected footage if necessary. Their built-in color-correction capabilities can be used during the editing session. Of course, this color correction is unnecessary for black and white film. However, contrast enhancement will be required to eliminate over- or underexposure.

4.13.1   Spliced Joints

There will be significant problems with spliced joints in this old material. The older stock was spliced with acetone glue that welded the two parts together. The same is true for any Supersound stripe that was attached to the film. Later materials were based on a polyester substrate, and during the 1970s various alternatives using short pieces of transparent tape were tried because there were no readily available solvents for polyester at the time. Significant cleanup and restorative attention will be necessary. When handling archive material, the telecine process must be very kind to the film and not cause it to be twisted or bent around tight pulleys and sprockets more than necessary. Modern transports carry the film gently and steadily through the scanning area with a smooth and flowing motion. This avoids damage due to the stop/start jerking movement that a projector has to deploy.

Figures 4-21 to 4-23 show a cross-sectional view of the film to illustrate some of the splicing techniques you will encounter when digitizing old film stock. The beveled-edge splice is quite weak and will break when the glue deteriorates. If this splice is done carefully at the frame boundaries, it is hard to detect in the projected image.

The undercut splice is stronger but damages a larger area of the film. In fact, it tends to completely ruin a frame of 8mm film. It is less likely to break due to the glue, but the film is quite weak at the ends of the joint.

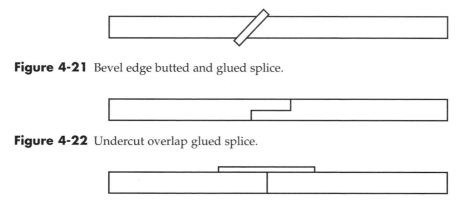

Figure 4-21 Bevel edge butted and glued splice.

Figure 4-22 Undercut overlap glued splice.

Figure 4-23 Adhesive taped splice.

The adhesive tape splice was introduced so that the polyester film could be edited. This was necessary because there wasn't a usable solvent available. Quite a large area of the film is obscured, but the tape is transparent enough that it is actually harder to detect than the glued undercut joint.

All of the splices will cause some gate weave and disruption to the smooth motion of the film through a gate. Specially designed gates or stepper-based movements will allow splices to go through without impeding the film movement. If you are building a telecine system, you must consider this issue, because otherwise the film will be displaced as it passes through the gate.

4.13.2 Fogging

Many amateur filmmakers were caught out when turning over the 8mm film to shoot the other side. The film occasionally slipped out of the roll, and unless you used a black bag to change the film, there was a risk of spoiling your movie. This caused many films to be exposed to some light as the film was exchanged. The result is a yellowish fogging effect down the first few feet of film. If this fogging is not too severe, some careful restorative image processing could clean it up once the film has been scanned in. Figure 4-24 shows what this looks like. It is usually fogged down the sprocketed edge of the film.

4.13.3 Surface Damage

When dealing with film as a source, you must consider the implications of dust and scratches. There used to be proprietary formulations that you could apply to films to clean them. They involved mixing all manner of carcinogenic chemicals (carbon tetrachloride—carpet cleaner—and paraffin wax for example) and applying them to the film. The wax dissolved in the carpet cleaner and as that evaporated, it left a waxy deposit on the film. It is sufficient to make sure the film is scanned in a dust-free environment rather than risk damaging your film with chemicals. Passing it between a pair of lightly sprung felt pads would remove any accretions. Any remaining particulate matter will become an integral part of the scan. This has to be removed using some image-processing code.

4.13.4 Physical Structure of Film

Before we consider how dust and scratches affect the film, we need to examine how film is physically structured. Up to now we've been looking through the film and discussing the imaging area in its normal viewing aspect. If we turn the film sideways and examine it from the edge, we can see that it is made up a series of layers sandwiched together. Figure 4-25 illustrates the structure.

Various depredations have been perpetrated on this piece of film, each one resulting in some reduction in image quality. The shortcut solution when restoring is just to isolate the area of damage and fill in the missing fragments by interpolation. A more scientific approach requires that each kind of damage be identified and treated accordingly.

Figure 4-24 Severely fogged 8mm film.

Table 4-3 describes the different kinds of damage shown in Figure 4-25. The item numbers in the table correspond to the numbers in the figure.

4.13.5 Dust and Scratches

A better-quality transfer will be achieved if the dust is cleaned off to start with. Figure 4-26 shows an example with some dust and scratches.

Because film is often passed through various positive and negative stages, dust will appear as white or black dots. Any dust on the negative will cause a white dot on the final output, and this is far more annoying than a dust particle on the positive film. Hairs in the gate of the telecine unit are also very annoying.

4.13.6 Severe Damage

Damage in the form of bad splices, tears, broken sprocket holes, and peeled emulsion require manual restoration to be applied. Once the film has been captured into the computer, much of this becomes quite easy to do. The process is sometimes arduous and time consuming, but a painstaking approach could yield a true gem of a movie from something that was simply unwatchable as projected film. Figure 4-27 shows a couple of examples. Both happen to be near the edge of the frame.

Being very gentle in the handling and scanning of film is of prime importance, and reducing the number of times the film is despooled and passed through a film transport

Table 4-3 Repairing the Damage

Item	Solution
1	Minor scratch to the film base substrate material on the side away from the emulsion. This will cause some light scattering and depending on whether the film is lit from the back or front, that will cause a spread of the illumination when the film is scanned. Lit from the back, a larger area of emulsion will be illuminated. Lit from the front, a few pixels will be scattered over a wider area due to the refractive effect. The result is a slight blurring over a localized area. De-blurring algorithms can usually correct this problem. Localizing them is somewhat tricky.
2	This is a minor scratch to the protective layer over the emulsion. Similar refractive problems occur. Because this scratch is nearer the emulsion, the blurring effect will be less. Use the same fix as for Item 1.
3	This is a very deep scratch through the protective layer and in this example, it has actually removed the yellow emulsion layer and partly damaged the magenta layer. Added to the refractive effects are actual color changes and loss of information. Blurring effects don't lose information, they just move it around, but this has effectively obliterated part of the picture. The only kind of repair you can do for this is reconstruction of the missing area.
4	This is a large piece of dust that prevents the light from getting through. Dust on the intermediate negative prints will show up as white spots. Reconstructing the missing pixels is the solution.
5	Fingerprints show as a distinctive pattern of light and shade. The oil in the fingerprint causes a refractive effect, but removing it is hard because the edges are complex and there is a large and odd-shaped area to correct. Blurring the edges might hide the effects, but you should make sure there isn't a noticeable difference between the frame with the fingerprint and the ones on either side. A temporal interpolation may fix this.
6	Films or smears of oily material or the results of getting the emulsion wet may show up as an area that is slightly discolored. You may only have to deal with the edges if the deposit has no color-changing effects. Temporal interpolation or manual rotoscoping the area to correct might be necessary.

is obviously a wise thing. Projectors that are badly adjusted will seriously damage a film. Lacing a projector incorrectly and turning it on will rip the sprockets. Not allowing the film to loop sufficiently on either side of the gate causes the claw mechanism to fight the drive sprockets and do terrible damage to the film as it is projected. All it requires is a little care and attention when projecting your film. Once your film is damaged like this, it is very hard to repair. Thankfully, as long as the imaging area is intact, film restoration can now take place in the computer.

Assembling a toolkit of software for this kind of restoration is likely to take some time and will be quite expensive unless you write the programs yourself. Some tools may be available as shareware or open source. Having Photoshop, After Effects, Final Cut, Commotion, Shake, Ultimatte, and various other graphics tools on hand will speed up the process. These tools range from a few hundred dollars to several thousand. Whether you should purchase them is partly dependent on your ability to use them to generate revenue from your film restoration work. You don't need to buy them all, but they can help you solve problems. Chapter 30 discusses some alternatives to add to your shopping list when planning your system. Appendix C describes a few more.

4.13.7 The RACINE-S project

The collaborative RACINE-S project is exploring how to restore historical footage with large sections of missing frames or audio. The project's goal is to be able to replace the missing material in real time. A variety of companies and academic institutions are involved and are publishing useful material about the project.

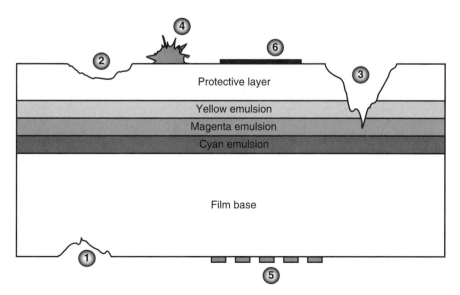

Figure 4-25 Film structure and damage.

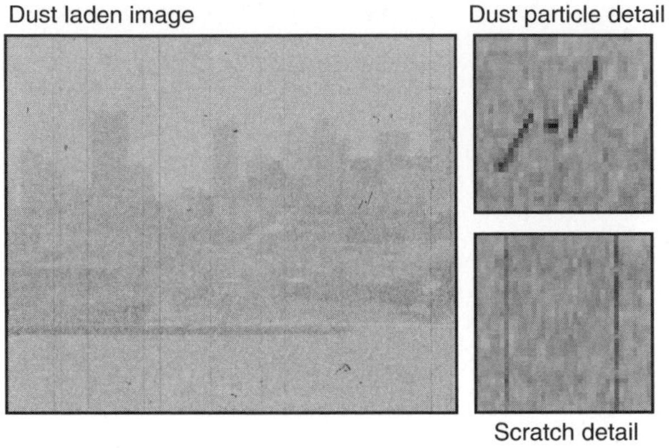

Dust laden image   Dust particle detail

Scratch detail

Figure 4-26 Dust and scratches.

Tears and punctures after scanning damaged film

Figure 4-27 Examples of film damage.

4.13.8 Hardware Solutions

The Cintel company that makes Telecine units has a product called Oliver that is designed to cope with damaged film as it is scanned. It fixes the effects of a scratch by looking for areas where the refractive damage has occurred and recombining the scattered light with a clever algorithm to restore the image.

Snell and Wilcox offer similar restorative equipment (Alchemist.PhC) for video content. This may be useful for restoring film as well.

4.14 Digital Intermediate Processes

The traditional way of making movies was purely mechanical. Splices were done manually and the color grading was done with filters and timed exposures. Although they are automated now, the processes have been fundamentally the same for many years.

Cintel International Ltd.: http://www.cintel.com/

Snell & Wilcox: http://www.snellwilcox.com/

Table 4-4 RACINE-S Project Participants

Company	Expertise
Arri	Developing a portable scanner for all available formats.
Pandora International	Developing the processing hardware required to run the restoration processes.
FSSG	Software to regenerate speech. They call this virtual dubbing. They are also looking at the acoustical enhancement of audio recording and reproduction systems.
Cineca	User interface being developed using VR techniques.
University of Glasgow	Interpolation software to replace or repair damaged and missing imagery.
Androme	Collaborating with the University of Glasgow on joint research projects to develop multimedia software and restoration techniques.
Limberg Univeritair Centrum (LUC)	Collaborating with the University of Glasgow on joint software tool development projects.
Cinecitta	Integration and bench testing to establish whether the restoration algorithms work satisfactorily, and feeding back to the researchers.

If the film is digitized and the color correction is done digitally, it can then be printed back onto film for distribution. This digital intermediate (DI) introduces an opportunity to improve the workflow and provide additional tools to the filmmaker.

Scanning the film in at the earliest possible point enables the editing to be done electronically. This is very beneficial. The integration of special effects or corrective "surgery" other than just grading the film can then be used to easily add or remove elements, or perform sky replacement or compositional adjustment to frame the content more attractively.

Shooting on HDCAM equipment eliminates the scanning process altogether at the expense of losing the organic quality of film grain. That quality can be reintroduced during the finishing phase. The process of shooting and editing a movie is shown in Figure 4-28. The top row of boxes is the traditional mechanical process and the bottom is

RACINE-S: http://www.racine.eu.com/ Arri: http://www.arri.com/

Pandora International: http://pogle.pandora-int.com/

FSSG: http://www.cini.ve.cnr.it/

Cineca: http://www.cineca.it/

University of Glasgow: http://www.gla.ac.uk/

Androme: http://www.androme.be/

LUC: http://www.luc.ac.be/

Cinecitta: http://wwwcinecittastudios.it/

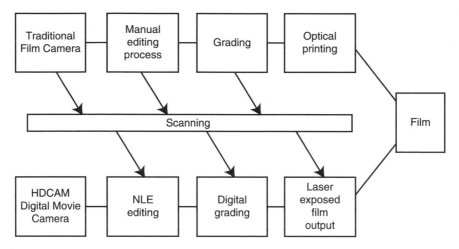

Figure 4-28 Digital intermediate workflow.

the all-digital workflow. You can see there are opportunities to move from the traditional workflow to the digital intermediate form whenever you need to.

The digital revolution is pervading and affecting every aspect of film and TV production, and video compression is critical to the success of the industry from one end to the other.

A significant advantage of the digital intermediate process is that an archival copy of the film is retained in a digital form. Since this was scanned from the original pristine footage, there is very little likelihood of damage, dust, scratches, or other artifacts being introduced. The colors in the picture will not fade over time the way the film emulsion would. Archiving becomes easier and repurposing to other formats such as DVD is a much simpler process. This also facilitates the migration to D-cinema and the electronic delivery of movies.

Archiving over hundreds of years is becoming an issue with digital content, and some current studies are examining the aging of storage media and the most reliable file formats to interface with systems that won't even exist for several hundred years. This might seem an odd subject to be talking about in a book on video compression, but it is quite important that future generations be able to decode the material that we store today. You should bear that in mind when choosing a codec for archival purposes.

4.15 Summary

This chapter has touched on a lot of different aspects of how filmed images work. There are, however, many film formats that have not been covered here. Studying this topic on the Internet reveals a large number and variety of Web sites that describe some very odd film formats. In addition, you will find some information in the appendices about frame sizes and formats.

As you work with archival film sources, keep in mind that the exact size and resolution of film stock varies considerably and that the values quoted here for picture sizes are nominal guidelines only. The chapter on digital imaging revisits the commonly used 2K, 4K, and 6K resolutions for digital film work.

The caveat stated at the beginning of this chapter applies here too: The resolution chosen for calculating image sizes is based on quoted values from a variety of sources. However, you may scan at a higher or lower resolution than the 115 pixels per mm used here. You will need to make adjustments to take that into account if you are doing any capacity planning. Your mileage may vary.

In the next two chapters, video and digital imaging are studied. A few minor issues having to do with film will come up again later on in the discussion of some of the more esoteric aspects of video compression.

5

Video

5.1 On the Matter of Video

During this segment of our journey we will examine the video source material that you might want to compress. We will start with the frame size and layout, and then move on to analog-to-digital conversion and synchronization of the video, all of which is related to the content of a line of picture information. The chapter is rounded out by considering color information and how it is converted from *RGB* to luma and chroma.

5.2 Video Is Not Film

Television is much more complicated than film. It involves several interlocking concepts that interact with one another. The way the picture is represented electronically and the techniques for color encoding influence how it is converted from an analog form into a digital form. This also has implications for how the compression works. The technicality of how video works is a book-length topic in itself. In order to cover it in just a chapter, a lot of the fine detail has to be put to one side.

The imaging mechanisms for film and TV are different. The technology requires that certain processing be done to deliver a satisfactory broadcast within the available bandwidth.

Television pictures are composed of a series of horizontal lines arranged in a sequence that scans down the entire screen from top to bottom. This is called a *raster*. The number of lines and how they are ordered in the scanning sequence depend on the kind of display being driven and where in the world the TV signal is being broadcast.

European TV is closer to movie film projection than the American system because the display frame rates are similar, but it is still different.

If only it were possible to go back in time and reinvent some of these things. Just changing the frame rate of projected film or adjusting the way that pictures are displayed to use progressive scanning instead of interlacing on TV sets would make the world a much simpler place for video compressionists. The following factors are all relevant to understanding how TV works and by implication how compression has to work:

- Picture sizes on different TV systems
- Frame rates in the United States, Europe, and elsewhere
- Aspect ratios and conversion between them
- Analog waveforms and how to code a digital image from them
- Coding of luma and chroma

5.3 Television Standards

There are a variety of standards that describe how TV is delivered. These have evolved over the years. New work is underway to accommodate high-definition formats and digital television delivery. The convergence between TV systems and computer imaging technology is also significantly affecting this. There are two principal standards for analog TV: *NTSC* and PAL. Some derivative standards are based on variants of these. In France, the *SECAM* system is used, but this is broadly similar to PAL.

5.4 Frame Rates

One of the things that you will encounter when compressing video is the capability to change the frame rate of the compressed output. You must be aware of the various source frame rates. If you are creating video to be played back on a variety of platforms, and they include TV systems, then choosing the wrong frame rate will detrimentally affect the quality of the playback experience.

Table 5-1 Analog TV Standards

Standard	Description
NTSC	NTSC is the way that analog TV is broadcast in the United States, although this does not actually describe a picture size, resolution, or frame rate.
PAL	The broadcasting TV standard in the UK is PAL. It is a coding and modulation scheme for transmitting video in the most economic bandwidth over analog broadcast systems. Therefore, it is an analog compression scheme and does not describe a physical presentation format.
SECAM	This is a transmission modulation technique used in some parts of Europe.

5.4.1 Comparing NTSC with PAL (60 Hz Versus 50 Hz)

To convert between NTSC and PAL services, the change in scan lines and the horizontal resolution is usually dealt with by simple interpolation in the X- and Y-axes. The frame rate is much harder to process because simply removing frames when going from 30 to 25 Hz leads to a somewhat jerky experience. Going the other way, from 25 to 30 Hz, requires the introduction of extra frames. Working with fields rather than frames does not solve the problem. Pulldown techniques that work for film do not work very well for video because the *interlace scanning* fields are not photographed at an identical moment in time. Therefore they cannot be averaged or repeated without some strange combing effects being introduced. Duplicating a single field is unsatisfactory because it has a spatial and temporal relationship to the adjacent fields before and after. Figure 5-1 shows these field-timing differences.

Digital systems with multiple frame stores provide the means to carry out the necessary temporal interpolation. Very good time-base conversion is possible with desktop tools such as Adobe After Effects and Apple Final Cut Pro. There are of course other alternatives to these, depending on the platform you use and the budget you have available.

5.4.2 Temporal Resampling

American TV transmissions run at approximately 30 frames per second—the actual frame rate is 29.97 frames per second. Because interlacing is used, this is really 60 fields per second. In the UK, Europe, and some other parts of the world, the values of 25 frames and 50 fields per second are applicable. Mixing content from both systems, or playing American content back in the UK and vice versa, causes problems.

Resampling the 2D raster image is simply a case of averaging or interpolating adjacent pixel values according to whether you are scaling down or up. Changing the frame rate is much more complicated because you must interpolate movement from one frame to the next and it is not happening uniformly across the picture.

Interlaced content is even more complex because pixels only correspond to one another in alternate fields, and adjacent fields are offset by the field time (one fiftieth or sixtieth of a second).

Thankfully you don't have to worry about this too much as there is now some very good software that makes changes to the frame rate. Products such as Final Cut Pro and

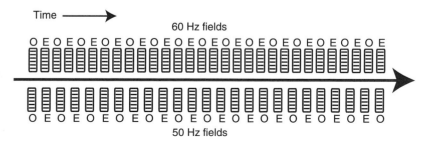

Figure 5-1 Frame rate relationships.

Adobe After Effects help with this problem. At the high end, professional users deploy tools such as Discreet Combustion and Pinnacle Commotion. All of these tools offer other useful capabilities as well.

5.4.3 Comparing Video with Film as a Source Input

When Hollywood movie films are broadcast on TV, the frame rates have to be adjusted so that the picture is played at a different frame rate. Film runs at 24 frames per second and opening the shutter twice for each frame reduces the flickering.

This is close to the frame rate of European broadcast systems, but it is a long way from the right frame rate for TV systems in the United States.

To change the frame rate without using the digital interpolation techniques is quite tricky, so a mechanical means of accomplishing this was developed that is called 2-3 or 3-2 pulldown. It is done differently for 60 Hz and 50 Hz field rates. (Chapter 4 discussed film formats and examined pulldown and telecine systems.)

5.4.4 Up-Rated Scanning

Some TV sets have a built-in frame store that is loaded with new pictures at a rate of 25 or 30 times per second. The output delivers the video to the screen at a 100 Hz frame rate. This significantly improves the viewing experience. The frame store also provides scaling and aspect-ratio correction. The digital scaling sometimes introduces subtle artifacts into the picture that are similar to those caused by over-compressing the source material.

5.5 Scanning Modes

In the descriptions of the different image sizes, terminology such as 1080i or 1080p is used to describe two alternative line-scanning patterns for HDTV. Standard definition (SDTV) generally has just an "i." This indicates whether the line scanning is interlaced or progressive.

> *The future of video everywhere is progressive, not interlaced.*
> *—Ben Waggoner, 2004*

This is certainly true, and the European Broadcasting Union (*EBU*) predicts that between 2009 and 2015, progressive HD-compatible displays will probably outnumber interlaced SDTV receivers.

Tests with H.264 and *WM9* encoders prove that they both encode progressively scanned video with a better efficiency (compression ratio) than they do interlaced video.

The delivery of progressively scanned content is preferable because it is easy to create interlaced material from it but much harder to go the other way. In any case, it is convincingly argued by the EBU that putting expensive and very-high-quality interlaced-to-progressive conversion equipment at the broadcaster's head-end installation is far better than deploying millions of less-capable, low-quality interlace-to-progressive converters embedded inside receivers in the home.

5.6 Interlaced Field Rasters

Interlaced scanning was introduced in the 1930s as a way to reduce the number of lines that must be transmitted to half of what was required for progressive scanning. This kind of presentation requires that the odd- and even-numbered lines be presented independently of one another. The presentation of interlaced lines is shown in Figure 5-2.

As the lines scan down the screen, the electron beam on a CRT display moves across the tube face, painting horizontal lines as it goes. When the beam reaches the bottom of the screen, it must go back to the top as quickly as possible to start the next downward pass. This fly back accounts for about 8% of the scanning time, so you end up losing some of the lines.

Note how a half line is necessary on each pass in order to properly interleave the lines in the odd and even fields. It is tempting to just crop those two lines when compressing the video. Very often the choices you make with a video processing operation will have consequences (or knock-on effects) later in the workflow. In this case, removing just a single line has a knock-on effect that potentially compromises the field dominance. Lines must be removed in adjacent pairs. So those half lines are actually going to cost 4 lines of image data. An alternative is to keep them, and work out how to fill the other half of each line. A simple copy from an adjacent line would probably be the best solution.

So the picture area is traversed twice, with one field being painted first and then on the second pass, the other field is painted with the lines filling in the gaps. Figure 5-3 shows how an object is painted on the screen.

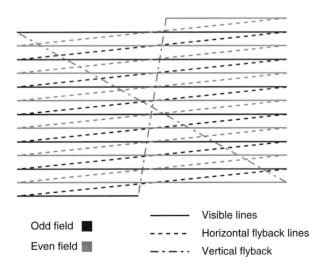

Odd field ■   ——— Visible lines

Even field ▨   - - - - - Horizontal flyback lines

                       — · — · · Vertical flyback

Figure 5-2 Interlaced scanning pattern.

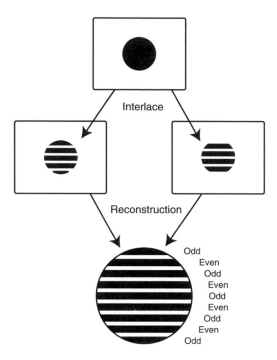

Figure 5-3 Interlaced field rasters.

Whether the odd or even field is painted first depends on what is called the field dominance. It is very important that this is maintained identically to how the footage was filmed because if it is not, a strange "twittering" effect is observed and all the motion seems very jerky. That is because every 25th of a second, the time base goes back by a 50th of a second—a "two steps forward and one step back" scenario—and it is not pleasant to watch. Figure 5-4 plots the time base for a correctly clocked field presentation and one that has its field dominance reversed.

5.6.1 Persistence of Vision

The time base of the picture movement is in a 50th of a second increment, based on the field times and not the frame times. The field rate is twice the frame rate, but none of the lines in the odd field are displaying a part of the image that exists in the even field. It is as if there are two separate but simultaneous and totally synchronized movies playing as far as any motion is concerned.

Because the tube phosphor glows for a little while after the electron beam has passed over it and our eyes have a "persistence of vision," you don't see this as two alternate scans. Instead your eyes aggregate it into a single image.

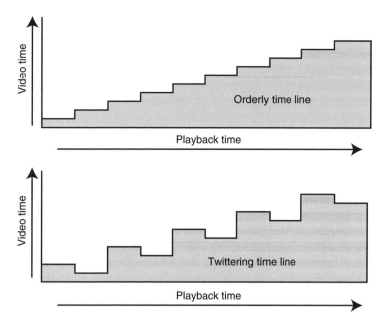

Figure 5-4 Time base twitter.

5.6.2 Horizontal Fine Detail

Interlaced video demands that certain fine horizontal detail gets special treatment. If you draw a 1 pixel-wide line across the screen, it will appear to flicker because for half the time it is not being displayed. If you increase the thickness to 2 pixels, it appears to bounce up and down because it is present in alternate fields at different times. This is called twittering. You must defocus the line in the vertical axis so it covers a slightly larger area, and the flickering effect is then reduced. See Figure 5-5.

   The top line will flicker at 25 Hz because it only appears in one field. The second line will appear to bounce 25 times a second because it appears in a different place in each field. The third line will appear stable because either a full-intensity line is visible or two half-intensity lines are visible, but the average position is always the center line. Hence the eye is fooled into thinking it is stationary.

5.6.3 Object Motion Between Fields

Another downside to interlaced video is that motion carries on between fields. A ball bouncing past the camera will be in different positions on the odd and even fields. Figure 5-6 shows the distribution of the object as it moves.

   If the original footage was shot on film and the telecine was transferred using a line-based algorithm rather than a pulldown, the effect is even grosser as shown in Figure 5-7.

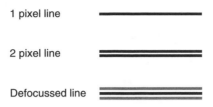

1 pixel line

2 pixel line

Defocussed line

Figure 5-5 Horizontal detail.

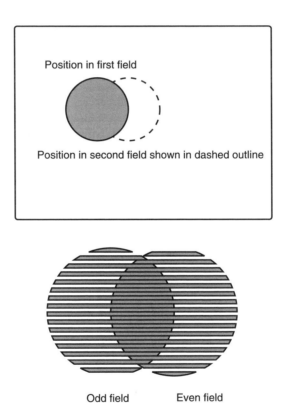

Position in first field

Position in second field shown in dashed outline

Odd field   Even field

Figure 5-6 Interlaced object movement.

Pausing the video so that both fields are displayed presents a very disturbed image with some detail twittering about all over the place while the background remains still.

Some of these effects are alleviated by only displaying one field when the video is paused, but this sacrifices vertical resolution. Averaging between the two fields is another possibility that works some of the time, but it is a compromise as well. Chapter 33 revisits that topic in the discussion about de-interlacing. This is an important part of the practical encoding process.

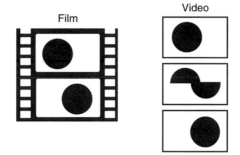

Figure 5-7 Line-based telecine object movement.

5.7 Progressive Scanning

Many of the problems with interlaced video go away completely when you use progressive scanning. You must progressively scan at twice the normal film frame rate (or at the field rate) to provide smooth motion. High-definition TV systems and computer displays are designed around a progressive-scanning model. Figure 5-8 illustrates the progressive-scanning line layout.

5.8 Picture Sizes and Formats

Television services transmit images of a markedly lower resolution than professional film formats. The frame rates are higher and the delivery process is often more complex. This is designed to reduce the transmission bandwidth.

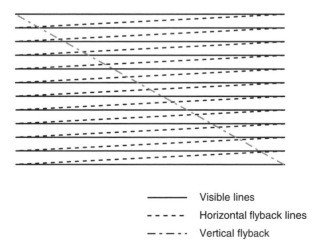

———————	Visible lines
- - - - -	Horizontal flyback lines
— · — · ·	Vertical flyback

Figure 5-8 Progressive scanning pattern.

5.8.1 Physical Raster Area

The physical raster is often described as if the image filled all the available lines. When a 525- or 625-line system is mentioned, this is a reference to the physical raster. You will not actually see 525 or even 625 lines on your TV receiver. The vertical blanking time required for the CRT electron beam to fly back to the top of the screen and the horizontal fly-back time accounts for about 8% of the raster. The raster is reduced from 525 to 480 in USA broadcasts and from 625 to 576 lines of usable picture area in Europe. The value of 480 has been argued about and is considered to be a nominal value. Other values are quoted in some literature. Anything bigger than 482 lines of visible picture may be cropped somewhere in the distribution process even when operating in Europe. This is because video equipment and processing software may be operated with settings that allow for worldwide distribution of the content.

In fact you lose some of the horizontal time because the imaging is only scanned from left to right, and about 15% of the horizontal time is lost to blanking while the beam goes back to start another line.

This is wholly an analog TV issue; digital TV systems don't require fly back or blanking time. However, they must make sure the image areas they work in are usable on analog systems.

This is probably best represented by drawing the physical raster and indicating where to place the blanking to see how much usable raster area remains.

5.8.2 Visible Raster Area

Within the usable raster area is a somewhat smaller picture area. The viewer normally sees an even smaller area than that. This is because TV sets are designed to stretch the image past the edges of the screen. This is called over-scanning. Studio TV monitors allow for this to be switched in and out so that you can see the entire raster. Computer monitors do not over-scan, and you should expect to see the whole addressable picture area on the screen.

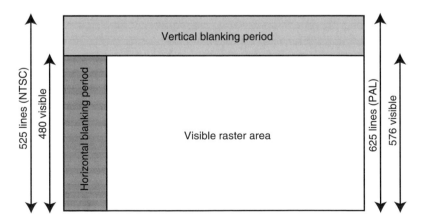

Figure 5-9 Physical and visible raster areas.

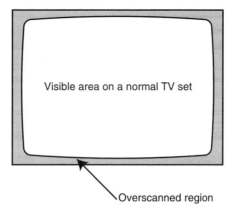

Figure 5-10 Over-scanned area on a normal TV set.

Over-scanning is used to avoid seeing noise and ragged synchronization down either side of the picture. It also hides the half line at the top and bottom of the picture. In addition, there is some hidden digital data that is not part of the picture intended for the viewer. Because of this over-scanning, television programs are designed so that everything happens within a safe area.

The human eye is amazingly forgiving of nonlinearity and curvature of perpendicular lines. Note that two safe areas are shown in Figure 5-11. One is the action safe area and the other is the text safe area. The text safe area is even smaller in order to cope with TV sets that are grossly misconfigured. The safe area ensures that text remains within the part of the picture that is most likely to be geometrically stable and linear. The safe area is the part of the picture that is least likely to be cropped or damaged by aspect-ratio conversion.

5.8.3 Legacy 405 Line Transmission

This format is no longer being broadcast, but it is important because some archival material was recorded off-air when this was the UK standard-definition service. The material will be monochrome because no color service was broadcast in this resolution. The BBC has publicly committed to making some of the archives accessible to UK citizens over the next few years, and very likely some valuable historical footage in this format will come to light. Any restorative processes will be performed digitally, so the first step is to convert the material from an analog form. The equivalent resolution for this service is 400 non-square pixels across 380 visible lines within a 405-line interlaced raster.

5.8.4 Standard-Definition TV

Standard-definition TV (SDTV) continues to be delivered differently in Europe and the United States. In fact there are many different variations to the size and scan rate of TV services all over the world.

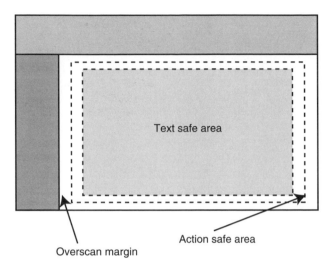

Figure 5-11 Safe areas.

The term NTSC is commonly taken to mean an image that is 720 non-square pixels wide by 480 visible lines high. This is delivered on a 525-line raster being presented approximately 30 times per second, again using an interlaced alternate field scheme.

For typical PAL TV transmissions, the picture size will be 720 non-square pixels wide by 579 visible lines delivered on a 625-line raster. This raster will be refreshed 25 times per second using an interlaced presentation of two alternate fields.

The SECAM system is structurally very similar to PAL, but the encoding frequencies and technical aspects of the color model are different. A special SECAM decoder must be used because a PAL decoder will not work. The signals are converted between the two formats relatively easily since they are physically similar in terms of raster size (625 lines) and image size (720 × 579).

Figure 5-12 shows the three most common physical raster sizes.

5.8.5 Source Input Format

Source input format (*SIF*) is a term that was originally defined in the *MPEG-1* standard to describe the format of the source video being compressed.

Beware. It is a similar size to that defined by the Common Intermediate Format (*CIF*) but is not the same thing.

CIF is defined in the basic form as a 352 × 288 pixels at a display frequency of 29.97 fps. SIF is defined as 352 × 288 × 25 fps or 352 × 240 × 29.97 fps. Where CIF jumbles attributes of the U.S. and European TV services, SIF keeps them separate and consistent.

SIF is very easily sub-sampled from TV signals. CIF is most assuredly not, since both the spatial and the temporal data must be interpolated with a non-integer calculation depending on the source format of the video.

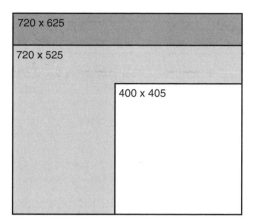

Figure 5-12 Common SDTV physical resolutions.

Table 5-2 enumerates some SDTV- and SIF-related resolutions. These are all taken from manufacturers' literature and the different variants are included to indicate the disparity between them. There are no clearly defined standards for this, so you should be very careful when selecting input and output sizes in your compression software. It will be more reliable if you specify exactly the size you want in pixels.

Notes:
- The sizes marked with an asterisk are considered to be canonical due to their integer relationship to the parent TV image size.
- The smaller sizes are often used when compressing video for use on the Web. They aren't the only sizes that are used but they are quoted in manufacturers' literature.
- Some of these sizes are based on multiples of 720, some on 704, and some on the base value of 768, which implies that some pixel aspect-ratio correction is happening as well.
- Note that for the 1/2, 2/3, and 3/4 sizes, only the horizontal axis is scaled. The line count remains the same.

5.8.6 High-Definition TV

High-definition TV (HDTV) is regularly broadcast in the United States now, and during 2003 and 2004 there has been a resurgence of interest in this medium in Europe. What is perceived as high definition depends on whether you are in the United States or Europe.

Historically, the earliest widespread UK broadcast TV service was delivered at 405 lines in monochrome. The United States introduced 525 lines, which was seen as superior, and it also delivered color-TV services to consumers well before the UK. In Europe, 625-line TV was engineered and delivered during the 1960s and color was introduced in the 1970s.

Table 5-2 SDTV-Related Picture Sizes

Description	NTSC		PAL	
	Width	*Height*	*Width*	*Height*
Physical raster	720	525	720	625
SQSIF	132	80	132	96
QSIF	160	112	176	144
QSIF	176	112	192	144
QSIF*	180	120	180	144
SIF	320	240	352	288
SIF	352	240	384	288
SIF*	360	240	360	288
1/2 D1 (HD1)	320	480	352	576
1/2 D1 (HD1)	352	480	384	576
1/2 D1 (HD1)*	360	480	384	576
2/3 D1*	480	480	480	576
3/4 D1	528	480	528	576
3/4 D1*	540	480	540	576
3/4 D1	544	480	544	576
FD1	640	480	640	576
FD1	704	480	704	576
FD1(4SIF)*	720	480	720	576
9SIF*	1080	720	1080	864
16SIF*	1440	960	1440	1152

In the past this was referred to as high-definition TV, which it is when compared to 405 lines. This is now referred to as standard definition. High definition now describes something with much larger vertical and horizontal dimensions.

The Beijing Olympics are anticipated to drive a significant uptake of HDTV receivers by 2008, with an additional 2 to 4 years before it is adopted as a mass medium. With the advent of H.264 encoding, there are amazingly few technical barriers to deploying HDTV in the very near future. Such obstacles that exist have to do with commercial issues and the penetration of the market by the existing MPEG-2-based SDTV set-top-boxes.

A range of HDTV picture sizes are shown in Figure 5-13 for comparison and are summarized in Table 5-3.

In the United States, HDTV signals are already being delivered with 720 lines, a major improvement over visible area provided with a 525-line service. When compared to

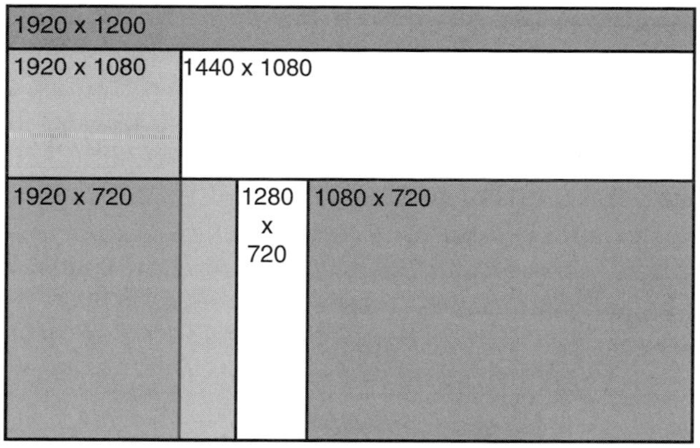

Figure 5-13 Common HDTV resolutions for HDTV.

625-line services it is not as large an improvement unless the implementation promises 720 visible lines. At the high end, image sizes of 1920 × 1080 are carried on a 2200 × 1125 raster and standards worldwide are converging on this format. This is a good choice because it is the same as that used for D-cinema, and therefore it is helpful to the distributors to only have to master their content into one format. Another popular resolution is 1920 × 1200, which is a multiple of the composite raster size for NTSC.

Note that some sources quote the HDCAM resolution as being 1440 × 1080. This may be one of the modes that HDCAM equipment supports, but the image dimensions of 1920 × 1080 are quoted in the Sony HDW-730S camcorder spec sheet.

In Europe the debate continues as to whether a 720p or 1080i format should be used for high-definition TV broadcasts. The 1920 × 720p 50 format is attractive because it fits with the available broadcast spectrum, but it is different from what is being adopted by the rest of the world. Progressive scanning is certainly more attractive than interlaced scanning.

Table 5-3 Common HDTV Picture Sizes

Description	Width	Height
Non-standard HDTV format similar to XGA computer display sizes	1080	720
SMPTE 296M HDTV format proposed for European trials	1280	720
Proposed European HDTV format	1920	720
Sony HDCAM format	1920	1080
SMPTE 274M HDTV format	1920	1080
Experimental high-def format that is a multiple of SDTV on NTSC systems	1920	1200

It is likely that early service launches in Europe will go with a 720p format but not pass up the opportunity of upgrading that to 1080p should the industry go in that direction with screen sizes and DVD formats in the future.

5.9   Aspect Ratio

Aspect ratio is a term used to describe the proportional difference between width and height. The values are often normalized so that the number on the right is 1. Sometimes they are normalized so that only integer values are used.

5.9.1   Common TV Aspect Ratio Formats

If you look at the back of DVD or video packaging you will see aspect ratios quoted. Normal aspect ratio is taken to be 4:3 and widescreen TV is 16:9. Some broadcasters compromise and deliver the content as 14:9. This allows for a small portion to be cropped on 4:3 aspect ratio TV sets, and a small black bar is present on either size of the picture on a 16:9 TV set. Figure 5-14 illustrates the various common aspect ratios in use.

Some common TV aspect ratios are summarized in Table 5-4.

5.9.2   Normal Aspect Ratio

Normal aspect ratio material is presented in a raster where the width to height ratio is 4:3. On a wide-screen monitor this is distorted to fill the screen, so a border is placed on each side to retain the original aspect ratio. Center cutout on a wide-screen TV sacrifices horizontal resolution. Letterboxing does the same when playing wide-screen content on a normal TV except that it wastes lines. In both cases, cropping is necessary to remove the wasted space if you are compressing for the Web. That will help to achieve the best possible compression ratio. There is an inevitable trade-off between quality and efficiency.

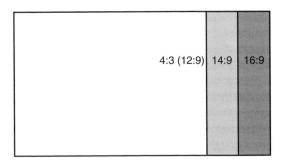

Figure 5-14 Aspect ratios.

Table 5-4 Common Aspect Ratios

Description	Aspect ratio	Normalized value
Standard TV	4:3	1.33:1
Widescreen TV	16:9	1.76:1
Compromised broadcast	14:9	1.56:1

4:3 image padded each side to fill 16:9

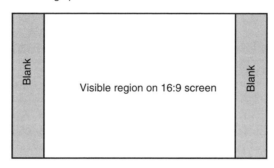

Figure 5-15 Ratio of 4:3 on a wide-screen raster (center cutout).

5.9.3 Wide-Screen Aspect Ratio

Wide-screen presentation is based on the width to height ratio being 16:9 and uses the full visible raster area. There is no additional picture detail being provided to add pixels to either side of the 4:3 aspect ratio picture. It is just the standard 720-pixel width image with the pixels being stretched horizontally even more than they were for normal presentation.

Fortunately, the human optical mechanisms are very tolerant of a loss of detail in the horizontal axis when watching TV.

5.9.4 Stretched Display Mode

Manufacturers of wide-screen TV sets added a "justify" display mode where the horizontal scanning is purposely nonlinear. This is another way to work the compromise between wide-screen and normal aspect ratio. The middle section of the screen is not stretched as much as the sides. A circle placed in the middle of the screen still looks roughly circular. Objects placed nearer the edges are stretched more and more as they move away from the center of the screen. Fortunately, you can turn this stretching feature on and off and select the viewing mode you prefer. The original linear geometry is shown in Figure 5-16 for reference.

The effects of the "justify" distortion are visible in Figure 5-17. This is fine most of the time but shows up when text crawls horizontally across the screen. It moves faster at the sides and slows down in the middle. Because you are able to see the whole screen,

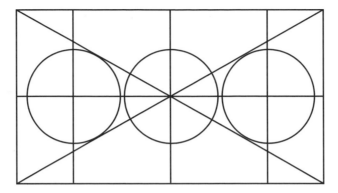

Figure 5-16 Original geometry.

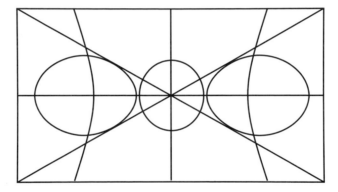

Figure 5-17 Example of warped nonlinear scaling.

your eyes focus on a single word at a time and it appears to squash and stretch as you follow it.

Sometimes a presenter will walk across the screen and appear to go on a very rapid slimming regime as the person reaches the center, and then experience a massive weight gain as he or she moves toward the side again. You are strongly advised to let the TV set do this and not try to implement this stretched mode in your content.

Oddly enough, the justify mode seems to work quite well most of the time and is an improvement over simply stretching the 4:3 raster across the 16:9 tube front. It is definitely better than a center cutout with black sides that look very odd after watching stretched 4:3 for a little while. However, purists may disapprove of this technique, and it will very likely offend experienced TV engineers.

5.9.5 Wide-Screen Signaling

Broadcasters transmit signals in hidden TV lines that the TV detects and uses to switch the display mode to a suitable setting for the program. It is quite disconcerting when the TV does this as the switch takes place in the scanning circuits in some models. Sometimes the electronics make a loud electrical crackling noise as the voltages change.

Ideally this would be done digitally and the TV scan circuits would simply continue scanning a constant-sized raster.

This is covered in more detail in Chapter 39, which discusses some advanced topics related to hidden data signals.

5.9.6 Film Aspect Ratio Formats on TV

Many movies are delivered on DVD in a wide-screen letterbox format that shows the entire picture. These days this is often standardized to cinemascope or Panavision format, which has an aspect ratio of 2.35:1. Adjusting the vertical zoom factor of the TV presents a larger picture, but it sacrifices consistent scaling in X and Y. Figure 5-18 shows how these formats are fitted onto a TV screen.

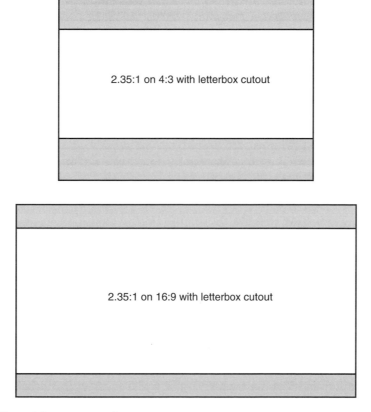

Figure 5-18 Panavision aspect ratio.

With the plethora of aspect ratios and built-in zoom and stretch modes on modern TV sets, it is very likely that almost no TV services and movies are broadcast in the aspect ratio that the program maker or movie director intended. But the human eye and vision system is remarkably good at compensating for this and consumers seem to not be unduly concerned. But viewers are occasionally surprised when meeting a celebrity face-to-face to find that the person is not in fact as fat or thin as he or she appears to be on TV.

5.9.7 Aspect Ratio Conversion

Compensation for aspect ratio is sometimes necessary when you compress the video. Broadcasters use a device called an aspect ratio converter (ARC), and while this is very convenient, it is possible for material to be converted backward and forward several times. The result is a rather low-quality picture that appears to be over-cropped. This is because the top and bottom are trimmed when going from 4:3 to 16:9, and the sides are trimmed when going back to 4:3. Figure 5-19 shows the commonly used ARC output settings when cropping the input to fit.

An ARC will also pad an image rather than cropping it. Figure 5-20 shows some commonly used padding setups.

5.10 Analog-to-Digital Conversion

The starting point is essentially an analog representation since the world at large is analog. It is very convenient to operate on video using digital techniques but in the end it is presented to a Mark 1 eyeball, which operates in an analog fashion. It is likely to remain that way unless the Borg collective from Star Trek assimilates us all. While we wait until that happens, let's examine the conversion process step by step.

5.10.1 Analog Video Source Format

A video signal is a continuously varying light intensity that is detected by the imaging electronics in the camera. Early cameras were monochrome (black and white) so there was just the one signal.

Later on, color cameras were developed so there were three signals to be processed and delivered. A color picture is composed of three monochrome rasters. The primary colors, red, green, and blue, are chosen because the display is composed of three light sources. Therefore additional color mixing is necessary. So green plus red equals yellow. Color information is reviewed again in more detail later in this chapter.

Video is most often represented as a black and white image (known as luma or Y') with some color components (known as chroma or C_B and C_R) described separately. This is quite a different and complex way to describe a picture compared with an RGB signal, which is very simple. The luma plus chroma representation is actually more compact and requires less information to describe it.

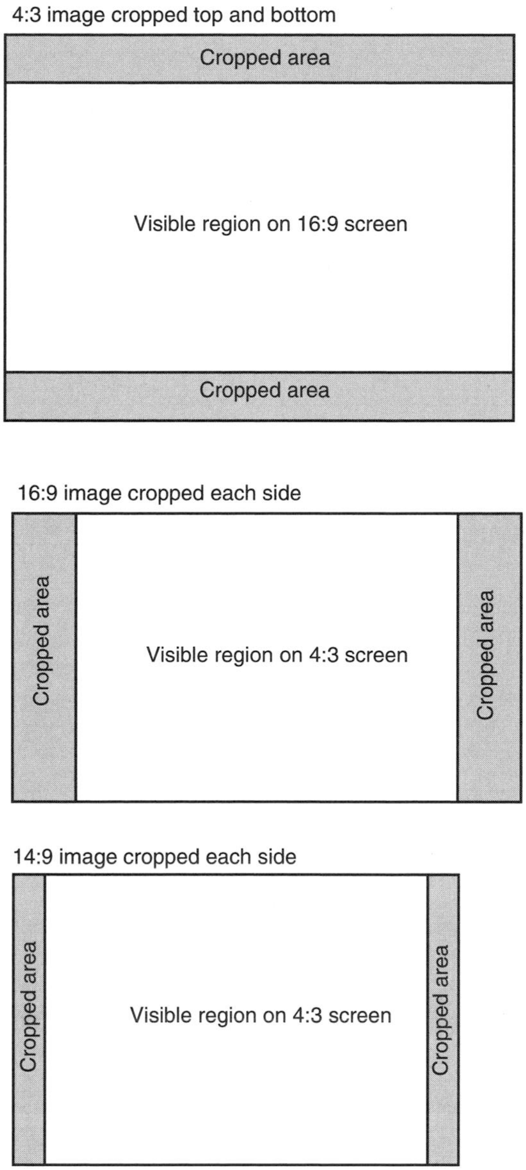

4:3 image cropped top and bottom

Cropped area

Visible region on 16:9 screen

Cropped area

16:9 image cropped each side

Cropped area

Visible region on 4:3 screen

Cropped area

14:9 image cropped each side

Cropped area

Visible region on 4:3 screen

Cropped area

Figure 5-19 ARC cropped frames.

16:9 image padded top and bottom to fill 4:3

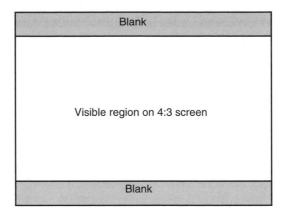

14:9 image padded each side to fill 16:9

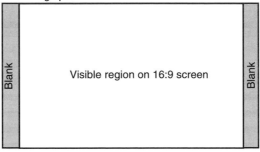

14:9 image padded top and bottom to fill 4:3

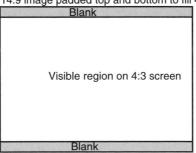

Figure 5-20 ARC padded frames.

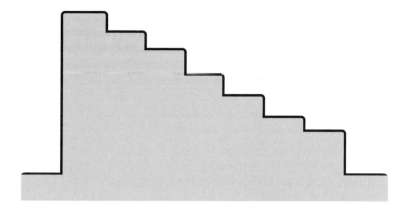

Figure 5-21 Analog waveform for one line of video.

5.10.2 Conversion to Digital Form

Video is converted from analog to digital form by measuring the height of the waveform at an instant in time and storing that number. The conversion takes place either in the red-green-blue domain, or the component signals are digitized and the conversion to separated color is accomplished in the digital domain. Information straight from a camera imaging charge coupled device (*CCD*) will already be in RGB but will be converted to other formats within the camera. Computer imaging is normally in RGB, but there are many alternative color spaces available.

5.10.3 Bandwidth and Sample Rates

Analog bandwidth determines the maximum resolution of the picture in the horizontal direction. Recording your content onto VHS videotape drastically reduces the resolution available to you in the horizontal axis. That is because the tape cannot record at the broadcast bandwidth and the higher-frequency information (the detail) must be discarded.

The basis for the relationship between bandwidth and horizontal resolution is this:

$$\text{Bandwidth} = \text{scan rate} * \text{lines per raster} * \text{sample rate}$$

The *Nyquist* theory indicates that the sample rate must be high enough to take two samples per cycle of the highest frequency of visible detail.

Some experts argue that significantly more than two samples are necessary to avoid aliasing artifacts. Refer to Chapter 7 for details of digital audio because it is more relevant in that area. The same theoretical arguments would apply to video, however. We would see aliasing artifacts in video as a moving pattern, for example, if a presenter is wearing a jacket with a particularly bold checkered pattern.

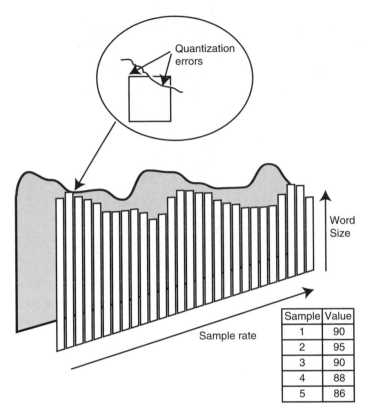

Figure 5-22 Digital waveform.

Interlacing halves this bandwidth requirement. The amount of detail is doubled at the expense of greatly increasing the complexity of the image in the temporal domain.

5.10.4 Resolvable Detail

Placing vertical black and white lines in front of a camera and zooming out will produce an increasing frequency gradient. Eventually the lines merge into an unfocused gray patch. At that point you have reached the limit of resolvable detail for this system. The resolving limits of the camera, transmission chain, or the display are all different. Resolution is a simple calculation based on counting the number of white-to-black transitions. You must take two samples at this rate to discriminate and capture a pair of vertical, one-pixel wide, white and black lines. Figure 5-24 illustrates how detail increases with frequency.

In Table 5-5, some typical values for the resolvable pixels with different kinds of video are enumerated.

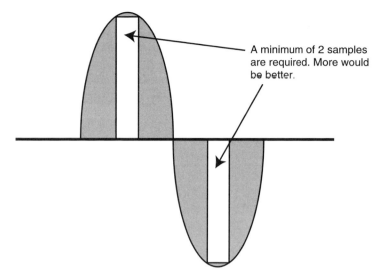

A minimum of 2 samples are required. More would be better.

Figure 5-23 Nyquist sampling.

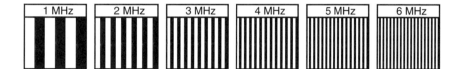

| 1 MHz | 2 MHz | 3 MHz | 4 MHz | 5 MHz | 6 MHz |

Figure 5-24 Resolvable detail.

Table 5-5 Resolvable Detail in the Horizontal Axis

Format	Horizontal pixels
VHS	240–300
Analog NTSC	330
Analog PAL	350
S-VHS	400
DV	500
Off-air digital TV	720
High definition	1920

5.10.5 Synchronization

An example of a single line of analog video picture information is shown in Figure 5-25. This is somewhat simplified and only shows the important aspects of the signal.

The dotted line indicates the area of interest to compressionists. We don't care about levels that are higher or lower than this and any video to the left or right is not picture information.

A synchronization pulse is visible at the left of the illustration. This is necessary for aligning each successive scan line so that the picture is reconstructed correctly. Note also that the only part that is interesting for compression purposes is the area occupied by genuine picture information.

The vertical position of each line is determined by its location in the sequence of scan lines making up the entire raster. Figure 5-26 shows a series of lines and how the vertical synchronization is coded with some much longer sync pulses. This is greatly simplified as the organization of sync pulses is very complex. Fortunately, the input circuits of the video cards deal with all of this.

Only the visible scan lines containing meaningful picture information are relevant to the compression process. However, it is important to find the right lines to compress. No part of the synchronization signal is included in the compressed video output. If this part of the picture is coded, it just wastes bit rate without conveying any useful picture information. Cropping at the input of the encoder effectively deals with this.

5.10.6 Genlock

The term *genlock* is jargon that is contracted from generator locking. It describes the way that multiple video services are synchronized together. It is also implemented on film

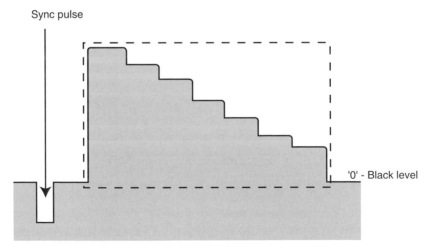

Figure 5-25 Waveform for a single line of video.

Broad vertical sync pulse

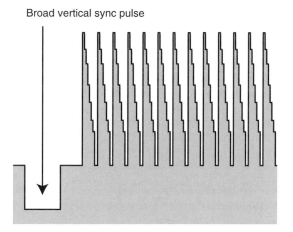

Figure 5-26 Lines and vertical sync.

cameras to synchronize the shutter with a video signal. This is the best way to eliminate rolling bars on TV screens when filming people surrounded by TV monitors. Figure 5-27 shows what the rolling bars effect looks like.

There are four aspects to the synchronization that must be locked in order for a source and destination system to operate correctly.

- Line sync (horizontal)
- Field sync (vertical)
- Frame sync
- Color sub-carrier sync

Figure 5-27 Rolling bars distortion.

Of these, the most difficult to keep synchronized is the color because any change in the phase of the color sub-carrier frequency will alter the hue of the color being displayed.

Problems occur if the synchronization of the color signal is compromised. Extra long paths for the analog signal cause phasing problems with the color information due to the propagation time. Color information runs at about 4 MHz. Wave shapes cycle every 250 nanoseconds. A cable run from one studio to another that is 100 yards long will introduce an appreciable delay. This problem is much reduced now that the studio is a predominantly digital domain.

5.10.7 Pixel Shape

When sampling analog video or outputting analog video from a digital source, square pixels are rarely used. The actual pixel map dimensions vary according to where in the viewing pipeline the raster is being extracted and the kind of signal being sampled. The physical raster is part of a transport mechanism while the image area is only a portion of that area.

Bandwidth available for recording devices such as VHS tape decks in a domestic environment limits the number of meaningful samples, and the way that color is encoded also affects the optimum sample rates.

The number of samples in the horizontal axis determines the fundamental data rate. The shape of the pixels must be taken into account for some applications.

In the U.S. TV standard with 525 scanning lines, only 480 of them contain picture information. Each line has 640 samples. This is commonly referred to as NTSC, but that merely describes the encoding of the color information.

European TV has 625 scanning lines but only 576 of these are active picture lines. While these will also be sampled 720 times for each line, that image must be stretched using interpolation to 768×579 so as to achieve square pixels. The 640×480 raster must be stretched to 720×480 to achieve the same effect. Square pixels are desirable because they make processing of any effects or overlays more straightforward. Computation of line drawing and circle algorithms for mattes and overlays work best with pixels that are spaced evenly in both axes.

The values quoted here are nominal, and this situation is actually far more complex depending on sample rates and whether component or composite source material is being digitized. Sample rates vary to preserve color information. This relates to the frequency at which color detail is modulated. The same Nyquist sampling constraints apply to color information. Sufficient samples must be taken to avoid aliasing and quantization artifacts. Nyquist states that digital sample rates must be at least twice the frequency of the highest frequency being sampled to avoid loss of information. Since color sub-carriers are modulated around the 4 MHz frequency range, sample rates in the region of 12 to 15 MHz dictate the spacing of samples when we want to record and reproduce the color sub-carrier frequency.

This complexity is dealt with by the input circuits of the encoding system or video cards and drivers. Most users need not be conversant with the fine points. Table 5-6 summarizes the values.

The most likely sampling will be based on the CIR Rec 601 component 4:2:2 format that yields a 720×480 or 720×576 image. Your working area would be 768×483 or

Table 5-6 Sampling Pixel Maps

Physical		Usable		Description
X	Y	W	H	
640	480	640	480	Square sampled image for VGA computer displays but not used in studio situations
780	525	648	480	Square pixel sample rates for NTSC 525i30 imaging systems used in the United States
944	625	768	576	Square pixel sample rates for PAL 625i25 imaging systems used in Europe
858	525	720	480	*Rec 601* component 4:2:2 sample rates for NTSC 525i30 imaging systems used in the United States
858	525	704	480	Reduced visible area variant of Rec 601 component 4:2:2 sample rates for NTSC 525i30 imaging systems used in the United States
864	625	720	576	Rec 601 component 4:2:2 sample rates for PAL 625i25 imaging systems used in Europe
910	525	768	483	Composite sample rates for NTSC 525i30 imaging systems used in the United States
1135	625	948	576	Composite sample rates for PAL 625i25 imaging systems used in Europe

948 × 576 in order to operate on square pixels, but the images must be scaled correctly when converted back to video.

This has implications for artwork that is used for DVD menus, for example.

5.11 Color Information

Three separate red, green, and blue (RGB) signals are combined in analog TV broadcasting using some very complicated modulation and matrix-mixing techniques. The RGB values are combined to generate a monochrome image. This is viewable on a black and white monitor and is referred to as the luma component. That same matrix calculation also generates two additional difference images that describe the color. Because the modulation frequencies are different, the luma and chroma signals are separated in the receiver.

Even in the analog world, there is some video compression being applied. The chroma information is filtered to remove high-frequency color changes so that the analog signal occupies less bandwidth. This works quite well because the eye is less sensitive to color changes than it is to light-intensity changes. The detail is preserved in the luma channel.

Extreme loss of detail in the chroma is sometimes apparent when you see a soccer player wearing a red shirt running across a green soccer field. The chroma signal is

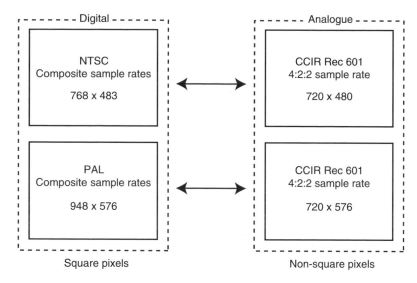

Figure 5-28 Working areas.

lower resolution than the luma, so the red color seems to spill out of the area of the player's shirt.

5.11.1 Luma and Chroma Component Signals

Reducing the video picture to component parts helps to process the video for compression. It certainly helps the transmission process at the expense of some of the information.

Deciding which way to componentize the picture is very challenging. The output of the video circuits will ultimately drive a red, green, and blue additive-light emission system in the display. Displays requiring reflective or transmissive illumination use subtractive color mixing that requires a conversion to cyan, yellow, and magenta (CMY) color components.

The TV industry decided a long time ago that the most versatile technique was to describe images with one lightness signal and a pair of color-difference signals that work together. The word luminance was used to describe the brightness of a video signal relative to a peak white value.

The Commission Internationale de l'Éclairage (CIE) defined the term luminance and chose the symbol Y to represent it in mathematical equations that describe color values. TV engineers and color scientists use the word luminance to mean quite different things.

Be mindful of your usage of the word luminance as it has been widely misused and its meaning has been somewhat ambiguous. Also be wary of the notation if you see it in a mathematical formula. The relative (to peak white) luminance value is indicated in mathematical formulas by the value Y but is rarely used in digital imaging systems. Luma, which is the most interesting quantity, is a weighted value derived from the gamma-corrected RGB intensities and is referred to by the symbol Y'. Note the prime mark that indicates it is a nonlinear property.

Charles Poynton describes at great length the historical confusion between luminance and luma. Refer to page 595 of his 2003 book *Digital Video and HDTV Algorithms and Interfaces* (published by Morgan Kaufmann) for further elucidation on this. Mr. Poynton also suggests that the use of the term luma is usually appropriate for discussing this quantity in digital video and computer graphics systems.

5.11.2 RGB

This is the primary form in which video content is represented. Because the human eye responds to these colors individually, it is a particularly appropriate way to represent images. The eye is most sensitive to the green channel, less so to the red, and least of all to the blue. Viewers suffering from color blindness may respond to these colors in a different way.

One possible compression approach, then, is to store the green channel at full resolution, remove some detail in the red, and remove even more in the blue.

The popular compression schemes developed by the MPEG standards body don't operate on the RGB value but on the component luma and chroma values, which are readily available in the video-production environment.

5.11.3 Color Difference Channel

Separating the RGB values into a brightness (luma) value and two color components requires a bit of math.

The RGB values are processed using a matrix calculation to derive a single luma value that presents the most accurate monochrome signal. The matrix values are selected so that displaying just the luma on a black and white monitor will present a pleasing and appropriately lit image.

Take the blue value and subtract the luma from it to generate a blue-difference channel. This is also done with the red to make a red-difference channel. The result is a pair of difference values.

Along with knowing a lot about how the human visual system works, the engineers who developed this technique also knew that reducing the resolution of these two color-difference signals would have little perceived effect on the reconstructed image when viewed under normal conditions.

Table 5-7 describes some common terminology that is related to this topic. Note that the Y' value always describes luma and not luminance.

5.11.4 An Experiment to Try at Home

Prove the importance of luma over chroma experimentally like this. First load an image into Photoshop and go to the channels palette. Apply varying degrees of Gaussian blur to

Table 5-7 Luma-Related Terminology

Terminology	Description
RGB	Original red, green, and blue source signals
Y'P$_B$P$_R$	Component analog video values. Matrixed luma Y' plus the two color-difference signals, which have been analog filtered to about half the luma bandwidth
Y'C$_B$C$_R$	Component digital video values. Matrixed luma plus scaled color-difference values
Y'UV	The blue and red difference components are combined and further down-sampled before being mixed with the luma signal to form the NTSC or PAL broadcast signal. This is decoded back into component values before your compression system operates on it.
Y'IQ	A legacy NTSC coding scheme that is obsolete but is referred to in older documents.

the red and blue channels. Provided the green channel is left alone, the effects are very hard to distinguish from the original, even if the blue channel is severely blurred. The most minimal blurring of the green channel is immediately visible. Reducing the detail in the red and blue channels also reduces the overall detail in the brightness channel and that is not desirable.

Changing the color space in the Photoshop application to LAB demonstrates the separation of luma and chroma. The luma channel is a monochrome image. The A and B channels are the chroma. They will withstand considerable blurring without affecting the apparent quality of the picture. There is no doubt that it is affected, because some information has been discarded, however, the human eye is designed to cope with this sort of degradation so the perceived effects are minimal.

You can use this knowledge to get better results when cleaning up the images before compression. If you want to sharpen the image, only apply the sharpening to the luma channel and not to the RGB image. That way you will avoid getting blotchy effects on skin tones.

5.11.5 What Does 4:2:2 Notation Mean?

If the luma and the two color-difference channels (chroma) are coded into a digital form, acceptable images are produced by sampling less information from the chroma. This is done by sampling a smaller number of bits-per-pixel or fewer pixels across the sampled area's chroma channels. The distribution of this sampling is not immediately clear from the naming scheme.

The first digit, "4," is an historical convention that means the sample rate is approximately 4 times the frequency of the color sub-carrier signal. These samples are taken of the luma signal and are considered to be one unit of sampling in the horizontal axis.

The second digit (which is often the value "2") means that during the same sampling period, only 2 samples are taken for each of the color-difference signals in the horizontal axis.

The third digit (which is also often the value "2") describes the sampling in the vertical axis but this *sub-sampling* involves some additional computation to halve the amount of data.

There is sometimes a fourth digit that represents an alpha channel-blending value. This becomes important for the more advanced codecs described by MPEG-4 and must be sampled at the same rate as the luma signal or else some unpleasant fringing effects will appear around the edges of the alpha-blended video object.

Table 5-8 lists some related formats that are relevant: In the table below, the first sampling pattern is called 4:4:4. The full range of values is preserved and this is essentially an uncompressed pixel map. Luma and chroma are both sampled at full resolution.

Some data reduction is achieved with 4:2:2 sampling, which reduces the amount of chroma information by only sampling half the pixels. The other pixels are ignored. Note that this is not an average value of two samples; it is selecting one of two samples.

A further reduction to a quarter of the chroma information is achieved with the 4:1:1 sampling pattern. This ignores 3 out of 4 color values and only records the fourth.

Table 5-8 Luma and Chroma Sample Sizes

Format	Description	Cell size	Chroma	Bytes	Factor	Fidelity
4:4:4	Luma and chroma sampled at full resolution	2×2	2×2	12	1:1	Uncompressed
4:2:2	Luma sampled at 4 times the sub-carrier frequency. Chroma sampled at half the resolution on the horizontal axis and down-sampled in the vertical axis	2×2	1×2	8	1.5:1	Lossy
4:1:1	Double-sized aperture cell to allow higher compression ratio for chroma. 8:2:2 is a more functional description of the sampling.	4×2	1×2	6	2:1	Lossy
4:2:0	Only one chroma sample for the whole *block* of luma samples	2×2	1×1	6	2:1	Lossy

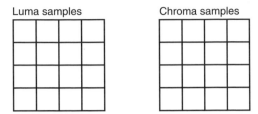

Figure 5-29 4:4:4 sampling.

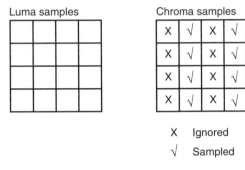

Figure 5-30 4:2:2 sampling.

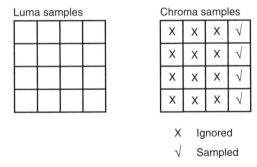

Figure 5-31 4:1:1 sampling.

This example is different. The 4:2:0 sampling pattern takes a group of four chroma values and averages them. Because this uses color information from two lines, some persistence is required to accomplish this kind of sampling because the lines are in different fields when an interlaced image is being sampled.

Another sampling scheme is the Y′UV arrangement, which averages the whole sample area for chroma into one large superpixel.

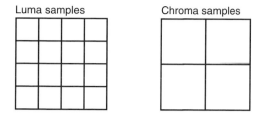

Figure 5-32 4:2:0 sampling.

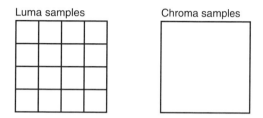

Figure 5-33 Y′UV sampling.

You will find further discussion on color models and color space in Chapter 6, which covers digital-imaging systems.

5.12 Video Formats

Video formats come in a variety of alternatives. Consumer formats are lower quality than professional formats and are stored on lower-capacity devices. While there is a performance difference between them at present, Moore's Law provides for ever-increasing processing capability. Eventually there is no economic reason why consumers should not enjoy studio-quality presentation in their own homes.

5.12.1 Transport and Delivery of Video

Broadcast studios and the transmission systems deliver the video in an encoded form that applies some analog compression. The luma value describes a basic black and white TV signal. Subtracting the luma signal from the RGB color values derives two color components. This color overlay does not have to be maintained at the same resolution because the human eye is better at resolving brightness than color, so some compression is already accomplished.

The delivery and transport mechanisms used to build TV systems are all based on transferring this luma and chroma component information. A camera will rarely produce an RGB signal directly, nor will a telecine machine deliver an output in an uncompressed form. While it is possible to design and engineer an RGB transfer system, it would be non-standard. Only large movie-effects companies would deploy the engineering effort to develop special-purpose hardware to do this sort of thing.

The rest of us will at best get a *DV50 bit stream* but more likely a DV25 bit stream in the studio. Downstream in the consumer or semi-professional world, it is more likely that a component signal in S-video format will be delivered. Otherwise, the best to expect is a PAL or NTSC signal off air. While the off-air quality is reasonably good when viewed directly, it has already been through several compression processes and converted back and forth between analog and digital several times. The analog output from a receiver is somewhat compromised compared to the original studio quality. The source material could be delivered on a VHS tape running in long-play mode that is only just viewable. These reductions in the quality all contribute to making the compression process more difficult. Many of the practicalities covered in Chapters 31 to 37 describe the remedial work before the actual compression process begins.

5.12.2 Broadcast-Standard Digital Video

If you are working in the broadcast industry, you encounter uncompressed material and serial digital sources that have some compression with invisible artifacts. The equipment manufacturers refer to formats such as DV50 or DV25. Video servers used for broadcasting allow these storage densities to be switched. The server will then trade off storage capacity against production quality. It is inadvisable to change this setting while the server is in use, as it will sometimes result in the server completely purging the video storage and reformatting the disk array. Note also that DV25 is sometimes loosely referred to as DVCAM.

5.12.3 Pro-Consumer Digital Video

At the top end of the consumer-grade equipment, in an area that is also populated by professional small filmmakers or semi-professional videographers, you will find formats such as DV. DV is slightly lossy compared with uncompressed video but the quality is a lot better than VHS. It is compressed at a ratio of 5:1 when compared with the raw, uncompressed footage. It is good enough for news gathering in many cases and the DVCAM format is widely used. DV is output by digital home video cameras (handycams) such as the Sony DCR PC 105.

These cameras readily connect to your Mac OS computer using the FireWire (a.k.a. *IEEE 1394* or iLink) cable and are controllable using iMovie, Final Cut Express, or Final Cut Pro. Other video-editing tools such as Adobe Premier are equally useful. Provided your Intel platform supports FireWire and you have the necessary applications installed, it all works similarly on a PC.

Although you often see DV and FireWire being used together, they are distinctly separate technologies. DV is a video-storage and transfer format and FireWire is a connectivity standard. Protocols that work on the FireWire interface have been developed for the control and transfer of DV material to and from compatible equipment. So the standards are used cooperatively with one another but are independent.

5.12.4 *Amateur Video Formats*

If you are dealing with legacy material, a lot of footage will be recorded on VHS or beta-max. You are going to experience some significant quality issues with the compression when it is applied to video that has been taken off a VHS tape.

In ascending order of quality, these home video formats are grouped like this:

- VHS—Long Play
- S-VHS—Long Play
- VHS—Short play
- S-VHS—Short Play
- betamax

5.13 Gotchas

These are the things that go bump in the night, or more likely during that rush job that you have to deliver first thing in the morning. Video is sometimes a royal pain to encode properly. Just getting it off the tape is difficult. That is when you discover some strange noise or artifact that causes problems. Some of these must be dealt with at source because they are much harder to remove later.

Dot crawl is an example that is fixed by using S-video connectors that separate luma and chroma instead of a combined composite connection.

Tracking errors are an issue to do with the quality of recording or the maintenance of your VCR. These and other gotchas are dealt with in Chapter 31 and the chapters immediately following it where the practicalities of video-compression processes are addressed.

5.14 Summary

This chapter has examined some fairly complex matters regarding video presentation. Refer to this chapter when reading about the video-compression algorithms in Chapters 8 to 14. It will give you some insights into why the encoding technology is implemented the way that it is.

The appendices summarize a variety of different formats and codecs for use with video. There is a whole zoo of formats described in Appendix L.

In the next chapter we will look at digital-imaging systems. These are where film and video converge in the same format. Most of the hard work involved with film and video is in trying to deal with their own special properties and wrestle them into a form that fits into a digital-imaging system.

Digital Image Formats 6

6.1 Are We There Yet?

Digital imaging is where all the technologies combine. It is also a domain where totally original material is created. Some of the animation that is realized with computer systems could not be done any other way. Nevertheless, digital imaging owes a lot to video and film before it. But this is not the end of the journey. It is only the end of the beginning.

6.2 The Power of Convergence

The convergence of computers, movie film, and TV systems provides opportunities to use the power of digital imagery to convert and combine content from celluloid and video. Completely new content is synthesized from scratch. The movies that Pixar makes originated wholly inside the computer and did not start as film or video. Digital imagery is now so sophisticated that it has become a completely new source of moving images.

In this chapter we examine computer displays and the revolution in computer graphics that has taken place since the 1960s when Dr. Ivan Sutherland developed his vector-based graphics systems.

Summarizing screen sizes will get some of the major differences between digital-imaging formats out of the way first. The sizes range from small handheld formats up to digital-cinema formats. The artifacts that affect the quality of the imaging are important, and there are opportunities to minimize them. Dithering techniques are also important. They might have been used in the image-creation process and will have serious implications for compression systems. There are several techniques that will compromise the quality and show up in the output. Digital camera functionality is important since that may be how you originate some content. At the end of the chapter we look forward to some interesting work being done to increase the dynamic range of the imaging model. This is likely to have a profound effect on the image quality we are able to source.

6.3 Computer Video Display Standards

In recent times, a variety of popular image sizes have become de-facto standards. These are related to the 640×480 image size that is based on the 525-line TV service. Other derivatives are based on a computer display known as VGA (video graphics adapter). These are also derived originally from TV standard sizes. In addition, a set of image sizes is defined for video conferencing by the *ITU* (the International Telecommunications Union). These screen sizes are also used in other contexts.

Computer video displays on personal computers were originally implemented by plugging in domestic TV monitors. The resolution and scan rates were related to the same picture sizes. Some modifications began with improvements to the computers, and the displays became a product that was more specialized and designed for use with a computer. The changes involved improvements to power-supply regulation so that the display would not breathe in and out as the content changed in brightness, and progressive scanning became popular. All of this was embodied in standard chipsets that started to be used on computer motherboards.

The earliest commonly used standard was called VGA (video graphics adapter). As successive generations of computers were manufactured, the standard evolved accordingly. Today's monitors are able to accommodate a variety of display standards, and the graphics adapters also allow you to define your picture size and scan rate in a very flexible way.

Table 6.1 gives the basic modes showing the names and dimensions of the screen display. Other modes are available but mnemonic names are not defined for them. The scanning rates are not standardized so rigorously.

Table 6-1 Standardized Computer Display Resolutions

Name	Width	Height
QVGA	320	240
VGA	640	480
SVGA	800	600
XGA	1024	768
SXGA	1280	1024
WXGA	1366	768
UXGA	1600	1200
UXGA-W	1920	1200
QXGA	2048	1365
Apple 30 inch	2560	1600
QUXGA-W	3840	2400

Digital Display Working Group: http://www.ddwg.org/

Computer video screens come in a variety of different sizes. A 15-inch diagonal screen is quite commonplace, and it is unusual to find CRT monitors smaller than this. LCD displays on laptops are usually smaller.

One of the benefits of this standardization is that monitor cables or the monitors themselves now have sensing pins. The picture information transmitted from the computer to the display does not require all the pins that are available in the connector. Connecting specific pins together creates a unique "'binary'" value. That value tells the graphics adapter card what resolutions the monitor is capable of supporting.

Many users have much larger monitors—17, 19, 21, and 23 inches are common these days. The larger sizes are available as computer-compatible LCD screens. Desktop screens are available that have a 30-inch diagonal and very high display resolutions. Plasma screens are manufactured with up to a 60-inch diagonal. Some large-format rear-projection displays are based on the Texas Instruments DLP chip that is also used in multimedia projectors.

The highest-performance screen that is widely available is the Viewsonic VP2290b. Laboratory prototypes of digital video cameras that operate at the maximum 8 megapixel resolution were demonstrated at the IBC by Olympus. These SH880 movie cameras will become more popular as HDTV penetrates the TV industry.

Experimental prototypes with up to 4,000 lines are being demonstrated in the NHK laboratories. This will show an incredible amount of detail but is unlikely to be in your living room in the foreseeable future. The display exceeds the amount of picture information presented in an IMAX frame.

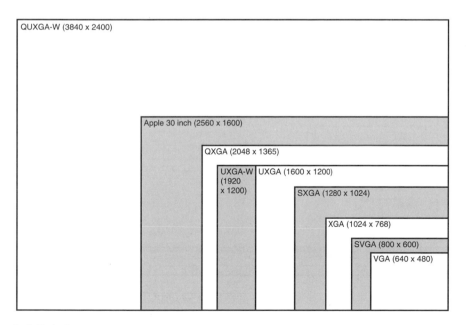

Figure 6-1 Relative screen sizes.

6.4   Screen Resolution

The size of the display and the chosen "'GA'" mode will determine the resolution. This is the number of dots or pixels per unit of distance measured horizontally across the screen. It does not correlate exactly with the screen sizes that are measured diagonally and the resolution depends on the aspect ratio of the screen. Vertical and horizontal resolution is not guaranteed to be identical. Setting up the geometry of a CRT display to get accurate, and straight/true alignment requires some practice. LCD displays don't require any geometry adjustment since they are a pixel-based display.

The resolution of a 640 × 480 display on a 15-inch monitor is computed using a little Pythagoras to find out the height and width of the display.

Screen display resolutions are described using dots per inch (*DPI*). In the discussions on film formats we specify sample resolutions as pixels per mm because the film sizes are expressed in mm. It is easy to convert between them using the 25.4 mm to the inch conversion ratio, so 10 dots per mm is equivalent to 254 DPI.

We know that the display is 15 inches measured diagonally. We also know that the aspect ratio is 4:3 (or 16:9). Pythagoras tells us that the diagonal of a triangle whose sides

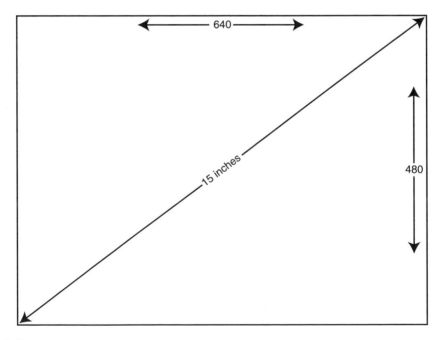

Figure 6-2 Aspect ratio to size versus resolution.

Viewsonic: http://www.viewsoniceurope.com/

Olympus SH880: http://www.olympus.co.jp/en/news/2004a/nr040414sh880e.cfm

NHK 4000 line display: http://www.nhk.or.jp/strl/publica/dayori-new/en/rd-0210e.html

measure 4 and 3 will be 5 units long. Multiply all the values by 3 to scale the diagonal to 15 inches and we learn that the width is 12 inches and the height is 9. This gives us a horizontal and vertical resolution of 53.3 DPI. This assumes that the picture is adjusted to exactly that size. But it is very likely it will under-scan slightly so the DPI value will be slightly higher. If the display is not set up correctly, some nonlinear distribution of the lines will cause resolution changes across the surface of the screen. This is a problem if you use the monitor to draw accurate diagrams.

At this resolution, there are significant issues with raster size, storage, throughput, and display. The solutions are all rather expensive. It is likely that this type of high-quality moving image will be useful to people making movies, compositing graphics assets, and rendering special effects, but the average users are not likely to require this type of output. Video editing is possible at much lower resolutions. Then, the edit decision list can be moved to a craft-editing workstation to conform the edit on a master copy of the video.

6.5 Video Conferencing Formats

When video conferencing systems were being developed, the International Telecommunications Union (ITU) defined a data rate and picture size that it thought was reasonable to accommodate within the transmission mechanisms being deployed.

6.5.1 Common Intermediate Format

The baseline standard was called common intermediate format (CIF) and is a quarter of the size of a generic TV display.

The ITU *H.261* standard defined CIF to be a progressively scanned 352×288 image with 4:2:0 chroma sub-sampling and a frame rate of 29.97 Hz. This is a strange combination because the size is based on the visible area of a 625-line TV service with the frame rate from a 525-line service.

CIF is sometimes called Full CIF (*FCIF*) to distinguish it from a related standard that defines a lower bit-rate service with a smaller display-image size. That standard is called *QCIF*. This is misleading because it implies that the picture is full size and somehow distinct from CIF, which it is not.

Some implementations change the number of lines or frames per second according to the geographic use. In PAL-based territories, the format is 352×288 and in NTSC territories, the line count is reduced to 240.

In some documentation the authors suggest that the "I" in CIF is short for interchange or image rather than intermediate. No common image format has ever been agreed upon so you should avoid using the term "common image format."

6.5.2 Quarter Common Intermediate Format

The quarter common intermediate format (QCIF or "quarter CIF") requires a quarter of the bit rate used by CIF image streams. It is designed to be suitable for video-conferencing systems that transfer their bit streams via telephone lines.

Again the data rate is based on 30 fps, but now each frame contains only 176 × 144 pixels. This is also part of the ITU H.261 video-conferencing standard.

As stated previously for CIF, some implementations change the number of lines according to the geographic use. In PAL-based territories, the format is 176 × 144 and in NTSC territories, the line count is reduced to 120.

6.5.3 CIF Versus SIF

Beware when you read specifications that describe screen sizes. The values for CIF and SIF are often mixed up and intermingled, but they aren't the same thing. SIF stands for source input format.

The exact sizes of these image formats depend on the underlying video standard that the content is derived from. Table 6-2 consolidates and summarizes the range of values for CIF-based images.

Figure 6-3 shows the relative difference between these sizes.

Prefacing with a Q quarters the area. The SQ size is smaller still, but not by an integer ratio and the scaling is not the same in X and Y. The names prefixed by 4, 9, and 16 refer to multiples of the area and are 2 × 2, 3 × 3, and 4 × 4 scaled-up sizes.

 The consequence of all the confusion over frame sizes is that your compression software may use terms like QSIF to describe a screen size, but you may not get a picture that is the size you expect it to be. It is a good idea to specify the X and Y values for your picture size explicitly and not rely on these settings.

Table 6-2 Intermediate Formats

Resolution	NTSC		PAL	
	Height	*Width*	*Height*	*Width*
SQCIF	128	80	128	96
QCIF	176	120	176	144
CIF	352	240	352	288
4CIF	704	480	704	576
9CIF	1056	720	1056	864
16CIF	1408	960	1408	1152

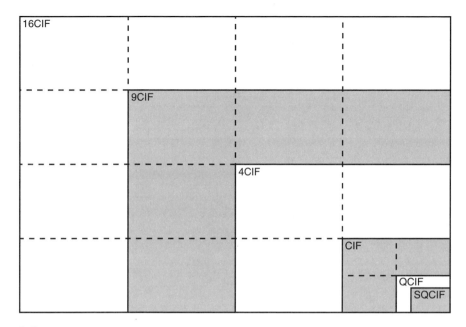

Figure 6-3 Relative imaging sizes for CIF and its derivatives.

6.6 PDA Formats

Ever since PDA devices first appeared, users have been working out ways to play moving video on them. The current state of the art is exemplified by high-end Palm OS-based Sony devices, although Pocket PC handhelds are also demonstrating strong capabilities in this area.

Earlier Palm OS devices supported very low-resolution 160 × 160 displays and some of these had very limited grayscale support. The display is only 4 bits deep, delivering 16 levels of intensity from black to white. Video is prone to look a bit "crunchy" on these earlier devices, but as the PDA devices have matured the current models do a remarkably good job.

Figure 6-4 illustrates visually how the screen size in PDA devices has gotten larger with each new generation.

Modern devices are equipped with good-quality cameras, wireless connectivity, and adequate capacity for removable storage. Sometimes phone connectivity is even provided as well. The cameras are equivalent to low-end digital still cameras, but the quality at 1.3 megapixels is more than adequate for shooting short video sequences. This will get better of course as the technology improves.

Typical resolutions for these devices are shown in Table 6-3.

The form factor is either square or portrait, but the devices support viewing modes where a landscape picture is presented sideways. PDA devices have screen sizes that are roughly 4 times the area of a video-capable mobile phone.

Video on Palm devices: http://www.manifest-tech.com/media_pda/palm_video.htm

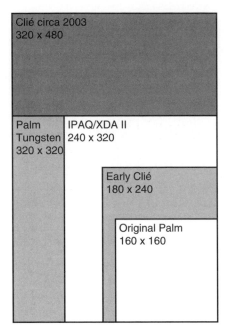

Figure 6-4 PDA screen sizes.

The modern codecs coupled with the storage capacity of the memory stick and Compact Flash cards provide up to 8 hours of viewing on the 2003/2004 models in the Sony CLIÉ product family. Display resolutions are approaching that of standard-definition TV, and you might choose between loading a movie into your PDA or your laptop when on long journeys.

Table 6-3 PDA Screen Sizes

Example model	Width	Height
Original Palm	160	160
Early CLIÉ	180	240
IPAQ	240	320
XDA II	240	320
Palm Tungsten	320	320
CLIÉ circa 2003	320	480

6.6.1   Kinoma Compressor

One of the most popular formats for compressing video for use on handheld devices is the *Cinepak mobile* video produced by the *Kinoma* codec. This has become widely available and is now being shipped within other compression systems. Later on when we start to experiment with compression systems, we can try out our test footage with the Kinoma Cinepak Mobile codec.

6.6.2   CLIÉ Video Recorder

Sony has introduced the VR100K video recorder that records television and video onto a memory stick in a format that is compatible with CLIÉ handhelds. The device also contains a TV tuner and supports a variety of input formats including the auxiliary outputs from other home video devices. It is very small and compact, roughly as big as a VHS tape box.

Computer systems with a video input jack will also be able to receive cable and TV signals through the TV tuner built into the VR100K. Viewing of recorded videos requires Apple QuickTime 6.

The CLIÉ VR100K recorder compresses video and stores it directly onto a memory stick. The utility software provided with it allows scheduled recordings to take place.

The video compression used in this device records nearly 17 hours on a 1 GB Memory Stick PRO in LP1/LP2 mode, or 4 hours in top quality. A 128 MB memory stick stores approximately 130 minutes in LP mode. This is just about enough for any major movie you are likely to want to record or possibly two episodes of an hour-long program.

The video is compatible with all of the Palm OS 5 Sony CLIÉ models, including the NX series, the TG50, NZ90, and the UX series. It uses the MPEG-4 Simple Profile video codec. This suggests that further compression efficiency is possible if the H.264 codec is deployed in the future.

This is a superb example of the kind of products that simply would not exist without video compression.

Sony has withdrawn from the PDA marketplace as of summer 2004, but the technologies they have developed will still be relevant to other similar devices.

6.6.3   Remote Video Monitoring

Aside from being able to play movies while on the move, other potential applications are being developed using video compression, handheld PDA devices, and the WiFi capabilities being built into these products.

The Firepad company is developing handheld video baby monitors that let you monitor your child from another part of the house.

Remote monitoring could use a mobile-phone service to deliver a video stream. Browsing via the Internet though an IP connection is another alternative. There are many possibilities for video conferencing and surveillance with these devices.

Kinoma codec: http://www.kinoma.com/products.html

Firepad: http://www.firepad.com/catalog/index.php?productID=2

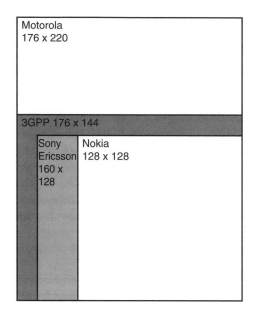

Figure 6-5 Mobile phone screen sizes.

6.7 Mobile Phone Formats

Mobile phones compatible with the 3G systems are designed to play back video as a fundamental capability. The screens are quite small and are fine for some services, but you probably would not enjoy watching a feature-length film at this resolution. High-end phones are based on PDA devices and there is a convergence between these two types of product. The functionality in both lends itself to being used in a single platform. Address books as sophisticated as that in the Palm or Pocket PC devices are very appropriate for use in a phone where the addition of a "dial this person" button provides exactly what you need.

Figure 6-5 and Table 6-4 describe the relative sizes of some video formats provided in phones and hybrid-phone PDA devices.

Table 6-4 Mobile Phone Form Factors

Format	Width	Height	Colors
3GPP	176	144	65536
Motorola	176	220	65536
Nokia	128	128	4096
Sony Ericsson	160	128	65536

The form factor is either square or rectangular just like the PDA devices and the phones support viewing in landscape or portrait modes.

The different sizes seem to be used on a per-manufacturer basis. The bulk purchase of display modules ensures that there is a generic Motorola screen size vs. a generic Nokia screen size.

Preparing your content for mobile phones will be quite an exacting challenge to preserve any kind of quality at these image sizes. Successful trials have proven that it is possible, however. One possible technique that saves significant bit-rate capacity is to reduce the frame rate. While the number of differences between frames will increase, the amount of data stored for each frame remains roughly the same. This is because of the way that compression systems reduce the image to a series of smaller tiles. These tiles are called macroblocks, and we will look at them more closely in Chapters 8 to 14 when we discuss how video compression actually works.

6.8 Physical and Visible Raster Areas

In the earlier discussion of how analog TV works, we saw that the picture was carried on a physical raster signal that had synchronization pulses and a defined area within which the picture is placed. Not all of the physical area is used for visible picture information, however. A little margin is provided at each end of the line scan, and a few lines are kept at the top and bottom as well, as those lines happen while the scanning circuits move the vertical position back to the top of the screen. That vertical repositioning is called flyback, and the stream of electrons to the CRT tube face is turned off while it happens. The time it takes for the flyback to happen is called the vertical blanking time.

So, for example, we have a physical raster of 480 lines with 720 samples. Converting an analog signal to a digital version sometimes leaves a small portion of black on either side of the picture. There are often some black lines at the top and bottom as well.

It is not necessary to compress these, but they must be there at the analog output if we are feeding a TV set or video recorder with our decompressed video. If we crop at the input stage, the playback system must ensure that the output physical raster is correctly sized.

If that is not done correctly, we will find our picture cropped more than we expect at the output stage. This is not fatal, but if we know about it, a safe margin placed around the image will prevent problems later.

Figure 6-6 illustrates how the physical raster is derived from the scanned TV signal.

6.9 D-Cinema

Digital cinema (D-cinema) is becoming more sophisticated and operationally easier to deploy. The IBC and *NAB* conferences in 2003 and 2004 featured more coverage of this topic than ever before, with special screenings of full-length feature movies. This included a digitally processed version of the old Robin Hood movie starring Errol Flynn. The processing worked from the original Technicolor separations and combined them digitally.

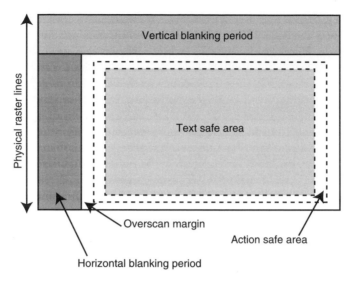

Figure 6-6 Safe areas.

Only a small amount of restorative work was done, but the vast improvement in quality came by working from a previous-generation master rather than simply digitizing a print that had been optically combined. With the advent of DVDs there has been a surge in demand for old movies to be restored and compressed using good-quality encoders in order to make them available to a new generation of consumers.

6.9.1 Dynamic Range

The imaging quality of the D-cinema format is improving all the time. When shooting this material with a completely digital video camera, the dynamic range of the content at the dark end of the intensity scale is still not as good as analog film. The detail is simply not there although it is improving year by year. Some compensation for this takes place in a film-to-D-cinema transfer. Where there is detail to be extracted, changing the gamma curve and adjusting the input-to-output intensity mapping will reveal subtle shading in dark-shadowed parts of the picture. Shooting must take place with strong lighting being carefully bounced into all the shaded areas of the scene.

Shortly, we will examine some of the work on high dynamic range imagery (HDRI). This technique will lead to some significant improvements in the quality of digital photography, especially where it pertains to low light conditions.

6.9.2 Film Grain

Cinematographers have fallen on either side of the fence regarding whether they like the quality of output produced with this technology. George Lucas clearly favors shooting straight to disk with a digital camera, while Steven Spielberg has gone on record to say he prefers the grainy texture of traditional film. Movies such as *Minority Report* achieve a good compromise by using digital effects to realize what the director envisioned while still preserving the film grain in the finished product by reintroducing it as a digital effect. As ever, there is clearly no right or wrong way to do this and the directors are likely to continue making movies with a mixture of technologies for some time to come. From the point of view of a compressionist, film grain is a bad thing.

6.9.3 Image Sizes

With the work that movie special-effects companies have been doing on fully rendered 3D animation, a third alternative of completely computer-originated material is now available. Two companies in particular represent the technological leading edge. Industrial Light & Magic (ILM) began work in this area in the 1970s. Some of the computer graphics work they were doing during the early 1980s was spun out to become the Pixar company. Both have continued to push the state of the art forward ever since.

Several companies are looking at resolutions for D-cinema that go well beyond the current 1920 × 1080-sized pictures we are becoming accustomed to. Barco, Sony, NHK, and Olympus all have interesting research and development projects underway.

6.9.4 Aliasing Artifacts

Pixar has consistently delivered computer-animated content that has a vibrant and realistic image quality. Pixar representatives have explained at conferences how they use many tricks and shortcuts in order to simulate some computationally intensive techniques to deliver something that looks as if it required far more computing power than was actually used.

Movies for cinema presentation are typically created at a 2.35:1 wide-screen aspect ratio. The resolution of an individual frame of 3D animation is rendered at 2048 × 862 pixels. The quality that Pixar produces appears to be that of a much higher resolution. This is because for every pixel being rendered, the computation averages an image that is drawn at a much higher resolution. This saves a lot of computation time when dealing with anti-aliasing artifacts. Figure 6-7 shows the effects of aliasing (jaggies) on lines, and how they are alleviated by anti-aliasing, which is covered in the discussion on visible artifacts.

Table 6-5 D-Cinema Display Resolutions

Name	Width	Height
Panasonic large-venue DLP projector	1366	1080
HDTV/D-Cinema	1920	1080
Barco D-Cine DP100	2048	1080
Sony high-performance D-Cinema projector	4096	2160
NHK Ultra-HDTV prototype	8000	4000

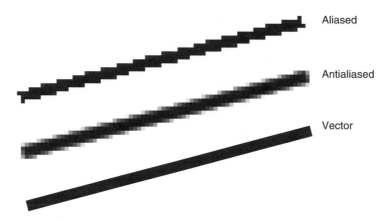

Figure 6-7 Anti-aliasing effects.

The industry is settling on some standard screen sizes for D-cinema that coincide with the HDTV specifications, so imaging areas of 1920 × 1080 will become popular.

6.9.5 Resolvable Detail

You would think that a cinema screen would require more than 1080 lines to provide an image of sufficient quality. Reducing the pixel resolution to 1080 lines is feasible, though, because the audience only resolves about 900 lines at the normal viewing distance—even in a good theater. IMAX theaters are a special case because the viewer sits a lot closer to the screen than normal. Using the best equipment, such theaters achieve approximately 2000 lines of resolution on a 35mm print. Since the detail is just not visible, it is pointless to put the extra information in the output image. While the justification is there for 35mm to be printed at that quality, the potential savings in storage capacity and bit rate for D-cinema are more compelling.

Figure 6-8 shows how the resolving capabilities of the human eye limit the usefulness of higher-resolution displays.

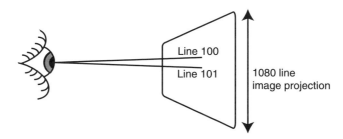

Figure 6-8 D-cinema resolving power.

Some compression is taking place as the movie is laser scanned onto film. This can be disappointing to hear if you have labored over an 8K square image. Nevertheless, an image that is created and worked on at 8K is going to look a lot better in the final low-resolution output than if you had worked at the lower resolution, so the effort is not wasted.

Knowing about this compromise in resolving power significantly alters the cost dynamics of the disk storage you buy when equipping the distribution and play-out systems in a cinema complex. It also helps facilitate the delivery and transmission of a movie via a network connection from the studio to the theater. Video compression helps some more, too, but it does not have to compress the image quite as harshly to accomplish useful bit rates.

Delivering an appropriately sized image directly to a D-cinema projector eliminates the intermediate process of creating a 35mm print. This improves the quality of the viewing experience for the customer and saves money for the distributor. Typical resolutions for this are 2200 × 1125 pixels, although 1920 × 1080 is also popular and is a size which coincidentally is also used for high-definition TV in some deployments.

6.9.6 Down-Sampling to SDTV Format

Let's say you are creating some program material in HDTV format, for example, rendered at 1920 × 1080 and interlaced at 25 fps. If this is intended for delivery at standard definition for broadcasting purposes, you must render a special low-resolution version unless you trust the broadcasters to convert it themselves. The visible area on a 625-line raster is only 579 lines, which does not have an integer relationship to 1080. Even more problematic is the 480 visible lines on the 525-line systems, which have added complexity of scanning at 30 fps. The change in time base causes more problems with keeping the motion smooth. This is especially tricky if the motion was rendered at field rate rather than frame rate. The interpolation artifacts are avoided by rendering two additional copies of the movie with the correct scale factor and frame timing. Most production companies will not have the luxury of time or computing capacity to do this so some shortcuts will be necessary.

6.9.7 Up-Sampling to HDTV Format

Time pressure being what it is, redesigning your rendering process could cut some corners off the time required to complete your project. For example, a raster only 720 lines high is probably detailed enough to be displayed at high definition. Up-sampling this 720-line image to 1080 lines is feasible for an HDTV output. A picture size that is 720 lines high is one of the HDTV standards currently deployed anyway. If you create content for multiple territories, then rendering at 25 fps will be less work than 30 fps. Pulldown will yield the 30 fps version as it does for movie film. Products such as Adobe After Effects will produce your up-sampled and down-sampled versions. The savings allow you to render 1080 × 720 × 25p instead of 1920 × 1080 × 60i, which reduces your render workload to about 30% of what it would be at full resolution.

Compression is not just about bit rates coming out of a tool like Discreet Cleaner; it is a mindset. You have to think about your entire workflow process and not waste time creating data that is going to disappear when the video is compressed.

6.10 Visual Display Artifacts

If you try to drive the display too hard by setting a raster size and scan rate that is near the performance limits of the display, the picture starts smearing in the horizontal axis and also ringing when hard edges are drawn.

Smearing happens because the scan circuits simply cannot change the intensity of the beam fast enough to cope with the resolution.

Ringing is seen as ghost copies of the image offset a quarter- or half-inch (depending on the display size) to the right. These are due to the electronic effects of throwing a high-frequency signal down a piece of connecting wire. At the very high pixel clock frequencies we use now, a bad joint in a cable causes a reflection of the signal that bounces back and forth to create the ghosting effect. The distance of each ghost image is related to the time taken for each reflection to go back down the wire until it hits another obstacle. If you want to know more about this topic, you'll need to study a physics or electronics book and seek out a description of transmission line theorems. Be warned, though: It is a very dense subject.

Making visual quality checks and reducing pixel clock rates to more realistic levels help to solve this problem. Using higher-quality cable and placing ferrite rings on the cables to increase the inductance will also alleviate the effects.

There are other artifacts that affect the geometry of the display but these are largely to do with the regulation of the scanning circuits in a CRT monitor. Using flat-screen displays based on one of the following technologies eliminates most of the linearity and color-purity problems:

- Liquid Crystal Display (LCD)
- Light Emitting Diode (LED)
- Organic Light Emitting Diode (OLED)
- Plasma
- Digital Light Projection (DLP)

6.11 Dithering to Improve Image Quality

Since the 1970s we have been using dithering techniques to improve image quality in situations where the color palette is limited, and the technique was known before that in the printing industry.

In the context of computer imaging, four techniques have been used widely. There are others that are less popular variants of these four basic techniques.

This information is important to anyone who renders images that are computer generated and then displayed on a TV video system. Some weird artifacts appear if you try and video capture newsprint or other dithered images on a rostrum camera. There are also implications here for preprocessing images and dealing with image data in the decoded output that yield harsh contouring artifacts. Adding a little noise to the image in order to perturb the contoured edges disguises the edges. That unfortunately makes the compression algorithms slightly less efficient. A little noise applied carefully helps to make the image look better at the expense of a little bit rate. Modern codecs such as H.264 deal with this by applying a deblocking filter in the player after the decoding is complete.

The main beneficiaries of dithering are people trying to get better results on lower-resolution printers, although it is also useful on displays where the available color palette is limited. Dithering is used in video cameras to allow them to operate with one CCD sensor array instead of three, which makes them a lot cheaper to manufacture. There are quality implications for video compression when this kind of camera is used: Because there are fewer imaging cells being used, the picture quality is reduced, and there is also a spatial displacement for each of the primary colors such that they are not all sampling the exact same pixel position in the image.

We will come back to this topic and discuss it further near the end of this chapter. First, though, let's explore a range of dithering techniques in order to understand how they work; this has implications for the camera designs we will consider later.

6.11.1 *Newsprint Half-Toning*

Photographs have been dithered ever since newspapers started publishing pictures. If you look closely at a black and white image in a newspaper or magazine you will see the effect. Figure 6-9 shows a closeup as an example. Choose an area where the shading changes from black to white to see how the intermediate greys are represented.

This effect is reproduced digitally by scanning images at a resolution much higher than the half-tone grating. Then, by clever image-processing techniques, the small

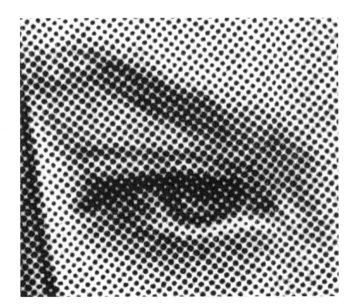

Figure 6-9 Newsprint half-toning.

diamond-shaped areas are produced. The size of the dots is made proportional to the average lightness of the image at that point. The human eye hides the detail of the dot pattern, so you perceive a continuously toned image and not a grid of dots. If you look very closely, the dots become visible.

6.11.2 Color Printing

Color printing techniques apply the half-toning trick but they overlay cyan, yellow, magenta and black (CMYK) to create the color. The half-tone mask is rotated by 15 degrees for each successive color so as to reduce any moiré effects. Figure 6-10 shows the four color separations.

The films for these prints are created in the same way as the newsprint half-tone images, but usually a finer grating is used for the half-tone mask.

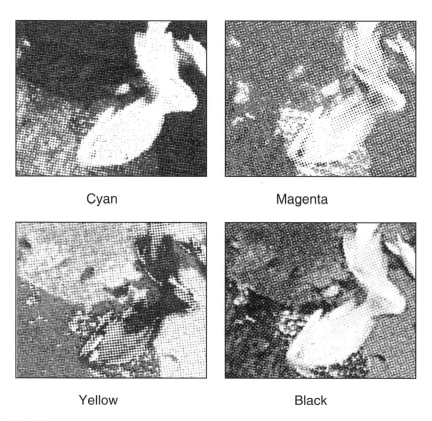

Cyan   Magenta

Yellow   Black

Figure 6-10 Color printing separations.

6.11.3 *Early Dithering Algorithms*

In the 1970s when the Apple 1 and II computers were introduced, one of their differentiating features was the so-called "hi-res" graphics. We don't call 320 × 192 high resolution now that we have screen sizes of 2560 × 1920, but back then it was good enough that scanned bit-map images of black and white photographs could be presented on screen.

The early compression technique developed for still images is important because it was the forerunner of the way we do video compression today.

The trick was to dice the image into small squares and look for similarity across the image. Then the image was reconstructed from a set of tiles that were stored in a more compact form to take advantage of duplication within the image. While generating the tiling, some smoothing effects were applied to distribute the dots evenly. This imparted a very pleasing quality to the images.

6.11.4 *Simple Checkerboard Dithering*

During the 1980s a lot of work was being done to move color printing forward so as to make color proofing available, and at that time a variety of different ink technologies were developed. Most of them could only deposit a very restricted number of colors. There was no intensity control—the colors were either on or off. Even with a four-color ink system this only yielded 16 solid colors, and half of those were unusable because they were alternative versions of black.

The resolution of the printer was sufficient that by using half-toning techniques, other intermediate colors could be realized. A checkerboard of red and yellow pixels yields an orange color. Figure 6-11 shows two checkerboard-patterned examples.

This works for some images but not all, and you get some weird artifacts around the edges of the colored shapes where the checkerboards don't mesh particularly well. Some patterns create the same color in two different ways, so there were ingenious phasing

 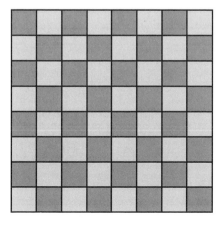

Figure 6-11 Simple checker dithering.

mechanisms developed to select the right checker pattern before other better solutions were invented.

6.11.5   Spiral and Bayer Dithering

The spiral dither approach takes a rectangle of pixels and orders the pixel drawing algorithm so that it draws a spiral pattern as you progress from one color to another. The image is colored more smoothly but has a somewhat grainy appearance. Because the grain is evenly distributed across the image, you don't get the edging artifacts that the checkerboard dithering gives you. The Bayer dither improves on this and yields a more consistent coverage.

This describes a variety of dithering spirals and incremental fill matrices. The values are used to determine a threshold against which to fill a pixel array. This is one of many so-called patterned dithering techniques.

6.11.6   Error Diffusion Dithering

In 1976, Robert W. Floyd and Louis Steinberg published a paper called "An Adaptive Algorithm for Spatial Greyscale." This described a new approach to dithering that scanned across the image and decided whether a pixel was light or dark not by simply slicing through the intensity graph, but by accumulating an error value from the surrounding pixels. It was developed to diffuse or distribute quantization errors over a larger area and it yielded some amazing results. Even when using 1-bit black and white displays, photo-

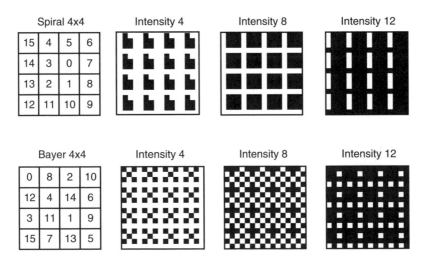

Figure 6-12 Spiral and Bayer dithering.

Bayer dithering (open source code): http://www.cs.rit.edu/usr/local/pub/pga/Graphics/GIF/gr/dither.c

graphic images can be presented in a very appealing way. Several people have offered improvements since then, and the basic technique is now used all over the world every day to create high-quality images on systems with limited resources.

Figure 6-13 shows a photograph, followed by a simple threshold mapping from grayscale to 1 bit and no dither. The third pane uses a pattern dither and the fourth uses error diffusion.

6.11.7 Albie Dithering

The Albie dithering technique is specially designed to deal with images that are going to be displayed on an interlaced monitor, which is what is required for TV imagery. The dithering technique is very similar to the Floyd-Steinberg error diffusion algorithm. Albie produces slightly better contrast but also exhibits some increased grain and contouring on

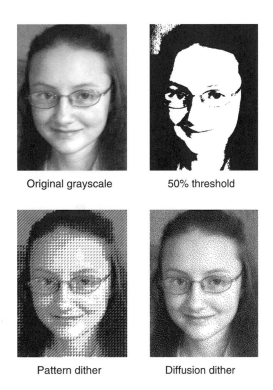

Original grayscale   50% threshold

Pattern dither   Diffusion dither

Figure 6-13 Error diffusion dithering.

Floyd-Steinberg derived algorithms: http://www.wellesley.edu/CS/pmetaxas/ei99.pdf

Modified Floyd-Steinberg algorithm: http://www.cs.indiana.edu/pub/techreports/TR458.pdf

ACM Digital Library article: http://portal.acm.org/citation.cfm?id=35039.35040

some subject matter. If you are eager to get the best out of your imagery, spending some time with Equilibrium DeBabelizer software and processing your pictures with different settings will be worthwhile.

6.12 Digital Imaging Processes in the Camera

The imaging process in a digital camera is fundamentally different from that in a film camera. The light is focused via the optics in the usual way, but the shutter is not a mechanical device at all. It is an electronic impulse that samples a CCD imaging array. From this a voltage is measured for each pixel and that is passed through an analog-to-digital converter to generate a digital sample value. Because the behavior of the CCD is not responsive in the same way as the human eye, a mapping function scales the values to enhance the detail in the image. Figure 6-14 shows this general arrangement.

Camera resolutions are increasing and costs are reducing. It is now possible to get cameras with 5 million pixels for just a few hundred dollars or less. Increasing the resolution does not materially help us with video cameras other than perhaps to offer high-definition video cameras to consumers. High-definition CCD devices operated at SDTV resolutions could use several imaging cells to sample a single pixel in order to average out any noise artifacts.

6.12.1 Color Imaging with a Single-Chip Camera

Getting a single imaging chip to detect color requires the placement of a filter over each picture element so that it only responds to the desired color. This is necessary because the imaging sensor is monochromatic and cannot tell the difference between a red photon and a blue one.

There are three techniques:

- Multi pass, one exposure for each color. This is not practical for moving images.
- Color filter arrays over a single sensor.
- Beam splitting via prisms to multiple sensors.

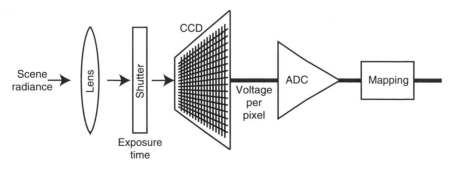

Figure 6-14 How digital cameras work.

Figure 6-15 Bayer color-filter array.

6.12.2 Color-Filter Array

Figure 6-15 shows a typical color-filter array with the green channel arranged in what is called a Bayer dithering pattern. This has two green quadrants for every cell and one each of red and blue. Because the eye is most sensitive to green and the dominant component of a luma signal is green, this enhances the perceived resolution.

This is fine for still cameras and for low-cost video cameras but it doesn't provide the desired quality for professional users. The main disadvantage is that the spatial resolution is traded off and the red and blue are recorded at half the resolution of the green, and that is only half the spatial resolution available on the sensor. The colored pixels are also offset spatially and fine detail may only be recorded in one channel or the other. The effective resolution is about a quarter that of the CCD array.

6.12.3 Prisms and Multiple CCD Sensors

The beam-splitting prism and 3 CCD chip arrangements are a much better solution. The 4-chip cameras are essentially similar but have a slightly more complex prism arrangement inside.

The main advantage here is that the three CCD sensors can operate at full resolution—there is no loss of detail and all the colors are spatially aligned. These cameras are more difficult to manufacture and the optical effects of the prisms compromise some of the lens choices that are available, but the qualitative gains are worth it.

You can find more information about how these color cameras and sensors work at the Dalsa Digital Cinema Web site.

6.13 Color Spaces

There are many other ways that color images are represented, some of which come from the still-image formats. There are implications for this when compressing video because

Dalsa Digital Cinema: http://www.dalsa.com/dc

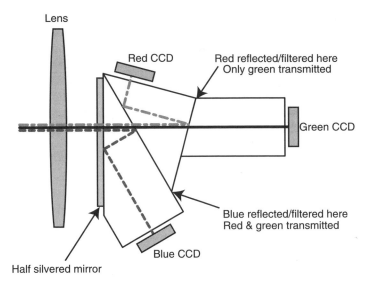

Figure 6-16 3 CCD camera internal arrangement.

moving images are represented as a series of still frames. Those frames originate from a variety of sources, not all of which use the same color space.

MPEG is not the same as Motion-JPEG, for example. The Motion Picture Experts Group (MPEG) incorporates motion-related processing into their standards. This requires some computation between frames, and each frame is represented by a description that is meaningful only in the context of its position within a sequence of frames. The Motion-JPEG format treats each frame as a discrete still picture.

Sequences of images are stored using image formats that are usually considered to be for still pictures. This is very similar to the way that uncompressed footage is stored. Color representations other than RGB or luma-chroma are often used.

Table 6-6 describes some alternative still-image formats

6.14 High-Dynamic Range Imaging

Eight bits per color (RGB 24 bit) is simply not enough to represent the full range of tones in an image. Digital cameras and video systems lose a lot of detail because of this.

Even worse are the hue-shifting effects that you get as a result of gamut clipping. Shooting directly into the sun shows up in the image as a darkened blotch in the area that is brightest. The rendered color is some strange hue that seems to bear no resemblance to the surrounding image. It is like a severe crushing effect on the peak value of the video. High-dynamic range imaging (HDR) allows a greater range of tones to be stored, and this leads to better quality video being created after it has been processed.

There is also a correlation among the range of colors that can be represented, what is available at the source, and what the human eye is able to resolve. In Figure 6-18 the lumi-

Table 6-6 Other Non-RGB Formats

Format	Description
CMY	Cyan, magenta and yellow. The blacks are not very dense and are often called brown-black.
CMYK	Cyan, magenta, and yellow with the K value representing an additional black channel. This value must be subtracted from the CMY values to achieve under-color removal.
GIF	Compressed-image format using Lempel-Ziv-Welch (LZW) compression originally developed for CompuServe. Unisys owns the patent.
HLS	Hue lightness and saturation
HSV	Hue saturation and value
JPEG	Joint Photographic Experts Group still-image format. Uses *DCT* transforms but no inter-frame computation.
JPEG-2000	A more recent version of the JPEG standard that allows for *wavelet* compression of still images.
LAB	Luma plus two color-difference values (chroma). The color-difference values represent the yellow–blue axis and the magenta–green axis.
PDF	Although not an image format itself, PDF files are being used increasingly as image containers with other formats embedded inside them. It is theoretically possible to convert between a movie file and a sequence of PDF files and vice versa. Since Mac OS X uses PDF for the display-imaging model, this will become more popular.
PICT	The Apple Macintosh picture format, revised and extended over the years to include compression.
Pixlet	*Pixlet* compression was developed by Apple and shipped in QuickTime 6.4 for Mac OS X. This uses a still image-based wavelet compression in a motion video container to provide compressed video with no observable artifacts. The name is derived from the words Pixar and wavelet.
PNG	Portable graphics format developed in response to the patent claim by Unisys. It was intended to replace GIF images on the Internet.
TIFF	Tagged image format originally codeveloped by Microsoft and Aldus for the pre-press industry. Various versions have been developed since.

nance of a scene is mapped to the behavior of the human eye, and the range of available brightness values for 8-bit and HDR are both shown on the same axis. In this case the word luminance is the lighting and color science value and must not be confused with luma values discussed elsewhere.

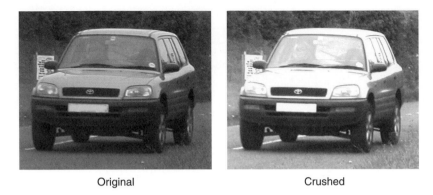

Original   Crushed

Figure 6-17 Crushing effect when white values exceed peak.

The extremes of digital imaging are explored when digital film and special effects work creates those blockbuster movie effects. Industrial Light & Magic has developed a technology called OpenEXR for the exchange of high-quality image data. Other high-dynamic range imaging systems use floating-point TIFF files (a.k.a. TIFF float). Visualization data stored in hierarchical data format (HDF) files may also end up being rendered using high-dynamic range techniques. The HDF files are most likely to be found in scientific research laboratories, but they are used in some other disciplines for storing complex graphical data.

Table 6-7 summarizes the popular HDR representations and shows some of their attributes.

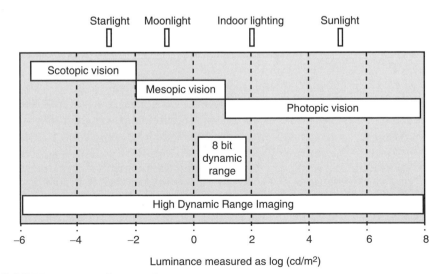

Figure 6-18 Human visual perception.

Table 6-7 Comparison of High-Dynamic Range Image Formats

Name	Sample size	Max value	Step size	Gamut
LogLuv 24	24 bits	10^5	0.11	Yes
Radiance	32 bits	10^{76}	0.01	Yes
LogLuv 32	32 bits	10^{38}	0.003	Yes
TIFF float	32 bits	10^{38}	0.003	Yes
Pixar log (TIFF)	33 bits	10^4	0.004	No
OpenEXR (ILM)	48 bits	10^{11}	0.001	Yes

Other formats that support HDR imagery include the following:

- Alias IFF
- Cineon DPX
- Mental ray
- Lightwave FLX
- Real Pixel

The most accurate representation is probably the Industrial Light & Magic OpenEXR format. Although it represents pixel colors with the maximum number of bits, the range of values is smaller than in the other formats. The true measure is the step size, which allows the most accurate gradation of tone across the image. All but the Pixar log format support the full gamut of colors.

By using a floating-point value to represent a pixel color, the dynamic range is greatly increased. All kinds of problems related to range limits, rounding errors, and issues with exposure under varying lighting conditions can be managed more effectively.

Here are some examples, first in Figure 6-19 a short exposure to show the backlight overexposure from the window, then in Figure 6-20 a flash photograph shot at night to eliminate the backlight. Finally, Figure 6-21 shows both images combined in Photoshop to eliminate the burn through and reveal the foreground detail as well as the trees outside the window.

The result I want is to have both parts of the view perfectly exposed. After all, that is what I see when I look at it directly. The final image was manipulated by hand with some careful masking and combining of the two previous images. HDR allows this to happen automatically.

HDR support allows photographs inside a darkened building to get the detail of the interior when the exposure time is so long that the backlight through the windows burns out the window detail and halos round the shape of the aperture. Setting the exposure time short enough to get the detail in a stained-glass window greatly underexposes the interior. HDR techniques allow the tonal range to be adjusted and the exposure setting to

Figure 6-19 Severely backlit photograph.

Figure 6-20 Backlight eliminated by using flash and shooting at night.

Figure 6-21 Combined low light and backlit images to show HDR possibilities.

be modified in a spatial manner so that areas of bright light are underexposed while dark interior walls are overexposed. This balances the two and you can see detail in both at the same time. It preserves the intent of what the photographer was trying to capture and is way beyond what cameras are normally capable of. This is why so much lighting is required to shoot movies on film sets.

It is possible to simulate the idealized HDR response with still photographs using existing low-dynamic range equipment, but it is necessary to take two or more pictures and combine them using sophisticated image-processing software. You can cheat with Photoshop like I did, which was fine for a monochrome-printed image but not good enough to realize the true benefits of HDR on movies. The goal is to build HDR into a camera that shoots high-definition TV pictures and still get all those nice details in the darkened corners of the room.

The color values in HDR describe the lightness over a range of values that is 4 orders of magnitude in scope. This includes the entire visible gamut for the human eye. Systems currently under development will at last allow us to realize the full range of human visible imagery within the production system for our video content. The consequence is that there will be an unprecedented level of image quality available to us and we must make sure that we don't throw away those benefits by using substandard compression on content that has been created using HDR techniques.

Figure 6-22 shows the CIE color space, with the triangle imposed on it representing the normal color gamut displayed by a TV set. HDR work will allow us to display the entire range of colors. This is the gamut that Table 6-7 described.

For more details, look at the ILM OpenEXR information on their Web site, and consult the Apple developer Web site for details of the HDR support in Mac OS.

If you are researching this topic further, also check out entries under the name "Munsell," which is another alternative color-space description method.

The implication for compressionists is that, if HDR gets implemented as a digital-imaging format on a wider basis, it will start to be used for moving images and we shall have

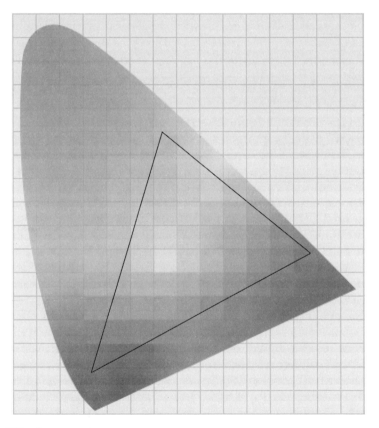

Figure 6-22 CIE color gamut.

ILM OpenEXR: http://www.openexr.org/

Apple Developer Connection: http://developer.apple.com/

HDR camera: http://www.spheron.com/products/SpheroCamHDR/hdri.html

to compress it. Currently we compress integer representations of pixel values. Floating-point pixel values will require some rethinking of how the compression algorithms operate.

6.15 Beyond HDR

Some scientists hope to go beyond high-dynamic range imaging by developing remote sensing systems. This work is called hyper spectral imaging and is designed to collect light from ultraviolet to the infrared end of the spectrum. While this isn't yet producing moving images, it will one day in the future.

Other scientists are looking at building imaging systems that operate at very high resolutions or at improbably rapid frame rates. The Cordin company in Utah manufactures a camera that can take 200 million frames a second. This can photograph an explosion as it happens.

So far no one is attempting to combine all of these into a supercamera—unless you know better, of course.

6.16 Summary: All Roads Lead to Rome

In this chapter we have looked at digital-imaging systems. Ultimately, whether our source footage originated on film or video, it is going to end up in a digital-imaging system on the way to being compressed.

Shooting some movie film, migrating it through a telecine box to a video format, and then ingesting it into a digital-imaging system is probably going to introduce artifacts from all three disciplines. Eliminating some of those stages by scanning the film digitally is obviously beneficial.

Film will have contributed grain; dust, scratches, and gate weave; and faded colors. You will then have lost significant amounts of detail and resolution as it was converted to video, and then as it became digitized, quantization and sampling artifacts came into play.

It may seem unlikely that we end up with anything worth watching, because we have not finished perpetrating all manner of punishment and depredations on that footage. Oh no, not by a long way. If you thought video caused some heinous damage to your images, just wait until you see what a badly set-up compression system is capable of.

But don't worry. It is possible to achieve some amazing (almost miraculous) results by taking care and minimizing the artifacts at each step. You might even make the result look better than the original if you care to apply some restorative efforts.

Before we leave the area of source-content formats, we'll spend a chapter looking at (or should that be listening to?) audio. While it might not seem obvious at first, many of the problems with compression affect audio in the same way as video. Because we use a different sense to experience audio, they seem to manifest themselves in a different way.

7

Matters Concerning Audio

7.1 I Hear the Sound of Distant Drums—and Voices

Compressing video deals with the visual part of the movie, but what about the sound track? This chapter covers the audio standards and formats that are used most often with compressed video. There are two primary scenarios to consider. There are others, of course, but these represent the extremes:

- Simple conversation with human voices as in telecoms or other low bit-rate projects.
- Very-high-quality music, background ambiance, and movie-quality sound tracks.

Before we go any further with our journey to perfect compression, let's divert from the straight and narrow path and spend a short while listening to the quiet rustle of pixels wafting gently in the breeze.

7.2 Blowing in the Wind

Audio is a moving pressure wave that the human ear interprets as sound. The change in pressure is plotted as a waveform and represented electrically as the output of a transducer. A waveform is a continuously varying value. Although the frequencies are higher, video is represented in the same way. All the discussion in this chapter regarding sample rates, word sizes, quantization errors, and digital filtering is relevant for video as well. The artifacts are the same but appear to be different because we see them instead of hear them.

7.3 Source Audio

With video, there are a variety of different sources for the moving picture content, and so it is with audio. The audio material could have been ingested from any of the following source formats:

- Vinyl or acetate disk
- 78 RPM disk
- Open-reel tape (a.k.a. reel-to-reel or quarter-inch magnetic tape)
- Cassette tape
- CD
- SACD
- DVD
- Off-air analog radio or TV
- Off-air digital audio broadcasting (DAB)
- Downloaded audio files
- Sound stripe from the edge of the home movie film
- Optical sound track from 16mm or 35mm movie film
- Surround sound audio from a synchronized audio source
- Live recording
- Embedded audio

Each of these recording mediums will introduce its own interesting features as well as very specific shortcomings/advantages such as noise, bandwidth limits, and quality of signal.

Refer to Appendix M for descriptions of the many kinds of connector you will encounter when connecting them together.

7.3.1 Analog Audio

Much of the legacy audio content is going to be delivered to you in the form of an analog signal. Ingesting it converts it from an analog continuously variable waveform into a discretely sampled format.

You must determine suitable parameter values for the following:

- The number of tracks to record in synchronization with one another
- The sample rate—bearing in mind the concepts based on Nyquist
- The bit value to indicate the resolution of the samples.

All of these will materially affect the quality of the audio that you record. Figure 7-1 shows the end-to-end path for analog audio.

7.3.2 Digital Audio from a CD

If you are taking audio directly from a CD, it will be sampled at 44.1 KHz and deliver 2 channels (or tracks) at a sample size of 16 bits. It is likely to be presented in an AIFF or WAV file container. The data rate of this content is about 150 *Kbps*. Figure 7-2 shows how the analog waveform is sampled periodically.

Other audio formats are emerging but have not achieved significant market penetration. Look out for SACD and DVD audio disks and high-density DVD formats based on blue laser technology. These may become dominant and will offer a greater capacity. This capacity can be used to store more material or increase the bits available for each sample.

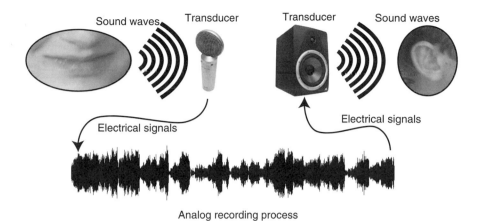

Figure 7-1 Analog audio capture and reproduction.

If you are planning to store much of this kind of material then a useful rule of thumb is that a minute of uncompressed audio requires about 11 Mbytes of disk space.

7.3.3 Digital Audio via FireWire

If you ingest audio from multiple analog sources, then a FireWire audio I/O (in/out) interface would be a useful addition to your equipment rack.

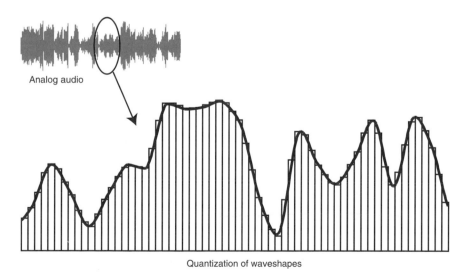

Figure 7-2 Digital audio samples.

The MOTU FireWire 828 and similar hardware products are not too expensive; there are also alternative products made by AJA and M-Audio, who provide audio input and conversion solutions too. There are several different models to choose from in the AJA Io FireWire interface family of products according to what your needs are.

M-Audio and Focusrite also make useful hardware. Certainly there are many other alternatives, and a search through the products available from your audio retail outlet will suggest some other alternatives.

FireWire is certainly a good choice because the throughput is sufficient to support the highest sample rate, bit size, and number of channels you are likely to want. For amateur or hobbyist requirements, USB is feasible but you may run out of capacity if you try to grab too many channels at once.

The entire audio mixing process in a studio is now available inside a desktop system. You simply have to get the sound in there in the first place. Figure 7-3 illustrates a MOTU 896 interface. M-Audio and other manufacturers make comparable units.

The MOTU 896 will sample 8 channels with 24 bits of resolution at 192 KHz. The rack-mounted unit has 8 outputs as well, so that offers some interesting possibilities for using it as part of a studio infrastructure. This unit also supports *AES* audio and SPDIF in/out via an optical interface.

7.3.4 Digital Audio via SPDIF

This is derived from the optical connectors that were deployed on hi-fi equipment when CD players were first introduced. The concept was that you would buy a high-end CD player mechanism and then separately install a digital-to-analog converter, or perhaps your very expensive hi-fi amplifier would have one built in. The SPDIF connection uses a short piece of optical fibre. It was popularized by DAT players that seem to have gone out of fashion now that you can record straight to your hard disk.

The SPDIF interface is used by semi-professional and professional sound engineers and is reasonably common in situations where you want to connect some high-quality audio equipment together.

Figure 7-3 FireWire 896 HD audio interface. Source: Image courtesy of MOTU.

One of the major benefits is that it electrically decouples the source and destination equipment. This means that problems such as ground loops, hum, mains-induced interference, and other nasty things that happen to electrical signals when they pass through magnetic induction fields are completely eliminated. Any potential difference in voltage between the two chassis is also isolated. These are all good things when putting together an audio installation. It is useful on location recordings when you are jacking a feed across from the house PA or the stage's main mixing console.

The Apple G5 computer now has SPDIF built into the motherboard and while there were some issues with "chirping" noise artifacts being propagated through from the power supply in a few of the 2003 early-vintage models, this has been eliminated in the updated products. A replacement power supply resolves the issue if you buy a second-hand machine that exhibits the problem.

If you are having trouble identifying an SPDIF connector on an unlabeled rack, consult Appendix M where a collection of audio and video connectors have been collated together for reference.

7.3.5 *Digital Audio via USB*

For some applications, taking digital audio in via a USB interface may be a satisfactory solution. As a general rule though, this interface is not as fast as FireWire although it is more popular on PC platforms. MIDI interfaces are often provided as a USB connection, and bear in mind that keyboard and mouse traffic also share this interface.

Instinctively I feel more secure putting multi-channel, high sample-rate audio down a FireWire interface but if USB is all you have and your audio transfer needs are modest, it should be fine, at least for a couple of channels at a 44.1 or 48 KHz sample rate.

If you plan to do your audio via USB, then an M-Audio interface would be a good choice. It has been engineered to deliver the optimum performance. A range of models are available to suit different requirements.

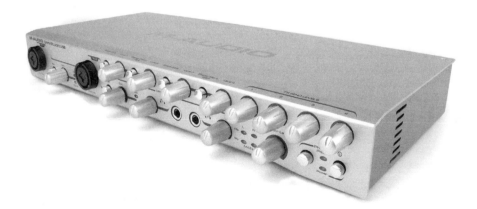

Figure 7-4 Omni studio USB I/O unit. Source: Image courtesy of M-Audio.

7.3.6 Radio News-Gathering

If you are ingesting from reel-to-reel formats, make sure the head arrangement is correct for the tape you are playing back because there are several ways the tracks could have been organized and some very old tape may not yield the audio you expect.

Back in the days of "steam-driven-wireless," radio news-gathering reporters used 2-track, open-reel tape formats. The portable kit only recorded on one track, which allowed the tape to be turned over. The tape reels were 5.25 inches and carried 15 minutes of tape running at 7.5 inches per second (ips). Using both sides allowed 30 minutes to be recorded in the field.

Back at home base these tapes could be played back on a 2-track machine but the "B" channel needed to be switched off to avoid playing back the other side in reverse while listening to the "A" channel. Turning the tape over was discouraged since there was often some cross-talk between the tracks when it was played back in the studio. The best-quality solution was to dub the tape while it was played back on the exact same machine as it was recorded on. This avoided any problems with head alignment and azimuth adjustment between decks. Cutting tape that was recorded on both sides was impossible anyway, so there was always this delay inherent in getting content to air.

It is only since the turn of the millennium that open-reel tape has been eliminated in favor of mini-disk formats. These transfer into a PC very easily and allow the content to be edited and aired almost right away. In the days of open-reel recording, editing in the field was always possible if the reporter had a razor blade and some splicing tape. These days, that is only possible if you have a laptop to download the mini-disk audio into so you can cut it with a sound editor.

7.3.7 Multi-Track Audio

If you are ingesting multiple audio tracks, you must be clear about what multi-track audio format you are using. Historically, reel-to-reel decks supported a variety of formats with 1, 2, 4, and 8 tracks of sound being recorded on a single quarter-inch tape. Studio formats on half-inch, 1-inch, and even 2-inch tape yield many more tracks. High-end studios have 48, 96, 128, or even more tracks.

Actually, number of tracks is no longer the problem it was in the past. These days, simply reversing the order of the samples and bouncing the tracks around in something like Bias Peak, Deck, or E-Magic Logic corrects a lot of that sort of thing. Pro Tools and Cubase are also candidates for this sort of work. Even those old news-gathering tapes could be ingested as a stereo pair and then split very easily with the sound editor. Figure 7-5 shows how to do this.

When equipping yourself for audio editing, look for products that allow you to use VST plug-ins on the PC. On the Mac OS X operating system the favored approach is now Audio Units. VST plug-ins also work on the Mac OS but are deprecated in Mac OS X while they are the preferred solution for Classic Mac OS. If your audio workbench supports VST or Audio Unit plug-ins, then obtain some shareware, freeware, or commercial tools to process all your audio tracks to remove undesirable artifacts.

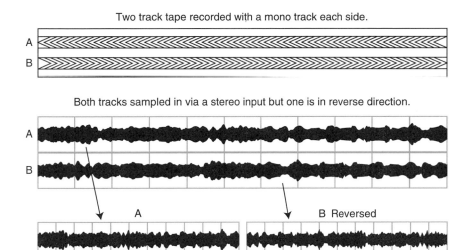

Figure 7-5 Multi-track audio swapping in sound editor.

7.4 How the Audio Is Coded and Synchronized

Audio is an analog waveform. The human ear responds to it as a change in air pressure and each ear receives a 1-dimensional signal. When we listen to sounds, we place them fairly accurately into a 3D space but this is still happening via just two 1-dimensional signals, one for each ear.

The relative phasing and arrival times of those waveforms are what makes sounds appear to move forward, backward, and up and down. The separation of the sounds and the panning is what moves them left to right. This is a very simplified description of what happens and if you need to know more, please consult some books on psychoacoustics.

Certain sound tracks are recorded with special attention to the placement of the microphones. This extends to using a dummy head to hold the microphones and placing them where the human ears would be. Even the shape of the ears is modeled to accurately pick up exactly what a human being would hear, although this can also be done by carefully selecting and positioning microphones with an appropriate frequency response and dynamic profile.

At playback time, the optimum experience is obtained by listening on a pair of headphones. This is called binaural recording and everything about the quality of the audio depends on the accuracy of the recording levels and the phasing of the channels. Lowering the sample rate or compressing the audio too much will destroy the subtleties of this recording and it will be impossible to reconstruct the missing information on playback.

7.4.1 Sample Rates and Nyquist (44.1, 48, 96, and 192 KHz)

Converting from an analog source to a digital storage medium requires an instantaneous measurement of the sound level and a notation of the value. These measurements are called samples. The time between each subsequent sample determines the highest recordable frequency. The Nyquist sampling rule dictates that a sample rate is able to record frequencies up to half the sample rate. Any higher frequencies will not be properly resolved.

At the sampling frequency, a peak and a trough may be recorded with two adjacent samples. With no intervening values the frequency is captured but the wave shape is nothing like what it originally was. The interesting wave shape is created by even higher-frequency overtones and harmonics that combine. So even though we can sample that very high frequency, we destroy the timbre.

When CD recording was first introduced, a sample rate of 44.1 KHz was thought to be adequate since the human ear cannot detect frequencies higher than 22 KHz. Higher-quality recording is achieved by sampling at 96 KHz and indeed sample rates of 192 KHz are used in very high-quality production.

Movie sound tracks on DVDs benefit from the slightly better sample rate of 48 KHz, and you will immediately see the relationship between 48, 96, and 192 KHz sample rates. Conversion among them uses an integer-based averaging so if the production system runs at 192 KHz, creating a 48 KHz track should be computationally easy.

Converting between 44.1 KHz and 48 KHz is not an ideal scenario, and a lot of work has been done on the conversion algorithms to reduce the unpleasant artifacts.

7.4.2 Word Sizes (8, 10, 12, 16, 20, and 24 Bits)

The word size describes the number of bits used to describe a sample. The more bits you use, the more accurate the sampling can be. The limited number of discrete levels or steps

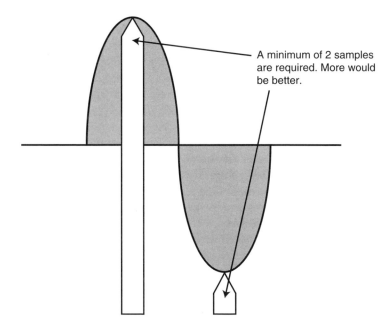

Figure 7-6 Harry Nyquist's sampling proposition circa 1920.

that a given word size allows determines the quantization. Allowing too few bits causes an audible artifact in the sound when it is reproduced.

As you increase the word size, it is harder for the human ear to discriminate the individual quantization levels. The extra detail enables the digital filtering algorithms to compute wave shapes more accurately and to avoid rounding and clipping errors. This helps to retain the highest-possible quality.

7.4.3 *Dynamic Range, Logarithmic Scales, and Decibels*

An 8-bit value has a range of levels from 0 to 255. Doubling the bits available increases this range to 65536 discrete values. A 24-bit sample has an even larger dynamic range. Having an increased dynamic range available is also useful for reducing the amount of noise. Even a silent passage will have some noise from the random movement of electrons in the digital-to-analog conversion circuits. Increasing the dynamic range by making the word size bigger provides a higher signal-to-noise ratio.

For many years audio signals have been measured on a logarithmic scale. This goes back to the days when telephony was a new invention. In order to measure impedance so that systems could be matched with one another (this is important for optimum performance), a means of measuring power dissipation across a known resistance was required.

Figure 7-7 shows a logarithmic curve. The X-axis shows equally spaced units. On the Y-axis, they are nonlinear.

The dissipation of 1 milliwatt (mW) across a resistance of 600 ohms requires a potential difference (voltage) of 0.775 volts. From this all manner of other calculations are derived, such as the root mean square (RMS) or peak power of a signal. This formula has been the bedrock of audio-level measurement. The Greek omega symbol (Ω) is used to indicate a value measured in ohms, and you will often see this used in specifications or on the back of a speaker cabinet.

The logarithmic scale is used to measure attenuation along a telephone cable because signals are reduced logarithmically according to the length of the wire. The human ear also responds logarithmically to the sound pressure level (SPL). This is the force that sound waves exert when they impinge on the ear.

The unit of measure on the logarithmic scale is called the Bel in honor of Alexander Graham Bell. The logarithm of the ratio between the measured power and a reference datum results in a very small value. For most practical purposes therefore, the Bel is too large a unit so the measurements are expressed in tenths of a Bel (or decibels).

The 1 mW across 600Ω is our reference and is defined to be the 0 dB reference value. All other values are measured with reference to that datum.

Taking two power values measured in watts, divide one by the other and then compute the base-10 logarithm of the result and multiply that by 10, because the measurement is in deci-Bels (dB). Here is the formula.

$$\text{Power Ratio} = 10 * \log \left(\frac{\text{Power1}}{\text{Power2}} \right)$$

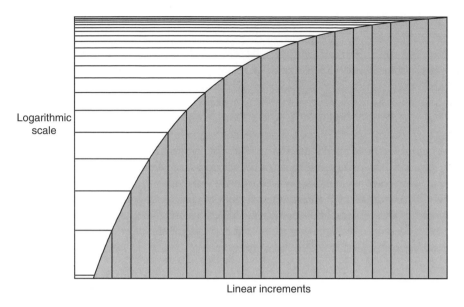

Figure 7-7 Logarithmic scale.

The value measured in dB is a ratio and therefore it only has meaning when described with respect to a reference value. Taking our 1 mW reference, any values for signal levels relative to that would be measured in dBmW, which is shortened to dB(m).

The formula for power ratios applies to power measurements in watts. Audio monitoring also measures voltage. Virtually the same formula is used but the result must be squared. Squaring a value that is converted to a logarithm is accomplished by doubling the result. Here is the formula for expressing voltage ratios in dB.

$$\text{Voltage Ratio} = 20 * \log \left(\frac{\text{Voltage1}}{\text{Voltage2}} \right)$$

Computing the dynamic range of the signal for a given sample word size is accomplished by adapting the voltage ratio formula like this:

$$\text{Dynamic range} = 20 * \log \left(2^{\text{word-size}} \right)$$

So for different word sizes in our sampling scheme a table of dynamic ranges can be computed as shown in Table 7-1.

So, the dynamic range describes the difference between the quietest sound and the loudest sound that is accommodated within the range of possible values.

Table 7-1 Dynamic Range Versus Word Size

Word size	$2^{\text{Word size}}$	Dynamic range
8 bits	256	48 dB
10 bits	1024	60 dB
12 bits	4096	72 dB
16 bits	65536	96 dB
20 bits	1048576	120 dB
24 bits	16777216	144 dB

The quietest sound would be total silence, but in fact there would be some kind of background noise introduced by the *DAC* even at that level.

7.4.4 Quantization Problems

Increasing the number of steps available also decreases noise that is due to quantization errors. A digitizer rounds the measured value to the nearest increment. It is possible to

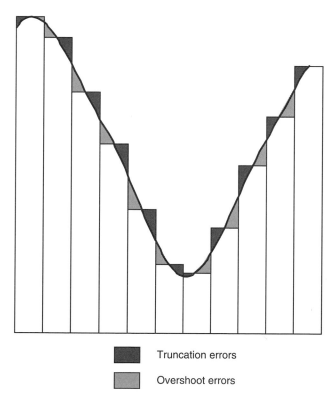

Truncation errors

Overshoot errors

Figure 7-8 Quantization errors.

miss the target value by as much as half a step. If the steps are smaller, the errors are smaller. Therefore the noise introduced by quantization errors will be less. Sampling with larger word sizes reduces the step size for the quantization.

Quantization errors occur because the sampling has not detected the correct level, or when converting back to analog, the correct output level is not generated. Some quantization errors happen because the timing of the samples was imperfect. If the sample clock is irregular then some samples will be taken at the wrong time.

Quantization errors are more severe as the highest frequencies are sampled. Figure 7-9 shows a 22.05 KHz sine wave being sampled at 44.1 KHz. In the lower part of the illustration the waveform is reconstructed using square samples and then, in the third waveform, joining it up with straight lines. None of these are reconstructing the original wave shape as it was. This introduces some harmonic overtones that alter the timbre of the sound. A sine wave sounds quite different from a square or sawtooth waveform.

It can get a lot worse than this. At or near the Nyquist limit, samples may miss entire waveforms due to phasing errors.

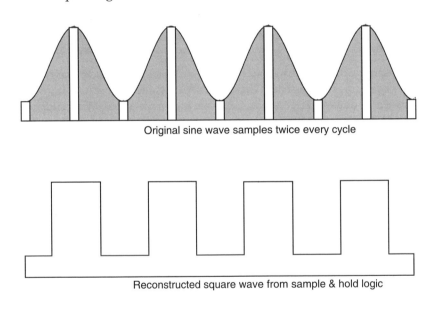

Original sine wave samples twice every cycle

Reconstructed square wave from sample & hold logic

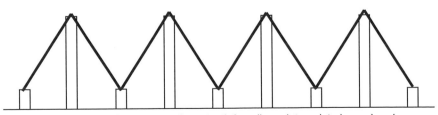

Reconstructed saw tooth from linear interpolated sample values

Figure 7-9 Waveform reconstruction from samples.

7.4.5 Aliasing Artifacts

Chapter 6 discussed digital-imaging systems and the aliasing artifacts that happen when you draw diagonal lines. These exhibit themselves as jaggies. The same effect happens on audio except that we cannot see it of course. We can hear it though. It is a horrible scratchy buzzing sound.

In the example showing severe quantization errors, the wave shape is reconstructed reasonably well if a sine curve-fitting algorithm is used. It is not such a good solution with frequencies that are slightly detuned from the sample rate. If that is not dealt with correctly, unpleasant sub-harmonics are introduced. The effects of that are far worse. At least with a square or sawtooth wave the added overtones are inaudible. An aliasing artifact generates frequencies that are lower than the sample rate and these are in the audible range. Figure 7-10 illustrates the effect.

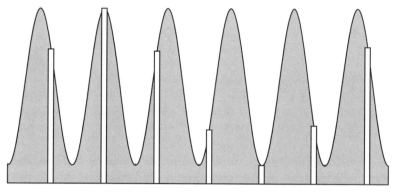

Samples taken from a frequency nearly at the sample rate

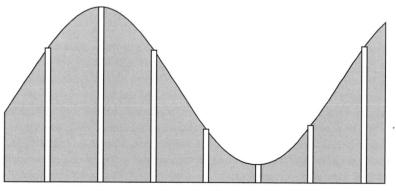

Reconstructed waveform is at a beat frequency

Figure 7-10 Aliasing waveform reconstruction.

In the second waveform, the decoder curve fits the output to the samples it has been given. In this case the period of the samples and the frequency of the audio being sampled yield a waveform reconstruction that is nothing like the original waveform. It fits the samples but it is not the desired waveform.

This is the case that is argued for sampling at a far higher rate than Nyquist suggested, and it is why audio sample rates go as high as 192 KHz. It is necessary to accurately capture the highest audible waveform without this aliasing artifact. In fact any aliasing that does happen at that sample rate is far above the audible range anyway, so it will not matter.

7.4.6 CD Sample Rate (44.1 KHz) Versus DVD Sample Rate (48 KHz)

Quantization problems may rear their ugly head when you are converting between CD sample rates (44.1 KHz) and DVD sample rates (48 KHz).

This is another example of when you should know something about the target output platform before you commence your processing. If the video is being encoded for a DVD product, you should ensure that your sample rate is 48 KHz (or a multiple thereof) when you ingest the audio. It may also be necessary to check settings in all the tools you use to ensure that the correct sample rate is preserved.

It is unlikely that the sample rate would get changed but it is possible if you flip a switch the wrong way inadvertently.

7.4.7 Digital Filtering Versus Analog Filtering

You may want to filter the audio as part of the preparation for encoding. Here you have a choice of doing some processing either before it is converted into a digital form or afterward.

The analog processing is going to be permanent and not easily altered after going through the digitizing process, so you may want to defer any processing until after you have the audio safely in a file on the hard disk and then use non-destructive *DSP*-based processes.

Analog processing is often said to have a certain warmth and personality while the digital processing is more harsh and cold. This may have been true of older processing solutions, but these days the analog world is very well simulated using digital-filtering algorithms that are very sophisticated indeed.

On the other hand, the analog hardware you have in your studio may yield better-quality audio than the available plug-ins on your computer. Your mileage may vary of course. The main advantage of applying the corrective filtering in the digital domain is that the process can be automated and undone. Some tools support key-framed control points. The processing is non-destructive.

In the end, it is likely to be a trade off between quality and convenience.

7.4.8 Removing Redundancy to Simplify Coding

Reducing the complexity of the sound so that it compresses better is virtually impossible to do in the analog world. This is something that modern codecs do automatically. Then at the decoding stage they reintroduce some harmonic content based on information that was coded in the bit stream.

The *AAC Plus* codec uses spectral band replication (*SBR*) to simplify the encoded signal and then recreate a very close approximation of the original sound artificially.

Other opportunities occur when there is a loud transient sound that masks all the others. Selectively removing the fine detail when a transient occurs will reduce the work that the encoder has to do.

7.5 Software Encoders Versus Hardware Encoders

Software encoders must be fast enough when processing audio data. Hardware encoders are useful in situations that require low-latency encoding. That is important in video conferencing, which requires zero latency.

If you have the time to carry out multiple passes, then hardware encoding does not provide any significant gains since you are in a non real-time scenario.

Your choice of hardware or software codec is likely to be mandated more by the video coding and what you need from that in terms of performance.

7.6 Source Audio Formats

Some of the issues you must deal with will relate to the setup of your studio. Routing analog audio around the system is optimal if your mixing desk is analog. If you are building a new and modern installation from scratch, it is very likely you will be totally digital with analog only at the input and output of the system. Appendix K has more information on the diversity of audio formats you will encounter.

7.6.1 Analog Audio

Analog audio is presented in a lot of different levels and formats. There are quite a few well-known connector standards for plugging things together, with minor variants on those providing some interesting interconnection problems.

Connecting digital equipment together is quite a bit simpler. It is a good idea to gather a collection of adapters and cables for interconnecting different pieces of equipment.

7.6.2 Balanced and Unbalanced Audio

Balanced audio is used in studios and in professionally constructed sound systems. This is designed to be very noise-immune because the cable carries two phase-opposed versions

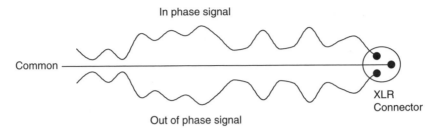

Figure 7-11 Balanced audio phasing.

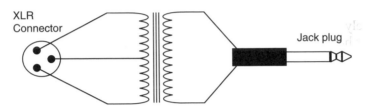

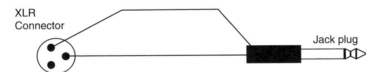

Figure 7-12 Balun versus cable.

of the same signal. Any inductive noise is then phase inverted when the signal is converted back to an unbalanced format.

In an emergency, wire the balanced cables so that they are compatible with unbalanced inputs just by connecting one of the two signals and the ground shield to a jack plug. This will not remove the noise. You must use a proper Balun transformer to do that.

When compressing audio or video, noise is your enemy. It consumes bit rate that would be better employed carrying the content you want to encode. Balanced audio is better than unbalanced since there is less induced noise.

7.6.3 AES Audio Formats

The Audio Engineering Society (AES) defines a standard for digital audio that is very popular with broadcasters. This is a good choice to make if you are building a new installation but not all equipment is compatible. Choose AES audio or balanced audio as your base format. Whichever you select, it is very likely that you will have quite a lot of hardware just for converting between them. This is affectionately called audio–visual glue and accounts for a large proportion of the cost of building a studio. It is very often not factored into the price of the build and will take you by surprise when you get the bill. Avoid this problem by selecting your equipment more carefully and making sure that adequate systems diagrams are drawn up to include a description of the types of signal being wired in and where the A–V glue must be inserted.

7.7 The New Standards: HE-AAC

The audio standards developed as part of the MPEG-4 standard are becoming popular. The name for the new kind of audio coding is AAC. The latest variant is called high efficiency *HE-AAC* but this was previously known as *AAC+*. It adds an extra layer of coding called spectral band replication. This synthesizes frequencies that are under the guidance of the coder. Those frequencies are then recreated and added to the output at the decoding end.

Figure 7-13 shows how the SBR coding takes place prior to the AAC coding. The SBR tool output is a coded data stream and the remainder is what gets coded with the AAC tool. At the decoding end of the equation, a decoder that only supports AAC will not see the SBR data. It will decode the AAC signal and deliver good-quality audio. If an SBR encoder is available, it will use the extra information to enhance the audio that has been recreated by the AAC decoder.

The coding pipeline divides the audio range into low and high frequencies. The low frequency components are coded by the AAC tool, and the high frequencies by the SBR tool. Adding this SBR tool to an audio coder improves the efficiency by 30% over what was being achieved with the AAC tool on its own.

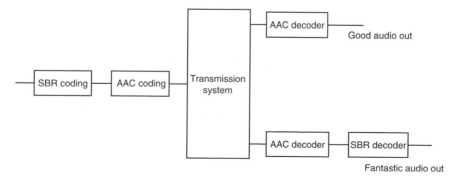

Figure 7-13 AAC and SBR pipeline.

The AAC+ or HE-AAC concept was developed by a company called Coding Technologies. Note that the nomenclature AAC+, AAC Plus, and MPEG-4 HE-AAC are all describing the same thing. The codec is becoming best known as HE-AAC.

7.8 Multi-Channel Formats

Here is a rundown of some common multi-channel formats. There are many more, and you must consult any records that may be attached to the source material and read the manuals for your encoding software to know how to map these to the output encoded media.

Table 7-2 Audio Track Arrangements

Tracks	Speakers	Description
Mono	1	Old legacy program material will only have a single audio track. You must duplicate this across both tracks of a stereo pair for most applications. It is very likely that home movie audio from magnetic striped film will only have mono audio.
Dual mono	2	This is the duplicated mono on two stereo channels.
Two-sided mono	2	The radio news-gathering format uses 2-track tapes but records one track in each direction, requiring that the tape be turned over to record the other track.
Stereo	2	True stereo recorded through a pair of microphones or mixed from multi-channel master tapes. Be careful to preserve the relative phasing between channels or sound will appear to move around.
Pseudo stereo	2	Sometimes old mono recordings will be reprocessed with filters to separate out various instruments that are then panned from one side to the other to create an artificial stereo effect.
Mix minus	2	Sometimes, the stereo signals are not a stereo pair in the true sense. One could be a backing track while the other is the same but with perhaps the vocals missing. In news gathering, one channel is probably ambient background noise while the other is the presenter. The two channels must be mixed carefully to turn them into a presentable stereo sound track.

Continued

Coding Technologies: http://www.codingtechnologies.com/

Table 7-2 Audio Track Arrangements (Continued)

Tracks	Speakers	Description
Dolby Surround	3 front and 1 rear	An analog-matrixed signal is decoded to create the extra surround channels. Too much compression will destroy the matrix information. Separate them out and then encode each independently.
Quadraphonic	2 front and 2 rear	An experimental analog surround format used for music in the 1970s. Not much content survives in this format.
5.0 surround	3 front and 2 rear	A modern surround format used for music applications and lacking the low frequency channel.
Dolby Digital (AC-3)	3 front, 2 rear, and 1 low-frequency channel	Surround systems constructed according to the Dolby model are configured in a variety of ways with anything from 1 to 6 channels being used. There are also complex matrix-encoding signals that must be preserved so the older Dolby Surround systems will work. This is critical, and you must have some knowledge of how this system works to be able to encode it competently. Most important, the sample rate must be high enough to preserve the surround information. There are many versions and variants of this system, and it is only Dolby Digital 5.1 if it says so on the box.
DTS Digital Surround 5.1	3 front, 2 rear, and 1 low-frequency channel	An alternative to the Dolby system is the Digital Theatre Sound system. This is often presented on major DVDs containing Hollywood blockbuster movies as an alternative to the Dolby sound track. It is not unusual for DVD video files to have 10 or more audio tracks associated with them. Every one has to be carefully encoded and precisely synchronized.
THX Surround ES™	3 front, 3 rear, and 1 low-frequency	This extends the DTS system from 5.1 channels to 6.1. All the earlier caveats apply. You must be confident about what you are doing when encoding this sort of channel complexity. Also known as DTS-ES 6.1.
THX Surround EX™	3 front, 3 rear, and 1 low-frequency channel	This is also known as Dolby Digital EX and supports 6.1 audio channels.
Sony SDDS	5 front, 2 rear, and 1 low-frequency channel	This is used in large cinema auditoriums and has 2 additional speakers on either side of the screen.

Continued

Table 7-2 Audio Track Arrangements (Continued)

Tracks	Speakers	Description
THX Periphonic	3 front floor, 3 front ceiling, 2 rear floor, 2 rear ceiling; a low-frequency driver at floor level and another at the ceiling level.	This is a system proposed by LucasFilm/THX that embodies dual 5.1 surround systems, one at floor level and the other at ceiling level, in order to convey height and surround information to the ear. It became known as Periphonic.

 Be sure to properly license any DTS Digital Surround decoding software you use from DTS. The open-source VLC player has had to remove DTS decoding support due to a threat of legal action over patent violations.

A lot of useful information about surround-sound systems can be found at the Time for DVD Web site.

There are some enhancements to the Mac OS at version 10.4 (known as the Tiger release) that will be useful when managing complex audio projects. The system has an audio-processing environment built in called CoreAudio. This manages the audio unit plug-ins on a systemwide basis; the audio processing is available to any application that cares to take advantage of it.

With the 10.4 release, the CoreAudio support provides much help with managing multi-channel surround-sound mapping, and a lot of the headaches to do with keeping tracks organized are now taken over by the OS and done automatically. This makes the Mac OS platform a good choice for some production work at the high end.

 Specialist audio processing tools such as Sound-Soap, E-Magic Logic, and ProTools are worth purchasing and keeping available nearby to run a quick audio-processing job when necessary.

Time for DVD: http://timefordvd.com/tutorial/SurroundSound.shtml
DTS: http://www.dtsonline.com/

7.8.1 Caveats Regarding Surround Sound

Over-compression of the audio with normal compression tools will lose any embedded surround-sound information. The consequence is that sound will come randomly from any speaker and may jump around as the compression factor changes. You may also hear strange bumps and whining noises from speakers driven by the surround circuits. This is due to the severe corruption of the surround-sound signal. In some formats, this is an analog-coded frequency or phase modulation that is outside of the normal range of human hearing and therefore is outside the range that some audio codecs are optimized for.

7.8.2 HE-AAC Surround

The Fraunhofer Institute has developed some very innovative approaches to compression, especially in the area of MPEG-4 and the related coding techniques for audio and video. At the IBC 2004 conference, they showed how the coding of surround-sound audio could be accomplished at 48 Kbps. This has profound implications.

The quality delivered is superior to that available from a matrixed analog audio signal. This announcement is innovative because it broadcasts a compatible signal that can be played back on both stereo and mono systems.

It is based on coding a down-mix as a mono audio signal and then adding difference information that can be *cascaded* onto that signal when it is decoded. You simply stop decoding when you have extracted the number of channels you need. It's a very clever solution.

Fraunhofer has also developed an *MP3*-based surround audio solution but while this is interesting, the *AAC*-based techniques will likely deliver a longer-term solution.

7.9 Pitfalls and Gotchas

Audio is much simpler than video, but there are still some nasty surprises for the unwary.

7.9.1 CD Versus DVD Sample Rates

CD audio is sampled at a rate of 44.1 KHz. DVD audio is sampled at a rate of 48 KHz and the difference is noticeable if the audio is clocked at the wrong rate. It also will not sync to your video. Converting from one to the other introduces audible artifacts at a frequency that is the difference between the two. A 3.9 KHz buzzing is very annoying if your audio is not resampled properly.

You need to know what the target output platform is for your program material. If you are planning to output to a DVD format, remember that the audio sample rates are not the same as on CD audio discs.

7.9.2 Sampling Word Size = Quality

Bear in mind that some older audio sources such as music synthesizers only offer 8-bit samples as their sound origination. Sampling analog signals that originated in 8-bit digital form with a 16-bit word size will not generate better audio than you started with. If you are using some kind of synchronized MIDI signal to generate a sound track, make sure it is being voiced out through hardware or software synthesizers that will generate a suitable signal.

7.9.3 Rights Issues on Re-Use

As rights protection is deployed more in the future, it is increasingly likely that you will encounter copy-protection issues with some source formats such as CD or DVD disks. Whether you can take music from commercial CD recordings depends on your rights to repurpose that material. You cannot simply dub from any CD you happen to have lying around. Stock audio libraries are designed to provide background music for programs, but special permission is necessary if you want to use well-known commercial material.

7.10 Open-Source Audio-Processing Systems

If you use the Linux operating system and want to experiment with digital audio, you can build a versatile home studio for much less than you would expect. Having the operating system and hardware built shouldn't cost a lot of money. Adding sound cards is also quite economical. The important glue that makes it all work is the software. Check out Ecasound, Audacity, and Ardour as potential candidates for recording and mixing your tracks.

The Ecasound application is a command line tool for recording audio via the sound card. This is useful for building automation systems because it is easy to incorporate into a shell script. Audacity is useful for editing sound files. This tool works on Windows or Mac OS as well as Linux. Mixing and mastering can be done with Ardour, which is free and is being ported to operating systems other than Linux. The Mac OS *port* is currently in progress. These are all available as source kits, which you can modify yourself.

7.11 Summary: Don't Tell Harry

Audio has some tricks and surprises just like video. Often it is written off as being of little consequence, but if you have perfectly compressed video with a truly awful audio track, that is no good at all. You have to be diligent with every aspect of the process whether it is video, audio, or other multimedia assets. It is all important.

Ecasound: http://www.eca.cx/

Audacity: http://audacity.sourceforge.net/

Ardour: http://ardour.org/

A simple three-step process when trying to compress and store or deliver audio as effectively as possible goes like this:

- First reduce the sample rate. This proportionally reduces the size of the bit stream. Encoding only a mono rather than a stereo signal saves half the capacity.
- Reduce the variation in the sound level. Even it out so the volume excursions are not so radical. Filtering to remove noise or unwanted frequencies helps, too.
- Shorten the clip somehow. Trim it. Edit bits out. Resample it a little faster with pitch correction but somehow reduce the total number of samples.

7.12 Continuing with Our Travels

So now we know how images are originated on film and video and are converted into a digital format. Computer graphics systems will contribute more source material, and we have also considered audio as part of the source of our compressed output.

We now know enough to start looking at the coding processes. We'll concentrate on video. Audio is interesting but our main focus is visual systems, and the compression of audio is a large subject in its own right, worthy of much attention. We will come back to audio near the end of the book when we set up some example compression processes. Chapter 37 deals with getting the best out of the sound track.

For now, let's journey onward into the depths of video-coding technology and examine some popular codecs.

Choosing the Right Codec 8

8.1 Where Next?

It is time to look at the map and choose a route. This chapter is all about choices. My choices would not necessarily be your choices. Some advisors may recommend that you buy products from one manufacturer to solve all your problems. I believe that the situation is more complex than that.

The major products all have benefits and disadvantages. Assessing their pros and cons here will facilitate your choosing the right compression tool and surrounding it with "best-of-breed" supporting applications.

No single product will be suitable for every occasion. Constructing a workflow from a selection of products chosen as the best for each part of the process will yield a better-quality result. Integration is the key, so checking out the import and export capabilities of your tools is very important.

Developing a clear strategy for your business goals is vital. Making an informed choice when selecting the most appropriate technology is the next priority. Do the necessary research well before placing an order and writing out a check.

8.2 Not All Codecs Are Created Equal

There are two main kinds of codec, and the information in this section applies equally to still images, video, and audio.

During the production process your focus is on workflow, re-use, archiving, and issues where quality is the dominant factor. To afford a large enough capacity in your storage system, some compression is likely to be required. The codecs you might use in a production workflow are lossless or so nearly lossless that it makes no difference. Compression is beneficial for more efficient archiving and quicker transfers from place to place. These are production codecs.

When you deliver a finished product, the consumer is not expected to continue working on the content, so the issues of quality recede and compression ratio or cost of storage and transfer becomes paramount. These are the codecs you use to squash your

Table 8-1 Codec Categories

Property	Production codec	Delivery codec
Compression ratio	Low – typically 4:1	High – typically 50:1 or better.
Quality	Perfect	Good but may degenerate down to sub-VHS quality.
Lossy	Zero for some codecs, for others it is very minimal.	Very
Bit rate	25 to 50 Mbps	Down to 800 Kbps for video and 24 Kbps or less for audio.
File size	20 GB per hour	Down to 0.4 GB per hour
Editable	Yes	Not really
Compositable	Yes	Only with alpha channel data provided and as an overlay at best.
Key frames only	Usually	Almost never.
Conversion to other formats	Easy	Further significant degradation likely.

content so that it can fit in the finite space of a CD or it can be transmitted through a broadband network. This kind of compression is somewhat lossy or even on occasion very lossy. These codecs would be grouped under the category known as delivery codecs. Table 8-1 summarizes the attributes of these codecs.

Most of the discussion in this chapter relates to choosing a suitable delivery codec. You don't have the same choices available when looking at production codecs since these are dictated by the infrastructure of your studio or the equipment you already have installed.

 Try several different manufacturers' codecs to see whether one suits your content better than another.

8.3 Why Are Standards So Important?

Many different codecs have been invented. They tend to be based around similar algorithmic approaches because the engineers all go to the same conferences and read the same technical papers. The differences are in the fine points of the implementations and the choices the engineers make when constructing them.

The current state of the art for players is to deliver architectures that allow different codecs to be plugged in at run time. The players are separated somewhat from the codecs. This is how it's done:

A player provides a framework and a foundation with code that is necessary for playing back all video formats. This framework and foundation include the user interface (UI), for example, with its play and pause buttons, menu and file-opening dialogs, and general look and feel.

Once all the generic handling of a particular video format is dealt with, any specialized code that deals with translating and decoding a specific video format is contained in a plug-in module. All of these plug-in modules support the same application interface, so the player can call for the same things to be done regardless of the format selected. The plug-in then deals with the specifics of a particular video-encoding or playback process, having been delegated with that task by the player application.

It's a very neat concept and allows codecs and players to upgraded independently. It creates opportunities for third parties to create their own plug-in modules or to make a player and then use a readily available library of plug-ins.

8.3.1 *Open Standards Versus Proprietary Implementations*

With an open standard, everyone gets to compete equally. Products are differentiated according to quality of manufacture, reliability, price, and functionality. With a proprietary implementation, you are locked in at the creative and consumption ends of the delivery chain. You have to justify for yourself whether this is good or bad. Decisions about this tend to be based on reach and market penetration of certain players or platforms.

Going with any of the proprietary codecs locks you into one or another company's future strategy. You are entirely at the mercy of any decisions the company might make to immediately cease support of its player on a particular platform. Companies do that sort of thing, often with little or no warning.

Real Networks video is available everywhere; QuickTime is available on Mac OS and Windows but is not available on Linux without your using special tricks. *Windows Media* support is likewise available on Mac OS and Windows but not on Linux unless you use those same techniques to run Windows dynamic link libraries (DLLs) in a Windows emulation framework.

A DLL module contains dynamically linked library software written in Intel machine code and is designed to be shared between several applications to avoid duplication of the same code every time. Linux operating systems can generally cope with this quite easily by running the DLLs inside a framework, and provided they are on an Intel-based computer, everything is fine.

Mac OS systems use a completely different processor that does not natively understand the Intel code without the necessary software support being provided. The PowerPC chip in a Macintosh needs to run a translation or emulation engine to interpret that Intel machine code. It is possible (Virtual PC does it, for example), but it is not very easy to set up. Ideally, the software inside the DLL should be recompiled for the PowerPC, but this is not always feasible.

The availability and the quality of the user experiences are not dictated by the technical ability to deliver them, nor are they defined by the resources available. The controlling influence comes from marketing strategies that attempt to impact the market share of the underlying platforms. The codec and player manufacturers often use their products as weapons with which to beat one another. Real Networks offers its products on all the major OS platforms. Even though they don't manufacture an operating system, they still make choices about how well to support a particular platform.

 Beware of lock-in with the coding platform and the client player tool. If they are both implemented correctly, you should be best served by getting each one from a different manufacturer.

The MPEG standards are deployed far more widely. They are readily available and are played back even by most of the proprietary systems that would compete with them. MPEG-1 was successful in its time and MPEG-2 has been resoundingly successful since then. H.264 is a worthy successor to MPEG-2 where it seeks to improve on the earlier state of the art. H.264 (MPEG-4 part 10) will be successful if the licensing terms for its use are made attractive enough. Early license arrangements for H.264 included per-copy fees and per-user charges, which the broadcasters found unattractive. The licensing process is still evolving slowly and the industry is optimistically anticipating terms that are similar to those under which MPEG-2 thrived. If program makers and broadcasters feel that patent holders are exploiting them unduly, they will not switch to the new standard.

More information about the H.264 licensing terms is available at the MPEG-LA and Via Licensing Web sites.

8.3.2 Why Standards Define Only a Decoder

In setting a standard, the MPEG working groups are seeking to provide interoperability between systems. Coders may be made by one company and decoders by another. If they both operate to an agreed standard then everything will plug together and work.

Therefore the standardization process typically defines the syntax of the bit stream to be decoded by the player. The specification does not usually mandate how that stream should be encoded. As coders become more sophisticated and powerful, they are able to squeeze more efficiency out of that syntax before they reach a point where no further improvement is possible.

MPEG-LA: http://www.mpegla.com/

Via Licensing: http://www.vialicensing.com/

MPEG-2 has improved in efficiency by a factor of about 2:1 since the original coders were introduced. Bit rates as low as 3.5 Mbps are routinely used for broadcast. There is still some room for improvements to the efficiency, but this is bounded by the need to remain 100% compliant with all the decoders that have been deployed. New opportunities for more radical improvement are presented when rolling MPEG-2 decoders out to "greenfield" situations where there is no prior deployment, although these are also candidates for H.264 and *VC-1* codec implementation.

By defining the characteristics of a compliant decoder, the encoder manufacturers are free to innovate in any way they like, so as to generate the most efficiently coded representation of the original video source material.

8.3.3 Profiles and Levels

Certain features might be allowed or disallowed by defining profiles. This helps to manage the complexity. Simple decoders check the profile of the incoming video and either attempt to decode it or display a message explaining why they will not.

Having defined a profile, the encoder must honor that and not create a coded representation that is any more complex than the profile allows.

Decoders are implemented up to a certain profile level and support content from the lowest to the highest they are capable of and everything in between. A maximally implemented decoder that supports everything MPEG-4 defines would be a very unwieldy and large piece of software that would be inappropriate for a lot of applications. A complete MPEG-4 encoder would be of no use in a portable device because you don't need the more esoteric features. The portable device would probably not have the memory or compute power to cope with it anyway. So profiles help to keep the software implementation under control as well.

8.3.4 Better Compression Factors

In general, the more modern the codec design, the better the compression ratio compared with the original source material. Longevity of the codec also comes into play. The longer a codec has been around, the more tricks have been developed to exploit the encoder.

On the downside, newer codecs or upgrades to existing models will require greater CPU power to leverage the improved algorithms. This is less of a problem for the decoding in the client because the algorithms tend toward techniques that are very easy to decode. So you may need to upgrade your processing hardware as you roll out new encoders even though they target decoders with a longer lifespan.

8.4 My Codec Is Better Than Yours

This is a game people like to play with one another, usually when discussing commercial issues.

You may find yourself taking a defensive position when discussing codec performance with other enthusiasts, especially when debating the merits of Windows Media over Real Networks, QuickTime, or H.264. All of the codecs are now capable of delivering good-quality content at useful bit rates. Content is carefully selected for demonstrations that play to the strengths of one or another codec, so the argument is never settled as to which is the best codec to use.

Very often the argument comes down to commercial matters such as licensing fees and the potential audience size. Choosing Microsoft Windows Media is a very easy decision to make but it is not always the optimum choice, nor are any of the other proprietary codecs. Note that I said codecs and not players. Exchanging content across different platforms is much easier with a mutually acceptable open-standard codec.

Bit rate and file size constitute an altogether different argument and your choice should be based on the desired performance at an available bandwidth. Here you would be looking at the more modern codecs. H.264 is a very strong contender and my personal view is that it will displace the others in the fullness of time, although there is no guarantee of that.

In the end, there is no substitute for running evaluation tests of all your main contenders. You may want to reduce the number of choices by looking at license fees and audience figures before running lots of tests on codecs that you'll end up eliminating for commercial reasons.

In order to test the codecs, you should assemble some representative sample video content and subject all the candidate codecs to a comparative test. This is sometimes called a "bake-off," and magazines such as *DV* or *Broadcast Engineering* periodically feature the results of these comparisons. Only after such testing will you have sufficient hard evidence to make the best possible choice.

8.4.1 *Choosing a Codec Is Not a Religious Pilgrimage*

You must look deeper than just examining a list of specifications. You should spend sufficient time running evaluations if you plan to "bet your company" or sink any significant investment into this area. You must understand the commercial reasons why the suppliers market these products and how your business fits into their overall strategy.

You must also assess the risks involved if you build a business around a product or service that is owned and survives only because another company chooses to sell a product. They may not have heard of you or even be aware of your existence. Nevertheless, they will make a commercial decision to upgrade, not upgrade, freeze, or cancel a product on which you depend for your livelihood.

The three major players, Apple, Microsoft, and Real Networks, all contribute valuable technologies and ideas. Each approach is different from a technical point of view. At times they are amazingly good at collaborating with one another and are a joy to work with. At other times, it is a challenge to get the different technologies to work cooperatively in the same environment.

8.4.2 Should You Choose Apple, Real Networks, or Microsoft?

Although some commentators make bold claims about one format having superior quality over another, this has to be seen in context and on the whole, the formats are roughly equivalent. Your viewpoint as to which is best will more likely be dictated by which platform you choose to encode and use for playback.

A proprietary approach is okay if you and your end users are already totally committed to a manufacturer's platform because you are not giving anything up or increasing the lock-in. I think it's a different argument if you are trying to evangelize a new service offering and are mandating that the client user must deploy it on a particular platform. The new service or product should just work with what the client already has or you are introducing an artificial barrier to acceptance, which will be reflected in your bottom line. Why would you choose to do something that reduces the chances of a successful business venture?

8.4.3 What Player Should You Choose?

On a Macintosh, there is absolutely no doubt that the very best player experience comes from using QuickTime. On Windows, the obvious choice is Windows Media Player. On UNIX platforms other than Mac OS X, the Real Networks media player option is the most widely available and is the optimum choice for Linux. Oddly enough, at major exhibitions such as IBC and NAB, I have observed that a lot of companies demonstrate their video prowess by using a Windows desktop but then they actually show you their video clips using a QuickTime player—at least it happens more than you would expect based on a statistical count of operating systems and the market share of QuickTime players in the consumer marketplace. This suggests to me that the QuickTime player experience on Windows is on the whole a happy experience, but you may draw other conclusions.

8.4.4 What Codec? There Are So Many to Choose From!

Which codec is the best? The cross-platform infrastructure and workflow benefits for the content producer lie fairly and squarely with the MPEG standards. My personal view is that the best codec is the one that works everywhere. On that basis, H.264 is a good choice given the amount of industry support it is acquiring.

Windows Media Series 9 might make some headway in its contest with H.264 under the VC-1 alias as an SMPTE standard. The VC-1 codec is a serious contender and is initially being adopted with H.264 as a requirement for next-generation DVDs.

During the latter part of 2004, the standardization process for VC-1 hit several bumps in the road. Some commentators have even ventured to suggest that it may be withdrawn as a requirement on DVD systems. We must wait for the outcome in the fullness of time. This delay introduces more uncertainty into the industry, because people don't want to choose a losing format as a foundation for their service offerings.

The *MPEG-4 part 2* codecs will most likely be deprecated in favor of H.264. My long-term choice would be to go with H.264 because the technical specifications are a superset of all the other codecs.

8.5 Codec, Platform, or Framework

There is a distinct difference between a video codec and a video platform. Many people who talk about digital video are ambiguous on this point. Knowing about this is important when you are selecting a technology to use as a foundation for your product or service.

A codec is simply concerned with delivering video in a compressed form. It deals with a single linear stream of media and represents it in a compact way that plays on a variety of devices.

A platform, on the other hand, provides a context in which that video is used. MPEG-2 represents a codec. The transport stream describes a platform that carries that coded video content. An MPEG-2 transport stream is still a linear presentation.

Examining QuickTime and the MPEG-4 systems layer reveals that the platform supports nonlinear experiences and an object-modeled representation of interactivity. Very nonlinear interactive experiences are built with both of these and they are significantly more capable than just a simple codec. Windows Media and Real Networks media are comparable to MPEG-2 when the systems layer (or the equivalent) is examined. They deliver quite adequate multiple-stream video quality under the right circumstances and also carry some linear data tracks, but they provide less-capable support for structured, object-based content. Multimedia systems are built with Windows Media but the containment and object management via the business logic is something your application has to deal with. QuickTime and MPEG-4 both provide support for this within the player, and that support allows the intelligence to be carried within the content.

8.6 Encoding Tools

There are a lot of coding tools available to help solve your compression problems. Appendix B lists hardware manufacturers and products, and Appendix C lists software manufacturers and products.

First let's untangle some confusing ambiguity that has arisen about what we mean by the phrase "encoding tools."

8.6.1 Tools Versus Tools

H.264 introduces some additional compression techniques. The standards describe these techniques as tools. But these should not be confused with the compression application, which might also be referred to as a software tool.

Discreet Cleaner is a software tool for compressing video with a variety of different codecs. The Object Descriptor framework is a tool in the context of the MPEG-4 *systems layer*. New Prediction (NEWPRED) is a tool that is used inside the coding mechanism for MPEG-4 video. Just referring to something as a tool is too ambiguous, and you will need to elaborate to make it clear what kind of tool you are talking about.

So you have a set of video-encoding tools available to the encoder for compressing the content. You don't have to use all of them, and if your encoding application provides an "expert mode," you can usually turn them on and off individually.

If you do use all the tools available to the encoder, the compression becomes increasingly efficient as the more sophisticated tools are deployed. The more tools you use in the coder, the slower the coder runs and the harder it is to achieve real-time compression. Using a simpler coder setup might deliver the compression ratio you need at the speed you can afford. This is what drives the need for faster computing systems when using later-model codecs.

8.6.2 Systems Design Choices

As a general rule of thumb, hardware solutions will be less versatile and will concentrate on coding one format well. They will be fast and efficient and usually deliver better results than you can get from software products.

On the other hand, software solutions will support a wide range of alternative coding formats and they will be very flexible.

There is also a sort of middle ground that has hardware-augmented software or software-controlled hardware compression. This would offer some of the advantages of each approach, possibly conferring the flexibility of software onto a piece of hardware or allowing a software framework to route compression jobs through a piece of very fast hardware, which it uses as a resource.

In addition to compression tools, there are transcoders such as Telestream Flip Factory and batch-oriented, server-based tools for enterprise-wide solutions.

 Be wary of lock-in to applications caused by your codec choice. If the application is killed or withdrawn, your service delivery could be severely compromised or, at best, unsupported.

8.6.3 Hardware Versus Software Coders

There are fundamentally two ways to implement a coder, hardware or software. Some companies build hybrid solutions with a combination of hardware and software.

If you have to encode a lot of video very quickly or you are intending to encode live video as it arrives, then you must consider hardware encoding solutions. Real-time performance is only possible with hardware assistance, and even then there is a time lag between the input and output of the encoder. This is because the encoding process must look forward and backward in order to do the best possible encoding job. Forward error correction and the reason why pictures are grouped together into sequences are both covered shortly.

Software encoders have the advantage that they are relatively cheap and work on general-purpose hardware. High-end Intel processors and the Apple G5 are well suited to this kind of task. The vector processing in a G5 does particularly well at this kind of computation. Hardware-based encoders are available from companies such as Envivio or Tandberg.

Regardless of whether you use a hardware or software solution to code your video, the processing creates the same sort of content. You get a sequence of packets containing fragments of video. Each one may just be a single tile in a mosaic that has to be assembled to reconstruct the raster.

8.6.4 Comparing Hardware and Software Performance

MPEG-2 hardware coders are very mature these days. The algorithm is well understood and specialized chip sets are manufactured and assembled into compact, rack-mounted systems. Video can be encoded between two and four times as fast as real time when processing cached material, and the hardware is easily able to cope with high-quality live encoding.

Software coders offer more flexibility for tailoring and customization. They run in general-purpose hardware (e.g., a desktop CPU) so they are slower than the hardware solutions. Moore's law takes care of this and as computers get faster, so do the coders. A hardware solution does not have as much opportunity to get faster since it cannot be upgraded as easily. Moving your software encoder to a faster CPU will yield immediate performance improvements.

The content will affect the compression speed on a software system. Hardware systems compress in real time, although they may allow for multiple simultaneous compression jobs if you buy a large enough system. Codec implementations vary widely and the computing platform will also make a difference. Your choice of codec implementation will also have an impact on the measured timings.

The following are some ball-park figures based on some compression runs with looped test footage of a waterfall.

I selected an MPEG-2 codec and compressed from DV to a standard that is roughly equivalent to what would go onto a DVD. The results are shown in Table 8-2. I have assumed that the hardware will compress in real time, so the values in that row of the table also indicate the clip duration.

The simple rule of thumb is that hardware encoding is generally faster than the software alternative because of the multiple parallel processing. Software encoding is cheaper to buy and works better if you are just processing one job at a time. Hardware comes into its own when you are compressing two or more live streams at once.

Table 8-2 Your Mileage May Vary

Platform	250 Kb file	3 GB file
Hardware	1.25 minutes	15 minutes
Software on slow PC	2 minutes	29 minutes
Software on average PC	1.4 minutes	20 minutes
Software on fast PC	45 seconds	10 minutes

Note also that some codecs may be faster or slower than others. During tests, the H.264 codecs I checked out were all prototypes, and they took a significantly longer time to compress the test video than the MPEG-2 encoders did. The Windows Media encoder took even longer. However, the longer processing times yielded smaller files, lower bit rates, and better-quality output.

8.6.5 Processing Without Compromising Speed

The speed at which you are encoding your video depends on how you are delivering the content. Mainly this will determine whether you buy expensive hardware solutions or much cheaper software solutions that run on commodity hardware. For example, you might be

- Streaming or broadcasting a service and playing out the original content live.
- Preparing a file to be downloaded completely before playback.
- Making material for playback from some local storage such as a DVD.
- Recording a live broadcast in a home recording machine.

At the broadcast end, the content is stored at a very high bit rate and this normally has only the slightest compression applied. That compression is visually undetectable anyway. Commonly the DV50 and DV25 formats are used. These store the video at bit rates of 50 and 25 Mbps respectively. DV25 is becoming popular as a consumer format as well.

The content is played out through a series of processing systems to compress and *multiplex* together a variety of different programs that are being broadcast simultaneously. This kind of system cannot drop frames. It must deliver the streams continuously, 24 hours a day, 7 days a week, and it must not exceed the budgeted bit rates or the transmission chain will break down. Chapter 14 examines statistical multiplexing, an important technique that drastically affects the coding quality. Simultaneously encoding several streams of video is a very hardware-intensive process and software is not often applied to that task. Faster computer architectures may change that assumption over the next few years.

Preparing content to be downloaded and played back locally is far less time-intensive. The processing is not constrained to operate at the same speed at which the video is watched. The process can go faster or slower. Here you have an opportunity to run the software on faster and more expensive commodity hardware and get more work done. Or you could save money and deploy just a single, slower machine and wait while it encodes. Examples of this kind of processing are the movie trailers that are posted on the Internet.

8.6.6 Scalability

Compression Master is a tool that has a lot more settings available for you to parameterize the compression process. Some tools simplify this to the point of giving you almost no control at all. Compression Master lets you fine-tune the coding and requires some expertise when operated at this level. It presents the settings in the foreground of the user interface in what I think is a more accessible way than having to bring up another window to edit the template. In terms of scalability, Squeeze and Cleaner are maxed out at the high end of desktop usage, while Popwire Compression Master and Flip Factory by Telestream extend into enterprise-level workflow systems.

8.7 Examples of Coded Video to Check Out Online

At the Apple Computer Web site, there is a large collection of trailers that are examples of achievable coding quality. The quality of the Apple trailers owes more to the skill and dedication of the people compressing the content than it does to the codecs themselves. As the trailer collection expands, it has become a series of snapshots of the coding techniques being used.

Right now, we are in a state of transition in the provision of video content online. In the fullness of time, online movie trailers (whoever they are provided by) will probably be encoded in the H.264 format. You may not notice this change because the quality of coding is already very high and will remain that way. What you might notice is that the trailers download in only a third of the time that you are used to when the H.264 codec is used. Of course, this cannot happen until everyone has upgraded his or her player to cope with the new codec. Even that can happen automatically if the player checks for a new version to download.

Searching Google yields many more collections of trailers and other interesting compressed video. Some of the results you will find are indexes to trailers rather than places where the trailers are served directly.

Probably the best-quality example I have downloaded from the Internet in recent times was the 2-1/2 minute-long high-definition trailer for *The Matrix—Reloaded*. This was available in a file that was 91.5 MB in size. The picture was 1000 × 540 pixels and used millions of colors. The codec for this trailer was *Sorenson 3* running at 24 fps. The bit rate for this was 4.8 Mbps, which is within the bounds of normal TV-broadcast capacity. This demonstrates that a larger image, progressively scanned, can be delivered efficiently if you are prepared to use a different codec. The quality of video encoded in this way is stunning and is way beyond what is possible with any currently transmitted TV format. Even stepping through one frame at a time reveals that there are virtually no visible artifacts as a result of the compression. This is in the realm of what we can expect to become commonplace with HDTV services.

Apple movie trailers: http://www.apple.com/trailers/

Internet Movie Database (IMDb): http://www.imdb.com/Sections/Trailers/

Jo Blo's movie trailer index: http://www.joblo.com/movietrailers2A.htm

Manga trailers: http://www.manga.com/trailers/

Cinemas Online: http://www.cinemas-online.co.uk/index.phtml

Go Movie Trailers: http://www.gomovietrailers.com/

DivX Digest: http://www.divx-digest.com/

Cinema Eye: http://www.cinemaeye.com/

Sci-Fi movie page: http://www.scifimoviepage.com/

Matrix trailer.http://whatisthematrix.warnerbros.com/

Table 8-3 Coding Formats for Different Applications

Description	*Potential coding formats*
DVD	MPEG-2, H.264
DVD-ROM	MPEG-1, MPEG-2, H.264
Offline	DVCAM, DV
CD-ROM	MPEG-1, MPEG-2, MPEG-4 part 10, Sorenson, H.264
Internet – dialup	MPEG-1, H.264, Sorenson, Real Networks, Windows Media
Internet broadband	MPEG-2, H.264, Flash, Windows Media, Real Networks, Sorenson
Video conferencing	H.261, H.263, H.264, H.320, H.323 and H.324
Mobile devices (3GPP & 3GPP2)	H.264

Table 8-4 Video Conferencing Standards Recommended by the ITU

Standard	*Category*	*Description*
G.72x	Audio	The ITU standards for audio compression.
H.261	Video	An ITU standard for videoconferencing video streams. H.261 uses the Discrete Cosine Transform (DCT) algorithm to compress video to fit within a bandwidth of 64 Kbps to 2 M bps.
H.263	Video	Another ITU video conferencing standard, that offers better compression than H.261. This is particularly well suited to compression down to the low bit rate available through dial-up modems.
H.264	Video	The telecommunications companies are experimenting with this codec for delivery of video content to mobile phones. For this application the codec must be used in a low latency real-time encoding mode.
H.320	Integration	A higher bit rate ITU standard for videoconferencing via ISDN or through a reserved portion of the bandwidth available on a T1 connection.
H.323	Integration	This is an ITU standard for videoconferencing that takes place over networks that don't guarantee an available bandwidth. The Internet is such a network where the traffic may be transferred in bursts and must be interleaved with traffic following completely different point-to-point connections. Compliant implementations must also support H.261 video content.
H.324	Integration	An ITU standard that describes video conferencing taking place over standard telephone lines with modems.

8.8 Fit for Purpose?

Table 8-3 lists a breakdown of some common encoding targets and the formats that are often used. Either the codec already exists and is selected because it is very suitable or the codec was specially designed for the application.

8.15 Video Conferencing Standards

A variety of standards are relevant to video conferencing. They are part of a series of related standards that are all concerned with video compression and they each address a particular niche or available bit rate.

Table 8-4 gives a brief summary of some of the ITU (International Telecommunications Union) standards that apply:

8.16 Conclusions

Going for an open standard such as H.264 is a very straightforward proposition. If the licensing terms are attractive enough to the content providers and carriers, then the standard could become widely adopted.

There are good reasons for choosing Windows Media or Real Networks as delivery codecs to audiences where the target platform is known and guaranteed to be compatible and has optimal support, i.e., Windows of one variant or another.

QuickTime is probably the most versatile when it comes to player design and the range of formats it can play. The only downside used to be that there was no Windows Media or Real Networks plug-in codec for QuickTime. Now that Telestream has dealt with the lack of a Windows Media plug-in and Real Networks has released its own plug-in, we have a unifying option that facilitates some powerful workflow solutions.

For encoding, you have to choose either hardware or software. For professional, high throughput, the best solution is hardware at whatever cost; and for the semi-pro, software is likely to do the job optimally and more important, at the right price.

In the end your decisions will most likely be commercially based rather than technology related.

 Choose your codec, then choose your compression platform operating system based on the available tools for that codec.

8.17 But How Do They Work?

I hope you are starting to get a feel for the range of coding alternatives that are available. We have quite a ways to travel yet. Over the next few chapters we'll develop an understanding of how the coder works internally.

It is not rocket science, and in fact we won't explore everything there is to know because it is not necessary to know how all the fine points work. We will, however, explore enough to be able to make good choices in how the parameters are set up when running the encoders.

9

How Encoders Work

9.1 Now We Are Getting Somewhere

Let's take a look at some of the issues that affect the whole video-compression process. Then you can make an informed choice about whether to go for speed or cost-effectiveness. This chapter sets the scene for a trip down memory lane, looking at some long-established codecs and then moving right up to date with details of the latest models.

9.2 Video-Compression Technologies

If you buy a software product such as the Popwire Technology Compression Master, Sorensen Squeeze, or Discreet Cleaner you can start encoding your video right away. By using the built-in templates you can begin without knowing anything at all about how the compression works. It helps to read the manual, of course, but often the quick-start guide is all you need to begin. Your next level of advancement is to edit the templates. Eventually you can create your own from scratch.

You are not going to achieve the best possible compression performance without knowing something about how it works. You don't have to know all the mathematical theories, but an overall appreciation of what is under the hood is a good thing.

I'll explain the mechanics of what compression does and the key concepts involved in it. I'll use pictures because arcane mathematical formulas are not very helpful unless you are in the business of implementing a codec. We should all be eternally grateful that the people at Popwire, Sorensen, Envivio, Apple, Real Networks, Microsoft, Discreet, and other companies already did that hard work for us.

There are many proprietary codecs available. These are closed systems and the inner workings are not generally accessible, so our discussions here will mainly be based around the MPEG standards because they are open and well-known.

A good place to start is with the earliest and simplest, MPEG-1, and then proceed through the enhancements that MPEG-2 provided, follow that with MPEG-4 part 2, and finish with the H.264 codec (otherwise known as JVT, *AVC*, or MPEG-4 part 10). This is currently the most advanced, standards-based codec available. Some alternative codec possibilities will be discussed later on.

9.3   A Short History of Video Compression

Video compression has been used ever since television was first launched as a publicly accessible service. The early compression was analog and was based on complex electronics inside the TV receiver. It was founded on the concept that interlacing the scanning lines reduces the transmission bandwidth by taking advantage of our persistence of vision, and the decay time of the phosphor in a CRT. Chapter 5 describes interlacing and the reduced sampling of detail in the color compared with the full sampling of brightness.

Standards that describe how digital video-compression works actually only define the decoder mechanism. If you produce a standards-compliant bit stream, then all past, present, and future decoders should display the video that you intended. This is a very important point. As encoding technology matures, better and better bit rates are accomplished without having to upgrade the installed base of decoders.

This has certainly been the case with the MPEG-2 standard, which is roughly twice as efficient as it was when digital TV was first being transmitted. The H.264 standard is easily twice as good as that and it is at the beginning of that maturity curve. The expectation is that H.264 encoders will improve to the point where high-quality video is delivered at better than 1 Mbps bit rates.

9.3.1   *Going Digital*

The digital revolution happened in the TV studios long before it ever became a consumer video format. In fact very different formats for TV production evolved.

Oddly enough, rather than store the unmixed red, green, and blue signals in a digital form, the engineers developed a way to digitally represent the luma plus the two difference components that comprise the chroma. This became known as digital component video and is often referred to as 4:2:2. There are other related formats also described in Chapter 5. These are essentially digital representations of an analog video format.

Nowadays the standards have evolved, and this digital video is stored using a variety of formats developed by SMPTE, MPEG, and other standards bodies. Most often it is moved around the studio in a serial digital interface (SDI) format that has become the most popular studio-quality interconnect standard for hardware.

9.3.2   *The Consumer Digital Video Revolution*

With the introduction of MPEG-2 video standards, products that were not feasible became economically viable to produce. The two notable outcomes from MPEG-2 are *DVB* standard digital TV services and DVDs containing films and TV programs in a very convenient portable format.

DVB services are delivered via satellite, cable and terrestrial transmission, and DVDs are manufactured in the same pressing plants that produce CD audio disks.

The industry is poised on the brink of further performance enhancements with the availability of the H.264 video codec, which improves the compression sufficiently to make mobile devices such as phones and personal digital assistants with video playback a realistic possibility. Handheld digital TV receivers are also facilitated by improved compression ratios.

9.4 Preprocessing Operations

Before running the encoding process, reducing the data size is beneficial. These tasks are called preprocessing because they are handled before the encoding stage of the compression. This accounts for the greater part of your time when compressing video. Although this is not strictly a compression process, the preprocessing is often dealt with by the workflow framework or application that the encoder runs in.

Sorensen Squeeze, Popwire Compression Master, and Discreet Cleaner all provide these facilities. Most other tools do as well.

You may apply these preprocessing operations in any order you like if you use different tools to work on the video. For example, After Effects is useful for tracking and stabilizing the video, and you can scale and crop it at the same time. Then you can import the processed footage into Squeeze for compression. There is an opportunity to introduce other processing outside of those two applications, too. For example, if you have some custom-built scratch removal software, it could be used prior to loading of the images into After Effects, and you have a chance to trim the in and out points (known as topping and tailing) before loading the video into Squeeze.

You do need to make sure that these preprocessing steps don't introduce any unwanted format conversion along the way, as that may degrade the quality of the output if it introduces visible artifacts.

We will discuss all of these techniques later in Chapters 31 to 38. Here is a brief summary of some preprocessing steps that help improve the quality of the output.

- Deinterlacing
- Frame rate adjustment
- Denoising (noise filtering)
- Sharpening
- Grain removal
- Color correction
- Cropping
- Scaling
- Aspect ratio correction
- Anamorphic squash

9.5 Frame Types

Both TV and filmed content consist of a series of still images called frames. TV reorganizes each image into a more complex structure and represents it as a series of synchronized scan lines. TV in its purest form is manipulated electronically in the analog domain. Film is just an image on a celluloid (or other) substrate and is manipulated using a combination

Table 9-1 Frame Types in MPEG-1 GOP Structures

Frame type	Description
I	Intra frames (key frames)
P	Predicted difference frames
B	Bi-directional difference frames
D	This is a low-resolution thumbnail image but it is used on its own and is not part of the animated movie sequence. Thumbnail images can be used in browsers to help indicate visually where scene breaks happen. We won't cover these any further here.

of chemistry optics and mechanics. Computer imaging is a matrix of pixels and is a far easier format to work on than either TV or film.

There are fundamentally four types of frame defined in the MPEG-1 standard. Table 9-1 summarizes the different types, which are discussed fully in the next few subsections.

9.5.1 Key Frames (I-Frames)

An intra frame (*I-frame*) is coded as a single, stand-alone frame. Everything that is required to render it is contained within that frame and it need not refer to any other part of the movie file. It is sometimes called a key frame since that is a handy, well-known concept.

If you think of a movie film, every single frame is discrete and you only have to project one to be able to reconstruct a viewable picture. So a movie film format consists just of key frames. There is no relationship between one frame and another. Editing is simple and straightforward and splicing happens during the gap between frames as shown in Figure 9-1.

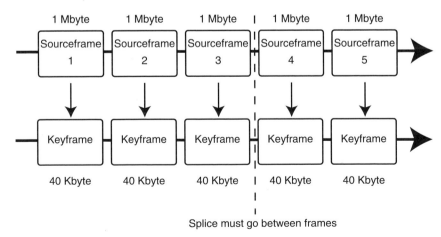

Figure 9-1 Key frames.

I-frames can be placed into the bit stream where there is a major change in the picture content, for example, at a scene change or editing cut point. Nonlinear editors such as Final Cut Pro introduce some hints when an edit or transition is placed into the finished product. The compression software may be able to make use of this help in choosing when to create a new I-frame.

9.5.2 Difference Frames (P-Frames)

A predicted frame (*P-frame*) is constructed using differences that are added to a key frame or the most recent P-frame and are not necessarily delivered immediately after the I-frame it is reconstructed from. The differences are assumed to be in the forward temporal direction as described in the earlier conceptual overview. Because P-frames cascade (one is built on another), any coding errors will propagate and eventually the accumulation causes visible artifacts.

Now take that movie film and compare two adjacent frames. Let's call them Frames A and B. To view Frame A, it is projected into the viewer. Frame B, however, does not exist as a viewable frame. It is a set of changes that must be applied to Frame A in order to reconstruct Frame B. You cannot simply view Frame B. If there are any visible pixels in the description of it, they will only cover a portion of the view screen. They must be drawn on top of the contents of Frame A to be meaningful.

Frame B is a difference or delta frame. Add two more frames, C and D. They can also be difference frames. The description of C is a set of visible differences between pictures B and C, rather like those "spot the difference" puzzles in the newspapers. The description of Frame D is the visible differences that must be applied to make Frame D from a fully reconstructed Frame C.

Figure 9-2 shows how this stacks up.

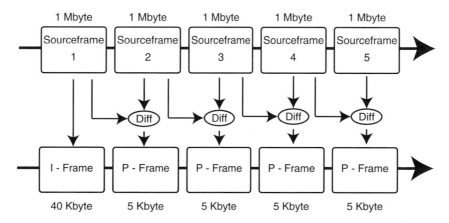

Figure 9-2 Difference frames.

Frame A is in fact the only completely described frame in the sequence, and to view any of the other frames it is necessary to traverse a series of changes, taking in all the intermediate frames between A and the target frame.

Random access to any frame in the movie is quite difficult. If 2-hour movies were coded like this, it would take a long time to accumulate all the changes to reach a frame somewhere in the middle. The reconstruction can run faster than 24 fps and a powerful computer will reconstruct frames more quickly. But it might still take 5 minutes, which is far too long.

Periodically placing a key frame into the sequence and allowing only a limited number of difference frames to be used before another key frame is called for provides more entry points for the encoder. This is fundamental to operating streaming systems efficiently as well.

9.5.3 Bi-Directional Playback Support (B-Frames)

A bi-directional frame (*B-frame*) is coded using the differences from the preceding I-frame or a following P-frame, whichever leads to the most compact coding.

Earlier implementations of video compression schemes only supported difference frames moving in the forward playback direction. To go back a frame required the video to be traversed from the most recent key frame, stopping one frame earlier each time. Playback in reverse was therefore somewhat time consuming and difficult to accomplish in real time.

Going back to our model of Frames A, B, C, and D, the description of Frame C is a list of differences that must be applied to Frame B, and the differences that are applied to Frame C to create Frame D will not create Frame C if they are applied to Frame B.

Some difference frames are designed to be applied in reverse. This facilitates reverse playback. Before that is possible, however, another kind of reference frame is necessary. This is a predicted frame that is some distance forward in time from the key frame. The difference between the key frame and the predicted frame is computed so that the sequence can be reconstructed from either end. The bi-directional difference frames are manufactured from the key frame at the start and the predicted frame at the end. This facilitates trick-play features in the player. Figure 9-3 illustrates how the relationships between frames are beginning to get complex.

Key frames are called I-frames; the predicted frames are called P-frames; and the difference or delta frames are called B-frames. Next we will see how those individual frames are coded.

9.6 Summary

What we've seen in this chapter can be applied to all the compression systems because it deals with the changes that happen from one frame to the next.

In order to dig deeper into the compression systems and how they work, we must look at individual codec designs. Over the next few chapters we will work through the MPEG family of standards because there is an evolutionary narrative to them. The earliest

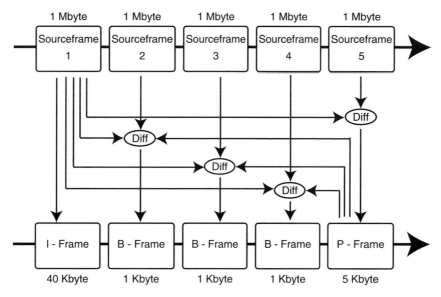

Figure 9-3 Bi-directional difference frames.

standard is MPEG-1, and it is comparatively simple. The next few chapters will also provide a basic understanding of how a frame of moving video is compressed, which is not too difficult to understand.

MPEG-2 builds on MPEG-1 and adds some useful features. MPEG-4 part 2 provides some additional tools, and the latest codec (H.264) offers major improvements in efficiency and performance.

10

The MPEG-1 Codec

10.1 MPEG-1

The MPEG-1 codec is still used for some legacy applications but the capabilities of MPEG-2 and MPEG-4 provide better compression ratios and more sophisticated coding techniques. New projects are unlikely to be based on MPEG-1. This was a popular codec when deploying video on CD-ROMs and is also used in games design.

10.2 How It Is Done in MPEG-1

The simplest of the MPEG video-compression formats is the best place to start. The others are all based on this model and just add some enhancements. The inventors of the MPEG coding schemes considered concepts of frames and luma plus chroma representation and worked out some techniques for compressing video that provide the most flexible but compact system.

The MPEG-2 and H.264 (MPEG-4) codecs are similar in many respects and will be easier to explain once MPEG-1 compression is understood.

The MPEG-1 standard was constructed around the limitation that the bit stream must be playable on a CD-ROM having a bit rate of about 1.4 Mbps. This must include compressed audio and video in a bit stream that previously was designed to deliver only digital audio content when CDs were first invented. This presents a significant challenge.

If you already know a little bit about how JPEG compression works, then you will understand the core of this topic. MPEG modifies the JPEG encoder slightly and adds capabilities to deal with sequences of frames containing motion pictures.

So let's now dig down deeper into the MPEG-1 compression system.

10.3 Bit-Stream Structure

The output of an encoder is a bit stream. The standards describe the syntax of this bit stream and the encoder must produce an output that is compliant. The syntax is structured

Table 10-1 Bit-Stream Syntax Organization

Layer	Description
1	Video sequence
2	Group of pictures (GOP)
3	Picture
4	*Slice*
5	*Macroblock*
6	Block
7	Sample

similarly in all the MPEG encoders although some naming conventions change. Table 10-1 summarizes the hierarchical nature of a bit stream.

Each of the layers, apart from the individual sample, has a header and an alignment bit pattern so they can be discerned within a bit stream. These headers carry various fragments of helpful metadata. The aspect ratio, frame rate, and interlacing method are all described in the header for the sequence.

10.4 The Sequence Structure

There is a nested structure to MPEG with increasingly detailed descriptions of the video being contained within each layer.

At the outermost level is the sequence. This contains your entire movie or program or just an individual segment of it. Figure 10-1 shows how a movie is broken into sequences.

10.5 The Group of Pictures

Sequences still contain a lot of video content, so they must be subdivided into smaller components. The MPEG-1 compression standard describes a series of frames as a group of pictures (GOP). This GOP will consist of a run of usually more than 10 but less than 30 pictures. Such a structure is also relevant to MPEG-2, MPEG-4, and H.264, the later codecs we will be discussing.

Figure 10-1 A movie segmented into sequences.

Sequence

Figure 10-2 GOP structures within a sequence.

The GOP structure is repeated as often as necessary to produce the sequence. Figure 10-2 illustrates the GOP sequence idea.

10.5.1 Inside the GOP Structures

The structure of a GOP is quite complicated because it is not just a collection of video frames. The frames have a very special relationship to one another within the GOP.

A GOP will always start with an I-frame because otherwise any successive difference information stored in the P-frames has no basis on which to build the deltas.

Note that the frames are organized at regular intervals with a constant number of *B-frames* between each I- or P-frame. Irregularly spaced key frames are permitted but this is not common practice.

10.5.2 Closed GOP Structure

A GOP file containing an I-frame, some related P-frames based just on that I-frame, and some B-frames coded only from pictures within that GOP is called a closed GOP structure. Using the letter notation, a closed GOP structure starts with an I-frame and ends with a P-frame.

In Figure 10-3, the arrows show the source of the difference data over several adjoining GOPs. Note that not all the connections are shown, otherwise it would resemble a ball of wool.

10.5.3 Open GOP Structure

An alternative structure dispenses with P-frames altogether and just alternates between I-frames and B-frames. Figure 10-4 shows several GOP structures and where the difference data is derived.

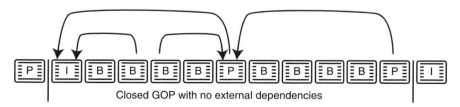

Closed GOP with no external dependencies

Figure 10-3 A closed GOP sequence.

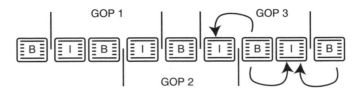

Figure 10-4 An open GOP sequence.

The GOP structures are quite short and there are no P-frames; GOP structures are all joined by the differences. This is called an open GOP structure, and there is no boundary between frames that does not have some kind of dependency joining that frame to another frame in the sequence. The I-frames are shared by two GOP sets and it is impossible to find a suitable point at which to break a sequence up.

Avoid this situation by using a P-frame at the end of each GOP so it becomes a closed GOP, or by eliminating B-frames altogether.

You may have all sorts of reasons for choosing GOP structures of one kind or another and you must determine what the appropriate format is for your target player. But keep in mind that a service provider may impose this structure on you.

10.5.4 Long and Short GOPs

Keeping the GOP small implies that the compression will not be as efficient. Increasing the number of difference frames makes the GOP bigger and the compression ratio is better. These two approaches are called short GOP and long GOP, respectively. A long GOP may accumulate more errors as the differences cascade. Sometimes using a key frame once every second will be fine. That would yield a GOP somewhere between 24 and 30 frames in length. For other content, a GOP every 6 frames may be called for. It depends on the picture content and the quality of the source, as well as the target platform on which you are putting the content. There are defaults in some compression tools that are set at 7, 12, and 18 frames for GOP length. It is a good idea to run some tests to exercise each setting and see if it makes a difference to your output. A selection of GOP structures is shown in Figure 10-5.

Figure 10-5 A simple GOP.

When creating MPEG-2 video content for DVDs, the length of the GOP structures should be set according to the guidelines established for PAL and NTSC DVD formats. For PAL you should not exceed 15 frames per GOP. For NTSC the value is 18 frames max per GOP.

If you exceed these values, then it is possible (likely even) that your content won't play correctly on a domestic DVD player.

10.5.5 GOP Transmission Sequence

Knowing about the different types of frames and the grouping rules, let's now examine the coding order and how the frames are transmitted.

The I-frame is compressed by itself, with no reference to any other frame. It is processed and placed in the first physical slot in the GOP. The GOP structure is defined beforehand so the encoder knows that it must jump forward a few frames to compute the forward differences required to make the next P-frame. The compressed P-frame is placed next in the physical GOP structure. Then the B-frames between the I-frame and that P–frame are computed using the bi-directional technique.

The frames are transmitted in a very different order from the playback sequence as you will see in Figure 10-6.

So the player must reorganize the received frames into the correct order so that the playback sequence is reconstructed properly.

10.6 Conversion from RGB to Luma and Chroma

If the video is not already in a luma plus chroma form, the RGB color values must be converted into the Y'CbCr components before the compression process starts in earnest. This can be done in memory if you have enough, or by converting from one file to another. The file-based approach costs you more in disk space consumed but is inherently more robust and is easily undone.

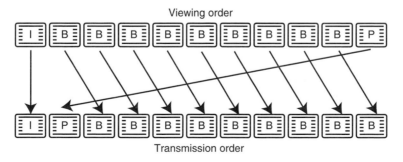

Figure 10-6 GOP transmission sequence.

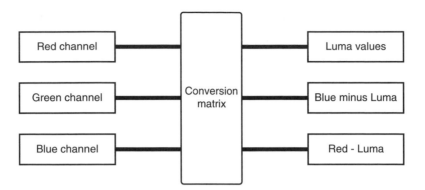

Figure 10-7 RGB-to-luma/chroma conversion.

The video may have been originally represented as luma plus chroma when it was digitized. If that is the case when you input the video, it is not necessary to convert it to RGB in order to store it in a file. A good rule of thumb is to avoid unnecessary conversion steps in your process. Such conversions will always lose some information due to the color gamut not being exactly the same in both formats.

Figure 10-7 shows an example of the processing pipeline for converting RGB to a compressible format that represents pictures as luma plus chroma.

The conversion matrix box takes a portion of each of the RGB values for each pixel and generates a luma value from it. The two color-difference values are also generated using different combinations of the same RGB values. The chroma information is reduced to a lower resolution at this stage.

10.6.1 Color by Numbers

Given a set of red, green and blue values,

$$Luma (Y') = (0.299* R) + (0.587 * G) + (0.114 * B)$$

The factors that are used to compute the luma are then negated and subtracted from blue and red to generate the B-Y' and R-Y' values.

Therefore,

$$Blue - Y' = B - ((0.299* R) + (0.587 * G) + (0.114 * B))$$
$$= (0.886 * B) - (0.299* R) - (0.587 * G)$$

$$Red - Y' = R - ((0.299* R) + (0.587 * G) + (0.114 * B))$$
$$= (0.701 * R) - (0.114* B) - (0.587 * G)$$

This computation is represented as an RGB-to-luma/chroma conversion matrix as shown below:

$$\begin{bmatrix} Y' \\ B\text{-}Y' \\ R\text{-}Y' \end{bmatrix} = \begin{bmatrix} 0.299 & 0.587 & 0.114 \\ -0.299 & -0.587 & 0.886 \\ 0.701 & -0.587 & -0.114 \end{bmatrix} \bullet \begin{bmatrix} R \\ G \\ B \end{bmatrix}$$

10.6.2 Testing the Luma Matrix Calculations

Now let's work that through with some test values. You can set the formula up in Excel if you want to test this yourself. The results are summarized in Table 10-2.

Note that the output values are usually substantially less than the maximum input values. The outputs are scaled in order to more effectively use the range of available values when converted to a digital form.

There are three images to pass on to the encoder. One is the luma image at full resolution and the other two contain the chroma information but at reduced (half) resolution in X and Y.

10.7 Macroblocks

In order to reduce the difficulty of manufacturing B-frames and to increase the likelihood of finding areas of the picture that are identical, the luma image is diced into squares of 16 × 16 pixels. These are called macroblocks.

Table 10-2 Worked Examples of RGB-to-Luma/Chroma Conversion

Color	R	G	B	Y'	B-Y'	R-Y'
Red	1	0	0	0.299	−0.299	0.701
Green	0	1	0	0.587	−0.587	−0.587
Blue	0	0	1	0.114	0.886	−0.114
White	1	1	1	1	0	0
Cyan	0	1	1	0.701	0.299	−0.701
Yellow	1	1	0	0.886	−0.886	0.114
Magenta	1	0	1	0.413	0.587	0.587
Black	0	0	0	0	0	0
Mid gray	0.5	0.5	0.5	0.5	0	0

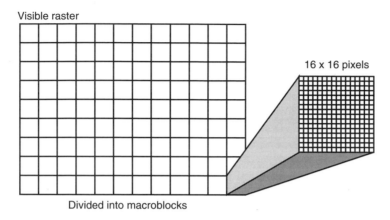

Figure 10-8 Macroblocks.

Figure 10-8 illustrates simplified macroblock arrangements for one frame.

The image array containing the pixels for the frame being compressed becomes a collection of smaller rectangles that are then operated on individually. For some images there is a good chance that there will be some areas of the picture that are similar to those already transmitted in an earlier I-frame or P-frame.

The techniques for creation of macroblocks depend on the kind of frame being created. I-frames must not refer outside the frame being worked on. P-frames refer to another frame, but only to the most recent I-frame or P-frame. The ordering of these must preserve the time sequencing of the frames. B-frame macroblocks may refer forward or backward in time to a P-frame or back to an I-frame, but in fact will only refer to a P-frame or I-frame that has already been processed.

10.7.1   Slices

Macroblocks are collected into slices. The slice is a standardized component and the decoder knows that if it loses synchronization at the macroblock level, it can reconstruct the picture starting at the next slice boundary. This helps the decoder in the receiver respond elegantly to dropouts in the signal and only a portion of the frame is then lost. Error recovery replaces the missing area of the screen with corresponding macroblocks from a previous frame in the playback sequence. Slices are a container for macroblocks (see Figure 10-9).

The slicing structure assists with the compression process. It is used to break up the image according to the average color of a macroblock. References between macroblocks are realistic only within the same slice. Slicing might also be used to balance the loading of the transmission channel.

Decisions on slicing depend on the content; the image in Figure 10-10 shows how the content helps the encoder make slicing decisions.

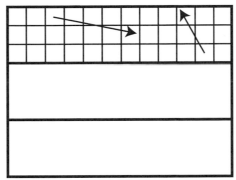

Can only refer to other blocks in the same slice

Figure 10-9 Macroblocks and slices.

At this point, encoders start to demonstrate performance differences because the way that slices are defined might differ between one encoder and another. Optimal choices such as selecting an area of the picture with many macroblocks that are similar will compress much better than an arbitrary slice structure with a fixed number of macroblocks in every slice.

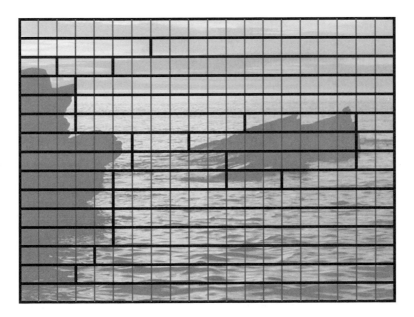

Figure 10-10 Slicing choices.

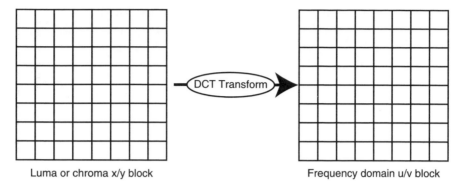

Luma or chroma x/y block   Frequency domain u/v block

Figure 10-11 DCT conversion.

10.7.2 Macroblock Coding

Before being compressed, the macroblocks are normalized by subtracting half of the full range value for the bit depth (Z-axis value). For an 8-bit image, the value 128 is subtracted because this is half of 2^8 (256). This normalization is done so that the encoder generates numbers within a controlled range. The core of the compression algorithm in MPEG-1 uses the discrete cosine transform (DCT) to convert the spatially organized pixels into an array of frequency values that are organized into the same rectangular shape. By organizing the image into a frequency graph as shown in Figure 10-11, the image is described more concisely.

10.7.3 Inside the Math—Aargh!

In the introduction I promised there would not be much math in this book. It is good to stay as far away as possible from the mathematical theories involved in compression. In order to frighten you just a little and to demonstrate why we don't want to get into this topic too deeply at a mathematical level, consider the DCT formula that is at the basis of the MPEG-1 encoder.

$$F(u,v) = 0.25^* C_u\, C_v \sum_{x=0}^{7} \sum_{y=0}^{7} f(x,y) \cos\left(\frac{(2x+1)\,u\,\pi}{16}\right) \cos\left(\frac{(2y+1)\,v\,\pi}{16}\right)$$

Where:

$$C_u = \frac{1}{\sqrt{2}} \text{ for } u = 0 \text{ otherwise } C_u = 1$$

$$C_v = \frac{1}{\sqrt{2}} \text{ for } v = 0 \text{ otherwise } C_v = 1$$

I don't know if this frightens you but it does me. Whenever I see sigma signs and functions of two variables like this I have to sit down and think very hard about what is going on. The u and v values represent the coordinates of the output array of frequency components. The x and y values are the input array of pixel values.

This formula is designed to operate on blocks of 8×8 pixels, so a 16×16 luma channel block is divided into 4 rectangles that are coded individually. The chroma channels in the macroblocks are sampled at a lower resolution and may require 1, 2, or 4 such 8×8 blocks to code them.

The first part of the formula (prior to the sigma signs) scales the result but applies a correction factor along the topmost row of pixels (when u = 0) and down the left row of pixels (when v = 0).

The two sigma signs indicate that a pair of nested loops computes a formula to the right of the sigma signs for each discrete value and then adds them together.

10.7.4 The Pseudo-Code Approach

In computational terms, the DCT algorithm could be implemented with a pseudo-code structure like this:

```
For (u = 0 to 7)
{
 For (v =0 to 7)
 {
 A = 0
 For (x = 0 to 7)
 {
 a = 0
 For (Y = 0 to 7)
 {
 {a = a + result of evaluating cosine formula
 }
 }
 multiply a by scaling factor
 assign a to appropriate cell (u, v) in output pixel array
 }
}
```

Every pixel in the x,y array contributes a value to every pixel in the output array. The DCT algorithm transforms pixels into frequencies using a fast Fourier transform (FFT) technique.

10.7.5 The Frequency Domain

The output array contains the average color of the macroblock at the top left corner. As you move through the pixel array toward the bottom right, the frequency components are based on ever-higher harmonics of the fundamental in both the horizontal and vertical axes. As the frequencies increase they have smaller magnitude. Fine detail is recorded at the lower right.

Figure 10-12 shows the frequency *coefficients* just on one axis:

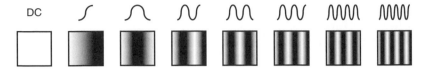

Figure 10-12 Frequency coefficients.

By arranging the coefficients into a 2-dimensional matrix, Figure 10-13 shows how the detail on the horizontal and vertical axes increases toward the lower right.

To compress the macroblock further, truncate the data working from the lower right toward the upper-left corner. This sacrifices fine detail in the decoded image but retains the overall average (nominal) appearance of that macroblock. This is why bit-starved transmission streams yield a very blocky appearance. They reveal the blocky structure because the fine detail is lost and that prevents the edges of the macroblocks from merging into one another perfectly.

The value at the extreme top left is a *DC coefficient* of the image, while all the other values represent AC (frequency) coefficients. Reconstructing the pixel values starts with

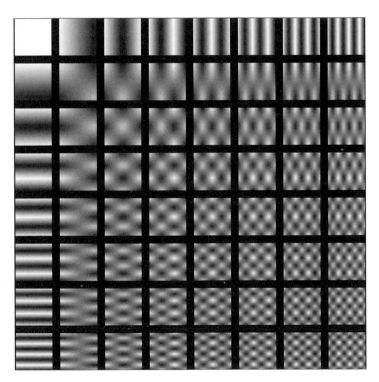

Figure 10-13 Frequency coefficient 2-dimensional matrix.

the DC coefficient filling the entire area and then the AC coefficients being added back on top to perturb the pixel values.

Sometimes the frequency domain is referred to as a power spectrum, and hence you may find the term "energy level" used when discussing the frequency components that contribute to the image detail in the DCT output graph.

This DCT compression process is applied to the luma and the two chroma pixel arrays independently of one another.

Phew! That was probably the most difficult part of the process. Everything else is a lot simpler to understand.

10.8 Post-DCT Quantization

Quantization artifacts as they apply to video are covered in Chapter 5 and more extensively in Chapter 7 in the discussion about digital audio. Quantizing to a word size that is inadequate to resolve all the intensity values causes contours. This is evident on a gradient shaded area. Figure 10-14 presents an example just to remind you about the effect.

This happens because the word size is trading off resolution in the Z-axis of the image. The Z-axis controls the intensity of the pixel illumination. Sacrificing resolution in the Z-axis reduces the range of colors or grayscale shades available to express the image.

The same data-reduction principle is applied to the DCT-coded version of the macroblock. Because that block of pixels has been transformed into a set of frequencies that describes the image, the loss of detail shows up in a very different way. It is called an artifact, a word that is used very often when compressing video and comparing outputs against inputs.

Truncating the higher-order harmonic frequencies will lead to a loss of detail in the image, but the overall appearance of the macroblock remains the same. At an extreme

Figure 10-14 Severely contoured image.

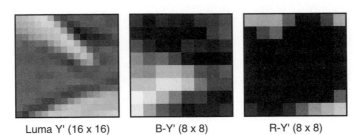

| Luma Y' (16 x 16) | B-Y' (8 x 8) | R-Y' (8 x 8) |

Figure 10-15 A picture of a macroblock.

level, the macroblock simply reduces to an average color across the entire block. This is the DC coefficient for that block.

To see why that is, you need to understand what data is actually in the DCT-coded version.

10.8.1 DCT—The Numbers Game

In Figure 10-15, a macroblock is shown as a series of pixels. Note that the chroma information is half the resolution of the luma. The pixel values (shown as hexadecimal values) are given in Figure 10-16.

B2	B7	C1	CB	CE	B0	7E	6E	75	7B	79	78	7D	7A	73	7B
AD	AE	B7	C5	D0	CE	A8	79	64	69	74	75	76	76	72	76
9F	A2	AE	B7	BE	C3	C6	A4	72	56	5C	63	6B	72	75	7D
89	8B	9C	A5	AE	B8	C2	CB	A6	6D	55	5A	5B	5F	66	74
84	79	80	85	89	9D	B0	C5	CF	AD	7D	68	65	67	69	6E
7E	78	7B	74	71	7E	8F	A4	C0	CA	B1	81	6F	78	79	7A
7B	77	77	78	75	72	73	77	8C	A9	C2	AA	7E	72	75	7E
7B	79	79	77	77	78	74	6B	66	79	98	A3	84	70	74	7C
7E	7A	79	77	78	7B	7D	7B	6F	6B	72	77	74	78	79	7E
80	7D	7D	77	77	77	7C	7E	7D	77	75	73	76	79	77	79
7D	7B	7D	7B	7E	7E	7D	80	81	7E	79	77	74	73	6D	6D
80	7B	7B	79	7F	80	7C	7A	73	6F	6C	70	71	78	7B	80
80	7D	7F	7B	7B	78	74	6D	6B	73	81	90	98	A3	A9	AB
81	7D	7B	74	6C	6B	76	7D	90	A1	B0	B8	B5	B7	B4	B4
82	75	6F	6C	6E	88	A3	B0	BC	BC	BA	B8	B4	B3	B1	B4
7B	6A	80	94	A6	BE	C2	C7	C5	BF	BB	B8	BC	BF	C4	CB

Luma Y' (16 x 16)

68	55	5E	59	56	60	67	77
57	49	4B	49	40	44	61	74
71	58	49	49	59	56	53	61
95	7A	7D	6D	58	4A	41	52
9F	98	B3	B3	9C	71	66	75
BD	BE	D8	D8	B9	89	69	6D
E8	D2	B0	90	6A	67	56	52
DD	AA	80	6B	54	5C	5C	67

B-Y' (8 x 8)

A3	A3	A4	77	4D	4E	67	99
54	6C	7A	4C	3F	3F	41	54
4C	40	40	3E	3E	3E	3E	4D
4E	3E	3C	3D	3E	3E	3F	4E
4E	3E	3D	3D	3E	3D	3F	4D
4D	3E	3D	3E	3C	3C	3E	4F
4B	3F	3F	40	40	48	51	76
5B	4E	4D	59	76	95	A8	B9

R-Y' (8 x 8)

Figure 10-16 Pixel values of a macroblock.

187	-29	-34	15	-2	7	5	1
190	33	-75	28	-6	-1	-1	1
-40	107	-59	22	-2	-7	-2	-1
-39	18	16	-13	14	-9	8	-3
3	-10	3	-9	10	-7	5	-1
-3	7	-5	-13	7	-5	-1	2
-1	2	10	-9	-2	1	-1	2
-4	3	3	1	1	3	-3	0

DCT output

Figure 10-17 DCT-coded macroblock.

DCT coding works on blocks of 8×8 pixels, and so the luma macroblock is composed of 4 DCT encodings while the two color-difference channels only require one each in this example. Figure 10-17 shows the output of a DCT-coded block of 8×8 pixels. This time the results are shown as decimal values.

Note that the values in the top left seem to be markedly larger than the ones in the lower right.

10.8.2 Coefficient Ordering

Now let's arrange those in a 1-dimensional array, ordering them according to the frequency of the coefficient. Traverse the coefficients in a zigzag fashion as shown in Figure 10-18:

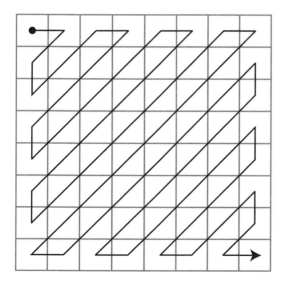

Figure 10-18 Zigzag scanning.

The zigzag scanning yields a single-dimensional array of DCT-coded values with the higher order and hence the smaller values sorted to one end of the array. At this point, no data have yet been lost and the DCT process is reversed using the same algorithm as the encoder. This is why DCT is mathematically so clever, but it isn't necessary to delve into the proof of that here.

There is a small caveat here with DCT and MPEG-1. Because MPEG-1 does not support interlacing, this 45-degree zigzag must be modified when interlaced content is being compressed. This only applies to MPEG-1 but the modification of this zigzag pattern enhances the preservation of vertical detail. It is useful to know that alternative mapping techniques for the coefficients will modify the compression behavior like this. Figure 10-19 shows how this traversal is modified for interlace support in MPEG-1. This is sometimes rather unkindly referred to as the "Yeltsin Walk."

The compression happens when this list of values is truncated. Any zeros that are discarded on the end will not make any difference at all. Dropping any values where a small coefficient is coded will lose some data and the recovered image will not be faithful to the original. This is where the encoder makes a bit-rate trade-off. Other techniques also reduce the run length of this sequence of numbers. Discarding more of the pixels to the right throws away the higher-frequency data.

The very top-left cell is called a DC coefficient. This is an offset value to set the average color of the macroblock. Everything else is then expressed relative to that value. In the extreme case, the block could be reduced to just that one value. For a pixel block that is 8×8 pixels, this is effectively reducing the resolution of the image by a factor of 8:1 in both the X and Y dimensions or 64:1 by area. Reconstructing a thumbnail image just by using DC coefficients is a neat shortcut and computationally very inexpensive. It might be used to show the video playing back as an icon on the desktop, for example.

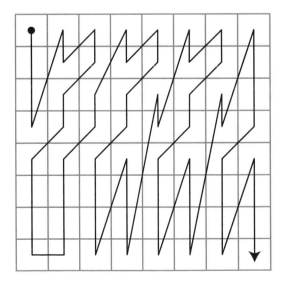

Figure 10-19 Modified zigzag scanning.

10.9 Entropy Coding

Entropy coding sounds like it's complicated. Implementing it well is a nontrivial task but as a concept it is quite simple.

If you recall how Samuel Morse designed his telegraphic code in 1838, you may remember that he first analyzed the frequency that different letters occurred in English-language texts. Morse found that the most commonplace letter was "E", and so he allocated the shortest possible code to it. The least often-used letter, "Z," was given a much longer code. This accomplished some compression of the message transmission because the more common parts of the message were coded with shorter representations.

Entropy coding does the same sort of thing for the DCT-encoded macroblock. Taking the linear arrangement of the sequence of coefficients, the message is parsed and converted into tokens that represent structures within the coded block. These tokens are selected so that the shorter tokens (measured in bits) describe the most common structures within the image data.

To understand the minutiae of entropy coding, you should consult one of the books on the theory of video compression. A useful keyword to search for on the Web is "Huffman," which is the name of the entropy-encoding technique.

If 100% of the entropy-encoded data is transferred to the decoder and is available for reconstruction of the image, then the codec is said to be lossless. The transfer route may require some physical reduction in the amount of data being delivered and so a truncation may happen. This truncation of entropy-coded data reduces detail in the image and the codec is therefore lossy.

Judging the optimum amount of entropy-coded data to discard is where the craft skill of the compression expert is concentrated. This is more of an art than a science and after you have compressed a significant amount of video, you will develop some instincts for the best settings given the source content that you observe.

Setting the truncation too harshly is probably the single most popular reason why coded video looks noisy. The artifacts become visible very easily and the effect is particularly noticeable because it does not remain stationary. Notice the coding artifacts around the edges of caption texts, for example.

If you remember the comment in the introductory paragraphs of Chapter 1, I suggested that you might be able to entropy-code your working day. The crux of the concept revolves around you completing all your tasks by the middle of the afternoon and having nothing else to do that day. So you might as well cut the day short and go home early. You just entropy coded your day in the office!

10.10 Motion-Compensated Coding

Motion compensation is another opportunity for reducing the data to be transmitted; it is applied after creating the macroblocks.

It is very likely that other blocks are identical. That data reduction should already have taken place. With a little more work, it might be possible to find a macroblock that is

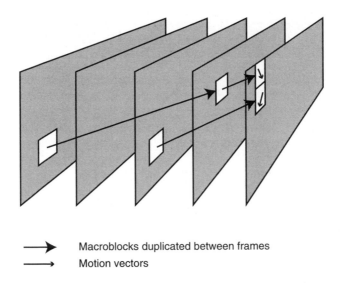

→ Macroblocks duplicated between frames

⟶ Motion vectors

Figure 10-20 Macroblock motion compensation.

similar. Then only the residual changes need to be stored. Macroblocks that are offset by some distance other than an integer multiple of the size of a macroblock are also candidates for this technique. Imagine an object moving through the scene (see Figure 10-20).

Pixels that cover the area of the moving object should appear elsewhere in the image but located in a spatially different position. This relocation is very unlikely to coincide with macroblock boundaries and therefore will not be spotted by the earlier identical-macroblock eliminator.

Describing our macroblock in terms of a previous image with some sub-macroblock movement should improve the compression if the extra deductive logic is implemented in the encoder. The accuracy of this depends on the codec. The most modern codecs support sub-pixel accuracy.

In the sequence of images shown in Figure 10-21 a car is moving through the scene. In the I-frame it is not there at all and in the P-frame it is partway across. The intervening frames gradually reveal more of the car.

The macroblocks in the P-frame that describe the car are already available when all the B-frames are being constructed. So those parts of the B-frame images that contain parts of the car will be taken from the P-frame while the background macroblocks will come from the I-frame. The background blocks in the P-frame will have also come from the I-frame originally. Figure 10-22 shows how the B-frame is composed from I- and P-based macroblocks. *Motion vectors* are applied in order to move the contents of the macroblocks by some small increment. Any residual errors that must be corrected are all that is coded and transmitted.

So our macroblock might be reduced to a reference to another macroblock-sized area in an image, plus a vector that indicates the movement necessary to reconstruct it after which any residual errors are corrected. Properly encoding the residuals leads to better

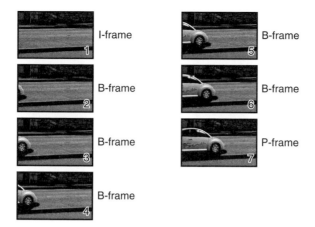

Figure 10-21 Moving components within an image.

quality. Leaving them unprocessed makes for a lossy coding output. This is where the complexity of video compression begins to bite. You probably don't need an analyzer unless you are building codecs but if you do, then one of the Tektronix models will do very well. A recent model is the MTM 400. You can also use the ADM953A or run the MTS4EA

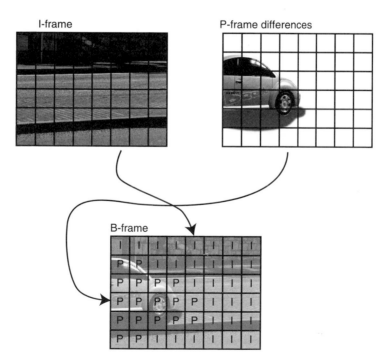

Figure 10-22 B-frame composition.

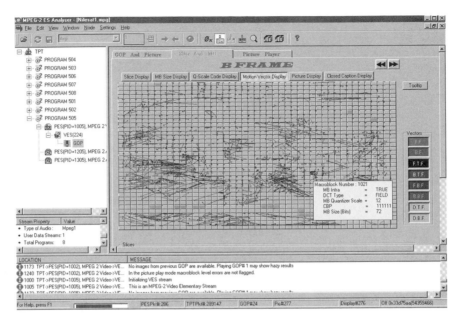

Figure 10-23 Motion vectors analyzer screen display. Source: courtesy of Tektronix.

software on your own Windows PC. Each of these is designed for a slightly different monitoring application. Figure 10-23 shows the motion vector screen display from an older MTS 300.

Figure 10-24 shows the motion vectors in close-up.

The encoder uses a process of *motion estimation* to extract the motion vectors. Coding the motion vector to eliminate motion artifacts is called motion compensation. The whole

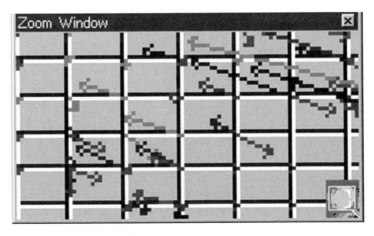

Figure 10-24 Motion vectors display zoomed view. Source: courtesy of Tektronix.

process is computationally quite expensive and to achieve the necessary performance, the coder may have a range limit on where it looks for blocks to motion estimate. There are a variety of techniques that codec implementers use to speed this up, and these will be the differentiating factors in their coder designs. Noticeably better results may be obtained with one encoder when compared with another, even though they purport to code the same standard model. As long as the bit stream they create is strictly standards-compliant, the decoder will be able to understand it. You may find that paying more for the encoder turns out to be money well spent in the end.

10.11 Tools

The concept of tools is introduced in MPEG-1 with there being just the one tool available to control the quantization scale factor (QSF). The QSF tool is used to manage the loading of the outgoing bit stream and is discussed in Chapter 14.

Tools are a way of describing components within the implementation of the standard that is used to define how much of the standard is implemented. In general, these tools describe techniques that are engineered into the encoding process.

10.12 MPEG-1 Caveats

Note that MPEG-1 has no capability to deal with interlaced content. Any processing or management of interlaced fields must be carried out prior to using the MPEG-1 encoder. Your application code has to work somewhat harder to de-interlace the content before MPEG-1 encoding starts, which is an additional processing overhead. The consequence is that the MPEG-1 coding efficiency is compromised.

Note also that the bit-rate specification for MPEG-1 places severe limits on how much data can be transmitted. The limits are defined in bits per second (bps) but if this is converted to macroblocks per second, there is not enough bandwidth to deliver a full-resolution TV signal at the full frame rate. It is only a little bit smaller than the 525-line raster used in the United States but it is significantly smaller than the 625-line raster required in Europe.

For these reasons, MPEG-1 has some continued use as a legacy format but for television applications it has been superseded by the MPEG-2 standard.

10.13 The Next Generation

While the MPEG-1 codec did a fine job in the past, the limitations forced the experts to develop an improved coding standard. Understanding MPEG-1 is important because all the advancements in MPEG coders after that are based on a lot of the same concepts. Yes, they are more complex and sophisticated but the underlying principles are the same. MPEG-2 uses the same divide-and-conquer techniques as we will see when we examine it in the next chapter.

The MPEG-2 Codec 11

11.1 Extending the Range of Capabilities

The MPEG-2 codec is credited with making the digital television and DVD industries possible. Certainly these were not feasible with MPEG-1. The coding support has been enhanced to include MPEG-2 HD for high-definition TV applications. The profiles and levels supported by MPEG-2 are summarized in Appendix F.

MPEG-2 is designed to run on a much wider variety of networks and carriage mechanisms than MPEG-1. MPEG-1 was designed to run in error-free environments such as CD-ROMs.

Although MPEG-1 was successful when it was deployed, it did not deliver all the requirements for broadcasting a TV service. To be fair, it was not designed to do that since it was intended as a delivery format for low bit-rate content for modems and CD-ROM disks.

MPEG-2 builds on MPEG-1 by adding some extra capabilities to the encoding process. Fundamentally, it works the same way but the enhancements produce better quality, larger picture sizes, and additional support for interlacing and film-to-TV transfer.

11.2 Interlace Tools

While the technical reasons for implementing interlaced video are largely eliminated when dealing with digital video and progressively scanned displays, there are still some technical experts that argue that interlaced video presents a smoother motion representation than progressively scanned content.

The MPEG-2 standard introduces some additional tools to cope with the coding of interlaced material. In particular, some variants of the I-, P-, and B-frames provide a means of coding individual fields. These I-fields, P-fields and B-fields are much like frames. Maintaining the correct ordering of them as odd and even fields is very important.

The correct sequencing of the fields as either odd or even lines in the picture and their temporal placement as first or second in the pair of fields that make a frame is referred to as field dominance. Sometimes these are referred to as the top and bottom fields.

While the physical implementation of odd/even first/second fields is the same for U.S. and European broadcasting, the signaling of the field dominance is not always the same and a weird twittering effect is evident if the fields are played in the wrong order.

Frame and field prediction is modified in MPEG-2. Instead of 16×16 arrays of pixels, there are 16×8 arrays (because of the interlace effect). Prediction is only operated on corresponding fields in another frame. The division of frames into pairs of fields continues on down into the macroblock and the DCT coding mechanisms, and all of this must be re-examined in the context of a field-based model rather than a frame-based model. The ordering of the DCT coefficients into a bit stream and the subsequent entropy coding is also modified to favor the vertical components.

The internals of the compression codec work similarly whether they are processing frames or fields. The complexity is about the same but the specifics of how the macroblocks are organized for luma and chroma coding is slightly different. The overall techniques are very similar to those already discussed for MPEG-1. You should consult the books on video-compression theory if you want to delve further into these more complex issues. All of this will be hidden deep inside your encoding software. It is likely to be activated by a single check box that selects interlaced processing.

11.3 Color Model

The color model is modified a little in MPEG-2 when compared with MPEG-1. Additional color coding is supported. The 4:2:0, 4:2:2, and 4:4:4 sampling schemes are all available. Profiles and levels must be understood in order to encode correctly, and those are discussed in a little while. Your encoding software should provide help with this.

Figure 11-1 shows the sampling windows for each of those sampling schemes:

When field-based coding is used, the color macroblocks are related to the upper one of the two fields. Color information is averaged both spatially and temporally. Some ghosting of the color may be evident in fast-moving objects having a saturated color. A common example is red-shirted soccer players against a green pitch.

11.4 Slices

MPEG-2 introduces a restriction on the slice organization. MPEG-1 allows slices to extend to several rows of macroblocks but MPEG-2 only allows those slices to extend to a full row. Slices can be smaller but must not span a right edge and wrap around as they could with MPEG-1. Figure 11-2 compares the two.

The benefit here is that dropouts in the signal cause much less damage and the reconstruction process stands a better chance of hiding the dropout if the decoder is smart enough.

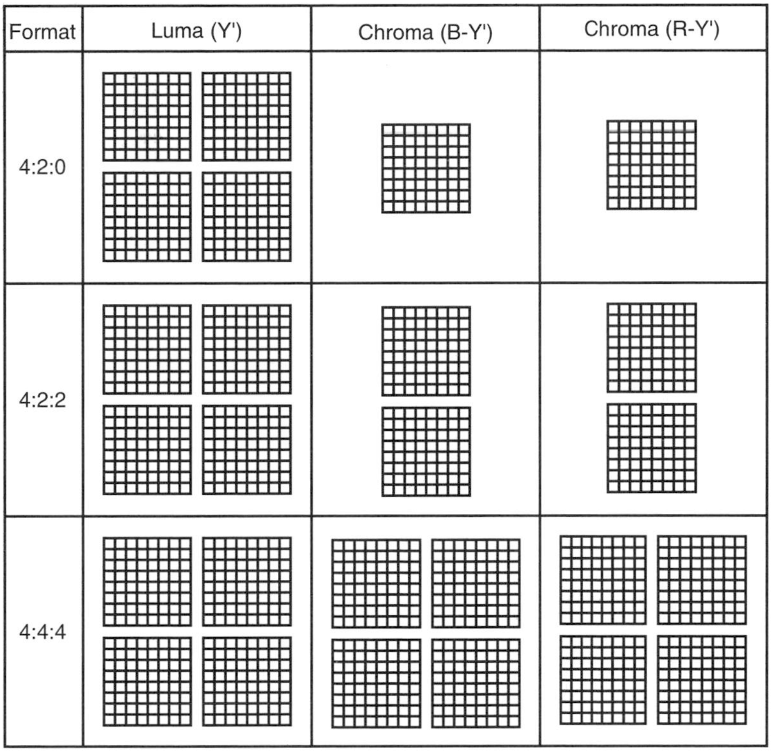

Format	Luma (Y')	Chroma (B-Y')	Chroma (R-Y')
4:2:0			
4:2:2			
4:4:4			

Figure 11-1 Sampling windows.

11.5 Quantization Improvements

Not much changes with quantization between MPEG-1 and MPEG-2 apart from the precision of the numbers used for coefficients. Allowing the coefficients to be specified to a higher precision will result in more subtle shading in the encoded image. This should reduce contouring artifacts, but it does not seem to eliminate them entirely since encoding

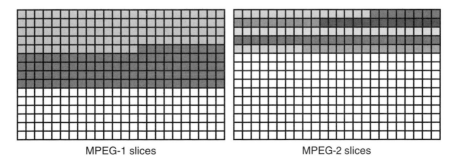

MPEG-1 slices   MPEG-2 slices

Figure 11-2 MPEG-1 and MPEG-2 slices compared.

companies are free to use less precision or compress more harshly at the entropy-coding and quantization stage if they wish.

Some widely available DVD titles exhibit particularly bad artifacts, but it would be unfair to single them out because most DVDs exhibit some artifacts when you inspect them closely. It may also be dependent on the player you are watching them on because some players only implement the very minimum functionality required to decode and display a basic image. They don't necessarily exploit everything that the encoder put there.

For examples that exhibit artifacts, check out scenes that are shot underwater with a searchlight beam in the shot. These are guaranteed to demonstrate contouring artifacts if the encoding process did not deal with them properly. Scenes with predominantly sky and sunset or a glaring sun also exhibit the same problem. Early DVDs with rapid scene movement such as car races demonstrate some very unpleasant motion artifacts. A lot of DVDs have been compressed with far too much edge enhancement applied during the telecine process.

11.6 Concealment Motion Vectors Tool

This is a useful tool to provide some redundancy in the coding. It works very much like the disk block reallocation technique in a hard disk. If a macroblock is lost, then the concealment motion vector in an adjacent macroblock may provide an alternative that is less optimal but still better than a total dropout in the reconstructed image.

11.7 Pulldown Support

Pulldown was explained in Chapter 4 when film formats were discussed. The MPEG-2 standard provides the tools to remove the pulldown frames to restore the 24-frame timeline. This is then compressed more effectively than the video might have been, but the information is added to the compressed data to instruct the decoder to recreate the 3:2 pulldown as necessary in order to play the content out again at 30 fps when it is viewed in a locale with 60-Hz displays.

11.8 Pan and Scan Support

A useful enhancement to MPEG-2 allows content to be displayed sensibly when the source aspect ratio does not match the playback aspect ratio.

A wide-screen image can be panned to center a 4:3 aspect ratio window where the most interesting part of the action is taking place. Figure 11-3 shows how wide-screen content gets cropped for a normal aspect ratio.

In the opposite situation, a 4:3 aspect ratio source image is scanned so that a wide-screen viewing rectangle is moved up and down to display part of the image (see Figure 11-4).

16:9 image cropped each side

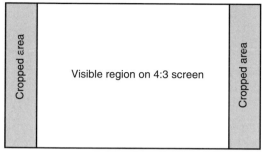

Figure 11-3 Panning across a frame.

Both of these techniques allow the entire picture area of the display surface to be covered. The pan and scan parameter values are transmitted for each field and allow the offset to be described to an accuracy of one sixteenth of a pixel. This allows for very smooth movement of the raster on the receiver so the viewer is never aware that it is taking place.

11.9 Aspect Ratio Conversion

An alternative approach is to aspect ratio convert (ARC) the content, but this normally leads to black bars at the top and bottom or at the sides of the screen. Although this is not specific to MPEG-2, the description is relevant at this point as part of the discussion about aspect ratio conversion techniques.

16:9 image padded top and bottom to fill 4:3

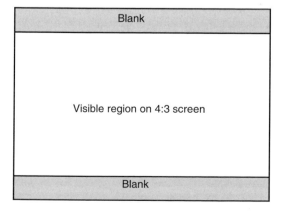

Figure 11-4 Scanning an image.

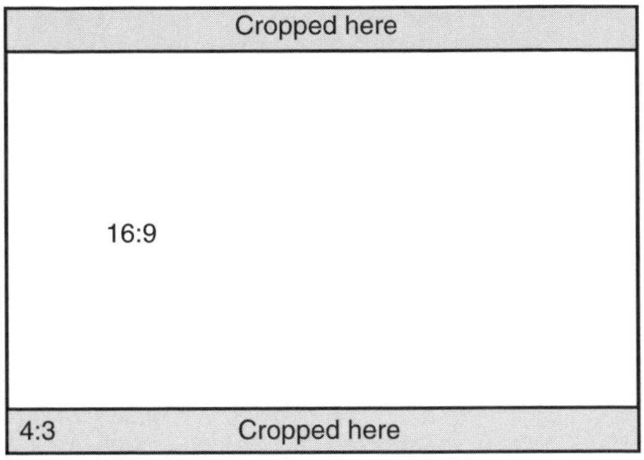

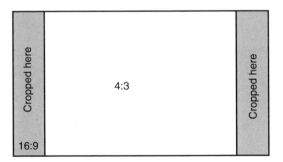

Figure 11-5 4:3 arced onto 16:9.

Figure 11-6 16:9 arced onto 4:3.

Converting 4:3 aspect ratio leads to a screen that looks like this:

Aspect ratio converted 16:9 content on a 4:3 aspect ratio TV after ARC processing looks like this:

Here is a compromise often used by the BBC where a 14:9 picture is displayed reasonably well on both a 4:3 and a 16:9 TV receiver.

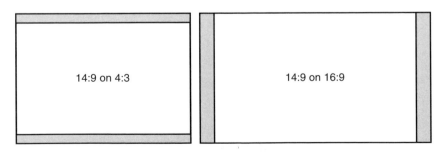

Figure 11-7 14:9 compromise.

11.10   Profiles and Levels

The MPEG-2 standard introduces the concept of profiles and levels. A profile is a way of describing a basic functionality or set of available tools that is easily described and unambiguous when mapping conformance between the encoding and decoding processes. The levels usually relate to the size of an image raster when applied to video standards.

A combination of profiles and levels is usually laid out in a 2-dimensional table and some cells are often left empty as the profiles and levels are not always meaningful in all possible combinations. For example, defining a level that uses very sophisticated compression tools on a very low-resolution raster is pointless.

The values in a standard would allow for video to be encoded with dozens of parameters that are defined independently of each other. The number of permutations would lead to hundreds or even thousands of slightly different video-encoding formats.

A profile defines appropriate limits or bands of values. This is most obvious when screen sizes are examined where the most common raster sizes are specified by the profile.

Sometimes the profiles are not specified by the standards organization that created the standard in the first place. Generally, profiles and levels are determined by the industrial application of the standards and are somewhat de facto in nature.

In the case of MPEG-2, some profiles and levels are defined but additional ones have been independently specified by SMPTE. Refer to Appendix F for a detailed summary of all the relevant profiles and levels for MPEG-2.

11.11   Scalable Coding

Scalable coding is a technique where the coded data is separated into two parts. A very low bit-rate stream (the base signal) is created and an extra supplementary stream (the enhancement signal) is provided to enhance the quality. For some applications, only the low bit-rate stream is used. For example, a previewing mechanism might use a low-quality video sequence.

The high-quality data augments the lower-quality version without repeating any of the information. It simply provides additional data so the decoder can then reconstruct a full-resolution picture with the extra detail.

There are two approaches to this. The SNR profile creates a so-called "moderate-quality picture" signal plus an enhancement signal with a "low-noise picture." The spatial and high profiles generate a low-resolution picture signal and a high-resolution picture enhancement signal. In both cases, combining the base signal with the enhancement signal yields the necessary information to recreate a high-quality rendition or the base signal can be used on its own.

The SNR profile is designed to allow the moderate-quality signal to be transmitted independently at a higher power than the enhancement signal. Receivers that have a good line of sight and therefore high-quality, noise-free reception should be able to decode the base signal and the enhancement signal to reconstruct the best-quality signal. Receivers that are further away on the fringe of the reception area may not be able to distinguish the enhancement signal from the background noise but may still be able to discriminate the base level and therefore decode a moderate-quality picture. This is all designed around signal-to-noise ratios and is thus called the SNR profile.

Another approach that might be available in the future is for manufacturers to build economically priced decoders that will only see the base signal. A premium set-top box might then be offered to deliver a better-quality service.

The spatial scaling is sometimes augmented by temporal scaling to double the frame rate. A wide range of potential service levels can be offered according to the bit rate available.

11.12 Systems Layer

The MPEG-2 standard introduces the systems layer. This provides mechanisms for combining the video content with audio and captioning. This carriage mechanism is called a transport stream.

The transport stream multiplexes program streams together. It carries other arbitrary supporting data streams as well as the programs. The streams can share a common time

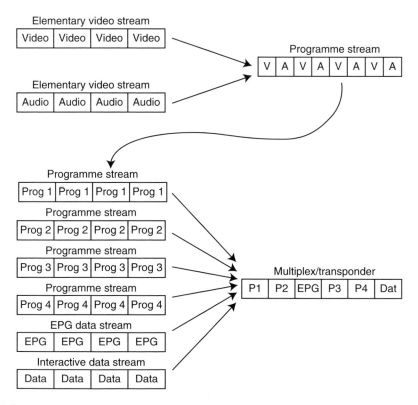

Figure 11-8 Nested streams.

base or they can play independently on separate time bases if necessary. The player separates (de-multiplexes) the streams and processes them individually as necessary.

Sometimes, this transport stream is called a multiplex (on digital terrestrial TV and digital audio broadcast radio). It may also be referred to as a *transponder* stream when discussing digital satellite or a channel on digital cable.

The transport stream is an important concept as far as the receiver is concerned because a receiver will have a tuner that acquires a single transport stream at a time. In a multi-channel broadcast environment that is delivered on multiple transponders or multiplexes, only one is acquired at a time unless you install multiple tuners. Channel hopping between program streams within a transport stream is almost instantaneous but going to a channel in another transport stream takes longer because of the retuning. Figure 11-8 shows how the transport stream is assembled from component streams.

Tuning into a program first involves the tuner in locating and locking onto the carrier signal for the transport stream. This may take a finite time and in analog broadcasting the picture will start to be delivered right away. On a digital broadcast, the transport stream must be buffered sufficiently that a segment can be reconstructed from the packets and then de-multiplexed into the packetized program streams. These are buffered and de-multiplexed to obtain the packetized *elementary streams*. Then the stream is decoded. The decoder must wait until the next I-frame before reconstructing a P-frame or B-frame from it.

This retuning process takes several seconds and is a major shortcoming when designing complex multi-channel content that is built into an interactive environment.

11.13   MPEG-1 Support in MPEG-2

When standards are designed in an evolutionary way, the earlier standards tend to still be functionally present but are wrapped with additional facilities. This is certainly the case with MPEG-1 and MPEG-2 because one of the stream constructs defined in MPEG-2 is identical to the MPEG-1 format. This is called a program stream and all the components within it must conform to the same time base as was the case with those in MPEG-1.

11.14   Designing a Better Mousetrap

For a long time the world was happy with MPEG-2. It did everything we needed at the time it was introduced, but though it was good, there is always room for improvement in video coding techniques. Gradually, year by year, MPEG-2 picture quality got better as the encoder technology was improved by enhancements to the coding algorithms. These improvements enable us to squeeze just a little bit more video into those already crowded transmission systems. Because we were just getting smarter and generating more efficient standards-compliant bit streams, the decoders installed in consumers' TV receivers and DVD players couldn't tell the difference. So they just happily decoded the more efficient bit stream without any problem at all.

Then folks started to wonder whether we had exploited all the possible tricks—were there some new approaches to try out? Soon there were groups of people in laboratories developing new and better codecs. Among others, Real Networks and Microsoft drove this forward in a competition to win market share. They were both inventing technologies that they claimed outperformed MPEG-2.

And so the MPEG-4 standard was born. This is a massive piece of engineering when you consider the range and scope that it covers. It is a complete and very comprehensive description of multimedia and interactivity; video compression is just a small part of it.

In the next chapter we will look at the improvements offered by MPEG-4 part 2. Again, this builds on the earlier work of MPEG-1 and MPEG-2, but it takes the algorithms a little further with the introduction of some new techniques.

12

The MPEG-4 Part 2 Codec

12.1 MPEG-4

The evolution of the video-compression systems designed by MPEG continues with MPEG-4. Some people assume that MPEG-4 is just another video codec, but it is much more than that. It includes a lot of multimedia capabilities for delivering a variety of audio–visual experiences as well as interactive support.

There are two video-coding standards included in MPEG-4 (part 2 and part 10). Up to the end of 2003, when people referred to MPEG-4 video, they were generally talking about MPEG-4 part 2, which describes the visual content.

Today it is too ambiguous just to say, "I am coding my video in MPEG-4." You must qualify that by specifying the following:

- Which version (1, 2, 3, 4, or another version)
- Which part (2 or 10)
- What profile
- What level

12.2 New Terminology Introduced

MPEG-4 video coding introduces some new terminologies based on the concept that every item in the stream is an object. Table 12-1 summarizes some of these new terms.

These groupings support the management of the video in a much more structured way than was possible previously. This allows arbitrarily shaped regions and alpha-channel coding to be managed very easily.

12.3 What of Wavelets?

Wavelet transforms are a new mathematical approach that is an alternative to using the discrete cosine transform (DCT). They work somewhat differently. Some codec

Table 12-1 New Terminology Introduced With MPEG-4

Term	Meaning
VS	Visual sequence. The top level of the hierarchical object-based representation.
VO	Visual object. These might be video sequences or static images. A VS object owns them.
VOL	Video object layer. These represent a layer within the display that contains some video. A VOL is owned by a VO.
GOV	Group of VOPs. These are similar in concept to the GOP idea but are extra layers of structure. VOL objects own GOV objects.
VOP	Video object plane. A single video sequence playing back in its own plane of existence. A GOV object is the parent object when the structure is visualized as a hierarchical tree.

manufacturers talk about them as if they are the Holy Grail, but wavelets are just another technique for encoding macroblocks.

MPEG-4 uses wavelet encoding with the discrete wavelet transform (DWT), but only for static textured images. It still uses DCT for compression of natural-motion video.

The difference between the Fourier-based DCT algorithm and the wavelet algorithm is minor but quite important. In DCT transforms, the higher frequencies are sampled across the same space so there are more cycles of the higher-order components. Wavelet encoding works on the principle of having a fixed number of cycles regardless of the frequency being used. So as the frequency increases, the area being considered gets smaller.

12.4 Further Improvements Introduced in MPEG-4 Part 2

This has yet to make a major impact in terms of deployments. Some manufacturers of mobile pocket devices are implementing video capabilities with MPEG-4 part 2. As a result, some very neat, compact, and cheap digital video cameras that store video on memory cards rather than tapes are starting to appear.

12.5 Coding Efficiency Improvements

When the MPEG-4 standard was revised to version 2, some new tools were introduced, which have a profound effect on coding efficiency. These tools include the following:

- *Global motion compensation* (GMC)
- Quarter-pixel motion compensation (QPMC)
- Shape-adaptive discrete cosine transforms (SADTC)

There is a hidden benefit to using the newer codecs once the problems of rolling them out are solved. The additional compression efficiencies will increase the broadcast real estate by a factor of at least 2:1. This will provide twice as much capacity for advertising revenues to be earned through additional channels. That alone is a very attractive option for commercial TV executives to consider.

12.5.1 DCT Improvements

A number of rather esoteric additions to the coding process improve its efficiency. These are in the area of how the coefficients of the discrete cosine transform are dealt with when processing P-frames. Quantization and variable-length encoding are also improved, so there are coding efficiency gains to be had simply by deploying the MPEG-4 part 2 codec.

The big problem is that there are a lot of MPEG-2 codecs already deployed in hardware and it is impossible to upgrade them so they will understand the MPEG-4 part 2 syntax.

12.5.2 Global Motion Compensation

The global motion compensation is useful because when it is applied to the object as a whole, the effects of motion compensation at the macroblock level are reduced, therefore reducing the encoding complexity.

12.5.3 Sub-Pixel Motion Compensation

By allowing motion to be calculated at the sub-pixel resolution, slow-moving objects are coded more accurately and the prediction frames are described with fewer errors and residuals.

Figure 12-1 shows the result of analyzing the motion vectors on a Tektronix MTS4EA.

12.5.4 Scaled Video

Recall that MPEG-2 introduces scalable video. The concept revolves around delivering a basic-quality and -resolution signal with a difference signal that is added to augment the bit stream to provide sufficient data for a higher-quality output. MPEG-2 is scalable in size, pixel density, and frame rate using this technique. MPEG-4 supports this, but at the individual-object level and it allows more than one enhancement layer if necessary. There are potentially many different permutations allowed and the spatial scaling is delegated to the decoder if necessary.

12.6 Shape-Coded Video Applications

The alpha shape-coded video support provides some interesting possibilities for deploying signing overlays for those who are hard of hearing. These would be carried alongside

Figure 12-1 Motion vector analysis. Source: courtesy of Tektronix.

the normal video channel and can be switched on and off. Set-top boxes that only have MPEG-2 players would not be affected because they would be unable to see the additional video stream. Special boxes provided for deaf viewers would allow a signing overlay to be switched on and presented during prime-time viewing for any and all programs. Currently, signed video is presented only at non-prime-time hours or for a few daytime programs on special-interest channels with smaller niche audiences.

12.6.1 Applications for Virtual Sets

Programs requiring virtual sets such as weather forecasts could be significantly improved by presenting them in an MPEG-4 BIFS framework containing several separate streams of content.

With codecs prior to MPEG-4, the entire picture had to be composited in the studio and broadcast as a full-frame moving video. Figure 12-2 simulates the kind of output created by a weather-forecasting studio. It shows how a presenter can be layered or composited over any arbitrary background.

This brings out a further issue regarding visual context. In this example, the presenter is dressed more informally than a weather presenter would normally be on a national network. However, for a program aimed at youth, this might be appropriate. Ensuring that the layers are coherent and are contextually or culturally relevant is an important aspect of the creativity in producing video. Sticking to a consistent visual grammar in your video productions is important. MPEG-4 allows you to support multiple presenter overlays if you wish.

Figure 12-2 Fully composited image broadcast as a single stream.

Separating the moving presenter and the static background is the first thing. This already happens when the presenter is filmed against a blue background. A matte or alpha-channel mask is easily created from that video. Degenerating the image into macroblocks provides a lot of help with this process. Take the example presenter in Figure 12-3. Note the macroblock subdivision grid superimposed on the image.

All the cells in the image are classified. Each macroblock is wholly inside, wholly outside, or partially within the alpha-channel masked area. This is determined by whether the edge passes through the macroblock. The two simple cases where the block is not intersected by an edge are eliminated trivially. The blocks that are completely inside must be coded, and those that are outside are ignored.

Blocks that are partially masked require the edge shape of be coded as an additional macroblock. The alpha-channel macroblock is coded quite efficiently, especially if the mask has no soft edges and is represented as a 1-bit value. Soft anti-aliased edges require an 8-bit value.

Comparing this with the MPEG-1 and MPEG-2 coding of macroblocks, an additional layer must be coded to carry the alpha channel if shape coding is used. In the decoder, the shape channel controls the blending of the decoded video as an overlay on the background layer to create a composited image.

Figure 12-3 Edge-detected and gridded layer.

12.6.2 Compression Efficiency for Shaped Coding

Pixels that will not be visible because they fall outside the object's boundary or outside the shape-coded boundary are processed to set them to the average value for the whole macroblock. They will be replaced by the DC coefficient value for that macroblock. Setting them to black or white regardless of the average value of the macroblock would require a lot of additional energy in the DCT coefficients to transform the pixel value from the average for that block to the default value we've specified. Figure 12-4 shows the breakdown into three kinds of alpha-coded block.

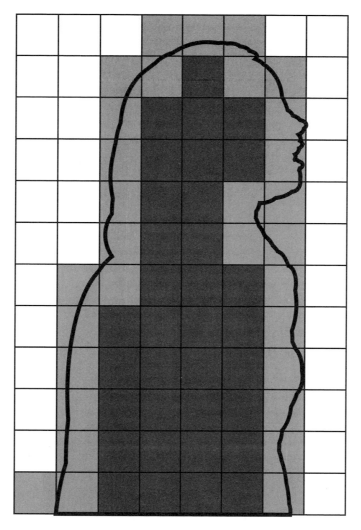

Figure 12-4 Shape-coded outline.

The white blocks are ignored. They are outside the mask and need not be coded in the mask layer or in the video. This conserves some bit rate. The light gray blocks straddle the boundary of the alpha-coded shape and contain masking pixels that must be coded. These blocks in the video must be fully coded even though they will be partially masked on playback. The dark gray blocks are wholly inside the masked area. No masking pixels are coded because those blocks will be displayed without masking.

12.6.3 Shape-Adaptive DCT

Version 2 of the MPEG-4 standard introduces shape-adaptive DCT coding. This is used when computing alpha channel-coded boundary macroblocks that may only partially cover the area occupied by the macroblock. By adapting the shape of the DCT window to better fit the area of interest, the amount of source data to be considered will be reduced, which improves the compression efficiency.

12.7 Profiles and Levels

The same philosophy regarding profiles and levels described earlier for MPEG-2 has been adopted for MPEG-4.

There are two profiles that have become focal points for compression for Web and mobile content, the simple profile (SP) and the advanced simple profile (ASP). The simple profile is intended for low bit-rate situations and the advanced simple profile has more advanced tools that improve the quality, but it isn't as well supported. Refer to Appendix G for more information on MPEG-4 profiles and levels.

Professor Jens-Rainer Ohm from the University of Aachen in Germany has developed a useful taxonomy. Other useful material on the subject has been developed by Ben Waggoner and published in *DV* magazine. See the appendices for a bibliography.

Professor Ohm's taxonomy divides the profiles into six regions on two axes. In one axis the profiles deal with rectangular or arbitrary shapes. The other axis is concerned with scalability. Here are the six regions:

- Arbitrarily shaped with temporal scalability
- Arbitrarily shaped with but with no scalability at all
- Arbitrarily shaped with spatial and temporal scalability
- Rectangular with temporal scalability
- Rectangular with no scalability at all
- Rectangular with spatial and temporal scalability

The standard is still evolving. There are profiles for studio systems and additional profiles optimized for 2D support. The natural visual profiles are used for conveying film or video content that has been digitized and will be viewed in a somewhat linear form.

Refer to Appendix G for more detail about the range of parts, profiles, and levels for MPEG-4 part 2 and MPEG-4 part 10, also known as H.264.

12.8 Licensing Issues

At the time when this codec was being launched, the licensing terms were not attractive to broadcasters and therefore there was little incentive to take this up as an alternative to

MPEG-2. These licensing terms have eased somewhat but there are some significant risk factors with licenses that you must assess. These are discussed in Chapter 18.

At the point where the MPEG-4 standard was ratified and beginning to get some interest, the licensing of patents suddenly became a hot topic. Broadcasters simply were unwilling to pay fees based on per stream, per user, or per minute of programming. They are well used to purchasing expensive equipment and software, with any licensing fees being recouped via a premium that is paid once when the technology is purchased. The European Broadcasting Union (EBU) stated in the fall of 2003 that it did not expect any broadcaster to find usage-based terms attractive.

The debate continued until the summer of 2004, and this gave a significant commercial advantage to proprietary codec makers. By making their proprietary licensing terms slightly more attractive than the H.264 terms, they won some converts.

A reasonable compromise seems to have been reached with encoder manufacturers paying a levy and content owners paying a small premium per copy that is distributed commercially. Charging on a per-copy-produced basis must be controlled to avoid hurting nonprofit organizations and small niche producers. As a result, nonprofit organizations and broadcasters are exempt from fees—at least for now.

12.9 Summary

The MPEG-4 part 2 codec is the one being cited when Windows Media Series 9 (WM9) and MPEG-4 are compared for performance and quality vs. bit rate and efficiency in marketing presentations. It is true that WM9 is superior to the MPEG-2 codec. However, when comparing WM9 with H.264, the contest is far more equal. Be very careful that the MPEG-4 codec being referred to in discussions is the one you intend to be talking about—especially when comparing performance with other codecs. The MPEG-4 part 2 and MPEG-4 part 10 codecs are completely different. Here are the main attributes of the MPEG-4 part 2 codec:

- Good quality
- Likely to be superseded by the H.264 codec
- Good file size at low bit rates
- Files get too large at high data rates
- Compatible across many player platforms, such as Real Networks and QuickTime (with some constraints)
- A useful general-purpose codec
- Sorensen version delivers marginally better quality but less-efficient compression
- *3ivX* is a good implementation available for Windows.

Now that the H.264 (MPEG-4 part 10) standard is available, regrettably the MPEG-4 part 2 codec has largely been superseded. It didn't offer sufficient advantage over MPEG-2, which has caught up with it in the latest implementations. H.264 goes significantly beyond MPEG-4 part 2 with its compression efficiency and lacks only the alpha-coded shape support. This feature is being added to the standard, at which point the MPEG-4 part 2 codec will likely become deprecated or at least be considered a legacy codec.

The next chapter looks at this exciting new codec (H.264), which has captured the imagination of the entire industry. In terms of raw performance, H.264 is the best codec there has ever been.

13

The H.264 Codec

13.1 H.264

H.264 is the most recently available codec. It is designed for general-purpose use and is known by several different names. This is a legacy of the various groups collaborating during the evolution of their standards and deciding in the end that they should work together as a single team.

H.264 is important because it incorporates the compression work done by several different industry bodies into the same standard. Thus, the same codec foundation is used across a much wider landscape.

H.264 is also known as MPEG-4 part 10. The MPEG-4 standard initially only supported the part 2 codec. Part 10 was added to include H.264 coding, which is also known as Advanced Video Coding (AVC).

13.2 Why Do We Need Yet Another Codec?

The H.264 codec is targeted at applications that previously would have used MPEG-2, H.263, and the earlier MPEG-4 part 2 video codec. It improves on a lot of capabilities that were available before and makes them more flexible and useful. Elements that were joined together and fixed are now more loosely coupled. Also, you can control certain aspects directly that were hardwired internally before. H.264-coded video runs at about half the bit rate that MPEG-4 part 2 requires. It has the added benefit that the image quality softens as the compression ratio increases.

13.2.1 Mobile Devices

Although the MPEG-2 codec performed very well at bit rates delivered by a domestic DVD player, it could not achieve the desired quality at bit rates available to mobile devices. This was a design goal for H.264. The new H.264 codec was designed to scale from very low bit rates to high-definition and digital-cinema applications. To do this, more tools were provided for the encoder to use when compressing the content. These tools are designed to cover those situations where the tools available in MPEG-2 were at their design limits for performance, thus creating a need for new tools.

13.2.2 Digital TV

The MPEG-2 codec is most often used for digital TV services; the H.264 codecs could be deployed to achieve better quality at the same bit rate or the same quality at a lower bit rate. Comparative side-by-side tests have shown that H.264 offers superior quality to MPEG-2 at less than half the bit rate. A very good-quality domestic TV service could be delivered at around 2 Mbps or better. This area is advancing technologically very quickly. Bulldog is now offering a 4-Mbps broadband service to UK homes and there is speculation that domestic services as high as 22 Mbps might be possible.

13.2.3 Main Features of H.264

Here are the main selling points of this codec:

- High quality
- Ultra efficient
- File size is efficient
- Scalable from 3G to HDTV and D-cinema
- Delivers full HD playback on contemporary hardware
- Open standard-ratified
- Cross-industry support for interoperability
- Elected as a standard for next-generation DVD, set-top boxes, and computing

The resulting codec delivers video at very low bit rates for devices ranging from mobile phones to high-definition TV and D-cinema formats. The mobile format is represented by *3GPP* 176 × 144 at a bit rate of 64 Kbps. High-def format would be 1920 × 1080 scanned progressively at a bit rate of about 8 Mbps or better.

13.3 What's in a Name?

The ITU and the *ISO* MPEG working groups combined to form the Joint Video Team so the codec is sometimes called *JVT*. Because it is ratified as an ISO standard, it is called ISO_IEC_14496-10 but this is hard to remember. The ISO 14496 standard describes MPEG-4 so this codec is sometimes called MPEG-4 part-10. The MPEG working group calls it Advanced Video Coding to distinguish it from MPEG-4 part 2, which is called the MPEG-4 visual standard. So the term AVC is used quite often.

Finally, the ITU recommendations are all coded with an H prefix so it is known as H.264. In order to distinguish the incomplete working status of the standard before it was ratified, the ITU replaces the last digit with a letter, so you may encounter the terminology *H.26L*.

The industry at large seems to be calling it H.264 when describing it in their product-feature set. If a video codec is referred to as MPEG-4, you should assume that it means the part 2 variant in the absence of any other qualifying details. The recommended nomenclature is H.264 or AVC.

13.4   Evolution to a Higher Form

The codecs have evolved gradually starting with MPEG-1, adding improvements for MPEG-2, and continuing with the enhancements for MPEG-4 part 2. Each one is slightly more complex than the one before.

A lot of people were involved in the design of this codec. Many of them were specialists in very narrow fields. They all set out to achieve the best possible image quality at the most efficient compression ratio that they could accomplish. At the extremes of the performance curve, you have very complex, high-quality modes at one end, but low complexity with some necessary quality trade-offs at the other end. The decoding process is unambiguous. All decoders should produce exactly the same output. Fine detail, gradients, and motion are all dealt with far more effectively than they have been in earlier codec designs.

13.5   Performance

Figure 13-1 shows a comparison of the bit rates achieved by the same quality video for MPEG-2 and H.264. The H.264 plot includes work done under the H.26L and MPEG-4 part-2 work streams. Note that MPEG-2 is now outperforming the early work on H.264.

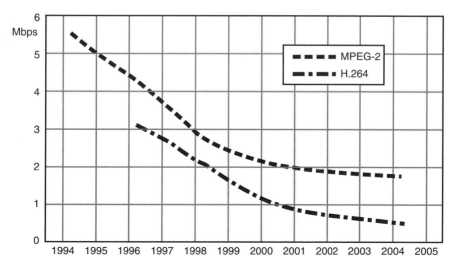

Figure 13-1 Relative compression efficiency between MPEG-2 and H.264.

Nevertheless, H.264 has always maintained its lead over MPEG-2 and has, for most of its life, been twice as efficient.

Envivio has produced H.264 video at 800 Kbps that would be good enough for consumers, and their research laboratory is chasing the goal of 600 Kbps without sacrificing quality.

This is in the ballpark of broadband-delivery bit rates. The industry is on the verge of delivering usable full-screen video via a telephone line. This has been a goal of the telecom carriers for a very long time, and earlier trials by British Telecom (BT) and Apple were pointing in this direction as early as the late 1980s.

13.6 Profiles and Levels

The profile and level organization in H.264 is much simpler than in MPEG-4 as a whole and the way it is defined for part 2. There are only three profiles currently defined:

- Baseline
- Main
- Extended

Within these profiles there are five main levels with some sub-levels also defined. In total there are 15 discrete levels supported.

The main profile (Level 3) is becoming the focal point of interest for H.264 encoder manufacturers that work in the broadcast TV industry.

Because H.264, AVC, and MPEG-4 part 10 are all the same codec, the profiles and levels are summarized together in Appendix G.

13.7 Tool Support

No other codec has as many tools as H.264. It is a superset of all the other codecs. You could develop a setup on another codec and optimize it to get good performance. Then, you could apply that same setup to H.264 and add the extra tools to gain even better performance than your original codec could possibly manage.

This is a short list of some of the feature enhancements in H.264 over the earlier codecs:

- DCT algorithm works at 4×4 pixels instead of 8×8 but also supports 8×8
- DCT is layered using Hadamard transforms
- Color sampling supported at 4:2:2 and 4:4:4.
- Up to 12 bits per pixel are possible
- Motion compensation blocks are variable sizes
- Arithmetic variable-length coding
- Built-in de-blocking filter and hinting mechanism
- Rate-distortion optimizer

- Intra-prediction mechanisms
- Weighted bi-directional prediction
- Redundant pictures
- Flexible macroblock ordering
- Direct mode for B-frames
- Multiple reference frames
- Sub-pixel motion compensation
- Proposed alpha-channel support as per MPEG-4 part 2

13.8 Coding Changes

H.264 is a quantum leap from earlier codec designs because it offers improved coding through the introduction of some new compression tools. The core compression algorithm is modified from a basic discrete cosine transform to support a hierarchical scheme. This refines the block structuring and reduces the macroblocks to smaller nested components.

By reducing the size of the blocks being considered, we create more opportunities to locate similar or identical macroblocks within the same image. This is where we make some great gains in the efficiency of the coding.

13.8.1 Hadamard Transform Tool

The transform algorithm in H.264 is modified to use a smaller (4×4) pixel area rather than the 8×8 or 16×16 macroblocking factors that earlier codecs used. This simplifies the math in the compression algorithm, allowing the transform to be implemented as a couple of basic matrix operations followed by a scaling operation. These are computationally quite easy to do and therefore the computing cost is reduced.

This is actually a subdivision of the 16×16 macroblock technique, so everything that has been described so far is still valid. It has just been refined to allow more detailed processing at the sub-macroblock level.

By arranging the 4×4 matrix as a subdivision of the 16×16 macroblock, obtaining a 4×4 grid of DC coefficients is very easy. Remember that this was the first item in the DCT transform output way back with MPEG-1 coding. Applying the transform again provides a two-level or tree-structured approach to the coding rather than a one-pass approach in the 16×16 DCT transform.

This technique is referred to as the Hadamard transform and is implemented with simple multiply-by-2 arithmetic in the CPU. Since this degenerates to a left shift of a binary value, it is computationally very easy to carry out.

The compression efficiency gains overall using this technique when compared with DCT are quite small but there are some significant advantages that improve quality for the same bit rate:

- The decoder behavior is replicated very exactly.
- Accurate decoding allows for much better predictive and scalability coding tools.

- The computational load is far less than with the DCT.
- A smaller computation overhead allows scope for other parts of the encoder to be implemented with more complex algorithms.

13.8.2 Entropy Coding Improvements

H.264 supports two methods of lossless coding, which are supported at the entropy coding phase of the coefficients provided by the DCT output. The following two enhanced operating modes are provided:

- Context-adaptive variable-length coding (CAVLC)
- Context-adaptive binary-arithmetic coding (CABAC)

The first (CAVLC) is based on a variable-length approach. The conversion tables that are used to compress the data are computed based on the content of the video. The second approach (CABAC) works by modifying the coding parameters to improve efficiency. These would be used in high bit-rate situations such as studio environments.

These new techniques vastly improve the compression available through entropy coding.

13.8.3 Logarithmic Quantization Improvements

Previous quantization tools used a linear quantizer. The H.264 codec implements a logarithmic scale in the quantization parameter settings. Each increment of the quantization parameter doubles the quantization step size. Figure 13-2 shows the logarithmic scale, which is oriented in a variety of ways depending on how the mapping must be carried out.

Logarithmic quantization has been used with audio for some time already because it plays to the strengths of the human ear and how it responds to sound. The ear is more sensitive at low amplitudes and so the logarithmic squashing of higher amplitudes allows the samples to be taken more evenly across the range of human sound perception. This technique is used to make telephone systems work more effectively. The coding schemes adopted by telecommunications companies are similar but not identical to those used in the media industry. Useful keywords for further research on the topic are Mu-Law, μ-Law, U-Law, M-Law, and A-Law.

The subjective effect is that an 8-bit sample sounds as good as a 14-bit sample on a linear scale. There is therefore some compression already implicitly going on here.

13.9 Block-Level Improvements

Many of the improvements to the coding offered by the H.264 codec take place at the macroblock level. Here, we highlight the more important additions.

Logarithmic scaling of samples

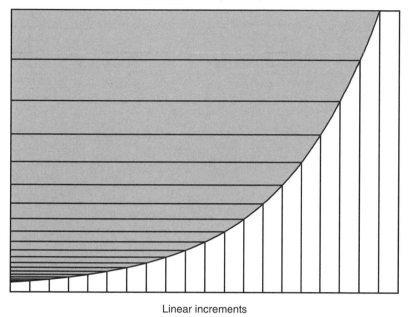

Linear increments

Figure 13-2 Logarithmic quantization.

13.9.1 Predictive Coding Improvements

The H.264 codec adds a spatial predictive tool for macroblocks within the same slice. Prediction allows the starting point of a macroblock to be based on an earlier block with only the residuals described as a series of changes to apply. This is slightly more efficient than simply defining an average color value since some kind of gradient across the macroblock might be usefully applied to make the residuals much smaller.

The prediction within a 16×16 macroblock is applied to the 4×4 sub macroblocks and is based on an earlier block to the left and above. Complete 16×16 macroblocks are predicted based on a block from earlier in the same slice and several modes are used to define how the prediction is applied.

13.9.2 De-Blocking Filter

H.264 adds a very useful postprocessing step that softens the artifacts caused by over-quantization. This artifact is exhibited as a very blocky appearance where the macroblock structure of the image shows through.

The de-blocking filter removes this artifact at the expense of some detail in the final image. Because it is now defined as part of the standard, the predictive coding process at the encoder extracts some residual information that is passed on to the de-blocking filter as hints to assist in de-blocking the image. That way the de-blocking process is not just a blind defocusing approach but an informed noise-reduction technique.

13.9.3 Motion Estimation Improvements

The improved quarter-pixel resolution deployed in MPEG-4 part 2 yielded some slight improvements in quality but these were not as good as they could be. H.264 improves the motion estimation by changing the way that sub-pixels are interpolated.

Up to this point interpolation has been a straightforward linear proportion between two end-point values. H.264 introduces a much more accurate interpolation of the sub-pixel value but degenerates to the simpler interpolation if the resulting output compresses more efficiently or accurately.

Motion estimation is applied at the 4×4 sub-macroblock level. A motion vector is described for the 16×16 macroblock as a whole and some additional motion vectors are described for smaller 4×4 parts of it. Those component parts within the macroblock are organized as non-rectangular shapes within the block.

13.10 Issues with GOP Structures, Frames, and Slices

The H.264 codec introduces a large number of new and complex mechanisms for referring between frames. This makes the group of pictures (GOP) closure very hard to do unless the encoder forces an initial I-frame and closing P-frame. The encoder must also prohibit some of the bi-directional references to target frames outside of the GOP.

13.10.1 Temporal Prediction Improvements

The I-frame, P-frame, and B-frame model used in MPEG-1, MPEG-2, and MPEG-4 part 2 is modified considerably in H.264.

The references are now made at the slice level rather than at the frame level. The slices are referenced in as many as 16 other frames rather than within a single frame as was the case with the earlier codecs.

As far as the decoder is concerned, this is only a trivial addition to the decoding complexity. At the encoding end of the process, much more information must be cached and for a longer time. In addition, the processing overhead requires motion-compensation searches to take place within several frames where it only used to have to search one. This is a significant computational increase and is one reason why the H.264 encoder is said to be slow compared with older codecs. When viewed in the context of the massive improvements in bit-rate efficiency, this increase in computational load is not as costly.

We take for granted that Moore's Law automatically deals with increasing computational loads imposed by desire for more sophisticated software algorithms. Moore's Law promised that processors would become faster at a steady rate over time, and the predictions have been true for 25 years. We appear to have reached some kind of performance boundary with the introduction of 90nm-chip manufacturing processes, and further progress in CPU speeds may come from parallelization and distributed processing techniques. Drawing circuits on silicon chips at nanometer resolutions has always been a challenge, and while some marginal improvements will continue to be made, new horizons are opening up with more efficient computer architectures and greater parallelization. Computer manufacturers will continue to develop new solutions to this, including totally new technologies based on biochips, quantum mechanics, and optical computers. Those are many years in the future, though, and in the short term, distributed processing across multiple processors looks to be the most promising approach.

The meanings of the "B" and "P" are slightly altered, as are some of the restrictions placed on them by earlier codecs. Previously, P-frames had to be derived from an I-frame. Now a P-slice might be derived from a slice in a B-frame that had been transmitted earlier on.

B-slices are referred to as bi-predictive, not bi-directional, in the H.264 codec. B-frames were bi-directional in the earlier MPEG-2 designs and could refer to just one frame earlier or one frame later in the temporal sequence. The frames had to have been transmitted earlier so they could be referred to, however. A macroblock in a B-slice may refer to one or two reference pictures that must have already been decoded and therefore also must have been transmitted already. They need not be from the adjacent frames in temporal order.

Figure 13-4 shows a frame whose macroblocks are composed of blocks that are referenced out of other frames. The intra macroblocks are local, the inter macroblocks are in another frame, and some macroblocks are static and not changing.

Because the references to macroblocks in other frames are much more complex, it is harder to accomplish closed GOP structures if you want to benefit from the highest levels

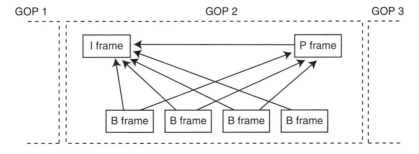

Figure 13-3 MPEG-2 macroblock references between frames.

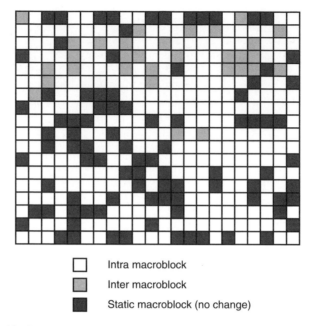

☐ Intra macroblock
▨ Inter macroblock
▧ Static macroblock (no change)

Figure 13-4 Macroblock composition of a frame.

of efficiency in the coding. The increased complexity is evident in the way that frames are derived in Figure 13-5. Even so, this diagram is a simplified example and the dependencies between frames are very complex.

As a sequence of frames is processed, the number of intra-coded macroblocks reduces as they change to static macroblocks. This is good because intra macroblocks are the ones that consume the most bit rate. Figure 13-6 shows a sequence of 4 frames displayed on a Tektronix analyzer. You can see that the number of intra blocks is significantly reduced in Frames 3 and 4.

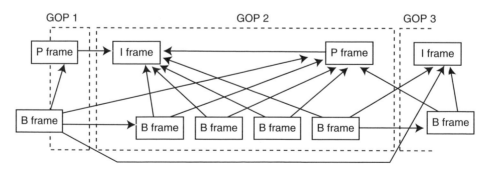

Figure 13-5 H.264 macroblock references to frames in different GOPs.

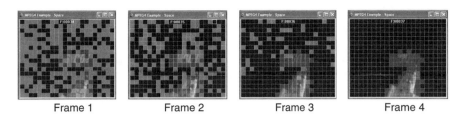

Frame 1   Frame 2   Frame 3   Frame 4

Figure 13-6 Intra macroblocks changing to static macroblocks. Source: courtesy of Tektronix.

13.10.2 Prediction Weighting

Earlier standards allowed macroblocks to be interpolated from two other frames. This is a straightforward averaging. H.264 supports an adaptive weighting so a greater proportion of the macroblock value is taken from one frame over the other.

13.10.3 Frame and Field Coding

The macroblock coding support for interlaced video is improved to allow pairing between macroblocks in each field, which improves the handling of motion that takes place between fields of the video sequence. This is provided as an adaptive technique, which is switched on and off as required.

13.11 Licensing Issues

At the beginning of 2004, the most worrying issues facing potential adopters of the H.264 codec were the licensing of the MPEG-4 part 10 intellectual property rights and how the revenues might be paid to the patent holders of any vital technologies.

Refer to Chapter 18 for a discussion about commercial issues, digital rights management (DRM), and related topics.

13.12 Ongoing Development of the Standard

Some further work is now necessary because in strict encoding terms, part 10 is far better than part 2. However, the technical capabilities of part 2 are more flexible than part 10.

There must be a merger of the two in order to render the older coding method completely obsolete. For the time being it may be necessary to code using part 2 if you want to take advantage of some of the additional capabilities such as alpha channel-shape coding. In the fullness of time, it is very likely that part 10 will acquire all of these capabilities but the working group must first incorporate the necessary changes into the standard. That will take a little time.

As of 2004, the JVT team is reviewing what is needed and the standard may be enhanced in due course to support alpha channels, shape coding, and some of the legacy color models that earlier codecs supported.

13.13   AVC Alliance and MPEG Industry Forum

It is a popular strategy for a group of interested companies and individuals to rally around a new open standard and form a collaborative organization. This leads to better interoperability and helps to promote the new standard in order to get things off the ground.

The AVC Alliance as well as the MPEG Industry Forum are now promoting the H.264/MPEG-4 part 10 standard and this will demonstrate to the industry that the participating companies are taking the standard seriously.

13.14   Risks and Benefits of Adopting H.264

The H.264 codec has been selected for next-generation DVD formats and European HDTV broadcasts so the risks of adoption are decreasing.

At this point in the MPEG-2 life cycle, bit rates of around 6 to 7 Mbps were being achieved for consumer-quality video. The MPEG-2 coders have improved over the last five years so that bit rates as low as 3.6 Mbps are possible with some compromises in quality. Envivio is aiming for a bit rate that will deliver H.264-coded video that is of excellent quality at well under 2 Mbps, and experts in video coding are optimistic that the same potential reduction of 50% of the bit rate is possible with H.264 over its life cycle (although that remains to be seen, and you should be careful of being too optimistic when using these values for capacity planning).

There is a risk that companies wanting to make an impact with AVC/H.264 encoders will launch products with less-than-optimally implemented codecs. While the new codec standard is becoming increasingly important, the software is entering the market more slowly than people would like. This careful approach is not necessarily a bad thing, but you should thoroughly test any codecs you purchase to ensure that they are interoperable and are delivering the anticipated quality and bit rate. Always remember that the standard defines only a legal bit stream for the decoder to process. How that was encoded is not specified in the standard, and two implementations of the H.264 encoder may deliver very different results even with the same parameter settings.

13.14.1   Implications for Linux

Let's examine this in the context of the Linux platform. There is no dominant de-facto standard on Linux and it welcomes all comers equally. The DivX codec, which is a derivative of MPEG-4, is available as an open source.

Oddly enough, Linux is used in products such as TiVo, and in fact quite a few TV set-top box manufacturers that are engineering interactive platforms are using a version of the Linux operating system optimized for TV. Linux is a useful platform to build streaming servers on, and certainly in the past it has been a very appropriate platform for building Real Networks encoders. It is still very good but Mac OS and Windows have caught up with it in the areas it dominated as an open-source platform. The H.264 standard would work very well with Linux and, provided a suitably performing player is available, H.264

offers Linux the opportunity to be on equal terms with the Mac OS and Windows platforms when it comes to video-based tools, servers, and players.

13.15 The Output of the Encoder

We need the encoder to generate a bit stream. This is what we transmit when we stream on the Internet or deliver via a digital TV system. All encoders deliver a similar output regardless of their internal algorithms. There are some similarities among the MPEG-1, MPEG-2, and MPEG-4 bit streams and the complexity increases as the later coders are introduced. The next chapter discuses bit streams and what you need to know about them as a video-compression practitioner.

14

Encoded Output Delivered as a Bit Stream

14.1 The Next Step

All codecs eventually produce a bit stream as their output. The bit stream is either multiplexed and transmitted live or packaged and stored in a file for later use. This is the end product of a coding operation, but just knowing that doesn't mean we will produce an optimum bit stream.

14.2 Producing the Output Bit Stream

A challenging aspect of producing the outgoing bit stream is to even out the flow of data so the available bit rate is used fully. The ideal situation is to use every last available bit but not run out of capacity. To do this, you have to develop a kind of "living-on-the-edge" mentality.

Taking the simplest case where I-frames are encoded to produce a bit stream, the amount of data in each frame will vary according to the amount of detail in the image. This is because even without coding in the differences and motion compensation from frame to frame, the entropy coding will yield frames of different sizes after each frame is encoded.

The encoding complexity will vary across the area of an image. Some parts of the image may code very easily while others may require substantially more information to describe the fine detail. Large areas of the same color such as sky or space scenes tend to encode very well indeed. Figure 14-1 shows a screenshot from the Tektronix MTS4EA video analyzer that you can install on a Windows PC. This example shows one of the statistical measurement displays that help you diagnose image-compression problems.

This topic crops up again in Chapter 20 in the discussion about streaming and again in Chapter 27 regarding digital TV systems.

The output is an elementary stream and requires further processing to be able to deliver it to an end point.

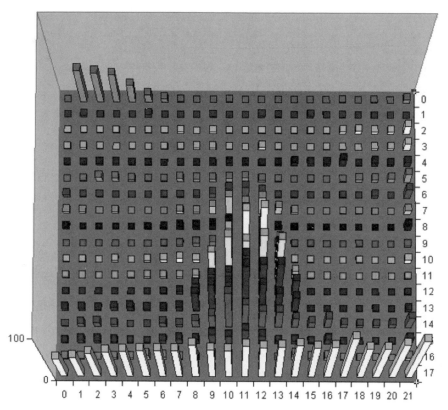

Figure 14-1 Spatial complexity shown by bit-rate usage per macroblock. Source: Image courtesy of Tektronix.

14.3 Bit-Rate Variability

When video is coded for delivery though a digital transport, the coding application allows either variable bit rate (VBR) or constant bit rate (CBR) to be selected. Both have advantages and disadvantages.

The video is arriving at the encoder ordered and synchronized to a steady frame rate. Perhaps it is coming from a file, in which case time is irrelevant at that point, but the video must be presented to the viewer on a strict time base. This has to be honored in both the decoder and the player. The player usually decodes on the fly since decoding to an intermediate storage format is not necessary unless you intend to edit the incoming video.

The frames may be delivered with a bit rate that goes up and down according to the content, or the bit rate may be constant. If it is permissible to deliver a VBR stream, then rate control is irrelevant unless the available bit rate has an upper limit. You can normally set that limit in the encoder. For example, Popwire encoders optimally code MPEG-4 video in a range from 60 Kbps to 2000 Kbps but you have to specify this, taking into account the bit rate needed for the audio, of course.

You have a variety of parameters in the compression engine that control the quality of the output. Chapters 31 to 38 discuss the optimum values for these as part of the step-by-step walk-through of the compression process. Whether CBR or VBR is selected in the parameter settings of your compression software controls the bit-rate usage.

A very useful bit-rate calculator is available at the DVD-HQ Web site. Also, Pioneer provides some DVD technical guidelines at their Web site.

14.3.1 Bursting

Bursting happens when the content being compressed momentarily becomes more complex than usual. This occurs when two scenes are lap dissolved from one to the other. A consequence of this kind of scene transition is that every pixel changes value on every frame, and any motion compensation is also compromised since subjects are partially transparent and may be moving in completely different directions in the two scenes.

This all becomes much harder to compress because there is far less chance of finding similar macroblocks in previous or later frames on which to base the delta information. As a consequence, virtually the whole frame must be recompressed as if it were an I-frame. Few of the gains associated with B-frames are available.

You should edit sympathetically in order to reduce compression artifacts like this. Editing sympathetically is when you avoid things like cutting abruptly and frequently (every couple of frames) or using transitions that create a lot of frame-to-frame difference information.

Straightforward cut edits are less attractive visually but compress much better. If you want to enhance the scene transitions, a wipe, possibly with a soft edge, would compress far more easily than a dissolve and is not unattractive. Figure 14-2 shows the two different transition effects.

14.3.2 Variable Bit Rate

With a variable bit rate (VBR), the video quality remains the same but the bit rate is allowed to burst occasionally in order to accommodate a more complex scene.

Some encoders provide a hybrid VBR that has a maximum bit-rate setting. The video will be compressed at a low bit rate most of the time. When it bursts, the bit rate is allowed to rise to a preset maximum value. This gives an all-around better performance if it is configured correctly. The quality will only degenerate when an extremely complex piece of video is presented.

Figure 14-3 also shows how a VBR signal uses more or less capacity but must remain below some arbitrarily defined threshold to avoid multiplexing problems.

Variable bit-rate streams have a major advantage in the area of video quality. Because they are variable, additional bit rate can be made available when a sequence of frames

---

DVD HQ bit-rate calculator: http://dvd-hq.info/Calculator.html

Pioneer DVD specifications: http://www.pioneer.co.jp/crdl/tech/dvd/4-3-e.html

Take 2 source images.

Transition with a disolve.

Every pixel changes at once.

A wipe, even one with a soft
edge is kinder to your bit rate.

Figure 14-2 Dissolves versus wipes.

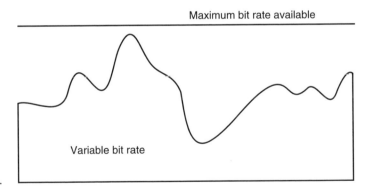

Maximum bit rate available

Variable bit rate

Figure 14-3 VBR bit stream.

becomes difficult to compress. Large areas of changing pixels cause compression systems a lot of trouble. Pop videos are notoriously difficult to compress because of the lighting effects. A simple change from red to green lighting forces every pixel to be changed. The differences from one frame to the next are therefore huge and this will severely spike the bit rate. Executing a lap-dissolve effect when editing video will do this as well. Straightforward cuts are much better for the bit rate than a dissolve.

14.3.3 *Constant Bit Rate*

It is possible to even out any bit-rate bursting by capping the available bit rate. The problem here is that bit-rate requirements may periodically and momentarily exceed the capping level. Those same dissolve and color-change effects will look quite different if the bit rate is capped at the average level. Figure 14-4 shows what happens if the same bit-rate pattern is delivered within a much lower threshold and that available bit rate is capped. The encoder might eke out the dips in the constant bit rate (CBR) if it is smart enough to move bits around and alter the buffering.

You will notice a severe blocking artifact at the points where the bit rate is capped because the compressor has to throw information away. The best solution is to reduce the information in the coded macroblocks.

A CBR setting forces the encoder to constrain the output so that even if the video compression becomes more complex, the maximum bit rate is not exceeded under any circumstances. During times of low complexity, the video quality will be better than when the encoder has to work hard. Because the bit rate remains constant, the trade-off has to be made with the video quality. In order to remain within the budgeted bit rate, more information must be discarded at times and this will lower the output quality of the resulting compressed video.

14.3.4 *Statistical Multiplexing*

A combination of variable and constant bit rate is available when statistical multiplexing is used. This is very useful in digital TV applications and is covered in Chapter 27 where digital TV services are discussed in detail.

The concept is essentially very simple. When two streams are transmitted together, it is statistically unlikely that they will both be bursting to their maximum bit rate at the same time. It is far more likely that one will trough while the other peaks.

The encoders are able to take advantage of this and create a multiplexed bit stream that maximizes both channels. In fact, the concept is extended to as many as five or six channels and still works very well.

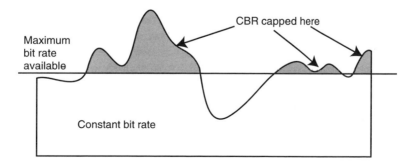

Figure 14-4 CBR bit stream.

14.4 Packetizing

The elementary stream just contains video. Somehow the audio must be added to it once that has been encoded separately. The result of the audio-encoding process yields an elementary bit stream similar to that of a video-compression process. These must be combined carefully so they remain synchronized.

The audio will very likely comprise several streams. This is because audio is played back through several loudspeakers to give a stereo or surround-sound effect.

It is not very sensible to deliver the video and audio separately, one after the other, because unless you intend to download the entire program, you will not have all the material available to start playing until the last stream begins to arrive. It is very efficient in terms of file-based storage but is no good for streaming.

The encoder postprocesses the compressed content by slicing it into smaller, unit sized packets. These are then shuffled together like a pack of cards as shown in Figure 14-5, making sure that packets belonging to the same real-world time frame are adjacent to each other.

Once these are interleaved, the stream is transmitted and at the receiving end, the player separates the packets out again to reconstruct the elementary streams. The output of this process is a collection of elementary streams that can be played together.

14.5 Audio Embedding

Once you have both the audio and the video encoded, some output targets will require that the audio be embedded into the digital-video bit stream. This is commonplace in the broadcast industry, as it is used to reduce the amount of additional cabling and routing equipment required.

If some of your source material arrives this way, having flexible embedding and de-embedding tools available will get you out of a hole. This falls under the general advice of always being on the lookout for useful tools.

14.6 Flattening Out the Bit Rate (Traffic Shaping)

You may have controls in your coding process that allow you to alter the buffering and bit-rate distribution during the encoding process. By carefully adjusting the buffering during times of low bit rate, more frames are delivered to the buffer in the client receiver. When some complex content is compressed, the encoder works within the available bit rate but allows the client to run slightly ahead and catch up a little with the buffered stream. Then, when the complex, high bit-rate content has been processed, the buffering begins to pick

Video	Audio	Video	Audio	Video	Audio

Figure 14-5 Multiplexed packets.

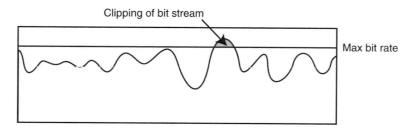

Figure 14-6 Peaking of content.

up and move ahead of the playback again. Figure 14-6 shows where a bit rate bursts past the capacity to deliver it, causing a momentary loss of quality.

This is complex to control and will require quite expensive encoders. The traffic shaping becomes more important when interactive services are packaged with the video. In that case, the interactivity is delivered opportunistically during the troughs in bit rate. The overall bit rate is then maintained at a constant level. Some interactive elements need to be delivered early in the stream so the user is able to interact with them right away. Figure 14-7 shows how the clipped bit rate is corrected by delivering some of the buffer a little earlier than originally planned.

This is effectively statistical multiplexing with the additional twist that some of the bit rate is allocated to non-video use. Interactive assets don't have to be delivered at specific frame times within the stream. They only have to be delivered before the interactivity calls them up for use.

 Higher frame rates will typically give a smoother motion, but they decrease the image quality. Lower frame rates result in crisper images but will probably cause jerky motion.

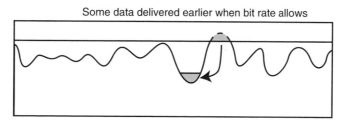

Figure 14-7 Traffic-shaped changes.

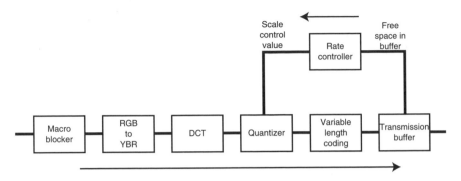

Figure 14-8 Rate control based on quantization scale factor.

14.6.1 Quantization Scale-Factor tools

The MPEG-1 standard provides a tool called the "quantization scale factor." This is used in a feedback loop that measures the buffering being consumed by the encoder. The feedback throttles the quantization level as necessary to stop the buffer from overflowing. This part of the encoding technology relates to the performance of encoders when you select variable bit-rate (VBR) or constant bit-rate (CBR) algorithms.

Being able to adjust the quantization scale factor allows us to more easily generate video that is delivered at a constant bit rate. The workings of this and the flow of feedback information are shown in Figure 14-8.

The feedback is quite sophisticated because it will affect the way that macroblocks are encoded. Knowing something about the complexity of the macroblocks will help you decide where to scavenge more bit rate with a quantization scale factor that increases the compression ratio. Performing some metrics on the original source image data provides a measure of the amount of detail. There are a variety of ways to do this. The best performance is achieved by carefully examining the source material before starting to encode the macroblocks.

This section of the encoder includes the video buffer verifier (VBV) and some compression tools (Popwire Compression Master, for example) allow you to control the behavior. Often it will not be called the VBV control. It masquerades as a minimum and maximum target bit-rate range control in the variable bit-rate settings. This is where traffic shaping and bit starving are controlled to even out the peaks in the bit rate.

If you have the analyzing tools, Figure 14-9 is a typical display showing buffer occupancy.

14.6.2 Bit Starving to Empty Buffers Just Prior to Complex Scene Switches

You will need to make sure that there is sufficient bit rate to cope when the video is complex. For example, the compression ratio will be less efficient when you are dealing with the following:

- Footage of fire
- Footage of explosions

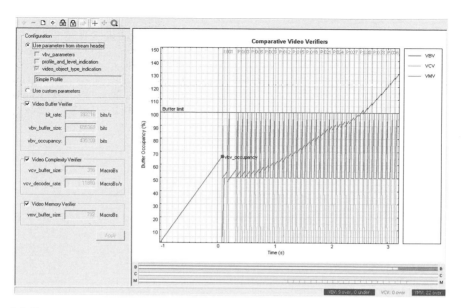

Figure 14-9 VBV buffer-occupancy analysis. Source: courtesy of Tektronix.

- Lighting changes in the studio
- Dissolves between scenes

These situations cause a massive increase in the bit rate required. If you have been unable to fill the buffer sufficiently, you may find that the available bit rate is insufficient to compress that section of video without introducing artifacts.

Figure 14-10 shows the effect of a buffer filling up as presented by a VBV analyzer that is able to evaluate the decoder capabilities.

If your encoder is well designed it will note the sections of video that require additional bit rate during the first pass of a two-pass encode. The encoder will wind down the bit rate prior to that scene. Then it can increase the available bits to allow the encoder to create a more complex description of that video segment without going beyond your maximum bit-rate settings. This measurement and compensation takes place in the VBV. Your editing system may have placed compression markers on cut and transition boundaries to facilitate this.

Figure 14-11 shows the same analysis as before, but in this case the bit rate has been throttled to allow the decoder time to consume the buffered content.

14.7 Joined-Up Systems

One of the useful features of Final Cut Pro is the insertion of compression markers whenever an edit or transition occurs. The Apple Keynote presentation application also marks its slide boundaries and transitions in an exported movie.

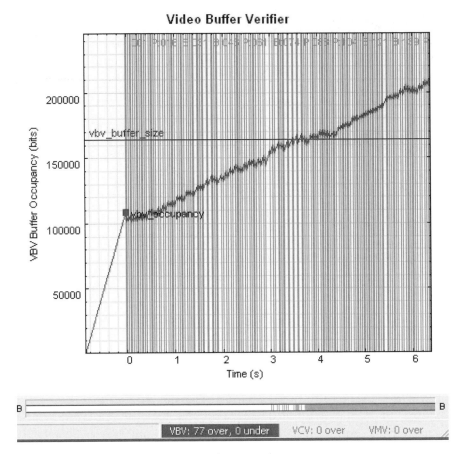

Figure 14-10 Buffer overrun. Source: courtesy of Tektronix.

This technique could be applied to graphics-rendering systems, to provide a macroblock-organized array of hinting values. Hinting could indicate how that portion of the scene was rendered and whether a part of it had come from the same place as a macroblock in another frame. In this way, we are structuring the hints to the compression process as part of rendering the scene. This obviously does not work for video being filmed on a camera, but rendered footage exists as a database model and it gets transformed into pixels along the way. We know everything there is to know about the provenance of that pixel.

For a workflow that produces a DVD, writing the compressed bit stream directly as an output of the rendering process allows optimizing decisions to take place as the rendering is processing. This improves the compression ratio at the source.

This idea is completely speculative and I am not aware of any systems that are available off the shelf with this level of integration. Architecting and building workflow

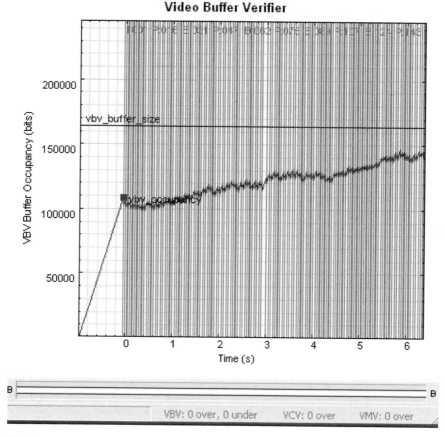

Figure 14-11 Carefully tuned client-buffer occupancy. Source: courtesy of Tektronix.

systems that reduce complexity by eliminating redundant steps would be worth research-ing, however.

14.8   The Final Result

In Figure 14-12 you can see something of the structure of the outgoing bit stream as it looks when displayed on a Tektronix analyzer. This is an example fragment of an H.264 bit stream at the start of the session.

The bit patterns are shown in the columns on the left and you can see clearly that some bit-stream fragments are longer than others. These of course have to be packed into bytes so they can be manipulated inside a computer more conveniently.

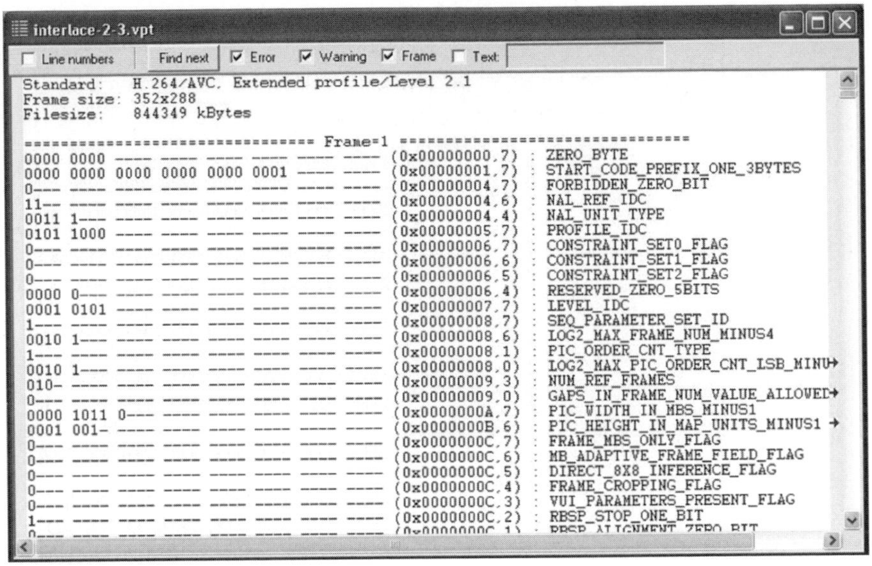

Figure 14-12 H.264 bit-stream output. Source: courtesy of Tektronix.

14.9 Summary of How Encoders Work

So to review where we have arrived now that we are at the end of this chapter, let's take a sequence of video and describe the step-by-step process of compression.

1. Divide the video sequence into groups of pictures.
2. Process the I-frame at the start of the GOP.
3. Locate the next P-frame in the GOP and code that.
4. Code the intervening B-frames.
5. Step forward to the next P-frame and continue until the end of the GOP.

For each frame,

1. Divide the frame into macroblocks.
2. Locate similar macroblocks nearby to reduce redundancy.
3. Separate the luma and chroma for each block.
4. Apply a transformation to each macroblock.
5. Quantize and entropy code the macroblocks.
6. Store the coded bit stream in an elementary stream.

Then,

1. Code the audio to produce the separate elementary streams necessary.
2. Packetize the video and audio elementary streams and multiplex them together to form the program stream.
3. Further packetize the program streams available and multiplex them into a transport stream.
4. Deliver to the broadcast head-end or streaming service and route them to the end user.

At the receiver, the streams are de-multiplexed and reassembled from the packets before decoding individually.

14.10 The Next Challenge

So we now have a bit stream. Before we delve into the storage mechanisms for bit streams let's just pause and look at live encoding. The next chapter will explore some of the issues involved. It is a good place to break off and do this because the output of a live encoder is a bit stream as well.

15

Live Encoding

15.1 Living on the Bleeding Edge

Streaming video efficiently is one of the biggest challenges involved in providing media services to the public. Video compression is an important part of the technology toolkit, but it is not the only thing that you need to consider. The challenges are extreme, especially when you are providing premium content to a large audience. Traffic levels can rapidly exceed any available bandwidth you can deploy from a single server, and so more innovative solutions are required. This is truly leading-edge stuff. This advanced technology is often called 'Bleeding Edge'—a play on words used because of the potential for failure and the somewhat large expenditure involved.

Whether you are encoding video for delivery via the web or for broadcast TV applications, the concepts are essentially the same. However, although the coding of the video is similar, the delivery format is different. Multiplexing is used for TV services in order to make maximum use of the transport stream by delivering several channels within the same stream.

Streaming content on a network is often used for delivery of live, encoded on-the-fly content. The issues involved with making content available to sufficient people are dealt with in Chapter 20, which discusses streaming. This chapter concentrates on issues to do with live encoding the master stream.

You have a large number of companies to choose from for your encoding hardware and software. As a general rule, encoding for the Internet is done with software running on a desktop PC and encoding for broadcast delivery is done with hardware. This difference is becoming blurred as some Internet and broadband service providers use hardware-assisted software encoders.

15.2 Streaming Basics

Let's briefly review the *packetizing* and serving mechanisms required to deliver a stream of digitally coded video.

Your video and audio are encoded separately and the audio is then merged with the video. This is sometimes called embedding or multiplexing. Multiplexing is a process that combines packets of encoded data from a variety of elementary sources and creates a single stream with them interleaved together.

That audio and video track pair might then have some data tracks added to carry URL and subtitle information and might then be prepared for streaming over the Web. The hinting process runs through a file-based version of the stream and adds information that the streaming server uses when delivering the content to the client player.

15.3 Live Streaming

For live streaming, all of the encoding has to happen on the fly. Moreover, it has to happen quickly enough that the outgoing stream keeps pace with the incoming video or you get a buffer overflow situation. That would cause the encoder to run out of capacity and either have to stop encoding or jump to a new location having missed a section. The resulting effect is a very unsatisfactory viewing experience.

To avoid this you need to make sure you are running the encoding and streaming process on a powerful enough computer. The modern codecs deliver a higher compression ratio than their older counterparts but this is at the expense of requiring significantly more compute power. Therefore the choice of codec and compute platform makes a lot of difference to your ability to serve live-streamed content.

15.4 Encoding for Broadcast TV

When encoding video for broadcast TV use, a hardware-based solution is used for most scenarios. The coding and multiplexing together of multiple program streams is a complex process and the architecture of your streaming service determines how effectively you utilize the available bit rate.

Broadcast TV services are delivered within a fixed bit rate for the entire multiplex or transponder. Within that fixed bit rate, individual streams may be coded with variable bit rates, constant bit rates, or statistically multiplexed variable bit rates. Figure 15-1 illustrates the complexity of a *DSat* broadcast and even this example is simplified somewhat. You can see that some channels are available only for part of the day and their capacity is used for quite different things, depending on when you are viewing.

15.5 Inserting Additional Data Feeds

Depending on where your streamed service is to be deployed, you may add supplementary data feeds to the outgoing stream. There are several likely alternatives here. Any data that must be synchronized with the video should be added as the video is encoded. Postprocessing is possible when encoding to a file since the content is managed offline, but when live encoding, the data must be coded at the same time. Subtitle streams, for example, may actually be typed by operators in real time or might be taken from the script that

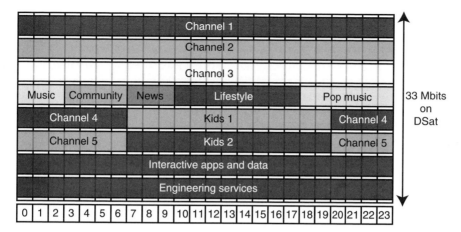

| 0 | 1 | 2 | 3 | 4 | 5 | 6 | 7 | 8 | 9 | 10 | 11 | 12 | 13 | 14 | 15 | 16 | 17 | 18 | 19 | 20 | 21 | 22 | 23 |

Figure 15-1 Transponder bit-rate distribution.

feeds an AutoCue unit. Sometimes speech recognition is used to track the autocue script and synchronize it to the audio track that is being encoded and added to the outgoing stream. This gets complex right away, without even trying to do anything very advanced.

Broadcasting services have the same requirements for synchronized data feeds. Some advantage can be gained by the fact that many programs are made well before broadcast. Although the output is encoded live, it is often being played out from a prerecorded source and is not very often "live to air" from an incoming feed. Many of the benefits of offline preparation are still available to the program creator. Some data will be synchronous to the real-world time and delivered once only, at the time of broadcast.

Other data feeds, perhaps having to do with the delivery of a text service or interactive application, are delivered at the same time as part of the transport stream but are played out independently. These would normally be driven from a carousel, which is a cyclically rotating buffer of data that is played out repeatedly. This is necessary because receivers typically do not have much cache memory available and it is quite likely that the viewer has come to the program some time after the most recent transmission of the data. Therefore, significant numbers of viewers may not yet have received the data and it must be transmitted periodically to ensure that they all receive it. This is of course a very wasteful technique in terms of bandwidth but is necessary in order to keep the costs of set-top boxes to a minimum.

15.6 Error Correction

The transport mechanisms convey the streaming data over a very long distance before it reaches your player. Internet-streamed video will have very likely crossed the Atlantic at least once and if you are a European user, it may have crossed the Atlantic several times if the routing is complex. It all depends on your ISP and how you are connected to the wider network. Certainly the content will have travelled several thousand miles and the routes may not always be the same for all packets. There may be delays or sequencing issues with the packets arriving at unpredictable times.

These effects are alleviated with buffering at the expense of latency. The simple rule of thumb is that TCP (transmission control protocol) guarantees the arrival and sequence ordering of the packets at the expense of their timeliness of arrival. Alternatively, *UDP* (universal datagram protocol) transports could be used, which guarantee timeliness but don't guarantee arrival or sequencing order.

Uplinking a feed to a satellite and downlinking to a dish connected to your set-top box involves a journey of several thousand miles through what may be turbulent atmospheric conditions. This introduces a delay and possibly some loss of information. The timeliness and sequencing is preserved, though, since the stream is continuously transmitted from the broadcast head-end.

Likewise, digital transmission systems such as terrestrial and digital cable may deliver the signal over some tens or hundreds of miles. Terrestrial transmission is susceptible to atmospheric conditions and there is also a possibility of co-channel interference and problems with receiver aerials that can "see" two transmitters separated by a narrow angle even though one may be a lot further away. Odd fringe effects come into play and this degrades the reception. *DCable* may be susceptible to network-balancing issues where the distribution is not ideally matched in terms of impedance at some nodes, or there may be substandard terminations in the cables leading to reflected signals.

All of these issues manifest themselves as dropouts or corrupted data in the delivered stream. The nature of the degradation varies significantly. While the transmission systems are designed to be resilient, extreme error conditions for lengthy periods may result in a loss of service. This is of course all predicated on the service being delivered perfectly in the first place, which is the norm, but occasionally a multiplex may be packed with too much data to be transmitted and the multiplex then breaks because it exceeds the capacity available to deliver the streams. That is quite rare and tends to happen when services are in pre-launch trials or when a major reorganization of the service is underway.

15.6.1   *Parity Protection*

One of the simplest forms of error resilience is parity protection. This is applied on serial connections on a byte-by-byte basis and is a somewhat costly way of protecting the stream content. Essentially a single bit is added to each *byte* and it is set to 1 or 0 in order to ensure that the total number of bits is either odd or even. This tells you when a single byte is corrupted. There is still an opportunity for undetected errors because two reversed bits cause the parity to read correctly. Parity protection at the byte level is resilient to a single error but no more.

15.6.2   *Cyclic Redundancy Checks*

A small amount of data is added as the packets are assembled to create a checksum value. By performing a simple calculation, a known value is generated for every packet. The calculation adds all the bytes together, throws away any carried-over bits, and then generates a value which, when added to the sum, yields a known constant value. This is very like the parity protection at the byte level. The technique of cyclic redundancy checks (CRC) is simple but has limited error-correction capabilities. It tells you that the packet is corrupted and if you have other countermeasures, they can be exercised only when necessary since they are too computationally intensive to apply to every packet.

15.6.3 *Forward Error Correction*

Forward error correction (FEC) involves a technique called Reed–Solomon that adds enough data to the packet that one can verify the correctness and also repair some errors. The number of errors that can be repaired depends on the amount of Reed–Solomon data that is added and the requirement for that depends on the transmission system. In a very noisy transport, adding more Reed–Solomon code may improve the reliability but it may also reduce the throughput since more redundancy has to be coded. That additional overhead does not convey any extra information; it just secures the existing data against potential corruptions. Figure 15-2 shows how the data is wrapped like an onionskin.

15.6.4 *Error-Correction Conclusions*

The error correction should be provided by the transport mechanism and this is not something you should have to concern yourself about when compressing video. You should expect the output of the transport process to deliver substantially what you put in at the head-end and any error-correction processes will be transparent as far as you are concerned.

15.7 Handling Signal Outages

During a live broadcast, the incoming signal may be interrupted momentarily. This also happens when transferring files around your system but the copying process deals with minor network glitches and any missing data is requested again. This is not possible with a live feed.

So the number-one priority is to guarantee that your incoming video arrives uninterrupted. One possibility is to interpose some equipment that buffers the signals. This buffer might also detect a loss of signal and substitute another recently delivered frame or fragment of an image. A simple dual-ported frame store with the input being fed from the live source and the output going to your compression system would do a lot to improve things during lossy transmissions. The movement might be a little jerky but at least you would have a whole picture to display.

The incoming video may be delivered from a live outside broadcast installation. That is likely to provide a very reliable feed but it might be doing this across a landline provided by a telecom provider or via a microwave link. These links suffer periodic interruptions.

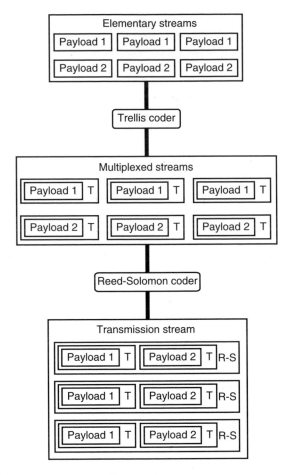

Figure 15-2 Reed–Solomon error correction.

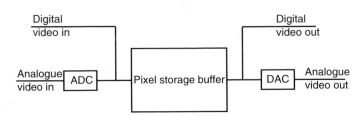

Figure 15-3 Dual-ported frame buffer.

Setting up a triangulated feed with an alternate leg will be important if your service is a high-profile and popular broadcast.

Your delivery to the end user may suffer glitches in the connection from their client to the service. Those service interruptions would only affect that user. Service interruptions on your incoming master feed will affect all users. The amount of time, effort, and cost you put into these links will vary accordingly.

15.8 Encoding Latency

Processing groups of pictures introduces a delay because the GOP should be processed from end to end before any of it is delivered for output. This allows the maximum encoding benefits to be gained.

Because of the way that video compression works, there is a built-in latency, which cannot be any less than the length of a GOP. Arguably, you might allow that latency to be reduced to the distance between an I-Frame and a P-Frame (see Chapter 10 for details of GOPs and frame types).

The H.264 (AVC, MPEG-4 part 10) codec has an even larger potential window for complex macroblock dependencies, and the motion-vector computations could be based on a macroblock that is a large number of frames in the past or future relative to the current frame being coded. This increases the latency.

15.8.1 Rate-Control Buffering

The rate-control process introduces a delay because it needs a buffer to measure in order to generate the throttling values for the quantization scale factor.

15.8.2 Consequences of B-Frames

Once you introduce B-frames, the bi-directional nature increases the latency because the look-ahead buffer must see a larger number of frames into the future in order to compute the bi-directional difference information and to reorganize the frames into the correct transmission order before loading them into the output bit-stream buffer.

Eliminating B-frames altogether allows the GOP to be assembled in transmission order and the latency to be reduced to a minimum.

Latency is the delay between the input video arriving and the output bit stream being transmitted and then received at the client playback device. Zero latency is achieved by eliminating B-frames altogether at the expense of coding efficiency.

15.8.3 Latency in Broadcasting Systems

The complexity of your content pipeline will also introduce some latency in addition to that caused by the coding process. Distance is not just a physical aspect of video systems. Buffers, repeaters, and communications links will all contribute small delays. These may be trivial on their own but significant when you cascade them together. For some program material, that may involve lossless compression from a remote OB (outside broadcast) or secondary studio delivering a feed to a transmission hub that aggregates several sources.

This presents some interesting issues with synchronization when locking the video to real-world time. The typical delay between analog terrestrial and digital terrestrial in the United Kingdom (where the comparison can be made very easily) is approximately half a second. For most program material this is not going to matter.

15.8.4   Latency in Videoconferencing Systems

Videoconferencing is deploying more video encoders as users get interested in the idea of seeing one another while they chat. The Apple iChat AV videoconferencing system is built around the H.264 codec. For this application the codec is configured to send the output of the video camera with zero latency. Zero latency is accomplished by eliminating the B-frames and sending a sequence that only contains I-frames and P-frames. Eliminating B-frames also reduces the size of the GOPs so they are effectively just one or two frames long.

15.9   Hardware Versus Software

In terms of sheer performance, hardware solutions are always going to deliver better quality than software, the major limitation being that they are hard to upgrade. This is being addressed by using specialized DSP chips that are reloaded with new codec algorithms. An upgrade can be delivered and rolled out very easily without needing to open the box. Another solution is hardware-assisted software. This will become more popular as graphics cards are deployed with embedded encoding and decoding support for video. Companies such as Texas Instruments, Ateme, Harmonic, and Equator are working on products based on this technique.

The graphics cards made by NVidia are already being manufactured with onboard video compression processing. It remains to be seen how software developers exploit this capability.

15.9.1   Hardware-Based Solutions

New versions of the chipset used in graphics cards made by NVidia now have video encode/decode for a variety of formats built in. This may lead to innovative solutions for encoder designs.

Texas Instruments: http://www.ti.com/

Texas Instruments Semiconductors: http://support.ti.com/

Ateme: http://www.adt-inc.com/products/ateme/ateme_prod_ov.htm

Harmonic: http://www.harmonicinc.com/

Equator Technologies: http://www.equator.com/

NVidia: http://www.nvidia.com/page/home

Ateme supplies a Texas Instruments DSP-based processor that is reprogrammed with different encoding/decoding algorithms on demand. That might lead to in interesting hybrid hardware/software solution. These codec reloads happen so quickly that they can be switched as the user changes channels. Demonstrations with the codec carried in the bit stream suggest that downloadable decoding software is feasible.

For high-performance modern codec implementations, Envivio manufactures a range of encoders, which are designed to yield very high compression factors with the latest H.264 codec. Encoder hardware is also available from Snell & Wilcox, Tandberg, Philips, and other manufacturers. Refer to Appendix B for a list of manufacturers of encoding hardware.

15.9.2 Software-Based Solutions

Your software solutions are obtainable from Real Networks, Popwire Technology, Sorenson, Apple, and Microsoft. The Popwire, QuickTime and Sorenson live encoders are used with the QuickTime streaming server while the other two are used with their own proprietary servers. As yet, there are limited options for live encoding with open source- and open standards-based solutions but that will change as the H.264 codec becomes more widely accepted and used.

Table 15-1 summarizes a list of products you should check out when you are looking for a live-encoding solution. Note that this list is not exhaustive but covers the most popular alternatives.

Table 15-1 Live Encoder Products

Product	Notes
QuickTime Broadcaster	Available as a free download.
Popwire Broadcaster	Runs on Mac OS X.
Popwire Live Engine	Runs on a Linux foundation.
Sorenson Broadcaster	A commercial product available across several platforms.
Helix live encoder	Real Networks encoding is done with Helix implementations.
Microsoft Windows Media	These encoding tools are the obvious choice for WM9 video.
Cleaner Live	Currently only available on Windows.

Envivio: http://www.envivio.com/

Digital Rapids: http://www.digital-rapids.com/

Tandberg TV: http://www.tandbergtv.com/

Philips: http://www.philips.com/index.htm

Thomson—Grass Valley: http://www.thomsongrassvalley.com/

Thomson: http://www.thomson.net/

Snell & Wilcox: http://www.snellwilcox.com/

Chapter 30 and Appendix C describe some more software-based encoding solutions; Appendix L describes the players and the formats they support.

15.10 Sizes of Live-Encoded Pictures

You should check the parameter settings on your live encoder carefully to ensure that you are correctly encoding the full picture. For performance reasons, some earlier models of the live-encoding tools will drop one or another of the fields when presented with an interlaced input. This yields a reasonably good quality output, but at half the resolution in the Y-axis. The X-axis will be scaled accordingly. If you are encoding from an analog source through higher-performance hardware, the encoding process may support full–frame, full-field encoding.

The lower-resolution encoding is fine for web-based video services but may not be what you require for the next generation of IPTV delivery.

15.11 Building Reliable Live-Encoder Farms

Live encoding on a small scale is generally easy to set up, since you just install a video-input card into a reasonably high-performance desktop computer and run one of the live encoders from Microsoft, Real Networks, Apple, or Sorensen. Envivio makes some very good and fast hardware-based encoders, but these tend to be out of the reach of small projects for reasons of cost. Appendix B lists some alternative hardware suppliers if you want to investigate their products.

Medium-scale solutions may be addressed in the same way by setting up multiple machines. If you have big powerful server-sized boxes with multiple processors you may be inclined to run several live-stream encoders on them at once. Running these in a UNIX framework with the encoder driven by a command line and enclosing that within an endless loop restarts the encoder automatically if it crashes. This works just fine for Real Networks encoders running on a Linux platform.

```
while(true)
{
    encode myfile;
}
```

This puts all your eggs into one rather large basket and if you prefer to offset the risks, then you could deploy multiple cheaper boxes, each one encoding a single stream. If some routing mechanism is provided at the input and the output stream files are named so that the content is mapped in a logical manner, then a failed encoder can be swapped out with a minimum of fuss. The video input is rerouted to another encoder and the configuration file of the stream server is changed to point at a different encoded stream. This adds to the resilience of the stream.

For high-end operations where you intend to stream hundreds of different programs simultaneously, there are large encoding systems available from a variety of manufacturers. Sun Microsystems builds massively distributed systems that might be good candidates, or you may want to rack mount hundreds of Linux-based encoders and run them with some centralized administration. If you are looking for low latency and high quality at high bit rates then a hardware solution is optimal, but it will be expensive. Over the next couple of years, as the H.264 codec implementations become more efficient when implemented in software, the hardware solutions may only be used for top-end TV broadcast distribution or high definition. This applies to D-cinema applications as well, because they operate at a similar resolution.

15.12   Eliminating Problems with Live-Encoded Output

The time that you are most likely to encounter problems is when you are encoding live-video sources. Some of these issues you may be able to avoid and others you may have to put up with or deal with in a remedial way. When evaluating your alternative encoder suppliers, be sure to run some tests with real-world services to observe what happens to the encoded output.

15.13   Summary: What I've Learned About Live Encoding

Live encoding is not very different from offline encoding. The main difference is that it cannot afford to slow down or stop, even momentarily. Latency is important to be mindful of because any delay leads to buffering issues.

Now that we've looked at bit streams in the previous chapter and live encoding in this one, let's move on and see how this compressed video might be stored in files.

16

Files and Storage Formats

16.1 Packing Your Bags

Squeezing everything you're bringing into your suitcase before a trip is not always easy. There's always more that you want to put in, and before long it is overstuffed. Part of the art of trouble-free travel is about packing what you need and not taking anything extraneous. The same is true for storing video in files effectively. A well-defined and structured file format gives you everything you need without having to deal with loads of things that you don't want.

16.2 Now Where Did I Put That Clip?

Movie data is often embedded into an interactive *package* or streamed over a networked connection. At some time in its life, the video will be stored in a file container unless the stream session is being encoded live. Some systems might create temporary structured storage in memory that resembles the format used for file-based storage. The streamed file may be stored at the receiving end by the client application.

This chapter looks at file structure and size and the implications of different kinds of file-based storage. Choosing the right type of file ensures that you output files that are easily imported into other tools. Later on, Chapter 29 examines storage systems as part of the systems-building process.

16.3 Basic Concept of Storing Video in Files

People have been storing video in files for a long time. In the very earliest days, the files were just a digital version of storing the video on an analog tape. The file structures were vestigial and the content was just a stream of video-intensity values. Storing video like this takes up a lot of space because it is not compressed. In addition it is hard to edit the video other than in a linear way. Storage like this is not very different from a straightforward waveform recording. It is much like an audio track that is recorded as a series of samples, except the video has a far higher sample rate.

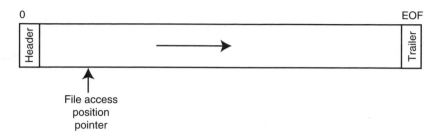

File access
position
pointer

Figure 16-1 Sequential file format.

Examples of early formats for use on desktop systems were the Cinepak and Indeo formats. MPEG-1 was developed at around the same time and QuickTime was launched with a structured video container that was primitive at the time but offered some useful capabilities.

Modern video file structures are designed for nonlinear access and modification. Inserting new content into a movie file is quick, easy, and economical in terms of CPU and disk-space requirements because the file structures are highly organized.

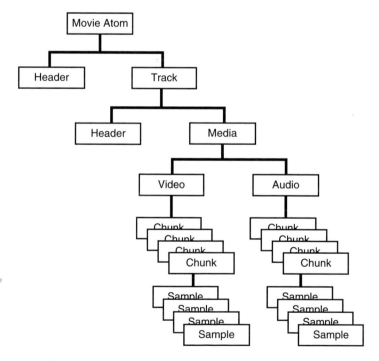

Figure 16-2 Atomic file structure.

Ligos Indeo: http://www.ligos.com
Cinepak: http://www.cinepak.com

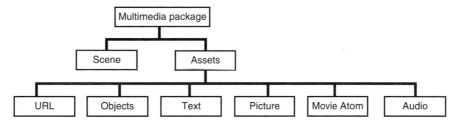

Figure 16-3 Multimedia object structure.

The basic idea is to store a sequence of data so that it can be recovered in real time. Then the video can be played back without glitches. Editing makes it necessary to change that sequence, perhaps removing some frames, adding some frames at an insert point, or moving some frames around, which is actually a special case of the previous two items anyway.

It is important to make those editing changes to the file structure without having to completely rewrite the file from beginning to end. That might be necessary at a final render stage but with a 2-hour-long movie file, the system will soon become unwieldy and difficult to use if you have to rewrite the file every time it changes.

Sound information must also be stored alongside the video. The minimum requirement is a monophonic sound track unless the movie is silent. It is normal these days to record a stereo pair. For feature film work and high-end drama production the file must cope with 6 or 7 separate tracks that are mixed independently for surround-sound presentations.

In recent times, text and data tracks have become useful additions, so the variety of information to be stored and synchronized is now quite complex.

Some efficiency savings at playback time are realized when the sampled macroblocks are saved in the file in decoding order. Buffering large amounts of the file ahead of time or seeking backward and forward in order to locate the required *atom* is no longer necessary, and performance is improved.

16.4   File Types

File contents are identified in several different ways and might depend on the operating system you are using. On a Macintosh, there are two hidden 4-character codes that identify the file type and also the creator. The creator is the application that is opened when the file is double-clicked. This has served the Mac OS very well since 1984.

If the file type and creator code are not set correctly on a file, then sometimes that file cannot be opened by a Classic Mac OS application. An example of this is the QuickTime Dumpster utility. It requires that the file type code be set to 'MooV' and the creator set to 'TVOD'. Without this, the older versions of Dumpster cannot "see" the file and won't open it for analysis.

This approach does not transfer well to other platforms, so the more recent versions of Mac OS also use the file extension to identify what kind of file it is. This is how most other operating systems determine the file type.

In the Unix command-line environment, the `file` utility can be used to determine the kind of file you are inspecting. This is rather clever because it looks at the beginning of the file and works out the file type from the content. The file extension is irrelevant because Unix considers the entire file name, the dot, and the file extension to be a single string of characters. Here is an example of how the `file` utility is used from the Unix command line:

```
$ file 0007.jpg
0007.jpg: JPEG image data, JFIF standard 1.02, resolution (DPI), 300 × 300
$ file 0010.ai
0010.ai: PDF document, version 1.4
$ file "Interesting article"
Interesting article: ASCII mail text, with very long lines, with CR line
terminators
$ file "tivo_1.pdf"
tivo_1.pdf: PDF document, version 1.3
```

The `file` utility uses a table of information stored in a special file called `magic`. If you use the Unix manual pages, the help file will tell you where this `magic` file lives so you can go and look at it. On Mac OS X it lives in the directory path at `/usr/share/file/magic`, which is a location you cannot normally get access to with the GUI interface because those sorts of things are hidden away in order not to frighten the unwary user.

Learning some power-tool tricks with the command-line interface is a very worth-while skill. You need not become tremendously adept at it before it becomes very useful. If you have a collection of files of unknown types, you might be able to write some kind of shell script and then go through them and add the correct extension.

The Unix `file` utility lets you manually select an alternative `magic` file. You can use the one that is provided to tell you what the mime type of a file is or you can roll your own and provide some custom file identification. Given that you have a file called `fred` in your directory, the following command will report its mime type to you as long as it is a known type of file.

```
file fred –m /usr/share/file/magic.mime
```

Since the list of files is quite extensive, the `file` utility knows about several hundred different file types. You can add your own, too, by creating custom `magic` files or recompiling the ones that are provided. Since this resides in the open-source part of the operating system it is quite easy to find out more about this. The manual pages in the UNIX command line are a good place to start. Just type man file and press return to get several pages of helpful information.

Appendix I summarizes some file types according to their file extension–type identifier.

16.5   File Formats

Generally speaking, the file content is organized into tracks. That logical arrangement is more important to us than the physical representation because it is similar to the way the compression and editing software presents the file content to us.

Internally the stream of video is broken into packets, and these are then interleaved with one another so that the packets from the various streams are stored more or less together with those from other streams that should be played at approximately the same time. That makes the synchronization process fairly straightforward and it is just a matter of buffering and sorting the packets on playback.

16.5.1   *Overall File Structure*

Files might be arranged sequentially, with content written from the beginning of the file to the end in a continuous session. Any file organization then takes place using the file manager software within the library that is used to create or modify the file.Because this library code is linked into an application, very often the software you are using does not have direct access to everything in the file. Some decisions are made by the library, and these may preempt things you would want to define yourself.

On other systems a random-access record-based structure might be used. This tends to be wasteful of space, though, and it is more useful for storing large amounts of metadata about many similar items in a structured manner.

The optimal form for storing media is a managed persistent-object repository. Objects are encoded and decoded as they are stored and retrieved. The application manipulates objects that are assembled using entity relationships. These relationships map directly to relational database management system (RDBMS) structures, although you would not normally store video in an RDBMS. You would use a database to store the metadata that describes the video.

These objects are sometimes called atoms and they exist in various flavors and types, each of which represents a different kind of content. This mechanism was popularized by Apple in the QuickTime file structures. Microsoft implemented a similar but more straightforward *chunking* mechanism in its early multimedia file formats. A similar structure is present in most kinds of video files you will encounter these days.

The QuickTime file format was used as a basis for the MPEG-4 file format and therefore they bear some similarity to one another. They are not identical enough that both formats' files can be parsed by the same player applications or codecs but the design is fundamentally the same. It is said that they come from "the same DNA."

A variety of file structures are used but all the major formats have settled on the idea of a structured chunk-based format composed of atomic objects. When video is streamed the technicalities are very similar for broadcast TV and Web delivery.

16.5.2 File Size

File sizes will vary greatly according to what you have contained in them. Raw footage that has been imported via a FireWire interface at broadcast quality will be the most bulky that you have to deal with. It is tempting to compress it right away and discard the original. This is probably a false economy unless that tactic is a necessary part of your workflow. It is better to provide sufficient disk space to work with uncompressed content for as long as possible. Very large disks with capacities in excess of 500 GB or more are available. Multiple disks can be assembled into a RAID array for reasonable sums of money and it is not very hard to put a couple of Terabytes (TB) on a desktop. Table 16-1 enumerates some file sizes for a 5-minute clip in various formats.

A more extensive table is provided in Appendix I. These file sizes might seem terrifying, but to put them into context, the spool files for wide-format plotters are orders of magnitude bigger. Large poster-size plots can be enjoyed at a single glance while a video file of the same size would run for a couple of hours even when stored in a high-quality format.

Table 16-1 File Sizes for a 5-Minute Video Clip

Format	File size
3GPP 64 Kbps	2.867 MB
ISMA Profile 0 (MPEG-4)	4.6 MB
ISMA Profile 1 (MPEG-4)	14 MB
AVI with Cinepak codec	124.3 MB
PAL MPEG-2	150 MB
DV 25	1.00 GB
DV 50	1.9 GB
525i30 NTSC raw	2.575 GB
625i25 PAL raw	3.106 GB
YUV420	4.5 GB
D-cinema, 24 fps 1920 × 1080 delivered on HDCAM	5.96 GB
D-cinema, 24 fps 1920 × 1080 raw	41.713 GB

16.5.3 Track Organization

The different kinds of tracks in the file-based container might include any combination of the different kinds of data. We'll look at those data types in this section.

16.5.3.1 Video Coded video is stored as a sequence of frames. This "video" category might also include groups of pictures chunked together and compressed or perhaps single frames stored uncompressed. This is the container for the video that is processed by the codec.

16.5.3.2 Left Eye/Right Eye Video IMAX and other cinema formats support a variety of interleaving schemes for mixing stereoscopic picture sequences and alternating the delivery so that each eye sees a subtly different image that simulates the camera as a virtual-eyeball point of view. The video might be stored as two independent streams or as an interleaved sequence of frames with left and right images delivered alternately. This would double the frame rate required in order to prevent flickering artifacts.

16.5.3.3 Mono Soundtrack Simple presentations might only require a monaural sound track, although it is commonplace to put the same mix on both the left and the right stereo channel.

16.5.3.4 Stereo Soundtrack A stereo soundtrack includes both left and right audio. This is probably the most common format for audio storage alongside the video. During playback and editing, the two must be totally synchronous with one another. Editing software must make a frame-accurate cut, but this might happen at an inopportune time in the audio. Audio and video may be edited independently and any synchronization or tracking problems are fixed later. Editors such as Final Cut Pro take account of this and maintain good synchronization even when you are performing complex edits.

16.5.3.5 Surround Sound Dolby 5.1, DTS, and AC3 formats are all varieties of the surround-sound format. Some of these are coded as interleaved audio with the data being stored in one single track, and during production the tracks might be held as separate mono streams so that they can be worked on separately.

16.5.3.6 Audio Description Track Broadcast regulatory bodies require that television companies deliver enhanced services to facilitate access by disabled viewers and listeners. An audio description track is an extra commentary that can be played alongside the normal audio and contains a description of what is being shown in the video. It is not a director's commentary, as you would find on a DVD, but it is a similar idea. The track must be carefully synchronized to ensure that the descriptions are placed between the spoken dialogue and don't obscure what is being said.

16.5.3.7 Structured Audio Track Structured audio is something that has been introduced with MPEG-4. It allows for sound samples to be delivered to the player and then reconstructed and mixed locally. Taking the speech-synthesis and MIDI information into account, very rich audio experiences can be created.

16.5.3.8 Phonetic Component Track With the advent of speech-recognition and search systems such as those developed by FastTalk, UI Speech, and DreMedia, it is likely that the audio signal will be processed and stored in other forms. FastTalk used a phonetic search algorithm, so to search the video file for phonetic matches, a track containing phonetic fragments decoded from the audio and synchronized with the time code at which that they are spoken might be searchable very rapidly.

16.5.3.9 Subtitle Track In video that is being prepared for mastering onto a DVD, there could be eight or more subtitle tracks. Although the delivery platform you deploy to is likely to have a strict limit on the maximum number of supported subtitle tracks, the master video file may be stored in a format that allows an unlimited number of tracks to be maintained. The rendering process for the target platform then merely selects those subtitle caption tracks that it requires. This is a specific variant of the simple text track.

16.5.3.10 URL Track This is another variant of the simple text track and contains a URL that is passed to a Web browser by the desktop video player when the video is clicked on. This has been underused so much that many people don't even realize it is available. Real Networks media producers can create a list of URLs with time codes and then process the file through an `rmmerge` utility to create a URL-tagged video file. Interestingly, the URLs can be in any form that the browser accepts, including `javascript:` URLs, which allow for very reactive synchronized content to be deployed.

16.5.3.11 Hotspot Track Sometimes hotspot maps are created and associated with the URL tracks in order to provide clickable regions on the screen. This is certainly used to good effect in QuickTime VR movies, where the hotspot map can be applied before or after the de-warping of the image. The hotspots can appear as positionally relative to the scene when applied before the de-warping, or as an overlay on the control surface if they are added afterward. This is a pixmap with the pixel values selecting one of several available links. Those links may be URLs for web pages, or they may be navigable links to other scenes or panoramas within the movie. Hotspots are also useful in linear-viewed video, and you could have a product placement that was clickable to a "buy me now" web page, for example. Hotspot tracks might be quite bulky, possibly similar in bulk to an alpha channel.

16.5.3.12 Sprite Track This is a track containing an animated object that is overlaid on top of the video. It is likely that there will be multiple sprite tracks.

16.5.3.13 Metadata Track Information about the video, such as copyrights, date of shooting, location, and camera settings, is called metadata. There is a wide variety of information that is useful to the production process and still more that assists the end user when consuming the final product. Adding this information to the video content is sometimes referred to as tagging. There is also some metadata that is outside the video file and relates to the location and use of the file as a whole. Internally stored metadata might describe individual scenes or actors. Tagging information about particular scene locations or edit points might be embedded into the video file in a special track within the movie or stored outside in a separate but related text file.

16.5.3.14 MIDI Track Music tracks are sometimes encoded as MIDI information. Obviously, an embedded MIDI instrument must be available in the playback device. QuickTime licenses the Roland GM sound samples as found in the original Sound Canvas synthesizer. Often the MIDI support will be labelled GM or GS depending on the manufacturer. A standard set of instruments located predictably at the same patch numbers will be supported. They might not sound identical, but if you choose a piano sound, you will get a piano and not a trumpet.

16.5.3.15 Warp Matrix Track QuickTime allows the video to be warped according to a matrix transform. By storage of this information in a track alongside the video, a frame-accurate animated warping effect can be applied during playback.

16.5.3.16 Alpha-Channel Track Cutting out a matte or alpha channel that moves with the video is accomplished using an alpha-channel track. This is frame-for-frame identical in timing and resolution to the video track but contains a value from 0% to 100% transparency. Application of a constant value across the entire surface of the video allows blending effects to be achieved. Wipes, transitions, and other compositing effects are also possible.

16.5.3.17 Color-Correction Track With the advent of very powerful systems, color correction might be applied in real time to the played-out video. This might be used for special effects or to correct the video after mapping of the transform to some ambient condition.

16.5.3.18 Effects Track QuickTime supports smoke, flame, fog, clouds, and rippled-water effects that are applied as a layer over the final composited video. These would be stored in a symbolic form as parameter settings that are applied frame by frame. They occupy almost no space at all.

16.5.3.19 Closed-Signing Track This is similar in concept to the closed captions. Closed captions are hidden subtitle data that require a hardware decoder to display them. Closed signing is the same idea, except that an overlay video is described using an alpha channel-coded image of sign language compressed using MPEG-4 part 2. This is turned on by the owner of a closed-signing decoder box but is not visible to other users. Assistance with access support like this is mandated in most broadcasters' licenses in the UK, and much useful work is done in this area by the BBC Research and Development department.

16.5.3.20 Hint Track This is used to assist the streaming process by providing help with the formation of packets and perhaps some information to insert into the headers of the streaming service. There may be multiple hint tracks allowing the content to be streamed through a variety of different services from the same source file. By the time the video is being streamed, any organization of the internal file structure as atoms or chunks is long gone, and the client player just sees a continuous stream of bits, which it must synchronize with, buffer, and then unwrap and de-interleave before decoding.

16.5.4 Atoms

Table 16-2 summarizes the terms that are commonly used to describe the different component parts of a video stream.

Accessing a file is accomplished (these days) by loading a chunk or atom of content. Sometimes these are organized into objects that are collections of video chunks. The video and audio streams would not be interleaved for the purpose of storage because it would not serve any useful purpose. The chunks merely have to be accessed in the correct order. Only those that are part of the current playback session have to be read from the file.

There is more information about atomic structures in the QuickTime file-format book published through the Apple Developer Connection, details of which are available on the Apple developer web site. Although it describes the QuickTime file format, the concepts are relevant to other video formats.

The ISO standards document ISO_IEC_14496-14_2003 describes the MPEG-4 file format but is rather thinner in scope. The URLs within the ISO web site are long and complex,

Table 16-2 Atoms and Chunks

Terminology	Description
Atom	An atom is used to describe the object-oriented breakdown of the video and multi-track audio when stored in the highly structured MPEG-4 and QuickTime files. These atoms also describe other kinds of data. A series of atoms would be assembled to form a stream containing one kind of content or another. Note also that atoms can be nested whereas none of the other component forms can be used in this way.
Chunk	Historically, the video is broken into chunks when it is stored in AVI files. These don't necessarily correspond to packets or groups of pictures. It is unlikely you would break a group of pictures across several chunks.
GOP	A group of pictures is the logical grouping of a series of frames that are treated as a unit when running a compressor over them. The compressed output is then divided into packets.
Packet	Normally taken to describe a fragment of transported content. The packetization serves to split the larger data items into pieces that fit within *TCP/IP* networking protocols, for example.

Apple Developer Connection: http://developer.apple.com/

Apple QuickTime developer information: http://developer.apple.com/quicktime/

ISO Standards: http://www.iso.org/

and the easiest way to navigate is to search within the ISO web site using the standard number as a key. You should be presented with a version of the site that is tailored for your browser's international language setting. You will have to purchase these specifications, as they are not available free of charge.

There are many other resources on the web that describe the available file structures for different types of video file. Some will be very hard to find, as they are proprietary.

Gunther Born published a very helpful book on file formats some years ago called *The File Formats Handbook*. This contained some useful descriptions of the AVI file structures that were sufficient to enable the reader to write code to parse the files. Other useful information has been published by Microsoft describing how to store DV streams in AVI movies.

Gathering and storing this sort of knowledge whenever you can is worth the effort because you occasionally get offered the chance to solve problems such as "here is a library of a million video files but we don't know what size the picture format is for any of them." You could write a small fragment of code to access the appropriate bytes within the file header and determine the information you are looking for. Then create the necessary Structured Query Language (SQL) instructions to load the database with the information corresponding to each file. The whole process can be wrapped in a shell script and left to run on its own.

16.5.5 Files Are Not Streams

A file on disk is not the same as a stream. If you have a player that is connecting to a stream, it can join and leave the stream at any point. There will be a few moments of buffering while it downloads some key frames for it to interpolate against.

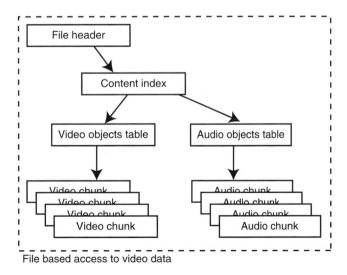

Figure 16-4 File access.

Microsoft DV-AVI spec: http://www.microsoft.com/whdc/archive/dvavi.mspx

Stream based access to video data

Figure 16-5 Stream access.

You cannot just open a file and jump in at random. You must honor the file structure. First, open the header to determine some basic characteristics. There is likely to be an index that provides random access to segments of the file. Not all file formats support this but those that are designed for nonlinear modes of interaction do.

Streams will arrive in packets that are arranged serially in sequence. The packets must be organized into a transport stream and then the contents must be de-interleaved to obtain the individual elementary streams so that the program content is reconstructed.

16.5.6 Hints

Hints are instructions that are added to a movie in order to assist a streaming server with the delivery of the video content across a streamed network connection. Because the hints

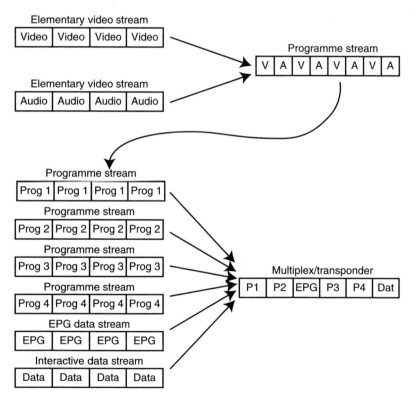

Figure 16-6 Stream structure.

are applicable to the movie in a synchronized and time-sensitive way, they are stored as an additional track. Hence the term hint track or hinted movie.

There will be more than one hint track added to a movie, typically, one for each of the target services the content is streamed to. The technical approach is to create a hint track for every stream. There would be one for the video and one for each audio track.

This is a useful approach to preparing videos for streaming because the same movie file can be downloaded and played locally. The player will just open the video and audio tracks in the normal way. The hint data will be ignored because it is concerned with transport and not playback.

A media packetizer tool adds the hints. This might be built into your compression software or it might be an additional tool that you must run over the file after it has been compressed. If you are buying a compression tool to use for creating streamed content, then you should check that the hinting support is available as part of the toolkit.

Be careful when flattening movies (a QuickTime operation) or doing other processing on them, as you might accidentally remove the hint tracks.

16.6 MXF Files

The MXF file format is emerging as an important interchange format for professional users. MXF encapsulates a variety of media formats in a container with the edit decision list (EDL) information and any relevant metadata. This is transferred to another system that understands the EDL and extracts the essence assets for further processing. MXF is format agnostic. That is to say, it does not care what the essence format is when you fill an MXF container with assets. There is no actual MXF video format because the standard only describes a container.

The MXF container format is derived from the *AAF* file format. This standard is managed by the *AAFA*. Data is wrapped in a three-part structure as shown in Figure 16-7.

The MXF file format specification allows for these key-length-value (KLV) fragments to be nested as shown in Figure 16-8.

This is very similar to the way that QuickTime and MPEG-4 files are structured with atoms and chunks. The metadata is described using an XML format so that implementations can use some already existing utility-code libraries to import and export the MXF

Key	Length	Value

Figure 16-7 A KLV fragment in an MXF file.

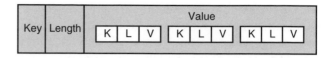

Figure 16-8 Nested KLV fragments.

data. Trials have been conducted at IBC and NAB for several years now and the interoperability is working very well.

Although this is a professional format aimed at broadcasters and high-end production companies, this sort of technology generally filters down to the semi-professional marketplace over time. MXF could also be very useful for exchanging material between media servers and desktop editing systems in the high-end domestic, educational, and corporate TV marketplace. MXF is going to be a very useful and important format. There is more information at the *Pro-MPEG*, MXF, and AAF Web sites. Snell & Wilcox have released the free MXF Express SDK toolkit for software developers to use when running interoperability testing. The SDK is available at their web site.

Recent developments include the AAF Edit Protocol, which allows the separation of edit decisions from the media content. This is somewhat akin to the reference movie technique that QuickTime supports, which is core technology within iMovie.

16.7   ASF Files

These are the files that are used to store Windows Media content. Sometimes they are referred to as Windows Media Files but this is not always strictly true because other media can be stored in them. The Advanced Systems Format file container stores the following kinds of content in one file:

- Audio
- Multi bit-rate video
- Metadata
- Index tables
- Script commands
- URLs
- Closed captioning

Pro-MPEG: http://www.pro-mpeg.org/

MXF: http://mxf.info/

AAF Association: http://www.aafassociation.org/

Snell & Wilcox: http://www.snellwilcox.com/

EBU: http://www.ebu.ch/

SMPTE: http://www.smpte.org/

The files are created through the Windows Media SDK and are structured according to a profile. These profiles are created and stored in XML files having the `.prx` file extension. The metadata support is based on `ID3` tagging protocols.

The file container supports files as large as 17 million terabytes (TB), which is way beyond anything you are likely to ever want to put in there.

Table 16-3 lists the file extensions used for ASF files depending on what is stored in them.

You can find out more at the Microsoft Web site on the pages that describe ASF and a TechNet security bulletin.

16.8 File-Related Gotchas

Sooner or later you are going to run into some file problems, and almost certainly they will have to do with file sizes or the space available to store them.

16.8.1 File-Conversion Issues

Sometimes converting from one format to another loses quality for no apparent reason. Going from one format to a supposedly better one might result in blocky or washed-out looking pictures. It might be the conversion software at fault so try an alternative tool to see if the compression is any better.

Sometimes this will not make any difference because the tools are built on top of a common application programming interface (API) and the only thing you are changing is the user interface.

16.8.2 2-GB Limit on Some Systems

Beware of the 2-GB file-size limitation. Some years ago, operating systems and PC hardware designs eliminated this, but many applications did not. Some still have this issue, and you have to be careful how you import movies into these packages.

Table 16-3 ASF File Extensions

File extension	Content
`.wma`	Audio compressed with the Windows Media Audio codec
`.wmv`	Audio and video compressed with the Windows Media Audio and Windows Media Video codecs
`.asf`	Content created with other codecs

ASF: http://www.microsoft.com/windows/windowsmedia/format/asfspec.aspx
TechNet: http://www.microsoft.com/technet/security/bulletin/MS01-056.mspx

The Apple iMovie application has this limitation, for example, and you cannot drag large files (bigger than 2 GB) onto the workspace. You can import bigger files, though, because the importer will segment the files as they are ingested. When taking the input directly from a camera or external drive, the files are also automatically segmented at or near the 2-GB boundaries and a reference movie is created to string them together.

When your project is complete, throw away any unused clips that remain in the clip bin and tell the application to empty the trash. This is not the same as the desktop trash—it is video that has not been included in the final edited sequence and that has been discarded. If you have many iMovie projects on disk, clearing out the trash yields a lot of disk space that would otherwise be wasted.

 Empty the trash in your video editing application if it has a trash bin. Lots of disk space can be wasted by unused video clips that are no longer needed.

Check the manual for your movie-editing software. These applications have many features in common and you might find that the same 2-GB file size limit applies to your application even if it appears to work quite differently from iMovie.

16.8.3 Reference Movies, Play Lists, and Self-Contained Files

The process of editing video involves cutting up the original and creating a new file. Some editing systems are able to do this non-destructively by creating a play list and storing it in a reference movie but leaving the original video intact, which means the edit takes up very little space. A reference movie is like a short cut. It contains pointers to the actual video, and when you play it back, the video-handling mechanisms in the operating system make it appear that you are playing a physical movie. The Apple iMovie and Final Cut Pro editors are good examples of such systems. They are able to do this so effectively because they are built on top of the QuickTime platform, which is designed to provide these services to any application that calls for them.

Eventually, you will want to save the movie as a self-contained copy without any dependencies (see Section 16.8.4). This will traverse the reference movie and clone the sections from the physical movies and create a new physical movie. This process will use significant amounts of extra disk space. Only the sections of video that are described in the reference movie will be copied. This would be one of the times when you are most likely to experience the "Disk Full" message and to have to abort the save. Fortunately, you still have your reference movie intact, but it is not the time when you are most prepared to go through your file system and remove redundant material.

There is a very high risk that as you create the space you need, you will remove something that you will later regret. The risk factor is increased because you will very likely be doing this 'save-as-self-contained-movie' just before you ship the finished product to a client—and probably very near a deadline! Panic sets in and you have to make some decisions very quickly. Keeping some spare disk capacity on hand to plug in at short notice is a very good idea.

Without a mechanism for referring to fragments of movies and creating edit decision lists as reference movie structures, the editing system would have to assemble all the clips in place as a physical process. This would involve massive amounts of copying and would fill disks up with lots of duplicate copies of the same footage. It would also be a lot harder to modify edit points in a nonlinear way and it harkens back to the old way of assembling an edit clip by clip. The productivity gains from nonlinear editors could not be achieved if they were working in the traditional way that a tape-based editor does.

16.8.4   Dependent Files

Large and complex systems can be designed to share media with each other or between projects. You may find that you have removed a file or project folder without realizing that it is referred to elsewhere. QuickTime is especially good at assembling the fragments from several files into a playback experience that resembles a complete movie. When you save that assembled file, it asks whether to save it as a self-contained movie or as a movie with dependencies on other files. Self-contained movies will not be affected if other movies are removed or relocated. Movies containing dependencies must be treated carefully until you have rendered down a self-contained version. A simple file dependency is shown in Figure 16-9.

16.9   File Management and Life Cycle

You must think about the life cycle of your video files. The content is first created, then stored, then accessed later and possibly eventually destroyed. Along the way it will very likely be transformed, and it is certain that the files will be moved from one place to another within the same system or to another system. Files might be placed offline and transferred across a network of some kind. Networks come in many forms such as a file

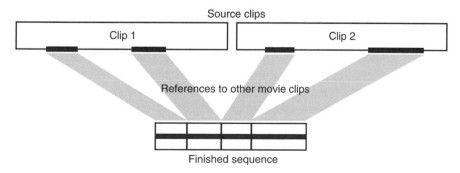

Figure 16-9 File dependencies.

transfer with a protocol such as FTP; or the content might be data that is broadcast as a package in a DVB transport stream or converted to a program stream and embedded as part of the output for a broadcast channel.

On arrival at the destination the client may convert the stream back into a file and store it in a cache. This is essentially what a digital video recorder (DVR) such as the TiVo does. Whether the file that is stored in the client is identical to the file that left the source server depends on the method of transfer. It is likely to be identical after an FTP file transfer.

Some topping and tailing will be necessary if the file has been dubbed and recorded from a broadcast or playback stream. Dubbing increases the manual effort and indirectly consumes more disk space. In addition, it expends valuable operator resources unnecessarily.

There are standards being developed (such as *TV-Anytime*) that indicate what parts of a broadcast stream constitute a program. These technologies are in the process of being deployed by broadcasters. They depend on all broadcasters supporting them fully in order for a consumer proposition to work reliably. In the not-too-distant future, the broadcast metadata and essence will be collected together and stored on a consumer hard drive and it will all work properly.

16.10   Examining File Structures

A lot of interesting information about a movie file can be deduced by opening the information window in the player application. Not all player applications support this but you should check yours to see if it does. This information tells you about the tracks stored in the file, the codecs used to compress them, and the data rate and throughput. Figure 16-10 illustrates one pane in the information browser built into the QuickTime version 6 movie player.

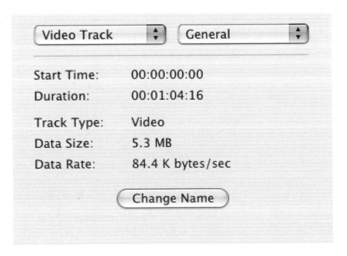

Figure 16-10 Information panel in QuickTime movie player.

Figure 16-11 Tektronix MTM 400 analyzer. Source: courtesy of Tektronix.

16.10.1 Hardware Analysis Tools

There are tools available from Tektronix, for example, for checking transport streams. Other companies such as Yokogawa, Snell & Wilcox, and Rhode & Schwartz also make tools that are used to diagnose problems. These are quite expensive and are only accessible to broadcasters. Here is a picture of the Tektronix MTM 400 analyzer.

You can learn a lot about the way your video-compression system works by analyzing the output. For example, the motion-vector display in some analyzers makes it immediately clear what the motion vectors are doing. You should be able to observe correlation between the underlying image changes and the motion vectors that are created by the compressor.

16.10.2 Software Analysis Tools

If you are analyzing QuickTime movie files, then the Dumpster utility is very handy. It is available as a download from the Apple QuickTime developer Web site.

The Dumpster tool provides a view of the internal structure of the QuickTime file container.

Currently it only recognizes movie files if they have the original Classic Mac OS file type and creator code set up. Just having a .mov extension is not sufficient. The file type must be 'MooV' and the creator should be 'TVOD'. You can set these with the FileTyper utility that is available on the Internet if you don't have it already.

Once Dumpster recognizes your file, you get a structured listing of the contents. Figure 16-12 shows a screenshot of a Dumpster session. Some of the header blocks have been unfolded by clicking on the bold keywords that identify each atom in the file.

Apple QT developer: http://developer.apple.com/quicktime/quicktimeintro/tools/

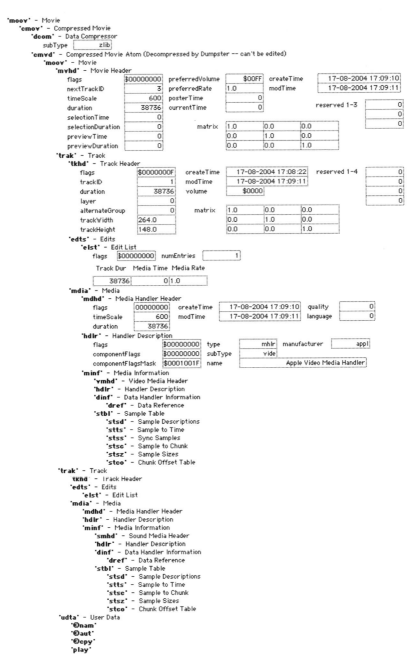

Figure 16-12 Screen shot from QuickTime Dumpster application.

Without the structured analysis that a utility like Dumpster provides, you have to navigate through a hex dump like the one shown in Figure 16-13. It is possible but it's a lot of hard work.

Figure 16-14 shows a similar display from a Tektronix analyzer application that you can run on Windows XP:

16.10.3   Viewing the Bit Stream

The listing on page 299 is an alternative display showing the beginning of an MPEG-4 bit stream decoded down to the bit level. You can see how the header contains a variety of useful information indicated by the symbolic names in the right-hand column. The area on the left shows the binary values for the bit stream.

16.11   Solving Problems by Using Compression Tools

If you are trying to record content off air, then it is likely to be arriving at your desktop in a transport stream and encoded using MPEG-2.

The El-Gato Eye TV boxes are neat solutions to delivering video off air straight to the Mac OS desktop. In record mode, the off-air program stream is dumped into a cache inside the Eye TV application. You can edit this to trim off the unwanted portions and export it to a QuickTime file. On the Windows platform, a variety of other alternatives exist such as Hauppauge WinTV PCI cards and its supporting software. With the growth in home-media systems, other alternative solutions are being released all the time.

```
000         Matrix 2.mov - Data
Len: $06159763 | Type/Creator: MooV/TVOD | Sel: $00000000:00000000 / $00000000
00000000: 00 01 00 F2 6D 6F 6F 76 00 00 00 6C 6D 76 68 64   ....moov...lmvhd
00000010: 00 00 00 00 BA BA 06 96 BA BB 01 EE 00 00 02 58   ...............X
00000020: 00 01 62 F8 00 01 00 00 00 FF 00 00 00 00 00 00   ..b.............
00000030: 00 00 00 00 00 01 00 00 00 00 00 00 00 00 00 00   ................
00000040: 00 00 00 00 00 01 00 00 00 00 00 00 00 00 00 00   ................
00000050: 00 00 00 00 40 00 00 00 00 00 00 00 00 00 00 00   ....@...........
00000060: 00 00 00 00 00 01 62 F8 00 00 00 00 00 00 00 00   ......b.........
00000070: 00 00 00 04 00 00 68 86 74 72 61 6B 00 00 00 5C   ......h.trak...\
00000080: 74 6B 68 64 00 00 00 0F BA B9 D8 B9 BA BA 06 9E   tkhd............
00000090: 00 00 00 01 00 00 00 00 00 01 62 F8 00 00 00 00   ..........b.....
000000A0: 00 00 00 00 00 00 00 00 00 00 00 00 00 01 00 00   ................
000000B0: 00 00 00 00 00 00 00 00 00 00 00 00 00 01 00 00   ................
000000C0: 00 00 00 00 00 00 00 00 00 00 00 00 40 00 00 00   ............@...
000000D0: 03 E8 00 00 02 1C 00 00 00 00 00 18 6C 6F 61 64   ............load
000000E0: 00 00 00 00 00 00 00 00 00 00 00 01 00 00 01 00   ................
000000F0: 00 00 00 24 65 64 74 73 00 00 00 1C 65 6C 73 74   ...$edts....elst
00000100: 00 00 00 00 00 00 00 01 00 01 62 F8 00 00 00 00   ..........b.....
00000110: 00 01 00 00 00 00 67 DA 6D 64 69 61 00 00 00 20   ......g.mdia...
00000120: 6D 64 68 64 00 00 00 00 BA BA 06 96 BA BA 06 9E   mdhd............
00000130: 00 00 02 58 00 01 62 FB 00 00 00 00 00 00 00 3A   ...X..b........:
00000140: 68 64 6C 72 00 00 00 00 6D 68 6C 72 76 69 64 65   hdlr....mhlrvide
00000150: 61 70 70 6C 00 00 00 00 00 01 00 D5 19 41 70 70   appl.........App
00000160: 6C 65 20 56 69 64 65 6F 20 4D 65 64 69 61 20 48   le Video Media H
00000170: 61 6E 64 6C 65 72 00 00 67 78 6D 69 6E 66 00 00   andler..gxminf..
00000180: 00 14 76 6D 68 64 00 00 00 01 00 40 80 00 80 00   ..vmhd.....@....
```

Figure 16-13 Screen shot from a hex dump application.

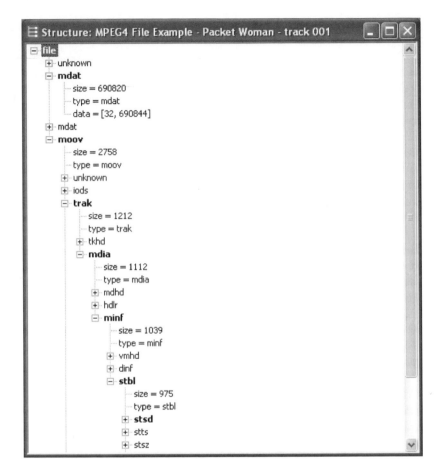

Figure 16-14 Screen shot from Tektronix analyzer application. Source: courtesy of Tektronix.

If you examine the saved QuickTime file by opening it with the movie player, you will see it only has one track. This is a multiplexed video and audio track. QuickTime will play it for you and will even honor the wide-screen signaling and display the correct aspect ratio.

If you then try and import it into iMovie or Final Cut Pro, and if you are lucky, you will get just the video. This is because the MPEG-2 codec plug-in does not support all the API calls that QuickTime expects to make on it in order to decode and translate it to the DV format that is used in iMovie and FCP.

You can convert the MPEG-2 stream with auxiliary tools and then you will have a complete workflow path from the broadcast chain right through your nonlinear editor and beyond. Figure 16-15 illustrates this workflow path. Note the DropDV and Popwire tools in the chain. These correctly decode the multiplexed stream into separate video and audio tracks, which can then be edited.

```
0000 0000 0000 0000 0000 0001 0000   (0x00000000, 7) : MPEG_4_START_CODE
0000 0000 0000 0000 0001 0001 ----   (0x00000004, 7) : START_CODE_PREFIX
0010 0000 ---- ---- 0001 ---- ----   (0x00000007, 7) : VIDEO_OBJECT_LAYER_START_CODE
0--- ---- ---- ---- ---- ---- ----   (0x00000008, 7) : RANDOM_ACCESS
0000 0001 ---- ---- ---- ---- ----   (0x00000008, 6) : VIDEO_OBJECT_TYPE_INDICATION
1--- ---- ---- ---- ---- ---- ----   (0x00000009, 6) : IS_OBJECT_LAYER_IDENTIFIER
0001 ---- ---- ---- ---- ---- ----   (0x00000009, 5) : VIDEO_VERID
001- ---- ---- ---- ---- ---- ----   (0x00000009, 1) : VIDEO_PRIORITY
0001 ---- ---- ---- ---- ---- ----   (0x0000000A, 6) : ASPECT_RATIO_INFO
1--- ---- ---- ---- ---- ---- ----   (0x0000000A, 2) : VOL_CONTROL_PARMETERS
01-- ---- ---- ---- ---- ---- ----   (0x0000000A, 1) : CHROMA_FORMAT
1--- ---- ---- ---- ---- ---- ----   (0x0000000B, 7) : LOW_DELAY
0--- ---- ---- ---- ---- ---- ----   (0x0000000B, 6) : VBV_PARAMETERS
00-- ---- ---- ---- ---- ---- ----   (0x0000000B, 5) : VIDEO_OBJECT_SHAPE
1--- 0000 0001 1001 ---- ---- ----   (0x0000000B, 3) : MARKER_BIT
0000 0001 1001 ---- ---- ---- ----   (0x0000000D, 2) : VOP_TIME_INC_RRES
1--- ---- ---- ---- ---- ---- ----   (0x0000000D, 2) : MARKER_BIT
0--- ---- ---- ---- ---- ---- ----   (0x0000000D, 1) : FIXED_VOP_RATE
1--- ---- ---- ---- ---- ---- ----   (0x0000000D, 0) : MARKER_BIT
0000 1011 0000 0--- ---- ---- ----   (0x0000000E, 7) : VIDEO_OBJECT_LAYER_WIDTH
1--- ---- ---- ---- ---- ---- ----   (0x0000000F, 2) : MARKER_BIT
0000 1001 0000 0--- ---- ---- ----   (0x0000000F, 1) : VIDEO_OBJECT_LAYER_HEIGHT
1--- ---- ---- ---- ---- ---- ----   (0x00000011, 4) : MARKER_BIT
0--- ---- ---- ---- ---- ---- ----   (0x00000011, 3) : INTERLACED
1--- ---- ---- ---- ---- ---- ----   (0x00000011, 2) : OBMC_DISABLE
0--- ---- ---- ---- ---- ---- ----   (0x00000011, 1) : SPRITE_ENABLE
0--- ---- ---- ---- ---- ---- ----   (0x00000011, 0) : NOT_8_BIT
1--- ---- ---- ---- ---- ---- ----   (0x00000012, 7) : QUANT_TYPE
1--- ---- ---- ---- ---- ---- ----   (0x00000012, 6) : LOAD_INTRA_QUANT_MAT
0000 1000 ---- ---- ---- ---- ----   (0x00000012, 5) : INTRA_QUANT_MAT
0000 1000 ---- ---- ---- ---- ----   (0x00000013, 5) : INTRA_QUANT_MAT
```

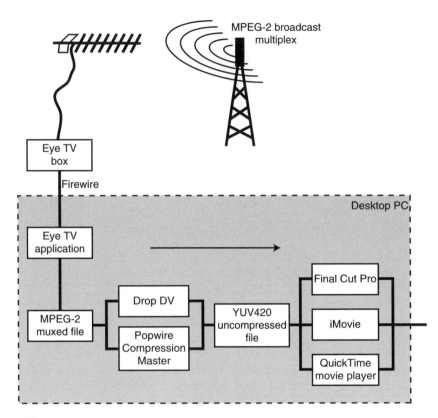

Figure 16-15 Using compression tools to solve conversion problems.

16.12 Summary of File-Based Video Compression

This chapter has explored some of the file formats and how they work and then looked at how to spend large amounts of money on disk storage. There are always cheaper solutions out there but you have to be prepared to compromise on quality or performance. There is an elastic relationship between cost, quality, and performance: changing one affects the other two. It is not feasible to have high performance and good quality at very low cost. Some savings are possible if you don't mind the job taking longer or if you are prepared to give up some quality to get it done in time.

In the next chapter we'll check out some tape formats, which are alternative storage mechanisms for video. They more naturally record the bit stream because they are a linear storage system. These days, however, the tapes might well be used to store files.

17

Tape Formats

17.1 Carry-On Luggage

Staying with our traveling analogy for a while longer, you don't just put things in a suitcase when you're packing for a trip. You also use a carry-on bag in order to have some things you'll need for the trip ready at hand. Similarly, files are fine for some types of storage, but they aren't the only solution. Video gets stored on a variety of removable-media formats—tapes, disks, memory sticks. Video is sometimes stored in these different media as files, but more often it is recorded as something more like a broadcast bit stream.

17.2 Input Video Quality

Some of your video may be of questionable picture quality. For example, pictures taken on mobile Webcams in remote news-gathering operations, perhaps in a war zone, may be very noisy. This is improving as the codecs for transmission back to base improve. Bear in mind that the best you will accomplish will be no better than that delivered by the remote source. Selecting the wrong coding parameters might actually produce artifacts in the coded output that are far worse because they are affected by artifacts in the incoming signal.

17.3 Grabbing an Analog Feed

A broadcast off-air signal encoded directly as an analog source might yield better results than recording to VHS as an intermediate step. Beware when recording off-air material though, as any material delivered via the digital TV services will have already been compressed to MPEG-2 format, and the bit-rate ceilings may already have compromised the quality at times. In that case, capturing the raw MPEG-2 stream is a better solution.

Even if you are encoding from an analog source these days, the origination and routing of the signals within the broadcasting infrastructure will occur via digital systems. If any compression were applied along the way, this might interact with your compression settings. It is important to understand the fundamental principle that you cannot get back any information that has already been discarded by a compression process. You may observe some digital compression artifacts in the analog service but it will be too late to remedy them by then.

17.4   Professional Recording Formats

Many different professional formats have evolved over the years. The current preferred format for high-quality work is Betacam, but even within that format there many varieties. The latest one is called IMX. This is an improvement over Digital Betacam but uses similar cartridges. Here is a list of common professional recording formats you might encounter:

- Betacam
- Digital Betacam (Digi-Beta)
- Betacam SP
- Betacam SX
- Betacam IMX
- DVC Pro
- DVCAM
- HDCAM
- XDCAM

17.5   Recording Off the Air

Analog broadcast quality varies considerably according to the atmospheric conditions, and periods of high pressure or very hot, dry days affect the signal propagation, which leads to more noise in the picture. Summertime weather conditions change the propagation such that reception of signals from transmitters that are very far away might cause co-channel or superimposed-vision artifacts. An aerial antenna that is surrounded with trees saturated by rain will cause ghosting of the image or echoes.

Once these artifacts are in the recorded material they are very hard to remove. Some of them (ghosting and co-channel artifacts, for example) will play havoc with your compression ratio.

17.5.1   NTSC Off Air

In the United States, outside of a studio environment, digitizing and encoding video that was taken off air from an NTSC broadcast results in a 525-line picture running at 29.97 fps. If we care enough to keep them rather than buy new DVD copies, any movies must have the pulldown frames removed. This content is also interlaced. If the original progressively scanned source material were available, encoding from that would be better than trying to recover the progressively scanned version from the interlaced broadcast. De-interlacing that movie footage by removing the pulldown is a vital first step. That may not be easy if the footage has been processed with edits and overlays being added after conversion to the interlaced format.

17.5.2 PAL Off Air

In the United Kingdom and Europe, off-air content will be from a PAL broadcast. The picture resolution is a little higher at 625 lines but the frame rate is lower at 25 fps. It will also be interlaced and will not have the pulldown since 25 fps is close enough to just run the 24-fps movie a little bit more quickly.

17.6 Generational Loss

Every time you re-record the video from one tape to another, there will be some degradation in quality. When you use analog video, the degradation is quite noticeable each time you dub the video. The generational loss is supposed to be eliminated when you record the video digitally. But this is only the case if no format conversion takes place during the digital transfer. Changing the encoding from one type to another results in generational losses even in the digital domain.

You should always work at the highest quality possible. Ideally your source will be uncompressed material. Apply the final compression down to the desired format in one step. Keeping the number of intermediate stages to a minimum helps improve the quality of the finished product.

Being aware of the compression process helps you make informed choices about what format conversions you are going to allow during the workflow.

17.7 Tape Formats and Recording Modes

Note that on your domestic players, the short-play and long-play modes may be called SP and LP, respectively. Always avoid LP when possible. SP will yield the best quality available.

You might argue that the Betamax format is actually better than the S-VHS short-play format but this might depend on the grade of the tape, how old the recording is, and all sorts of factors including the source of the tape recording.

Other important considerations are tape tension and head wear. The playback/record head in the VCR might be worn by overuse. The age of the tape heads and the tape tensioning will materially affect the quality of analog playback. Tape tension will affect the synchronization and time-base correction may need to be applied in order to get a reliable signal. You may also get those horrible little tearing patterns in the bottom few lines of the raster.

17.7.1 Quality Issues With Different Source Formats

There are many different formats from which you might source your original material. Some will present you with no problems since they are high quality. Where you will experience some difficulty is in trying to get the best out of the lower-quality consumer formats that you might be sourcing your content from.

17.7.2 DVCAM Format

If you are using any of the DVCAM formats or even DVCAM HD you will be down-converting from a 25-Mbps or even higher bit rate to your target. The signal will be clean and noise free. Everything should perform well because the encoder is working at compressing clean picture information and not wasting time trying to encode the random hash that the lower-quality formats deliver.

17.7.3 DV Format

At the top end of the consumer or pro-consumer range is the DV format that you get from digital handycams such as the Sony DCR PC 105. This format lets you drag the digital bit stream off of the 8mm-tape cartridge, but since there is no generational loss involved, it is going to be as clean as it was when you shot the footage. This is optimum for consumer and semi-professional because the price point of the equipment and its capabilities are a good compromise all around.

Another advantage of devices such as the PC 105 is that you can dub analog sources into it. It is not as good as a studio-grade analog-to-digital converter but taking analog TV off air usually results in quite good quality. It is not recommended as the best solution but it is often good enough. Obviously one way you can improve on that is by grabbing the MPEG-2 bit stream off air and staying in the digital domain.

When you import video from the DV format, it might be stored in a QuickTime file if you use a Mac OS–based computer or in an AVI file if you are running Windows. It all depends on the software being used. The difference is only in the containment; the DV content should be identical in size and quality, it is just stored differently. This may cause you some problems if you have to move the content around, because your applications will need to open and understand the file contents. This is really a cross-platform issue, and if you remain on one platform for the entire workflow, you shouldn't have any problems with unrecognized files.

17.7.4 S-VHS and VHS Formats

Moving down the scale in terms of quality, you might be taking a dub from your video recorder. This could be an S-VHS, a VHS, or even a TiVo device. You will get varying levels of quality, and the TiVo running at the lowest (basic-quality) recording mode will deliver some fairly bad video in terms of something that you might want to encode.

Converting a collection of Hollywood movies recorded on VHS is a complete waste of time—quite apart from the legal arguments about fair use. It is always better to go out and buy or rent the DVD because you will never come close to achieving that level of quality. It has already degraded too far in the VHS recording.

If the recording is a one-off, never-to-be-repeated program, then you might justify using whatever source quality you have available. Footage of your children growing up or some very rare live events on TV that are never going to be broadcast again are worth encoding—even from a low-quality original.

Keep in mind that the lower the quality of the original, the worse it is going to look after it has been encoded. You must be prepared to put in a lot of extra work and to be disappointed in the results, at least on the first try.

17.7.5   *Quadrature And Edits on VHS*

The Phase Alternate Line (PAL) system depends on the correct phasing of the color information with respect to a reference signal. When the video is recorded onto a VHS recorder, the combination of PAL coding and the modulation of the signal onto the tape causes a rotating phase relationship that takes 4 frames to cycle. It is like the cadence effect on NTSC pulldown footage. You cannot cut with anything more reliable than a 4-frame accuracy in PAL on VHS. Footage that has been edited on VHS might have been done on a 4-head machine but at the edit point, there may still be synchronization irregularities. These could cause some tearing of the video as it is ingested. You should carefully inspect the footage if you think it has been edited in this way, and you might have to make some remedial cuts to clean it up before compression.

17.8   Are Tapes Dead?

It might appear that tape formats are defunct and no longer of any use but they are still useful because they are good for large, bulk storage at very cost-effective prices. Their dominance in this area is being challenged by removable-disk formats and it will be interesting to see the effects of second-generation DVD formats such as Blu-Ray when they become available.

17.9   And Now for Something Completely Different

Let's now change direction completely and discuss some business and commercial issues, some of which are sometimes uncomfortable to talk about. In the area of money, video compression brings up some significant issues regarding the cost of using the technology and the rights of consumers when they have access to the content. In the next chapter we look at some of the challenges that DRM and intellectual property present to us.

18

Commercial Issues, Digital Rights Management, and Licensing

18.1   Visa or Green Card?

Traveling with inadequate documents not only is foolish but also can lead to serious trouble. So it is with digital media. A quick trip around the block without your passport is not an issue. But longer trips are simply not feasible without the proper licenses, visas, and tickets.

Nobody likes to be under surveillance or monitoring, but there are so many people who are prepared to try to rip off the rightful owners of content that the movie companies and content-creation industry understandably have very little trust in human nature.

We are approaching a time when playing music or watching a film does not take place without some kind of authentication from a central server. Many people consider this to be intrusive and an attack on personal liberties and privacy.

It is because there is so much money at stake that we find ourselves in this position. There is profit to be gained from selling rights to view as well as rights to use intellectual property. The downside to this is that it enfranchises those who can afford to pay and closes out those who cannot. This socioeconomic aspect of the licensing regimes is not usually factored into the equation.

This whole area is complex and fraught with legal pitfalls. Here we can examine only some of the issues. This discussion is meant to start you thinking about implications that you may not have considered previously, but you will need to seek out your own solutions depending on the factors that affect you. A happy few will have no consequences arising from this at all, while the bulk of us will need to consider some or all of these issues whenever we distribute our products.

18.2   What Is Digital Rights Management?

Commercial exploitation is an important concept to understand. This chapter looks at some of the issues regarding protecting your content and managing the rights of use—a very complex subject that affects every stage of the production process.

Digital rights management (DRM) comes into play in several fundamental parts of the creation and use of digital content.

1. Right to use source material
2. Licenses to use production tools
3. Codec licenses
4. Distribution rights cleared
5. Right to receive content
6. Right to play back content
7. Right to repurpose content
8. Right to engage in peer-to-peer sharing and super-distribution

See Figure 18-1 to see how these relate to each other in the end-to-end food chain. The numbers in the foregoing list are keys to the illustration.

No system can ever be guaranteed to prevent copying. However, there is increasing legal protection for content owners to wield if they detect that someone has tried to work around the protection. The Digital Millennium Copyright Act (DMCA) in the United States is one such example. Japan also has legislation in place and a number of European countries will follow in due course.

Nevertheless, content pirates still offer bounties in the order of $10 million or more for good-quality digital masters of movies, sometimes even before those movies have been released. That is a lot of money involved and a significant temptation to people working in the industry to compromise the security. Very few companies would pay that much to build a secure system let alone implement one on a per-movie basis.

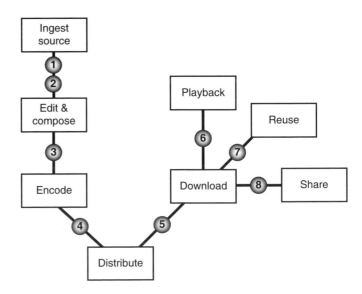

Figure 18-1 DRM food chain.

18.2.1 *Content-Sourcing Issues*

To begin with, during the production process, you must know whether you have the rights to include some content in a program you are making. This applies equally to the use of still images, pictures on the wall at the back of a studio set, and even the video footage playing on a TV in the corner of a room behind the actors. Indeed, even the music being played on that TV set must be rights cleared. Digital rights are complex and become even more so when older material is being recycled. That might invoke residual rights, repeat fees for actors, and royalties to the copyright holders and owners of the material, so it becomes a nested problem with additional layers of rights that have to be cleared.

18.2.2 *Implications for Encoder Users*

The emergence of the new codec implementations has thrown some licensing issues right to the foreground of the business planning process.

There are implications for encoder users with respect to the intellectual property rights and patents on technologies implemented in the encoder. The historical licensing model is one where the purchaser of an encoder pays a certain percentage of the purchase price to secure a right to encode. The encoder manufacturer then passes on that royalty to the clearinghouse.

Today, a new model is emerging where content owners or providers are expected to pay on a per-user or per-copy basis as the material is delivered. Certain not-for-profit organizations enjoy some exemption from this, but producers of CD or DVD products could be met with a nasty surprise and a demand for royalties.

18.2.3 *Content-Consumption Issues*

The second major part of the equation is at the consumption end. This controls whether an end user is able to play back the content based on the rights that have been purchased or granted. There are no completely satisfactory solutions although there are some propriety technologies that give you some temporary peace of mind. This rights protection must work flexibly and without stopping legitimate use while placing an enormous barrier in front of people who would steal content wholesale.

18.3 Commercial Considerations

Digitizing and compressing video allow new distribution models to emerge. Some of these may allow video to be distributed to audiences that previously were too niche-oriented to merit production runs of tapes or disks. The following are two particularly good examples of commercialization or distribution of content to niche markets.

18.3.1   *The Apple iTunes Music Store*

The first example is the massive success of the Apple iTunes music store. This company is so successful that many other companies are launching similar initiatives. While the profits from each sale are small, they are tangible, and in such bulk that the long-term business model is sustainable. Ultimately, every single recorded piece of music could be available online. At present only the most popular material is being made available legally, and some tracks are exclusive to iTunes or other competitive services. Of course much material is also available through illegal sources, which in the long term will only serve to damage everyone's interests.

The iTunes DRM system allows the user to make some limited copies of the track on several computers and to burn a list of songs onto a CD. Based on the fact that you can never put back information that has been discarded, those CDs will carry audio with some compression artifacts. Apple uses the MPEG-4 AAC audio format, so high-quality content is still delivered. It is not an exact copy of the original CD recording, however. This DRM

Figure 18-2 Apple iTunes Music Store.

system is a good example of how the content can be secured without getting in the way of a normal user's listening habits.

18.3.2 BBC Creative Archives Project

The second example is the stated goal of opening up the entire BBC archives to the UK public on terms that are similar to an open-source software license. This makes the raw material available, and if people so desire, they can restore or aggregate the content together in new ways. All of that adds value to the archive as a whole. This is of great benefit to schools, for example, as supporting material for their curriculum, and new television program ideas may emerge as a result of this material's being accessible to a wider public.

18.4 Inconsistent Licensing

The iTunes music store and other similar services run by Real Networks, Microsoft, Virgin, Napster, and their competitors have negotiated licensing arrangements with the owners of the copyrights. These licensing arrangements are slightly different from each other, and aside from the formats possibly being incompatible, there is the problem that authentication facilities may not be available to everyone. If you download a track from one service, you may not have the same rights as you would if you obtained it from a different source.

This comes down to the issues of fair use and right to copy. Clearly the laws must be designed to prevent piracy and the selling of content whose copyright is owned by someone else. This must be accomplished without significantly affecting the convenience and right to fair use that a legitimate purchaser should enjoy.

Needless to say, this is an area of much debate. At the one end of the spectrum is the desire for total control and measured distribution that the recording and movie companies deem important. They have every right to protect content where they have funded the creative process. At the other end of the spectrum is the public's desire for total autonomous freedom to transfer a legitimate copy of a music track to an MP3 player or a movie to a laptop hard disk so that it is available while traveling.

18.5 Struggles Between Copyright Owners and Pirates

DRM is seen as the main weapon that the copyright owners in the recording and movie industries have to protect their assets. While DRM may well hinder determined piracy operations, it will not stop them completely.

This is because the large revenues that the pirates make from stealing content are sufficient to fund "cracking" teams with more resources than the people protecting the content are willing or able to spend on protecting it.

The problem is analogous to making your home or car burglarproof. In the end, the best you can hope for is that the thief is deterred or discouraged and moves on to another victim. This works fine for the casual theft of rights-protected material. For some enthusiasts, there is an essence of challenge involved in this process. To the determined cracker, for example, the challenge is all the more rewarding if the system is difficult to break into. If it is very hard, the bragging rights are huge if you are the first one through the door. So there is an ever-increasing spiral of move and counter-move by each side.

18.6 Consumer Issues

If video compression is going to prosper as an industry, then it is important to protect the rights of content owners so that they can control who accesses the content they are making available.

From the consumer point of view, a somewhat unhealthy disrespect for content ownership has evolved over the years. This is because duplicating someone else's content is so easy that the barriers to copyright theft are very low. Whatever arguments each side puts up, they cannot develop a commercially viable relationship unless a compromise delivers what they both need.

The copyright owners need protection but the purchasing user who buys a legitimate copy must also be allowed some fair-use rights. Providing a barrier sufficient to deter casual copyright theft is appropriate. But building a scheme that cannot eventually be cracked or circumvented by determined software pirates is unlikely to succeed and isn't technically possible anyway.

The Digital Living Network Alliance seeks to provide interoperability but recognizes that this must start through a focus on the consumer's needs. This an interesting change of emphasis.

18.7 What Rights Do We Need to Protect?

Protecting the rights of the content owners to ensure that they get a fair return on their assets is paramount; otherwise they will not make content available. However, this protection should not be at the expense of the fair-use rights of the consumer. Describing fair use in a legal sense is very hard because it must take context into account. Ripping a CD into iTunes for eventual playback in an iPod seems to be acceptable. Ripping a CD into iTunes for eventual playback in someone else's iPod is not. Ripping a DVD for playback in a laptop seems to be frowned upon under all circumstances.

18.7.1 Yours to Own Forever?

Media companies are prone to see a new platform as an opportunity to generate an additional revenue stream by republishing old content in that new format. They feel no burden

---

Digital Living Network Alliance: http://www.dlna.org/home

of obligation to support prior purchasers of their product, even if collectively they make obsolete a redundant format such as vinyl, 8-track tape, or audiocassette. The days of the VHS cassette are certainly numbered, but no one would suggest that the record companies should offer an upgrade to a DVD copy at a nominal charge. We take low-cost upgrades for granted with software purchases, but it doesn't seem to apply to music and video.

Customers that purchased titles in older formats have the right to continue enjoying them. The industry must decide whether it is reasonable that media companies charge the full price to someone who already owns the Betamax, VHS, LaserVision, or DVD version of a movie when it gets released on some holographic storage format and the legacy players for the old formats have become obsolete or have worn out and are no longer working.

18.7.2 Rewarding the Content Creator

The arguments become a moral issue when the original author, artist, or director receives no additional reward or residual royalties because the original contract is interpreted to only include the originally available distribution channels. It is outrageous that large organizations retain 100% of the profits from re-releases without passing any of them on to the creator of that content. Not making allowances for the customer already having purchased the product in previous formats while criminalizing the last few fair-use rights we have is also unreasonable.

Thus, what might seem to be the morally correct and honorable approach is in fact the exact opposite of the way that recording contracts and copyright law are interpreted.

18.7.3 Control Systems Need to Allow Some Slack

If the copy proofing and duplication restrictions are too draconian then they start to affect legitimate duplication processes. While the interests of the large corporate copyright holders are protected, small independent rights owners find they are disadvantaged. This happens when levies are charged on blank media, for example. Implicit in those levies is the right to copy but this gets charged to people who are copying home movies they've shot and edited themselves. Video recorders have many uses that are outside the sphere of copyright infringement.

18.7.4 Why We Need It

At the other extreme, the ease of copying commercial content dramatically reduces potential revenue earnings because fewer "master" copies are sold through the retail channels. This is blatant theft. The excuse that the perpetrator was not ever going to buy a copy anyway doesn't hold any water. It certainly causes loss of revenue, although some of the assertions by the industry as to how much revenue is lost are absurd. They are calculations of what they might have sold but these are probably somewhat idealized. Because the figures are speculative they can be exaggerated without any burden of proof.

18.7.5 Rented Movies

Some viewers only need or want to rent movies for a couple of nights. That business model has helped found huge chains of video-rental stores and for these consumers, some kind of digital duplication process with embedded rights control would be ideal. You might purchase 10 plays of a movie or rights to watch it an unlimited number of times during a certain period.

For this to work, the system must be closed and inaccessible so that the material cannot be extracted. That is very hard to do but streaming the content and charging on a user account basis might be a way forward.

Some people will like this. Those who would rent movies are likely candidates. Those who purchase the copies to keep will probably not be interested in this model.

18.7.6 Public Performance

Theoretically, public performance should be the most secure way to present movies to people. In practice, it is likely that this is the preferred point of attack for piracy attempts.

Much wringing of hands and bemoaning of revenue loss have come out of Hollywood, accusing the public of theft of movies which have found their way onto DVDs that are sold in markets in the Far East and on street corners in Western cities.

Unfortunately, that does not tell the entire story. A significant number of these pirated disks carry films that have not yet been released in the cinemas, let alone published on publicly accessible media. Some of the originals that have been compromised are samples sent out for preview by the movie companies (a.k.a. screeners). They are working on making this process much more secure, but it is not the public that is at fault when a film is "borrowed" from the projection booth at a cinema and duplicated on a telecine machine without the distributor knowing.

18.7.7 Mobile Applications

Tracking people on the move and securing the content being delivered to their mobile device adds some complexity to the problem. Properly identifying a device and user who is authenticated should be no more complex than with a fixed-client system. It might be more difficult if the mobile device moves to another commercial territory, which is certainly possible when users travel to another country.

Companies are beginning to develop products that address the needs of this market. For example, DMD Secure offers a DMD mobile DRM system.

18.7.8 Broadcasting

The whole point of broadcasting is to deliver a single stream of content to as many households as possible. This is a very efficient distribution technique. In terms of rights control,

---

DMD Secure: http://www.dmdsecure.com/

however, there are mechanisms for scrambling the content so it cannot be decrypted without the necessary permission. That permission is often embodied in a card that is inserted into the front of the receiver.

In practice, these schemes are compromised by people buying cards within the legitimate territory and using them outside of it or by nefarious activity that leads to the cards being hacked and distributed illegally.

18.7.9   Broadcast Flags

In the United States, content owners are pressing the broadcasters to adopt the "broadcast flag," an embedded signal that recording equipment must obey. This functionality is part of the Advanced Access Content System (AACS). It is being promoted as a means to allow consumers free and fair use but will prohibit onward distribution of the content.

There is an insidious move toward the ultimate goal of having total control of the consumers playback system. In due course the broadcast flag will no doubt be extended to prevent recording of any kind. It is the thin end of the wedge to handing control of your playback experience to a company who will build a revenue stream out of granting you permission to play content that you have already purchased. When we have bought content in the past, the contract implied or implicit is that we have purchased a right to play that material in perpetuity. Handing control to the content owner like this seems to contradict those fair-use rights, especially if there is a possibility that they will deny access after a certain time or a limited number of plays.

The broadcaster must ensure that the customer get the rights they think they are paying for. If I think I am purchasing perpetual rights and later find that I was actually only renting a limited permit to access, then I will be a very unhappy customer.

18.7.10   Implications for Video Libraries

This is a variant on the rented-movies scenario. The charging model is different for video libraries, but it deals with media that is ephemeral and duplicated as needed from a master copy. There is no need to return the assets like there would be in a physical library but there are also zero production costs.

This is potentially useful on a streamed delivery system as well. Is it possible to prevent people from capturing and recording the streams? I doubt it. Do you need to? Why would you want to? If a library is publishing some archival footage and it is never planning to take it offline, and the footage is going to be freely available in perpetuity, is there any reason to bother trying to protect it? Before buying and implementing a sophisticated and complex DRM system, you need to think about whether you actually need one at all.

Advanced Access Content System: http://www.aacsla.com/

18.8 What Is Fair Use?

Fair use is the right you have when you purchase a media asset to view it or listen to it wherever you happen to be. This is very simple in the case of an individual viewing a program in private. If you think of the original tangible object as a license, then as long as you have possession of that object, you should be able to enjoy playing back the content on any device, at any location of your choice, for your own personal pleasure provided you are only playing one copy at a time and no one else is participating.

Then we need to consider a family viewing a DVD that is owned by the household. That is fine. It's fair use, and I don't think anyone would argue. But what about an enlarged family, or a family that lives in multiple locations? Once we move beyond the simple scenarios, it is hard to clearly define the boundaries and becomes an argument about whether there was an intent to defraud.

Copying your vinyl record collection to tape for listening to in the car seems to also constitute fair use.

Copying your DVD movie to your laptop hard drive for playback on an airplane is no different, but it is singled out as being questionable. That digital copy on your hard drive is a bone of contention for Hollywood movie companies. They are worried that it might be converted, duplicated, and given away without them earning any revenue on the copy. Provided you still own the DVD and it isn't disposed of while you retain the copy on your hard disk, there is no indication that a theft has occurred.

The crux of the matter is the unauthorized duplication and redistribution of content without payment of royalties. You should have no doubt at all that this is theft, whereas duplication for one's own personal convenience and enjoyment is "fair use." Unfortunately, fair use has not been framed in any legal sense and no one wants to become the test case to establish exactly what the scope of fair use extends to.

18.8.1 Private Viewing of Purchased Media Assets

Purchasing a DVD or other movie file in order to watch at home includes the rights to watch the program an unlimited number of times. Indeed this was the promise on the front of many VHS movies. "Yours to keep forever," the movie publishers said. That may be true, but with the imminent demise of VHS players and the rapidly declining amount of new VHS material being published, this promise has become rather empty. Forever did not turn out to last as far into the future as we thought.

The issue, then, is how do we protect the interests of the purchaser without removing all copyright protection and control? Perhaps it is permissible to allow that user to ingest his or her movies into some kind of jukebox system but only allow them to be shared within a household. Defining the limits of that household or private network needs some careful consideration, however.

18.9   Hidden Benefits of Allowing Casual Copying

You could think of this as a distributed backup solution. We are only able to enjoy some archival content because someone did bend the rules a bit and keep a private copy of a classic TV program. When that copy is later "donated" back to the owner, it turns out the owner lost or destroyed the original. The so-called pirate copy turns out to be the only one in existence. This has happened several times in the case of classic and important BBC-TV programs from the 1960s.

It is also possible to lose recordings through human error or because the tapes are labeled ambiguously. Archivists should take note and check a tape before recycling it. Users who are about to record over a used tape should check before pressing the record button. But we are always in such a hurry, aren't we?

18.10   Background Music in Home Movie Audio Tracks

If you plan to digitize and redistribute your home movies, you may not have the rights to use the audio on the soundtrack. Rights management was far less sophisticated and onerous in the 1950s, 60s, and 70s when some of this footage might have been shot and edited. It is very likely that some background music from non-authorized sources will have been used, and you may need to re-record some of the audio to clear up the rights issues before selling copies of your films.

If this problem rears its head in a professional environment, then some extra leverage may be possible if funding is available to apply a technical solution. Fuji Television Network has developed some software that erases music from the background of an audio track but leaves the speech intact. This is a useful tool because a lot of archived material cannot be reused until the music rights are cleared for secondary use.

18.11   Where It All Breaks Down

All of the techniques that might be deployed have a means of circumvention. It may sometimes be challenging but it is always possible given sufficient effort and willingness to break into the protection system.

Those people with the most to gain from the break-in attempt are those who will steal the content, blatantly duplicate it, and distribute pirated copies. This problem will persist as long as the public is willing to buy these pirated copies.

No amount of policing will completely eradicate it because there is a public perception that this content has a certain value and to buy it legally, the cost is somewhat higher than the public is prepared to pay, and the illegal copies are available more cheaply.

Fuji TV Network: http://www.fujitv.co.jp/en/

While this situation persists, the organized criminals will be prepared to invest far more time, resources, and effort into cracking a system than the content providers are prepared to invest in protecting their systems.

The current climate is a no-win situation, so a new kind of strategy must be developed, one that offers the content in a way that can be purchased legitimately at a more reasonable price but also makes each copy of a movie unique in some way and therefore traceable.

If consumers feel that they are somehow accountable, then maybe they will be less willing to offer casual copies to their friends. If a pirated copy can be traced back to the person that purchased the original from the supplier or the official that was responsible for the safekeeping of a master copy, then this might make people pay more attention to the rights of the content provider.

But if this continues to prop up artificially high prices for the media, it is more likely that the pirates will work out how to remove this tracing data in order to protect their own revenue streams.

18.11.1   *Bolting Stable Doors When the Horse Is Long Gone*

Some experts are beginning to argue that stopping people from copying the material is a wasted effort. Arguably, the content providers are ignoring the status quo—the fact that every household capable of watching digital content probably has an analog VCR. Connecting up the equipment such that the digital box is routed through the VCR and then to the TV set allows an analog copy to be made very easily.

Some analog protection mechanisms might impede this but techniques for circumventing that have been in existence for a long time and are well known.

Some rights-protection proposals suggest that keeping the signals digital all the way to the loudspeakers and video display will secure the content. They fail to realize that you simply have to impedance-match and attenuate the level of the speaker drive signals and feed them into your recording apparatus. Then you can make a perfect analog copy of the audio. The process is not much harder for the video. The industry is in some kind of denial about the fact that the human sensory organs are all analog. But these protection systems are all a waste of time and effort because they won't stop the pirates.

18.12   Re-Use

All of the broadcasters and movie-content owners become concerned about the potential reuse of their footage. This also applies when segments are extracted and used for other purposes.

This is a difficult area to police because some content is intended to be reused. Stock footage from video libraries and now the BBC creative archives initiative make available a vast quantity of historical material.

The rights-control system must determine whether a particular fragment of video is allowed to be copied or must be prohibited from being used as part of another program.

This is already being addressed within TV production systems. The BBC news organization has a system that manages the usage rights on footage received from other providers. This becomes very complicated with territorial issues; number of plays permitted; and whether the usage is internal, external for a limited audience, or available to the public at large.

18.13   Peer-to-Peer Sharing

The whole peer-to-peer file-sharing issue has been brought into disrepute by the use of sharing as a way to steal music files and redistribute them without authorization. People should be made aware that this is illegal and contravenes the copyright ownerships of the material being shared.

Peer-to-peer sharing has some significant benefits. It can significantly reduce the burden on a service provider because fewer copies need to be delivered from a central server. However, access control is much more complex.

Allowing the media to be copied but encrypting it such that those copies will not play without authorization might be a solution.

18.14   Encryption and Access-Control Techniques

The first step in combating the casual use of your content is to decide what kind of protection you need. There are a lot of choices and deciding how to boundary limit that control is a necessary first step. Of course, having a working control system in the first place is important, too.

18.14.1   Open Access

Maybe you don't need to provide any protection at all. The BBC has taken the step of broadcasting in the clear on the digital terrestrial and satellite services in the United Kingdom. BBC content being broadcast by other TV companies elsewhere in the world may not be as freely available. Such rights may apply only for a certain time frame and while end users might video record the program off air, they most certainly don't have the right to redistribute that copy in any way whatsoever.

18.14.2   Geographical Access

The funding of the BBC-provided services is a main factor in determining their availability to various geographically organized audiences. BBC license fee-funded broadcasts are supposed to be viewed only inside the United Kingdom, and BBC broadcasts funded from other sources are supposed to be seen only outside of the country.

As it turns out, the BBC is extremely popular with viewers in continental Europe, especially in Holland, France, Belgium, and Denmark. In the coastal regions nearest to the

British Isles, a large aerial antenna carefully sited will ensure you can receive BBC broadcasts well outside the boundaries of the United Kingdom.

The European viewers tuning into the UK transmissions are watching the BBC content illegally because they don't have a TV license. If they are watching BBC services that are delivered through a redistribution arrangement with their local broadcaster then everything is cleared. Such arrangements are made from time to time but may be limited to certain regional variants of the BBC services. There are some BBC services that are broadcast outside the United Kingdom that are intended for non-UK viewers and these are not made available within the country.

Constraining the viewing territory is very easy to do with cable systems. It is a little harder with terrestrial transmissions but it is almost impossible with satellite broadcasts.

18.14.3 Conditional Access

If you meet other conditional criteria that are embodied in an access card or conditional-access account that is keyed to the receiver, then there is at least some physical access control.

The Sky Satellite systems enable the unique identification of users who pay for subscriptions to keep an account running. In the case of default, transmitting a secret code in the broadcasting service will disable an account.

People buying access cards and exporting them to territories where they are not marketed compromise these card-based models. Other people attempt to break open the access control mechanisms and neutralize them. They then sell cards that provide free access with no revenue return to the service provider. At least with a card that has been legitimately purchased and exported there is some revenue stream going back to where it should be.

18.14.4 Subscription Models

Subscription models based around a regular fee seem to be attractive to a large proportion of the population. Bearing in mind that UK residents must pay for a TV license in the first place, somewhere around 10 million of them are also prepared to pay a subscription in order to receive premium content such as soccer matches and first-run movies. These used to be available free to air but the rights go to the highest bidder, therefore the pay-TV services could afford to outbid the free-to-air channels.

The access control provided by a subscription service also gives access to T-commerce (television commerce) and interactive services that may yield additional revenue to the service provider. Indeed, you will often hear the term ARPU being used. This is a contraction of "additional revenue per unit" and service providers set target levels for this number and base their business plans on it.

Finding that your access control has been compromised is a serious problem when you have built a business model around the concept of secure and reliable identification of your consumers. Anyone using a purposely compromised access card on a pay-per-view service who is stupid enough to try and access T-commerce using that card probably deserves to be caught and penalized.

18.14.5 Authentication

All of these control mechanisms depend on authenticating the users. Knowing that they are who they say they are is important, but this proposition is not as simple as it appears. It is very easy to determine that someone in a particular household is using the pay-per-view service, but it is a lot harder to determine exactly which family member that is. Minors could be viewing totally unsuitable content without the knowledge or permission of their parents.

In the end, access control probably comes down to managing the viewing rights at the level of a household and then relying on parental supervision after that.

Thus we need to determine exactly what a household means. This is important because it sets the boundary limits for a network. The technologies for watching TV in a domestic setting are converging toward a streamed model built around household servers and gateways.

18.14.6 Territory Management/Region Codes

The movie industry has attempted to manage territorial distribution by using region codes on DVDs and then mandating that players must honor those codes.

Figure 18-3 shows the organization of the regions, and Table 18-1 lists their names and identities.

Within 12 months of the introduction of DVD players, chips to get around region coding were devised; they have been available ever since. You can even buy region-free "chipped" players that retain the manufacturers' warranties.

Region code enhancements (RCE) have been added by the film companies to defeat this chipping of players. The enhanced disks play in multi-region players but not in the chipped units. Disks with this additional regional coding protection are beginning to enter the market.

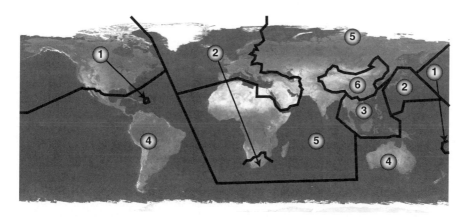

Figure 18-3 DVD region code map.

Table 18-1 DVD Regions

Region	Sub-code	Countries served
0		No region coding applied to disk or player is region free
1		The United States, its territories, and Canada
2		Europe, Japan, the Middle East, Egypt, South Africa, Greenland
2	D1	Only released in the United Kingdom
2	D2	European disk not sold in the United Kingdom
2	D3	European disk not sold in the United Kingdom
2	D4	Available across Europe
3		Taiwan, Korea, the Philippines, Indonesia, Hong Kong
4		Mexico, South America, Central America, Australia, New Zealand, Pacific Islands, the Caribbean
5		Former USSR, Eastern Europe, India, Africa other than RSA, North Korea, Mongolia
6		People's Republic of China
7		Unused (reserved for future use)
8		Aircraft and cruise ships

This territorial control is largely unnecessary. The majority of people in Europe don't care enough to go to the trouble of importing DVDs from the United States. Those few people that want to do this would have found a way around the region coding anyway.

The arguments in favor of region coding might be supportable if the digital-video formats had been made compatible everywhere in the world. We had a chance to do that with the introduction of digital TV but it slipped away. We have another opportunity with HDTV and it is marginally possible that the whole world will end up adopting a common format for that.

If the distributors had genuinely made all their material available in every territory, the region-coding scheme might have been vindicated. Unfortunately they did not. In fact a significant proportion of DVD-based material can only be purchased in the United States. It is not distributed worldwide and the only way it can be viewed in Europe and elsewhere is to watch Region 1 disks on chipped players. The excuse that region codes control distribution is undermined by the fact that there is no distribution. Rather than strangling the distribution process you would think that the content owners would be seeking to maximize distribution in order to yield the largest possible revenues.

Blockbuster movies are not the problem because they are made available worldwide. The more interesting, esoteric cult films or documentaries are hard to obtain in some markets. Thankfully, some distributors do understand this and they code their disks as Region 0, which ensures compatibility worldwide. The distribution in Europe is patchy but imports are not hard to organize, and a Region 0 disk will play in an unchipped player.

Related (but probably necessary) stupidity persists in the way that computer DVD disk drives are set up to control the regionalized playback with limited numbers of region changes and abrupt lockouts, which render the drive inoperable.

18.15 Watermarking Techniques

Some content owners are realizing that their money is better spent on watermarking the content so the original purchaser who allowed his or her copy to be compromised is traceable. The Recording Industry Association of America (RIAA) has already begun to use this kind of legal tactic to pursue people who illegally downloaded and then shared music tracks. People who offered up music archives for others to download wholesale were effectively painting a large target on their forehead.

Closing the circle by adding a unique watermark when a track is downloaded from iTunes or Napster is an optimal way of tracing pirated content. Virtually all the other DRM mechanisms that prevent fair use could then be set aside because they are not going to stop determined pirates.

Watermarking must be robust enough to remain intact throughout any compression and transcoding process. It is feasible to bury an encoded version of the transaction record in the sample data so that wholesale piracy can be tracked back to the original purchaser. So if a pirate rips off a CD from iTunes or the video equivalent of it, there could still be some traceable identifying data embedded within it.

It is a matter for conjecture whether such a scheme has or might be implemented in the future. The service provider should never disclose the details of when or where it is used. Indeed, the very fact that it is technically feasible should work in favor of the content owners because if people were made to believe that they could be traced, they might be more circumspect in their willingness to pass on "free" copies of tracks they have bought for their own personal use. In the end, a propaganda war may be more cost-effective than trying to reliably secure the content.

The Sarnoff Corporation has devised a watermarking scheme that is very resilient to movies being duplicated, compressed, or even filmed with a handheld camera in the movie theater. A digital signature is encoded into the movie and can be recovered to trace back through the distribution chain and identify exactly where the compromise occurred. This is especially useful for D-cinema applications.

In general, consumers instinctively know the difference between right and wrong. A passive DRM system that helps to keep them honest is likely to be more useful in the long term than a draconian technique that renders material unplayable in some devices.

18.15.1 Hiding the Crown Jewels in Plain Sight

In the end, the most practical way to secure content is to mark every copy indelibly with some code that records a transaction identifier. That code can be used to trace back to where the unauthorized copy was first duplicated. A few casual copyists will be very alarmed to find that the copy they gave away to an old friend ended up being pressed on hundreds of thousands of illegal DVD disks and that they are culpable and liable for millions of dollars of lost revenue.

To accomplish this, visible and invisible encoding techniques must be used for the identifying codes, including data values inserted directly into the stream. Techniques such as hiding information in what looks like film grain or dust particles on a film print may also be used, and if this becomes known, then changing the audio or removing and adding frames to the edited movie might also be used to differentiate one copy from another. Subtly shifting the subtitles to a new time code might be sufficient to encode some values. Comparing them against the master might then yield the coded information. If enough different techniques are used, there should still be some trace of the transaction ID left even after the video has been duplicated and passed on several times.

18.15.2 Problems With Artifacts

One of the issues with watermarking is that it must be robust enough to survive the video content being reformatted and compressed.

Watermarking is very similar to the technique known as steganography, which hides data within the complexity of the picture information. Hidden messages are encoded into images and can be extracted if the key or cipher is known.

This is very similar to the code based on a series of holes cut in card, which is then placed over the correct page of a book so that the message can be read.

Steganography just hides a message somewhere in an image. Watermarking must be hard to remove but must also be invisible. This is easy to do with a still image and much harder to do with a moving image. The watermark becomes visible occasionally because it appears to be a stationary noise pattern while the rest of the underlying image is moving.

During 2002–03, the BBC Research and Development laboratories demonstrated motion-tracked watermarks that were designed to move with the video. The difference when viewing watermarked video with a slow pan was remarkable—the watermark was much harder to detect. This technique is somewhat related to the motion detection and compensation in the video-compression systems.

Hiding codes and watermarking information in the deeper recesses of the compression data may be another useful technique. In addition, many other techniques are available to hide unique identifying codes in movies.

18.16 Patent Pools and Technology Licenses

You must be diligent in determining whether or not you have to pay a license to use some footage. Even if you are simply providing a compression service, there may be some licensing issues to deal with.

You should consult the licensing terms for the encoder you are using if you think there is an issue. Older encoders such as MPEG-2 probably have all the licensing embodied in the purchase of the encoder software and hardware. The manufacturer pays a portion of the sales price as a levy.

Read the licenses on your more recent software carefully to know whether you have permission to distribute the encoded files you create. On installing Squeeze 4, the licenses are presented and you are warned that certain codecs must not be used to create distributable copies of your content without seeking a further license from the encoder manufacturer. You may have to shell out some more cash, and that doesn't even count any clearance fees you will have to pay for your content replication. Such hidden costs will kill your business model if you don't know about them at the outset.

Newer codecs such as H.264 definitely have terms that could include your activity within the community of fee-paying users. It will generally come down to whether you are deriving commercial benefit from broadcasting or selling the content.

The two organizations whose licensing terms you should consult are MPEG LA and Via Licensing. The *MPEGIF* organization also has much useful information on this topic.

18.16.1 Multiple Licenses

You may not realize the extent of this licensing complexity. If you use H.264 codecs, you may be liable to pay a license fee to MPEG LA (the licensing authority) to satisfy the holders of the patents that they administer in their patent pool. This will not cover you for the licenses in the patent pool administered by Via Licensing. You must consider both licensing pools independently of one another. Their terms are different and so are their qualifying thresholds. Your administration will have to run two audit trails to ensure both licenses are covered.

18.16.2 Audio Licensing Is Not Covered by Video Licenses

So you've been diligent and have covered the necessary licensing for your H.264 encoded video. This allows you to ship a silent movie! What about the audio?

If you want to add a sound track coded using the AAC technology, you come under another licensing scheme that you must also administer. Via Licensing also handles this license pool. And licensing AAC does not include the SBR support in AAC plus. You have to license that separately as well.

So where you thought you might have to pay 50 cents on every copy you ship, you might find you have to pay $1.50, plus you may also have to employ someone to administer your licensing process because it is three times as complex as you thought.

18.16.3 It Gets Really Crazy Sometimes

This will get even worse as you deploy more diverse kinds of multimedia. A BIFS-based presentation containing several kinds of media might fall foul of a half-dozen different

---

MPEG LA: http://www.mpegla.com/index1.cfm
Via licensing org: http://www.vialicensing.com/
MPEGIF: http://www.mpegif.org/patents/

license regimes and cause some nightmare licensing problems. It probably invokes others if it uses metadata as a means to search and discover TV programs via *MPEG-7* or *TV-Anytime*, and more still if *MPEG-21* is used to rights-protect it.

It is important to be able to license only the technology that you are using. The scenario outlined above is beyond any reasonable complexity that you should expect to deal with as a product developer or content supplier. Certainly if you are only shipping AAC audio, a simpler license would be required than if you ship video and audio products. BIFS-based multimedia will force the licensing authorities to develop a simpler approach or risk killing off the very technology generating the revenues for them.

18.16.4   At the End of the Day

If licensing of open-standards technology becomes too complex or expensive, it will drive people into the arms of the proprietary or patent-free open-source codec manufacturers and we will lose the opportunity to gain all the interoperability advantages of an open standard.

The licensing situation is better than it was but is still out of control. It is right that folks who have genuinely invented something should get some revenue for their hard work. That's not the issue. It is all the middlemen that are demanding their piece of the action that I find hard to justify.

The problem is the way that licenses have been divided up according to the technology components and then split between two separate and mutually incompatible licensing bodies. This needs to be harmonized—urgently.

We need a single place that we can go with one set of rules and criteria. Then we need to just be able to check the boxes to indicate what technologies we are using. This isn't a hard system to develop. It has been done for years with the MCPS scheme that clears royalty payments to composers, which is considerably more complex.

What we will get in the short term, at least, is a third company getting involved and writing a suite of software that you have to buy to work out all your clearance fees. From the point of view of the small independent producer, that's another bunch of people having a slice of your pie and your share is getting smaller all the time.

This is ultimately going to kill the whole thing unless these people who aren't actually contributing anything constructive stop trying to carve out their own piece of the action in what is an emerging and potentially interesting set of technologies.

The fact that we are even in this situation is, in a very perverse way, an indication that the standards will become dominant, or at least very important. If that were not the case these middlemen and intermediaries would not waste the time and effort. The lengths they are going to suggest that their projections of revenue earned from licensing are significant.

18.17   Making Money

The following are the relevant questions to pose when analyzing the commercial side of compressed-video distribution. The first list relates to factors contributing to positive cash flow:

- Who pays me?
- How much?
- How do they pay?
- When do they pay?

These are negative cash-flow items, which are equally important:

- Who do I have to pay?
- How much do I pay them?
- How do I pay them?
- When do I pay?

It looks fairly simple, doesn't it? Answers to these questions will determine how you construct your business model, and the efficiency that you are able to muster will make the difference between a successful business and one that fails.

For a business model to work, you need to be sure that people pay you money for your products before you have to pay the royalties on the content and technology licenses. Getting some business administration knowledge is vital, and having some kind of credit-control process to chase in the revenues will ensure that your cash flow is positive.

18.18 Examples of DRM and Rights-Control Systems

A few schemes are becoming used in a widespread manner. They are still proprietary but more generic approaches are being developed.

18.18.1 Apple Fair Play

This is a scheme currently deployed in the distribution of music via the iTunes service; it is embodied in the iPod hardware.

The system allows the user a certain amount of freedom to duplicate tracks. There are limitations on how many computers are authorized to play the track back. You are permitted to burn a CD audio disk of an iTunes play list. The Fair Play system intervenes so that the same play list can only be duplicated a limited number of times.

The Fair Play system is designed to recognize a user whose activity is legitimate and only intervene when the fair-use boundary is crossed. Most users will never be presented with a warning message that they have contravened the Fair Play rules. How many copies of a play list burned onto a CD would you legitimately need to create?

There are limits to the formats that this protection scheme will support at present but it may be licensed to other organizations in the future.

18.18.2 MPEG-4 Content Protection Specification

The Internet Streaming Media Alliance has published an initial draft of the specification for the protection of MPEG-4 content. This is quoted as being the first step toward an open standards-based DRM system. There is a long way to go yet but some progress is beginning to be made. The encryption mechanism is a 128-bit NIST/AES standard, which is free of any patent liabilities.

This is not a solution in itself but it is a move toward an interoperable system.

18.18.3 Windows Media DRM

Windows Media DRM protection is somewhat different from the Fair Play system. The Windows Media solution depends on a message going back to an authentication service to request permission to play. This worries some people, and with good cause. The control over whether I can watch a program that I own, in my own home, on my own system is not something I relish handing over to a third party. Asking someone else for permission to watch a program that I have recorded or purchased is something that I find very intrusive. I would much rather it either be allowed without intervention or that I would be denied the original recording process.

As with all proprietary systems, there are limits to the scope of formats that this mechanism will protect. WM9 DRM supports these formats:

- Windows Media Audio
- Windows Media Video
- Microsoft MPEG-4 Video
- Windows Media Screen
- ISO-MPEG-4 version 1

18.18.4 Macrovision

Macrovision has a variety of copy-protection technologies that they have developed over the years. The CDS-300 scheme is designed to apply copy protection to CDs and this remains intact on the audio all the way to its destination in an iPod. This is interesting because to do this, the scheme must work collaboratively with iTunes and the Apple Fair Play system.

This level of interoperability is vital to the success of any DRM system. All DRM products must exchange information about rights and permission with each other. It is only then that users will enjoy the rights to easily move their content around between the various repositories they are licensed to use.

At present, the favored approach is to implement one single DRM mechanism in all systems. No single system has proven to be robust or portable enough. Interoperability is the key and if DRM systems utilize the MPEG-21 mechanisms, there may be an opportunity to do this.

---

http://www.microsoft.com/windows/windowsmedia/drm/default.aspx

Windows Media Series 10 DRM:

Macrovision: http://www.macrovision.com/

The ActiveRea©h products comprise a three-part strategy that stops content from being compromised. Part 1 prevents DVDs from being ripped the way that CDs are converted into MP3 files. Part 2 protects streams and part 3 is called Hawkeye and is a peer-to-peer movie-sharing intervention tool.

These three tools are designed to work together to protect the content that might be compromised by piracy operations and to improve the longevity of a marketing campaign.

18.18.5 Nagravision

Nagra is another manufacturer with a portfolio of its own and collaborative links to other companies with complementary technology.

Their systems are designed to work with the emerging IPTV and Video-on-Demand (VOD) systems and digital video recorders (DVRs), and also include the Lysis DRM server-based systems. These interoperate with the Microsoft DRM mechanisms in Windows Media. The Lysis DRM system will allow you to aggregate DRM control of Windows Media 9, Real Networks Video, MPEG-2, and MPEG-4 content.

18.18.6 MPEG-7 and MPEG-21

The MPEG-7 standard is developing a set of description tools for multimedia. These are used to manage the metadata associated with multimedia essence that is stored in MPEG-4 containers, for example. The term essence is used to describe the viewable video content as opposed to the metadata which describes it. The tools provide a way to identify content and provide a framework for personalized filtering and reuse of content across multiple platforms. The information stored also pertains to copyright details but rights control is left for MPEG-21 to manage.

An example of how MPEG-7 metadata can be searched is presented by the IBM research center at their Research and Development Web site.

The MPEG-21 standard is all about the design of rights-control mechanisms. This unifies all the different schemes that are used to control access. MPEG-21 has information about individuals, their rights of access, and what they are allowed to do. It matches this with what it knows about the accessibility of an asset. In a compliant implementation, the combination of the two is the strictly Boolean answer to the question, "Can I access this asset, on this system, at this instant in time?"

So MPEG-4 allows us to create some essence, MPEG-7 helps us find it, and MPEG-21 grants us access to use it. You can find out a lot more about this from the MPEGIF organization.

Nagravision: http://www.nagravision.com/

Lysis: http://www.lysis.com/

IBM R & D: http://mp7.watson.ibm.com/marvel/

18.19   Alternative-Rights Approaches

Some organizations are developing new ways to define rights that allow more open access to end users. These are designed specifically to allow content to be copied and reused. An interesting definition and quite detailed explanation of copyrights and public-domain ownership can be found at the Fact-Index Web site.

As copyrights expire or materials are found to be out of copyright, a growing community of Web users are assembling archives of material that is freely available. An interesting archive of movies and video content is accessible through the Internet Archive project. A large number of movies are available here for downloading at no charge. They are presented in a variety of formats, which are compatible with home media systems that you might construct with the currently available technologies.

18.19.1   Creative Commons

This is a completely alternative rights-control mechanism. Creative commons is new and evolving, but the idea is that you might want to share your work in a less restrictive way than the traditional copyright technique. There is no active software component; this is more of an honor-based approach.

A series of rights with special marks similar to the © copyright mark are being developed. Table 18-2 highlights a few of them.

18.19.2   GNU Copyleft

"Copyleft" is a system designed for protecting free software and making sure that any derivative works are also free software.

Table 18-2 Some Examples of Creative Commons Rights

Model	Description
Attribution	Others are permitted to copy, derive, distribute, display, and perform your copyrighted work only if they give you credit.
Noncommercial	Others are permitted to use your work for noncommercial purposes only.
No derivative works	Only verbatim copies of your work can be used. No derivative works can be based on it.
Share alike	Others are permitted to use your content but must pass on their content with the same rights attached.

Definition of public domain: http://www.fact-index.com/p/pu/public_domain.html

Internet Archive: http://www.archive.org/

Creative commons: http://creativecommons.org/

You could choose to just put your software in the public domain, without any copyright attached at all. This allows anyone to share the code. It also allows commercial users to appropriate the code and profit from it without paying you a cent.

The GNU project aims to give users the ability to redistribute and change GNU software, at the same time preventing commercial exploitation from stripping the rights from derivative works.

In order to "copyleft" a program, it is first copyrighted. Then distribution terms are added to give everyone the rights to use, modify, and redistribute the code. These rights are inherited by any derivative product.

The term copyleft was coined because it does the opposite of copyright. Copyright takes freedom away from end users; copyleft gives those same freedoms back again and ensures that users get to keep them.

The specific distribution terms used by the GNU project are enshrined in the GNU General Public License, or GNU GPL for short. A similar licensing mechanism exists for manuals and documentation and is called the GNU Free Documentation License (FDL).

18.20   Can We Ever Make Money from This?

End users are open to being convinced of the need for digital rights management provided it allows them to legitimately enjoy the products they have purchased. A certain amount of fair use must be allowed. I believe that people are generally honest and understand the concept of a fair reward for the effort put in.

The system must be robust enough to prevent massive copyright infringements by pirate duplicators without making the general public out to be criminals as well.

If you intend to do any encoding for profit, in particular encoding products to be replicated and sold on a retail basis in quantity, check all of the small print. This includes reading the encoding licenses for your tools in addition to knowing that you have done your research and ensured that you have the rights to use any source material. You must know where you stand at the outset rather than discovering a liability later on when you have a successful product. The standards documents may include an annex listing the IPR holders that are relevant. Search out any license holders and patent pools for details of how to obtain clearance or to find out whether you are exempt. In the end, you may find no license is necessary.

DRM systems are still in a constant state of flux and are likely to continue like that for some time. The main focus is on securing audio formats at present. If this is accomplished effectively, securing video formats should not take as long. At this time, no one can predict the delivery of a reliable and completely satisfactory solution. It could take another 10 years to reach a workable compromise.

GNU Copy Left initiative: http://www.gnu.org/copyleft/copyleft.html

18.21 Letting the Cat Out of the Bag

Assuming we can deal with all the rights issues and actually get permission to deploy some content, we need to understand what those deployment opportunities are. The technical issues will seem very simple, straightforward, and finite when we return to them after this diversion into commerce. In the next few chapters we will look at networks, streaming, and the implications of choosing one player over another.

Network Delivery Mechanisms $\qquad$ 19

19.1 Time to Show and Tell

So we have some content that has been lovingly crafted and carefully compressed. Now it is time to ship it out to the consumer. How is it going to get there?

This chapter examines how to deliver your video clips once you have encoded them. There are a variety of ways to do this. Principally, this comes down to a small number of possibilities with variations on the following basic themes:

- Broadcast them over a digital TV network
- Stream them over the Internet
- Download them over a network as files

A number of transport mechanisms that exist to deliver video content are based on digital-transmission techniques and all of them are remarkably similar. Where they differ it is in the amount of bit rate or the way that content is unicast on some and multicast on others.

Table 19-1 summarizes some common bit rates available on different kinds of connections.

19.2 Delivery on Multipurpose Networks

Delivering video services over telephone networks is becoming possible as the available network bandwidth into the home increases. Multipurpose networks provided by the digital TV cable companies are also supporting data services and the number of telephone services being provided through the same wire is also increasing. That is quite apart from the voice over IP services. Within a few years, most communications services will be delivered to the home over a TCP/IP-based infrastructure. Routers instead of telephone-exchange switchgear will be far easier to maintain and cheaper to deploy. However, some work remains to be done to make sure it is all resilient and reliably implemented.

It is certainly feasible to eventually deliver totally integrated Web, radio, TV, and telephone functionality to a variety of devices in the home via a single connection.

Table 19-1 Typical Connection Speeds for Networks

Connection	Speed
Analog modems	9.6, 14.4, 28.8, 33.6, 56 Kbps
ISDN (1 channel)	64 Kbps
ISDN (2 channel)	128 Kbps
T1	1.544 Mbps
ISDN-32	2.048 Mbps
ADSL	8 Mbps down,1 Mbps up
Ethernet LAN -10Base-T	10 Mbps
ATM25	25.6 Mbps
Ethernet LAN -100Base-T	100 Mbps

19.3   Dial-Up Telephone Services

Internet connections have used dial-up modems for many years. Back in the 1970s the connection could only manage 1200 baud. Modems supporting 56K baud and broadband connections running at better than 500 Kbps are now becoming commonplace. Note that broadband is measured in bits per second (bps) and modems are described in baud rates.

The baud rate is a measure of physical bits per second, but they are not all usable bits for our payload. Figure 19-1 shows how the bit pattern in a single frame uses some bits to manage the data flow.

The 7-bit character requires a start bit to synchronize the delivery. The format has a parity bit for error correction and in this case it has 2 stop bits to allow characters to be sent continuously. Parity might be on or off, the stop bits might vary, and the data size might change. So the frame is 11 bits long in this case but the payload is only 7. For a baud rate of 9600, the usable transfer speed would only be 6109 bps.

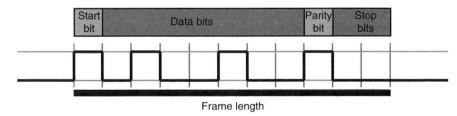

Frame length

Figure 19-1 Serial bit streams in telephony.

19.4   ISDN Connections

The next advance in performance beyond the 56K modems is an ISDN line. This is a digital connection using the same cables as a 56K modem, but the equipment at the exchange needs to be configured properly. You also have to have an ISDN termination at your premises.

ISDN delivers a dual-channel connection. This provides two simultaneous 64K bit streams, although each connection is charged as a separate call. Therefore, if you duplex them to get a 128K connection you will be charged twice as much. But then your call will last half as long. This is good for when you have a large, bulky file to transfer but not great if you normally only make short calls. ISDN includes voice circuits as well.

It is a good idea to connect a router to an ISDN line so that all your systems can share the connection. This can form the basis of your office network because it will probably have an integral network hub. The other major benefit is that it can block incoming connections and act as a barrier to virus infections.

19.5   Broadband Connections

Broadband technologies provide novel and sometimes more effective solutions to propositions that previously required a broadcast infrastructure. The peer-to-peer distribution model is an example that is normally only suited to downloading files. The protocols could be extended to pass on a stream as long as the connectivity is assured. One feed could be delivered to a household and the receiver could route it onward through the local *LAN* to multiple client players. This model would also work for schools, hospitals, campus settings, and corporate environments.

Using a router to share a broadband connection is a good thing to do. Like the ISDN router/hub concept, hardware is available for broadband connections with all the same advantages of sharing and virus protection if the router is properly configured.

Fast network connections like this are beginning to be tested by companies such as Netflix and TiVo, which are both perfectly positioned to take advantage of networked rentable video as a commercial possibility. This might result in services being offered to the public during 2005 or 2006.

 Be wary of running beta versions of software unless they provide features that you absolutely MUST have.

This kind of networking is also where the IPTV services will grow from. Prototype H.264 set-top boxes are already in evidence, as seen at the National Association of Broadcasters conference in 2004. The DG2L Neuron and the MediaReady 4000 unit are typical examples.

19.5.1 Nailed-Up Connections

A nailed-up connection is when your router connects via broadband and doesn't hang up. It just holds the line up all the time. This is good for browsing because you don't have to incur the delay of a dialup when you link to another page.

ISPs often bulk-purchase lines from a telecoms provider and bundle the call charges with your monthly subscription. You may still need to pay the line-rental fee to the telecoms provider.

If your desktop PC is directly connected via the broadband line, then it has to handle the routing for any other machines that you have networked at home. Keep in mind that the network is "down" when your PC is shut off. Intrusion protection takes place in that directly connected PC, and it is a weak point in your security whenever the broadband link is connected and you are online. This is especially true if you have a nailed-up (always-on) broadband line and you leave your PC on all the time. Unprotected machines can be detected and compromised with malware within minutes of being connected to the Internet.

An ideal solution is to place a router on that broadband line and turn off any responses to incoming connections. This does mean your ISP cannot PING your router for diagnostic purposes, but if they need to do that you could allow them access for a short while and then switch the router back to a silent mode. That would be a very rare occurrence, though. Boundary protection like this is a good policy for broadband users, but you should still turn off any unnecessary ports and services on your machines inside your network.

19.5.2 Contention Ratios

You may encounter this terminology when discussing bandwidth available via your ISP. It most commonly relates to consumer connections. The contention ratio describes the number of available input connections versus the number of requesting connections.

In terms of broadband-modem connections you often find that the number of users to available modems at the ISP is perhaps 2:1 or even 4:1. Therefore, you might have a 1 in 4 chance of achieving a successful connection.

Contention is also used to describe the available bit rate. When you purchase 2Mbps of bandwidth and share that between all the members of your household, as long as you only use the Internet one at a time, you all have 2Mbps of capacity. If four members of the household begin to watch streamed movies on separate computers, you have a contention ratio of 4:1 and all of you on average get about 500Kbps. Your client player should do some content negotiation with the server to select a lower bit rate if necessary.

19.5.3 Bit-Rate Aggregation

You might design your connectivity to the outside world using multiple redundant connections, each delivering a proportion of your total bandwidth. By connecting sophisticated routers across these multiple links, their bandwidth is aggregated together so that they behave like a single virtual link.

19.6   Networking Basics

For a start, servers and clients are situated long distances away from one another in the geographical sense but also in the networking sense. A network is connected using a series of smaller sub-networks joined together by routers. The router knows about other routers that it is connected to but knows nothing of the network beyond them. A process of discovery is involved when you make a connection. The number of routers that need to be traversed from your local network to the one where the target server lives will determine the shortest route.

19.7   Transport Protocols

The networking protocols are built using a technical structure that is referred to as a stack. This describes the way that protocols manage different parts of the process starting at the very lowest level where the physical cable connects two devices together. The TCP stack is based on the ISO Open Standards Interconnect layering scheme, although some layers are merged together in the TCP stack, so there is not a complete 1-to-1 correspondence between the two models. They are ordered the same, however, and the counterparts are shown in Figure 19-2.

The electrical signals along that wire are defined as voltages and impedances, and on that a means of coding binary digits is imposed. This describes the bottom-most layers of

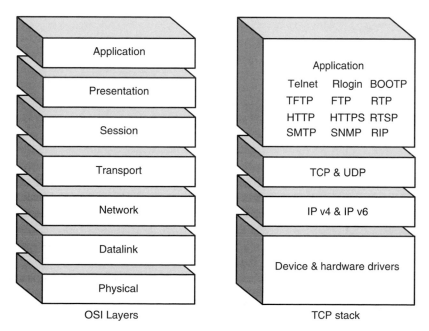

Figure 19-2 TCP stack.

the stack, sometimes called the physical layer. This layer is also sometimes referred to as the transport but that embodies some higher-level functionality that helps correct for errors.

The data become wrapped in increasingly structured containers as the layers are traversed, and each layer adds some small overhead in order to manage its specific responsibilities. Figure 19-3 shows how this works.

19.7.1 TCP Versus UDP

Somewhat higher up in the stack is a layer called the universal datagram protocol (UDP). This UDP describes an interface that guarantees a timely delivery of a packet from one node to the next. It does not guarantee 100% reliable delivery of a complete series of packets in a session since some may be delivered via another route and may not reach the destination. The UDP also does not guarantee that they will all arrive in the right order.

A further layer in the protocol referred to as TCP addresses the shortcomings of UDP. The TCP acronym is short for Transmission Control Protocol and this layer guarantees that all the required packets will be sent and that they will be delivered to the calling application in the client in the correct sequence. This layer implements sophisticated buffering algorithms to ensure that sequencing is correct and also supports acknowledgment messages to the sender. If necessary, it can request that a packet be retransmitted to fill any gaps.

The downside is that TCP will guarantee delivery but not necessarily in a timely fashion. This is why your client player offers you the opportunity to select TCP or UDP connections in the preferences panel.

19.7.2 Irregular Packet Delivery (Jitter)

Delayed packets when using the UDP protocol may manifest the problems in a different way from when you use TCP. A delayed packet in TCP simply slows down the transfer.

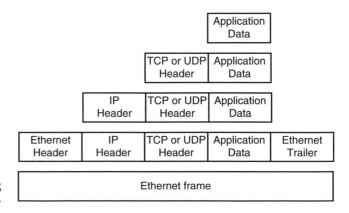

Figure 19-3 TCP packetizing structure.

A delayed packet that arrives too late with UDP will be out of sequence and cannot be used. The consequence is dropped frames and a rather jittery viewing experience.

19.7.3   Packet Sequence Errors

Packets arriving out of sequence might be handled gracefully if you are downloading or buffering rather than playing live to the window as packets are received. Players are getting better at handling this sort of problem. Network latency and error handling is also being designed into the transport protocols so that the players do a better job under extreme situations.

These artifacts are not evident in broadcasting systems because the flow of bits through the system is uni-directional and not subject to routing and transfer problems. The transmission chain is simply a first in–first out (FIFO) buffer. This preserves sequence order and guarantees delivery. Momentary dropouts will be error-corrected but will result in some latency.

19.7.4   Lost Packets

Packets that get lost completely and never arrive present the player with a problem. Handling the dropout in a graceful manner that the user won't notice is challenging. The forward error-correction support may help by providing sufficient redundancy coding to allow the missing data to be reconstructed. This imposes some load on the CPU but the dropouts by nature are infrequent and if they do happen often, the content negotiation could kick in and force the streamer to deliver at a lower bit rate. This might help to alleviate the problem if it is due to bandwidth limits somewhere in the route between the client and server.

The codec has some additional strategies for dealing with missing parts of the image; newer codec designs are far more resilient when faced with data loss and may have a variety of alternative strategies for locating a suitable fragment of data to replace the missing part.

The H.264 syntax specifies that the decoder should cache a large number of frames that it can refer to for missing data. The structure is organized so that the P- and B-frame references can also be computed at the slice level. A single reconstructed frame might use component slices from several different source frames. Older codecs refer to entire frames. This fine-grain approach helps H.264 video handle dropouts more effectively. When a dropout occurs, the reconstructed error correction will be less noticeable.

19.7.5   Dropped Frames

The TCP guarantees delivery of all packets in the right order but with the penalty that there may be some delays. On the other hand, UDP delivers all the packages it can within the lowest latency but will occasionally lose a packet.

To avoid problems when this happens, the streaming protocols add error-correction support to the transport and the parity algorithms help to fill in missing parts of the data stream. The H.264 codec introduces a certain amount of error resilience and there may be some smart things the decoder can do to help. Strangely enough, loss of data in the audio is actually more disturbing to the viewer than the visual artifacts when data is lost from the video channel.

If severe data loss occurs, you may notice jerky movement since the player is dropping frames in order to make its best effort to play the video. The player may also drop frames if the available bit rate falls so low that it cannot preserve the time base unless it sacrifices a frame occasionally. The player will attempt to preserve the time base because this ensures that the video remains synchronized with the sound track and any other streams that may be playing.

19.7.6   *Resource Allocation and Management*

If you have a sophisticated gateway, you might be able to reserve a certain amount of bandwidth for priority use, such as for the main view screen in the lounge, while arranging that the downloading process consume less bandwidth since a human being is not watching it. Large enterprise-sized servers provide resource allocation that that can be measured and throttled under operating system control. This allocates disk space, CPU time, and network bandwidth according to a scheme of priorities.

19.8   Firewall Issues

Getting your streamed content through a corporate firewall may present a significant challenge. There is no technical reason why this should be difficult but the security staff may be justifiably paranoid about opening any chinks in the armor. Allowing outgoing connections on certain ports for streaming protocols should be quite safe. The ports listed in Table 19-2 are relevant for consideration although you should not just blindly open them all without careful consideration.

Alternatives to opening firewall access include the deployment of proxy servers. A proxy and a firewall are carefully configured to work cooperatively. If outgoing connections are always proxied, then the firewall knows that traffic from other machines should not be allowed through. This should provide adequate security for even the most paranoid systems administrators.

19.9   Diagnostic Tools

If you have a computer equipped with some basic networking diagnostic tools, the `traceroute` utility will display a series of connected devices between the two endpoints. An example screen dump is shown in Figure 19-4. Another useful tool is the `ping` utility that sends messages to a remote machine and tells you how long the round trip took when it receives a reply.

Table 19-2 TCP Port Numbers for Streaming

Port	Usage
80	You can tunnel RTSP and RTP traffic through port 80 as if it were an HTTP connection.
554	This port number is used for RTSP.
7070	This port number can be used for RTSP instead of 554. This avoids using a number in the lower 1000 port numbers that are considered special from a secure-access point of view. Firewalls may be configured to disallow connections to ports in the lower 1000 range.
6970–9999	These ports can be allowed for UDP connection but on a requested basis. You may want to ensure they are only requested by authentic sessions that may have been initiated on another port first.
1220	This port number is sometimes used for Web administration.
8080	A high-numbered port, this is occasionally allocated for HTTP use as an alternative to port 80.
311	This port number is sometimes opened for Mac OS X Server Admin.

Other useful tools that help you to look up network addresses are listed in Table 19-3.

19.10 Virtual Private Networks

In times past, large organizations would lease landlines from telecoms suppliers to connect their various offices together. This meant that even though they had a somewhat physical connection to one another, the networks were secure and very hard to penetrate because they were not connected to the rest of the world at any point outside of very secure switching centers.

Then the corporate organizations began to put Internet gateways on their networks, and so different companies were able to send e-mail and exchange files.

With the advent of the World Wide Web in the early 1990s, the Internet took off and companies then deployed firewalls and proxy servers in order to facilitate Web browsing from within the corporate network. This also provided the opportunity to connect their sites to one another via the Internet. As this required a much more secure connection, various protocols and services were evolved into virtual private networks (VPNs). These are secure connections between two sites belonging to the same company and are delivered on the basis of a guaranteed minimum level of bit rate that is reserved for that VPN.

A typical use for a VPN is to connect a Web content-creation HQ to the server farm, which is normally located in a bunker for resilience.

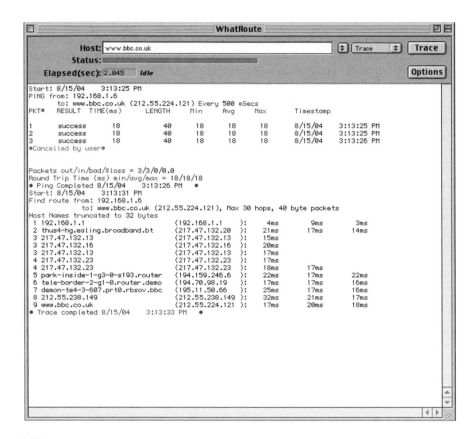

Figure 19-4 Traceroute display.

19.11 Networked Files

Video stored in files and shared around a network , among members of a workgroup, or even across a wider community requires that compression make the best use of the available storage. Even working at television resolutions rather than those of D-cinema, you will encounter very large files.

Sport and news departments in major broadcasting companies such as the BBC share content widely across the organization. Working practices that involve passing around a single tape simply don't work in the high-pressure broadcasting environment.

The BBC News organization has developed a system in which incoming video is written straight to disk as it is ingested and as soon as it begins to arrive. Editorial staff can begin to assemble edits with that incoming video right away. This is operated from a normal desktop computer running a standardized Windows environment. You can find out

Table 19-3 Useful Networking Utilities

Utility	*Description*
ping	Useful for determining whether you can reach a target node and examining the quality of the service in terms of latency. This will also tell you if you are barred from reaching the target device. This tool and others may be compromised when trying to use them to penetrate a firewall or proxy service.
traceroute	A tool for examining routing complexity between your client and a target server. Certain "hops" may take lengthy times to resolve and this will help you to diagnose a "stale" route, that is, one that was previously established and has somehow become locked in but is no longer valid. This tends to happen with dialup connections and can be resolved by your ISP.
whois	One of the tools for determining the domain name for an *IP address*.
nslookup	A useful tool for decoding a DNS domain name into an IP address and vice versa.
netstat	Tells you what connections your machine has made since it was last booted.
tcpdump	A tool for examining traffic between your machine and another. You can determine ports and message status over the connection.
snoop	A widely available utility that sets your *Ethernet* interface to a special mode (promiscuous) where it will be able to examine traffic on your sub-net regardless of whether it is to and from your client node or not. Switched hubs may prevent this from being very useful but having a machine equipped to share a network via a hub will help diagnose very hard-to-find problems. You can also observe traffic and build bandwidth-monitoring, error-detection, and logging tools with this approach.

more about this by contacting BBC Technology (now part of Siemens Business Services) and asking about Colledia.

Architecting a system such as this is quite challenging. In the BBC News 24 studio, there may be thousands of hours of video retained online at any one time. Several hundred journalists are working on this content at once so the architecture of the shared-file system is very important. Large server engines with storage area networks and proxy copies of the video for desktop browsing enable this system to be built and deployed with current technology although quite a lot of specialized coding has taken place to join it all up.

_____

BBC Ventures Group: http://www.bbcventuresgroup.com/
Siemens Business Services UK: http://www.sbs.siemens.co.uk/

Moving content around a network causes some significant problems with saturation. One user can move a DV file on a 100-Base/T Ethernet without much hindrance. Possibly two users can move files at the same time. Allowing more users than that will reduce the network throughput and the sessions will be compromised. Using Ethernet switches only provides limited help because the files are very likely to be pulled off the same storage medium. Therefore, the network connection for the server that supports it will be saturated. Providing Gigabit Ethernet connections to every desk is an unsatisfactory solution because it just defers the saturation until the team grows bigger. When very large numbers of people are operating on shared video storage you have to consider deploying fiber-channel connections and a storage area network (SAN).

19.12 Streaming It Out

While we can deliver content across a network in the form of a downloadable file, a lot of service offerings are more attractive when deployed as a stream. It is a commonly held misconception that streaming content cannot be recorded. This is a silly assumption because it is just one software application talking to another.

As a server application, your system may think it is talking to a client player or Web page plug-in but you only have the evidence provided by that player to indicate that this is the case. How do you know the client isn't lying to your server and is in fact recording the whole stream for playback later? Someone who wants to record your stream and redistribute it for their own profit might very well do this and you would never know.

It's a mystery why people should imagine that recording a stream is difficult when that's exactly what a digital video recorder does. Let's examine steaming a bit more in the next chapter and find out a bit more about it.

20

Streaming

20.1 How Do I Get There from Here?

Streaming is the major means of delivery for digital video since the technique works for television as well as networked systems. Obviously some content is downloaded, but the bulk is delivered as a stream.

This chapter discusses how streaming systems work and what you need to know to optimize your video for them. Streaming is also used for TV systems but we will deal with that when we talk about digital TV in Chapter 27. For the time being we'll stick with streaming on the Net.

20.2 Internet-Streamed Media

Streamed content is normally associated with Web-based AV services. It has its heritage in the Real Networks, QuickTime, and Windows Media formats. Over the next few years, more streaming content will be delivered as H.264 compressed video. The H.264 codec is being considered as a realistic format for carriage of high-definition broadcast TV. Using the same format for both TV and web delivery has some clear advantages over using the earlier proprietary formats:

- Coding farms are shared.
- The differences are only in the fine points of the format.
- Workflow is virtually identical.

Two areas of particular interest are gaining in popularity, although they have taken a while to mature since they are technically challenging to accomplish:

- Multicast streaming from one stream to all connected users
- Peer-to-peer onward delivery of content

A very useful technology solution would be to reduce the traffic so that it is not necessary to deliver the entire file. Ideally, only that fragment the user requests should be transmitted. A streaming server might do that, provided the requesting client can indicate a starting position or in-point for the browse session. The metafiles that encapsulate video streams for linkage to Web pages have a very sophisticated syntax that allows play lists, combinations of clips, and specific in-points to be defined. This level of complexity isn't always necessary, but it is worth reading the documents provided by your streaming vendor in order to better understand what capabilities you have at your disposal.

20.3 How Streaming Works

The core idea behind streaming is that a server on a network for which your playback client machine has rights to connect a session will deliver a sequence of bits through that connection that are decoded and reconstructed to form a moving image and soundtrack.

For this to be useful, this sequence must be accurately synchronized and delivered continuously without any break in transmission, and the amount of data must be sufficient to make the viewing and listening experience enjoyable.

Given the way that the Internet is designed, this is quite a challenge from a technical standpoint.

The Internet was not designed to deliver content in real time, nor was it designed to deliver thousands of TV channels to millions of users. Originally, the Internet (or ARPANET, as it was known then) was intended to reliably deliver e-mail between users on different networks. Networking became progressively more advanced with the addition of the file transfer protocol (FTP). Then web-based services were introduced using hypertext transfer protocol (HTTP). More recently, streaming audio and video via the real-time transport protocol (RTP) and real-time streaming protocol (RTSP) provide media services on the web.

The greatest strength of the Internet is the resilient nature of the connections and the way that alternative routes between two end points are discovered automatically. The downside is that it is actually quite hard to get a guaranteed level of throughput between two points because a sudden burst of traffic between two other end points might saturate the common parts of the link and consume all the available bandwidth.

Other protocols exist to help solve this, and you can operate the connections in a variety of ways. Recent innovations allow for a single streaming service to be shared by many users so that the number of listeners does not affect the outgoing bandwidth from a streaming center.

20.4 Streaming Protocols

Using the user datagram protocol (UDP) and transmission control protocol (TCP) as a foundation, the HTTP or RTSP protocol is layered on top to deal with higher-order functionality. These describe content to be delivered, and in the case of RTSP, you can choose TCP or UDP connections to improve the viewing experience. UDP is feasible because the RTSP protocol supports buffering and skipping. The stream encoding has sufficient error correction built in that an occasional lost packet can be handled without the viewing experience being severely compromised.

20.4.1 HTTP

HTTP was originally designed for the delivery of Web pages, and those comprised a mixture of text-based HTMP, CSS, and other varieties of marked-up content and code. Various binary formats containing images, executable code objects, and other assets that help create the human readable page are also delivered using HTTP.

The technique known as progressive downloading was developed in the mid-1990s. It allows the HTTP connection to remain open, and the client continues to process the stream incrementally as it arrives. This seemed to work for delivering audio and video content, but because it was designed to operate on top of TCP, the delivery is not ideal for real-time live broadcasting. Progressive downloading works reasonably well for delivering movie trailers or other short clips, since these are being sourced from a previously encoded file and the client is simply electing to begin playing the content before it is fully delivered.

20.4.2 RTSP

Early implementations of streaming servers and clients used RTP, but this has been superseded by RTSP. RTSP is an application-level protocol to control the delivery of data in real time. The protocol is designed for on-demand delivery of real-time data, such as audio and video. This includes live data feeds or stored clips. Multiple, simultaneous data-delivery sessions are also supported.

RTSP is better than HTTP when long-form content is being delivered. Capturing streaming protocols to disk is not usually possible in consumer-oriented applications unless the broadcaster allows it, and even then the facilities are not obvious to an untrained user—so the consumer is less able to capture and retain a copy of the content than if a downloadable file based protocol were used. This is seen as a benefit from the content provider's perspective. Capturing RTSP sessions is not overly difficult if you know how, but it requires a solution that is beyond the average consumer user's technical capabilities to deploy. So casual copying is less likely with RTSP than it would be with HTTP. Relying on RTSP isn't a bad approach to security, but a properly developed DRM policy would be better.

Refer to RFC 2326 for full technical details of RTSP and to RFC 1889 for details of RTP. RFC documents are mirrored in many locations on the web. The most authoritative source is the Internet Engineering Task Force (*IETF*). Other sources can be located via Google. Additional information about RTSP is also available at the Real Networks web site.

Real Networks: http://www.real.com/technology/rtsp/index.html

IETF Org: http://www.ietf.org/

FAQs Org: http://www.faqs.org/rfcs/

RFC Archive: http://www.rfc-archive.org/

20.4.3 *Session Description Protocol*

Session description protocol (SDP) describes multimedia sessions in a way similar to an electronic program guide (EPG) for TV channels. SDP is also used to advertise new services and invite clients to initiate a session.

20.4.4 *Stream Control Transmission Protocol*

A new standard is being worked on for streaming; it is called stream control transmission protocol (SCTP). SCTP works extremely well in conjunction with the network-friendly H.264. They are very flexible and adaptive, and well suited for delivery of uni-cast solutions. This combination is apparently very robust and adaptive when faced with a transmission route that is prone to packet loss. This topic is also being discussed by the Audio Video Transport working group at the IETF.

20.4.5 *Proxies and Firewalls*

Certain port numbers are defined as well-known ports. Your security advisors will have configured access through the firewall for some of these ports when you are working within a corporate environment. Access through the firewall may involve a proxy server that acts as your intermediary when connecting to the remote server. Your connection then involves traversing the internal corporate network to reach the proxy server; thence through the corporate firewall and across the Internet, possibly traversing further firewalls as the connection enters the network belonging to the streaming company before hooking up to the target server. A lot of things can go wrong if the preferences are set incorrectly. The player must be configured correctly; otherwise it will be unable to connect to the server with the streamed content.

   The principal settings are the name and port number for the proxy server within your corporate network. This is defined centrally as part of your network setup on the desktop computer. There may be additional proxy settings in the various applications you use and these obviously must be consistent. If you have an opportunity to use an auto-proxy, that is likely to be the most correct set of configuration data. Not all applications honor the auto-proxy settings and will fall back to the static settings or to their own preferences.

   It is vital that you define these proxy configurations consistently. Otherwise, when they come into play and are mutually exclusive, you may not even reach the right proxy-server port, let alone penetrate your corporate firewall and reach the streaming server.

20.5 Delivery Standards

With the increase in the amount of streamed and downloadable content over the last decade, the number of available standards and alternative formats has become bewilderingly large. This has prompted companies to found organizations to help control this complexity and agree on some common profiles.

The standardization process is driven by several factors. Some *de facto* standards evolve first as a result of a new innovation by a proprietary service that has been developed by a single company. This leads to competitive products from other manufacturers, and soon there is sufficient interest that a standards body forms a working group to develop an open-standard-based alternative. Then the manufacturers of proprietary players recognize this and add that open standard to their players. Gradually, the proprietary formats decline in use, since none of them guarantees 100% penetration. At least that is how it should work in an ideal world.

With video-compression standards, certain functionality is defined as being mandatory and other capabilities are grouped into bands of features that are likely to be useful as the sophistication of a service increases. Basic streaming of simple rectangular content might be defined as a base level, while multiple streams of non-rectangular video are something that a basic player does not need to support but a premium player might well be able to play back.

This leads to the standards working groups' defining some profiles of functionality that player manufacturers must support in order to be able to claim compliance. Within those profiles, different levels of performance specifications are addressed. For example, a basic functionality profile might define that a single rectangular video be played, but a variety of different sizes and bit rates might be defined as alternative levels.

20.5.1 *Internet Streaming Media Alliance Profiles*

The Internet Streaming Media Alliance (*ISMA*) defines some constraints on performance and bit-rate requirements to facilitate streaming services. Two profiles were published some time ago known as Profile 0 and Profile 1. At the beginning of 2005, the version 2.0 draft standard was released, which adds Profiles 2, 3 and 4.

There is a degree of compliance between ISMA and MPEG, for example. The MPEG standards are mapped to digital video broadcasting (DVB) and Digital Television Group (DTG) specifications and standards for television defined by the Advanced Television Systems Committee (*ATSC*) and the European Broadcasting Union (EBU). With the VC-1 codec under consideration, SMPTE should also be included. The version 2.0 ISMA standard further integrates the work with 3GP and DVD next-generation formats and provides more DVB harmonization.

Refer to Appendix H for technical details of the ISMA Profiles 0 to 4.

The previous version of the specification was 1.0.1, which also includes the version 1.0 Authentication and Encryption standard. A version 2.0 document has been released for comment and should be approved by the spring of 2005.

ISMA Web site: http://www.isma.tv/

20.5.2 MPEG-4 Fine Grain Scalable Profile

The MPEG-4 Fine Grain Scalable (FGS) profile is well suited to streaming situations because it is designed to be resilient to the way that available bit rate changes in capacity during a session. The available bit rate might decrease to almost nothing and then suddenly burst at full capacity again. The FGS profile allows the encoder to build a very low bit-rate foundation video stream and then deliver an optional enhancement layer. The minimal bit-rate situation allows the base level through but the enhancements can be discarded. Thus, a minimum level of performance is maintained while allowing better-quality video to be delivered when the bit rate is in plentiful supply again.

20.6 Multi-Stream Embedding and Multiplexing

The services delivered to the client user need to combine many separate streams of information. Figure 20-1 is a diagram showing the way that streams are nested together.

20.7 Streaming Servers

These are something of a commodity application now. Originally, there was a market for streaming servers that could generate significant revenue streams for a company. Real Networks made some useful capital from it in the 1990s. However, the free and subsidized Windows Media content servers mortally wounded this business model. The coup de grace was delivered by the open-source Darwin Streaming server. Real Networks responded by making the Helix project open source and hence freely available.

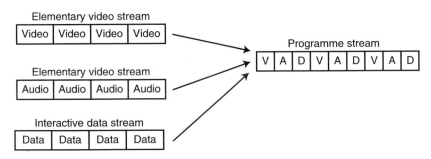

Figure 20-1 Packets and streams.

Darwin server: http://developer.apple.com/darwin/projects/streaming/

Darwin home page: http://developer.apple.com/darwin/

Helix server: https://helixcommunity.org/

Windows Media servers: http://www.microsoft.com/windows/windowsmedia/9series/server.aspx

QuickTime Streaming Server: http://www.apple.com/quicktime/products/qtss/

Live Channel streaming service: http://www.channelstorm.com/

20.7.1 *Managing the Risk by Buying a Service Instead of Running Your Own*

Other alternatives are available to purchase, and there is also a business model built by Akamai and Kasenna around the concept of a streaming service. They add significant value to the proposition because of their infrastructure. Refer to the discussion about edge servers in Section 20.12.

20.8 Areas of Difficulty and Streaming Tricks

Because the design of the Internet is not optimized to support streaming services, technology implementers need to be ever more inventive when trying to extract the maximum performance from the available network capacity.

20.8.1 *Hinting*

Hinting is a process that is applied to files after they have been compressed. It adds time-coded annotations on a separate track, which the streaming server can use to optimize its performance.

There are several common hinting mechanisms described by standards bodies as well as proprietary schemes developed by manufacturers:

You should consult your streaming-server documentation to find out what kind of hinting is required and how to include it in your files. The open standards are likely to be more widely supported, and products such as the Popwire encoders will insert the non-proprietary hints as part of the compression process.

20.8.2 *Buffering*

Because of the generally unreliable way that packets arrive across the Internet with respect to their sequencing and timeliness, streaming players will buffer a certain amount of

Table 20-1 Hinting Strategies

Format	Status
IETF	Open standard
ISMA	Open standard
3GPP	Open standard
QuickTime	Proprietary
Real Networks	Proprietary
Windows Media	Proprietary

Vara Wirecast: http://www.varasoftware.com/

content before commencing the playback. The player observes the packets arriving from the server and is able to calculate the amount of buffering required. The QuickTime plug-in, for example, will wait until it has buffered sufficient material so that when it commences playback, it has a reasonable chance of continuing through the movie without pausing to buffer more content. This is very necessary with low-bit-rate networks or high-bit-rate content. If the two are carefully adjusted to match, then optimum conditions are created for minimum buffering.

The user may request that the player jump forwards in the buffer to a point beyond what has been delivered. The RTSP streaming interface will go to that new location and begin buffering from that point. However, progressive downloading with HTTP doesn't support that kind of access. It is strictly linear.

20.8.3 Fast Start

Fast start is a QuickTime feature that allows a downloaded file to start playing before it is fully downloaded. This feature is called progressive downloading in other video players. When a browser requests a movie file using the HTTP protocol, the download does not have to be completed before playback begins. Previously the download and playback processes could only take place sequentially because the cached file could not be opened for playback while it was still being written. As long as the playback speed is equal to or less than the download speed for the content, fast start is a neat solution and plays the video in real time. See the discussion on buffering for what is required when download speeds are slower than playback speeds.

Another advantage of progressive HTTP-based streaming is that an ordinary Web server can serve the files. This saves you having to install and deploy an RTP or RTSP server.

The main disadvantage compared with streaming is that you cannot seek ahead and only the content that has already downloaded is playable.

20.8.4 Content Negotiation

Smart players will negotiate with the streaming server to establish the available bit rate for stream delivery. This is called content negotiation. The player requests a low bit rate (lower quality) stream if network faults or high traffic levels compromise the networking bandwidth. Sometimes this feature is called Sure Stream or Smart Stream.

20.8.5 Bandwidth

All of the advanced streaming techniques have evolved out of a need to deal with bandwidth issues. There is simply not enough bandwidth to deliver video and audio without carrying out some very complex compression and delivery management.

Since the beginning, innovations in the reduction of bandwidth required to deliver video and audio at quality worth watching have been matched by the telecoms' research into more efficient modulation techniques over a wiring system that was originally designed to deliver only limited speech service using a narrow band of analog frequencies.

It was only as recently as 1975 that figures of 1200-baud (approximately 1 Kbps) download and 75-baud upload were provided by British Telecom for the Prestel Teletex system. Since then, modem speeds have increased to 56 Kbaud. Dialup modems were displaced by ISDN services with dual 64-Kbps lines. Today, asymmetric DSL (*ADSL*) communicates down that same original analog copper wire, achieving speeds in the region of 500 Kbps. In optimal conditions, broadband connections deliver potentially as much as 8 Mbps to the home.

Coupling a 500-Kbps connection with the improvements in codec design that yield good-quality video at 800 Kbps brings us close to an interesting threshold. That critical point where TV can be delivered via broadband infrastructures is not very far off.

Table 20-2 illustrates some data rates to which content should be compressed when being delivered over various Internet connections.

20.8.6 Reach

With video that can be encoded at a lower bit rate and achieve the same quality, it is possible to reduce the footprint of that service on the cable connecting the subscriber's home to the exchange. This reduced bandwidth means that a usable signal can be delivered over a longer distance. Therefore, your signal reaches more people because the radius of your catchment circle is increased. Only people within your catchment circle can subscribe to your service. Therefore, making it bigger for little or no cost will improve your revenues without requiring you to massively re-engineer your infrastructure. In fact, for an increase in reach distance of 33%, your catchment expands by 44% due to the effects of πR^2, which is a very good return.

Table 20-2 Bit Rate for Encoding Based on Connection Type

Connection	Target encode bit rate
28 Kbaud modem	20 Kbps
56 Kbaud modem	32–28 Kbps
64 Kbps ISDN	40 Kbps
128 Kbps dual ISDN	80 Kbps
Corporate LAN	300 Kbps
UK Domestic Broadband (e.g., Demon Internet)	350–500 Kbps
Fast Home Broadband (e.g., Wanadoo)	1 Mbps

Wanadoo Broadband: http://www.wanadoo.co.uk/
Demon Internet: http://www.demon.net/

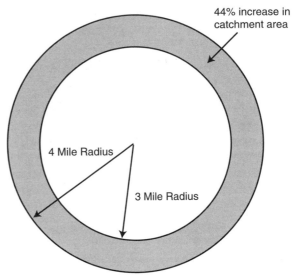

Figure 20-2 The effects of πR^2 on your catchment.

20.8.7 Buffering

When the movie is played back on a PC or TV set-top box, the player expects that the data will be made available in a timely manner. The output video runs on a timeline, and as long as the data is provided (at least as fast as that timeline is being traversed) then the playback experience will be smooth. Of course, the smoothness depends on the frame rate that was selected when the video was compressed, but in any case it should be continuous and consistent.

If you are streaming the video and cannot deliver the stream either continuously or at a fast enough rate, then some kind of buffering becomes necessary. Modern client players are smart enough to negotiate with the streaming server to select a content stream that is deliverable within the available physical bit rate. This bit rate is measured across the connection during the session, and the content can be negotiated up or down as the available bit rate changes.

The calculation may involve some computation based on the length of the video and should also take into account the buffering space available and the delivery speed. This yields a buffering time that loads perhaps 30 seconds of video before the playback commences. Figure 20-3 shows a partly loaded buffer where the playback has already commenced. The buffer must be filled with new material until the end of the transmission without the playback process catching up.

Once playback begins, the content continues to be delivered from the streaming server while the player uses the buffered bit stream from the other end. Ideally, the playback will just about catch up with the download at the end of the video.

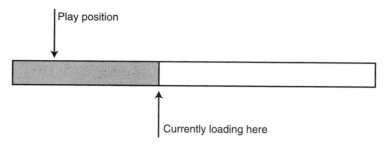

Figure 20-3 Buffering.

This is fine for short video clips such as trailers and advertisements but is not likely to yield a satisfactory experience for a movie. For a start, the buffer has to be much bigger and the buffering time much longer.

A DVR device with a hard-disk cache is an optimum solution here. The content is downloaded to the local hard disks so it can be played back from there.

This does not solve the immediate viewing-on-request of a movie but in a scenario where you are booking or selecting movies ahead of time it is a very good solution. For real-time, live viewing of a stream, the only solution is to reduce the bit rate and hence the quality of the video to that which can be delivered in real time over the available link.

QuickTime has some especially smart look-ahead computation built in to allow the auto play to calculate whether it is likely to catch the buffer loading. When the player is sure that it can play all the way to the end of the clip uninterrupted, the movie begins playing. This assumes that nothing interrupts the delivery or substantially slows down the buffer loading in the meantime. A "lumpy" network would cause this technique some problems. We describe a network as being "lumpy" when the throughput changes unpredictably and suddenly. Imagine a garden hose with a mixture of water and mud being delivered under pressure. Each clod of mud causes a momentary blockage that then clears and lets the hose run freely again for a while.

20.8.8 Rebuffering

The session may go into rebuffering mode when you are viewing streamed video on a very congested network. That congestion may be anywhere in the route between you and the target server you are streaming from. It is most likely to be in your local network or your connection to the Internet, which is often through a single "pipe," or proxy server. That connection can easily be overwhelmed by the traffic demands in large corporate networks.

So your player may be happily chomping its way through the incoming data while the connection handler that is receiving packets from the remote stream server constantly refreshes the buffer. Then something interrupts or slows down the traffic. Before your player is able to negotiate a lower bit rate, your buffer is exhausted and the player cannot proceed until you have rebuffered.

This is one of the most frustrating experiences for a viewer, possibly only exceeded by getting disconnected when too many people try and reach the same streaming server and it runs out of available connections.

20.8.9 Delayed Packets

The client player may receive an occasional delayed packet. If the session is using TCP, you may observe the effects on the player window. If it indicates the play position and the amount of buffered video, the playback indicator continues to move while it is within the buffered content, but the buffering indicator will not stay ahead of the playback indicator.

> Note: The playback indicator is sometimes referred to in the documentation as the play head. This is a throwback to the old analog recording tape days when the tape passed over the play head on the tape deck.

20.8.10 Joining a Stream Partway Through

One of the things that a streamer and client have to cope with is when a user joins a live stream part of the way through. This is a very similar problem to when you tune a digital TV set to another channel.

Step 1 is to acquire the transport stream and synchronize with that so that the client is framing the data correctly and is then able to unpack the various program streams.

Step 2 is to locate the desired program stream and synchronize to that in order to locate the beginning of a segment so that the elementary streams can be unpacked.

Step 3 is to extract and reassemble the audio and video streams and locate suitable starting points where the viewing experience is reconstructed. For audio this tends to be quite straightforward since it is a much simpler protocol. For video the codec must be determined, initialized, and an I-frame acquired before decoding commences.

All of this takes some time and explains why it changing channels on digital services and streamed internet AV seems less responsive than on the older analog solutions.

20.8.11 Too Many Users

Although it is a nice problem to have, when your service becomes very popular and the whole world hits your servers you may run out of licenses. This tends to happen to people who stream major sports events through a single Real Networks streaming server, for example. That is not to imply there is anything wrong with a Real Networks server, but one pricing model is based around a licensed number of simultaneous user streams.

So when you purchase a license for a streaming server from Real Networks or anyone else, you should check out the licensing model and ensure that you purchase enough streams. This model becomes expensive very quickly. Above a certain level (you will have to calculate that based on the terms you are offered) you may prefer to base the license on a number of CPUs.

With an open-source streaming server, the licensing issue may be less of a problem. But there you run into a capacity problem. Soon, your traffic levels exceed the bandwidth that you have purchased from your ISP. You may have a very happy relationship with your ISP, and as long as they are warned in advance, they may allow your service to burst to multiples of your normal total outgoing bit rate and not charge you a great deal of money. On the other hand, they might require that you purchase additional bandwidth to cover the expected overload. Be careful not to purchase a service level that has capacity for your high-traffic times when the average traffic levels never reach this most of the time. If your traffic is "bursty," it's a good idea to work out a deal based on bandwidth actually used rather than budgeted capacity that may be underutilized.

20.9   Streaming to Large Audiences

Distributing video to large numbers of people over broadband connections is growing very quickly as an industry. Now that codecs are efficient enough to deliver good-quality video at about 1.2 Mbps and reasonable quality at 800 Kbps, broadband comes into its own. That is not to say that broadcast TV will ever go away. Broadcasting has some compelling advantages compared with the uni-casting approach of a streaming service, such as the way you can broadcast just one copy of a program and everyone receive it at once. Building video-on-demand services with a broadcasting system that lacks a return path and only has one outgoing stream is impossible. Some interactive, multi-stream services have been rolled out and are successful, but that isn't truly video on demand.

20.9.1   Uni-Casting

Uni-casting is a technique in which a client makes a connection to a media streaming service and the server delivers an individualized bit stream. This is how Internet video streaming used to be done in the very earliest implementations, and it is truly a video-on-demand model. You get exactly the content you requested, and you have it delivered at the time you request it. Someone else may request that same content only a second later, or even at the same time, but he or she will get a separate and individually delivered bit stream with no relationship to yours. The uni-casting model is illustrated in Figure 20-4.

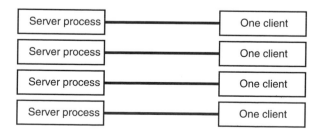

Figure 20-4 Uni-casting model.

There are very few opportunities at the server end to make this more efficient. Some servers will cache the content so that, when it is requested again, it can be delivered from local memory rather than from hard disks. This model is used in edge-server architectures.

20.9.2 *Multicasting*

The technique of multicasting has been developed over the last few years to provide a way to deliver the same stream to many users at once. This brings the benefits of the broadcasting model, where everyone receives the same content even though the loading on the master server is just one stream. With a combination of the multicasting and uni-casting models, you achieve the ideal situation, where you can serve video on demand but also gain efficiencies through shared streams when the opportunity presents itself.

The multicasting model is illustrated in Figure 20-5. It is more efficient than the uni-casting model.

20.10 Implications for Codec Choice

A DV file is already somewhat compressed but not enough to stream it to a desktop. There are two commonly used bit rates for DV files in broadcast studios. DV50 runs at 50 Mbps. DV25 is compressed to half that but the compression is fairly light and you cannot see the artifacts. But this is not compressed enough for deployment to the public. A more compact format must be used. Your application determines what compression trade-offs you make. If you share video during the production process and need to synchronize accurately for edits and audio dubbing, then you must ensure there are no dropped frames. You may be able to tolerate some picture degradation, however.

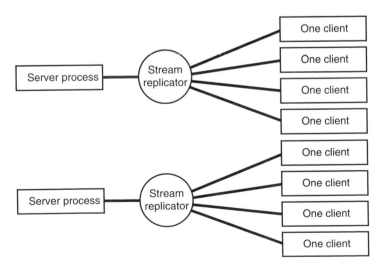

Figure 20-5 Multicasting model.

This is a problem that Pixar encountered in its workflow. Apple introduced a new QuickTime codec they had developed to deal with the issue. The new codec is called Pixlet, which is a contraction of "Pixar wavelet." The Pixlet compression is somewhat like a motion JPEG file because it only codes I-frames. Pixlet is designed to compress efficiently but without dropped frames and with no visible artifacts at all. This yields sufficient compression to get the bit rate down to about 1 Mbps. At that scale, the video can be played across the network with no dropped frames. This is sufficient to be able to post-sync the sound, for example.

The Pixlet codec now ships as a standard component in QuickTime (version 6.4), which is an integral part of the Mac OS X 10.3 (Panther) release.

20.11   Very-High-Performance Solutions

Some important work is being done by companies such as Kasenna and Akamai in the area of distributing the streaming servers out to the edge of the Internet. Kasenna in particular has some very interesting ideas, and, as a member of the Internet Streaming Media Alliance, (ISMA) is clearly committed to making this work with open standards. You can choose proprietary standards and stream them through the Kasenna architecture as well.

20.12   Edge Servers

A major problem with serving content across the Internet is the long distance between the client and the server. The distances are large in geographical terms but also in logical terms. The signals have to travel a long way though the wires, and the logical connectivity describes the number of different sub-networks and routers that are involved in the connection. Recall that these are called "hops."

Kasenna and Akamai have worked hard to address this problem. Although they both deploy edge servers, the way each company connects them to the central repository is slightly different.

An edge server is a CPU that is placed near the end user's connection, close to the edge of the Internet. This reduces the distances involved, both physically and logically. As a consequence, the service enjoys reduced latency. Locally cached content is delivered more rapidly and responsively. This works especially well for streamed content and for very high-traffic loadings when serving static content. It divides the audience into smaller communities and avoids everyone in the world hitting your server at once. This model is illustrated in Figure 20-6.

Because there are many edge servers involved, the loading is spread across more machines and distributed over a wider part of the Internet. Multiple connections become effectively aggregated into a single request from the edge server back to the central repository, and in many ways it looks like a proxy server connected in the reverse direction.

Kasenna and Akamai have solved replication of streams and delivery of content, and some very innovative work is being done to enable broadband services to make full use of

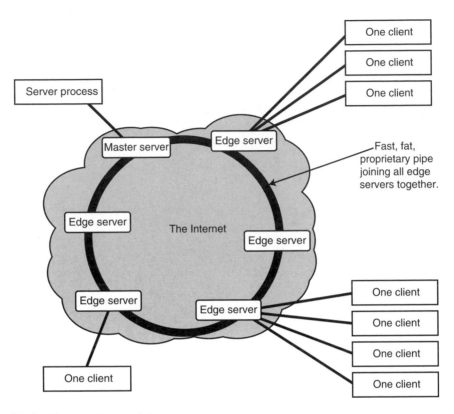

Figure 20-6 Edge-serving model.

streamed content. These are the two principal companies that provide this capability. They operate with slightly different emphases, and you may find that one or the other fits your requirements better.

20.12.1 *Akamai*

Akamai has developed a very large infrastructure around the world. Some thousands of Akamai servers have been deployed into the data centers run by the various ISP companies. Akamai has then connected all of its machines together with its own private network that runs extremely quickly. Because it is Akamai's own network, it controls all of the traffic and essentially has encircled the globe and connected its servers to a very large and fast ring.

As soon as an end user hits an Akamai server for a file or stream, that edge server checks the local repository; if the file does not exist, it requests a copy from the central store. This is delivered so quickly that it does not hold up the download to the end user whose connection is running much slower. That content may then be cached there for a while on the grounds that it is likely to be needed again soon by another user.

Following the terrorist attack on the World Trade Center in New York, all the news-based Web sites found that their serving capacity was exceeded by orders of magnitude. As a consequence, some of them now have an arrangement with Akamai to deliver their sites through the edge servers at times of extremely high traffic. This has proven to be a very good solution to providing Web-based coverage of other major events, such as the Olympic games, other international sporting events, and the wars in Afghanistan and Iraq.

So the strategic opportunity that Akamai is exploiting is a service-based offering. You can rent capacity from them when demand for your content exceeds your ability to serve it.

20.12.2 Kasenna

Kasenna operates in a different way from Akamai. The company is interested in selling a solution for you to deploy. You buy the hardware and software from Kasenna and run your own installation. This is not the same as the service model that Akamai promotes. Typical applications for Kasenna systems are major TV services to local community areas, corporate organizations, campus TV systems, and distribution of pay-per-view services within a condominium.

Kasenna also provides an interesting technical solution that pre-caches just the first part of a large file on the edge servers. This is immediately delivered to the user as soon as the user connects while the back end requests the remainder of the file from a central repository.

This has the advantage of making all of the content seem to be available immediate at all of the edge servers without the need to replicate the entire archive and install massive disk stores everywhere.

20.12.3 Which Edge Server Should You Choose?

If the content is not already fully cached in your nearest edge server, Kasenna's performance might be slightly better in terms of an "instantly on" start-up of a video-on-demand stream when compared with Akamai. The Akamai solution is popular, reliable, and it serves a large number of users simultaneously and efficiently from the same source by virtue of the major back-end network support.

If you have a large number of users in several locations, you might even benefit from a hybrid approach in which multiple Kasenna networks are set up with central repositories but are connected to a central publishing system via the Akamai network. This might seem expensive as an approach right now, but if the current trend for delivering TV services through the Internet continues to expand, some kind of major architectural shift will need to happen because the TV viewing audience is far larger than the Web-browsing audience. The bandwidth requirements are also magnified for delivery of a predominantly streamed video experience rather than a few pages of text and graphics to each viewer.

20.13   **International Webcasting Association**

Although not a standards body, the International Webcasting Association (IWA) provides a forum for a number of companies who are involved in webcasting to collaborate and ensure that their services are interoperable. They exist to promote streaming on the Internet and other networks, and they operate a mailing list to inform subscribers of news and announcements.

Television services are beginning to be delivered over broadband connections with an IP protocol. This format is sometimes called IPTV. As IPTV becomes more popular, the IWA may be a useful place to start your enquiries when trying to locate webcasting companies.

20.14   **Summary: Now I Know About Streaming**

We have now looked at the implications of streaming servers—the implications of low and high traffic levels and the underlying technologies that streaming depends on.

Of course, a stream needs to be played back to a user's TV or PC screen unless it is being recorded to hard disk. That means a stream player is required. But which one shall we use? In the next chapter we'll assess some possibilities and find out about the players that are available.

International Webcasting Association (IWA): http://www.webcasters.org/

21   *Players and Platforms*

21.1   Any Color You Like, as Long as It's Black

We might like to think we have a lot of choice about which format to use, but in actual fact that choice is quite limited. Mostly we are limited by the platforms we choose to operate.

21.2   *De Facto* Playback Standards

Until now, streaming has been dominated by several *de facto* standards. They have been important in generating interest and penetrating the consciousness of the buying public. The different formats are proprietary. Some of the major proprietary formats are developed by companies whose primary interest is something other than video compression, save one – *Real Networks*. The availability of the formats on operating system platforms is subject to commercial decisions that are dictated by platform dominance and market share. Generally speaking, *de facto* standards cannot deliver on a promise of 100% market penetration, since they are limited by the market penetration of their hosting platforms.

    For example, QuickTime is unavailable on Linux. To choose QuickTime as a streaming solution facilitates delivery to Mac OS and Windows users, but you cannot reach any users who operate the Linux platform. The same argument applies to Windows Media (WM).

    The Real Networks video format is widely available. The user experience is less satisfactory on some platforms and the latest version of the player is not available everywhere. This is true of Windows Media players as well. QuickTime releases are better synchronized for delivery on Windows and Mac OS, but the user experience is compromised on Windows when other media players are installed.

21.3   Choosing Players and Codecs

Some service operators will choose WM9 on the grounds of market share. The Windows platform is allegedly used by 97% of the world's population. The player is installed with the operating system, making it a good format to choose. This argument was called into question by the Frost & Sullivan findings that Windows Media and QuickTime have a roughly equal share while Real Networks trails some distance behind. But none of them has anything approaching a 97% installed base.

There are no reliable statistics on what people actually have installed. The arguments are also unreliable, because market share figures and installed base are not the same. So, many of the assumptions are simply not reliable enough to state authoritatively that most people use a particular player and codec. There is no substitute for doing your own research and surveying your target user base properly.

21.3.1 Performance

Codecs of a similar vintage will generally deliver about the same performance under optimum conditions. Note the word "generally" and the word "vintage." MPEG-2 is clearly not going to deliver similar performance to H.264 and WM9. But WM9 and H.264 are reasonably similar in performance. There are some minor differences between them, and there will be compression tools that are available only for one or the other. But you will be able to put HDTV onto a DVD disk with either codec, and you can compress SDTV for around 1.2 to 1.5 Mbps.

21.3.2 Choosing Open Standards

A good strategy is to look at an open-standards approach. Your preferred player may support some open standards anyway, so if the player is the overriding technology selection criterion, opting to use an open-standard video codec rather than the proprietary one may be a good compromise. An example of this might be to select the QuickTime player but elect to deliver H.264 video. Of course, that is oversimplifying things, and you must ensure that the profile and levels are compliant as well.

 Open standards imply choice of suppliers for each part of the end-to-end process, and therefore they prevent lock-in.

Because you are using open-standard video codecs, you don't have to purchase your encoder from the same company as you did the player. This allows you to test a range of encoders to see which one produces the best quality for the smallest file (for downloads) or lowest bit rate (for transmission/streaming). As long as the profiles and levels selected are standards-compliant and your player copes with them, you will gain some strategic advantages. Components within your system can be replaced with alternatives as new and higher-performance versions are delivered, and you will completely avoid the lock-in associated with a proprietary solution.

21.3.3   *Portability and Compliance*

In the end, compliance with standards leads to better portability and less lock-in to a proprietary set of products. Portability is a very desirable thing from the perspective of broadcasters and content providers. The analogy about not having to buy a different TV set to view each channel is often rolled out to support this argument and is profoundly true. The world of broadcasting would not have become such a huge industry if not all TV receivers were immediately compatible with the broadcast service regardless of the manufacturer.

The owners of proprietary systems imagine that somehow they can achieve that 100% total market penetration. This is a vain hope. There will always be some detractors who will choose not to buy into a platform simply because it is the dominant one.

It is important to realize that "never" is a very big and difficult word for proprietary player manufacturers. They might say today that their player will "never" play some particular open format or be available on operating system X. Two years later this could change completely. Be wary, though, because support is withdrawn just as easily as it is given.

21.4   Computing Platforms

The platform describes the computer type or the genre of device that the video is being played on. Including the computer operating systems in this category is sensible because they are indeed platforms and each supports a very different combination of video playback systems.

21.4.1   *Microsoft Windows–Based Computers*

There is no argument that currently the most popular operating system is Windows (in all its flavors and variants). Viable player choices for this platform are Windows Media, RealNetworks, and QuickTime, all of which work acceptably well. There is a range of open-source players that work very well on the Windows platform if you want to use other formats.

Unless you particularly want to use another proprietary solution or you have a preference for an open-source player, it is a very easy choice to go for Windows Media Player and the Series 9 codec. For a Windows-only scenario, this is the best choice. It locks you in to Microsoft from one end to the other, but if you are deploying to a large network of Windows machines, you are already committed to Microsoft and this will not significantly affect the risk factors.

21.4.2   *Apple Mac OS–Based Computers*

The optimum choice for Mac OS users is QuickTime. Because Apple engineers QuickTime as part of the overall platform experience, the level of integration with the operating system is excellent. QuickTime performs at its best on the Mac OS platform.

The Windows Media Player is also available on this operating system but tends to lag behind the Windows version somewhat and often lacks a few features that the other has. In particular, the Microsoft advanced video codec is not supported by Windows Media Player on Mac OS. Windows Media is probably not the best choice for Mac OS–based applications. The Real Networks player used to be well supported on the Mac OS Classic operating system, but the support on Mac OS X has been less robust. Recently, however, the support for Mac OS is improving dramatically; coding Real media is now possible due to the release of a Real Networks codec plug-in that works with QuickTime.

You still have the option of going for the open-source solutions if you choose. In some cases, the codecs are made available as QuickTime-compatible plug-ins, which is a good way to go when using the Mac OS platform. Telestream took this approach when they introduced a Windows Media codec for the Macintosh (called Flip4Mac).

21.4.3 Linux

Historically, Apple has been reluctant to port QuickTime to Linux. This is probably because Linux could be seen as a competitor to Mac OS X since they are both variations of UNIX. Likewise, Microsoft has been reluctant to port Windows Media Player to Linux because it would cut into Windows sales. Fortunately, the open source MPlayer provides some solutions, and there is no shortage of people working on the Linux platform creating applications to play video.

A variety of video players have been implemented on this operating system. Indeed, the TiVo DVR units are implemented on a Linux-based operating system. You may need to upgrade your kernel to support real-time video playback. Some open-source kernel modifications were posted on the TiVo Web site in 2003 and should still be available there if you need access to this level of support. The optimum choice for Linux is to go for an open-source solution.

Note that some devices are called personal video recorders (PVRs), a category that includes all digital and analog devices. Many newer units are being referred to as DVRs, which may mean "digital video recorder" or "direct video recorder" depending on whose marketing hype you are reading. This digital recording may be a digitized analog TV service (classic TiVo style) or a recording of the digital bit stream (ElGato EyeTV). The recording of a digital service is going to be of a better overall quality.

21.4.4 JavaTV

Sun Microsystems' JavaTV is poised to offer the same cross-platform advantages to interactive TV services as it did to computer platforms. This is attractive inasmuch as the development programming skills for JavaTV will not be as scarce as those required for OpenTV, for example.

TiVo kernel patches: http://www.tivo.com/linux/linux.asp

Library code has been developed to integrate the so-called Xlets with the transport stream, which is represented as a collection of objects.

Further support is provided for tunnelling an IP stream within the video transport mechanism to provide data services over and above those already described by the DVB specifications.

21.4.5   Set-Top Boxes

As mentioned above, the TiVo DVR units are built on Linux and implement video encoding/decoding in a very neat package. There is a community of users who upgrade the TiVo unit to store much more video, and this does tend to put the user interface under some pressure since it was originally designed around a small disk store that might hold a few dozen programs. Upgrading the disk on a series 1 TiVo to a 240-hour capacity challenges the way that the TiVo interacts with the user through the user interface (UI), which is what the application draws on the screen for you to interact with. With a large 240-hour video store, this will have to manage hundreds of programs.

Other set-top box systems are gaining in popularity, such as the circa 2000 Convergent design and Linux TV, which is a contemporary design for integration into your own original equipment manufacturer (OEM) system. An OEM will buy kits of parts, component software modules, or unbranded systems and will add some value by integrating them in a unique way before shipping them as their own product—in fact, an OEM probably manufactured the computer you have sitting on your desk

The DirecTV and Sky+ units also provide video-storage capabilities. In the case of the Sky+ unit, there is no need to code the video because it is just storing what it extracts from the digital bit stream delivered from the satellite transponder.

During 2003–04 there was a significant increase in the number of boxes offering IPTV delivery over broadband connection, and as of spring 2004, the H.264 video codec is growing quickly in popularity. Microsoft is also very keen to develop other product offerings in this area.

21.4.6   PDA Devices

The main contender here is the Kinoma video format, but it is likely that H.264 will rapidly gain in popularity. The principal operating systems in this marketplace are Windows Mobile and the Palm operating system. The most video-oriented devices are probably the Sony CLIÉ models, but Sony has discontinued these in markets outside of Japan. PDA devices are rapidly converging with cameras and phones. All of these AV capabilities are being squashed into a box that is roughly the size of a pack of cigarettes.

Kinoma: http://www.kinoma.com/

21.4.7 Mobile Phones

The H.264 standard was explicitly designed for delivery on mobile phones. Some experiments with H.26L codecs took place in the United Kingdom in 2002–03 to prove that video could be delivered to mobile phones known as *2.5G* devices. Now that the 3G devices are rolling out, video is becoming an important selling point for the new handsets. This is attracting subscribers to those providers who deliver video alongside the other voice and data services.

21.5 Players

Let's look at the part of the equation involving the players. When compared to each other, they have some similarities and also some important differences.

 Note that some players may not implement all of the decoding they could. The standards may describe a minimal level of decoding, but more sophisticated players and decoders may work harder to display a better-looking picture. If you think your encoding is set up correctly but you still see artifacts on one player, test the content on several others, if you can, to see if it is a player issue rather than an encoder issue.

There are fashionable trends that come and go, and it is currently a popular design gambit to style the players as if they were made of brushed aluminium. Changing the appearance of the players or reducing them to just a video window is easy to do. Embellishing them with your own borders and controls is also a popular pastime for video enthusiasts. They call this 'skinning,' and the product is called a 'skin.'

Examine the technology that supports this appearance-tuning support in your player. It is far more useful to deliver this appearance code with the content rather than load it as a property of the player. Players implement support for this in different ways. By the way, this decorative matter is sometimes referred to as "window chrome"—a term that was probably derived from the material on 1950s automobiles.

There are four players in common use today:

- Apple QuickTime
- RealNetworks
- Microsoft Windows Media
- *Macromedia Flash*

Of the first three, each is covered in a chapter of its own following this one, while Flash is covered in Chapter 25 together with some other alternatives.

21.5.1 Open Standards

The trend seems to be for players to move toward the support of open-standards content formats. If this continues, they will lose some hold on the customer base since the proprietary lock-in is no longer in force. This is good news for the service providers, because they can deploy the best products for the task at hand—for example, Windows Media production tools running on Intel hardware or QuickTime tools running on Mac OS X feeding content to a Helix or Darwin server running on Linux or Solaris. In the long term, the market should find its own level, based on the suitability and quality of the tools, if the customer is allowed to choose the most fit-for-purpose products and integrate them into a systematic workflow.

The open-standards support is good for consumers because they are able to use the player of their choice. It would be ludicrous to mandate that consumers must watch a particular TV channel on one manufacturer's TV. The parallels are very similar, and many online video providers are forcing users to make exactly that choice. Proprietary formats are not well enough supported by the competing players, so there is an opportunity to solve that problem by using open standards.

There are some robust, emerging open standards for multimedia and some very advanced video coding technologies available as open standards. Let's examine how that might look from the standpoint of the three major companies and the Linux operating system with prior *de facto* standards that might be threatened.

The most encouraging possibility is that all three dominant players and those whose market share is minuscule by comparison appear to be willing to embrace the open standards. It is anticipated that the H.264 standard will be supported widely. If that happens, you will have a better chance of reaching viewers on all platforms regardless of the player or platform they choose.

21.5.2 Postprocessing in the Player

De-blocking filters are the most common postprocessing operation that the player applies to the decoded output. This is designed to hide the edges of the macroblocks when extreme compression ratios are used.

Some codecs just allow the player to apply de-blocking blindly and whenever they feel like it. There is no finesse to this approach because it is just a blurring operation.

More recent and advanced codec designs insert de-blocking hints into the file to assist with the de-blocking process at the decoding stage. The hints are worked out based on the errors and residuals in the encoded input.

In addition to de-blocking, some decoders support a de-ringing or de-fringing of edge artifacts. These get introduced by the DCT transform. They may be there in the first place because too much sharpening was applied when the video was scanned on the Telecine unit. Refer to the chapters on video formats and quality issues, as well as the practical encoding discussion in Chapters 31 to 38. If the image quality is rubbish to start with, it will be impossible to fix it up at the decoding stage with some trivial post-processing.

Frame rate interpolation at the decoder is only supported by the Real Networks player. Apparently no other players do this. These postprocessing tasks are executed subject to the availability of sufficient CPU power remaining after the decoding process. If there is insufficient capacity, these processes will be skipped regardless of hinting or configuration parameters.

21.5.3 *Advertising-Supported and Ad-Free Players*

When you buy a client player you will be offered a variety of different deals. Some of them give you a reduced feature set but a free player. Others will give you more features but at the expense of surrounding the video playback area with ads. In a few cases, you will be presented with interstitial ads before playing a clip.

Some content providers object to the placement of advertising material immediately prior to or after their content. There is also the added complication of ensuring that the ads comply with advertising standards that pertain in the territory where the content is being viewed. These may be far more strict than those imposed where the content is created or broadcast from.

You have to do a lot of work to your transmission systems to ensure that advertisements are targeted culturally, territorially, and to a relevant audience at the point of consumption. If the ads are part of the program material, this may not be as difficult, but if the ads are served independently and are displayed under control of the client player it becomes more complex to administer.

21.6 The Main Players' Market Share

Of course, figures produced by any of the three player manufacturers must be weighed very carefully, but it is possible that there are even more copies deployed than even Apple is claiming since they are only backing their statements with statistics measured by logging the number of downloads.

Frost & Sullivan published statistics during the early part of 2004 that indicated QuickTime and Microsoft Windows Media were at almost identical market penetration, with Real Networks trailing some distance behind. A commentator remarked that the two leading platforms were nearly equal and that Apple was poised to take advantage of any opportunity for growth that presented itself.

I am inclined to believe figures published independently like this more than those published by the manufacturers themselves.

The introduction of the MacMini at MacWorld 2005 with the new upgraded iLife 2005 software suite certainly demonstrated that Apple is seriously interested in serving a wider customer base. Every single one of the computers Apple markets comes with some very-high-quality software that is ready to edit and compress video right out of the box.

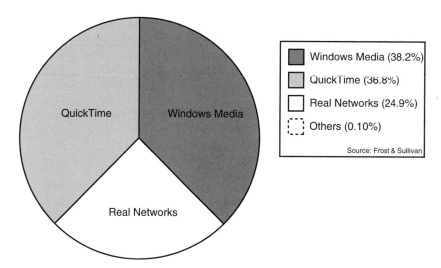

Figure 21-1 The main players' relative market shares, spring 2004.

21.7 So Many Players to Choose From

No single player or technique will solve all of your deployment problems. There is a variety of factors that will affect your strategy and choice.

Which is the best one to choose? Well, you will have to decide. There are continuing arguments on the World Wide Web about whose codec is better. Some say that Windows Media is best. Others say that H.264 is better. But the truth is, none of the codecs is best in all situations. Windows Media is adequate for many deployments, but your reasons for choosing it will more likely be due to your preference for the Windows platform or the way it ties in with an existing information technology strategy. H.264 is a good choice for consumer-oriented services because it is an open standard and should in theory work on a far wider range of platforms and devices. In strict terms of video quality, it depends on how smart the encoding operator is and how well suited the encoder is to the content being compressed. It is possible to work out demonstration cases to prove that any one of the mainstream codecs is the best performer.

Judging from interviews with several implementers, there is a consensus that the computational workload for decoding appears to be slightly less for H.264 than for Windows Media, and the market seems to be leaning towards the adoption of H.264 in preference to Windows Media.

In the next few chapters we will look in detail at the three main players and then consider some alternatives.

Windows Media 22

22.1 Why Choose Windows Media?

If your target audience is entirely Windows based, then it is a very easy decision to go with this player. It will deliver everything you want to do if you are deploying a video-led service or implementing something that integrates with the media center products.

22.2 WM10

If you predominantly use Windows-based machines in your organization and you are sure that your end users also use them, then Windows Media is a good choice. Microsoft goes to great lengths to ensure that the media player is available when you install the OS and that the performance is as good as possible.

There are commercial downsides to using Windows Media, but the upsides in a controlled and closed Windows-based environment probably outweigh the benefits of choosing another platform. I will make exactly the same argument for using QuickTime-based video delivery if your organization is built around a Macintosh desktop deployment strategy.

WM10 is released as a public beta trial for the Windows platform only. It introduces a new player and some upgrades to the codec support but no radically new coding engine or algorithms. There are other new features related to the Microsoft music store and some DRM changes. Also, there is a more advanced Series 9 encoder that supports interlaced video. It provides more sophisticated support for building media applications around the SDK as well as a lot of support for audio, play lists, and the new online music store service. Additional support for transporting WM9 content on other systems such as broadcast networks and DVD players is also introduced.

Windows Media home: http://www.microsoft.com/windows/windowsmedia/default.aspx

Table 22-1 Windows Media Coding Performance

Type	Format	Codec	Bit rate (min)	Bit rate (max)
Vision	720 × 480 × 24p movie	WMV Pro 9	1.3 Mbps	2 Mbps
Vision	720 × 480 × 30i video	WMV Pro 9	2 Mbps	4 Mbps
Vision	1280 × 720 × 24p HDTV	WMV Pro 9	5 Mbps	8 Mbps
Sound	2 channels, 20 bits sampled at 48 KHz	WMA Pro 9	128 Kbps	128 Kbps
Sound	6 channels, 20 bits sampled at 48 KHz	WMA Pro 9	192 Kbps	256 Kbps
Sound	6 channels, 24 bits sampled at 48 KHz.	WMA Pro 9	768 Kbps	768 Kbps

22.3 Performance

The performance of the Windows Media coding is optimized for the kind of media you would use in a home entertainment system. Table 22-1 summarizes some bit rates taken from Microsoft publicity material. The video and audio bit rates are specified separately, so you should combine them depending on the service you are offering.

Running some compression tests suggests that these figures are optimistic.

The sweet spot for this coding technology is in the high-end broadband video market. Compression times increase dramatically as image resolutions get higher, and significant hardware support is required to attain any performance at HD quality. Interlaced video is not well supported as far as compression algorithms are concerned, and standard–definition, broadcast-quality TV is difficult to compress in real time without the assistance of expensive dedicated hardware.

Reducing the picture size, selecting progressive frame display rather than interlaced, and lowering the quality threshold will not ruin your project; if you use a broadband network or corporate LAN, you can take these steps and still get very good results at reasonable bit rates.

22.4 The Player

Like Real Networks and QuickTime, the player appearance is flexible enough to allow you to add your own branding to the browsing experience. This is now a feature of most players. There are examples of different skins at the Microsoft Windows Media web site. Figure 22-1 shows the media player 10 in the default state as it appears on the Windows platform.

The player integrates a lot of audio support similar to that found in the Apple iTunes application. Play lists and access to the Microsoft music store are prominent additions. The UI also manages the library of video clips as well as audio.

The Series 10 player is not supported on Mac OS X right now, so your viewing experience continues to be with the Series 9 player shown in Figure 22-2.

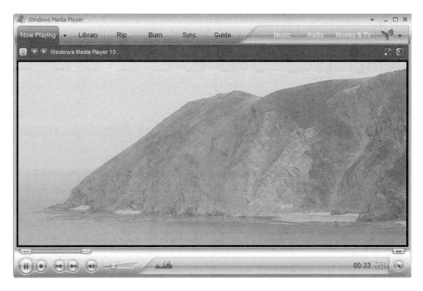

Figure 22-1 Windows Media Player Series 10 on Windows.

Figure 22-2 Windows Media Player Series 9 on Mac OS.

22.5   Digital Rights Management

An area where Windows Media excels over all the other platforms is in digital rights management (DRM). This is probably its most significant capability and the thing that endears it to Hollywood and the TV companies, because they would like to control exactly how the browsing and viewing experience is made available to the end user. Creating scenarios where you can make content playable only for a specific time is where Windows Media outshines the other players. These are the scenarios that Microsoft points out in the DRM documentation:

- Direct license acquisition
- Indirect license acquisition
- Subscription services
- Purchase and download single audio tracks
- Video and audio rental services
- Video-on-demand
- Pay-per-view

DRM is a probably another significant reason why you would adopt this technology. It is available to some extent on QuickTime (as evidenced by the FairPlay DRM implemented in iTunes). Real Networks provides rights management on the basis of access control to the content. However, that rights control evaporates once the content has been downloaded and stored locally.

The Microsoft model depends on the player's being able to check back with the rights owner for permission to play. This is an area of concern for privacy advocates and civil liberties groups, but the important thing is that it works and is available now. The rights-access control need not be a Microsoft-provided service—for example, the Lysis DRM server is an example of how third-party suppliers are getting involved with DRM.

22.6   Adding Multimedia Support

Windows Media is less capable on its own than Real Networks when it comes to adding multimedia capabilities to the content. The QuickTime and MPEG-4 platforms are far beyond what either Windows Media or Real offers in non-video support.

22.6.1   Multimedia Plug-Ins

The Envivio TV plug-in works with the player to deliver MPEG-4 systems-layer interactivity. Other plug-ins, such as Anark, provide 2D and 3D capabilities within the context of the media player. Anark is also available for the Mac OS, and if you prefer another alternative, you should consider the AXEL modeler from Mind Avenue.

This approach to providing functionality via plug-ins is a good way to open up the architecture to third parties. Theoretically, any kind of media can be added to Windows Media. The infrastructure is less sophisticated in the management of multimedia objects and QuickTime is still an optimum platform for this kind of thing.

The other downside to delivering multimedia experiences within Windows Media Player is that you need to integrate playback mechanisms from a variety of manufacturers, and while you might know that your audience has the Windows Media Player installed, it is much harder to predict whether they have the extension plug-ins available and working.

22.6.2 HTML-Based Multimedia

Windows Media does support some synchronized HTML presentations. For example, you can embed the video in an HTML page. This allows for some of the combined video and HTML tricks that you might have done with the Real Networks video player, as well as for use of the embedded event model, which *triggers* URLs to the web browser. However, you would implement them differently on Windows Media Player. Another alternative is to embed some HTML content inside the Windows Media Player. By use of this approach, a more coherent user experience is possible.

22.6.3 Multimedia Packaging Mechanisms

Windows Media does support a packaging mechanism wherein a Windows Media Download (WMD) package file is downloaded to the local client and then unpacked so that the assets are distributed around your file system as needed. With this approach, delivery is accomplished to the Windows Media player with a single download.

This solution is inferior to the packaging provided by the MPEG-4 Part 1 systems layer and wired QuickTime movies. They both maintain the object collection within the packaged files, and the package remains intact when being played back. There is a potential security issue with Windows Media delivering arbitrary files in video packages and then strewing them around your hard disk under someone else's guidance. Very tight controls should be exercised over who is able to arbitrate where those files should be placed and what they may contain.

22.7 Supported Codecs

Apart from the older Series 7 and 8 codecs, the following Series 9 codecs are provided as part of the Series 9/10 support:

- Windows Media Video 9
- Windows Media Video 9 Advanced Profile
- Windows Media Video 9 Screen
- Windows Media Video 9 Image
- Windows Media Video 9 Image Version 2

22.8 Support for Other Formats

Windows Media Player used to support the `.ra`, `.rm`, and `.ram` files that are used by the Real Networks player, but that support has been withdrawn in recent versions.

You have to understand that proprietary player manufacturers are in the business of making money from their products. It is unreasonable to expect any of them to support and promote their competitors' formats unless there is some perceived gain or benefit for them. Microsoft is often accused of eliminating competition, but this is just the company's way of increasing business.

Here is a list of the popular open standards or proprietary formats that Microsoft supports in Windows Media Player. This list evolves according to the emphasis placed on different codecs and Microsoft's commercial needs:

- MPEG-1
- MPEG-2
- MPEG-4 Part 2
- CD audio files (`.cda`)
- MIDI
- Wave files (`.wav`)
- QuickTime audio (`.aiff`)

22.9 Implications of the SMPTE Standards Process for WM9

Interestingly, in the autumn of 2003, Microsoft lodged the specifications of WM9 with SMPTE in order to get the codec ratified as an open standard. Cynical commentators noted the suspicious timing of this news with respect to the release of the H.264 codec standard. However, if there ever was an intention to compromise the chances of the emerging H.264 standard becoming dominant, it appears to have backfired.

The extent to which the standard is open depends on the conditions that surround the licensing. This is not the first time that a proprietary standard has been passed into the public domain. To date, the standard has not been ratified and the licensing terms have yet to be defined. This process is taking longer than Microsoft predicted at the outset.

SMPTE is an unusual choice for standardizing this codec; this kind of work has generally been undertaken by MPEG or the ITU. But then they already had H.264 nearly ratified, so they would have been unreceptive to another codec design at that time. Nevertheless, SMPTE has expertise in the area of moving images and is well qualified as an organization to back this process.

If the standard is ratified and adopted, it could become quite popular, possibly at the expense of H.264, and there are some very concerned people in the broadcast and streaming industry who have already invested a lot of time and money into H.264 implementations. The SMPTE standard is sometimes incorrectly referred to as WM9 or *VC-9*. SMPTE has announced that they will call it VC-1.

Once the standard is ratified and adopted, nothing will prevent Microsoft or anyone else from trumping it with improved versions and providing even better performance with a future proprietary codec. The VC-1 codec may be important for some time to come because of its adoption into new platforms—that is, provided it can complete the standardization process without falling by the wayside.

22.9.1 *Licensing Issues*

Note that the SMPTE VC-1 and Microsoft WM9 codecs are not the same legal entity. The licensing of WM9 is available from Microsoft under its commercial terms. That does not grant permission for you to use VC-1, which must be licensed through SMPTE or the agents that it appoints. The two standards are similar, but not one and the same, and they could diverge somewhat over time

DRM support is a facet of Windows Media and not VC-1. Only the video coding is being standardized by SMPTE, and it's wrong to assume that the entire Windows Media functionality portfolio is being offered up as an open standard under the VC-1 heading.

Microsoft provides a Web page with details of Windows Media licensing costs as well as sample contracts you can download.

22.10 Playing Windows Media on Non-Windows Platforms

All non-Windows operating systems (of any significant market share) are now UNIX based. They are sufficiently similar that the engineering effort to achieve *porting* between these systems is not massive. Windows Media Players are available on Mac OS and Solaris. For now, at least, there is no Linux player. This might change in the foreseeable future as Linux gains market share. History demonstrates that the availability of any particular revision of Windows Media Player on non-Windows platforms tends to be released later than it is for the Windows platform and often lacks some features. For example, WM9 playback on Mac OS X does not support playback via the Windows Media advanced codec.

WM9 is currently supported on these platforms:

- Windows—all current variants
- Mac OS X—10.3 is considered normative (older versions are not recommended; 10.4 is in the process of being adopted)
- Solaris

Windows Media 9 (or the equivalent, SMPTE VC-1) video is one of three mandatory formats to be supported by consumer HD-DVD players as the next generation of DVDs is

---

Microsoft Licensing:

http://www.microsoft.com/windows/windowsmedia/licensing/licensing.aspx?displang=en-us

being prepared. The standardization process is running more slowly than was anticipated, however, and there is a possibility that the WM-based codec requirement could be withdrawn if it is not ratified in time. The Hollywood movie studios are somewhat ambivalent about this new DVD format as yet.

22.11   Producing Content

If you are working with Windows Media, it is best to build your workflow around a suite of Windows-based PC systems. One of the arguments for using open standards is that you are then free to choose the production platform that most suits your workflow process.

Creating WM7 and WM8 files on Mac OS with Discreet Cleaner is possible, but the format options are limited and it is not an optimal solution.

22.11.1   The Telestream QuickTime Plug-In

If you decide to deploy Windows Media Player and want to also use the WM9 or VC-1 codec, tradition dictates that your production system would be a Windows machine. Creating WM9 files on Mac OS as a direct export from Final Cut Pro has just become possible with the Telestream Flip4Mac plug-in exporter for QuickTime.

Microsoft has chosen to make the Windows Media codec available on Mac OS and Solaris only as an embedded codec inside its own player. However, you cannot operate it on the same peer level as all the other codecs that QuickTime supports.

At IBC 2004, Telestream announced Windows Media codec plug-ins for playback and export of standard and high-definition Windows Media on the Mac OS platform. This is a very significant development and is possibly one of the first fruits of the SMPTE VC-1 standardization process, although they may be unconnected.

You should still maintain some Windows machines in order to test the content.

It is possible to build a farm of Windows-based encoders and administer them through a Web-based administrative interface. This has been supported since the Series 7 release. With the Telestream codec embedded in a Mac OS X-based QuickTime installation, all the UNIX scripting and AppleScript support can be used to create an automated workflow.

The Flip4Mac plug-in is very well designed. It installs very easily and the user interface obeys all the correct rules of Mac OS software design. This provides an export to Windows Media from any application that uses QuickTime. Although it will encode to the advanced codec, that process does require some heavyweight computing power, and if you are intending to encode Windows Media with it, you should consider using the fastest available machine you can find. It does work fine with lower-specification hardware.

22.12   WM9 Risk Factors

There is always some risk that goes with selecting a proprietary system, and that goes as much for Real Networks and QuickTime as for Windows Media. You are at the mercy of the manufacturer, which will choose to drop a particular product or cease support for it whenever that suits its commercial needs.

The conventional wisdom is that, if you choose not to deploy WM9, your potential reach to consumers is restricted. The argument is often used that a considerable number of Windows users have the Series 9 support already installed when they buy their computer and are not prepared to upgrade or replace it with Real or QuickTime.

That argument might be true of consumers that are not computer literate. Inside a corporate environment where the IT department creates a standard desktop environment, that argument is not as compelling. The IT department might choose to install Real Networks or QuickTime players everywhere, and there is no additional installation overhead since it is likely the hard disks are prepared by cloning/ghosting a standard image or running some automated installation process.

You should establish an accurate profile of the target user base before committing to one format or another.

22.13   Benefits of Adopting Windows Media

With a Windows Media–based service, you know for certain that a lot of people will be able to play your content. You can offer rich media services with the knowledge that there is a large potential audience.

You should still survey your target audience because a lot of people might be running older versions of Windows. Some of them might not have the media player installed by default, or they may be running older versions of the media player.

This could determine the codec that you use. For example, you might choose WM7 codecs because they will play back in Series 8 and 9 players as well.

But you still have to decide what to do for those people who don't have Windows Media Player and will never install it.

22.14   Implications of H.264 for Windows Media

Does MPEG-4 and in particular the H.264 codec threaten Windows Media in any way? Choosing the Windows Media technology is a good solution if you plan to reach all of a captive audience who you know will have that player installed.

It is not yet clear how this situation with media players, dominant codecs, and market leadership will play out. Microsoft must see H.264 as a threat to its dominance of the streamed-video and TV marketplace. It has been trying to win that market over for some time now. The WebTV, Ultimate TV, eHome, and xBox products are examples of the technologies Microsoft has developed as part of that strategy. For now, the VC-1 codec being worked on by SMPTE seems to be the Microsoft response to the potential threat of H.264 dominance. This has not gone as smoothly as first anticipated, and the expectation of a rapid turnaround for the standards documents in a 6- to 12-month time frame now seems to have been too optimistic. There is as yet no clear indication of when the standard will finally be ratified.

Windows Media will not be completely displaced by any other codec. As long as Microsoft manufactures it, the WM9 codec is likely to be a successful codec and a good choice. However, beware of committing yourself totally and irrevocably—you could be painting yourself into a corner.

The H.264 codec is becoming more widely supported. DVD standards bodies are selecting H.264 for use in delivering HDTV, but to be fair they are also considering support for VC-1 at the same time. So you have two codecs to choose from. The H.264 codec is much more likely to be well supported on all platforms. It remains to be seen whether VC-1 will be deployed at all.

22.15   Summary of Where Windows Media Is Most Useful

So, if you want to deploy to a large audience known to be using the Windows platform and you intend to deliver to them a service comprising small clips or reasonably sized linear-video programs and movies, the WM9 codec is a good choice, given that by using it you will potentially reach a large proportion of the available audience.

Take note, though, that Microsoft has been ordered to unbundle the media player from the operating system package when sold in Europe. This doesn't make the media player less available, but users will have to install it separately and will also therefore have an easier choice to replace it with an alternative.

22.16   Other Alternatives

But what if you don't want to use Windows Media? In the next chapter we'll look at the strengths and weaknesses of the Apple QuickTime system before considering RealNetworks in the chapter following.

QuickTime

23.1 Hello, QuickTime

QuickTime has been around probably as long as any video playback system on desktop computers. Originally, it could only play small-format video and it had no streaming capabilities until the mid-1990s.

QuickTime was the first of the video frameworks to support the idea of pluggable codecs, and Apple has continued to innovate in the way that components are downloaded automatically when needed.

With the introduction of the new Telestream and Real Networks codec plug-ins, QuickTime is the only platform that can export video in its own format, many open standard formats, and those of all its competitors. This is a significant advantage.

QuickTime also introduced de-interlace and inverse-telecine support earlier than its competitors, and in 1996 it added the capability to play MPEG video in reverse at a time when the video format did not support it. We take these capabilities for granted now, but this was revolutionary back then. QuickTime is very mature and robust because it has been available for a very long time and is constantly undergoing revision and re-engineering of various parts of the infrastructure to support more advanced capabilities.

Some good examples of the quality that can be achieved with QuickTime can be found at the QuickTime trailers web page on the Apple web site and at the Warner Brothers Matrix web site.

23.2 How Is QuickTime Different from Other Formats?

QuickTime is quite different from the other two major players (Real Networks and Windows Media) in that it is a framework (or platform) on which a rich, diverse, and interactive experience can be built. A totally nonlinear playback can be constructed that allows the deployment of portable multimedia experiences to everywhere that QuickTime is supported.

QuickTime movie trailers: http://www.apple.com/trailers/

Matrix trailer: http://whatisthematrix.warnerbros.com/

When people talk about a QuickTime video codec, they are describing one of the Sorensen codecs that is supplied as a part of QuickTime. A QuickTime movie file might contain any one or more of a large variety of video formats. Other kinds of media might also be present in the file.

Over and above normal linear playback, QuickTime supports the following additional capabilities that are not found in the other players:

- Massively parallel numbers of tracks
- A wide variety of non-video/audio track content types
- Internal object base
- Real-time effects layers
- Real-time warping and transforms
- Object movies in QuickTime VR
- Scene/panorama movies in QuickTime VR
- Embedded movies within movies
- Wired script control
- Sprites
- QuickTime Music architecture
- Image conversion and translation
- Multimedia data codecs

Most of these capabilities have been available in QuickTime since about 1998.

Interestingly, a lot of these capabilities have now become available in MPEG-4, and that sets MPEG-4 apart from MPEG-2 in a very important way. Creating packaged interactive multimedia experiences that play across multiple platforms is possible and is now available in an open-standards format. So if you are already able to create a nonlinear experience in QuickTime, you should be able to translate that content quite easily.

QuickTime also has a valuable toolkit of image conversion and compression tools as well as multimedia data converters.

23.3 The Player

When you use the QuickTime player, it looks the same on Windows and Mac OS. The release strategy ensures that the same version is supported everywhere and the upgrades are synchronized as closely as possible so that the viewing experience and API support are consistent.

Figure 23-1 shows the QuickTime 6 movie player in the default state. The QuickTime 7 movie player looks slightly different in appearance.

23.4 The QuickTime Applications Programming Interface

The QuickTime player is available as an applications programming interface (API) that you can invoke from within your own application. You are responsible for setting up the

Figure 23-1 Movie player.

environment and placing the player window into the display screen. Most often you will be coding in Objective C, Java, or C++, depending on the platform. You might use 3GL tools such as Visual BASIC or LiveStage Pro. All of the multimedia-authoring tools, such as Director and Flash, will let you play QuickTime movies within their presentations.

23.5   Trick Play Capabilities

QuickTime allows you to do some very tricky things, such as set up non-rectangular windows and warping operations on the video being played back. You can do this yourself if you have installed a QuickTime Pro license.

With your movie open in the playback window, get the movie properties panel up. Then select the video track and inspect the properties.

The size panel has a button labeled "Adjust." Click this and some handles will be placed on your movie in the player. You can then drag these to resize the movie and rotate it. Sizing after rotation causes a skewing effect. QuickTime does all this while the movie is playing and applies the distortion matrix to the live output.

23.6   Player Skins

Because QuickTime supports alpha-channel blending of the output, some very interesting non-rectangular players are possible. QuickTime supports player skins, and re-skinning a

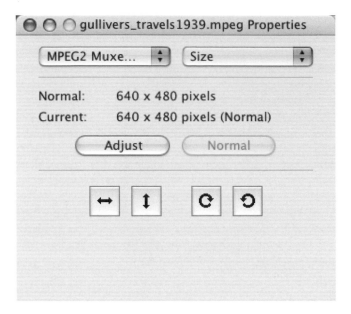

Figure 23-2 Display adjustment panel.

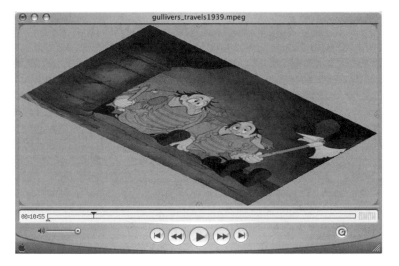

Figure 23-3 Distorted playback window.

QuickTime player is actually a function of the movie being played rather than the player configuration. This is a subtle difference from the approach of other media players. The media player appearance is totally under your control as the movie provider.

Lately the other platforms have begun to support skins and non-rectangular playback apertures. There are some extreme examples of user interfaces built around player windows that are shaped like fish or circular designs like portholes with the controls placed around the periphery. Some of those are triumphs of artistic design over functional use, but it is clever all the same and it could be useful in some situations.

Here is an example of an AXEL animated 3D track playing inside a skin using an automatically downloaded component.

23.7   Using Open Standards Within Quicktime

QuickTime has always been well endowed with support for open standards. Because the architecture has always allowed for pluggable codecs, adding a new standard has been relatively easy whenever it becomes necessary.

To be fair to the Real Networks and Windows Media platforms, they also support multiple codecs. QuickTime also provides a music architecture containing a MIDI GM-compatible software sound synthesizer based on the Roland Sound Canvas. This allows you to open and play MIDI files and save them as CD-ready AIFF files, rendering in the synthesized audio without the user intervening.

Recent versions of QuickTime have concentrated on support for open standards used in 3G mobile devices. Building an authoring system for mobile content becomes much easier when one is using QuickTime as a foundation.

The number of different formats supported by QuickTime is amazing. It is huge. You can convert between more diverse formats than with any other media platform, and not just video—diverse audio and image formats are also well supported.

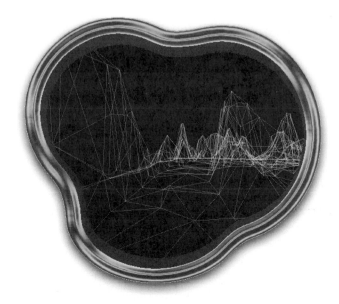

Figure 23-4 3D content in a non-rectangular skin.

QuickTime and MPEG-4 have some interesting parallels. When the MPEG-4 standards group called for technologies to be suggested for use, Apple put forward the QuickTime file format and Microsoft offered AAF. In the end, QuickTime was adopted as a starting point. Some minor structural changes were made to the file format by the MPEG working group, so QuickTime and MPEG files are not identical. Recent updates to QuickTime add support for some of those changes to the MPEG-specific file format differences; this suggests that some convergence between them may be underway.

23.8   Other Video Formats

You can save RealVideo 10 format files with the RealExporter plug-in and create WM9 movie files with the Telestream Flip4Mac Windows Media plug-in. With the Telestream importer plug-in, you can also import Windows Media files. Both of these plug-ins enfranchise the user of Mac OS, bringing her or him broadly into line with the Windows operating system users as far as available output formats are concerned.

23.9   Mobile Applications

QuickTime is strong in the area of mobile applications. Apple has worked hard to ensure that there is good support for the 3GPP and 3GPP2 standards. The Internet Streaming Media Alliance (ISMA) standards are also well supported, and with the introduction of ISMA 2, the additional profiles should show up in the QuickTime parameter settings in due course.

23.10   Non-Video Format Support

QuickTime copes well with a lot of other formats, both video and non-video, including Macromedia Flash and MIDI. The MIDI format is especially well supported due to the built-in Roland GS sound set. This is derived from the popular Sound Canvas synthesizers.

The movie player provides sufficient support that you can at least re-voice the instruments in a MIDI track so that it sounds different when played back. This MIDI support is relatively unsophisticated, so you are not able to do much more than edit instrument assignments.

You access this through the movie player's property inspector. In Figure 23-5 we see the music track selected and the instrument properties pane on display. Each instrument corresponds to a separate MIDI part within the music track. These are usually assigned to separate MIDI channels but need not be.

Real Video Export Plug-in: http://www.realnetworks.com/

Telestream Windows Media plug-in: http://www.flip4mac.com/

Figure 23-5 MIDI instrument list.

If you select one of the instrument tracks, you can change the sound for any MIDI part with the instrument selector panel, seen in Figure 23-6.

The QuickTime support for MIDI is sufficiently flexible that a MIDI track can be imported into iTunes for playback, as can the music tracks you make with the GarageBand and SoundTrack tools. The iTunes player can play MIDI as easily as it does CD audio, MP3

Figure 23-6 MIDI instrument selection panel.

files, and other music formats such as AAC. When you come to burn a CD from iTunes, it renders these MIDI tracks and loops into AIFF format so that they can be played back on a normal CD player. You don't have to do anything—it just happens.

Many other audio formats (including the AAC format) are supported in QuickTime as well. QuickTime also works with surround-sound multi-track audio for movies as well as the very low bit rates required for mobile audio services.

23.11 Downloadable Extension Components

You can install the Mac OS X version of the Envivio TV plug-in with your other QuickTime components and play back MPEG-4 BIFS multimedia. You will have to contact Envivio directly to obtain the plug-in. QuickTime players will automatically download other component modules from the Apple web server as the media being played calls for them. These are listed in Table 23-1 and are supported on both the Mac OS and QuickTime for Windows:

23.12 QuickTime VR

QuickTime offers VR capabilities as well as navigable movies and wired sprites. These capabilities lean toward what MPEG-4 has to offer in the systems layer. QTVR elementary movies come in two varieties, panorama and object. You would 'move around' inside a panorama, which from your point of view is an environment. You can 'pick up' and turn over an object to inspect it from all sides. Panoramas are just cleverly constructed sets of individual frames within a movie with an additional layer of playback control that allows the movie to be navigated in a totally nonlinear fashion.

They use compression at the frame level, but because the experience is nonlinear, P and B frames have no meaning in this context.

23.13 Effects

QuickTime contains some special effects for creating additional enhancements to your content without consuming large amounts of bit rate. These effects are described using parameters and are then rendered at playback. Examples include ripple, fire, fog, and clouds. The effects are stored in a separate track that can be enabled or disabled separately as needed.

23.14 Embedding Videos into Wired QuickTime Movies

QuickTime wired movies come in a variety of different forms. QuickTime VR presentations can be wired with additional movie panes playing inside the VR environment. This

Table 23-1 Add-On Components for QuickTime

Component	Description
Be Here	A 360-degree live streaming VR technology.
Digital Anarchy Microcosm	A 32- or 64-bit lossless video codec.
EnvivioTV	An MPEG-4 BIFS extender for playing "wired" MPEG-4 packages.
Ipix	Immersive 360-degree VR designed for real-estate applications and other similar projects.
Kaydara FBX 3D	FBX for Apple QuickTime allows any FBX file to be viewed and interacted with using the Apple QuickTime player on either Macintosh or Windows computers. The file format is supported by a variety of 3D modeling tools.
Mind Avenue AXEL	An interactive 3D modeling system with a very compact 3D-model format. This format allows scripts to be built into your models so they animate while still being viewed in 3D space.
MPEG-2 playback	An optional extra component that you can purchase from Apple to enhance the playback of MPEG-2 content. It is provided free with the DVD Studio authoring tools.
On2	A full-screen, TV-quality codec.
Pulse	A rich media 3D-animated technology platform. This is designed for e-Learning and e-Marketing applications.
Real Networks	During the latter part of 2004, Real Networks launched a plug-in for exporting RV10 content from QuickTime on Mac OS. This plug-in is not an importer but any application that can save as a QuickTime movie can now save its video in Real Video 10 format.
Streambox	Advanced Compression Technology level-2 video codec.
Windows Media	At IBC 2004, Telestream launched a plug-in for exporting Windows Media content from QuickTime. Any application that can save as a QuickTime movie can use this to create Windows Media on Mac OS. The Flip4Mac plug-in is not automatically downloadable like the other components because you have to buy it, but it is an extension component all the same.
Zoomify	A zoomable image codec. Download a small-scale image and then as you zoom, in the portion in view is downloaded as needed.
Zygo Video	A good-quality Web video codec.

makes use of the QuickTime live-warping and morphing capabilities that transform the movie while it is playing. Demonstrations from the 1990s showed QuickTime movies being played back as a texture map on various topographic shapes. The most extreme was a movie projected onto a doughnut shape, and rotating cubes were also used to show off this capability.

Creating an environment and mapping the video onto the surfaces of that environment is clearly technically achievable and was shown at several developer conferences in the mid to late 1990s. The implementation was technically challenging, and not very many developers used the technique. This kind of presentation is likely to become popular again, since the improvements to Mac OS 10.4 provide an OpenGL-based canvas onto which QuickTime projects its movies. The improvement in computing power and tools for authoring will also facilitate its wider use.

23.15 QuickTime Utilities

There are many tools available for manipulating QuickTime movie content. A collection of utilities is provided for download at the Apple QuickTime web site. See Table 23-2 for a summary list.

23.16 Cross-Platform Portability

The major caveat here is that you can only use QuickTime on Macintosh and Windows systems and naturally it works at its best and smoothest on the Macintosh. Nevertheless, it is quite popular on the Windows platform.

There is currently no Linux version available. When Apple QuickTime management was questioned about that at a developer conference in 2003, the indication was that there could never be a Linux version for commercial reasons.

It may be possible to play QuickTime movies inside something like M-Player, which hosts the QuickTime dynamic link libraries (DLLs) in such a way that they think they are running in Windows. This is a clever technique for porting binary code from Windows to Linux. The DLLs provide a library of code that supports the QuickTime functionality. Because they are available as a library, you have only a single copy in memory and it is shared by all applications that are playing a QuickTime movie. Getting these DLLs to work in Linux with a PC simulation tool will likely stay the only way to get QuickTime support on that platform unless Apple decides to port QuickTime there themselves.

If you choose to use QuickTime on Linux, your decision is probably based on a desire to build your workflow around a UNIX-based environment. But because Mac OS X is UNIX based, putting QuickTime onto Linux would not gain you very much from a

---

QuickTime utilities: http://developer.apple.com/quicktime/quicktimeintro/tools/

M-Player: http://www.mplayerhq.hu/

Table 23-2 QuickTime Utilities Available From Apple

Tool	*Description*	*Availability*
Dumpster	A tool to view and edit moov resources. There are versions for Mac OS X and Mac OS 9.	Mac OS and Windows
Effects Teaser	This utility explores the effects architecture in QuickTime.	Mac OS and Windows
FlareMaker	A tool to explore Lens Flare effects that are built in to QuickTime.	Mac OS
HackTV	A simple movie-capture tool to record audio and video.	Mac OS and Windows
Hint Track Profiler	A diagnostic tool that graphs the hint packets in a streaming movie as it is played.	Mac OS
MakeEffectMovie	Takes the video tracks from two movies and creates a new movie with an effects track for them.	Mac OS and Windows
MakeEffectSlideShow	Makes a slide show movie with an effect as it switches from one video track to the next.	Mac OS
MakeRefMovie	Creates alternate movies for various Internet connection speeds, CPUs, languages, etc. You will need this tool to make reference movies that you can refer to from Web pages.	Mac OS and Windows
Plug-In Helper	Associates URLs as well as stores QuickTime plug-in settings inside a QuickTime movie.	Mac OS and Windows
QTStreamSplicer	This tool adds an image to an audio-only live stream (or to the beginning of a streaming track).	Mac OS and Windows
RTSP/RTP Proxy	Users of Mac OS X Server 1.2 and earlier versions can give client machines within a protected network access to streaming servers outside that network.	Mac OS and Windows
Streaming Info Plug-in	This plug-in adds an information panel to the QuickTime player. It shows packet-transfer information for streamed video tracks.	MacOS and Windows

technical point of view. In fact, you'd likely lose some functionality. AppleScript, for example, is only available on Mac OS. Building workflow automation systems without it would be much harder work, and you also would lack many of the other popular applications and tools that Mac OS supports.

So actually the question "Does QuickTime work on Linux?" applies mainly to players on personal desktops. If open-standards video is deployed, even this becomes moot; if you choose to build on a Linux platform there is more support available. Open-source projects such as M-Player may provide a solution if you want to have a Linux client playing proprietary formats.

23.17   H.264 Implications for QuickTime

How does the emergence of a new open standard for video coding and multimedia affect Apple? Many people are unaware that MPEG-4 is related to QuickTime through the file format that Apple allowed the MPEG-4 standards body to adopt. At that point, the file format diverged slightly from the QuickTime model, but the fundamental object-based nature of it remains largely the same. Architecturally, QuickTime is very well placed to take advantage of everything that MPEG-4 has to offer.

A wired QuickTime movie and an MPEG-4 systems-layer interactive package are very similar in capability. The authoring process is functionally similar. The differences mainly lie in the data structures rather than the platform architectures. Since Apple has already stated that it supports open standards wholeheartedly and has already implemented some MPEG-4 capabilities, it is possible that the company will provide further support in future operating-system releases. But this, of course, is speculation until such a release is announced.

This is important because a lot of software manufacturers have built tools on top of the QuickTime architecture. All of these capabilities are available to tool builders on the Windows platform once they install QuickTime there as well.

With the release of Mac OS 10.4 and QuickTime 7, Apple supports the H.264 codec as a built-in component within the QuickTime architecture. This makes it available to anyone who wants to take advantage of the improved coding capabilities.

23.18   QuickTime Risk Factors

If you use a codec that is proprietary and only available in QuickTime, you are implying that the only audience you are aiming for runs Mac OS or Windows. In fact as QuickTime goes forward, it will be increasingly difficult to retain compatibility with the version running on the old Classic Mac OS. Careful choice of codecs will stave this issue off for a while, but eventually it will become compelling to use newer codecs, and these are unlikely to ever be ported to Classic Mac OS.

Choosing QuickTime containment for your media somewhat disenfranchises Linux users. Interestingly, the operating system core and the streaming server have both been open-sourced by Apple, so if you wanted to do the necessary work, getting the streaming server to run on Linux would not be that difficult. Before embarking on a porting exercise, check the Internet for implementations. Someone else has probably done it for you already.

Making a QuickTime player for Linux presents some issues, too. The QuickTime file format has been published, but any proprietary codecs will likely be stored in those files as chunks of opaque data that you will not be able to interpret.

There are video formats and codecs that are best processed with a workflow built around the QuickTime architecture. Most of the non-Apple proprietary formats may be available as external, application-driven codecs, but no other system embodies the range and flexibility of QuickTime.

When you deploy applications such as Final Cut Pro, iMovie, Adobe Photoshop, Adobe Illustrator, Media 100, and Microsoft Excel, you can wrap the process in AppleScript and achieve a high degree of workflow automation. You'll find coverage of this at the Apple web site under the heading of "Showtime." It makes a very compelling case for AppleScript, which is not available on any other platform.

23.19   Situations in Which QuickTime Is Useful

While Real Networks and Microsoft cut deals to distribute massive quantities of their products, it is worth noting that QuickTime has been available on enhanced CD products for years. Huge numbers of CD singles are shipped with QuickTime for Windows installers. It has even been given away on free CDs mounted on the front of cereal packets. The distribution and reach of QuickTime must be more ubiquitous than any other video player, and yet it shows quite low on any industry-based measurements. This is very strange.

QuickTime is embedded in a couple of hundred different digital camera models, and this is evident when you shoot those 15-second movies with a still camera. They upload to the computer as `.mov` files because that is the format used in the camera.

QuickTime provides a lot of translation services for image formats and all kinds of media handling. This support facilitates applications such as iMovie, iTunes, iPhoto, and Keynote on the Macintosh platform. The iTunes for Windows application could not be delivered without the underlying QuickTime support. Installing iTunes onto a Windows machine also ensures that a library of very useful media tools is there for other application writers to take advantage of.

23.20   Other Alternatives

So in the previous chapter we considered Windows Media and in this one we've looked at QuickTime. The other major player in this game is Real Networks, which has been at the forefront of streaming audio and video since those formats first started to become popular. In the next chapter we'll look at their strengths and weaknesses.

Real Networks

24.1   Introducing Real Networks Media

The Real Networks story began with the delivery of audio at low bit rates in the mid-1990s, when the company was called Progressive Networks. This became attractive to music-based Web sites and radio stations all over the world, which started to live-encode their programs and broadcast them on the Internet.

In 1997 the first examples of streamed video were delivered, and we were all astonished by this low-bit-rate, low-quality, postage-stamp-sized video at very jerky frame rates. Nevertheless, it was the precursor of the present online video services. Some experts consider this to be the future of TV delivery. There were a few other small companies doing similar work during the 1990s, but Progressive Networks quickly became dominant. Over the years, the company has evolved and is now known as Real Networks.

24.2   RealOne Player

Real Networks media version 10 is the latest incarnation of the codec and was released in January 2004. The company claims it is more efficient than all the other codecs, including WM9 and the H.264 codec. Although unverified, this is possible, because the Real Networks encoder does a very good job of exploiting the compression tools it has available. The improvements all take place in the version 10 encoder, allowing the content to play back in the version 9 player. Going on the assumption that a coding standard defines the bit-stream syntax for a decoder, this doesn't really warrant calling it a new codec. It is just a more efficient model of the previous one.

The RealOne player is available on a wide variety of platforms. Figure 24-1 shows what it looks like on a Mac OS X system:

The player now plays back QuickTime movie files courtesy of the QuickTime SDK. This is interesting because the only way you can create Real Networks video files is through their SDK or through the QuickTime codec plug-in that Real Networks launched during late 2004.

Real Networks: http://www.realnetworks.com/

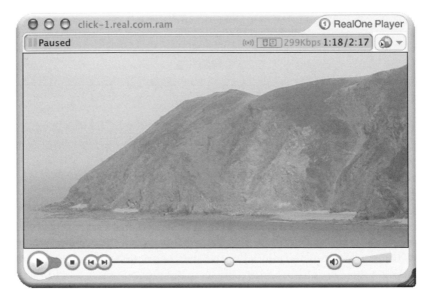

Figure 24-1 RealOne player.

The player is available in several alternative formats. The free version supports fewer features. It used to be quite hard to find, but lately the link has been prominently displayed on the front page of the RealOne player site.

24.3 Cross-Platform Portability for Players

The Real Networks products are a good solution for general streaming and video-delivery tasks. They have a wide portfolio of products available. The support is very good on Windows, and some tools also work well on Linux. There are other alternative compatible players for Real Networks video available for Linux. The Real Networks experience on Mac OS has been much improved in recent times.

If you want to run a "user-supported" player, then Real Networks offers just about the widest possible platform support of all the major streamed-video companies. Real Networks players are supported on the following platforms:

- Linux/Alpha (Debian)
- Linux/Alpha (Red Hat 6.2)
- Linux/Sparc (Red Hat 6.2)
- Linux/PPC 2000

RealOne player: http://www.real.com/

- Silicon Graphics Irix 6.5
- Silicon Graphics Irix 6.3
- IBM AIX 4.2
- IBM AIX 4.3
- Sun Microsystems Solaris 2.6 (Sparc)
- Sun Microsystems Solaris 7 (Sparc)
- Linux 2.x (libc6 i386)
- Linux 2.x (libc6 i386) RPM
- HP-UX 11
- Unixware 7 (i386)

All of the currently shipping CPU types are supported, and just about any combination of OS and hardware that you'll likely encounter is covered.

The Helix initiative was created by Real Networks when they published the source code for their player and streaming server as an open-source project. This has enabled other people to take that player and server and add extra features. Real Networks is then able to absorb those changes and improve their own products.

Figure 24-2 and Figure 24-3 show two view of what the Helix player looks like on Linux. You can see that some alternative appearance themes can be used to change the styling:

Figure 24-2 Helix movie player on Linux.

Helix web site: https://helixcommunity.org/

Figure 24-3 Alternative appearance of Helix player.

24.4 Mobile Deployment

The Helix player is an alternative to using the Kinoma player on some mobile and PDA platforms. The Helix web site contains examples of the player being used on the Symbian mobile operating system. Figure 24-4 is an example of what the player looks like in that context.

24.5 Interactivity Support in RealPlayer

With the Real Networks player, you can construct some very rich interactive propositions. These can include multimedia developed with the following technologies:

- HTML and JavaScript
- ActiveX controls (only on Windows platforms)
- SMIL
- Macromedia Flash

The JavaScript control offers some very sophisticated possibilities. The player plug-in is accessible to scripts contained in a web page. Real Networks also supports URLs embedded inside the movies. JavaScript URLs call back to script functions in the enclosing web page to trigger actions at appropriate times during the movie playback.

By adding extra support such as the Envivio TV plug-in, your Real Networks player also supports MPEG-4 Part 1 systems-layer multimedia content. This is similar to wired

Figure 24-4 Helix movie player on the Symbian mobile operating system.

QuickTime and also does a lot of the things that you might have implemented in Macromedia Flash.

Real Networks products are a good choice if you are creating video-led content with some reasonably unsophisticated interactivity. Manufacturing SMIL files with Web-based production systems is quite straightforward, and the components in them are just graphics files and video streams, so the workflow is reasonably easy to set up. SMIL is only marginally more complex to create than HTML-based web pages.

There is a small downside to this approach. The components are gathered together in a loosely organized collection but are not aggregated into a package in the same way as QuickTime or MPEG-4. If your publishing system experiences a momentary outage preventing an asset from being delivered to your server, the SMIL experience will be compromised. The missing asset would result in a broken link in your presentation. You may be able to work around that by packing things into zip archives and then transferring them as a whole. The public-facing server unpacks them for deployment. But this is more work for your content-system engineers to do.

For those times when you want to produce something more complex, you have Macromedia Flash or even MPEG-4 BIFS.

There is a comprehensive metadata package built into the player that allows you to re-skin the appearance to produce some very distinctive designs.

The introduction of Real Networks video version 10 coding improves on the state of the art but still plays back on the version 9 players. Real Networks has been consistently good at continuing to support their older players and codecs, which is good for the end user who prefers not to reinstall the player every few months.

24.6   Producing Content

The Helix family of products includes Helix Producer Plus and the Helix server. These are available with all the other tools from the Real Networks web site. You can choose to run the Helix producer tools or the Real Producer kit which is also available.

Primarily, the Helix producer tools let you create Real Networks–format video output and some standards-based output. You can also create MPEG-4 audio (AAC) and video (Part 2) and H.263-coded video.

The matrix of what works where is increasingly complex as new formats are developed and the commercial decisions that proprietary video-format manufacturers make carve out different, incompatible, and mutually exclusive niches. It is incredibly frustrating trying to build workflow infrastructures that cope with the diversity of formats and achieve that with the minimum number of machines and operating system variants. This complexity will ultimately drive people toward using open standards.

Interestingly for a company that gets no direct benefit from one operating system over another, Real Networks only supports production tools on Windows or Linux machines. Support for Solaris has been withdrawn with Real 10 encoders. Until recently, Real Networks support for Macintosh was based on the older Classic operating system. The implications of this are that tools such as Cleaner that use the Real Networks SDK would only produce Real Networks–format video when running in the Classic environment on a Macintosh.

Popwire Technology has engineered its own codecs for some formats rather than using libraries provided by the operating system. These codecs are embedded in its compression products. They support RealVideo and RealAudio output on Mac OS X at version 2 of the Compression Master software independently of any other support that is installed for that format.

It is possible that some additional Real Networks–oriented production tools could be put together using the Helix open-source kits as a starting point.

Real Networks and Apple have agreed to serve each other's content on their streaming servers. This makes it possible to stream QuickTime on a Real Networks server and stream Real Networks content on a QuickTime or Darwin streaming server. You cannot yet create QuickTime content on a Linux system, although you can create it on Windows. You can create Real Networks content on all three operating systems.

Real Networks developer resources: http://www.realnetworks.com/resources/index.html

24.7   Real Export Plug-In for QuickTime on Mac OS X

With the release of the Real Export plug-in codec for QuickTime, Real Networks has solved most of the integration problems and also made its format available to any application that integrates with QuickTime. So, where Cleaner would have had to drive the Real Networks SDK directly, it can now access it through the QuickTime API, which it already uses.

A list of applications that are supported is provided by Real Networks, but these are just the ones that have been tested. Others will probably work without any problems provided they implement the QuickTime APIs correctly. The plug-in is available as a free download.

You will need to have a QuickTime Pro license installed for the Real Export plug-in to work, but the license doesn't cost much, and you should probably have already purchased it as a matter of course. You will have received a license with your Final Cut or DVD Studio applications, and QuickTime Pro licenses are also provided with some books.

Note that this is an export-only plug-in. You cannot use this to ingest content that is already encoded into Real format.

The following export formats are supported:

- Real Video 10—Single pass (medium complexity)
- Real Video 10—Two pass (high complexity)
- Real Video 10—Single pass (high complexity)
- SureStream (multiple bit rate)
- Real Audio 10—Voice
- Real Audio 10—Music

24.8   Real Networks Video Tools

If you are making Real Networks video-output files, use Real Producer 10 or Helix Producer. The tools developed by Real Networks are optimal for creating its proprietary files, although there are other alternative applications. Those alternatives must use the Real Networks SDK so there is little benefit in buying them. On Linux platforms this may be the only tool available anyway. The RealProducer software works very well with the Osprey video cards.

24.9   Useful Utilities

A variety of useful tools are listed on the tools and plug-ins page at the Real Networks Web site.

Real Export plug-in: http://www.realnetworks.com/products/realexport/index.html

Real Networks tools and plug-ins: http://www.realnetworks.com/resources/toolsplugins/

These companies and products are listed next, although this list is not exhaustive and other tools that aren't specific to processing Real Networks content will also be useful as part of your kit.

- MPI Media Publisher
- SofTV.net ShowAndTell
- SofTV.net Presentation Maker
- Serious Magic Visual Communicator Pro
- Adobe
- Accordent PresenterONE
- Candesent software
- SMILGen
- Macromedia
- Sonic Foundry
- Oratrix Grins
- Viewcast Niagra SCX software and hardware encoders
- Camtasia Studio 2

Plug-ins from a variety of manufacturers are also listed on the same page.

24.10 Streaming Servers

Another important revenue source during the 1990s was the sale of streaming servers. That marketplace is now supported by a variety of other companies, and, when deploying streamed content on a massive scale, you might now select Akamai or Kasenna rather than Real Networks.

Media Publisher (MPI): http://www.media-publisher.com/

SofTV.net: http://www.softv.net/

Adobe: http://www.adobe.com/

SMILGen: http://www.smilgen.org/

Accordent: http://www.accordent.com/

Macromedia: http://www.macromedia.com/

Sonic Foundry: http://www.sonicfoundry.com/

Oratrix: http://www.oratrix.com/

Serious Magic: http://www.seriousmagic.com/

Viewcast: http://www.viewcast.com/

Techsmith Camtasia: http://www.techsmith.com/

One interesting initiative is the Helix server. This is an open-source project and is becoming quite popular among the academic and scientific communities, which have a history of participating in open-source initiatives.

24.11   Risk Factors in Adopting Real Networks Media

The biggest single risk here is that end users must download a player that is not automatically installed when they buy their computer. Microsoft Windows Media Player and the Apple QuickTime player both have a significant advantage over Real Networks media because they are already installed on their home platforms.

This is actually not such a downside as it appears to be. Consumers will download a player if they are assisted through the process. If you provide content in Real Networks format and also test for the necessary plug-ins with some JavaScript, then a very easy introduction to the process of downloading and installing a plug-in is possible.

If you do use the Real Networks format and player, you will reach a segment of the viewing audience on the Linux platform that neither Microsoft nor Apple is serving. You can get Windows Media players for Solaris, but not for any other UNIX platform.

Probably the most significant benefit of using Real Networks is that it is more portable across different platforms than the other players. Its production tools used to lack some portability to the Mac OS X platform, but this is no longer the case and it does support Linux very well.

Because other companies like Popwire Technology are also implementing production tools on Mac OS for Real and Windows Media video formats, you are no longer limited to using just a Windows platform if you would prefer to use an alternative.

24.12   Using Open Standards Within Real Networks Players

Like the other proprietary offerings, the Real Networks players are also capable of supporting open-standards playback. Appendix L summarizes the available format and player combinations.

24.13   H.264 Implications for Real Networks

Does the emergence of MPEG-4 threaten the position of Real Networks in the market? For some time, Real Networks has made little revenue from players, and its server market now generates far less revenue than it previously did. The company recognized that this was happening and decided to go the open-source route with the Helix server.

The MPEG-4 standard represents more of an opportunity than a threat to Real Networks, and while the company may yet make some money out of its proprietary technologies, reaching a wider audience for a subscription-based service is likely to yield better revenues in the future. Real Networks is well positioned to evolve into something very similar to a broadcaster.

24.14   Summary of Where Real Networks Is Most Useful

Real Networks has always been and continues to be available across the widest range of platforms. Real Networks media is a good choice provided you make the player-download process easy for your users. In a corporate environment you might need to acquire a site license to get an "advertising-free" player and install it everywhere in your organization.

24.15   Are There Any Other Choices?

We have now considered the three main contenders for video playback on computers. In the next chapter we will look briefly at some niche players whose offerings are unique and therefore address the needs of small markets. These niche players are generating some business because they offer capabilities that the big three do not.

25

Other Player Alternatives

25.1 The Other Players

Having devoted a chapter each to the main player products, let's spend a few pages look-ing at some other alternatives. These may help if your requirements are somewhat niche oriented.

25.2 Macromedia Flash

The indications are that Macromedia Flash is probably more ubiquitous than any of the other multimedia players. Macromedia has done a very good job of delivering its plug-ins with the major operating systems. The Flash playback integrates with QuickTime and RealNetworks players as easily as it does with web browsers.

You can make players any shape or size and they embed into web pages very nicely. Note that the controller in Figure 25-1 neatly spans the bottom of the video and has only the controls that are necessary. The close box is inset into the video area, but it needn't be because you can completely determine the controller size, placement, and appearance. With some of the other players, you can only turn the controller on or off.

Because you have total control over the look of the player and because the appearance is an aspect of the content, it should look and behave the same on all supported platforms.

The Macromedia Flash player has become more important lately since the introduc-tion of Flash video. This allows the same video to be played within the content on Windows and Mac OS platforms. Many of the situations where you might have consid-ered using MPEG-4 BIFS could be addressed by the Macromedia Flash format. It is only when you get to the very advanced multimedia capabilities of MPEG-4 that the Flash player requires too much programming to accomplish the same result.

You should be looking to deploy content that is at least Flash 6 compliant, but Flash 7 is probably a better base level to start with if you want to do serious amounts of video and mixed media. Flash player is available for Linux, but only on the vanilla x86 variant. The PowerPC and x86 64-bit versions of Linux aren't currently supported and you should contact Macromedia directly for further advice if you need to support those platforms. You can also get Flash player support for the Pocket PC platform.

Figure 25-1 Flash movie player.

Your choice will revolve around what you know about your end users and what they have installed on the target client systems.

Creating content for Flash-based players is straightforward. You can create content manually using the Flash tools available from Macromedia, export from a variety of applications that support Flash, or download the Shockwave file specification and create the files directly yourself with your own content-creation tools.

To encode Flash video, you will need a copy of the *Sorenson Spark* Pro codec. This is available as a stand-alone tool or as part of the Sorenson Squeeze compression suite software.

25.3   Forbidden Technologies

The *Forbidden Technologies* player is implemented as a Java applet, so it works in most situations. In the examples on the company web site, the controls are shown inset into the video. Figure 25-2 shows an example of the player.

This compact player is very well suited to deployment in mobile applications.

This is an interesting video-compression system because the company decided to implement a coding technique that is completely new and original. The video is coded using edge and fill compression. What this means is that the codec seeks out the sharp edges and codes them efficiently and then the areas inside them are coded as a fill. This gives the video some intriguing characteristics. As the bit rate falls, the video quality does degenerate but it doesn't exhibit the normal blocky appearance of a macroblock DCT-coded video stream. Instead, it just looks more like an animated facsimile of the original. This is generally kinder to the content. You can see the effect in the zoomed-in portion of a video frame in Figure 25-3.

Linux Flash 7 player: http://macromedia.mplug.org/

Shockwave file format specification: http://www.openswf.org/

Sorenson Spark Pro Codec: http://www.sorenson.com/solutions/prod/mx_win.php

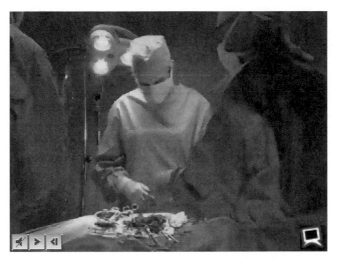

Figure 25-2 Forbidden Technologies movie player.

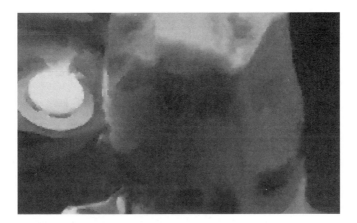

Figure 25-3 Forbidden Technologies coding artifact.

At the resolution of a mobile phone or over a slow dialup connection, this yields a quite pleasing video experience. There is some audio-sync slippage, but when video is compressed spatially and temporally the whole experience is compromised, and worrying about totally accurate lip sync on low-frame-rate video is a lost cause.

Forbidden Technologies: http://www.forbidden.co.uk/

25.4   VideoLAN's VLC Player

This is a remarkably popular player because it is available as a totally open-source kit, which you can modify yourself if you wish.

Figure 25-4 shows what the player looks like on the Windows platform. Note the unusual placement of the controls at the top of the screen.

The player looks somewhat different on Mac OS. In this case (Figure 25-5) the controller is displayed in a separate window like the DVD player that ships with Mac OS. This is a nicer way to implement the controller.

The following operating system platforms are supported by downloadable pre-built binaries, which you can install and run straightaway:

- Windows
- Mac OS X
- BeOS
- Debian GNU/Linux
- Mandrake Linux
- Fedora Core

Figure 25-4 VLC movie player in Windows.

VLC player: http://www.videolan.org/

Figure 25-5 VLC movie player in Mac OS X.

- Familiar Linux
- YOPY/Linux
- Zaurus
- SuSE Linux
- Red Hat Linux

These next few operating system platforms are also supported, but you will have to download and build the player from the source code yourself:

- NetBSD
- OpenBSD
- FreeBSD
- Solaris
- QNX
- Gentoo Linux

25.5 M-Player

The M-Player project is another interesting open-source initiative. It won the 2004 Linux New Media award for best media player, and the recognition is well deserved.

If you are interested in the internals of codecs and digital video, the M-Player project web site is a good place to look for code that you can download and modify to suit your requirements. Related to the project are a large number of encoders, plug-ins, UI kits, and various gadgets that you will find interesting.

M-player supports some intriguing output models, including some text-based displays that are very low resolution but create a "matrix"-like effect very easily. If you can play these out on a display that you can record, you can generate some interesting special effects.

M-Player rather cleverly wraps the Windows DLLs for a variety of codecs so they work on Linux or other x86-based operating systems. The code has also been ported to a very large number of different UNIX platforms, including Mac OS. Thus, it might be interesting as a way to play back video formats that are not otherwise supported.

The internals of the player are undergoing a complete overhaul, and the current player is referred to as the Generation 2 software.

More details are available at the M-Player web site.

25.6 Java Media Framework

The Java Media Framework (*JMF*) is interesting because like the MPEG-4 scenario, it offers extreme portability. Provided you have an up-to-date-enough Java virtual machine (VM) installed (and any other necessary low-level libraries), you can add the media framework and play back various video formats.

When that is coupled to the low-level support on your platform, the video playback is delegated to an existing media framework via an SDK connection though the API.

Experiments in the Interactive News development group at the BBC have proven that portable multi-screen playback can be accomplished via JMF. In fact, the JMF application that was written did not actually care whether it was controlling QuickTime or Windows Media and worked exactly the same regardless of whether it was installed on a Mac OS X system or a Windows workstation. Total portability!

A combination of JMF and MPEG-4 would give you "author once-play everywhere" capabilities. You should be able to construct a basic player with JMF that works the same on all platforms.

You can find out more about the JMF at the Sun Java Media web site.

The code snippet below is all that's required to run the Java TV applet in a web page and get it to play back a movie clip. The applet just displays a rectangle containing the movie playback area with no controller.

```
<applet code=TVApplet.class width=587 height=510>
<param name=file value="media/playme.mov">
```

The JMF is for those who wish to develop some more complex video playback solutions that cannot be implemented with a standard player.

M-Player homepage: http://www.mplayerhq.hu/

Sun Java Media: http://java.sun.com/products/java-media/jmf/2.1.1/formats.html

25.7 Still More Codecs and Players

These are some other players or codecs that you should look at if you are interested in trying out alternatives beyond those that have been covered so far. Some of these are vehicles for a new codec, so player support might be limited or dependent on other products.

- Ogg Vorbis
- DivX
- *Emblaze*
- *Dirac*

25.8 Just Put It on the Web

The one common destination for all these formats is the web. It is a big market, but the consumer TV market is bigger still. There is an attempt to get web-based systems to drive TV sets. It works (sort of), but it is not totally convincing yet. The main shortcoming is the style of presentation. Web content just doesn't transition well from page to page. It still needs a lot of work to engender the same design principles as TV graphic design manages. And yet TV design is not inherently interactive. We need a style of design that combines web interactivity with TV presentation. In the next chapter, we will explore the deployment of audiovisual assets onto the web to see if that helps us understand the technical challenges involved.

Ogg Vorbis: http://www.vorbis.com/

DivX: http://www.divx.com/

Emblaze: http://www.emblaze.com/

Cinepak: http://www.cinepak.com/

Ligos Indeo: http://www.ligos.com/

Dirac: http://www.bbc.co.uk/rd/projects/dirac/overview.shtml

MP3 (Audio): http://www.iis.fraunhofer.de/

26

Putting Video on the Web

26.1 Web Delivery

Web-based video delivery presents the digital video in a compressed form as a stream that you can join at any time. This is like jumping on a train as it passes through the station without stopping.

There may be multiple streams, as with a broadcast TV multiplex, but in this case the streams are synchronous and only relate to a single program.

26.2 Adding Video to Your Web Pages

Over the last few years, it has become popular for broadcasters to augment their TV services by providing web-based services. This has been particularly true of news broadcasters. Having come from the TV world, they naturally have a large body of video content available for repurposing. Many broadcasters' web sites provide links on the relevant story pages so that the clips can be viewed on a PC screen.

The BBC News Online web site uses a very complex content-management system with a database-driven model of the web site and all the video assets. This allows up to 200 clips of video to be embedded every day, although the site doesn't always deploy that many.

Often, just placing a link on a page will be sufficient to call up a player application and display the video. More sophisticated approaches involve embedding the video content in a web page. Usability studies indicate that the best way to approach this is to create a separate console in which the video is played. The console is designed to take up only the space required for the video and some helpful supporting graphics or text. This is much smaller than a normal web page. The console can be parked in the corner of the screen and you can carry on with other work while it is on display.

Embedding the video directly into the body of the main web site can be problematic because the user is then unable to continue browsing. With a separate console, the user is free to browse while the video is buffering or loading, and the whole experience generally runs more smoothly.

Real Networks video embedding: http://www.realnetworks.com/resources/samples/embedded.html

RealOne player: http://www.realnetworks.com/resources/samples/realone.html

26.3   Player or Plug-In—You Choose

If you are building a video-enabled web site, you must decide how you are going to present the video within your content. Some say the best approach is to embed the video within the web page with a plug-in, while others suggest that it is better to call up an external player.

You must look carefully at this; the choice may determine whether your engineering needs will be trivial or complex, and that will affect your bottom line.

Using a player is generally more portable. The player would have already been installed and is mapped using the MIME-type mechanisms within the web browser in order to select the helper application. This works similarly, regardless of the platform you are playing back on. So long as there is a player available for all the target platforms, this is fine. Some players force the viewer to read advertising that the player manufacturer controls. You may be able to get extended developer licenses and re-skin the player to reduce this effect.

26.4   Plug-Ins and JavaScript

If you decide to go with the plug-in approach, you may have to do significant amounts of work to ensure that the plug-in works on all browsers and platforms. Back in 1998, the BBC News Online web site deployed an audio/video console that uses frames and JavaScript in order to solve these problems, but the implementation was technically challenging. Certain approaches did not work well. For example, changing the name of a clip worked on some plug-ins but not on others; the page containing the plug-in had to be reloaded from scratch because the JavaScript command to select a new URL was not honored. On some browser and platforms it was necessary to use an <EMBED> tag, while on Windows it was necessary to use the <OBJECT> tag. Further challenges led to the Windows code having to be created dynamically when used in the MSIE browser but not in the Netscape browser. Creating HTML dynamically with JavaScript causes object bindings to happen after the page begins loading. Those bindings are not properly resolved until some time after the page has finished loading. Any onLoad event triggers might cause scripts to run earlier than intended. They will then cause errors because the target objects are not yet properly created (the technical term is instantiated).

Object creation and destruction on any dynamic basis is also prone to memory leaks because it is an unusual thing to do and seems to slip through the Quality Assurance testing processes when browser code is developed.

Another disadvantage of embedding is that the page with the video object must remain loaded. Therefore, putting the video on a page that has any links to another location takes the viewer away from the video very soon after accessing it. The optimum approach is to create a pop-up window with the video object in it. The pop-up (console) remains on-screen as long as the user needs it, without affecting subsequent browsing.

In 1998, another major problem was that the plug-ins supported different APIs for JavaScript control. This is still not standardized. It would be very helpful if there were a

Table 26-1 Media Delivery Protocols

Method	*Description*
file://	File on locally attached file system.
http://	HyperText Transfer Protocol.
https://	HyperText Transfer Protocol—Secure.
mms://	Microsoft Media Streaming.
pnm://	Progressive Networks Media.
rtp://	Real-Time Protocol.
rtsp://	Real-Time Streaming Protocol.

standard set of controls that video and audio plug-ins were expected to use. This would lead to more portable JavaScript code.

26.5 Protocols

The video content may be delivered in various ways. These are indicated by the protocol method, which prefaces the colon in a URL. Table 26-1 summarizes some common protocol methods.

26.6 Metafiles

Most of the player implementations use a reference- or metafile, which is referred to in the HTML of the web page. This file doesn't actually contain any media, but it points to a file or stream that does. This allows the media to be served in a variety of alternative ways. By using an intermediate file, it avoids the user's having to republish the web pages when an alternative server is used.

Another benefit is that some of these metafiles allow the construction of playlists or the attachment of header and trailer clips. You can also usually define the in and out points so that one clip file can serve several uses.

As you would expect, the different platforms support mutually exclusive file name extensions, and the syntax of the metafile content is also different for every player family.

26.7 File Extensions

Table 26-2 summarizes the file-type extensions for the different metafile file formats. A more extensive listing of file types that are relevant to video-compression activities appears in Appendix I.

Table 26-2 Metafile File Name Extensions

Extension	File type
.asx	Windows Media Advanced Stream Redirector metafile
.m3u	MPEG media queue file
.mov	QuickTime reference movie
.ram	RealAudio Redirector Metafile
.rmm	RealMedia Redirector Metafile
.rpm	Real Plug-in Redirector Metafile
.smi	SMIL
.smil	SMIL
.wax	Windows Media audio redirector
.wmx	Windows Media redirector
.wpl	Windows Media playlist
.wvx	Windows Media video redirector

26.8 Windows Media Metafiles

Advanced Stream Redirector (.asx) metafiles provide information about a file stream and its presentation. The .asx files also define playlists and provide Windows Media Player with instructions for presenting media items in the playlist.

Windows Media metafiles are implemented with an XML-based syntax and can be encoded in either *ANSI* or UNICODE (UTF-8) format.

The listing below shows the contents of an .asx file as used by Windows Media players.

```
<asx version="3.0">
<entry>
<ref href="mms://stream.contactright.com/media/clip.wmv"/>
<starttime value="00:00:00"/>
<abstract>Describing abstract text</abstract>
<title>Title text</title>
<author>Content author</author>
<copyright>Copyright 2004 ContactRight Ltd</copyright>
</entry>
</asx>
```

The example `.asx` file is set up for playing a Windows Media video clip. It could be stored with a `.wmv` extension. The `.wax` files are almost identical except that their file references are to `.wma` files containing audio.

The benefit of having almost identical `.asx`, `.wvx`, and `.wax` files is that each kind of metafile can be associated with a different helper application or plug-in.

26.9 Real Networks

The metafiles for Real Networks are rather simpler. They are just a list of URLs for the media to be played. In this example some progressive downloads via http files are invoked. A Synchronized Multimedia Integration Language (SMIL, pronounced "smile") presentation is streamed and some local files are played. Then the metafile stops. The media item at the end of the metafile after the stop won't be played.

The listing below shows a Real Networks metafile.

```
http://www.contactright.com/media/video1.rm
http://www.bbc.co.uk/media/video2.rm
http://www.contactright.com/media/sample1.smil
rtsp://server.real.com:554/sample.smil
file://mymedia/video1.rm
file://mymedia/video2.rm
file://mymedia/sample1.smil
—stop—
pnm:// server.real.com:7070/sample.rm
```

26.10 QuickTime

QuickTime uses a reference movie, which has the same file extension as a normal movie. The nature of the file is not apparent until the file is opened, at which time it turns out to refer to other files. This is an integral feature of QuickTime movies: they can refer to video content in other external movie containers.

To make reference movies you will need to download the `MakeRefMovie` tool from the Apple QuickTime web site. With this you will be able to compile the binary QuickTime ref movies that you'll refer to from the web pages.

Apple QuickTime: http://www.apple.com/quicktime/

26.11   MPEG Media Queue Files

The `.m3u` files are a media queue format. These are otherwise known as a playlist. This is the default playlist format used by Winamp and many other media players. The listing below shows what an example `.m3u` file might contain if it just has a single entry. The first line, "`#EXTM3U`," is the format descriptor. This one describes an Extended M3U. This line is mandatory.

```
#EXTM3U
#EXTINF:350,ELO — MrBlueSky
/Music/mp3/ELO/Best Of/MrBlueSky.mp3
```

The song entries are indicated by pairs of lines. The first line is information that will be presented to the user; the second describes the location of the media to be played.

The first media item line must begin with "`#EXTINF:`," and this denotes the start of a record. The number after the colon is the track time in seconds. A delimiting comma separates this from the track name. This track name should be consistent with the `ID3` tag inside the MP3 file.

The second media item line is the file path of the media to be played. This is a standard UNIX-style file-path description. In the example it is rooted in the local file system.

26.11.1   SMIL

The SMIL containers perform a very similar function but are format neutral. They can support a mixture of media types from different manufacturers. It is living dangerously to mix different kinds of media players in a single session, but the Oratrix Grins player was reputed to be able to cope with mixed format SMIL files when it was launched. This operates as a plug-in container, which can involve any of the installed video players. The risk is involved if you start having overlapping areas of the screen being owned by different players—that is, assuming they will all run cooperatively in the first place.

A safer course is to implement your SMIL container in such a way that it doesn't mix formats and only uses one kind of media.

The listing that follows illustrates an example SMIL container for multimedia.

26.12   The Fine Points of Web Delivery

When you insert a video into a web page, it is preferable to use the `<EMBED>` and `<OBJECT>` tags. There are some significant issues with using an `<A>` tag and an `HREF=""` reference to your movie.

```
<smil>
<head>
<!--Presentation attributes. -->
<meta name="author" content="www.contactright.com"/>
<meta name="title" content="Title text"/>
<meta name="copyright" content="© 2004"/>
</head>
<body>
<audio src="http://www.contactright.com/soundtrack.rm"/>
<video src="http://www.contactright.com/visual.rm"/>..
</body>
</smil>
```

Linking to a movie with an <A> tag bypasses the MIME-type matching and the browser cannot properly invoke a plug-in. Some browsers cope with this more elegantly than others, but it is never ideal. Even if the browser does intercept this loading mechanism and create a virtual page with a plug-in, there is no way to control that plug-in viewing experience. Appendix I summarizes some useful MIME-type values. Note that some of these must be defined in your web server configuration files.

If the file extension is not mapped, the file contents may be presented as text in the browser window. A movie presented like this is not going to impress a consumer!

Some file types, such as .mp4, .smil, .swf, and the rtsp:// protocol, will not properly invoke QuickTime or other handlers; if you don't have a plug-in that maps to the kind of data being downloaded, the whole thing might even crash.

The <EMBED> tag works with all browsers across different platforms. One of the attributes is the MIME type of the content. The browser uses this to select a playback application or plug-in. The <EMBED> tag also has failover mechanisms that lead you to a download page if there is some content being embedded for which you don't have a plug-in installed. Table 26-3 lists the download addresses if you want to include them in your web pages.

Table 26-3 Download Pages for Popular Player Plug-Ins

Player	*Download URL*
QuickTime	02BF25D5-8C17-4B23-BC80-D3488ABDDC6B
Real	CFCDAA03-8BE4-11CF-B84B-0020AFBBCCFA
Window Media 9	6BF52A52-394A-11D3-B153-00C04F79FAA6
Window Media (legacy)	22D6F312-B0F6-11D0-94AB-0080C74C7E95
Macromedia Flash	D27CDB6E-AE6D-11cf-96B8-444553540000

Table 26-4 Class ID Values for Plug-In Objects

Player	Class ID value
QuickTime	02BF25D5-8C17-4B23-BC80-D3488ABDDC6B
Real	CFCDAA03-8BE4-11CF-B84B-0020AFBBCCFA
Window Media 9	6BF52A52-394A-11D3-B153-00C04F79FAA6
Window Media (legacy)	22D6F312-B0F6-11D0-94AB-0080C74C7E95
Macromedia Flash	D27CDB6E-AE6D-11cf-96B8-444553540000

The <OBJECT> tag is defined as a *W3C* standard and should be implemented consistently by all browsers on all platforms, but it is not. You have to use the <OBJECT> tag in MSIE on the Windows platform, but on all other browsers the best choice is the <EMBED> tag. The <EMBED> tag in MSIE on Windows does not support the PLUGINSPAGE attribute, so the failover mechanism for fetching the plug-in does not work. If a QuickTime movie is called for, then the <EMBED> tag only works in MSIE Win if the QuickTime has been installed. On the other hand, the <OBJECT> tag lets you specify an ActiveX control and this does not depend on the MIME type. Furthermore, if the ActiveX control has not been installed, MSIE for Windows knows where to go to get it and offers to fetch it for you. Table 26-4 lists the CLASSID values for the <OBJECT> tag.

Yes, I know—CLASSID values are intended for computers to understand and not human beings. Nevertheless, it seemed like a good idea to collect this information into one place. Note that this only applies to using the <OBJECT> tag on the Windows platform. Table 26-5 lists the CODEBASE values for ActiveX downloads.

When you use the <EMBED> or <OBJECT> tag, include some height for the controller. The amount of allowance to make for this depends on the plug-in type. QuickTime, Real Networks, and Windows Media players all look slightly different when rendered into the display buffer. The movie itself may have switches set internally that activate or deactivate the controller, or the movie may have an alpha mask or skin that changes its shape to something other than a rectangle. You must be aware of what you are embedding to ensure that sufficient space is set aside for it when the browser manufactures the page layout.

Table 26-5 Code Base Download Values for Plug-In Objects

Player	Code base values
QuickTime	http://www.apple.com/qtactivex/qtplugin.cab
Real	http://www.real.com/player/index.html
Window Media	There are no .cab files supported for Windows Media Player. The necessary support is delivered automatically within the operating system installation. Note that this may now not be true in all European versions of Windows.
Macromedia Flash	http://download.macromedia.com/pub/shockwave/cabs/flash/swflash.cab#version=6,0,0,0

Controlling the <EMBED> and <OBJECT> tags with JavaScript is a time-consuming and sometimes frustrating experience. All the major companies have shipped video player plug-ins for some time. Nevertheless, there is still no standardized set of properties and methods that can be called up from JavaScript. A work-around solution can be manufactured, but it requires extra JavaScript code to be written to wrap the plug-in APIs so that they behave consistently with one another.

Coding an <EMBED> tag nested inside the error handling of an <OBJECT> tag is a neat HTML trick. It will allow the browser to failover to the <EMBED> if the page is loaded into a browser that does not support ActiveX <OBJECT> embedding.

Below is an example that will play a QuickTime movie through an ActiveX plug-in in MSIE on Windows but that on all other browsers will play via the <EMBED> tag.

```
<OBJECT WIDTH="120"
HEIGHT="100"
CLASSID="clsid:02BF25D5-8C17-4B23-BC80-D3488ABDDC6B"
CODEBASE="http://www.apple.com/qtactivex/qtplugin.cab">
<PARAM NAME="src" VALUE="MyMovie.mov">
<PARAM NAME="autoplay" VALUE="true">
<EMBED WIDTH="120"
HEIGHT="100"
SRC="MyMovie.mov"
TYPE="video/quicktime"
PLUGINSPAGE="http://www.apple.com/quicktime/download/">
</OBJECT>
```

More information on these techniques and some utilities is available at a number of third-party web sites.

26.13 Windows XP Service Pack 2 Implications

There have been changes to Windows XP that are installed with Service Pack 2. These have a major impact on web browser functionality, especially in the area of ActiveX controls, which are now often blocked.

PAGEot: http://www.qtbridge.com/pageot/pageot.html

Qtilities: http://www.qtilities.com/

Adobe Go Live: http://www.adobe.com/golive/

Windows XP SP 2: http://www.microsoft.com/technet/prodtechnol/winxppro/maintain/winxpsp2.mspx

MSIE browser changes: http://www.microsoft.com/technet/prodtechnol/winxppro/maintain/sp2brows.mspx

If you have installed the Service Pack 2 onto your Windows XP machine (and you should), you may find that the behavior of certain ActiveX controls is modified. This is in the interest of enhanced security. Scripts and plug-ins that would previously just run without your consent will now be blocked completely or may ask your permission before being executed. The following is a list of the main points relating to web browsing that you will need to check out. More detailed information is available at the Microsoft web site.

- Download modifications
- Attachment modifications
- Authenticode enhancements
- Add-on management
- Crash-detection improvements
- Binary behaviors security setting
- Modifications of code to support URL security zones
- BindToObject mitigation
- Information bar enhancements
- Using feature control registry settings with security zone settings
- Feature control settings in group policy
- UrlAction security settings in group policy
- Local machine zone lockdown
- MIME-handling enforcement
- Object caching enhancements
- Pop-up blocking
- Untrusted publishers mitigations
- Window restrictions
- Zone elevation blocks
- Network protocol lockdown

Be aware that some software may just stop working altogether. This could be due to the closure of ports in the firewall and resultant inability of these applications to talk to the server.

Sometimes software is supposed to respond to incoming connections, and you may have to purposely open certain ports to allow other computers to connect to yours. Mail, file transfer, remote desktops, and file sharing are obvious examples. If you run a server with a database or web site on it, the clients will need to gain access, which may be denied until you do something about it.

26.14 Porting to Linux

Running web browsers on Linux is becoming increasingly popular. Not all the plug-in manufacturers agree, so they don't all provide a Linux-compatible version of their plug-in. However, you can run the Windows plug-ins within a special package so that they think they are running in Windows when they are actually running in Linux. Check out the Codeweavers web site for a variety of porting options that might help you with this sort of problem.

26.15 H.264 on the Web

To deploy video with web and online services, our most popular choices are Real Networks and Windows Media. QuickTime is another possibility, and while it is excellent and is deployed on many platforms, there are not as many services running QuickTime as there are running Real Networks and Windows Media.

It is very likely that support for H.264 will become dominant. In the fullness of time, Real Networks, Windows Media, and QuickTime will all very likely support it in their players. That does not prevent them from supporting their proprietary formats but allows them to interoperate. This is already happening with some players. When all three players offer H.264 capability and AAC+ audio support, there will be no reason at all to go with a proprietary format. This suggests that H.264 is a good choice for going forward.

An open-source implementation of an open standard gives you total freedom to buy the server from one party and the client player from another and to use authoring tools from a variety of vendors. The server is then deployed on any of the three major platforms (Windows, Linux, or Macintosh). Users can view your content on any platform that has a viable H.264 player.

26.16 If It Won't Go on the Web, Let's Broadcast It Instead

The other major audience for our content will be TV viewers. They may be receiving our video through a broadcast TV system or over a broadband network connection. The broadband solution is becoming more likely as a future mainstream TV conduit.

In the next chapter we will look at how digital TV services work. This is important because it deals with issues of what happens to video after a compressor encodes it.

Codeweavers: http://www.codeweavers.com/site/products/

Digital Television

27.1 Digital TV Broadcasting

This is probably the most common way that compressed video is delivered, at least when measured by the number of receivers being viewed by end users. The main benefit of broadcasting is that although just one copy is transmitted, everybody can see it by receiving it on an aerial antenna and then decoding it into a form that can be viewed on a TV set.

The UK digital TV industry has rolled out three fundamentally different platforms, and a fourth is rapidly gaining acceptance.

27.1.1 Digital Satellite TV

Digital satellite (DSat) services in the United Kingdom are based on MPEG-2-coded video contained within MPEG-2 transport streams and some additional support for Open TV-coded interactivity. The DSat services are delivered to a dish antenna mounted on the roof or exterior wall of your dwelling.

The Digital Video Broadcast (DVB) Organization has looked again at the specifications for the DSat delivery protocols and evolved a second-generation approach. The DVB-S2 transmission techniques are 30% more efficient than the previous DVB-S delivery protocols. This, coupled with the improvements in coding offered by H.264, means that HDTV delivery is now a realistic proposition.

27.1.2 Digital Terrestrial TV

Digital terrestrial TV (DTT) broadcasting in the United Kingdom uses a DVB-based packaging technique very similar to the satellite service. A transport stream carries the programs and other data in the same way but deploys interactivity with the MHEG standard. The DTT broadcast uses the same spectrum as analog TV but simply uses some of the channels in a more efficient way.

Confusingly, MHEG is named similarly to the MPEG standard but is an altogether different thing. MPEG describes video in a compact and coded form; MHEG describes interactivity in an object-based scene structure. There are similarities between MHEG and MPEG-4 part 1 multimedia, but MPEG-4 is far more sophisticated in what it offers.

27.1.3 Digital Cable TV

The same DVB-based MPEG-2 transport stream model as DSat and DTT is used for digital cable TV (DCable) services in the United Kingdom. The interactivity is implemented using a variant of HTML that was developed by Liberate. DCable TV is delivered though a network of copper cables connected through a series of distribution amplifiers direct to your house. Cable operators also provide telephone connections and Internet services. This is sometimes called a "triple play." With suitable head-end infrastructures, they are also rolling out video-on-demand services. This method has the highest chance of being superseded by broadband connectivity.

27.1.4 Broadband TV

Broadband delivered via the telephone service provider is gradually being investigated as a possible way to distribute broadcast TV signals. This is sometimes called IPTV (after the Internet Protocol, which is the basis of its delivery) or video on demand (VOD). The strengths of broadband-based TV solutions are in the area of unicasting rather than multicasting. The main limiting factor of broadband is the last mile of connectivity, which is most often provided by legacy copper wiring. Signal attenuation affects the reliability and integrity of the data stream. Some broadband suppliers guarantee availability only up to a limited distance away from an optical-fiber transducer.

27.1.5 Hybrid Services

Combining digital satellite or digital terrestrial broadcasting with broadband for auxiliary services provides the optimal service. Combining broadband with DCable would seem to be redundant, since you would be putting in twice as many wires as necessary. If you are going to the trouble of wiring at all, then why not put in high capacity with a return path on the same connectivity?

27.1.6 Multimedia Home Platform

European digital TV services are being prepared and launched on a multimedia home platform (MHP)–based platform. This is being made available in the same way across the different kinds of transmission, so the receivers are very similar, as are the opportunities for adding interactivity.

27.2 The Set-Top Box

In the United Kingdom and elsewhere that the DVB standards are deployed, the MPEG-2 codec is used for video coding. This is embedded in silicon so that receivers can be built inexpensively. The carriage occurs via a transport stream that multiplexes several channels together into a single bit stream.

27.2.1 DSP Technology in Set-Top Boxes

Here is a possible alternative strategy that revolves around developing set-top boxes with video digital-signal processors (DSP) instead of application-specific integrated circuits (ASIC) containing the codec. The DSP can be loaded with a replacement codec on the fly, but ASICs are hardwired when they are manufactured. Texas Instruments has demonstrated that the codec could be delivered as a header on the front of the program and then loaded into the DSP when needed. That requires a closed system to work effectively. This is an attractive solution for box manufacturers who are uncertain whether to deploy the VC-1 (Windows Media) or the H.264 codec in the short term. The codec is swapped in the field by reloading the DSP chips with the new software.

Equator Technologies and Hitachi Semiconductor are demonstrating similar experimental work. Many other companies are also working in this technology area. These DSP chips are designed for real-time processing with algorithms as complex as that described by H.264.

27.2.2 H.264 on TV Set-Top Boxes

Rolling out H.264 compatible coders and set-top boxes is no small challenge. In the United Kingdom there are in the region of 10 million MPEG-2 boxes in consumer households. These devices are not going to be replaced quickly.

Upgrading the firmware is not a viable solution because the computing overhead for decoding H.264 compatible and the necessary memory is more than these boxes have available. This legacy situation comes about through delivery of free boxes to the consumers with the hope that the subscription revenues over several years would pay off the cost of the box. Those with the deepest pockets achieved the largest market penetration. So, in the United Kingdom at least, no one is in a hurry to replace the receivers.

27.2.3 HDTV

New markets for TV services have the advantage that they have no installed base and so a new standard is a viable option.

Electronics Weekly DSP special issue: http://www.electronicsweekly.com/Issue200.htm

EDN DSP companies listing: http://www.ednasia.com/dsp2003.htm

Hitachi Semiconductor: http://www.hitachisemiconductor.com/

Texas Instruments: http://www.dspvillage.com/

Equator Technologies: http://www.equator.com/

During 2004, the relevant standards bodies agreed that the H.264 codec would be ideally suited to delivering HDTV transmissions in Europe. It had already been ratified as one of the additional codecs for use on DVD, Windows Media being another.

High-definition TV is becoming more popular and the same techniques and infrastructures as are used for standard-definition TV are applicable. The bit rates for HDTV are somewhat higher for uncompressed material. This is where new coding standards such as H.264 or VC-1 facilitate the transmission of HDTV in existing SDTV networks.

27.2.4   Convergence with the PC

With receivers becoming essentially just PCs in brushed aluminium cases, and PCs becoming more powerful all the time, good receiver-application design in the future should allow some degree of prediction. For example, if the user is channel hopping, some sense of what the user is doing may allow the receiver to buffer the multiplex on which it expects the next selected channel to be located.

Simple one-tuner devices such as the El-Gato Eye TV 400, when plugged into the UK Terrestrial Freeview service, deliver a very good viewing experience, and the technology allows for some interesting home media server development if you connect the tuning and recording processes to an automation system.

27.3   Broadcast Streams

Digital television services all over the world have been deploying MPEG-2 video content embedded within a transport stream. These transport streams are specified by the MPEG-2 standard and are compatible with satellite, terrestrial, and cable systems. Indeed, it is technically possible to deliver the same transport stream to all the platforms provided that it carries a superset of the necessary supporting data streams suitable for all three. This would not be practical for public consumption but is useful in a test and prototyping environment when researchers are developing interactive content and attempting to preview the result.

27.3.1   Evolving the Transport Stream

Because the MPEG-2 transport stream mechanism is sufficiently well evolved, the MPEG-4 standard did not seek to introduce any changes. The MPEG-2 standard allows MPEG-4 content to be carried alongside the MPEG-2 streams in the existing infrastructure. This allows new services to be developed and tested without complete replacement of the broadcast systems that are already working, which have required a significant investment in time and money to develop.

Organizations such as DVB govern the broadcast mechanisms and decide what may be carried. The H.264 codec is likely to be deployed for broadcast HDTV deployment in Europe. It may be that other standards will be deemed acceptable as well, such as SMPTE VC-1 (based on Windows Media), if and when that is finally ratified as a standard. However, it is looking increasingly unlikely that VC-1 will be ratified in time.

27.3.2 Resilience in Transport Streams

Digital-video broadcasts must deliver the content without dropping frames and at a quality that is satisfying to watch for long periods. Commercial pressure dictates that video quality be reduced in favor of broadcasting more channels.

The carriage of the video is quite complex because the transmission medium is designed to carry multiple channels. In the old days of analog video, each channel would only be one video signal. Digital TV carries a bundle or multiplex of TV services on each channel that your receiver is able to tune into. A breakdown of this is shown in Figure 27-1.

A multiplex may carry 6 video signals with stereo audio plus additional language channels and other streams of supporting data.

Digital cable is slightly different because although the same multiplexing technique is used, the cable companies also offer telephone and broadband Internet connections down the same cable.

27.3.3 Switching to Another Stream

In analog TV sets, this happens instantaneously. There is no buffering required before the presentation continues. There may be a slight frame roll or bounce as the display synchronizes, but modern TV sets do this very rapidly.

Switching channels on digital TV sets is quite arduous by comparison. Leaving aside all the issues with tuning and then extracting the program stream from a multiplexed

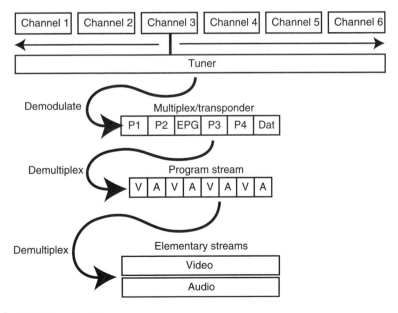

Figure 27-1 Multiplexed data.

transport stream, just switching from one local stream to another seems to take longer than it should on some viewing equipment. The amount of delay depends on the buffering techniques and whether the receiver is smart enough to do some work for you before you decide to change channels.

Sony is developing high-definition products with as many as 7 tuners. These will all decode simultaneously so that switching from one stream to another merely connects the output to the display instead of some kind of sink or null device. Having extra tuners allows multiple simultaneous recordings.

27.3.4 *Statistical Multiplexing*

When the bit rate is fixed, it introduces some inefficiency to your coding system. The video may not always require that amount of bit rate. Reserving that capacity is wasteful when several streams are multiplexed together.

Statistical multiplexing is a more advanced variant of the CBR/VBR approach. It assumes that at any instant in time, some streams are encoding very efficiently, yielding high compression ratios and requiring low bit rates. Others may be bursting at high bit rates.

The theory works as long as the channels are bursting at different times. This does not work when you simulcast the same channel several times (perhaps with regional variants on some kind of opt-out basis for an hour each day).

Statistical multiplexing allows the streams to breathe in and out so that bit rate is constant overall. Each individual stream is able to consume more bit rate while the others are momentarily starved to provide the extra capacity. This technique is used in broadcast systems where multiple compressed video streams are packed into programs and then into transport streams.

Figure 27-2 shows the bit rates for two programs whose bit rate demands peak at different times. Conveniently in this case, one peaks when the other dips.

So when Channel 1 is bursting to a high-bit-rate requirement, Channels 2, 3, 4, and 5 are probably broadcasting something far less complex and requiring fewer bits. Figure 27-3

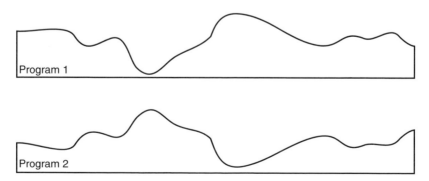

Figure 27-2 Multiple channels.

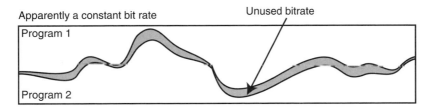

Program 1

Program 2

Apparently a constant bit rate

Unused bitrate

Figure 27-3 Statistical multiplexing

shows what happens when you stack the bit-rate graphs for 2 channels. The bit rate for program 1 has just been plotted from the top axis downward.

There may be times when this technique doesn't deliver the required bit-rate savings. For example, making sure that the type of material being broadcast on each channel is very different is a good idea. Grouping 5 music-video channels together or 5 sports channels that are all likely to be showing content with a lot of motion may detract from the benefits gained by statistical multiplexing.

From a broadcast engineering point of view, the downside of statistical multiplexing is that the coding of all 5 streams must take place at the same time in the same system. Uncompressed content must be delivered, so the feeds to the coder and multiplexer must have a high bit rate and be of good quality. This increases the amount of wiring that is necessary.

Statistical multiplexing is more useful to TV broadcasters than to anyone else. The source material is likely to be delivered to the coders as *SDI* video running at 25 Mbps (also known as DV25). There are higher-bit-rate formats, such as DV50, but these tend to be used for production processes.

27.4 Analog Switch-Off

Digital TV has been broadcast in the United Kingdom for a number of years, and the penetration into households passed 50% in 2004. Analog TV is in declining use and will likely be discontinued in the foreseeable future. Predictions about when analog TV will be turned off vary from one country to another, but already citywide TV distribution in Germany and community-wide broadcasting in Wales have switched to all-digital delivery. Most other broadcasters are predicting between 10 and 15 years before the demise of analog TV.

27.5 DVD Publishing

DVD is a random-access, file-based storage container. The video is compressed using MPEG-2 and is then encrypted with the content scrambling system (CSS) algorithm. Applications that decode this video are widely available for all types of PCs and operating

Table 27-1 HD-DVD Formats and Bit Rates

Format	Bit rate
MPEG-2/HD	15–20 Mbps
H.264/AVC HD	6–10 Mbps
WM9/VC-1 SD/HD Video	7–12 Mbps

systems. The encoded video may be PAL or NTSC. A high-definition format called MPEG-2/HD is available as one of the alternative formats for next-generation HD-DVD disks. The three selected formats and bit rates are shown in Table 27-1.

The interactivity on a DVD is reputed to be based around MHEG, which might provide useful opportunities for content creators who are able to target multiple platforms. However, finding documentary evidence to confirm this is very difficult, and you will need to purchase the DVD specifications to find out the exact details. These specifications are available only from Phillips and cost $5000 each! The information you need is going to be expensive and hard to obtain, which probably explains why there are not many DVD authoring systems available. Those that are available have been produced by large companies with deep pockets. No doubt this pricing is necessary to discourage casual hacking of DVD content, but it also probably makes very little difference to a determined piracy organization.

27.5.1 H.264 on DVDs

DVDs implemented with H.264 could be manufactured as a single-layer disk and still carry about the same duration of content as a dual-layer disk does now. That should reduce the manufacturing costs that are based on the cycle time of producing each disk. Reducing this from 3 seconds per disk to 2 seconds cuts the production costs significantly.

H.264 is one of the selected alternatives for delivering HD video on next-generation DVDs. This would run at a bit rate of around 6–10 Mbps.

27.6 Digital Video Recorders and Video on Demand

Digital video recorders (DVRs), such as the TiVo device, have begun to mature and to include more useful integration with other services.

TiVo is now able to connect to OpenTalk-enabled services being shared by a Mac OS system on the same network. This potentially allows it to display the iPhoto pictures and play the iTunes song libraries on your TV. It is the beginning of an integrated home-media network that doesn't revolve around a single device and works in a distributed fashion due to the interoperability provided by different manufacturers.

The alternative is the eHome or Media Center approach that Microsoft is promoting. That system would be built around a set of devices that are all running the Windows operating system.

There is room for both approaches, although at this stage in the game everyone is trying to carve out market share at each other's expense. This will all evolve and unfold over the next few years as the technologies are developed. For any of them to succeed, mutual interoperability must ensure that they all succeed. It won't work if one company is dominant.

27.6.1 Downloadable Files

Downloadable files are a potential delivery mechanism for low-bandwidth situations. They might also be used to download content to a DVR device in something less than real time. It may not matter how long it takes to transfer this material. It could be delivered quickly, on a fast broadband or broadcast-transport mechanism, or slowly, via a modem link. Table 27-2 enumerates some delivery times for the same broadcast-quality content over several alternative links. It assumes H.264 video compression at 2 Mbps and transferring a clip of 5 minutes' duration.

It is clear from this table that DVR devices connected via dialup modems are not going to have sufficient throughput and that a broadband connection at 500 Kbps or significantly better is what is required.

27.6.2 Peer-to-Peer Opportunities

The peer-to-peer model applies here. Some systems have a built-in limitation because the delivery might be processed asynchronously due to the fact that upload speeds on ADSL lines are lower than download speeds. This impedes the delivery of a stream but does not matter for shared files unless the transfer is charged by the minute.

27.6.3 Trick Play

The trick-play capabilities tend to be implemented at an application level and are special decoding modes.

Recall our earlier discussion on GOP structures. To reconstruct every 8th frame in order to play the video in a fast-forward mode will still require significant amounts of work to decode the delta frames. Obviously, no processing power is required to display

Table 27-2 Delivery Times Versus Bit Rates

Bit rate	Estimated delivery time
Broadcast at 4.5 Mbps (normal MPEG-2 bit rates)	2 minutes, 15 seconds
Broadcast at 2 Mbps	5 minutes
Broadband 1 Mbps	10 minutes
Broadband 500 Kbps	20 minutes
Modem 56 Kbaud	4 hours

7 of those 8 frames, but that task was likely delegated to a graphics co-processor anyway. Your CPU is still going to be working quite hard.

The trick-play features inform the way that you set up the encoding. You might, for example, place I-frames at useful intervals and shorten the GOP length in order to improve the fast-forward playback quality.

27.6.4 Double Speed

This is implemented in a very simple way. It is only necessary to discard every other frame. The computational effort involved depends on whether it is necessary to decode only a single I-frame or several P- and B-frames to extract the required image. Encoded video should be played forward; later versions of the standards allow for bi-directional playback, so reverse play is also supported as a trivial engineering task.

27.6.5 Pause

Implementing this is easy because you simply stop the decoder. Pausing digital TV services presents a very stable and high-quality paused picture when compared with the performance of a VHS player. If you recall the kind of artifacts that analog suffered from when being paused, you will see that even gross digital artifacts yield a still image of superior quality.

27.6.6 High-Definition DVRs

Already, companies are starting to investigate delivering DVR technology, which will cope with HDTV services. Pace is a company that makes set-top boxes that other companies can then brand with their own logo and add value to. They have introduced an HD-capable DVR product for cable and satellite broadcasting.

27.7 Receiving TV on Your PC

Increasing numbers of hardware suppliers are packaging TV tuners in a way that is convenient for attachment to your PC. This enables you to display the broadcast TV in a window on the desktop or perhaps think about building your own media center and DVR system.

Alchemy TV, Hauppauge, and ElGato are three companies whose products are particularly successful. ElGato is an interesting case because it is attached by FireWire to a Macintosh. This suggests that you could connect it to a laptop and receive digital TV in a mobile situation. This is practical for DTT or might lend itself to DVB-H compatible mobile services. Obviously DCable and DSat are non-starters in mobile situations because of the dish size required or the permanent connection to a cable.

ElGato also offers receivers for DTV services as well as analog, and you can connect to just about any kind of TV service you want. Some of their products are also

Table 27-3 Some Examples of PC-Based TV Receivers

Receiver	MacOS	Windows
Miglia–Alchemy TV	Yes	No
Hauppage–WinTV	No	Yes
ElGato–Eye TV	Yes	Not currently but technically feasible

HDTV ready. This is a neat solution because it basically just receives the DVB transport stream and any decoding and presentation is done by the application. This allows you to write your own plug-in modules and intercept that decoding process to extract data feeds.

Some varieties of these TV tuners also receive radio, and if you don't want an outboard box then a PCI card is a viable alternative.

27.8　TV on the Go and Mobile DVR Products

Another area that is growing in interest is the use of the DVB-H standard. This gives mobile-equipment manufacturers the opportunity to build TV services that can be enjoyed by viewers on the move.

Pace has anticipated the demand for recording this kind of material and viewing it in a time-shifted manner. At the IBC 2004 conference, they introduced a handheld DVR product that features a 40-GB drive and a 5-inch widescreen display.

Another contender in this area is Nokia, with its very unusual-looking portable media-player device. The next chapter explores these mobile video technologies.

Alchemy TV: http://www.miglia.com/

Win TV: http://www.hauppage.com/

El Gato: http://www.elgato.com/

Pace Micro Technology: http://www.pacemicro.com/

Nokia: http://www.nokia.com/

28

Digital Video on the Move

28.1 Mobile Phone Delivery

Delivering content to mobile phones is technically feasible with third-generation (3G) mobile devices. These use 3G Partnership Project (3GPP) profiles based on an MPEG-4 derivative using the H.264 codec. At the available bit rates, every transmitted bit must carry useful data. The consumer or the operator is paying by the packet; thus, a compression system that wastes packets also wastes money. Customers will not put up with that for very long.

28.2 Bit-Rate Limitations

Bear in mind that the available bandwidths for mobile devices are as low as 64 Kbps. Reducing the frame rate of the video you encode will allow more bit rate to be retained for image quality. Keep the clips short. Thirty seconds is plenty. You might find that a streaming solution is preferred to a downloaded video solution because the handset memory is somewhat limited. Check the network provider specs and also be aware that not all handsets support downloading content. It may be a 3GPP2 issue anyway, and not relevant to your customer. Streaming is not the same as progressive download, which also may or may not be supported. Do plenty of investigative planning and then lots of testing.

28.3 Quality Issues

If you are creating content for this medium, you must use source material of the highest quality available. Because the compression renders the video down to a very low bit rate, the codec must deliver the best possible averaging of the image, and it can do this more effectively if the video is clean to start with.

Ideally, the source should be Motion JPEG, or raw uncompressed video. MPEG-2 or MPEG-1 is fine as long as it is cleanly compressed in the first place, and DV format is good too.

Try to avoid sourcing 3GPP material from already compressed, Web-based content. Noisy VHS tapes are also a bad source format, and anything that's been produced for TV consumption must be looked at carefully because it is probably not ideal for mobile devices.

 When streaming to GRPS, 3G, and dial-up modems, use Frame Skip Probability—this sets the priority to sustain the bit rate, sacrificing the frame rate in return.

When encoding content for use on mobile devices whose screens are very small, consider the following points:

- Compose the shots so the picture is framed tightly on the action.
- Avoid cuts between scenes.
- Use large, clear text.
- Make the packages short.
- Use mono audio.
- Pre-emphasize the audio for small speaker size.
- Gamma-correct video for the display characteristics.

Typical size for packages used to be 90 KB, but this has increased to 300 KB now that the networks can transfer downloads more quickly.

28.4 Encoding Formats

Encoding formats for 3GPP include H.263, AMR, MPEG-4 Simple Profile—Level 0, and AAC audio. Make sure to check on the kind of packetizing that the network requires.

For 3GPP2, H.263 is okay with audio in QCELP format. AMR, MPEG-4 Simple Profile—Level 0, and AAC are also fine.

Also check out the Kinoma codec and player. They have been designed with mobile applications in mind, although they are aimed more at PDA users than mobile phone operators.

28.5 3GPP Versus 3GPP2

The differences between the two 3G file formats are subtle and are best shown in a tabular form. Table 28-1 enumerates the various properties of both standards.

Kinoma: http://www.kinoma.com

Table 28-1 3GPP Format Specifications

File format	3GPP	3GPP2
Network type	GSM	CDMA2000
Video coding	MPEG-4, H.263	MPEG-4, H.263
Audio coding	AAC, AMR	AAC, AMR, QCELP
Text coding	3G Text	3G Text
Physical file format	QuickTime	QuickTime
File extension	.3gp	.3g2

28.6   Different Kinds of Networks

The mobile community supports a variety of different types of networks, depending on your operator and where in the world you are using the device. Some networking technologies are used more widely than others. The more efficient the networking technology, the larger the video payload you can deliver. Larger payloads mean better quality.

Table 28-2 lists several kinds of network technologies and suggests some bit rates that might be appropriate as starting points for testing content on them.

Table 28-2 Mobile Network Technologies

Network type	Generation	Bit rate	Quality	Resolution	FPS	90 KB duration	300 KB duration
GSM	2G	9.6 Kbps	Bad for video	n/a	n/a	n/a	n/a
HSCD	2.5G	28 Kbps	Good for stills	128 × 96	4	27 sec	90 sec
GPRS	2.5G	24-50 Kbps	Good for stills	144 × 120	6	19 sec	63 sec
EDGE	3G	64-200 Kbps	Good for streaming	160 × 120	8	11 sec	37 sec
UMTS	3G	128-384 Kbps	Excellent	174 × 144	10	5 sec	17 sec

Third Generation Partnership Project (3GPP): http://www.3gpp.org/
Third Generation Partnership Project 2 (3GPP2): http://www.3gpp2.org/

28.7 Production Workflow

You should build an automated workflow for mobile-service content creation. The Popwire Compression Engine supports watch folders and server-oriented solutions that are ideal for this application. If you have live content to be streamed, then Popwire Broadcaster may be just what you need. You can find out more about all of the Popwire products at their web site.

The Compression Engine product is meant to be used for "industrial strength" encoding systems. This product is designed to work in a server-based environment and will automatically distribute work around a cluster if you have one. As part of the process, you can apply filters to clean and de-interlace the content prior to compression.

28.8 Other Technologies to Explore

There are some important technologies and emerging standards relating to mobile systems. If you want to investigate these further, then searching the Internet for certain keywords will lead you to some useful documents. Depending on the territory you are targeting with your content for mobiles, these terms may be relevant to your operation:

- DVB-H
- DMB
- ISDB-T
- WiMAX
- BSAC
- HSDPA

HSDPA (High Speed Downlink Packet Access) is a faster delivery technology developed by Motorola. This delivers 2 Mbps to the mobile device and Siemens has plans to introduce capacities of up to 1 Gbps, which is about 20 times as fast as current technology allows. Useful information about the technologies used by mobile operators and the companies that develop them can be found at the Global mobile Suppliers Association (GSA) Web site.

28.8.1 Digital Video Broadcasting—Handheld

The Digital Video Broadcasting—Handheld (DVB-H) standard has been developed by the DVB Organization for the broadcast of content that is like traditional TV to handheld devices such as mobile phones. It has previously been known as DVB-M and DVB-X.

Popwire Technology production workflow: http://www.popwire.com/

DVB-H information: http://www.dvb.org/index.php?id=278

IPDC Forum: http://www.ipdc-forum.org/

BMCO-Berlin: http://www.bmco-berlin.com/

RTT: http://www.rtt.tv/

DigiTAG: http://www.digitag.org/

Open Mobile Alliance: http://www.openmobilealliance.org/

Nokia: http://www.nokia.com/

Wireless Multimedia Forum: http://www.wmmforum.com/

GSA: http://www.gsacom.com/

The DVB-H devices have very different characteristics from normal TV receivers in terms of power consumption, screen size, and mobility. Even portable TV receivers are more like the static sets that you have in your living room. The DVB-H standard also describes data services.

Manufacturers such as Nokia and Pace are already showing prototype products based on this standard.

Draft documents and initial versions of the standard are published on the DVB web site. Other DVB-H material is available at IPDC, BMCO-Berlin, DigiTAG, and RTT.

28.8.2   *Digital Multimedia Broadcasting*

The digital multimedia broadcasting (DMB) service is a satellite-based system that is designed to deliver TV and radio to mobile devices such as phones and laptops. It is very new and still being developed but is currently being rolled out in Asia. Because it is satellite based, there are gaps in the service, such as when the user is underground. These are being dealt with by installing gap fillers to ensure that service is uninterrupted.

The design takes account of users who may be in transit, and so it is still usable at speeds up to 150 km per hour (or about 90 miles per hour).

Initially delivering as many as 12 visual and 26 radio channels, the service is expected to reach 8 million subscribers by 2010. The services are based on MPEG-4 standards and use H.264 coding for the video. The audio and video presentations are combined in a BIFS container, which describes the scenes.

28.8.3   *Integrated Services Digital Broadcasting—Terrestrial*

ISDB-T has evolved from the digital terrestrial TV (DTT) services. It is another example of how these technologies are adopted very early on in the Far East. ISDB-T is designed to scale from audio only up to HDTV applications in mobile situations.

This service is similar enough to DVB-H that the two might converge in the future, but for the time being they are moving forward independently of each other.

28.8.4   *WiMAX (IEEE 802.16)*

This is the next step onwards from the Wi-Fi IEEE 802.11 standards, which have become popular for wireless networking over short ranges.

The WiMAX standard addresses similar needs to the DMB services in the Far East. It is also designed to cope with the receiver's being on the move at rapid transit speeds. The goal is to deliver broadband connectivity speeds to mobile devices over a range of 25 to 30 miles. This is far greater than the 300-foot radius of an 802.11 hotspot.

This is also known as Mobile-Fi as opposed to Wi-Fi; Mobile Broadband Wireless Access (MBWA) is yet another name for it. It's the usual 1 concept to 300 different names ratio just to confuse the innocent.

Samsung DMB chips: http://www.samsung.com/

This is being touted as an alternative to wiring everyone's home with optical fiber in order to cover the last mile from the exchange to the consumer. While this is all very exciting stuff, it also increases the spectrum of radio-frequency energy that we are constantly bathing ourselves in.

28.8.5 *Bit-Sliced Arithmetic Coding*

BSAC is the part of the MPEG-4 Part 3 audio coding standard that allows the data transfer to be scaled in increments when delivering audio over a wireless network. It is used in the DMB platform that's currently being developed in Asia.

28.9 So How Do We Make It Work?

We now have a pretty good idea of where our content comes from, how it works, where it is going, and how we might get it there. That positions us very well to design and build a system to process the video. We might be a small outfit or a large enterprise. Either way, we'll probably use the same coding techniques and the difference will just be in the scale of the system and the amount of money we are prepared to spend on it.

In the next chapter we will find out how to construct the hardware foundation for our systems.

Building Your Encoding Hardware

29.1 Let's Spend Some Money

This chapter is about the components that you would use to build a system as well as the process of designing and building a system with those components. Building a system with sufficient capacity to store your video is important, and there are a variety of disk storage alternatives.

In this chapter, the emphasis is on video. Setting up audio equipment was covered thoroughly in Chapter 7. To give this some real-world context, at the end of the chapter, the summary plans the construction of three different systems:

- Single-user, home-based system—built on a budget
- Small workgroup sharing some storage—medium cost
- Large-enterprise-sized system—money no object

You should plan and build your system to as high a standard as possible. The more diligent you are in designing your system, the better it will work in the long term. Even if you are running a very small system, pay attention to the systems administration. Document your system, do your backups, and take out the trash periodically.

29.2 Planning Your System

There is no substitute for sitting down and working out your plans before you start. Probably the first question to ask yourself is how much money you have available to spend on this project. The more complex you build it, the more it will cost. It helps to organize your system building if you break the process down into separate steps or phases:

- Phase 1—Planning
- Phase 2—Purchasing
- Phase 3—Building
- Phase 4—Commissioning
- Phase 5—Day-to-day operational matters

- Phase 6—Upgrading
- Phase 7—Emergencies and disaster recovery

Working on it like this helps you to focus on the requirements of each discrete part of the planning and building process.

29.2.1   Dream Your Dreams

It's a good idea to dream of the maximum scope your system will scale to and then work out how to build it in stages. Then you can avoid painting yourself into a corner that prevents future upgrades. An example of thinking in a scalable fashion would be to build a 2-node cluster. It is so small that it scarcely qualifies as a cluster, but because it is in fact a cluster, adding a third node is very easy. If your ultimate goal is to build a 10-node cluster, start with one master and one slave. As the money comes in from client jobs, add the subsequent nodes when you can afford them.

29.2.2   Foster Good Habits and Reliable Working Practices

You should study and implement good practices, such as archiving and backup. Making sure this is considered at the outset is very important. Later on when you realize you need backup facilities, it is hard to justify the cost when the entire budget has already been spent. Larger installations should build this into a tiered storage strategy with faster and more expensive storage closer to the users. A rule of thumb is that the cost of storage is correlated to how fast the access is.

Document everything, even if you work on your own with a small system.

 Keep track of your dongles. These are the little plug-in hardware keys that are supplied with some software. They might plug into serial ports, parallel ports, or USB interfaces. Identify and label them or record their serial numbers so you know what each one is and where it is. Lose them and you have to buy another copy of the software. They are your license to use it, so be careful!

29.2.3   Building a Custom System from Scratch

You might enjoy the challenge of building the system for fun and profit from scratch. There are open-source projects available on the Internet with some very good video encoders. The industry is learning a lot from these open-source communities. The question is whether the extra work involved is worth it. Of course, the pleasure is sometimes in the journey, and building a system just exactly how you want it may be a very satisfying experience. It is not always about the money—or the performance.

29.2.4   Decide Your Priorities Before Spending Any Cash

When you build your system, it is important to set out what your priorities are. If you are building a large corporate-sized workflow solution, then the productivity is going to be important. Factors that affect this will make a significant difference to the bottom line. Everything must be designed to reduce latency and increase the throughput.

On the other hand, if you are building a system to process your collection of home movies or videos, then performance may be less critical and it is likely that the cost factor will be the most important.

Semi-professional or independent filmmakers might deem quality of output to be more important than cost. Improvements in productivity bring in more dollars because you can get more chargeable work done in less time. Therefore, it is worth a little more investment up front.

Obviously, the most desirable outcome is a system that is dirt cheap but will process everything you throw at it instantly with no effort involved in setting up new compression jobs. In reality, however, you are going to have to compromise somewhere.

So start with this list of basic requirements, add your own ideas to it, and put them into priority order. Only then should you start to scope out your system and work up your shopping list.

- Target consumer platform
- Quality of output
- Ease of use in workflow
- Scale of production (throughput)
- Needs for automation and batching
- Codec choices
- Cost of building the system
- Ongoing running costs
- Operating system choice

29.2.5 *Understand the Life Cycle*

The life cycle of your digital video starts at the point where the incoming video is connected to your computer. You may have a variety of source formats and playback devices for that.

In a broadcasting environment, the video will almost certainly have already been digitized and will arrive in one of the industry-standard digital formats, most likely a serial digital interface (SDI). Note that European and American SDI formats may differ from one another and you need to ensure that the equipment you buy is compatible.

News organizations are very interested in the possibilities offered by the material exchange format (MXF) container format, and so news feeds might arrive as MXF-packaged files in the not too distant future.

If your incoming video is analog, then the video input card is responsible for sampling and converting that video to a stream of digital values. The least processor-intensive method is to just store the stream in a file.

The most likely scenario is that some kind of encoding takes place. In edit suites, it is common practice to ingest a proxy or low-quality version of the video, being careful to note the time-code location of that material on the source tape. This is called logging.

Edit the proxy copy and transfer the edit decision list (EDL) with the original tape to a more expensive system where the EDL is used as a control script to carry out the same edit process on the full-quality, high-resolution original. This is called conforming. Between the two processes may be a step that involves a skilled editor's making sure the edit points are clean and visually attractive. This is called craft editing. An example life cycle is illustrated in Figure 29-1.

This life cycle is obviously built around a reasonably large organization. Draw up your own workflow charts even if you are planning small systems and working on your

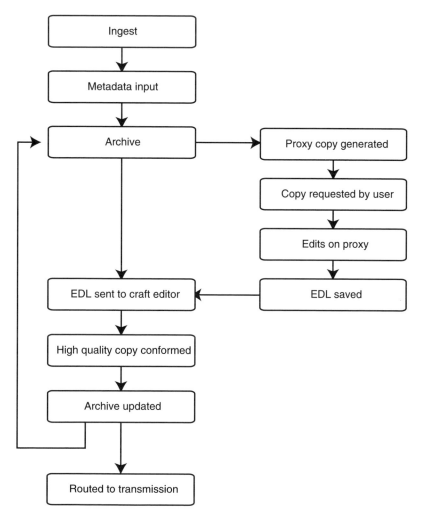

Figure 29-1 Editing life cycle.

own. It will get you thinking in the right way, and that will pay dividends when your business grows larger.

29.2.6 System Design

Work out the various connectivity requirements of your system. What equipment will you be installing? What sources and destinations do you have? Decide on standards for video and audio delivery. Make lists of equipment and ascertain whether each one has an Ethernet connector on the back. If it does, then it will need an IP address allocated. Draw up lots of lists and make diagrams to help you plan.

It is not necessary to create many complex diagrams. A few sketches of your system connections will be helpful if you need to do some maintenance later on. The main reason for this level of detail is to help you see what you are building and plan it properly. We will come back to this example and build on it later. You should prepare at least the following documentation:

- Connection layout diagram showing major equipment and cabling required.
- A summary of your wiring circuits.
- A list of sources and destinations with details of their format.
- A set of competitive price quotations for each major component.
- A budget plan with capital, building, commissioning, and maintenance costs.
- For larger installations, a summary of power requirements.
- Also for larger installations, a summary of heat dissipation.

29.3 Purchasing Strategies

Be realistic about what you actually need and what you can get by with for now if money is scarce. You can probably do without that fastest and best new CPU that has just been launched. In 6 months' time it will not be the fastest anyway, because a better model will have been launched by then. Staying just behind that technology curve can save you thousands of dollars. The same applies to disk storage and versions of software.

29.3.1 Good Deals on Hardware

If you are buying Apple Computer hardware, there are several reliable refurbished-systems suppliers. A refurbished machine comes with a factory guarantee and has nothing substantially wrong with it. So what if there is a small scratch on the case?—these are good deals.

Look for end-of-life product lines. Right around the time a manufacturer is about to introduce a new model, the old lines are often sold at reduced prices. The prices decline even further after the new model comes out. This happens because the distribution channels need to be cleared of old stock before the new machines start shipping. This is the smart way to stay just behind the leading edge. These systems are a good value because they have been around awhile and any bugs and shortcomings they might have had when new have usually been solved.

29.3.2 Good Deals on Software

The same trick works for software, as long as the purchase works on your version of the OS you select. Waiting for version 8 (Creative Suite) of Photoshop to come out and then buying a copy of version 7 on a closeout deal saves several hundred dollars. Sometimes you get deals where the upgrade to the current version is free or at least at a reduced cost. The old version's price plus the cost of an upgrade is still likely to be less than the cost of the new version. So you have to install it and then put in an upgrade. That is a half-hour's worth of inconvenience versus a couple of hundred dollars of extra cost. What's more, maybe that later version has features you don't even need.

29.3.3 More Information on Suppliers

For a list of compression-hardware manufacturers, consult Appendix B. Software manufacturers and products are listed in Appendix C.

29.4 Video Connectivity

There is a variety of different video-hardware interfaces you will often encounter when connecting your system together. Each interface has advantages and disadvantages. The connectors on the back of your equipment are specific to each one. They are either professional or consumer oriented, although some professional equipment such as the Sony DSR DR 1000P hard disk recorder supports both kinds. Higher-spec connectivity implies more expensive equipment.

29.4.1 Serial Digital Interface

A serial digital interface (SDI) is a digitized version of the analog component signals. Virtually all of the video connections within a studio environment will take place with SDI signals. Beware of the specifics of the SDI interfaces on your equipment, because there are differences between the American and European bit structures and the hardware may support one or more of a variety of SDI-based protocols. The SMPTE 259M standard specifies four basic variants:

- Composite NTSC transferred at 143 Mbps.
- Composite PAL transferred at 177 Mbps.
- Rec 601 4:2:2 component video transferred at 270 Mbps.
- Rec 601 4:2:2 component video (16:9 format) transferred at 360 Mbps.

Connections are made with 75-Ohm coaxial cable fitted with BNC plugs/sockets. Some equipment allows tee splitters to be inserted, while other equipment may be extremely sensitive to a drop in the signal level. This connection is good for about 100 feet of cable. Racks that are further away can be connected with fiberoptic transducers with only a local signal being carried via coax.

Bear in mind that audio signals may either be embedded in the serial digital stream or be supplied separately.

29.4.2 Composite

This is an analog signal predominantly used as a consumer format. Some older offline studio systems and desktop-monitoring equipment may use this format as well. Composite video is delivered on a single-screened cable and connector using an RCA jack (i.e., a phono plug).

29.4.3 S-Video

S-video is designed as a superior connection for consumer equipment that delivers the luma and chroma signals down separate wires. It is connected together with a 4-way cable that has special mini-plugs at each end. In an emergency, an Apple ADB keyboard cable will serve as an S-video connector. This signal may also be delivered via a SCART (Peritel) connector.

29.5   Audio Connectivity

Audio comes in several flavors, depending on whether you are connecting consumer or professional equipment. In broadcasting systems, the audio may be supplied in a variety of formats:

- Unbalanced mono
- Unbalanced dual mono or stereo
- Balanced mono or stereo
- AES digital audio
- SPDIF
- Surround DTS, THX, Dolby, AC3, 5.1, 6.1, 7.1

29.5.1 Consumer Audio

Stereo audio from line-out sockets on domestic hi-fi equipment connects using RCA phono jacks. Originally designed for connecting hi-fi separates, it is now often found on computer audio input/output (I/O) panels and mixing desks. Each wire carries an unbalanced analog mono signal.

29.5.2 Balanced Analog Audio

Refer to Chapter 7 for a discussion on balanced audio and how it works. The signal is transmitted down two wires with a common ground. External USB and FireWire interfaces and mixing desks will all likely support this. Many will also supply the 48-volt phantom power required by some condenser microphones. Professional-grade equipment has latching XLR connectors. Balanced audio is not usually available on low-cost, consumer-oriented computer I/O panels.

29.5.3 AES Digital Audio

TV studios will likely use balanced analog audio or AES digital audio. The benefit of using AES is that up to 8 channels can be embedded in the SDI video signal, thus significantly reducing your cabling infrastructure and the costs of providing it. This is more significant when routing via fiberoptic circuits, as it reduces the number of circuits and transducers required. Circuits are expensive and the transducers cost many hundreds of dollars each—and you need one at each end, on every circuit. Your alternative is multiple-fiber circuits, which makes the cost of embedders and de-embedders very trivial by comparison.

29.5.4 USB Audio

New equipment is being developed all the time. If your audio needs are modest, then check out the M-Audio FastTrack interface. It's designed to be small and economical, and it just plugs into an available USB port on your computer. This makes adding a good-quality audio input to your system very easy.

29.6 Choosing an Operating System

An encoding platform can be built on any OS. Some operating systems lend themselves more easily to this than others because of the additional software that is installed along with the OS. All of them are equally viable. It is just as realistic to build your system on Mac OS X as on Linux, Windows, or any other mid-range system such as Solaris or IRIX.

There may be some limitations on the support for a particular proprietary codec as a result of marketing choices made by the supplier. Certain codecs may be built into the operating system and therefore whatever tool you choose is irrelevant since the same codec machinery is invoked each time. Some tools may provide more controls than others, so it is worth investigating the alternatives. Getting something that is simple to operate but not very flexible might be better than having to acquire in-depth training and knowledge to get the best results out of a complex and detailed parameter set.

29.6.1 Building Around a Mac OS Architecture

On the Macintosh platform, the Sorenson Squeeze 4 product or the Popwire Technology compression tools are the current state of the art. Discreet Cleaner may still be useful for some work. The current version is getting a bit old now and has not been upgraded for some time. The product is apparently not discontinued, but no announcements have yet been made about future upgrades.

29.6.2 Building Around a Windows Architecture

On the Windows platform, you have the Microsoft Windows Media tools, which are clearly going to work at an optimum level on this platform since they come from the same manufacturer as the operating system.

If you prefer, there are other specialized tools such as Canopus ProCoder, and as was the case with Linux, you may have some open-source alternatives available as well. Sorenson Squeeze 4 is also available for Windows.

29.6.3 Building Around a Linux Architecture

On the Linux platform, your choice is likely to be one of the open-source solutions. Obvious candidates are DivX (which is a derivative of MPEG-4) or maybe the *Ogg Vorbis* codec. There are others, too. If you want to go with a proprietary solution, the Real Networks products are quite popular, although their penetration of the market is declining in favor of Windows Media and QuickTime compared to the market share that it used to enjoy.

29.7 Choosing a CPU

In the end, the amount of computing power that you deploy is what dictates the through-put of your encoder. You might build a system in a suboptimum way and bottleneck it by badly configuring your storage or keeping everything on remote network drives and writing back to a remote device. Assuming you have not done anything stupid with your system design, the raw CPU power is what counts.

29.7.1 Single or Dual Processor?

A fast single-CPU computer may compress faster than a slightly slower dual processor because the codec may not have been optimized for dual-processor operation. If it has, the technical specs should mention that as a feature. Match the codec hardware requirements to the CPU. Checking the manufacturer's online knowledge base (if they have one) will often direct you to a Frequently Asked Questions (FAQ) or specifications with the information you need. Alternatively, if you telephone the manufacturer of the codec you want to use, the technical support staff for the product in question should be able to answer questions about choosing an optimal CPU for their codec.

29.7.2 Processor Architecture

It is a mistake to base your assumptions purely on GHz clocking speeds for the CPUs. Some CPU architectures lend themselves well to video compression for very subtle reasons.

High-end IBM PowerPC architectures have a roughly equal computational through-put to equivalently priced Intel CPUs, even though the clock speeds differ by as much as 33%. All manufacturers claim to deliver the fastest systems. These claims should be viewed with some suspicion unless independent test laboratories produce the results. This is a moving target in any case, and while a particular brand may be fastest on the planet today, competitors will develop and launch products in the future that beat that perform-ance in order to gain a competitive edge.

29.8 Compression Workstation Memory

Recall the discussion in Chapter 10 where macroblocks and different kinds of frames were described. If you think about how the algorithm is implemented, you will soon realize that a very large amount of data must be kept around for some time in order to allow the encoder to look backward and forward in time so that it creates efficient B-frames.

This requires a lot of memory, and the fastest memory is in RAM. Building your sys-tem with larger physical memory capacity rather than depending on virtual memory being paged in and out will result in much better performance when compressing video.

Rule of thumb: Put in as much memory as you can afford.

 Get lots of memory.

29.9 Disk Storage Architectures

This is a book-length topic on its own, so we are only going to hit the high points here.

Whether you build a cluster of tightly coupled machines or simply network some nodes in a loosely collaborative way, you will need to design some storage mechanisms that will provide sufficient space and also allow the storage to be accessible and shared among several machines. The challenges you face are as follows:

- Keeping it cost effective.
- Scaling it larger when necessary.
- Backing things up regularly and reliably.
- Recovering something from the archives.
- Keeping everything online and running smoothly.

Storage systems are built from these components:

- Memory
- Virtual memory (on disk)

- Internal disk-based file systems
- External disk-based file systems
- RAID stores

You can organize your storage architecture like this:

- Direct-attached storage (DAS)
- Network-attached storage (NAS)
- Storage area networks (SAN)

 Get enough disk space. You'll be up a creek if you run out just in the closing stages of a lengthy compression job.

29.9.1 *Direct-Attached Storage*

DAS is the storage that you attach to the CPU. You can share it with other users if you like. The storage gets powered on and off when your workstation does. It is only available for other users to share when your workstation is turned on.

If you are running a small single-user system, there is little point in building huge shared-storage arrays. Just max up a compression workstation with a couple of terabytes of storage.

Attaching extra disk capacity with FireWire or SCSI is a good idea. External disks are better than installing more drives inside the main computer case. Using RAID arrays instead of single drives provides fast and large storage capacity. Installing RAID systems is not a good idea for archival storage unless they are part of a SAN. Archive systems should have sufficient parity protection that they can auto-recover the lost data if a drive goes bad. A reliable and functioning backup strategy should be deployed, too.

Go for RAID 0, which gives you more and faster disk space. RAID 1 gives you resilience through mirroring (duplication). Unfortunately, you only end up with 50% of the capacity you buy. RAID 3 is quite good if you have a sufficient number of drives, because the resilience costs you just one extra drive to store parity data on.

DAS is appropriate for small setups, for adding to individual workstations in a workgroup. If you go enterprise-sized and install a SAN, it is unnecessary to add DAS over and above what is already there.

29.9.2 *Fiber Channel–Connected Drives*

If FireWire in single or duplex configurations is too slow for your requirements, then put a fiber channel interface card in a PCI slot and use an optical fiber-connected storage system. This is a fast way to move video or in fact any bulky data set around. It is also a fast way to empty your bank account because it is very expensive. The high-performance drives can only be connected to computers fitted with a fiber-channel interface. The ubiquity of a FireWire connection is just so much more attractive (and cheaper). Fiber-channel connection might be used to attach large amounts of storage to a centralized server that shares the content out across a network.

29.9.3   Network-Attached Storage

Network-attached storage (NAS) is disk space that you mount via the network. Network File System (NFS), Samba, and file transfer protocol (FTP) are all ways to access files on NAS. Bear in mind that what looks like NAS to you is DAS on another machine that is serving you. All the arguments about resilience of DAS storage apply back at that home base. Figure 29-2 shows the basic NAS concept. NAS is a fashionable name for file sharing that has been around for some time. It has networking bottlenecks, but it is good for 3 to 10 people to share things, provided you put in a fast network, like gigabit Ethernet.

NAS systems commonly use NFS or the Common Internet File Systems (CIFS) to share the drives. Mac OS systems can also use the AppleTalk protocols, and when integrating systems together with a mixture of operating systems you might use the Samba protocol.

Choose whether to install dedicated NAS servers or just serve the space with a spare CPU. This is a good use for an old machine that is being retired after having been replaced by a faster machine for your compression work.

NAS is a good solution for a system composed of several nodes. If you have a half-dozen systems configured optimally for different tasks, then a central shared store is a good idea. You could do daily backups and also keep archives and project reference information there. Don't write compressor output directly to NAS. Write it to DAS and then copy it across when the job is finished.

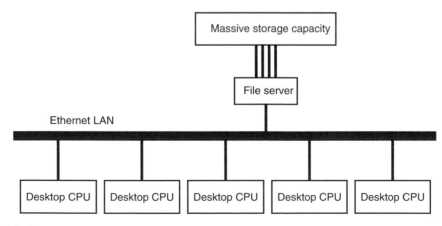

Figure 29-2 File server–based network topology.

29.9.4 Storage-Area Networks

Storage-area network (SAN) systems have been evolving for several years, and they represent the current state of the art for high-end workgroup storage. A SAN is fast, low latency, and shareable across a few dozen people (any more than that and you start to get traffic problems). Where the performance improvement has been added is in the area of metadata. Figure 29-3 shows how these are all connected together.

If a SAN is properly designed and implemented, it will look to the workstation user as if he or she is accessing an internally mounted, direct-attached drive even though the drive is remotely coupled by optical fiber.

A SAN requires a fiber-channel switch in order to connect it to the workstations and get the required throughput. This is fundamental to getting it working; trying to save money here is a false economy. The switch is easily the most expensive part of the whole SAN system.

Normally, you enquire about the state of a file system from the network-attached server. This is the same place that the files are stored. The SAN architecture delegates a lot of this work to a secondary node called a metadata controller. This SAN file system catalog is stored here and is accessible quickly because the network is not saturated with file I/O. The client talks to the metadata controller, finds out where on the SAN disk the files are stored, and requests the physical file space via the fiber-channel link.

Other positive aspects of SAN systems include the following:

- Backup can be built into the SAN back end.
- Metadata controllers can be backed up with a secondary controller—the cost is incremental and you are already spending a lot.

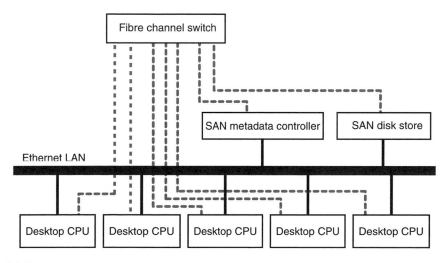

Figure 29-3 SAN systems' organization.

- Storage is aggregated into one block rather than separate blocks on a per-user basis.
- Bandwidth can be allocated and reserved.

So you have several items of significant cost to add to your system in order to make a SAN system work. The SAN storage systems are not intended for single-user or small workgroup situations. They are justified if you have a group of people working on Hollywood movie production or commercials with massive throughput and fast workstations.

Some projections of enterprise deployments suggest that SAN installations will be twice as common as DAS installations by 2007. Right now the DAS approach outnumbers SAN by 2 to 1.

The biggest disadvantage of SANs is that they are very expensive to install and out of the reach of everyone apart from the high-end users. This may change, because Apple has been driving down the cost of this kind of enterprise-level computing for several years now and the xSAN product is another step in reducing the cost of ownership of the SAN. Even so, the cost requires a solid business case to justify it.

29.9.5 High-End Solutions

If your requirements are at the top end of the performance spectrum, you might want to look at products by companies such as Apple, Rorke Data, or Storage Tek. These and other companies in the same market have storage architectures that are optimized for the storage and delivery of video, which must have large capacity and very rapid access with low latency. Unfortunately, this performance level costs a lot of money.

29.9.6 Storage-Capacity Planning

The memory capacity necessary when building systems is predicted to more than double each year. When this growth is compounded, it is easy to reach astronomical sizes of disk farms within just a few years. That presents some very interesting problems. For instance, how do you back it all up?

 Digitize some known reference or test content (squares and circles, perhaps) to calibrate your sample rates to your working canvas. Get the geometry right.

Apple XSAN: http://www.apple.com/xsan/
Rorke Data: http://www.rorke.com/
Storage Tek: http://www.storagetek.com/

29.9.7 Planning Storage Capacity Around DVD Projects

Suppose you are planning to deliver a DVD product and want to assemble a collection of assets into a disk image before burning it. DVD media comes in a variety of sizes. You could choose to master to a single-sided, single-layer disk and store 4.7 GB on it. Dual-layer disks hold approximately 9 GB. Double-sided disks are multiples of these capacities according to how many layers there are in total.

You need to allow for the content to be processed and stored at each stage of the production process. Creating a 4.7-GB disk requires much more space than that to retain all the intermediate copies.

Burning the disk is going to be based on copying an image of it from your hard disk to the writable media. Whether you create that image or the software that writes the disk does it, you need the space reserved. It is a good idea to build the image yourself to run it in preview mode for testing. Professional software like DVD Studio Pro maintains that image as a project that you can modify and preview before committing to a burn.

Make sure to keep at least one backup copy so the changes can be reverted. You won't have worked on the assets in place in the project, so there must be at least one more equivalent DVD's worth of space for the assets in their raw form before they are assembled into the DVD project master image. Most of the content of a DVD will be video. The 4.7 GB is compressed video. The uncompressed footage will occupy significantly more space. Five minutes of MPEG-2 video at a quality equivalent to DVD consumes about 150 MB. At DV quality, which is what you might use for editing, that same footage occupies at least 1 GB. At broadcast-studio quality, it might consume 5 or 6 GB. Multiply that up from 5 minutes to 2 hours and you have video files in the region of 100 to 150 GB in size. And that's just for one copy! Table 29-1 enumerates some capacities for a variety of DVD-layer formats and assumes that the storage calculations are based on professional studio-quality mastering. You may get away with less storage for editing home movies.

The uncompressed video component uses the bulk of the space. You should choose an editor that will perform non-destructive edits on this using an EDL or reference movie that retains all the source components intact. Even then there will be unused footage in our editing project, which increases the storage requirements by perhaps another 50%. By the time you have completed a 4.7-GB DVD, you can easily have used 250 GB of space.

Table 29-1 Project Sizes for Storage-Capacity Planning

Item	Single layer	Double layer	Two sides (four layers)
Master copy	5 GB	9 GB	18 GB
Raw assets	5 GB	9 GB	18 GB
Uncompressed video	150 GB	270 GB	540 GB
Total	160 GB	288 GB	576 GB

Now multiply this by the number of projects you want to work on. This is without building archival space and allowing additional workspace for storing video-editing sessions, building special effects, and any other ancillary tasks.

The simplest answer? Just buy as much space as you can afford. Don't even bother buying less than a 500 GB disk as your main workspace unless you are only working on small projects, and think about how you are going to get all that material offline to a backup medium to make space for the next project. The best solution might be to just use a LaCie big disk for each project, then put them on the shelf and plug in a new drive for each job.

29.9.8   Storage Cost

The cost of storage measured in dollars per GB reduces as you purchase bigger disk drives. Table 29-2 lists some representative prices per GB from companies selling disk products. These are provided for comparison and may change, although their proportional costs with respect to each other will probably be more stable over time.

These prices are approximate and will fluctuate as market conditions change. The prices are more likely to go down rather than up. What is more important is the relative pricing. Buy the right sort of disk space for your system (and your budget) as well as the required capacity. NAS storage is about twice as expensive as RAID storage on its own. Pocket drives are cheaper if you buy the larger-capacity units. Simple FireWire 400 drives are the cheapest of all, so going on these figures, I would recommend purchasing 500-GB desktop drives because they are a reasonable size for working on projects and the cost per GB is about the best available value. Paying more for RAD storage, however, buys you performance, throughput, and error resilience.

Table 29-2 Dollars Per GB

Description	Size	Per GB
Xserve RAID	1.00 TB	$3.8
	1.75 TB	$2.8
	3.5 TB	$2.1
HP StorageWorks NAS	320 GB	$6.05
	640 GB	$3.76
	1.00 TB	$2.95
Portable pocket drives	60 GB	$2.03
	160 GB	$0.66
	200 GB	$0.70
Formac FireWire 400	160 GB	$0.60
	250 GB	$0.53
	320 GB	$0.50
	500 GB	$0.52

29.9.9 Disk-Capacity Conclusions

An 80-GB disk is going to be barely big enough to execute a project on. 160 GB is readily available in build-to-order systems. Larger 250-GB hard disks come at a premium, and if you are prepared to spend the money, LaCie Big Disks at 500 GB are a useful size for video-project workspace.

FireWire lets us add 10 disks quite easily, so let's think about maxing up a system with 10 LaCie one-terabyte disks. In a broadcast environment, that is about 4 days' worth of DV50 workspace in a large newsroom. It's a quick and dirty solution and those disks can be organized as a RAID using software built into the Mac OS operating system. With disks of that capacity you probably wouldn't need them all online at once and FireWire lets you hot plug them as needed.

29.10 Networking

Structure your cabling when you create your studio. Wire your network wall sockets back to a patch bay in a central location. Then patch in the interconnections with jumper cables as you need them. Upgrading your network is a lot easier if you set it up this way (see Figure 29.4).

It is very important to carefully label all your cables and sockets and to document the wiring when it is put in. Be sure to keep it updated if there are any changes. Use color codes to identify which cables are important. Use green cables for video and yellow for audio. Or use red cables for parts of a live system that must never be disconnected and green cables for less important connections. You choose, but make sure you apply the regime consistently.

 Don't read files across the network. Copy them to a hard disk that is physically attached via the fastest interface possible. The same applies to writing files.

Done neatly, your cabling will be an asset. On the other hand, if you create a spaghetti-like rat's nest of cables, soon you will be tearing out your hair trying to find out what is connected where.

If you take care, it should be nice and neat, like the fully populated *ADC* Telecommunications Ethernet Distribution Frame in Figure 29-5.

ADC Communications has a full range of structured cabling solutions that all work together so you can build a cabling system for audio, video, fiber, and Ethernet. The whole system will be coherent because the products are compatible. At the ADC web site you will find lots of information in addition to the product details. In particular there are very useful white papers and tutorial materials about networks.

ADC Telecommunications: http://www.adc.com/

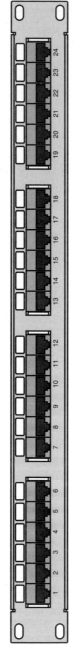

Figure 29-4 Rack-mounted Ethernet patch panel.

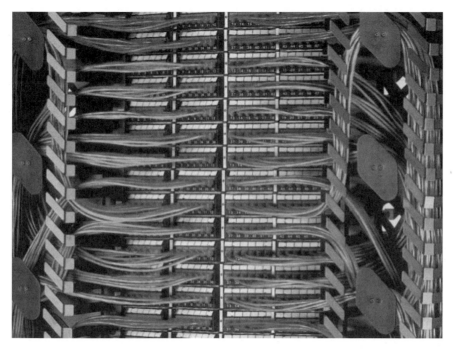

Figure 29-5 A job done well is a job done right. Source: courtesy of ADC Telecommunications.

29.10.1 *Ethernet Speed (10, 100, or 1000 Base-T)*

Networks are fast. But they may not be fast enough. Oddly enough, networks can be faster than disks although they are often assumed to be slower. A 10 Base-T Ethernet network will not deliver the performance you need unless you are prepared to do your file transfers overnight.

A 100 Base-T Ethernet network is probably capable of servicing a pair of edit workstations from some shared storage so that two editors can be working at once.

If you have a bigger team and a bit more money for better-quality wiring and a larger number of machines, then 1000 Base-T or Gigabit Ethernet is desirable. Beyond that, you get into crazy money spent on fiber-optic networks and switches, and at that level you probably care less about the cost as long as the performance is good enough.

 Don't write to a network-mounted drive. It is very slow. Every line that is written to a file is another network transaction. Copying whole files across the network is far more efficient.

At the very least, you should be wiring with a cabling system that is rated at Category 5 (CAT-5). This is a specification of the quality of the cable, connectors, and other active components.

You also need to ensure that the four pairs of wires in the unshielded twisted pair (UTP) cable are wired correctly. There are two well-known formats, T568A and T568B. They are different, for historical reasons having to do with legacy telephony systems. If you mix telephone and Ethernet systems so they can share the same structured cabling, be careful to keep them separate when you patch them or you will fry your Ethernet interfaces in any PC that is accidentally connected to the telephone network.

You must also be careful to use crossover cables only where appropriate. They are normally used to join stackable hubs together. Crossover cables are occasionally useful for connecting two Ethernet-equipped devices together. It's all you need to create a network of just two nodes. Keep a crossover cable handy in your toolkit just in case you need it.

29.10.2 Hubs or Switches?

Make sure that your network is connected together with switches—avoid the use of hubs. Look at Figure 29-6 to see how all the traffic is directed along a common signal path inside a hub.

Contrast the way a hub works with the direct port-to-port connections inside a switch. None of the traffic between two ports affects any other ports because there is no shared signal path (see Figure 29-7).

Hubs present all the network traffic on all the ports. A switch connects one port directly to another and bypasses all the others. The traffic is direct and private and does not interfere with any of the traffic going between other port pairs. For video delivery, this is very good.

29.10.3 Transfer Speeds

One of the issues with video is that the data is bulky. Storing video requires a lot of space to describe just a few seconds' worth of content. Moving the footage around your system takes more time than you thought it would. Within the bounds of your own system, run

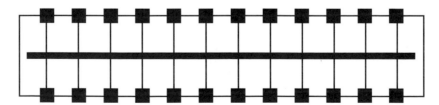

Figure 29-6 Network hub internals.

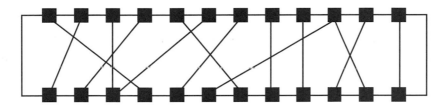

Figure 29-7 Network switch internals.

some tests to establish just how long it takes to move an hour's worth of video from one machine to another. Then, when a client presents you with a rush job, you will know what the workflow implications are.

29.10.4 SneakerNet

There is one cheap, quick, and effective solution for small outfits. You plug a FireWire drive into one machine and copy the file to it. Then, because FireWire is hot-swappable, dismount it, disconnect it, and carry it across to another machine where you can reconnect it again. (You should read the instruction manuals to ascertain whether your drive can be removed while the power is on.)

The downside is that there are security risks to this approach and anyone might just as easily plug in his or her own drive. You could counter this with drives that carry security codes and software that checks on mounting that an authorized drive has been connected.

So why is this technique called "SneakerNet"? It's because someone wearing sneakers transports the data across the room.

29.11 Monitor Displays

If you want to see what the picture is going to look like when it's displayed, you should connect up a monitor that is similar to the one your footage will be viewed on. It is a waste of time looking at video on a high-resolution progressive monitor if it is going to be delivered on standard definition with an interlaced display. You need to view it on a TV monitor. This is also a good idea if you are previewing MPEG-2 content for broadcast or DVD output.

ATI Radeon cards come equipped with an S-VHS output. This is useful for previewing video to get an idea of what it will look like. But don't be fooled by playing a good-quality master through that output. Compressed results will look worse by comparison. Try to get the preview to be as close to the technology that the end user will be using to view your content. Otherwise there is no point in previewing.

Make sure you get a monitor and cable that match your video card connectors. DVI cables come with and without the analog circuits connected.

Refer to Appendix M for examples of a range of video-card connectors.

29.12   Video Cards

This is an area that has seen constant innovation for the last dozen or so years. If you have good video-recording equipment that has a FireWire interface, you may not even need a video card for ingesting. But if you do, here are some popular video cards.

29.12.1   Osprey

The Osprey video cards are popular with Windows-based systems. You may also find that video cards supplied by Bluefish, Matrox, and Digital Voodoo are useful if you use the Windows platform. Pinnacle and, of course, NVidia and ATI also offer solutions that deliver what you need. Some of the ATI Radeon video cards include VGA outputs for your desktop and secondary S-VHS outputs for video recording or monitoring.

29.12.2   AJA

At the IBC 2002 exhibition, AJA demonstrated the Kona video card. This was attractive to broadcasters because it had SDI video output. With the correct drivers installed, up to 8 channels of audio can be embedded into the outgoing bit stream.

29.12.3   Blackmagic Design

At the IBC 2003 conference, Grant Petty (formerly of Digital Voodoo) launched the Blackmagic Design (BMD) range of video cards. These have made an incredible difference to the whole video card industry.

The card works in Mac OS X and Windows environments. There is a family of cards ranging from those that only support SDI or analog video up to the top-end cards that cope with high definition and multiple formats. The most astonishing feature of these cards is the pricing. They are an order of magnitude cheaper than the average price of the rest of the market. It is possible to build an SDI video device with an $800 computer fitted with a $250 video card and write some software to do things like captioning and graphics overlays. Building video servers for about $1000 per channel with commodity hardware negates the conventional wisdom that video-server hardware is expensive.

At these prices, you can deploy as many channels as you need and have some cash left over to put backup machines into storage or alongside the live system as hot spares.

BMD has made a truly incredible contribution to the embedded-video-card customer base. This will ultimately lead to some very innovative product solutions when combined with creative software.

29.12.4 *Optibase*

Optibase has been making video hardware and software for a long time and has some useful products. Most of its offerings have been for the Windows platform, but the MPEG Movie Maker 2000 now provides an MPEG-2 hardware encoding solution for the Power Macintosh user. This is particularly useful if you are creating content for eventual deployment on a DVD. This board is quite expensive for the non-pro user but is still cheaper than previous solutions, which were priced at $20,000 or more.

Deploying a hardware encoder like this can save you a lot of time because you can process the content far more quickly this way. The alternative is to use a software compressor.

29.13 Hardware Encoder Solutions

This is likely to be of interest to you if you are a broadcaster or large organization with a lot of money to spend. Hardware solutions are appropriate when the quality and reliability of the outgoing video are more important than the cost.

Appendix B summarizes some example hardware encoder manufacturers for you to investigate and speak to about your requirements.

29.14 Analog-to-Digital Conversion Alternatives

Depending on the equipment you have available, there are various ways to convert your analog footage into a digital format.

If you have a DV handycam, you may be tempted to ingest your VHS video into that via the analog input connector. However, the quality of the analog-to-digital conversion is less than ideal. If it is the only ingest method you have available, that may not matter. A better solution is the BMD DeckLink video card. This will provide the highest-quality ingest at the best price. AJA I/O boxes are also good, and they come in a variety of configurations and prices to suit all pocketbooks.

Although a DV deck may not provide very good conversion of analog to digital, a DVCAM deck might. Sony DSR 11, DSR 45, and DSR DR 1000 units are all good options

---

Blackmagic Design: http://www.blackmagic-design.com/

Optibase: http://www.optibase.com/

for low-budget studios. The DSR 11 is very cheap. The DR 1000 is interesting because it has an 8-hour hard disk store fitted into it instead of a tape drive.

Having said that, DV handycam devices are not particularly good at analog-to-digital conversion, although they are very good as acquisition devices for direct shooting. They offer a very good price–performance combination.

29.15 Cabling Your Studio

The cabling in studios and also in pro-consumer setups has for a long time standardized on 75-Ohm coax (coaxial cable). This is used for analog composite video and also for the serial digital signals that professional studios deploy.

Avoid the use of radiofrequency (RF) connections. RF is only designed for connecting a VCR to a TV set for playing back VHS tapes. It is a truly awful way to connect anything else if you are trying to do transfers. The results will always be totally unsatisfactory and not worth compressing.

Use SCART or S-VHS if you are connecting analog. RCA phono jack connectors are okay but you will be using composite video. The SCART and S-VHS systems deliver the video at a better quality. Ideally, you should get the video into a digital format as soon as possible with the minimum of generational copying or conversion.

 Label the power plugs on the distribution board or you will unplug a power supply from an online hard disk instead of the laptop when you are rushing out to a meeting. This does bad things to the disk, not to mention that it stops your 3-day-long compression job dead!

29.15.1 Routing Video and Audio

Trying to route video around a small studio is fairly easy. It is easy to disconnect cables from one place and reconnect them somewhere else, which is fine for just a few computers and video decks. However, in a production environment or in a major broadcast studio it is physically impossible to create circuits by hand patching with cables.

Instead of cabling, an electronic switching system called a router is used. This is sometimes referred to as a matrix because it is a grid of inputs and outputs arranged so that the crossing points are joined to make a connection. This allows any output to be connected to any one of the inputs. Any of the inputs can be simultaneously connected to more than one output. Everything is synchronized so that the switching happens during the blanking time and the new source is then available on the next frame. So it is a combination of a switcher and a distribution amplifier.

Common sizes for these are 8 × 8, 16 × 16, and 32 × 32. If you are prepared to spend big money, then 64, 128, 144, and 256 square units are readily available. If you need to go bigger than this, then gang them up in multiples.

Blackmagic Design has introduced a workgroup routing solution that is economical and may do just what you need: the Workgroup Videohub (see Figure 29-8).

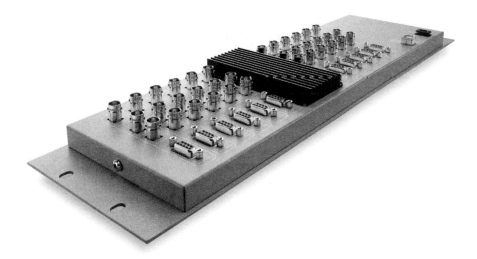

Figure 29-8 BMD Workgroup Videohub. Source: courtesy of Blackmagic Design.

Although you may want to route audio and video separately sometimes, you will probably want to switch them together so that they are routed to the same place most of the time. On a very big matrix, you will have a video layer plus two audio layers, and if you are providing surround sound, you might potentially require five or even seven layers of audio switching along with the video. This gets quite expensive, and the control system increases in complexity accordingly.

29.15.2 Embedding Audio Versus Separately Routed Audio

A very neat solution to the massive wiring costs in a big studio is to embed the audio inside the video signal, thereby removing the need for more than one layer in the switcher. This allows economies in cabling systems and also reduces the number of fiberoptic links you need to provide. Embedders and de-embedders should be placed adjacent to where the audio and video need to be processed separately.

Modern SDI video cards such as the AJA Kona and the Blackmagic Design DeckLink products support audio embedding within the driver that feeds the outputs of the card.

The audio your equipment is compatible with might be in digital AES format, or if it is analog, it is likely to be balanced audio. You will need to convert back and forth, so some AV glue ware will be necessary. This sort of I/O conversion is available from companies such as Vistek or Miranda. There are many others as well.

29.15.3 Loop Back

When you wire your studio, there are times when you will need to test something. Putting in a few extra circuits and leaving them unconnected is a good idea. Use these for loop-back

---

Vistek Electronics Ltd: http://www.vistek.tvt/

Miranda Technologies Inc.: http://miranda.com/

tests. If you go to the end of the circuit and join it to a cable that seems to be faulty, test it from the other end to see if you get a satisfactory signal. You also gain a spare circuit, which is helpful when you need to mount a new service quickly. Part of the diagnostic process is to eliminate a bad wire. Substitute a known good circuit for a suspected faulty circuit in order to isolate the problem.

29.16   FireWire Interfaces

FireWire carries DV video and multi-channel audio, and it also connects hard disks to your computer using dual twisted pair cabling. It is a very versatile and powerful peripheral connection system, also known as IEEE 1394 and iLink. Refer to the 1394 Trade Association's web site for more details.

29.16.1   Connectivity

The 6-pin connector supplies bus power and the smaller 4-pin connector does not. There are variants of the connectors for use on proprietary equipment.

 Buy some cheap FireWire disks for storing completed projects on. That way you can remount the project again very quickly. Disks with capacities of less than 40 GB are very cheap.

You can get patch bays for FireWire, which allow you to rack-mount a lot of FireWire equipment and bring the connectivity out to the front of the rack. ADC makes a useful product for this market, as shown in Figure 29-9.

Figure 29-9 ADC FireWire patch panel. Source: courtesy of ADC Telecommunications.

1394 Trade Association: http://www.1394ta.org/

29.16.2 Auxiliary-Powered FireWire Interfaces

Another good approach is to have a spare FireWire drive sitting idle on the shelf just ready to be plugged in, assuming that you have a FireWire interface available. FireWire is fitted to most new computers or can be added easily with a PCI card. If all your available FireWire ports are used, add an auxiliary-powered FireWire hub. This gives you extra connectivity and reduces the current load on the FireWire ports in your main logic board since some additional power is provided separately. Because the same FireWire bus is being shared, the throughput will remain the same. That is only increased if additional FireWire buses are installed.

Providing additional sources of auxiliary power is always a good thing when equipping your computer with extra FireWire PCI cards and USB or FireWire hubs. It is possible to blow up a FireWire bridge chip on your logic board very easily if you try to draw too much current. The same applies to FireWire bridges on PCI cards that don't have the auxiliary power connector. Belkin offers a useful FireWire PCI card that has a socket for the same kind of power supply that you might provide to an extra internal drive. An example of this card is shown in Figure 29-10. So long as you have sufficient spare power-supply capacity inside your PC, you can use it to drive the FireWire interface.

29.16.3 AJA Io

AJA also offers a range of I/O products called the Io (Figure 29-11). These come in several models—analog only, digital only, and multi-channel audio/video. They offer very good performance if you are looking for a FireWire bridge. The Io will also deliver uncompressed video down the FireWire interface. This is a very good solution when combined with a Macintosh G5 running Final Cut Pro. Having some xRAID storage on hand in sufficient quantity provides somewhere to store the massive amounts of video that you will be tempted to ingest.

29.16.4 Blackmagic Design Multibridge

Another new product from BMD is the Multibridge. Combining this with the workgroup router and DeckLink video cards allows you to build a very flexible and articulate workgroup solution. The bridge is extremely compact and can be mounted within a video rack in a variety of ways (see Figure 29-12).

29.16.5 Other FireWire Bridges

Other cheaper FireWire bridge solutions have been around for some time, such as those made by Datavideo and Miranda. The Miranda hardware is also marketed under other brand names, such as PrimaVideo, Dazzle, and Hollywood. These are good for capturing short sequences. Check that you have the latest drivers for them.

AJA Video: http://www.aja.com/

Figure 29-10 Belkin-powered FireWire card.

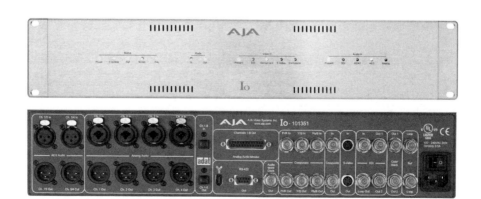

Figure 29-11 AJA Io FireWire interface (front and rear view). Source: courtesy of AJA Video Systems.

Figure 29-12 BMD Multibridge. Source: courtesy of Blackmagic Design.

29.16.6 DV Cameras

The FireWire interface is particularly popular because some DV cameras and decks come already equipped with a connector. Video-editing software like Final Cut Pro or iMovie is aware of this and of how to drive it with the correct protocol. Just plug in and away you go.

On Sony equipment, you will find that the interface is labeled iLink and may require a special connector at the camera end of the cable. These connectors are small and fragile. Oddly enough, you will often find that these cables are supplied separately from the cameras. Cables with the 6-way FireWire connector at one end and the mini iLink connector at the other are available in photography stores. Check when you purchase the camera, because you may get home only to find that another trip is necessary to obtain the necessary cables.

29.17 Removable Media

The original intent of the MPEG-1 codec was to deliver video at bit rates that would allow a movie to be compressed sufficiently to fit on a CD-ROM. That's about 650 MB in size. The codec was not good enough to do that job as convincingly as consumers wanted, but it has turned out to be useful for other low-bit-rate applications.

MPEG-2 deployed on DVDs makes MPEG-1 on CD-ROMs totally obsolete. Systems based on H.264 allow movie-length content to be compressed down sufficiently to fit onto a CD-ROM. The DivX codec is also designed for reducing movie-length projects to CD-ROM-sized files.

Sony is deploying video cameras that use Memory Stick technology, and Panasonic was showing cameras at the IBC show in 2003 that supported multiple memory cards that were used together rather like a RAID array of disks. Their camera is manufactured with very few moving parts, which improves the reliability. The same memory sticks are used to deliver video to Sony CLIÉ PDA devices and currently store up to 8 hours of video using the MPEG-4 Part 2 codec.

29.17.1   External FireWire Drive

This is rapidly becoming very popular as a way to move large video projects around the workplace. A big selling point is that FireWire devices are hot-swappable. Not all operating system drivers allow this, however. Mac OS supports hot swapping by default and you should check the device manufacturer's guidelines for any caveats on other systems.

The video could be ingested on a machine that has high-quality digitizing hardware attached and then taken off to a more modest desktop editing system for further work. A range of disk sizes is available. The largest is the LaCie terabyte-sized disk. This is actually a quad array of 250-MB drives presented as a single device via a FireWire connector. Pocket drives come in sizes from 10 GB to 80 GB, and bigger sizes are on the way. The pocket drives are excellent for storing client projects and keeping the entire thing not only intact but filed away offline in the fire safe until you need to work on it again. This is cheaper than backing up to DVD or CD-ROM disks, and much more convenient. Clone the drives if you want a safety copy.

29.17.2   Dual FireWire Connectivity

Apple has continuously upgraded the FireWire capabilities, and you can now connect its enterprise-level systems together using dual FireWire 800 interfaces. This allows transfer rates of 1.6 Gbps. This technique is sometimes referred to as Gigawire, which is a trade-marked name. You might go down this route if you are configuring a cluster of XServe boxes to share a FireWire RAID unit.

29.17.3   RAID Storage and Firewire

FireWire is a convenient interface for all sorts of video-related activities. It is quite good for attaching a RAID storage system to a domestic or semi-professional system. A RAID set is managed from within the standard Mac OS disk utility. Just attach 6 drives and assemble them into a RAID set. Whenever the Mac boots, the RAID set will mount as a single volume on the desktop. This is very robust and will mount automatically if you power up the FireWire drives after booting the computer. Figure 29-13 shows a screen shot of the disk utility in the process of setting up a 6-disk RAID set.

In this case the striped option was selected. A mirrored alternative could have been chosen, which would have halved the capacity and improved the redundancy factor.

There are two caveats with FireWire drives that are important to keep in mind:

- Dismount the disks before disconnecting or powering them off to avoid getting errors from the operating system about drives having failed.

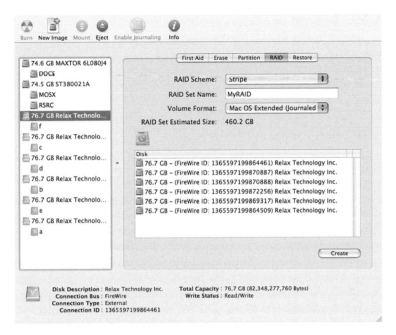

Figure 29-13 Mac OS disk utility RAID setup.

- Don't connect too many devices to a FireWire interface unless they are powered separately. A FireWire hub helps distribute auxiliary power, but it cannot supply enough to run a 6-drive RAID array. Those drives should be independently powered.

29.18 USB Connectivity

USB is primarily used for connecting keyboards, mice, and other low-throughput auxiliary devices. It is used for digital still cameras and scanners and for synchronizing PDA devices. FireWire is used for higher-resolution or higher-performance systems and is favored for digital video (using the DV protocols).

As USB gets faster, it is being developed as an audio and video interface. For example, some domestic TV on PC receivers will deliver its output to the USB port on your PC.

29.18.1 Video on USB

The USB Implementers Forum is developing video capabilities, and they publish their work as a USB Video Device Class specification. Other standards cover the use of USB as a bridge to Ethernet connectivity.

The video interface specification supports the following:

- YUV422
- Motion JPEG
- DV
- MPEG-1
- MPEG-2
- MPEG-4 (H.264) is being worked on.

29.18.2 USB Caveats

Don't confuse FireWire with USB. They are different, although many of their uses are similar.

Keyring USB storage devices, smart-card readers, digital cameras, and some PDA devices use a protocol that identifies them as mass storage devices. The operating system should recognize this and just treat them as a disk. So when you plug in a digital camera via USB, it may look like a disk drive on the desktop.

The same eject-and-dismount caveats apply to USB mass storage devices as apply to FireWire. Dismounting before unplugging makes sure that everything that must be flushed to disk has been done and there are no incomplete data records.

The capacities available on keyring-mounted USB disks are reaching useful sizes. 256 MB is just about enough on which to build a bootable Linux operating system. It is not enough capacity to be very useful for video yet, but as capacities increase, within a few years it might be viable for transferring video from a camera to a computer in the field.

29.19 Systems Administration

In this area, you can avoid a lot of problems by anticipating what is going on and then generating some kind of warning.

Try not to read video from the same hard-disk drive that you are writing the output to. This can cause the hard disk to thrash. This is because it is trying to read and write to two or more different parts of the disk surface at the same time and has to move the head a long way back and forth. Drives are built to withstand this, but treating your system kindly gives it a longer lifetime. You can tell when a disk is thrashing because you can hear it. The noise is alarming and you'll have no doubt that it's happening.

For example, write a script that will measure the amount of disk space that you are using and calculate the rate at which it is being consumed. Compare this against the space remaining and compute a simple projection of when that space will all be filled.

Run this automatically on a regular basis and set it up to warn you with an e-mail message when you exceed a certain threshold, measured either in terms of percentage used or in days/hours left before the disk is completely full. This then gives you the choice of continuing (and living dangerously) or doing something about it before the situation gets critical.

All of these metrics and measurements will help you watch over the general state of health of your system. This is what systems administrators do for a living in large corporate installations, and it is no less applicable to a system you are running just for your own benefit.

You may be able to buy the tools you need off the shelf, as there are an increasing number of admin utilities being made available on the market.

The UNIX `df` command probably tells you most of what you need to know about any mounted disks. Following is an example of the output from it.

```
<BAB>$ df
Filesystem 512-blocks Used Avail Capacity Mounted on
/dev/disk1s10 41678080 28207800 13053504 68% /
devfs 278 278 0 100% /dev
fdesc 2 2 0 100% /dev
<volfs> 1024 1024 0 100% /.vol
automount -nsl [311] 0 0 0 100% /Network
automount -fstab [314] 0 0 0 100% /automount/Servers
automount -static [314] 0 0 0 100% /automount/static
/dev/disk0s10 77854288 19931944 57922344 26% /Volumes/PROJ
/dev/disk1s12 31192320 8083576 23108744 26% /Volumes/APPS
/dev/disk1s14 82628944 11227016 71401928 14% /Volumes/DOCS
/dev/disk2s10 149859424 43396656 106462768 29% /Volumes/WSHP
/dev/disk5s9 150121664 126235224 23886440 84% /Volumes/PEND
/dev/disk7s10 149859424 147592992 2266432 98% /Volumes/REFS
/dev/disk4s10 149859424 108382560 41476864 72% /Volumes/TRLR
/dev/disk6s9 150121664 136207512 13914152 91% /Volumes/CLNT
/dev/disk3s10 149859424 17153760 132705664 11% /Volumes/PICS
```

29.20   Documenting

Keep track of what is happening on your systems: Document things thoroughly. At least record the following for reference:

- Network wiring
- Network addresses of all items of equipment
- Ethernet MAC addresses (this is a unique hardware reference number)
- Machine serial numbers

- Disks, when they were purchased, what systems they are attached to, serial numbers, etc.
- Machine configurations
- Software you have bought and the version numbers
- Authentication keys and licensing codes for software so you can re-enter them if necessary
- What software is installed where
- Where the manuals are (make sure you read them!)

 Be sure you make a permanent note of all license keys and any other information necessary to install. You might need it when you have to re-install or claim upgrades.

29.21   Systems Plans

Now it is time to draw up some concrete plans for what the example systems will look like. At this stage, it is only about the hardware requirements; software comes up in the next chapter.

Three example scenarios will be covered here. They are all realistic and based on genuine environments. The smallest is a home or semi-professional system intended for use by filmmakers working on their own. The mid-sized system is a small production company creating an animated TV series and having to produce several variants of the finished product. The last and biggest system is deployed in a newsroom producing a 24-hour rolling news service and many other bulletins on a national network.

29.21.1   *Single-User, Home-Based System— Built on a Budget*

This system is typical of what you might build in order to process home movies. A small independent filmmaker producing short documentary projects between 30 and 50 minutes long might also use it.

Input material will be DV edited with Final Cut Pro. On the basis of a 30-minute program involving about 8 hours of footage and wanting to keep (let's say) 4 rough cuts of the finished film, that is a total of 10 hours of DV footage for a 30-minute film. From experiments with compression software, the measurements suggest that 5 minutes' worth of DV consistently uses about 1 GB. So 8 hours would consume slightly less than 100 GB. Remember, this user also makes longer programs, and these might require 200 GB each.

That editing workstation should probably have a couple of LaCie 1-TB disks attached. To start with, a single 500-GB LaCie Big Disk would suffice. Add bigger drives later on (Figure 29-14).

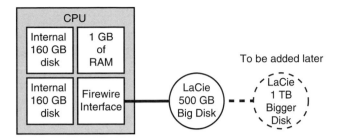

Figure 29-14 Small compression system for a single user.

As far as processing power is concerned, a G5 would be nice, but this user can accomplish what is needed with a late-model G4 that would be priced competitively now that it has been discontinued. Fitted with 1 GB of memory and a couple of 160 GB internal drives, it should provide fast-enough local storage and sufficient memory to run the compression jobs in a reasonable time.

An alternative would be a Windows workstation running at about 2 GHz and similarly equipped with memory and disk space. That same workstation could easily run Linux if it were preferred.

29.21.2 Small Workgroup Sharing Some Storage—Medium Cost

This system is a little more complex because it has to serve the needs of a team. These folks are cranking out a 30-minute animated film every 2 weeks and they need to run some automated processes on it. Those processes are identical and include some up-sampling and compression.

The input material is a raw render-output file. The program is 30 minutes long and the raster size is designed to broadcast as one of the low-spec HDTV resolutions, so it is rendered at 1080×720 progressive at 25 fps. There is no editing necessary, but the file must be up-sampled to 1920×1080 at 25 fps. Then a 30-fps pulldown master must be made, and finally NTSC and PAL SDTV versions must be down-sampled from the original. The up- and down-sampling and frame-rate changes can be accomplished with Adobe After Effects.

The files then need to be compressed for DVD (region 1 and region 2) and also a low-bit-rate comp must be made for demos on a laptop.

Our input file will be 100 GB to start with. Table 29-3 lists the output files that must be created for just one episode.

That compression workstation will require a workspace of 1 TB per episode being processed. A FireWire drive is a good alternative to use. Attach it to the render station and move it to the compression system when you need to.

Because these folks are cranking out these episodes every fortnight or even week and they plan to make 26 or 52 of them, there is a good case for building a huge RAID-based

29-3 Output Formats Required

Format	Size
H.264 low bit-rate demo copy	350 MB
European MPEG-2 compressed copy for DVD	900 MB
American MPEG-2 compressed copy for DVD	900 MB
Down-sampled U.S. SDTV master $720 \times 480 \times 30$ fps	52 GB
Down-sampled European SDTV master $768 \times 579 \times 25$ fps	56 GB
Original source-rendered movie	100 GB
Up-sampled European HDTV/D-Cinema master $1920 \times 1080 \times 25$ fps	261 GB
Up-sampled U.S. HDTV/D-Cinema master $1920 \times 1080 \times 30$ fps	313 GB
Total working space required	Approx 785 GB

store. That would allow the master render copies for all 52 episodes to be retained while the rest of the re-versioning is recorded to tape.

It is possible for frightening amounts of disk space to get consumed even with quite modest projects. A proposed solution with a bulk store and offline tape backup is shown in Figure 29-15.

The same specification used for a compression machine would be fine here. In this case, a top-end machine might be affordable within the available budget, for example,

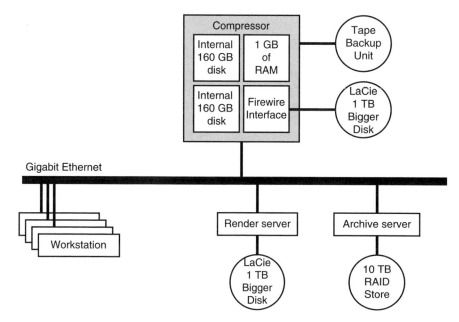

Figure 29-15 Mid-range system for rendering-team use.

a dual-processor G5 Macintosh running at 2.5 GHz or a 3-GHz Intel or AMD machine running Windows XP or Linux. Such a configuration has the option of moving files by Gigabit Ethernet or by hand-carrying of the FireWire drive across to the compression machine.

There is also an opportunity here to completely automate the process by wrapping the conversion tools in AppleScript controlling scripts. It is possible to build a system to accomplish this kind of production workflow that only requires a human being to drop the original file into a watch folder and to run some Q/A inspection over the final result.

29.21.3 Large Enterprise–Sized System—Money No Object

This is a completely different ballgame. A big newsroom creates a huge amount of content every day. Hours of video will be delivered through a variety of ingest points. Sometimes it is file based; other times it a live video feed that must be captured to disk on the fly.

 Run multiple compressors as one with different parameter settings on each and choose the best resulting quality from all the finished products.

This system will need to store thousands of hours of video in a format that is easily repurposed and edited as needed. Among the system's needs are browse-quality proxy copies at 1 Mbps and 56 bps for the web, as well as the DVCAM editable master. The browse-quality images allow an intranet to be used to check out video footage. You would not want to saturate the network by using the full-quality video for that.

A system like this has to be implemented as a SAN. The 1-Mbps and 56-Kbps proxy copies may be stored in separate repositories. Figure 29-16 illustrates part of the network setup that is relevant.

This system has significant amounts of automation built in. When a new DVCAM clip is deposited in the SAN, the Solaris server spots it and grabs a copy, which it then passes through the Flip Factory software. The resulting output is dropped in the two target servers.

It is not necessary for the directory servers to be on the fiber-channel network. The files in them are trivially small compared to the ones that are held in the master system. Money may be no object when building these big systems, but there is no excuse for wasting it.

29.22 Summary: I Can Now Build a System to Encode Video

The factors that affect performance of a compression system include the following:

- How much memory is fitted?
- Can it read and write to disk without thrashing?

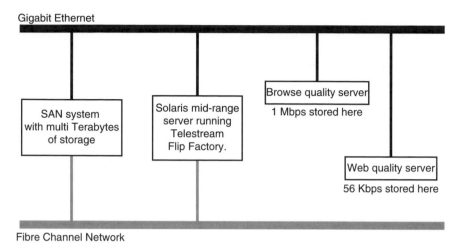

Figure 29-16 High-end system with massive storage and automation.

- What kind of CPU is being used, and does it have vectorization and other processing enhancements that are good for video transformations?

We have explored what is involved in building the hardware. Now it is time to look at the software aspects of the systems-building process. In the next chapter we'll examine some software tools for compression and for the other activities that we need to carry out around the compression process.

30

Setting Up Your Encoding Software

30.1 Introduction

Chapter 29 looked at the various hardware components and subsystems that comprise our compression systems. Most of that is generic hardware and it is a question of working out how much disk space and what accessories are required. Your system will not do any video compression until the vital software components are added. This chapter examines your software alternatives. The following categories of software are relevant:

- Video-editing tools
- Video-compression tools
- Power tools for modifying video
- Gadgets and widgets (small, special-purpose tools)

There are many video-compression tools to choose from. Those few that are included here are not an exhaustive selection, and you may know of other alternatives. You will not have to buy all of these tools, although a fully configured system equips you to tackle any job that crops up. You may find a lot of what you need is available as shareware, freeware, or open source. It need not be as expensive to set up a system as you first thought.

 Note what you installed—where, when, and especially if you changed anything. This is very important if you have a farm of machines. They can easily get out of step with one another.

30.2   Portability Across Platforms

If you want to run the same software across different platforms (e.g., Mac OS and Windows), then select Discreet Cleaner or Sorenson Squeeze. Beware, however, that you will not necessarily have the same range of codecs available across the different platforms.

30.2.1   Will I Get the Same Output Regardless of Platform Choice?

If you invoke the same codec on Mac OS as on a Windows platform, the output will likely not be identical. It will be somewhat similar, but because the standards processes only describe the decoding of the video, the encoders have a lot of scope for adding features that yield better compression factors and still remain compliant with the decoder specification. So apart from minor differences due to software development issues (bugs), there may be differences due to implementation features. If you are using a proprietary codec, it is more likely that a consistent file would be created.

As they say, "Your mileage may vary," and if you end up doing more than a casual and occasional video-compression job, you will develop some skill at selecting the best encoder and settings for the job regardless of the platform or toolset you happen to be using that day.

30.2.2   Open-Source Solutions

There are very few mainstream video editors, FX tools, or compressors available for Linux other than the Real Networks Producer tools. This may change as the market share of Linux desktop systems improves. On the other hand, Linux is well served by open-source alternatives to proprietary tools and there are many codecs supported on the Linux platform. Linux is also a good platform on which to build automated systems.

 Open-source and shareware resources are not free. Put back what you get out of the relationship. Someone donated a lot of time; reciprocate somehow.

As an alternative to Linux, the Darwin open-source project also provides a way to build a streaming server on top of an open-source, kernel-based operating system. This is the basis of the Mac OS operating system, and while its users lack some of the fine points of the user interface and the higher-level tool kits such as QuickTime, this might be a useful foundation on which to build video-processing server engines. More details can be found at the Darwin web site.

Darwin: http://developer.apple.com/darwin/

30.2.3 *Why Some Codecs Are Available and Others Are Not*

Choosing one computer operating system over another will affect the available codecs due to the commercial policy of video-compression companies. For example, certain codecs are only available on the Windows platform. Tools that provide compression frameworks such as Sorenson Squeeze or Discreet Cleaner appear not to support some codecs in their Macintosh version of the product. This is not because they did not port the code from Windows to Mac OS but because the software development kit (SDK) provided by Microsoft for Windows Media and by Real Networks for its codec was previously not fully supported on the Mac OS operating system. Because they are both proprietary formats, the availability across different computer platforms is dictated by Microsoft and Real Networks, not by Sorenson or Discreet.

In the case of the Real Networks encoder, you may be able to address this shortcoming of Squeeze and Cleaner by installing the Real Networks QuickTime codec plug-in. Then you should be able to export using the QuickTime API. Support for encoding Windows Media on Mac OS systems is possible when you install the Telestream Flip4Mac plug-in.

30.3 Automation

Unless you are only doing some small amounts of video compression (say, one file every day or so), the task is likely to become repetitive and boring. This activity is not well suited for a human being. People are best at making decisions. Robots and computers are very good at carrying out the same set of instructions many times without making mistakes, provided they are given the correct instructions in the first place.

Therefore, deploying sufficient automation in your workflow is a worthwhile investment. Your operators can set up and initiate batches while the compression system works through the boring repetition on its own.

Products such as Flip Factory by Telestream or the Popwire Technology Compression Engine software are examples of that sort of architecture. It is worth wrapping additional metadata and workflow control around these systems in order to manage your business logic with some labor-saving automation.

 Think about workflow automation from the word Go.

On the other hand, if you have done some work with your business logic and workflow, deploying diverse encoding platforms lets you encode the widest possible range of formats. You have only to ensure that the job goes to the correct machine.

30.3.1 Batch-Mode Operation

Some compression tools will provide a way to queue several jobs to be processed one after the other. This is called batch mode and comes from the old days when programmers created batches of punched cards to be processed. It is sometimes referred to as offline operation because it does not involve an operator in an interactive session.

Batch mode is very useful when projects require a collection of video files to be processed. A DVD, for example, may have several extra programs apart from the feature presentation. These would be accessed in a special-features menu, but they still have to be encoded just like the main feature.

30.4 Buying Encoders

When you are choosing and purchasing a codec or encoding application, go for the "Pro" versions if they exist. They will invariably give you better control and are less likely to have everything locked down in presets. Presets are fine for demystifying everything for an inexperienced user, but they get in the way when you want to tweak one of the settings.

 Buy and then download electronically. It is often cheaper.

30.5 Compression Software Products

When you decide to install your compression software, you might have to purchase several coding applications in order to cover all the formats that you want to target. Some of the more esoteric encoders will only be available with one particular tool.

The more popular codecs might be provided by the operating system. If your compression tools are built on top of QuickTime, it is unlikely that you will get significantly different results when comparing the output of one compression application to that of another. QuickTime includes the control-panel interfaces. Any tool that exports via QuickTime will be able to provide as much parameter setting as necessary without adding complexity to the application itself. Some tools (such as the Popwire products for example) implement their own codecs. These are engineered from the ground up and contained within the application. You can use the embedded codec or you can use the QuickTime

 Check the online support for the latest version of the software you just installed.

codecs provided by the operating system as well. This is true of other applications that run on Windows, too.

Keep an eye out for tools that allow you to control additional aspects of the process that differentiate that tool from the others. Table 30-1 shows the tools you should acquire, as you need them, and it summarizes what is available for each platform. Bear in mind that this may change as new products are released.

Table 30-1 Compression Tools and Platforms

Tool	Windows OS supported	Mac OS supported	Linux supported
Cleaner	√	√	No
Squeeze	√	√	No
Popwire Technology	No	√	Live encoding
Real Networks Producer	√	Only in Classic OS	√
Real Networks QuickTime plug-in	No	√	n/a
Windows Media Tools	√	No	No
Telestream QuickTime plug-in	No	√	n/a
Telestream Flip Factory family	√	No	No

 Negotiate bulk deals for software if you want many copies. On a per-seat basis, multiple-seat licenses should be cheaper than single seats. Site licenses should be cheaper still. Enterprise licenses for big organizations should be the best possible deals.

30.6   Discreet Cleaner

The Discreet Cleaner application is aimed at the semi-professional and professional users. It provides a lot of powerful features. The main window is shown in Figure 30-1.

When choosing a clip for processing, you can preview it and set up some preprocessing parameters in a separate popup window (Figure 30-2).

The progress indication during the encoding is very detailed on this program, with a lot of statistics being displayed. Most similar tools only show a progress indicator.

Cleaner is ideal for creating QuickTime material. This is probably because it was originally developed as a QuickTime-based application known as Terran Media Cleaner. The ingest algorithms are particularly robust and will cope with some sub-optimal input source material. If you are having trouble getting good results with other compression tools, it may be worth trying Cleaner to see if it does a better job.

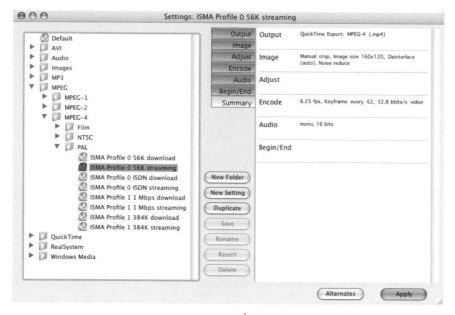

Figure 30-1 Discreet Cleaner 6 main window.

This software has been around for a long time and was originally known as the Terran Media Cleaner. Back in 1996 it already supported a lot of very powerful noise-filtering and video-improvement tools. De-interlace, gamma correction, and audio re-sampling were also in evidence even then. That software evolved and later became known as Discreet Cleaner.

Table 30-2 Video Formats Supported by Cleaner

Format	Import	Export
DV	√	√
Kinoma (PDB)		√
MPEG-1	√	√
MPEG-2	√	√
MPEG-4 Part 2		√
QuickTime (see separate list in Table 30-5)	√	√
Real Networks		Classic Mac OS only
Video for Windows (AVI)	√	√
Windows Media (WMV)		Limited support for WM8 only on Mac OS, WM9 on Windows version

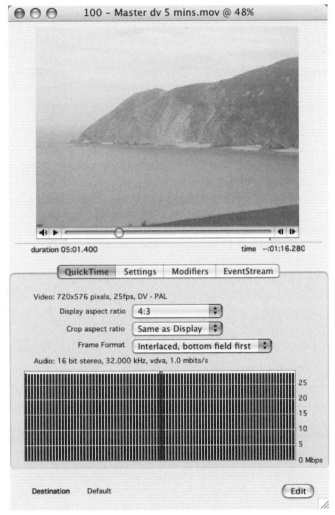

Figure 30-2 Discreet Cleaner 6 preview window.

Cleaner 6 on Mac OS and Cleaner XL on Windows are very similar. Real Networks video is supported natively in XL, while on Mac OS the support is only available when it is running as a Classic application. Windows Media encoding is better supported on the Windows platform because the SDK includes a WM9 encoder that is not available on the Mac OS platform. That is an issue with Microsoft's support of Windows Media, not a Cleaner shortcoming.

Some batching and workflow support is provided. Cleaner supports watch folders, which is a useful feature for building automated compression systems. Cleaner also has some AppleScript support, which provides opportunities to build workflow that integrates

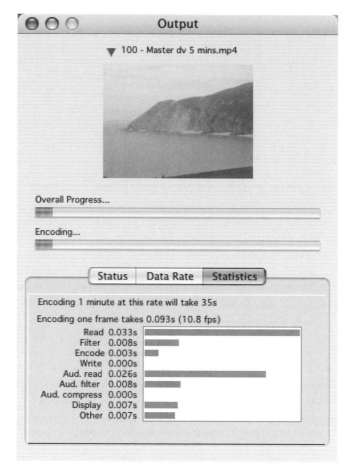

Figure 30-3 Discreet Cleaner 6 progress and statistics window.

with other applications on the Mac OS platform. Table 30-2 lists the formats that Cleaner supports.

In addition to the video formats listed in Table 30-2, Cleaner also imports and exports a variety of audio files, still images, and animation files.

The future availability of Cleaner is unclear. There have not been any updates for some time, and although the software works fine, there are new formats coming along (such as H.264), which may require an upgrade for Cleaner to be able to take advantage of them. It is unconfirmed but likely that we shall see new Discreet video-compression tools during 2005. In the meantime, version 6 of Cleaner is still a usable and robust tool.

More information is available at the Discreet web site.

Discreet: http://www.discreet.com/

30.7 Popwire Technology Compression Master

The Compression Master application from Popwire Technology is a more recently engineered product than Squeeze and Cleaner. It is part of a family of products aimed at the semi-professional and professional user. The complete suite of tools can be scaled up to large multi-processor or clustered enterprise-sized systems. The Popwire Technology products are an alternative to Flip Factory by Telestream. You would choose one or the other according to whether your workflow is Mac OS or Windows based. The complete suite of Popwire products includes the following:

- Compression Master
- Compression Engine
- Ingestion Engine
- Broadcaster (Mac OS)
- Live Engine (Linux)

The user interface for Compression Master is constructed around a main window, which is shown in Figure 30-4.

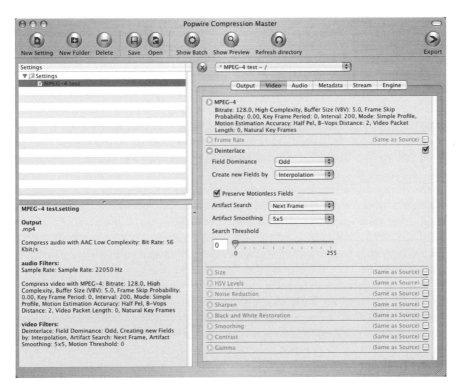

Figure 30-4 Compression Master main window.

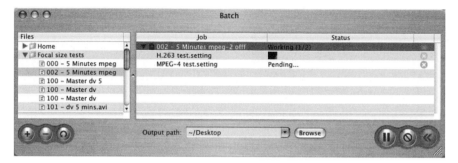

Figure 30-5 Compression Master batch-control window.

You can see that one of the parameter-settings panels has been opened. This unfolds rather than popping up another window, which keeps the user interface nice and simple. In this area you will find more parameter settings than I've seen in any other compression tool.

Compression job control is managed through the batch window (see Figure 30-5). There is also a preview window to see the effects of the compression settings.

Popwire Technology is strong on open-standards support and has a well-thought-out batch and server infrastructure design. It provides a lot of powerful features. The level of detailed control over parameters is probably more sophisticated than in any other tool available. This fine-grain control lets you tune the preprocessing and encoding process very precisely.

This is an area where Popwire encoders exceed the performance of many other competing coding tools. Some applications have to rely on the underlying support provided by the operating system. All of the tools that work like that provide a little more parameterization and some surrounding job control to add value to the foundation support. They also provide preprocessing, but they are hostage to the quality of the encoder implementation with which they are provided.

Because Popwire Technology engineers its own encoders from the ground up, it can provide hooks to control parameters that are inaccessible on other products. Implementing its own encoders significantly differentiates Popwire from the rest of the pack and allows it to extend into the enterprise-based systems more easily. The fact that Popwire has done this without sacrificing access to the operating system-provided support is a major benefit.

The strength of this approach is that the encoders provided by the platform (via QuickTime, for example) are still available as an alternative. This gives you two completely different encoders for a single format in some cases, which is useful when one encoder "chokes" or underperforms on a particular piece of video. The other codec implementation may well be able to process that footage without any trouble.

Generally speaking, the encoders in Popwire Technology applications produce a higher quality than those generically available in the QuickTime layer. They have a more sophisticated preprocessor and many more fine-tuning parameter settings. This is not to imply that the QuickTime codecs are in any way bad. They are useful across a wide spectrum of applications and in disciplines where the user interface must be simplified. The Popwire Compression Master user interface allows you to control just about anything you would want to while the encoders in QuickTime are optimized for ease of use. But here we have both alternatives available, so it's the best possible scenario for the compression engineer.

The fact that QuickTime is integrated as well as the embedded encoders is also important because this dramatically increases the number of audio/visual formats that can be imported. So while you can export via QuickTime, it tends to be used more as an input mechanism with the output going through the Popwire encoders.

Compression Master has some very sophisticated noise-filtering and de-interlacing support. If you have footage with severe interlaced artifacts, this tool might process them out where other tools would try to retain the detail and waste bit rate. You can also convert between NTSC and PAL formats as part of the temporal processing support. Unusual for a compression tool, you can also add watermarking. This can be taken from another movie file to make it even harder to detect and remove.

The Popwire Compression Engine supports server-based workflow control with watch folders. You can build powerful compression-processing farms by deploying compression engines on servers and making them available as a service to the client users.

Popwire Technology products run on a variety of hardware. For performance reasons, some applications need to scale to hardware beyond that which desktop manufacturers can deliver. For example, server software may need to run on a Sun Microsystems Solaris machine to attain the required computing leverage although similar performance might be achieved with distributed processing on Apple X-Server clusters.

The client tools are available on Mac OS X. Popwire's Compression Engine is deployed on Mac OS X or Solaris servers, and Broadcaster is available on Mac OS. Live Engine (Broadcaster) runs on a modestly powerful Intel PC running Linux if you need it on that platform.

Table 30-3 lists the main formats that Compression Master supports. The baseline support is considered to be version 2, but some new codec support has been added for the version 3 release (November 2004). This is indicated in the table. Notably, this is the first released product on Mac OS X that encodes WM9. Other manufacturers are following this route as well.

Codecs that were available in previous releases of Compression Master have been improved. Some new filters and preprocessing options have been added, as has 2-pass coding on codecs that only supported 1-pass coding previously. There is also support for transcoding between NTSC and PAL in the new version. In the press release, special attention is drawn to the transcoding between DV and MPEG-2 that preserves the interlacing. This is useful for postproduction work. It was a solid product before, but now it's even better.

More codecs are being added, and a further release is scheduled to coincide with the NAB conference in April 2005. The spring 2005 release is expected to include an H.264 encoder.

In addition to video formats, Compression Master also imports and exports a variety of audio files, including RealAudio. The Popwire Technology products take input from

Table 30-3 Video Formats Supported by Compression Master

Format	Import	Export
MPEG-1 multiplexed streams	√	
MPEG-1 program streams	√	√
MPEG-2 transport streams	√	
MPEG-2 program streams	√	√
MPEG-2 elementary streams	√	√
MPEG-4 Part 2	√	√
ISMA—MPEG-4		√
3GPP—MPEG-4	√	√
H.263	√	√
DV 25 stream	√	√
DVCPro 25 stream	√	√
DVCPro 50 stream	√	√
QuickTime (see separate list in Table 30-5)	√	√
AVI—wRAW	√	
AVI—PCM	√	√
AVI—DV	√	√
AVI—MJPEG	√	√
AVI—RGB		√
3GPP—MPEG-4	√	√
3GPP—AAC	√	√
3GPP—AMR	√	√
3GPP—H.263	√	√
3GPP2—QCELP	√3	√3
3GPP2—EVRC	√3	√3
Windows Media 7	√3	
Windows Media 8	√3	
Windows Media 9	√3	√3
RealVideo 8		√
RealVideo 9		√
RealVideo 10		√
RealAudio 8		√
RealAudio 9		√
RealAudio 10		√

Table 30-3 Video Formats Supported by Compression Master (Continued)

Format	Import	Export
WAV	√	√
MP3	√	√
GXF	√	
M4A		√3
AIFF		√3

some video formats that are not supported on other platforms and have some interesting and novel design features. The encoders include 2-pass and VBR support for compact output files. Because Compression Master imports MPEG-2 Program and Transport streams, it is happy to decode multiplexed video files. This saves you the trouble of using DropDV to convert your El-Gato off-air files to the DV format that Final Cut Pro operates on.

If you are compressing video and audio for 3GPP applications and need an automated workflow, Compression Master together with a rack of servers running the Compression Engine software could form the basis of a versatile and powerful system.

If you require more performance than a single machine can deliver, you can move up to the Compression Engine deployed on a server. You can continue to use your existing Compression Master application to create settings templates and associate these with watch folders on the server.

Your live-encoding needs are addressed with Broadcaster, which runs on Mac OS X (use the Live Engine application on Linux). This creates a live stream of encoded video. These products are aimed at telecoms operators running mobile networks and are optimized for that kind of format.

If you are building a large, industrial-strength workflow (for a newsroom perhaps), then you probably need to ingest a lot of material from archive or daily tapes. The Ingestion Engine provides the point of access for your media-porting activities, whether they are tape based, analog, or digital via SDI.

More information is available at the Popwire Technology web site.

30.8 Sorenson Squeeze

The Squeeze application is aimed at the semi-professional and professional user, more specifically at folks who want to condense their video down so that it can be deployed on the web (hence the name Squeeze perhaps?).

Figure 30-6 shows a screen shot of the session window. Everything takes place in this cockpit view.

Popwire Technology: http://www.popwire.com/

Figure 30-6 Sorenson Squeeze 4.0.

Sorenson Squeeze looks very similar on Mac OS and Windows. The main difference is the encoders and formats that are supported. Windows Media encoding is not well supported on the Mac OS platform because the Microsoft WM SDK is incomplete and out of date. Sorenson does absolutely the right thing by dropping it entirely on Mac OS and only supporting it on Windows, where it works fine.

The most obvious change with version 4.0 of Sorenson's Squeeze Compression Suite is that the application has radically altered its appearance from the earlier versions. The new version has had a major user-interface overhaul, and the result is a lot better than the previous version. However, you should look for the latest updates periodically and ensure that you have your software as up to date as possible.

There are some additional filters in the new release for preprocessing the video before compression, but also some legacy file formats for import and export that have been dropped.

Version 4 now supports H.264, which is becoming more widely available in new releases of coding tools. Sorenson calls it AVC and makes no mention of H.264. At this stage, the support is fairly basic and built around the Advanced Simple Profile (ASP). Alternative coding support is available by invocation of a QuickTime processor and selection of the Apple H.264 codec shipped with Mac OS 10.4.

It is too soon to draw any conclusions about which of the available H.264 encoding tools produces the best results. There are some slight differences in how they have both interpreted the standard, causing some minor interoperability issues. This should be able to be corrected by an update patch by the time you are reading this. So make sure if you buy Squeeze that you run all the available updaters as well.

This encoder is good for creating web video, but it is an early implementation and not ideal for TV-quality use yet. This is somewhat typical of a lot of early implementations of H.264 encoders. These issues will be solved in the fullness of time as the H.264 implementations improve and mature.

The defaults in the menus don't include European TV resolution settings; the range and scope of the settings appear to be optimized for Internet delivery. Selecting the default settings seems to be the way to go for fast and reliable encoding. However, the parameters can be set manually to larger values. This will operate the codec out of its optimal range, so while it might work, compression jobs might take an abnormally long time or might crash the encoder. Short compression jobs using default parameters move along quite quickly.

Running some simple experiments with an initial release of Squeeze Compression Suite version 4 suggests that there is still some work to be done but that it will be a very good tool once it matures. Some batching and workflow support is provided, and watch folders are implemented for building automated compression systems. Table 30-4 lists the formats that Squeeze supports.

In addition to the video formats listed in Table 30-4, Squeeze also imports and exports a variety of audio files, still images, and animation files.

Version 4 of Sorenson Squeeze was released in summer 2004. You may still find version 3 to be useful, and since it is mature it will work reliably. In fact, it is worth having both versions, 3 and 4, installed on your system if you spend any amount of time compressing video. Version 4 will improve as updates are released.

Running H.264 compressors on Mac OS 10.3 is an interesting experience. The file is manufactured, but you cannot play it back because QuickTime does not natively support H.264 on versions prior to version 7. The "play" button in Squeeze does not do any better, because it delegates the playback to QuickTime. The moral of this tale is that you must make sure everything is upgraded if you are going to do any serious work with H.264. Solve this particular problem with an upgrade to Mac OS 10.4 or QuickTime 7.

When you are encoding media on the Mac OS platform and you know that it is going to be played back on the same platform, then Sorenson Squeeze and the Sorenson Pro codec are the right choices for getting the best possible quality in your output file until H.264 is stabilized and fully supported.

There is more information about Squeeze at the Sorenson web site.

 Buy version 2 installations just as version 3 is released. You get good close-out deals on the old version, and upgrades may be free or quite cheap.

Sorenson: http://www.sorenson.com/

Table 30-4 Video Formats Supported by Sorenson Squeeze

Format	Import	Export
MPEG-1	√	√
MPEG-2	Windows only	√
MS ISO MPEG-4 video 1		√
MS MPEG-4		√
Real Networks video codec 8		√
Real Networks video codec 9		√
Real Networks video codec 10		√
RealVideo G2 (with SVT)		Windows only
Sorenson MPEG-4 Part 2		√
Flash MX (Sorenson Spark)		√
AAC audio	√	√
MP3 audio	√	√
MPEG layer1, layer2 and CM audio		√
Qdesign Music		√
QUALCOMM PureVoice		√
Uncompressed raw audio (AIF/AIF)	√	√
ASF	√	
AVI	√	Removed in v4
DV	√	√
MPEG-4 AVC/H.264 (Sorenson AVC Pro)		√
DVD		√
WMV	Windows only	Windows only
WMA	Windows only	
SVCD		√
VCD		√
SWF	√	√
WAV	√	√
Windows Screen 7	Windows only	Windows only
Windows Media 7	Windows only	Windows only
Windows Media 8	Windows only	Windows only
Windows Media 9	Windows only	Windows only
Windows Media audio ACELP and series 8	Windows only	Windows only
QuickTime (see separate list in Table 30-5)	√	√
FLV 1.1		√
Sorenson Video 3.1		√

30.9 QuickTime-Based Tools

The QuickTime framework adds multimedia and video import/export to any application that calls on it for assistance. Many applications use QuickTime to hide the complexity for inexperienced users. QuickTime works similarly on Mac OS and Windows.

You can get quite a lot of compression work done with the simplest of tools. The media player supports exporting via QuickTime. The same settings panels are provided by all applications that export via QuickTime.

The movie settings are applied first (see Figure 30-7). This lets you select whether to export audio, video, or both.

Clicking on the settings button brings up an extra sheet of parameter settings. The individual codecs may also provide some settings via additional preference dialog panes. QuickTime is purposely designed to simplify all these parameter settings so that users with very little compression experience can apply the process.

Note the preview rectangle at the right-hand side of the panel. Although it is quite small, the preview is updated as parameters are changed, so you can see the effect of dialing in different settings.

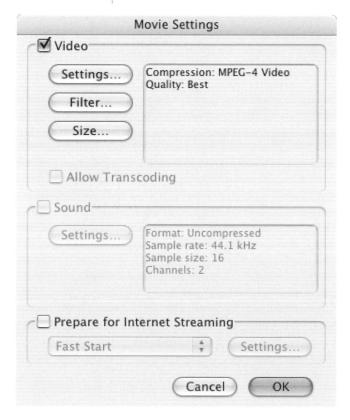

Figure 30-7 QuickTime 6 movie player export.

QuickTime 7 now supports the H.264 format. A large number of other formats for video, audio, still images, and animations are also supported.

QuickTime does not do anything by itself, since it is just a library of functionality. It is the applications built on top of it that unleash the power. Even simple applications like the movie player are useful for converting file formats. QuickTime is built into compression tools like Cleaner, Compression Master, and Squeeze to add functionality. These invoke the QuickTime mechanisms, which will deliver the same coding process regardless of what tool was used to call it. Some encoding frameworks may provide additional functionality and a finer degree of control over the parameters (see Figure 30-8). Occasionally, they also provide some extra codec plug-ins.

Table 30-5 lists the formats that QuickTime supports.

Although QuickTime 6 includes an MPEG-4 encoder, it is MPEG-4 Part 2 only and not a very sophisticated profile. However, it is good enough for web video or mobile phone applications. The encoding is reasonably quick but there are better implementations. The H.264 codec will supersede this implementation in due course.

 Do purchase the QuickTime Pro license. It is well worth the fee to get the extra features.

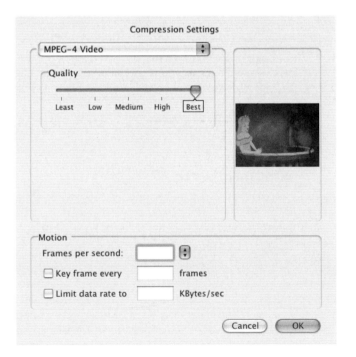

Figure 30-8 Codec parameterization.

Table 30-5 Video Formats Supported by QuickTime

Format	Import	Export
Image Sequence movie exporters		√
3GPP	√	√
3GPP2	√	√
H.264 (supported in Mac OS 10.4 onward)	√	√
Animated GIF	√	
AVI	√	√
DV	√	√
FLC	√	√
Macromedia Flash 5	√	
MPEG-1	√	
MPEG-2	√	
MPEG-4 Part 2	√	√
PICS	√	
QuickTime Movie	√	√
SDV	√	
VDU (Sony DU1)	√	
Animation	√	√
Apple BMP	√	√
Apple Pixlet	√	√
Apple Uncompressed Video	√	√
Cinepak	√	√
Component video	√	√
DV25 NTSC	√	√
DV50 NTSC	√	√
DVC Pro NTSC	√	√
DV25 PAL	√	√
DV50 PAL	√	√
DVC Pro PAL	√	√
Graphics	√	√
H.261	√	√
H.263	√	√
JPEG 2000	√	√

Continued

Table 30-5 Video Formats Supported by QuickTime (Continued)

Format	Import	Export
Microsoft OLE	√	
Microsoft Video 1	√	
Motion JPEG A	√	√
Motion JPEG B	√	√
Photo JPEG	√	√
Planar RGB	√	√
PNG	√	√
Sorenson Video 2	√	√
Sorenson Video 3	√	√
TGA	√	√
TIFF	√	√
Uncompressed 10-bit 4:2:2	√	√
Uncompressed 8-bit 4:2:2	√	√
On2 VP3		√
ZyGoVideo		√
Streambox		√
Microcosm		√

If you want to encode to Real Networks video format from within a Mac OS–based QuickTime-enabled application, install the Real Exporter plug-in. Likewise, adding Telestream's Flip4Mac will allow you to output Windows Media files directly.

More information is available at the Apple QuickTime web site.

 If all you need is full-screen mode, there are alternative solutions that don't require a QuickTime Pro license. The application that plays the movie through QuickTime can measure the screen size and draw a movie rectangle to just fill it.

30.10 Apple Compressor

The Compressor utility is shipped with DVD Studio Pro and Final Cut Pro for creating MPEG-2 and MPEG-4 (Part 2) compressed files. The user interface is constructed around a main window, as shown in Figure 30-9.

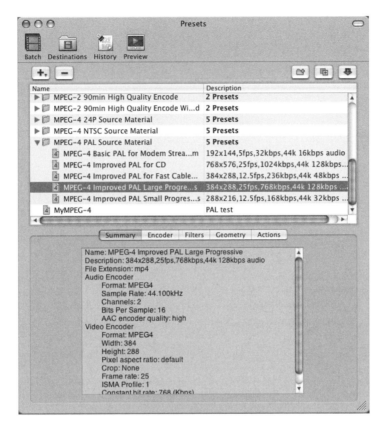

Figure 30-9 Apple Compressor main window.

The compression process can be inspected in the preview window where preprocessing, crops, and the effects of the compression process can be seen before and after by moving the sliding bar. The effects have been exaggerated in the example shown in Figure 30-10.

Job control is managed through the batch window (see Figure 30-11).

The MPEG-2 output is used when mastering DVDs, for example. The MPEG-4 support is for creating web streamable ISMA profile 0 and 1 files. Compressor will also use QuickTime and supports a TIFF-based export as well.

Compressor is the best tool for making MPEG-1 and MPEG-2 coded video packages on the Mac OS X platform.

Apple QuickTime: http://www.apple.com/quicktime/

Figure 30-10 Apple Compressor preview window.

Figure 30-11 Apple Compressor batch window.

The application is designed as a framework for initiating batch-compression jobs. It is OpenTalk (previously known as Rendezvous)-aware and has queue master support, which it has inherited from Apple's compositing tool—Shake. This allows it to automatically identify other machines on the network that have compression support. It will then distribute the compression work around the LAN to any machines that have unused computing capacity.

At the end of the compression job, the application sends an e-mail alert and/or runs an AppleScript. This allows some postprocessing to take place after the compression job is complete. It is useful for chaining workflow systems together so that they operate in an event-based way rather than polling watch folders all the time.

Droplet applications, which live on your desktop, are another useful feature that the Apple Compressor supports. If you drag and drop a movie file onto the droplet icon, it will initiate a compression job. These droplets are manufactured from the settings items in the presets list.

30.11 Telestream Flip Factory

This is a major transcoding server product family. The idea is that it will deconstruct a compressed file and reassemble it in a new format. It has some original approaches in that it does not completely decode a file unless it has to. The following software products are part of a coherent enterprise-ready system:

- Traffic Manager—Media gateway
- Publish—Automation for streaming media publication
- Flip Factory Pro—Universal format translator
- Flip Factory News—News content ingest
- Flip Factory News Manager—Workflow automation
- Flip4Mac—A plug-in for QuickTime on Mac OS that creates Windows Media output files.

The Flip Factory software has been available for some time as an enterprise-level transcoding engine. It has a variety of interfaces for job submission and it can be integrated into an automated workflow and provided as a service to client users.

It is designed around a workflow that fits very well with news and sports organizations that have remote feeds and outside broadcast content being delivered. These arrive via the ClipMail and Media Application Platform (MAP) interfaces.

The architecture is fairly complete and well thought out, and it runs on a Windows-based infrastructure, integrating with the .NET technologies.

While this isn't a compression system, it will transcode content from one format to another. There is a point at which transcoding becomes compression (when you are transcoding from a raw digital format to a highly compressed one), but we would be arguing fine points. Generically speaking, all compression tools transcode the content.

In fact, when you look at the range of I/O formats, Flip Factory looks a great deal like other products such as Compression Master and Cleaner, but it offers far more in the way of workflow integration and isn't intended to be used as a stand-alone application on a single desktop.

Telestream has started to venture into the Mac OS platform by providing some QuickTime support for Windows Media. This is a welcome addition to its product range and is a major step forward for the integration of Mac OS systems into the Windows Media–oriented video-transcoding business. It remains to be seen whether Telestream will port further products to the Mac OS platform.

Table 30-6 lists the formats that Flip Factory supports.

Table 30-6 Video Formats Supported by Flip Factory

Format	Import	Export
MPEG-1 4:2:0 System stream	√	√
MPEG-1 IPV SpecterView		√
MPEG-2 4:2:0 <15 Mbps	√	√
MPEG-2 4:2:2 Program streams <50 Mbps	√	√
MPEG-2 4:2:2 Transport streams <50 Mbps	√	√
MPEG-2 DVD-compatible elementary streams		√
DV25 (.dv)	√	√
DVC Pro 525 lines	√	√
DVC Pro 625 lines	√	√
AVI	√	√
Matrox AVI	√	
Avid QMF	√	
QuickTime—Apple Video	√	
QuickTime—Sorenson Video	√	√
QuickTime—DV 525	√	√
QuickTime—DV 625	√	√
QuickTime—Avid MJPEG	√	√
QuickTime—Media 100 MJPEG	√	√
QuickTime—MJPEG A	√	
QuickTime—MJPEG B	√	
QuickTime—Cinepak		√
QuickTime—DVC Pro HD	√	
QuickTime—IPV FMA	√	√
QuickTime—Raw PCM	√	√
QuickTime—Qdesign Music 2 (ver 4)		√

Table 30-6 Video Formats Supported by Flip Factory (Continued)

Format	Import	Export
QuickTime—Qdesign Music 2 (ver 5)		√
QuickTime—Qdesign Music 2 (ver 6.5)	√	√
QuickTime—MPEG-4 part 2		√
Windows Media —6.1	√	√
Windows Media—7	√	√
Windows Media—8	√	√
Windows Media—9	√	√
Windows Media—9 HD		√
Flash animation (.swf)	√	
DPX/Cineon	√	
Audio—WAV	√	√
Audio—MP3 elementary stream	√	√
Audio—AC3	√	√
RealVideo—6		√
RealVideo—7		√
RealVideo—8		√
RealVideo—9		√
RealVideo—10 (Helix)		√
Clipstream playerless Java streaming		√
RealAudio		√
Windows Media Audio		√
QuickTime—Audio		√
MPEG-4—PacketVideo		√
DivX (AVI)		√
MPEG-4—AAC		√
MPEG-4—3GPP		√
GXF DV50		√
GXF DVC Pro 50 (PAL)		√
GXF DVC Pro 50 (NTSC)		√
MXF/IMX	√	√
HD 1080i		√
GXF DV50		√
GXF DV50		√

In addition to the formats in Table 30-6, Flip Factory will access many common broadcast- and production-compatible edit systems. Video servers allow access to the file stores with whatever protocols are supported. These are often Ethernet based protocols such as FTP. For this reason you should try to find equipment with an Ethernet or Firewire connector as well as video I/O. Then you can bridge between the two worlds of IT and video production more easily.

30.12   Other Available Tools

There are many other tools available for encoding, but it is impossible to cover them all here. Appendix C provides details of some other companies and their products.

30.13   Ancillary Tool Kits

There is a variety of tool kits available for manipulating files. You might buy some expensive and powerful tools, but it is more likely that you will find all you need by searching the web for some open-source alternatives. I have highlighted several here but there are many others. It is a good idea to build up a toolkit of utilities like these to dig yourself out of a hole when you have to.

 Download trial versions. There is sometimes a promotional code for a price reduction on the full version.

If you want to do some video and audio editing, there are a range of tools that are either provided with the operating systems at no charge or are quite inexpensive to buy.
Don't forget that you may need some audio-editing software, too.

30.13.1   Video-Editing Tools

There will be many occasions when you must trim or modify some video before encoding it. Having one of the various nonlinear editing tools around will solve the problem, and it need not be expensive. Table 30-7 lists some popular video-editing tools.
You should install one of these on your compression system. Final Cut Pro would be ideal on the Macintosh although you already have several other alternatives installed there by default as factory-fitted items. Adobe Premier is a good all-around choice for Windows users. Avid DV Express may also be appropriate, but you will probably not need to install both.

 Buy all the options you think you might need when you purchase the software. The supplier may no longer offer them if you later decide you want them.

Table 30-7 Video-Editing Tools for Compressionists

Product	Description
Apple Final Cut Pro	A leading video-editing tool used for TV and movie production. Unless you need all the features of the Pro version, then Final Cut Express will probably do most of what you want at a reduced price. This is the optimum choice for Mac OS-based systems if the expense is justified. More information is available at the Apple Web site.
Apple Final Cut Express	For straightforward video editing and simple work this will do just fine although it is a DV editor only and does not support HD or film frame rates. You must upgrade to Final Cut Pro for that. There is a lot of useful information at the Final Cut Planet Web site.
Apple iMovie	If your needs are unsophisticated and you want to cut some home video or handycam footage, the free iMovie application is very powerful. This is a good place to begin learning about video editing. An amazing amount can be accomplished with iMovie even though it is relatively unsophisticated. The 2005 version now supports different aspect ratios.
Adobe Premier	Now only available on the Windows platform, this is a well-known and much-used editor that has been available for some time and is now mature. This is a good choice for the Windows platform if you only plan to buy one video editor. More details are available at the Adobe Web site.
Avid Xpress Pro	This is available for Windows XP and Mac OS but does not offer any advantages over the Apple products on Mac OS. It has some interesting image-stabilization features that will be useful for eliminating gate weave when you process telecine source material. More details area available at the Avid Xpress Pro Web site.
Avid Free DV	A downloadable free DV editing application. This may be useful to Windows users. A version for Mac OS was shipped but does not offer any significant advantages over the copy of iMovie that you already have.
Media 100	This is a family of video-editing tools at varying prices. Some products are available on Mac OS but most are Windows based. A key feature of Media 100 on the Macintosh is the AppleScript support. Nothing else currently equals this automation framework. Some very highly detailed and automated edits can be done with this. It is possible to join up Adobe PhotoShop, Illustrator, Microsoft Excel, and Media 100 into a totally hands-off workflow.

Continued

Table 30-7 Video-Editing Tools for Compressionists (Continued)

Product	Description
QuickTime movie player	If you install QuickTime it is well worth the small fee to upgrade to the Pro license. It unlocks all kinds of extra features in the player and your QuickTime installation. The movie player application is capable of editing files and then exporting them in other formats. QuickTime has a lot of codecs built in, although it is fair to say that some of them are not the best implementations available. A lot of them are unique and not available anywhere else.
Windows Movie Maker	A Windows-only equivalent to the iMovie application. Movie Maker supports similar functionality allowing you to add transitions and effects. It has built-in titling capabilities as well.
Ulead Video Studio	This tool is useful for editing and assembling video files. It can also translate files for archive in DVD, VCD, or SVCD format.
Ulead Photo Explorer	Useful for viewing and trimming video files. It can also be used for viewing and editing photo files.
VideoReDo	This is a Windows-based MPEG file editor that may be useful if you just want to cut some video without having to convert it first.

30.13.2 Power Tools

Sometimes when you have an especially nasty input file, you will have to deploy some heavyweight tools. Maybe the video you are producing has tears, jaggies, bad sync, and so much gate weave that it is hard to focus on. Or maybe it's just in the wrong format, has the wrong frame rate, or needs some restoration. Fixing some of those problems is not for the faint of heart unless you have the help of some power tools.

Table 30-8 lists the kind of tools you might find useful. If you only buy one tool, make it Adobe After Effects. Each has unique and useful capabilities, however, and if you cannot solve your problem with one of them it is likely that one of the others could do it.

The thing is to think laterally. Any application that imports or exports a QuickTime movie is a candidate for adding to your power tools collection.

Windows Movie Maker: http://www.microsoft.com/windowsxp/using/moviemaker/default.mspx
Apple: http://www.apple.com/
Final Cut Pro Planet: http://www.dvcreators.net/finalcutproplanet/
Adobe: http://www.adobe.com/
Avid Xpress Pro: http://www.avid.com/products/xpresspro
VideoReDo: http://www.drdsystems.com/VideoReDo/?src=dvdrHelp1

Table 30-8 Power Tools for Compression Assistance

Product	Description
Final Cut Pro HD	Although this is a video editor it also provides other capabilities such as effects and title-sequence compositions. A totally neglected feature of Final Cut Pro is the FXScript language. This does some amazing damage repair on your video. Areas of an image can be copied between frames under script control to do garbage removal. The express edition is also useful but has some limitations.
Cinema Tools	This is an add-on for Final Cut Pro so that it can manage a database of time codes and edit decisions. This enables you to import film and edit it as if it were video. Then the editing decisions can be exported back to a film editor for cutting. Once the film has been properly ingested and the database set up, Final Cut maintains all the metadata via Cinema Tools.
Motion	This is a new application that provides some very easy-to-use effects and motion-graphics rendering. It is very inexpensive to buy but is only available on Mac OS. Motion is a useful add-on to a studio running Final Cut Pro but is cheap enough to appeal to people who only use iMovie.
Apple LiveType	This ships with Final Cut Pro and you can use it to create replacement titles.
Adobe After Effects	After Effects has some powerful analysis mechanisms built in for motion tracking. This fixes gate weave, especially the compound gate weave that is introduced by the camera and telecine fighting one another. By carefully setting up the necessary key frames and defining expressions at those points in the sequence, you can ensure that parameters will be adjusted as the movie progresses. Another particularly strong area is the time-base correction and video scaling. This program also works for high-definition formats. Extra functionality in the form of plug-ins can be purchased from third-party developers. These are incredibly powerful and some contain entire script-driven rendering engines. Connecting them to your key frames with expressions allows you to replace just about any pixel in the image under script control.
Discreet Combustion	This is an alternative to After Effects that is designed to do similar things.
Pinnacle Commotion	Another alternative to After Effects, this is also very powerful.

Continued

Table 30-8 Power Tools for Compression Assistance (Continued)

Product	Description
Apple Shake	If money is no object, you might use Shake to fix some problems. It is designed as a compositing tool for Hollywood movies but it also has capabilities in the video realm. It supports complex compositing filters and of course it is key-frame controlled so you could use it to make that vital correction on your movie clip. However, it is probably not worth buying Shake to use as an occasional fix-it tool. But if you already have it installed, you might not have thought of it as a power tool for fixing problems in your video.
Ultimatte	You may be able to pull a moving matte off of the presenter and do a background replacement to get rid of some unwanted motion complexity. That would reduce the bit rate required to compress your footage.
Apple Keynote	Since Keynote can create a movie as an export, you might use it to render insert sequences and title fragments.
Microsoft PowerPoint	See Keynote above. PowerPoint exports to a QuickTime movie when it is being used on the Mac OS platform There are some issues with transitions not rendering properly if the frame rates are not high enough and getting the slide duration timings correct is tricky.
Motion Director	An image-stabilizing application for Windows that reduces the movement due to handheld shooting by detecting unwanted camera movement in your video files. It uses a statistical analysis technique to stabilize the image during playback.
MPEG2Works	This is a general-purpose, "Swiss-Army-knife" kind of tool for converting a variety of formats. It also converts between NTSC and PAL, but it is currently only available on Mac OS X.
Womble Multimedia	MPEG Video Wizard and MPEG-VCR are two tools, which are designed for fixing up MPEG files. MPEG-VCR is reputed to have a very good GOP fixer for when you want to prep files for burning onto a DVD. This software is for Windows only.
Mireth MacSVCD	This is a suite of Mac OS-based tools for manipulating video so it will fit the SVCD format. There are various MPEG-2- and DivX-based encoding utilities provided, including the Apple MPEG-2 playback component.
Digital Film Lab	This is a suite of tools that plug into Final Cut Pro and provide a way to create film like effects. It is made by a company called Digital Film Tools.

Table 30-8 Power Tools for Compression Assistance (Continued)

Product	Description
iStabilize	This is a very useful stabilization tool at a good price point. If you only need to steady some video, buying After Effects may be overkill and something like this may do everything you need.
altShiiva	This is an MPEG-4 encoder designed to creating content to be delivered to a Sony PlayStation Portable (PSP). It is based on the Open source Shiiva video tools.
Kino	Kino is a quite basic alternative for Linux users. You need to install other packages to get special effects, but the scriptable command line provides access to a lot of video processing power.

30.13.3 FFmpeg

One interesting tool called FFmpeg is available as an open-source utility on SourceForge.net.

FFmpeg is a complete solution for recording, converting, and streaming audio and video. It includes the libavcodec, the leading audio/video codec library. FFmpeg is primarily developed on Linux, but it is supported on most operating systems, including Windows.

 Pay shareware fees. It encourages the developer and leads to more new software for you to download.

A recent addition to FFmpeg is support for Sony's portable PlayStation handheld unit (PSP). Table 30-9 summarizes the component parts that are provided with FFmpeg. The download kit is available at the FFmpeg web site.

30.13.4 DropDV and Embedded Audio

Some systems will expect the audio and video to be stored in separate files. This has some advantages if you want to work on them separately and then combine them later on.

MPEG2Works: http://www.mpeg2works.2ya.com/

Womble Multimedia: http://www.womble.com/products.htm

Mireth MacSVCD: http://www.mireth.com/pub/mac-svcd-bdl.html

Digital Film Tools: http://www.digitalfilmtools.com/index.htm

IStabilize: http://www.iStabilize.de/

altShiiva: http://hetima.com/psp/altshiiva.php

FFmpeg download site: http://ffmpeg.sourceforge.net/

Kino: http://kino.schirmacher.de/

Table 30-9 FFmpeg Components

Component	Description
ffmpeg	A command line tool to convert one video file format to another. It also supports grabbing and encoding in real time from a TV card.
ffserver	An HTTP multimedia-streaming server for live broadcasts
ffplay	A simple media player
libavcodec	A library containing all the FFmpeg audio/video encoders and decoders
libavformat	A library containing parsers and generators for all common audio/video formats

When digital TV broadcasts are delivered, the audio and video are multiplexed together, and if you capture and save the transmission in order to keep the footage you just get one file, an MPEG-2 multiplexed audio and video file. This presents some problems because you need special tools to unwrap the two streams.

Recording the MPEG-2 multiplex off air with an El-Gato Eye TV gives you this sort of file. Although this file plays back through QuickTime on a Mac OS system, when you import the file into Final Cut Pro it separates out the video but loses the audio. This is a shortcoming of the MPEG-2 codec implementation in QuickTime, and it is unlikely this will be remedied in the near or distant future.

The solution is to get a copy of the DropDV utility. This will separate the multiplexed tracks and convert the MPEG-2 into a DV-format file, which is quite a bit larger.

30.13.5 Gamma, Color-Sync, and Video Compression

During a test for this book, some off-air footage was moved into Final Cut Pro and then exported as an MPEG-4 file. The MPEG-4 output was virtually identical to the DV copy, but the conversion from MPEG-2 to the DV format seemed to lose a lot of clarity and vibrancy. This might have been due to a misinterpretation of some gamma-coding setup. Either the MPEG-2 player made some compensation that the DV did not, or the gamma settings got lost along the way. This situation is still being investigated.

Initial research suggests that there is a disjoint in the gamma-correction area. Graphic arts use Color Sync to adjust colors to a calibrated setting. Historically, QuickTime-based video compression has ignored Color Sync. Therefore, if you have calibrated your display and are using a special profile, it does not reflect what happens in the compression system. Compressors typically use a Generic RGB profile with its inherent gamma setting. So perhaps it would be a good idea on your compression system to make sure any color calibration is set to a Generic RGB profile before compressing any video. At least then any gamma correction you apply in the tool won't be compromised by settings in the operating system.

Further testing will be necessary to get optimal results, and as a word of caution, you probably want to get these conversion tools installed and tested well before you must deploy them on a paying job.

Note that if you already have a compression application that decodes MPEG-2 multiplexed files, you probably don't need DropDV. For example, the Popwire Compression Master does a very competent job of de-multiplexing MPEG-2 files. This is sometimes referred to as demuxing.

30.13.6   AsfTools

If you want to operate on ASF files outside of your video editor, then the AsfTools application is what you need. It is a free utility for working on ASF, WMV, and WMA files. These are the sorts of things it helps with:

- Joining files together
- Splitting files apart
- Repairing broken files
- Converting ASF or WMV format to AVI
- Extracting audio to WAV files
- Converting WMV1 or WMV2 format to MP43
- Making stream files "seekable"
- Creating ASX files

This application will only work on Windows platforms. There is more information about AsfTools at the MyAsfTools web site.

30.13.7   AVI Joiner

If you have MPEG content stored in AVI files, then AVI Joiner may be useful. It will join multiple AVI, DivX, MPEG, MPG, and WMV ASF files together into one large movie file and create slideshows with music from photos and images.

The application is not free, but it is not very expensive either. AVI Joiner will allow you to accomplish the following kinds of tasks:

- Output AVI DivX, MPG, MPEG, WMV ASF, VCD, DVD, and SVCD compliant formats.
- Join any AVI/MPG/WMV/ASF files into one file.
- Preview the output before joining.
- Change the order of items.

My ASF tools: http://www.geocities.com/myasftools/

- Merge an unlimited number of items.
- Import audio files as background music.
- Add transition effects.
- Create a custom photo slideshow.

For more details, check out the AVI Joiner Web page.

30.13.8 RE:Vision Effects—Plug-Ins

The FieldsKit plug-in, made by RE:Vision Effects, works with After Effects, Final Cut Pro, Combustion, Premier Pro, and GenerationQ editing and other effects tools. It provides more sophisticated de-interlacing tools than you normally find in any of these tools. Check their web site for details of platform compatibility, as this can change as new support is added.

Other useful tools in RE:Vision Effects' library include pixel repair, image smoothing, and creative text effects.

30.13.9 Red Giant Plug-Ins

Two of the Red Giant plug-ins are particularly useful for compressionists. The FilmFix plug-in is designed to help cure problems that happen during processing of film footage that has already been ingested. Seams and tears can be repaired. Stabilization, dust, scratches, sparkles, and non-severe flickering can be dealt with as well.

The Magic Bullet plug-in is designed to soften the harsh nature of video to make it look more like film. More details of these and other tools can be found at the Red Giant web site.

30.13.10 Audio Tools

You may need to think about doing some remedial work on your audio. Table 30-10 lists some tools to consider for use on Mac OS X.

30.14 Analyzers

If you are doing a wide variety of work with different codecs and have a reasonably large and complex setup, then it would be worthwhile to invest in some analysis tools. These might be hardware or software tools. You will want to analyze the analog input signals as well as the encoded outgoing digital bit stream.

AVI Joiner: http://www.hitsquad.com/smm/programs/ AVIJoiner/

RE:Vision Effects: http://www.revisionfx.com/

Red Giant: http://www.redgiantsoftware.com/

Table 30-10 Useful Audio Tools for Mac OS X

Tool	Description
GarageBand	A useful add-on tool for Mac OS that provides a way to create rights-free audio backing tracks
SoundTracks	A more sophisticated audio loop and backing-track compilation tool
Logic Express	A cut-down version of the professional editing tool. This is now at version 7.
Logic Pro	The version 7 release of Logic adds many useful features for the professional musician and sound designer. As is the case with Compressor and Shake, the Logic application is able to distribute work to other idle processors on your network using the OpenTalk technology.
BIAS Sound Soap	An all-in-one noise-reduction tool. It is available as a VST plug-in, an audio unit, or as a stand-alone application.

The analyzers can usually cope with a variety of formats, and the more modern products also support H.264, which you should look for as a supported codec if you are buying a new analyzer. That way you will future-proof your investment as much as possible.

Table 30.11 summarizes some companies whose products you should investigate further.

Table 30-11 Hardware and Software Analyzer Tools

Product	URL
VISUALmpeg	http://www.mpeg-analyzer.com/
DekTec StreamXpert	http://www.dektec.com/
Hamlet waveform monitors	http://www.hamlet.co.uk /
Synthetic Aperture test gear plug-in for Adobe After Effects	http://www.synthetic-ap.com/
DMB Monitoring systems by onTimetek	http:// www.ontimetek.com/
OmniTek digital video monitoring	http:// www.omnitek.tv/
Thales H.264 analyzer	http://www.thales-bm.com/
Pixelmetrix preventive monitoring	http:// www.pixelmetrix.com/
Cinegy Cinelyzer	http://www.cinegy.com/

30.15 Summary

Combining the systems discussed in Chapter 29 with the software from this chapter should result in a totally killer video workstation and compression system.

While you may be interested only in compression today, video rendering, editing, and manipulation are part of a process that precedes compression. Having an appreciation for these other arts will help your compression processes because you will have additional skills and tools to bring to bear on the video you are compressing.

The result should be a far higher quality of output than what you get when you just "whack" it through a coder without any attention to detail.

Table 30-12 summarizes the tools you should select as priorities for coding particular formats.

Table 30-12 Optimum Coding Tools

Format	Optimum production solution
Real Networks	Real Networks encoder running on Linux or Windows. On the Mac OS platform, consider the Real Networks QuickTime plug-in as a priority item to install. You could also buy the version 3 Popwire Technology Compression Master application if you want to code RealVideo on Mac OS X.
Windows Media	Windows Media tools running on Windows XP. As of the fall of 2004, you should also check out the Telestream Flip4Mac codec plug-in that includes an encoder for Windows Media that runs on Mac OS X. The Popwire Compression Master 3 is also a candidate for Windows Media production on Mac OS X.
Sorenson (a.k.a. QuickTime video)	Sorenson Squeeze 4 running on Mac OS 10.4 or Windows XP
QuickTime-based codecs	Any QuickTime-compatible application running on Mac OS 10.4
MPEG-4 Part 2	Sorenson is considered to be one of the best coders for this. Cleaner or QuickTime as reserves might be appropriate. Platform is probably irrelevant, but bear in mind this might become a deprecated codec as H.264 encoders mature.
H.264	Best quality is obtained with Envivio products, but for a more modest budget use QuickTime on Mac OS 10.4 or Sorenson Squeeze 4 on Mac OS or Windows XP. Be prepared to install updates, as this is still a maturing codec and only the initial releases of products are currently available.
MPEG-2	Can be created with many of the available tools. The format is very mature. Use Apple Compressor on Mac OS. The easy choice is Cleaner XL on Windows.

If you want to encode Windows Media on a large scale, buy Windows XP and run the tools on that. It is unrealistic to do it on any non-Windows platform until or unless the SDK is revised so that it is complete on all platforms. The Telestream plug-in may negate that argument in the future, though, because it allows workflows to be built on Mac OS X for the production of Windows Media content.

30.16 My Favorite?

If I were to express a preference, it would be for the Popwire tools, especially the Compression Master encoding product. It is very easy to use and yet is potentially the most powerful of all the encoding applications, scaling from a single desktop to an enterprise-sized server solution. Popwire Compression Master is available only on Mac OS, and to get a comparable experience on the Windows operating system, you should consider the Telestream Flip Factory application and its related tools.

30.17 Can't Wait Any Longer

You've been very patient all this time while we've looked at a whole raft of issues that surround video compression, and I know that you are just bursting to begin compressing some content.

Well, in the next chapter that's what we are going to start doing! We'll prepare some content and in the following chapters we'll carry out the preprocessing. Then, finally, we'll have that coded video delivered.

Preparing to Encode Your Video

31.1 Introduction

This chapter (as do the ones that follow) covers the practicalities of encoding good-looking video. The consensus among compressionists (experienced practitioners in video compression) is that this is a mixture of art, craft, and science. The bulk of the work involves preprocessing the video before the compression begins.

31.2 The Workflow

The process follows an ordered sequence that is broken into several major sections:

- Bringing the video into the system—ingesting
- Temporal preprocessing—dealing with timing
- Spatial preprocessing—dealing with sizing
- Color correction—grading and picture quality
- Noise removal—cleaning it up
- Audio preparation
- Encoding the content
- Postprocessing and delivery

Figure 31-1 shows this in a little more detail, and each of these topics is covered in the following chapters.

If all you want to do is remove some noise from the video and everything else is OK, then go straight to Chapter 36, where we discuss noise removal. Likewise, if you are just restoring some old footage, then go directly to Chapter 34. That's where we cover scratches, tracking errors, and repair of damaged film.

Performing the preprocessing operations in the right logical order is key to reducing the encoding workload. If this is all happening inside the one tool, then these operations will be done in the right sequence. However, if you are using different tools for each step, then it is important to do the right things first. What you choose do at the preprocessing stage will materially affect your output.

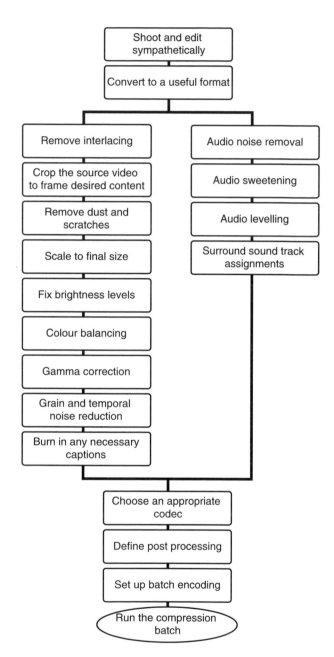

Figure 31-1 Compression workflow.

31.3   Step by Step

In the next few chapters we will work through the practical steps in preparing some footage for compression, many of which are considered to be preprocessing. The sequential ordering of these steps is suggested because it tends to reduce the amount of work being done.

If you have good reasons for doing it, you can change the order of these processing steps to suit your workflow needs. You should try to stay within the domain of processing being carried out. That is to say, you should do temporal processing before spatial processing. However, within the spatial processing, you may want to crop and then scale or scale and then crop. You should avoid defining a processing order that undoes something that was done at a previous step. For example, setting consistent audio levels throughout should be done after mixing down to assign sounds to different surround channels. Otherwise, there is a risk of altering the overall loudness and then having to level-compensate again. That could introduce more noise.

1. Planning
2. Shooting
3. Ingesting
4. Editing
5. De-interlacing
6. Stabilizing
7. Restoration
8. Scaling
9. Sharpening
10. Cropping
11. Luma correction
12. Gamma correction
13. Color correction
14. Noise reduction
15. Caption replacement
16. Audio trimming
17. Audio–video sync
18. Audio-noise reduction
19. Audio sweetening
20. Audio normalizing
21. Surround-sound tracking
22. Codec setup
23. Postprocessing
24. Batch control

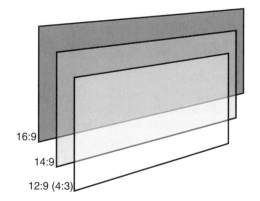

Figure 31-2 Aspect ratios 4:3, 14:9, and 16:9.

31.4 Be Prepared

When you are deciding what preprocessing operations are necessary for your video, consider the source material as well as the target that you plan to deploy it onto.

Preparing content to go onto the Internet as a downloadable or streamed video presentation requires more preprocessing than most other ways you might deploy. On the other hand, taking existing interlaced video footage and processing it for use on DVDs may require almost no work, since it is already in a usable form. Don't forget that MPEG-2 provides some interlace-compression support, which is what makes it viable for use on DVDs.

Likewise, preparation for broadcast may require very little in the way of preprocessing before compression begins. Some aspect-ratio conversion might be applied, for example, when you are mixing 4:3 and 16:9 aspect-ratio content (see Figure 31-2). A good compromise to use here is 14:9, which is midway between the two.

All of these preprocessing steps are optional. Your footage may be ready for compression right away without needing any preprocessing.

Also bear in mind that you might enter this preprocessing workflow at various points and that the processing need not all be carried out in one tool.

31.5 Picture Quality

The quality of the source pictures you are trying to compress may vary greatly according to where you acquired them.

Off-air broadcast of analog video is of noticeably better quality than that from a VHS recording. It will still need to be digitized, but if you can capture directly from the air, this is better than using a tape.

Digital broadcasts should be recorded digitally if possible. Products that capture the streamed MPEG-2 video are often only available to high-end users, and then the extraction of the video content is still technically challenging. Recording the transmitted bit stream to a file is straightforward. However, this then needs to be de-multiplexed to extract the program stream. Before you can use this in an editor, it then has to be separated into audio and video streams (further de-multiplexing). A format conversion may also be necessary, at which point there is a risk of gamma value corruption.

Most of the issues to do with video quality will relate to the bandwidth of the video content. That equates to the resolving capability in the horizontal axis.

31.6 The Results Have to Look Good

The next few chapters will examine the effects of encoding different kinds of content to see what artifacts are introduced. Cuts, wipes, dissolves, and so forth will all introduce different encoded bit-rate loadings and artifacts. Video content that has been created with some knowledge of the compression consequences will produce a compressed output that streams more evenly.

31.7 Content That Is Hard to Encode

Occasionally, you are going to find that some of your video content is difficult to encode.

Race cars, for example, move at a very high speed. If the camera shutter is open for any length of time, there will be significant amounts of motion blur. Because the point of view and attitude of the car changes from frame to frame, the number of reusable macroblocks diminishes drastically. The background is blurring differently from the car when you are shooting from the side of the track. Cameras mounted in the car are subject to all sorts of movement, but the interior of the car would be stationary with respect to the camera. This might actually compress better than the output from a track-side camera doing lots of pans to follow the cars. A lot of new information has to be coded for almost every frame. In Figure 31-3, the train has been motion-blurred on purpose to look like it is speeding through the stations. This shows that the image contains some very rapidly moving objects as well as some stationary ones. The boundaries of the two kinds of object are especially hard to code.

Moving seascapes and waterfalls are another example. There is a lot of motion (although in the case of a waterfall, a very good simulation might be generated at a low bit rate because the movement is cyclic and repeating). Moving images of waterfalls can be looped without the viewer's noticing. The structured and object-based approach that MPEG-4 provides might be used to good effect here if it is considered early enough in the scene-building production workflow. Figure 31-4 shows two frames from a movie about waterfalls. These are cyclic and repeating when you watch them; they would loop very easily. The frame-to-frame changes are considerable from the compressionist's point of view, however.

Figure 31-3 Extreme motion blur.

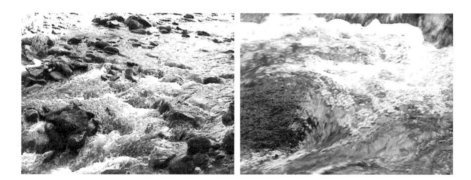

Figure 31-4 Moving water.

Video compression is not normally taken into account when the movie is being shot. Having some sense of the entire process, from the output medium all the way through the workflow from the earliest stages, will yield worthwhile results in the long run.

Clouds moving against stationary foregrounds should compress quite well because the motion is steady and the shapes are relatively unchanging. Although they do change, the change is gradual and only a small part of the cloud is altering between frames. As a whole, the cloud is simply traversing the frame. The motion detection and compensation

Figure 31-5 Gently moving clouds.

come into play with good effect here (see Figure 31-5). The clouds would compress very easily, although the seagull flying around in the foreground would pose some more difficult challenges to the encoder.

Large fires, close-ups of flames, and explosions will cause some significant increase in the bit-rate requirements because the movement is rapid and large areas are changing simultaneously (see Figure 31-6). Video of a fire will have some cyclic activity going on in the picture, much as with a waterfall. Whether the codec can take any advantage of that depends on whether the group of pictures (GOP) is long enough and whether the codec buffers sufficient frames.

Figure 31-6 Fire.

31.8 Local or Global Scope

Knowing whether the tool you are using applies an effect globally throughout a whole movie file is important. Sometimes you will want to apply the process just to a localized portion of the footage, or perhaps you want to apply the processing differently in each part of the movie. You must use tools that allow key-frame control of the parameters if that is the case. Experience will teach you how to import and export footage between tools in a non-destructive way. Moving the footage in and out of the tools should not perform any processing as part of that export unless you have told the tool to do that. You should keep control of what is going on and allow the system to intervene only under your supervision.

31.9 What's Next

The next step is to import some video into the system. We'll try that in the next chapter. Now that we know the implications of the footage we just shot or edited, we have some idea whether it is going to be compressible. Or at least we'll understand why it looks horrible when we try to compress it.

Ingesting Your Source Content

32.1 Incoming!

Well, it should be obvious that you can't compress video until you have some in your system. You must either provide a means of ingesting it yourself or have someone else do it for you. Small outfits will be shooting and inputting content on their own, whereas larger organizations may be receiving feeds from outside.

32.2 Preparing Your Content for Easy Encoding

PLANNING
There are many benefits to be gained by preparing your content beforehand so that it is more efficiently compressed.

Apply these rules when shooting video for compression. They will all affect your source quality for the better:

- Use the best cameras available.
- Put the best-quality tape in them that you can afford.
- Lock down your camera on a tripod and keep it still.
- Avoid panning the camera.
- Avoid zooming in or out.
- Make sure your live-sound recording is as free of background noise as possible.
- Stand your presenter in front of a stationary background.
- Have the presenter dress in solid-colored clothing. Patterned jackets cause moiré artifacts.

- Make sure that the presenter's clothes are a different color from the background.
- Light the scene with a diffuse, even illumination that minimizes shadows.

When you edit the video, take these points into account:

- Make your transitions short.
- Remember that straight cuts will be fine.
- Avoid cutting between scenes too often.
- Avoid the use of special effects.
- Avoid having scrolling text over moving video.
- Avoid scrolling text in any case.
- Do not fade the text in and out.
- Make sure text is large and readable.
- Use blue or green screens and substitute your own backgrounds.
- Minimize the number of pixels that change from one frame to the next.

32.3   At the Shooting Stage

Making sure you shoot optimal video is a good first step. Footage from the archives may not have been photographed under ideal circumstances. Knowing that the video is going to be compressed should ensure that new footage is properly photographed.

Completely avoid using that contemporary hand-held style where the camera jigs about in the presenter's face all the time. It is not nice. It is not clever. It compresses horribly. It is just some fashionable fad that some amateur cameramen decided to use because they were too lazy to set up a tripod and shoot a scene properly. Everyone else just copied it because they thought it was a cute new technique.

Movies with a lot of fast-moving action are hard to compress even with a locked-down camera. Moving the camera around at the same time only adds to the problems the compressor has to deal with.

Figure 32-1 Presenter against static background.

32.3.1 Talking Heads

Minimizing the movement of the presenter and using a totally static, but still visually interesting, background gives the encoder a very good chance of maintaining a low bit rate. In Figure 32-1 the presenter is set against a static, draped curtain.

If you have facilities to chroma-key the background behind the presenter, then you could set up a workflow that introduces moving or static backgrounds as required by the output platform. This could be added to the workflow control in your content-management system so that broadcast output takes advantage of the higher bit rates. Low-bandwidth versions of the video can have still backgrounds so that they compress more efficiently.

32.3.2 Rapid Movement

Any rapid movement in the picture over a large area will introduce a peak into the bit-rate coding requirements. A stationary scene with a truck driving across it will introduce some movement that the compression system must deal with, but motion compensation should cope with that. A slow pan will introduce movement as well, but the compression algorithms have motion detection and compensation built in so as to take advantage of pixels that may have moved from another position in the frame.

32.3.3 Choosing the Codec Before Shooting

Another important thing to decide before proceeding is which codec you will eventually use for coding the video. This might determine some of the preprocessing steps and how you set them up.

Certain codecs are mandated if you decide to present your content on particular devices. DVDs, for example, mandate MPEG-2. Mobile 3GPP phones require MPEG-4 constrained within a particular profile defining the bit rate and picture size.

The kind of material you are compressing may require certain quality-of-service metrics that dictate a particular codec. A browsable-quality copy of the video is used as a proxy in a modern IT-based newsroom to create an edit decision list (EDL) in the production workflow. This requires a coding scheme composed entirely of I-frames. The pixlet codec was designed with this sort of application in mind.

32.4 Video Capture

Capturing the video can be done in several ways. If the video was shot on a digital camera or is already in a digital format, then the ingest process is fairly easy. DV cameras can be accessed with FireWire, as can digital decks.

 When ingesting video from an analog source, pre-roll your source material to avoid syncing issues.

Broadcast equipment may support an Ethernet port that you can access with an FTP client.

Analog video presents a few more difficulties because it needs to be converted. If it is possible to transfer to a digital format using broadcast-quality or professional equipment, then that is preferable. Otherwise some kind of bridge or video-input card will be necessary.

A bridge is preferable to a video card because it is optimized for transfer and does not load your CPU as heavily. An AJA Io would be an ideal solution. Video cards such as those made by Blackmagic Design have built-in video-bridging capability and can convert from analog to digital as the video is played back.

32.4.1 Low-Quality Domestic Tapes

The quality of what you feed into the input of the compression system will have an enormous effect on the output compression result.

For example, compression of a low-quality VHS recording will always be compromised by the inherent noise that is a "feature" of that format. Old Betamax tapes will fare a little bit better, as will S-VHS recordings, but if you have the higher-quality production master tapes available you will achieve better results if you work from them.

32.5 File Conversion

You should avoid any unnecessary file conversions due to the risk of coding artifacts' being introduced. The source material might be presented in a format that cannot be operated on in the way you want. Perhaps you want to change the clip length or splice two segments together that are presented in different formats. Converting to an uncompressed format will allow you to edit the content and then recompress again with minimal artifacts. This is not ideal, but it may be necessary.

32.6 Editing Styles and Implications of Different Transitions

If the film editor knows something about the compression system used to create the finished program, some editing decisions can be made to avoid compression artifacts. The edited program will suffer far fewer problems when it is delivered through a low-bit-rate transmission system.

Video editing is only feasible on video that is coded with all I-frames. DV25, for example, is a motion JPEG format, and there is no dependency between one frame and the next. This is a format that can be edited without any problems. Editing of any format where there is a cadence or structure to the frames should be avoided. In these cases, you should convert the format first and then edit. If you must restore the original format, then do so when the editing is complete. For example, removing 3-2 pulldown from telecine footage before editing is vital. Otherwise, the cadence will be compromised during editing and the pulldown cannot be removed properly after that.

32.6.1 Cuts

Cutting from one scene to another is an example of an editing technique that is sympathetic to the compression process. Because the audio is dealt with separately, so-called L-shaped edits are feasible. Figure 32-2 shows an L-shaped edit where audio and video are cut at different times.

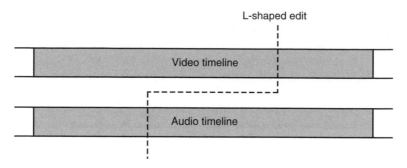

Figure 32-2 An L-shaped edit.

Cutting so as to place the scene change on a group of pictures (GOP) boundary might help some compression engines, but the main thing is to minimize the number of frames whose pixels are drastically different from the preceding and following frames (Figure 32-3).

A human being is unlikely to be able to place an edit in the right place, but an editing system could provide a lot of help. Final Cut Pro implements an extra track of hinting information that is maintained as you edit your sequence. The compression-markers track contains details of cut points, transitions, and edits as well as user-inserted data. This informs the compression engine that a complex section is about to be processed, and the encoder optimizes the process accordingly.

32.6.2 Dissolves

Avoid dissolves whenever possible—anything that causes a large area of the picture to change from one frame to the next and continues that change for a few subsequent frames is very bad for the compressor. If you want a special transition, use a wipe instead.

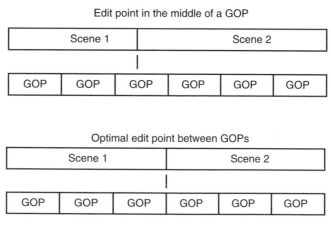

Figure 32-3 Cutting around group of pictures (GOP) structures.

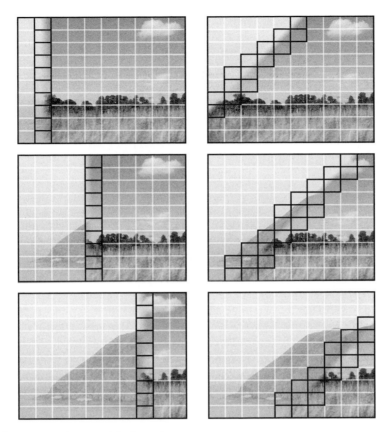

Figure 32-4 Wipes with macroblock grids.

32.6.3 Wipes

Wipes are less harsh on the compression process. If the edge is softened, it will increase the amount of picture area that is changing. When you create a soft-edged wipe, try to ensure that it spans as few macroblocks as possible. Figure 32-4 shows some wipe transitions and draws macroblock grids over them to indicate the area of change.

A diagonal wipe affects more macroblocks than a perpendicular wipe. These blocks are guaranteed to change from frame to frame. Other blocks may also be changing due to the moving pictures being wiped.

32.7 Using Video That Has Already Been Compressed

Recompressing footage that has already been compressed with a lossy codec leads to the introduction of some very nasty artifacts. For a start, unwrapping a compressed video clip may yield some blocky effects that are a result of the macroblock-compression process on a previous compression pass. If your macroblocks are the same size and position, this artifact can be minimized. If you move the uncompressed image and recompress according to a different macroblock layout, things may go bad very quickly. So, uncompressing and then moving or scaling need to done with care.

Telestream Flip Factory transcodes video clips by decompressing only as far as necessary before recompiling into a new format. When translating from one format to another where both use a discrete cosine transform (DCT) algorithm, it is not necessary to fully decode the image. The conversion may just require a repackaging of the macroblocks.

 Use transcoders such as Flip Factory rather than cascading (or concatenating) encoders.

32.8 Avoiding Other Problems During Capture

Depending on the hardware you use, you may experience synchronization problems when capturing footage from legacy analog formats. Video recorded on VHS, Betamax, and Video 8mm formats may have an occasional timing glitch in the recorded video. The capture card needs to maintain synchronization with the video and may have trouble following these timing instabilities.

You could try inserting a time-base corrector between the playback machine and the capture card. Some capture cards are designed to be upgradeable. Blackmagic Design video cards are loaded with firmware operating code every time the computer is restarted. This allows a new revision of that software to be deployed to the video card without needing to change firmware ROMs by hand. This will improve the performance of your capture card as later revisions are published.

Making sure that the signals are as clean and robust as possible is always the best solution. Be watchful for problems due to electrical noise, video, sync levels, and time-base glitches.

Sometimes, routing the video through another piece of equipment and using a monitor output or capturing to a DV camera will give a more stable input. While DV cameras are generally not ideal analog-to-digital conversion devices, sacrificing a little detail is probably better than losing complete frames due to an unstable time base.

32.9 Time and Relative Dimensions in Space

Getting the time-based aspects of our video sorted out is the next task. Dealing with that right now is important because we want to get the frame rate correct and get rid of any nasty interlacing artifacts if we can. This is probably the hardest part of the preprocessing to deal with, so let's crack on with that in the next chapter.

Temporal Preprocessing 33

33.1 Introduction

Temporal preprocessing is an important part of the preparation for compressing your video. Getting this wrong will significantly compromise your compression ratios and waste bit rate by preserving unwanted artifacts in the video in order to describe the content you do want to deliver.

The main area we are concerned with here is removing interlacing effects when converting the images to a progressively scanned format. This operation will also remove any redundant frames that contain duplicated fields. This is also good for compression purposes. We can eliminate the pulldown that is introduced when playing 24-fps movie film on a 60-Hz TV service such as that used in the United States. However, in territories like Europe where the display runs at 50 Hz there is no pulldown and therefore no reduction in frame count. Nevertheless, converting from an interlaced to a progressive display regime is still valuable and helps the compression process.

33.2 Interlace Removal

Broadcast SDTV has two fields per frame, with the lines interlaced. This is not the same as computer video, which is progressively scanned in one pass. If you are deploying the video to the web, you must remove the interlacing. If you leave the interlacing intact, then the coded video treats moving objects very poorly and you get double images of things appearing. Because of the interlacing effect, you get lots of alternating single horizontal lines on the image, and these are very hard to compress. Check whether you have to remove the interlacing from your content, because if it is already in a progressive format then this step is unnecessary.

 Take into account the eventual picture size you are aiming for when selecting a de-interlacing technique.

This step is sometimes called interlace removal or de-interlacing. The user interface on your compression software might use both terms interchangeably.

Interlaced video contributes a large amount of horizontal detail to your video and makes the encoder spend all of its effort on compressing this artifact instead of the image that you want to compress.

If you are using an MPEG-1 encoder, you must de-interlace first. The later encoders generally support interlaced content internally. They may de-interlace in order to do this, but you don't have to care.

Figure 33-1 shows a ball moving across the screen that moves a significant distance between one field interval and the next.

If we zoom in close enough to see the interlacing effects, the two fields look like this when they are viewed at the same time (as they would be on a progressively scanned movie).

Removing interlaced artifacts (see Figure 33-2) will become more important in the future because TV display is moving rapidly toward a progressively scanned presentation. In addition to up-converting standard-definition video to high-definition, it must be changed from interlaced to progressively scanned content.

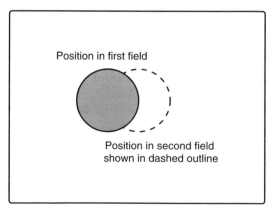

Position in first field

Position in second field
shown in dashed outline

Figure 33-1 Rapidly moving ball.

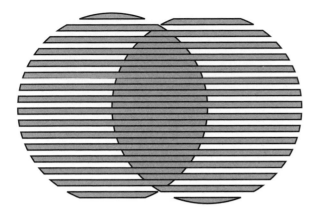

Figure 33-2 Interlaced video artifact.

 If your target platform does not display an interlaced signal at two fields per frame, then it may be worth the processing overhead to de-interlace the video before compression. You should get a more compact file. It will play better, and it will look nicer too.

There are five fundamental techniques for removing the interlaced effect. Selection of the best one depends on the kind of source material you are using. Table 33-1 shows the alternatives.

Figure 33-3 shows a sequence of four frames that we shall work on to demonstrate the effects of these different de-interlacing techniques.

Note how the second and third frames look like they have been double-exposed. They are actually a combination of fields from two frames. There is a frame of motion between the first and the last, but it has been combined in two different ways to make two frames where there was originally only one.

Table 33-1 Alternative De-Interlacing Techniques

Choice	Description
Averaging	Combining both fields into a single raster. Not a preferred way to go.
Field drop	Throwing away either the odd or the even field
Adaptive	Averaging the stationary parts of the image
Inverse telecine	Only applicable to 24-fps film transferred to NTSC
Do nothing	Output to DVD and broadcast need not be de-interlaced.

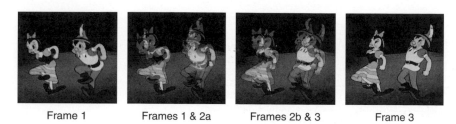

Frame 1   Frames 1 & 2a   Frames 2b & 3   Frame 3

Figure 33-3 Pulldown fields.

33.3 Using Averaging to Remove Interlacing

Averaging the fields together might seem like a good idea, but this just moves the problem of the horizontal interlacing artifact. Instead of having odd and even fields, there is a single field per frame and this converts readily to progressive scanning. However, this only solves the mechanical problem. The image has not actually been de-interlaced at all. It is going to compress very badly and waste bandwidth. So we see that a simple averaging technique yields unsatisfactory results and is therefore not recommended (see Figure 33-4).

If you look closely, you can see that there is some grain reduction and the lines in the interlaced images are blended out by the averaging, so the compression may spend less time on the horizontal detail but the superimposed effect is still evident. In this case the averaging involved simply taking pairs of lines, one from each field.

This is obviously not a good solution.

33.4 Dropping a Field to De-Interlace

The simplest technique is to just drop the odd or even field. This preserves the horizontal resolution but throws away half of the vertical detail. The eye is amazingly forgiving of this, but there are implications.

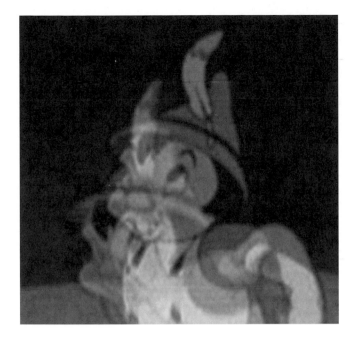

Figure 33-4 Field averaging.

So an image size that has a resolution of 720 × 480 becomes 720 × 240 pixels, and unless some line-doubling or aspect-ratio correction takes place, this looks rather strange. Consider the scale of the output when doing this. There are significant implications if you want to retain a full-sized raster.

Now look at the example of what happens to our four-frame sequence (Figure 33-5) if we discard a frame.

In the second and third frames there are some residual noise artifacts. This may be due to the format used to deliver the video. In this case, the original video was presented

| Frame 1 | Frames 1 & 2a | Frames 2b & 3 | Frame 3 |

Figure 33-5 Field-dropping artifacts.

as an MPEG-2 file and some pixel values have migrated from one field to the other during the MPEG-2 coding process. This is a good example of why you should avoid re-encoding footage that has already been compressed with another codec.

Note also that although we have eliminated most of the double exposure, we have in fact lost a field of motion and the third frame closely resembles the fourth.

This technique eliminates interlaced motion artifacts, but for film-based content, it is going to result in jerky motion and wastefully duplicated frames.

So this is not going to work with film-based content, although for normal video-shot footage being transferred to the web it might be fine.

33.5   Motion-Adaptive De-Interlacing

A more sophisticated and better method of de-interlacing uses an adaptive technique.

Adaptive processing treats only the moving parts of the picture. The stationary parts are left alone. For locked-down shots this might be OK, but it's not very good on pans unless the adaptive processor is sophisticated enough to detect the motion.

Technology has not yet been invented to simulate the effect of the human eyeball in translating an interlaced image into a clean, progressively scanned format; however, it is an area that computer science is working on all the time. The performance of video-processing tools will no doubt continue to improve, and the resulting output will only get better.

The major benefit of adaptive de-interlacing is that it effectively doubles the resolution when compared with the basic field-dropping approach.

There are some downsides to this technique, however, as it introduces errors with some content. For example, anything that is gently and smoothly panning vertically is not handled sympathetically by this approach.

Notably, this adaptive technique makes a mess of on-screen credits. The recommendation by expert compressionists would be to retype the screen credits as stationary frames.

Screen credits also get clobbered by the Gibbs effect (also known as mosquito noise). This is a cross-color artifact that shimmers around areas of text.

It might be a good idea to apply a combination of techniques to separate parts of the program and then join them up again.

This helps to explain why the preprocessing stage of a project accounts for such a large proportion of the time you spend working on it.

24 FPS film

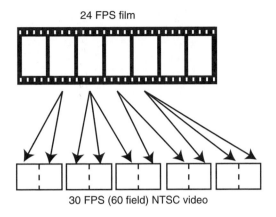

30 FPS (60 field) NTSC video

Figure 33-6 Telecine pulldown.

33.6 Inverse Telecine to Remove Extra Frames

This technique is relevant to those situations when you are removing the interlaced arti-facts from footage that was originated on film. Note that this is relevant only to NTSC 525i30 and it is not required on PAL 625i25 versions of movie film footage.

When converting 24-fps movie film to the near 30 fps used on NTSC TV broadcasts, some frames are scanned more than others to increase the number of fields.

This is easiest if two media are viewed side by side, as shown in Figure 33-6.

The first frame of the film is imposed on two fields of video while the second frame is imposed on three fields. This 2-3 pattern is repeated in a cycling pattern of five fields, distributing them uniformly across an odd and even field structure. The two formats are in synchronization every 10 fields, during which time only 4 frames of movie film have passed through the gate. This cyclic pattern is called the cadence, and it is illustrated in Figure 33-7.

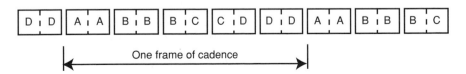

Figure 33-7 Telecine cadence.

Figure 33-8 Pulldown removed correctly.

Frame 1   Frame 2   Frame 3

Recovering the correct frames is theoretically possible by dropping those fields that duplicate one another and combining the correct pairs of the remaining frames.

Now let's revisit our original four-frame segment and see if we can recover three perfectly intact frames by taking the odd and even fields from different frames.

You can see in Figure 33-8 that we have successfully reconstructed the original Frame 2 that was divided by the pulldown. There are some residual artifacts, but these would be eliminated if a better-quality master-input format were used instead of the MPEG-2 original that was used for this test.

33.6.1 *When It Gets Nasty*

Some significant problems present themselves if more advanced telecine approaches have been used.

One problem occurs because the technology companies that develop telecine machines have introduced some cleverness into the scanning process. The film is scanned into a frame store at 24 fps, and when that frame store is dual ported the output is clocked at a different frequency. The output may combine the top half of one frame and the bottom half of the next. The pulldown is applied not at the frame boundaries but on a line-by-line basis. This is much harder to de-interlace, which is apparent in the middle frame of Figure 33-9.

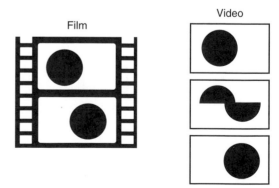

Figure 33-9 Line-by-line pulldown.

33.6.2 Cadence Issues

There are conventions for mapping the cadence to the time code of the video. Your encoding preprocessor that does an inverse telecine operation may look for this mapping in order to do the best possible job. The frames are named A, B, C, and D. The A and C frames are repeated twice; the B and D frames are repeated 3 times. The cadence is therefore 2-3-2-3, so the name "3-2 pulldown" is slightly misleading.

The clip may have been edited after the telecine conversion. This editing should be done carefully to avoid interruption of the cadence. If the cadence is compromised, the de-interlace code must offset the cadence detector from the beginning of the clip and attempt to re-synchronize if necessary when there is an edit.

The solution is to perform the inverse telecine operation before importing the footage into your nonlinear editing system (Premier, Avid, or Final Cut Pro) so that what you are cutting is a sequence of progressively scanned video frames with no interlace artifacts or pulldown cadence embedded in them.

Some encoding tools will make an attempt to detect this cadence slippage. Discreet Cleaner, for example, is reasonably robust if it is not given a sequence where the cadence is seriously damaged. It will cope with minor corruptions.

Some earlier versions of Adobe After Effects experience problems with this, and you must check the processing of the footage and do some remedial work in order to get the effect you want. While After Effects is not a compression tool, it is a very useful "Swiss Army knife" for fixing things in video clips, so this may or may not be an issue that you confront. If the cadence is correct and undamaged, After Effects will have no problems processing continuous sequences of video several hours long. A cadence error in the middle will cause a problem. If this happens, fall back to Cleaner for that part of the processing task.

It's useful to have a variety of tools available to analyze the footage to inspect the pulldown on NTSC content that may have originated at 24 fps.

33.6.3 Compromised Telecine Pulldown

Pulldown removal works best when it is processing telecine footage that has not been processed any further once it has been converted to the interlaced format. You will have problems where some telecine footage has been overlaid with a moving caption that was rendered using interlaced motion because then you have a combination of both interlaced and pulldown content within the same frame. Adaptive de-interlacing might be the only way to process this properly.

33.7 Field Dominance

Make sure you synchronize the sampling inputs on your video digitizer to the correct field on the source. If this is configured incorrectly, the wrong field is drawn first. This causes a nasty twittering artifact. There are two possibilities (Figure 33-10). How your video system responds depends on the hardware implementation. Neither possibility does the

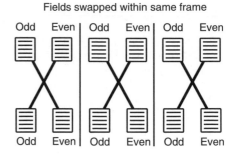

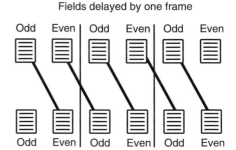

Figure 33-10 Field-dominance errors.

quality of your compressed video any good. The synchronization must be correct in order to digitize the video properly. The compression algorithms work very inefficiently with video that has the field dominance accidentally reversed, and the resulting output is unattractive at best and will normally appear to be seriously degraded.

33.8 Other Frame-Rate Issues

There are also time-base artifacts that may be introduced during modification of the time base. Figure 33-11 shows the difference between the 50- and 60-Hz field rates. You can see

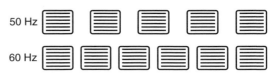

Figure 33-11 525i30 and 625i25 timing.

that the timing positions of the frames line up at regular intervals but the frames in between are located at quite different times. Converting between them requires some complicated motion interpolation to take place or else the resulting output will suffer from a strange jerkiness in the motion (which is hard to see clearly, but very disturbing to watch for any length of time).

33.8.1 Frame-Rate Selection

Slightly reducing the frame rate will yield some capacity to improve the picture quality. This is not appropriate for TV broadcasting, but Internet-streamed video will benefit from it. Reducing the frame rate below 18 fps is going too far unless your bit rate demands that you deliver a very low-capacity stream. This minimum value is chosen because it was used for many years as a domestic (home movie) frame rate for 8mm film. Frame rates as low as 15 or even 12 fps are usable in extreme cases. At these frame rates, any rapid movement causes objects to disappear because they are moving too quickly. This artifact is sometimes called submarining.

33.8.2 Strobing Artifacts

The wheels on a moving vehicle may appear to be going in reverse, possibly due to a strobing artifact on the original movie footage. Pulldown is going to make this look rather messy. Unfortunately, there is very little you can do about it. If you are expecting to play back the footage on a non-TV platform, reducing the frame rate might help.

Avoiding any kind of flickering effect is a good idea. Flickering objects that flash between 3 and 49 Hz will exhibit some unpleasant effects on the screen. Apart from the general unattractive appearance, there is a possibility of affecting viewers who suffer from epilepsy. It is known that certain flashing video artifacts can trigger a seizure.

Some strobing may be visible if TV pictures are filmed with a 24-fps camera. The picture will either flicker or exhibit a darkened bar that rolls in the vertical axis. It is possible to fit film cameras with a genlock sensor that forces the camera shutter to open and close in sync with the video. In fact, this genlock approach is used with video cameras as a matter of course.

33.9 Spaced Out

So that's the temporal processing dealt with. It's a relief to get it out of the way, because it is quite tricky to get right. Now we can deal with the spatial elements. That's the X- and Y-axes; we just did T; and we'll get to Z later. In the next chapter, we'll find out about cropping and scaling and all that spatial interpolation stuff.

34

Spatial Preprocessing

34.1 Introduction

This stage of the preprocessing workflow is all about the content of the frame. Here we set the overall dimensions of the frames and move the content around in them so that it compresses effectively.

We want to clean up any noise around the edges and frame the interesting part of the video so that we don't compress any more area than we have to. Scaling and cropping to clean up the edges is very worthwhile.

There are some quality gains to be had if you can avoid stretching or shrinking the image. Pixels can be interpolated or averaged when this scaling happens, and that leads to loss of detail. A crop is always preferable to a scaling operation.

The same aliasing effects that we discussed in the audio sampling (see Chapter 7) can exhibit themselves in video if you are shooting strongly patterned material. Scaling the image when someone in the shot is wearing a checked shirt can lead to some very nasty-looking artifacts.

34.2 Stabilizing Film and Telecine Content

If you are coding some old film footage that has been transferred via a telecine machine, then it is worthwhile to make sure the film is clean before the telecine process takes place. If you forget to do that, then later you might be able to apply some noise-reduction filters to remove dust and scratches from the digitized film.

Unless your telecine system is of especially high quality and the footage was shot on a stabilized camera platform with a good-quality camera, the subject matter will move around. It is common for filmed content to suffer from gate weave. This happens during shooting and also during playback. Several different aspects of the film process cause unwanted movement. Video is less susceptible to these, and modern cameras have built-in stabilizers to reduce the effects of handheld movement.

Figure 34-1 shows various axes of movement. There is a modern style of camera operation much favored by trendy TV programs wherein the camera is operated in a handheld fashion, even in situations where a locked-down and tripod-mounted camera would have been better. So, this handheld movement relative to the frame may be purposeful. Now, shaky movement may be acceptable when one is newsgathering in a war zone or presenting a point of view from a rollercoaster. It is completely unnecessary when one is filming a chef demonstrating how to cook a meal in a lifestyle program.

Introducing any additional movement is a bad thing to do while shooting content that is intended to be compressed. Inadvertent handheld movement can be tracked out and removed. Movement due to camera gate weave and movement of the substrate in the projector or telecine gate can be eliminated by tracking the exposed edges of the frame. Tracking the exposure edges will leave any handheld wobble in the shot if that is what you want to achieve.

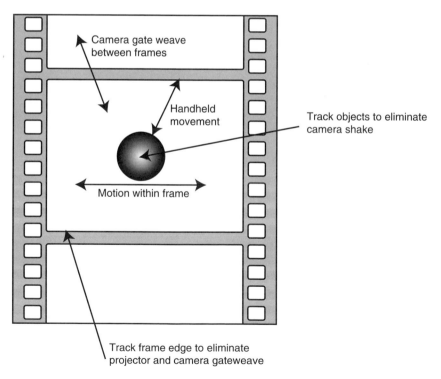

Figure 34-1 Instability within the framed area.

Some of these artifacts also apply to video, but you don't have the frame edge to track against. You can still track objects in the frame in order to remove camera wobble, but there is no gate weave because the pictures are not imaged on a physically moving stock.

Tools such as Adobe After Effects are useful for stabilizing the shots so that the camera movement and telecine gate weave are eliminated. The cost here might be a few pixels around the edge of the shot. These would need to be cropped, but they are probably in the over-scan region of the image so they would not have been visible anyway.

Well-stabilized, cleaned footage should compress much better than raw filmed shots.

This is also a good opportunity to grade and color-correct the footage. If the content was imported from very old film stock it will have a purple cast to it. Applications such as Final Cut Pro have very good color-correction facilities these days. If you use Windows, then Adobe Premier is useful for this kind of work. There are also many useful plug-ins to incorporate into your suite of tools to enhance the whole process.

 Be careful not to oversharpen during the telecine transfer from film, as this will compromise your compression efficiency.

If you have the money, then high-end tools such as Shake give you a lot of leverage for applying complex processes to your footage. However, they are financially out of the reach of most users.

Stabilization should be done before dust removal so that the chances of copying pixels from adjacent frames to repair the damage are improved. Scratch removal may be a bit more tricky, because the scratch is prone to move as the video is stabilized and that might make it harder to eradicate. This kind of restoration needs to be done painstakingly, and dealing with very specific artifacts might have to be done one step at a time.

The tools listed in Table 34-1 may be useful alternatives to Shake or After Effects.

Table 34-1 Motion-Tracking and Stabilization Software

Tool	URL
DeShaker:	http://home.bip.net/gunnart/video/Deshaker.zip
Dynapel SteadyHand:	http://www.dynapel.com/
2d3 Steadymove:	http://www.2d3.com/
iStabilize:	http://www.istabilize.de/

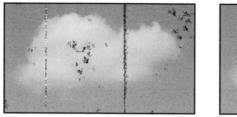
Scratched and dusty

Restored

Figure 34-2 Dust particles before and after media filtering.

34.3 Removing Dust and Scratches

If you have sourced your material from film, it may suffer from scratches as well as dust particles. The analog noise removal that averages pixels over a couple of frames may not remove the speckles. There are image-processing filters that are designed to remove dust, and the median filter would be appropriate here. You could also run the digitized film through After Effects to remove the dust. Figure 34-2 shows dust and scratches on a piece of film before and after filtering has been applied.

Scratches are a bit more difficult to deal with. Because this is mechanical damage to the film, it might have a repeating pattern that is cyclic but not in sync with the frames. If the pixel maps are arranged as they would be on the film, applying some kind of matte and repair algorithm might help. It depends on how bad the damage is. The dust filter might remove fine scratches, but tears and severe damage might need manual repairs. Badly repaired film breaks, and old splices may also require some special attention. Figure 34-3 shows a cyclic scratch on the left and a torn film on the right.

Speckles and scratches may be lighter or darker depending on whether the dust is on a positive or negative master and whether a scratch damages the substrate or the emulsion.

This all falls under the heading of restoration, and it is arguable whether that kind of work should be done at this stage or earlier on before the cropping takes place. It is best to do this as early in the process as possible, because the more you scale and process the video that you do want, the more you are blurring the edges of any dust and damage. A blurred dust particle is going to be much harder to remove than one that is crisp and well focused, so whenever you choose to deal with dust and scratches, you should always do it before the scaling step. Figure 34-4 illustrates the effect of scaling on dust particles, which makes them much harder to remove. Which of the three dust particles shown do you think will be the easiest to remove?

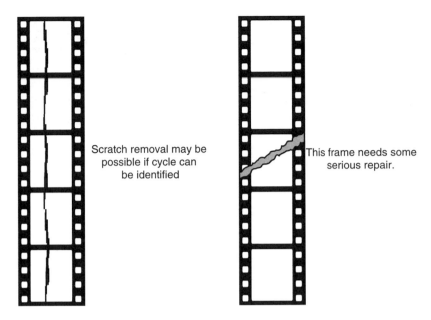

Scratch removal may be
possible if cycle can
be identified

This frame needs some
serious repair.

Figure 34-3 Cyclic scratch and tear.

34.4 Scaling the Input Source

The scaling operation makes the image the correct size for the target output. If you have been processing video for output on broadcast TV or DVD, this stage may not be relevant, but it is important for getting your Web video into the right size and shape.

Some applications allow the scaling to take place in the client. If you decide to use that approach then this step is not necessary. Better results are obtainable by applying

If you are really lucky, the
dust is well focussed.

Its more likely to be
like this though.

This is what it looks
like after scaling.

Figure 34-4 Sharp and blurred dust particles.

higher-quality image-processing algorithms during the compression. This will always achieve a cleaner result than a low-powered handheld device is capable of.

34.4.1 Scaling Down

Scaling down is worthwhile because it will lead to a lower bit rate. Scaling up increases the bit rate and is only necessary if the target platform cannot scale video while it is being played.

This step may be necessary to correct the aspect ratio of the raster or the aspect ratio of the pixels. These are two very different things. For TV output, your working image size might be 640 × 480 or 768 × 579 in order to let you work on square pixels. For broadcast, the image must be scaled to one of these sizes so that it looks right on the TV set:

- 720 × 480
- 720 × 486
- 720 × 575

These are all non-square-pixel display sizes. Some production tools, such as Adobe Photoshop, are introducing support for non-square pixels. New features introduced in Photoshop are often added to After Effects as well (which is actually Photoshop for movies).

When scaling the output video, web video does need to have a strict 4:3 or 16:9 aspect ratio. Movie players and plug-ins don't have specific requirements for this, and you can play any size of video within the constraints of your display size.

It is a good idea to make the output aspect ratio match the cropped source unless you are applying some correction.

If possible, make sure that both axes are scaling down or remaining at unity ("unity" is a common way of describing a 1:1 scaling—i.e., no change). This should feed back to some decisions you made earlier when you selected a de-interlacing technique or applied cropping. For example, if you know what the final size of the image is going to be, then your cropping operation may force you to scale the image up when you reach this step. Scaling up is a "bad" thing to do and should be avoided. Choosing a more optimal cropping area might help you avoid this scaling up and hence would result in a better-quality image in the finished product.

Bear in mind that applying the basic de-interlace technique that discards one of the alternate fields also reduces the vertical resolution to half what it was and discards alternate lines. It does not average between the two rasters, so fine detail may be lost if it only occupies a single line in the field that was thrown away. This approach yields a raster that is 720 × 240.

If you are preserving the 4:3 aspect ratio and desire a width of 360, you must make the vertical height 270. The 240 pixels must be scaled up, and this is a non-integer relationship. There will be some very nasty artifacts introduced if you do this. The horizontal axis is scaling down and will average nicely but the vertical axis is scaling up and will not.

A raster whose size is 720×240 should be scaled down to 320×240 for a 4:3 aspect ratio or 432×240 for 16:9.

If you must scale a raster down or interpolate between lines or pixels, use bi-cubic algorithms or sine curves. The nearest neighbor introduces some blocky artifacts that don't look good on a still image and on a moving image they are gross and very distracting. The implications of these interpolation methods with regard to quality are discussed in a little while.

Honor the pixel aspect-ratio rules—they are important to remember:

- Use non-square pixels on TV.
- Use square pixels on computers.

Some input sources are so close to the desired output size that applying a sensible crop is better than trying to scale the image.

Input taken from 486 line sources should be simply cropped to 480 lines. The obvious default crop to apply would seem to be removing 3 lines from the top and bottom of the image. This will move the video up or down an odd number of lines, and this could switch pixels from the odd to the even field, which might lead to field-dominance issues (that is, which field is broadcast first) later on in the broadcast chain.

The best approach is to crop using an even number of lines at the top and bottom, as in the following examples:

- Remove 0 lines at the top and 6 at the bottom.
- Or crop 2 and 4.
- Or 4 and 2.
- Or crop 6 and 0.

The even number ensures that field-dominance problems will not show up later.

Because you may be using various different tools to perform the stages of preprocessing, it is worth knowing that on the Mac OS platform, the Compressor application that is shipped as part of the Final Cut and DVD Studio tool kit is superior to QuickTime when scaling because the processing algorithms are better. But if you have only the basic QuickTime tools available, that will have to do.

A simple rule of thumb is that for 320×240 or higher, you should minimize cropping and use adaptive de-interlace processing or inverse telecine to keep as many lines intact from your original source as possible.

34.4.2 *Scaling Up*

Scaling the size of the video to a larger format is likely to introduce artifacts that appear as jaggies in any non-vertical edges. Horizontal edges may also show a tendency to bounce a little. Using high-quality interpolation algorithms in the scaling system will alleviate this.

There are several occasions when this scaling technique would be used when rebroadcasting archived material, for example, when transforming NTSC 525-line standard-density (SD) video into European 625, which is shown in Figure 34-5.

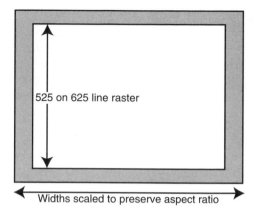

Figure 34-5 525 lines on 625-line format.

The second quite common example is when 405-line UK transmissions are being displayed on 625-line TV (or being shown in the United States). The output quality will be better if the picture size is reduced so that it occupies a 405-line window in the middle of the 525-line raster rather than scaling it to fit. Over-scanning of TV sets will account for some of the margin around the edges. The relative sizes of these margins are shown in Figure 34-6.

This leaves an unacceptably large blanked region around the picture when it is broadcast in Europe, so 405-line TV is often scaled up to fit 625 lines. Otherwise the margin around the image is probably too wide. The 1:1 scaling is too small and 1:2 is too large. So a non-integer scaling factor is used. This yields some very nasty line-based artifacts. Oddly enough, 405 would probably look better on HDTV because a 1:2 scaling in the vertical axis would be feasible.

The third case is when you are just enlarging an area of picture. Obviously, non-integer scaling factors will be problematic.

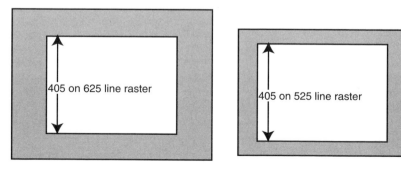

Figure 34-6 405 lines on 525 and 625 rasters.

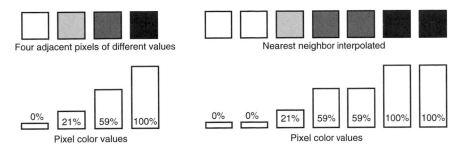

Figure 34-7 Nearest neighbor.

In all of these cases, some form of interpolation is necessary. The spatial interpolation must be processed separately from the temporal interpolation. A variety of different algorithms have been developed to deal with spatial interpolations.

34.4.3 Nearest-Neighbor Interpolation

Taking into account the relative positions in the raster of each line, the nearest line to the correct position is simply duplicated. Figure 34-7 shows how a 4-pixel-wide area is scaled to a 7-pixel-wide area.

34.4.4 Linear Interpolation

This technique refines the nearest-neighbor approach. It calculates a proportional difference between two adjacent pixels and selects a value that is a blend of the two. This is not a discrete computation just based on two pixels; it is a curve-fitting exercise based on the rate of change of the pixel values. A line is fitted to the values on the input grid and the output values are calculated proportionally according to the output grid positions. Figure 34-8 shows the same group of 4 pixels scaled using a linear interpolator.

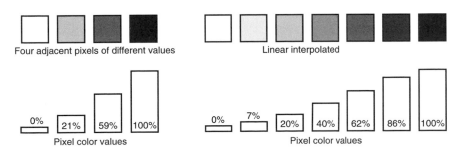

Figure 34-8 Linear interpolation.

Where the scaling is applied in two dimensions, the interpolation is calculated on two axes and a value is selected according to the X and Y positions. This is also a curve-fitting process and is called bi-linear interpolation.

34.4.5 Cubic Interpolation

The curve-fitting process is used again here, but a more complex algorithm is used than in the linear interpolation. This approach is a little more computationally complex. It derives a spline curve that models the intensity value and ensures that it passes through the intensity values of the pixels in the source image. The position for the output value is calculated proportionally as a distance along that curve but the interpolation of intensity values is nonlinear. Figure 34-9 must be compared carefully with Figure 34-8 to see the difference in the output values.

A two-dimensional variant of the cubic interpolation technique is used to interpolate across an X–Y grid of pixels. This is called bi-cubic interpolation.

34.4.6 Separate Interpolations in Different Axes/Color Spaces

In situations where limited CPU capacity is available, it may be worth applying a bi-cubic interpolation in the luma channel and a computationally less intensive bi-linear algorithm in the chroma channels. This would improve performance when a high throughput is required. The color information is stored at a lower resolution, but that's fine because the eye is more sensitive to light intensity than color. The compromise occurs where the effects are least likely to be noticed.

34.4.7 Scaling Issues

Converting video down from higher to lower resolution throws away information but still results in good quality at the target-picture size. This is sometimes called sub-sampling. Scaling up cannot introduce any extra information. But good results can be achieved by interpolation when the scaling is less than 150% of the original size. Going larger than this will result in a compromised picture.

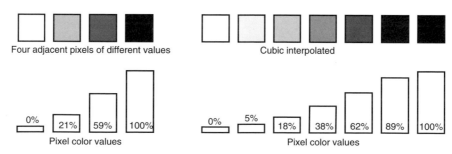

Figure 34-9 Cubic interpolation.

34.5   Edge Enhancement

Smoothing or softening the image with a little blurring might remove some noise artifacts and lead to better coding. But that may reduce the bit rate a little, since the coding of sharp edges requires high-frequency coefficients to be included in the coded output. It is important to understand how edges work in digital imaging before we can make informed decisions about how to optimize them for compression.

If you are working on edges, apply the correction just to the luma channel. The chroma channels can remain untreated unless the distortion is gross.

34.5.1   Slew Rate

The slew rate is the capacity of your input circuits to adjust to a sudden and drastic change in the intensity levels. If the slew rate is insufficient, the edges will become blurred. Figure 34-10 shows two slew-rate scenarios; one depicts going from black to white and the other from gray to white. The slewing distance may be different, but because of the edge, the slewing rate is just as fast because of the sharp transition. It is only the excursion that is reduced.

A poor slew rate will look as if the picture is blurred in the horizontal direction and fine detail may be lost altogether. Thin vertical lines, for example, just disappear altogether. This is evidenced in the example waveforms shown in Figure 34-11.

34.5.2   Sharpness

Applying additional filtering may control the sharpness of the detail in the video. But you need to be careful to avoid overshooting. There are several artifacts that are undesirable, and the wrong sharpness-filter settings will actually make your compression less effective.

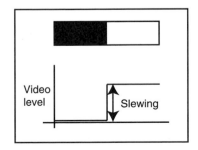 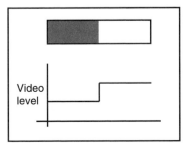

Figure 34-10 Slew rate.

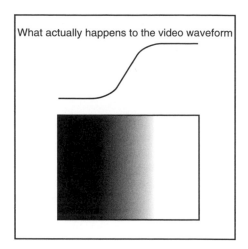

Figure 34-11 Slew-rate waveforms.

Figure 34-12 shows the effect of an overshoot in the transitions around the edges. There is a risk of this happening when the film is processed through a telecine unit that is incorrectly calibrated.

The effect is obvious if a small part of the picture is reproduced as a waveform. This is illustrated in Figure 34-13.

Just enough sharpening should be applied to restore the clean edges.

34.5.3 Edge-Sharpening Damage

Don't turn on any automatic sharpening filters, as this increases edge detail but also introduces more noise artifacts, which are harder to compress effectively. If you are going to do this at all, then it needs to be done manually and with care.

Original grayscale image   Severe edge enhancement

Figure 34-12 Sharpening halos.

This was the unfocused blurred edge you started with.

This is the perfect sharp edge you wanted.

This was what the edge enhancer did.

Figure 34-13 Sharpening-halo waveform.

Avoid applying any edge enhancement if possible. It leads to ringing effects where the edge detail overshoots if it is not applied correctly.

A lot of edge enhancement tends to be applied when movie film is transferred to video. This is necessary because a low-pass filter is applied to remove aliasing and flicker artifacts, which sacrifices some detail that can be restored by using some edge enhancement. Beware, however; often, far too much edge enhancement is added and a halo effect around dark objects is created. This is very difficult to remove later on.

34.6 Cropping the Input Source

The next step is to crop the picture to include the desired part of the image. This is necessary for several reasons:

- Video monitors and TV sets are designed to over-scan.
- Computer displays do not over-scan.
- It is necessary to crop off edge-blanking areas.

When cropping, keep the following points in mind:

- Cropping asymmetrically is permitted to remove noise.
- Low-resolution output is cropped to the safe area.
- Crop off any letter boxing and center-cutout blanked areas.
- Crop to the final aspect ratio if it is not going back to TV.

If you are exceeding your desired bit rate, it is preferable to shrink the frame size in order to keep the frame rate up.

34.6.1   Cropping for Aspect-Ratio Correction

For output to the web, you may be processing some wide-screen footage with black bars at the top and bottom of the frame. There is nothing to be gained by encoding these areas of the frame, and they will only consume valuable bit rate that is better used on genuine picture information. Figure 34-14 shows how to crop these.

You should leave in the letterboxing effect when you are encoding wide-screen footage with an aspect ratio wider than 16:9 for eventual deployment on a DVD since a complete raster must be encoded. The overall cropping outline should be set to 16:9 for a DVD but may be anamorphically scaled to 4:3 for encoding.

34.6.2   Ragged Edges

Another reason to crop is that the edges may be ragged due to timing issues when the footage was ingested at the digitizer. This might show up as noise at the extreme left and right edges and some tearing at the bottom of the picture. Often there is also a half line at

Figure 34-14 Cropping to correct aspect ratios.

Figure 34-15 Crop to remove data lines at the top.

the top of the picture and one at the bottom. This half line is required to adjust the timings in the horizontal axis so that the interlacing works correctly. These half lines can be cropped as well.

Figure 34-15 shows a snapshot of the top four lines of a captured frame of video. After being scaled vertically by a factor of 10:1, the top line is blank and the second line has some digital signaling superimposed. This must be cropped.

If you are creating some encoded footage for a very-low-resolution target platform such as a mobile phone, then it is permissible to crop into the subject matter as closely as possible.

34.6.3 Safe Areas

Crop down to the safe area, which is a boundary that is approximately 10% of the screen size around the border. This is important for content being viewed on a TV set because it is designed to over-scan the picture in order to hide any nasty edges. Other devices that show you the entire raster do not require this precautionary framing of the content. Figure 34-16 shows where the safe areas are.

There are other safe-area designs, depending on who made the content and what it was eventually intended for. Figure 34-17 shows a safe area graticule designed for

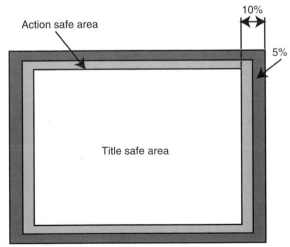

Figure 34-16 Safe areas.

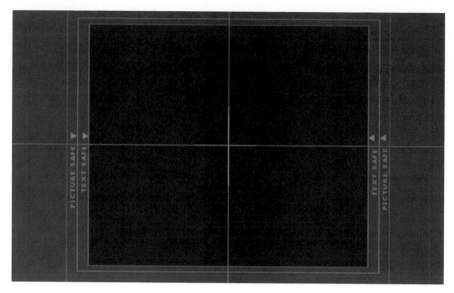

Figure 34-17 Mixed aspect-ratio safe areas.

framing content into a 4:3 aspect-ratio area within a 16:9 aspect-ratio raster. This is important because some broadcast-TV channels are output on a variety of services, some of which are wide-screen 16:9 and others of which are 4:3. By framing the picture carefully like this, a simple cropping process is introduced at an appropriate point in the broadcast chain.

Be aware that cropping rectangles might be pulled in slightly when content has been edited from a variety of sources. The top and bottom blanking on a wide screen may float up and down. Loading your film into After Effects to correct some of the framing may be helpful. The location of the cropping rectangle can be key-framed to pan and scan the optimum pixel area. Motion tracking can be applied at the same time to steady any gate-weave artifacts. The amount of effort expended will depend on the time you have available and the importance of the footage.

Check out the Creative Mac web site for an article on safe areas and details of a downloadable plug-in action that you can install into Photoshop to generate them.

34.6.4 Raw Viewing Mode

Beware of viewing modes offered by the encoding tools. Always try to display in raw format so that you see an unscaled image when setting up crop regions. Your cropping will then be more accurate.

Creative Mac safe areas: http://www.creativemac. com/2002/11_nov/features/download8021122.htm

34.6.5 *Local or Global Cropping Set-Up?*

Be aware that Cleaner and other compression tools usually only give you a global setting for any of the parameters. If you want to apply preprocessing in a key-framed way, you must load your footage into another tool such as Adobe After Effects.

Scrub through the video to check that the framing of the crop is correct at all times. All frames should fit your crop. If necessary, pull it in for the lowest common denominator. If the movement of the area of interest is more than you are prepared to accept, then run the file through Adobe After Effects. Take advantage of the motion-tracking and key-framing features to reposition errant video segments so they fit your crop window better.

The first lines at the top and possibly as many as 10 lines at the bottom of video that has been sourced from a consumer format are usually badly synchronized. This is where you get tears, luma levels going funny, and half lines. You occasionally see some digital text data and what looks like one line of color-bar video. This is a mixture of Vertical Interval Time Code (VITC) and Vertical Interval Test Signals (VITS). You don't want to have any of this in your compressed video, and unless you introduce better-quality equipment or some kind of time-base correction and VITC/VITS line blanking, you will have to deal with it by cropping.

After Effects allows frame-accurate cropping and repositioning. You could track the edges and correct gate weave and misalignment due to multiple sources being edited together, but this is very time consuming.

34.7 Alpha-Channel Coding

In Chapter 39, there is a discussion about shape-coded outlines that enable the video to be encoded in layers and composited with a non-rectangular outline. This is one of the capabilities of MPEG-4 Part 2. So far, none of the commercially available tools supports this capability, but it is likely that they will in the future. It remains to be seen whether this capability is added to H.264 or will remain a differentiating feature between H.264 and MPEG-4 Part 10. Companies are likely to be reluctant to commit to an implementation until the appropriate standard is revised.

When this capability is implemented, it would seem appropriate to deal with it at the same stage as scaling and cropping since it is essentially a cropping operation.

34.8 Catching Some Zs

No, it's not time for a nap yet. It is all about that Z-axis now. We've sorted out T, X, and Y with the temporal and spatial corrections. It is all scaled and cropped the way we want it, but maybe the colors aren't quite right or it has lost some of its sparkle. That's all Z-axis stuff, and we'll find out how to fix it up in the next chapter.

Color Correction

35.1 Light and Shade

Now that the preprocessing has sorted out the temporal and spatial adjustments, we can turn our attention to the overall lighting and coloring of the image. It is helpful to separate adjustments to the brightness from those that modify the color, so first you'll need to get the luma values right. Then the color can be tweaked if necessary. The luma may need to be checked again and very slight adjustments made after color correction is taken care of.

35.2 Correction Is Sometimes Mandatory

Sometimes the footage you are processing requires some color correction simply because of the kind of material involved.

Old home-movie film is almost certain to have a purplish cast to it because some of the dyes in the emulsion will have faded more than others. The magenta dye seems to hold an image for the longest time.

Shooting underwater lends a bluish cast to the whole color balance, which darkens with the depth that the diver is at when the film or video is shot. This is because the reds in the illumination are lost faster than the greens and blues. Some experiments have been done with logging the depth in a data track stored with the video. This is then used to select a color-correction filter according to the depth that was recorded for that frame. This seems to work very well, although it probably requires some calibration.

35.3 Compensating the Luma

This preprocessing step takes place here because if luma correction were applied earlier, the scaling algorithm would alter some individual pixel values. The new red-green-blue (RGB) values generated would change the intensity values. Altering the luma at this point leaves it unchanged by subsequent processes unless you apply large amounts of color-correction and hue-rotation effects.

It is this interplay between the different preprocessing stages that tends to make it appear more complex for the beginner. Once you break down the process into a series of discrete steps, everything becomes easier and more predictable. At that point you are well on the way to becoming a proficient compressionist.

35.3.1 The Range of Legal Values

Lowering the overall brightness of an image adds contrast and color saturation. That makes it appear stronger and less washed out. It also corrects the black levels. Black and peak-white levels must be checked when adjusting the luma range.

The video standards define a range of legal color values. That range forces the blacks to be somewhat higher than 0 and the peak-white values to be somewhat less than 100%. It is important to preserve this legal range of colors when broadcasting video. All adjustments of the luma must remain within that range. The values of black below the legal level are called footroom and the white values above peak are called headroom.

The exact values you will find will depend on where the image-sampling values are taken. For most purposes, you will be working with an 8-bit value. Very-high-quality systems use a 10-bit resolution, but it is rare to encounter that outside of a studio setting.

The 8-bit values range from 0 to 255. You will normally only see these values if you are recording the serial digital interface (SDI) video values. These are not the same as the analog values. The 0 and 255 are reserved to carry synchronization pulses. So any video information will be range-limited to between 1 and 254. The analog black level is defined as 16 increments higher than the SDI 0 value. The blacks will be a very dark grey, but not absolute black. The peak-white values are limited to 219 increments above the base-black level. In terms of the interface, this is a byte value of 235. The full range at the extreme of the legal values within the interface values is 254. If the 16 increments of black-level offset are subtracted, the maximum white value is 238. The space between 219 and 238 in the analog-video domain is the headroom. This way, any filtering operations that cause a pixel value to exceed the peak-white level of 219 do not get crushed because they fall into the headroom and are corrected.

This is a lot easier to see in a picture (Figure 35-1).

You don't have to adjust these settings if you have a clean source and the video looks good. If you are working wholly within a broadcast system, these level corrections will be taken care of for you.

35.3.2 Compensation

It is in the area where your footage is being moved between the video world and the computer world that you must compensate the luma values.

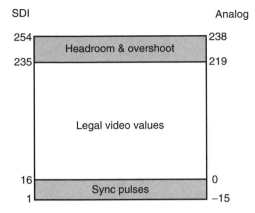

Figure 35-1 Luma range.

If you have some video and intend to broadcast it on the web or via a broadband link to eventually be viewed on a computer screen, you must bring the black level down. You must also increase the range.

Some color correctors allow you to simply grab the black and white levels on a visual histogram graph or via some dial wheels on a color-correction user interface. On a simpler system, you will have to use the brightness and contrast controls. If you are using QuickTime-based tools, a lot of this compensation takes place automatically and you need not worry about it.

We adjust the various properties of the video by applying an operator. This term just describes a tool that modifies a particular part of the video information, usually without affecting any other property. For example, color and lightness are separate operators, although they are actually adjusting the separate red, green, and blue values to accomplish their respective tasks.

To get the appropriate value for the background, first adjust the brightness level. Figure 35-2 shows that reducing the brightness will cause the loss of some information. It is an offset operator, not a scaling operator. Contrast correction is a scaling operator.

35.3.3 Measuring Tools

Figure 35-3 illustrates the levels palette from Photoshop. It presents a histogram of pixel values in the image and lets you pull up the black value, white value, and mid-tone setting. It is a little more complex for video because you must integrate over a series of frames. Similar controls are available in After Effects, and because they are key-framed, the settings can be altered while the movie is playing.

Note in this example that two colors in particular show up as spikes in the histogram chart.

Final Cut Pro provides some very sophisticated color-correction and monitoring tools. Figure 35-4 is a screenshot of the vector scope, histogram, and waveform monitors

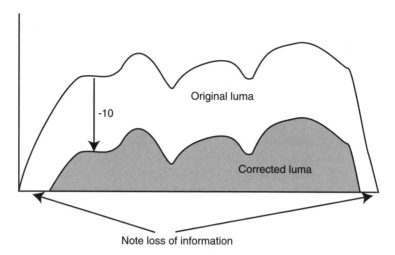

Figure 35-2 Brightness correction.

showing the measurements for a video picture containing a female face that almost fills the screen. The skin tone is set correctly and the exposure, luma, and contrast are all optimal:

Once the black level is set correctly, use the contrast control to open up the range of values to pull the white level up to an optimal setting.

Be careful with the contrast setting. Too much contrast enhancement causes crushing. Figure 35-5 is a screen shot of the vector scope for the same picture but shows the effect of a gross over-adjustment of the contrast. In this picture, the skin tone is all washed out to white.

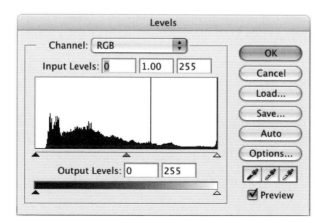

Figure 35-3 Photoshop's levels palette.

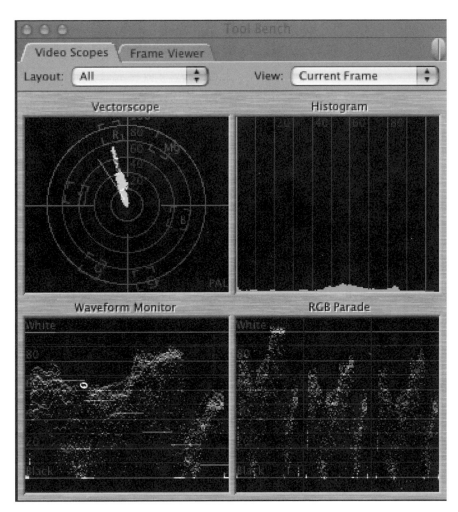

Figure 35-4 Final Cut Pro video scopes.

Note that the vector scope has not changed significantly. The color balance is unchanged. The waveform monitor shows that nearly all of the video lines are at peak white. Note also the histogram chart at the top right. This shows a major peak in the number of pixels whose value is near the maximum peak setting.

Because the brightness and contrast interact, you must modify them together. A good technique is to reduce the brightness and increase the contrast by an equal amount. Typical settings at this stage might be Brightness −10 and Contrast +5 to +10. This would reduce the black level to lose any inherent noise and leave the peak-white level pretty much where it was at the start.

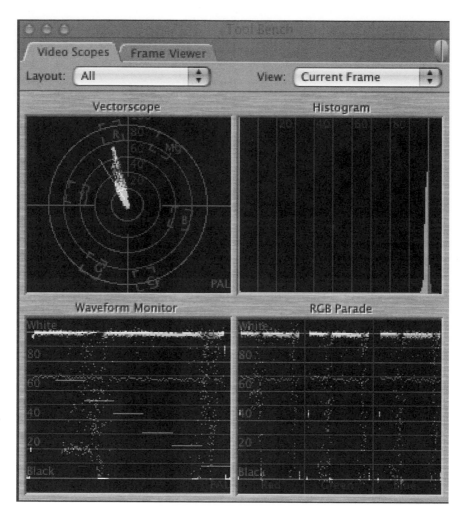

Figure 35-5 Crushed whites.

You should use measurement tools to check this. If you are not using something as sophisticated as Final Cut, After Effects, or Premier, you might be able to open a preview window in your compression tool to see the effect of your settings. The preview window shows the result, and you can compare the source and preview values with a color-measurement tool.

In Mac OS X, in the Utilities folder inside the Applications folder you will find a digital color meter tool. To help you find it, Figure 35-6 shows you what the application icon looks like.

Figure 35-7 shows you what the tool looks like when you run the application.

DigitalColor Meter **Figure 35-6** Digital color meter tool icon.

This tool is only available on a Mac OS, but there are other equivalent tools for Linux or Windows. There are also open-source tools you can download for nothing. You might be able to use the color-dropper tools in paint applications. Check out your copy of Photoshop or Paint Shop Pro to see if the color dropper works when the cursor is outside of the painting canvas. Then use it to measure the preview window in your compressor.

35.3.4 Adjusting for the Optimal Setting

Now that you have a way to measure the values, adjust the brightness and contrast to get the optimum black and white settings for the frame being viewed.

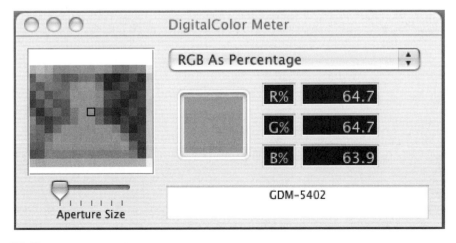

Figure 35-7 Digital color meter tool.

A word of warning, though: Note that none of the currently available compression tools will allow you to key-frame the settings. These values tend to be applied globally by the compression tool. Use Final Cut or After Effects if you want to process the luma and key the changes to different segments of your movie.

Here are some final rules of thumb that apply when planning your luma correction.

Bear in mind that increasing the brightness also increases the noise floor, so any noise in the black area of your image will become visible as you raise the overall luma level.

Brightness adjustment should not be needed for a clean source. But lowering the brightness to correct the black levels also has the benefit of improving the coding efficiency because of the noise reduction.

It used to be commonly recommended that the contrast should be increased by +27 before compression. Modern codecs should not need this adjustment since they have built-in compensation. Any automatic compensation will be taken care of and you need not worry. If you and the codec both apply +27 contrast enhancement, that is a 2 × 27 adjustment, which will lead to a severe crushing of the white levels.

35.4 Correcting the Gamma

The gamma value is not the same as the luma, although they are related. The luma property describes the overall range, while the gamma property affects the linearity of that intensity gradient. Often, the gamma value is adjusted upward on material being processed on the Macintosh to make the mid-tones show up better on Windows PC displays, which have a different gamma setting.

Gamma correction is used to change the shape of the graph that maps the output intensity levels of the luma signal and how they correspond to the input levels. This is necessary because the apparent brightness of a pixel is not necessarily proportional to its numeric value. The emissivities of CRT, Plasma, LED, OLED, TFT, and LCD display devices are different. This is because the nature of the chemical or electromagnetic effect that generates the light emits different wavelengths and intensities. While your eye may see what you think is white, the actual value may vary considerably from one kind of device to another.

The sensitivity of the human eye is affected by the perceived brightness. The entire chain of processing, from the initial photography to viewing, will influence the apparent brightness of a scene.

35.4.1 The Effects of Changing the Gamma

The area that is most affected by gamma settings is the lower mid-tones down to the extreme blacks. As the gamma value is increased, any detail that is hidden in the darker regions of the image will be exposed. It is in this area that modern digital cameras are least successful when compared to film. So if the footage you are digitizing has been shot on a digital device as opposed to a film camera, gamma correction may help to reveal detail that was hitherto invisible.

Some codecs do this gamma correction between platforms automatically. The Sorenson codec does not automatically gamma-correct. The MPEG-4 Part 2 codec does.

Gamma changes have no effect whatsoever on the extreme black and extreme white value. It is designed to affect the linearity and hence the mid-tones. This correction must be applied after the brightness and contrast setting have corrected the luma.

These are some common gamma values:

- Macintosh has a standard gamma setting of 1.8.
- Video has a gamma setting of 2.2.
- Windows has a gamma setting of between 2.2 and 2.5 but it is not rigorously defined.

Increasing the gamma value makes images appear to be brighter, which is what people want when they say they want a brighter image. It is only necessary to adjust the gamma; leave the brightness and contrast settings untouched.

Figure 35-8 shows some example gradients with changes to the bit depth and the gamma values.

In the top strip of pixels, the intensity is shown as a linear gradient from black to peak white. Because the color depth represents a 10-bit value, there are no contours or steps.

In the second strip of pixels, the effect of reducing the bit depth from 10 bits to 8 bits has been exaggerated. The reduction in bit depth does not actually cause such a gross contouring but it is there. It is exaggerated so the effect is visible in print. The contouring can be removed by adding a little noise to the image before the thresholding takes place. Subtle application of a static dithering pattern will not affect the compression process very much, but if you apply a moving noise pattern it might decrease the compression efficiency.

The third strip of pixels applies an exaggerated gamma correction in order to show it on the printed page. In reality, the effect is very subtle and when you see it on the screen, the image becomes more pleasing as the gamma is increased.

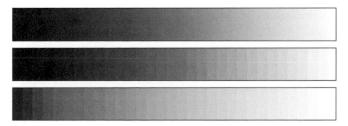

Figure 35-8 Grey-scales and gamma.

Charles Poynton's gamma FAQ: http://www.poynton.com/PDFs/GammaFAQ.pdf

35.5 Color Correction

The luma and chroma settings should already have been equalized throughout the whole movie as part of the grading process during the movie production. On the other hand, you may be working on some original footage that you shot yourself. That grading process must still be done to average out the overall picture brightness and color throughout the movie.

35.5.1 Color-Correction Tools

Figure 35-9 shows a screenshot of the color corrector from Final Cut Pro. An amazing amount of control over the video is possible. This will rescue grossly underexposed footage that might have been unusable otherwise.

If you are getting into color correction, this must be applied sparingly and in different ways at different times in the movie.

This color corrector operates on the video content by working on blacks, mid-tones, and whites as separate ranges. Other color correctors have fewer controls and work in different color spaces.

For each range, you have control over the hue and brightness and the overall saturation. On this control pane, you will see other buttons and presets. You can pick a color in the image with the eyedropper and use that as a handle to pull the pixel value to a desired setting. Other color values for the remaining pixels in the image have their values interpolated from that. To remove a yellowish cast from an image, choose the lightest pixel that is a pale yellow but that should be white. Then use that as a reference pixel and the color corrector will compensate by removing that amount of yellow from the image. The effect will be applied proportionally to darker values.

35.5.2 Color Calibration

Find the Mac OS X digital color meter in the utilities folder that was discussed earlier. This is useful for getting RGB values in the raw and preview windows in order to adjust the brightness and contrast settings. Measure the blacks and the whites and check that there is no crushing.

If you can only afford one moderately expensive tool apart from your compression software, then buy Adobe After Effects. Version 6.5 is especially good for processing bad video. Even though it is a tool designed for creating special-effects shots, it does give you some leverage with corrective filtering.

International Color Consortium: http://www.color.org/

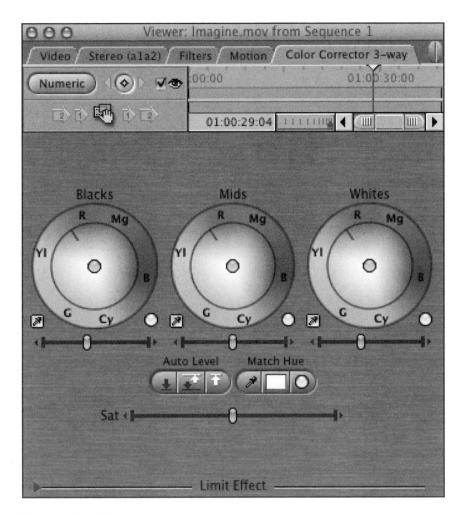

Figure 35-9 The Final Cut Pro color corrector.

35.5.3 Calibration Issues

It might help to have some calibration frames at the start of a tape reel. These will give you some reference points when setting things up.

Check to make sure that any color correction and video processing is done in the correct color space. The recommended color space for this work is RGB. Sometimes you might find that your monitor or other equipment is set up to a special device-based color space. The effect of this is visible if you mix moving video and still images in DVD menus.

If you have a still frame and then start rolling a video clip from an in point containing the same frame, the color appears to change as the video starts to play. This is an indication that you have processed the video in the wrong color space at some point in your workflow.

35.5.4 Color Saturation

Color saturation affects the RGB values of a pixel, but when the video is stored in a componentized form, the color saturation should have no effect on the luma. So if you de-saturate the color, the only savings will be in the compression of the color macroblocks.

35.6 Color Legalizers

Analog video is designed so that synchronizing pulses are interleaved with the video signals. Certain signal levels need to be reserved so that the sync pulses are properly discriminated. These reserved values cannot be used to represent a visible video intensity value. Therefore, they must not be legal video levels. Figure 35-10 shows how this video waveform fits into that legal range.

Sometimes when video is scaled or cropped, certain values result from the pixel averaging that fall outside of the legal range of colors. This sometimes happens around the edge of the frame. For example, someone wearing a bright red jacket walking off the framed video area causes some very bright red values to be generated at the screen boundary. These values push the intensity past the peak value and into the overshoot area, which is illegal. Analog systems are forgiving of this and it will get clamped, clipped, or crushed further downstream. But this kind of thing absolutely kills digital services. Some digital-video processing equipment is so devastated by the arrival of illegal values that it completely seizes up. If this is on the critical path to air, your service goes down.

Add more resilience to your system by placing color legalizers in the circuit. These will substitute acceptable values for the illegal excursions. It is a little more expensive, but far more preferable than going off air.

Your video capture card may provide protection against illegal color value generation. The Blackmagic Design video cards scale 255 RGB values to 100% video white and restore the correct values on output. Not all video cards do this, and you should check the specification of all the items of equipment in the video workflow path to find the problem if you see illegal color values in the output.

Eyeheight LegalEyesHD: http://www.eyeheight.com/
Blackmagic Design: http://www.blackmagic-design.com/

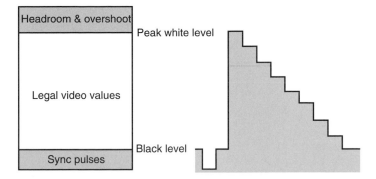

Figure 35-10 Legal video values.

35.7 Hue-Rotation Consequences

Rotating the hue of an image causes some severe bit-rate problems. You will see this in footage of music concerts where the lighting director changes the stage lights from red to green. Every pixel in the image has changed color. Because luma is computed using a matrixed RGB value, there will be some small changes to the luma but most of the change will be to the chroma. The lighting positions will cause slightly different shadows to be cast, also affecting the luma channel. The perceived effect for the viewer is a major increase in macroblock artifacts.

The same argument applies if you are using color correction as a special effect.

35.8 Kill That Noise

So a few chapters back we sorted out the T-axis. Then we wrestled with X and Y. Now we just got Z to toe the line. But our image still has some noise in it. Let's try to find some ways to eliminate that noise and get it looking just right. In the next chapter we'll cover de-noising techniques.

36

Cutting Out the Noise

36.1   Can't See the Forest for the Trees?

Removing noise from your content is akin to film restoration; whether it is worthwhile depends on the value of the footage. Removing the noise will help reduce the work the compressor has to do to attain a low bit rate.

36.1.1   Weird Artifacts and Problems

There are a few nasty "gotchas" that may present themselves when you are processing source footage ready for compression. They have been known and identified for years. Most of them are inherited from the analog domain that older footage is derived from. I will enumerate them here and describe what causes them and whether anything can be done to alleviate them.

36.1.2   Vision Problems and Imaginary Artifacts

Some visual artifacts are imaginary, and others are due to defects in the viewer's vision such as color blindness or astigmatism. A few are consequences of the way that the human eye works and therefore cannot be compensated for or corrected.

36.2   Noise in the Source Image

The noise in any source material is going to be seen by the compression engine as difference information. There is a certain level of random white noise that creates a twinkling effect in the intensity of an analog video signal. This is apparent when you look closely at a locked-down shot of a studio. The background is supposed to be unchanging, but on a per-pixel basis, it twinkles all the time. Removing this noise before applying the compression is well worth the effort, as it reduces the amount of work that the compressor will have to do.

Preserving hard edges but softening a large area of continuous tone in the luma channel should yield a useful improvement. Ideally, the smoothing should take place in the temporal domain, that is, at a single X–Y point but also from one frame to the next. This is analogous to grain removal when processing films, and the same grain-removal filters might help if you have them.

Removing the noise within a single frame is a compromise but achieves nearly as good a result. It might cause some average-intensity changes from frame to frame but these will be small.

De-noising an image effectively is computationally very expensive. A reduced CPU loading is achieved by applying a high-frequency cutoff filter that operates only in the horizontal axis since this corresponds to the transmitted line of video, which is what the noise is being imposed on. The cutoff might destroy some edges that you want to preserve.

36.3 Different Kinds of Noise

Certain kinds of noise, such as dust and scratches, should have been removed earlier in the process. Some filters are introduced to remove ringing artifacts and also to average pixel values between frames so as to remove the inherent white noise that is present in analog transducers (cameras).

Analog noise cannot easily be removed because the effects extend over an area of the picture, and decisions about where edges of the noise pattern are situated are difficult to build into an algorithmic framework. The human eye does a remarkable job of discriminating between noise and genuine picture information. If you concentrate you can observe the noise, but after a while you tend to tune it out and ignore it. While it's good that the eye and brain work cleverly together like this, it is rather tiring for the viewer and it's better to remove the noise if you can. Your video compressor will do a better job, too.

Repeating and cyclic noise artifacts can be removed algorithmically if you can identify the cycle and pattern. The effects of signal interruption and interference from other radio-frequency sources generate these cyclic effects. If you live near an airport, for example, you may notice a repeating pattern of dashes that scrolls down across the picture periodically. These are the radar pulses that interfere with your TV service reception, causing momentary loss of signal.

For the amateur or semi-professional who may actually be working in a domestic environment, there are a lot of noise sources to cope with. You may be able to alleviate some of these effects by making sure your systems are running on a clean mains supply, so introducing mains filters could be worthwhile.

Electrical noise from appliances, car engines, lawn mowers, electric shavers, and central-heating systems all contributes impulse noise that can be removed by careful application of dropout compensation. You might take a few pixels from a previous or subsequent frame and paint in the missing detail.

There are also various herringbones and dot-crawling artifacts that might be introduced by the analog production processes on older footage.

36.4   Noise-Reduction Techniques

Noise reduction is the final stage of video preprocessing, and it will always cause some blurring to be introduced. In fact, some cheap noise-removal algorithms just apply a blurring function. This is unscientific and not the best approach.

If you are operating on video that has been converted into luma and chroma, then apply noise reduction to the luma channel and blur the chroma channels. Don't de-noise an image and then sharpen it afterwards, because it just brings the noise back again.

Sharpening in the luma without including the color information works well for skin tones and faces. If you are working in the RGB domain, then switch the image mode to LAB and work on the L channel only.

Reduce the analog frame-to-frame twinkling noise artifacts by passing the content through Adobe After Effects and applying a film grain-removal process. This works because the noise is similar to film grain even though the footage is totally electronic and has never been rendered on film at all. Some compression tools provide this as a built-in feature.

At the end of the noise-removal process, the images should look as if they have had a layer of dirt removed without damage to the underlying image. Think of it in the same way as a conservationist working on a piece of important art.

36.4.1   Convergence Errors

Effects such as convergence errors, barrel distortion. and blooming happen when your TV monitor is not set up correctly. These effects don't exhibit themselves on LCD monitors, because you don't have to adjust the linearity. See Figure 36-1.

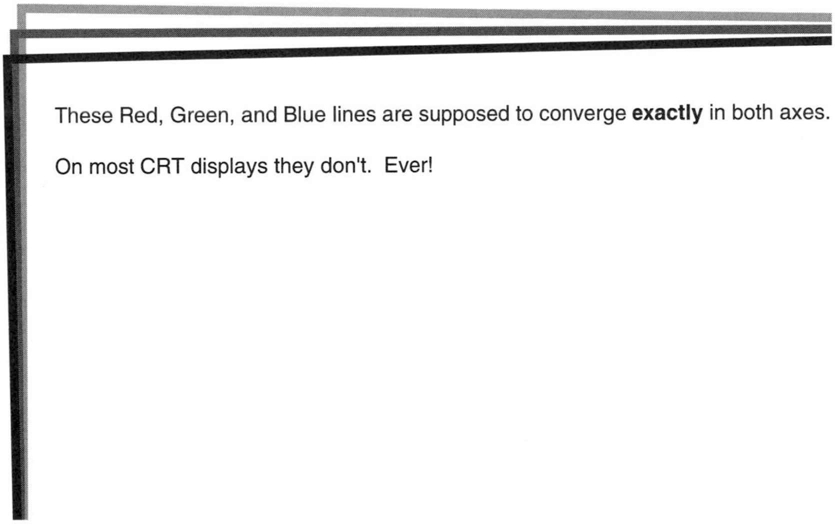

These Red, Green, and Blue lines are supposed to converge **exactly** in both axes.

On most CRT displays they don't. Ever!

Figure 36-1 Convergence errors on CRT displays.

Solution?

1. There is no software solution to apply. Do not try to compensate by altering your video content.
2. It is not your video that is at fault but your display monitor. Switch from CRT to LCD flat screen.
3. Recalibrate the convergence settings on your CRT.

36.4.2 Hanging Dots

Areas of red and blue appear to shift even though the pixels are lined up precisely. This is an artifact of the human eye that appears to place blue and red objects at different distances on the Z-axis. It is not actually a displaced portion of the image but a consequence of the human eye's having a different sensitivity to blue and red (Figure 36-2).
Solution?

What is really in the display.   What the eye thinks it sees.

Figure 36-2 Hanging dots.

1. This is not actually a fault but an illusory artifact. You cannot fix it by modifying your video content.
2. It is a property of the display. Replacing your CRT with an LCD monitor may help.

36.4.3 Comet Trails and Dark Pixels

Older video cameras with plumbicon tubes used to suffer from a persistence effect where a bright point source would desensitize the phosphor in the camera tube for a short period of time. This would cause the phosphor to act as if it were still lit for a few frames after the light source was removed, and the camera output would continue to show a ghost image. A related effect would be if the middle of a large bright area saturated the tube and momentarily burned it out so that the middle of a light source would appear dark.

Figure 36-3 Comet trails.

Camera operators were trained to point the camera away from a bright point source because this could permanently damage the camera tube. The consequence was that you got comet trails (Figure 36-3) showing up whenever some stage lighting came into view.

You might also see dark patches in images a few minutes later when the producer switched back to the camera and the plumbicon either had not settled back to the normal sensitivity across the whole surface or had been permanently damaged (Figure 36-4).

Modern professional CCD video cameras don't suffer from this, and it is rare to see the problem other than in older analog footage that is being repurposed. It sometimes shows up in cheaper cameras, which have longer exposure times, and it is also an issue with digital still cameras under certain lighting conditions. You may see a strobing effect on the comet trail due to the lighting being fed with AC electrical current.

This artifact is an integral part of the imaging process. You cannot easily remove it, because it's a camera defect and therefore a part of the original recording.

Figure 36-4 Simulated camera-tube burnout.

Solution?

1. Use a better camera.
2. Hand-retouch every frame in the video you are restoring.
3. Live with it.

36.4.4 *Tracking Errors*

Tracking errors (Figure 36-5) happen when the heads in your video player don't properly line up with the recorded tracks of video information on the tape. The fix is to properly maintain your tape players and ensure that you play back footage that was recorded properly in the first place. Tracking correction might be applied manually if the tape was recorded on a VCR whose tracking was maladjusted.

Figure 36-5 Tracking error.

Solution?

1. Don't even bother trying to encode something that has tracking errors; it is going to look horrible.
2. Apply extreme dropout compensation if you have it.
3. Crop off the offending part of the frame if you can.
4. Live with it and bear the consequences of a compromised compression ratio and a gross artifact onscreen when the video is played back.

36.4.5 *Bad Horizontal Sync*

Correcting bad horizontal sync (Figure 36-6) may be possible if it isn't too extreme. Some special-purpose software may need to be written, so the value of the footage will determine whether it is worth the effort.

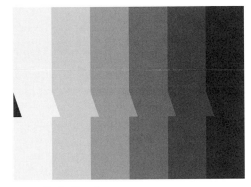

Figure 36-6 Horizontal tearing.

Solution?

1. Hand-edit every frame to line up the edge again.
2. Write some software to fix it.
3. Crop the edges to hide the worst of it.

36.4.6 *Ghosting*

Ghosting (Figure 36-7) is caused by analog signals reflecting from another surface and arriving at your antenna somewhat delayed with respect to the original signal. Wet leaves on trees and large buildings may cause this. It is theoretically possible to remove ghosting effects using sophisticated image-processing techniques, but in practice it is hard to deal with. Sometimes it's just best to wait and record the program at a later time.

Figure 36-7 Ghosting.

Solution?

1. Discard the footage.
2. Have a rocket scientist process your footage through the NASA JPL space mission imaging system.
3. Live with it.
4. Re-record the program at a later date.
5. Re-orient your antenna to receive from a different transmitter.
6. Relocate your antenna so it doesn't receive its line-of-sight signal through the trees.

36.4.7 Co-Channel Interference

Co-channel interference (Figure 36-8) is probably the hardest kind of noise to remove. It is the consequence of atmospheric conditions causing a transmitter elsewhere to broadcast over an exceptionally wide range at the same frequency as the channel you want. The video is usually almost synchronized, but slightly offset from the one you are watching and recording.

Figure 36-8 Co-channel interference.

Solution?

1. Discard the footage.
2. Blur the image a little if the effect is not severe.

3. Live with it.
4. Re-record the program at a later date.
5. Re-orient your antenna to receive from a different transmitter.

36.4.8 Dropouts

A dropout occurs when there is a momentary loss of signal. How it appears on the screen depends on whether it is an analog or digital effect. Blocks of randomly placed checker patterns and lines indicate a digital dropout. Streaks or dots of white or black affecting only one horizontal line at a time indicate an analog dropout (Figure 36-9).

Figure 36-9 Analog signal dropouts.

Solution?

1. Apply a dropout compensator.
2. Apply a median convolution filter.
3. Blur in the horizontal axis only.
4. Use a threshold filter to identify the white dots, select them, and reduce their brightness.

36.4.9 Appliance Noise

This is caused by noise generated by home appliances breaking through via the mains circuits. If it is there in the recording, you can't do much about it. Filters that work with tracking and dropouts might help. For noise caused by washing machines, lawn mowers, and hair dryers (Figure 36-10), the correct solution is the obvious one: Turn off the appliance while ingesting video from your VCR.

If the problem is caused by your neighbor mowing the lawn, then either wait for the mowing to stop or ask your neighbor (politely) to avoid doing this at critical times when you want to record or ingest some footage. Moving to a remote location is another solution but is usually too expensive or impractical. Installing some mains filters might solve the problem more cheaply.

Because this is electrical noise from the same mains supply that the TV picture was displayed on, it is likely that the noise will be synchronous with the frame rate and therefore more or less stationary on the screen. If you are lucky, it will be located near the top or bottom and might be removed with a crop.

Figure 36-10 Washing machine noise.

Solution?

1. Turn off the offending appliance.
2. Install a mains filter.
3. Apply a dropout compensator.
4. Crop if possible.

36.4.10   Radar Noise

Living near an airport may result in some interference from the ground-approach radar. This noise is very distinctive. If the atmospheric conditions are right, you may suffer from this even if you live a long distance away.

The noise pattern (Figure 36-11) is distinctive because it's a set of well-defined pulses that cause quite lengthy dropouts in the signal. The cyclic nature may help you to set up a filter, but it is rare for the cycle to be in sync with the video, so the effect will roll through the frame.

Figure 36-11 Radar noise.

Solution?

1. Apply a dropout compensator.
2. Create an RF-shielded room (expensive).
3. Re-orient your antenna to receive from a different transmitter.
4. Hand-retouch if really necessary.
5. Live with it.

36.4.11 *Aliasing*

This happens when the interlacing interferes with the presentation of moving objects on the screen. It is most obvious with near horizontal edges moving vertically, and it appears suddenly during a pan.

The artifact will be most obvious on NTSC versions of 24-fps movies because of the pulldown effect. Where it is evident in the output from a playback device, using progressive scanning instead of interlaced presentation should cure it. Figure 36-12 shows what might happen during a pan.

Figure 36-12 Aliasing during a pan.

Solution?

1. Carefully de-interlace or inverse-telecine the footage.
2. You may be able to reconstruct the broken frames by taking fields or parts of them from the adjacent frames. This could become quite laborious, and whether it is worth the effort depends on the value of the footage.
3. Manually cut and paste parts of frames that get through the inverse telecine pass.

36.4.12 *Moiré Patterns*

This happens when some repeating pattern in the image almost lines up with the scan lines or pixel grid in the display. It is virtually impossible to remove, but applying some selective blurring may help to disguise it. The example in Figure 36-13 is made by overlaying two fine gratings, each alternating from black to white on every line, and slightly stretching one of them just by a couple of pixels. It's the same as if you try to shoot some fine regular detail that is nearly on the same axis as the scan lines in the camera. You get an interference pattern between the two gratings and it moves and strobes as the subject shifts against the fixed scan-line raster.

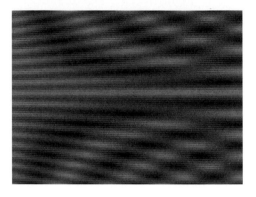

Figure 36-13 Moiré effect.

Solution?

1. Apply averaging or blurring to one or both axes.
2. Drop one field of video. It won't solve the problem completely, but it might reduce the effect at the expense of some video quality.
3. Eliminate the source of the patterning and re-shoot.

36.4.13   Bleeding

This is where the area of a brightly colored object floods adjacent objects with the same color. It occurs because the color resolution is lower than the luma and there may be some oversaturation of the color information. De-saturating the image might help. If the effect is very localized, some manual retouching might be the only solution.

The dark circle indicates the area covered by the object, which should be colored. The area outside should not have any color. The blurred area to the right shows the color bleeding across the screen due to loss of chroma bandwidth.

Figure 36-14 Color bleeding.

Solution?

1. Reduce the color saturation.
2. Get a better color decoder.
3. Manually retouch the image.

36.4.14 *Cross-Color Artifacts*

This happens when some horizontal fine detail occurs at such a high frequency that it leaks through the filters and the color circuits act as if some chroma information is being coded. It is luma information, though. This occurs when you use composite connections and send luma and chroma down the same cable. Component systems that keep luma and chroma separate don't have this problem. It is difficult to show in printed form because the effect changes color rather than brightness. It is very like the moiré effect, but there will be twinkling areas of blue and yellow that shimmer as the image moves.

You might overhear a video engineer referring to someone wearing a 3-MHz shirt. Newsreaders at the BBC used to wear checkered jackets and houndstooth tweed, and this caused cross-color artifact problems when the BBC started to broadcast in color during the 1970s.

Solution?

1. Use a better PAL, SECAM, or NTSC decoder.
2. Get the presenter to change clothes and then reshoot.
3. De-saturate the color.

36.4.15 *Chroma Noise*

This is where an area of solid color looks blotchy. It is due to noise's being introduced into the chroma channel and seems to affect the blue component more than any other. When compressed, the appearance is very blocky because the codec is working hard to render the fine detail. The trouble is that the fine detail is noise. It will show up when processing legacy analog footage and is less likely to cause problems with modern, digitally processed content.

Solution?

1. Apply film grain removal to the chroma channel only.
2. Blur the chroma channel.

36.4.16 *Dot Crawl*

This is a strange effect that shows around the edges of objects where the color changes abruptly. It is caused by the color information leaking into the luma channel and is the worst when you are connecting equipment together with a composite video signal. Using S-video connectors to deliver the luma and chroma down separate wires eliminates this problem.

The area shown in gray on either side of the object in the illustration is where the dot-crawl effect will be worst.

If some video has been transferred and recorded with dot crawl in evidence, it is there forever and you cannot remove it. Keep your luma and chroma separate. Having said that, grain removal might help reduce it slightly.

If you don't remove the dot crawl, it will increase the bit rate on your compressed-video output. You will be wasting a lot of that bit rate preserving the crawling pixels. Their motion will be perfectly rendered when the compressed video is played back.

ATI Radeon video cards offer an option to switch between stationary and moving dot crawl. Ideally, you would like to click a check box to turn it off completely, but that is not possible. This is your only option on a composite output signal carrying this artifact.

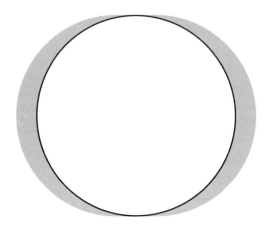

Figure 36-15 Dot crawl.

Solution?

1. Reduce the color saturation.
2. Apply grain removal.
3. Modify the parameters of your video capture or source device if they provide stationary/moving dot crawl selection.

36.4.17 *Temporal Noise Removal*

If your processing system is designed to cope with film artifacts, it may have a grain-removal filter. Random noise is similar enough to film grain that the filter does a good job of removing it.

This does a sort of averaging between frames, but be careful because it may lead to blurring if it is overused. It is sometimes called temporal noise because it is due to changes at the same pixel from one frame to another. Hence it is on the time axis rather than X or Y.

An example from a cartoon movie is shown in Figure 36-16.

The picture shows a zoomed-in rectangle cropped out of two adjacent frames of a 1939 animated movie, which has been converted via telecine and compressed using MPEG-2. The background changes subtly from frame to frame due to grain and fading of the emulsion. The compression didn't introduce the background noise, but it did introduce some macroblock artifacts. The differences between one frame and the next were calculated using Photoshop and exaggerated by equalization of the resulting image.

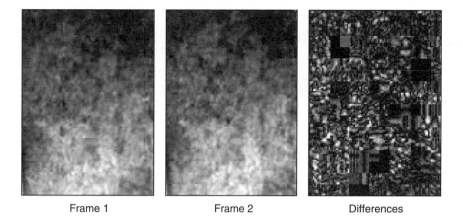

Frame 1   Frame 2   Differences

Figure 36-16 Temporal noise and its compression effects.

Solution?

1. Apply grain removal.
2. Apply blurring.
3. Motion-compensated averaging across frames might solve this, but you would need expensive or complex restoration software/hardware in order to deploy that capability.

36.4.18 Gibbs Effect

An artifact similar to dot crawl and cross color that is evident after compression is known as the Gibbs effect (Figure 36-17). This is where letters acquire a shimmering cross-color effect around their edges. It is a consequence of losing the high-resolution detail when the entropy filtering is engaged. Screen credits must be processed separately from the rest of the content. It is worth completely redesigning and retyping them to eliminate the problems arising from processing them like normal moving video. The Gibbs effect is also known as mosquito noise.

The example shows the word ENGLAND originally drawn on a solid background. The Gibbs effect has caused some harmonic effects of the DCT transform to introduce resonant frequencies that have added detail that was not there in the original. This might be due to the entropy coding having compressed the data too much. The effect often happens around the edges of text. To fix it, you have to sacrifice some compression efficiency or draw the text in a way that compresses more easily.

Figure 36-17 Example of the Gibbs effect on text.

Solution?

1. Give up some compression efficiency.
2. Replace the footage with stationary text pages.
3. Try different colors and aliased edges on the text.
4. Replace the text with a clean version against a more neutral, stationary background.

36.5 Burned-In Captions

Encoding video with burned-in captions is not ideal. There are nasty artifacts (such as the Gibbs effect) that cause horrible fringing patterns around text when the DCT transform is applied. In many cases, the size of the video is such that any text you burn in will be unreadable.

If there are already burned-in captions that didn't survive the compression process before, then use the cropping mechanisms to remove them.

If you cannot avoid burning captions into the video, try to make them sensibly large so they can be read on the screen at the resolution at which the image will be playing back. If they have to be added as part of your processing, make sure it is the last thing you do before compression begins. Then any scaling, noise filtering, or other operations will not have spoiled the clean edges of the text.

The ideal scenario is to encode an extra text track and let the player subtitle the video in a separate area of the screen. This can be done with a Real Text track in an `.rt` file, a QuickTime text track in a `.mov` file, or a Windows Media `.smi` or `.sami` file.

36.6   A Sound Proposition

So the video preprocessing is now complete. It should be looking very good by this stage. Of course, if we are using a tool that includes all these facilities, we shan't actually be able to see the intermediate stages of the preprocessing.

We just have to get the audio sorted out and we will be ready to press that "GO" button! In the next chapter we will run through some processing on the audio to tweak it up to the best possible condition.

Preparing the Audio for Encoding

37.1 Audio Preprocessing

Now that the video is preprocessed and ready for encoding, the audio must be processed. There are several things that need to be checked, although there is no set order to doing these. Obviously, you want to make sure that each step removes unwanted artifacts without undoing what you did in the previous step.

37.2 Trimming and Cropping

The audio usually accompanies some video, so their durations must be cropped to the same length. The editing software should be maintaining the edits on the audio track as the video is cut; otherwise the lip sync is broken. There are occasions when the video and audio digitizing processes are carried out independently. In those cases, the audio must be laid alongside the video and carefully trimmed to fit after it has been aligned.

37.3 Synchronizing

Any independently digitized audio must be synchronized; an offset of even a couple of frames is enough for lip sync to be lost, and that makes for a very unsatisfactory viewing experience. Check at the start, at the end, and at intervals throughout the movie. Ideally, you should play it all the way through to check. Depending on how you are doing this, you might perform the synchronization before the cropping. You need to check that the audio is in sync at the start and the end and in the middle of an insert. There are so many ways that the video and audio might have been worked on that you'll have to work some of this out for yourself. Playing through the whole piece if the video and audio were created separately should reveal any sync problems that you need to correct. Be careful that in synchronizing one section you don't accidentally push out another. Using multiple tracks in the editor can help a lot and you'll need to down mix again later to finish it off.

37.4   Audio-Noise Removal (Hum, Rumble, and Hiss)

Leaving noise in the signal just wastes compression bit rate. The encoder is supposed to be spending time compressing the audible sound that you intend to be heard. If it is encoding the noise, it is wasting some of its capacity.

In this description, the noise removal is placed before the normalizing step. However, normalizing the audio levels could bring up the noise levels in quiet passages. You might revisit the noise-removal process again or place it after the normalization.

It is possible to get tools such as BIAS Sound Soap that will remove all this noise at a single stroke. For the price of these products, it's a very cost-effective solution and probably deals with most of the problems you'll have to solve.

37.4.1   Hum Cancelling

Use notch filters (Figure 37-1) to remove hum and cyclic sounds. Set the notching as tightly as possible, around 50 Hz in Europe or 60 Hz in the United States. These are the mains

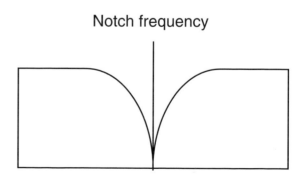

Figure 37-1 Notch filter profile.

BIAS Sound Soap: http://www.bias-inc.com/soundsoap

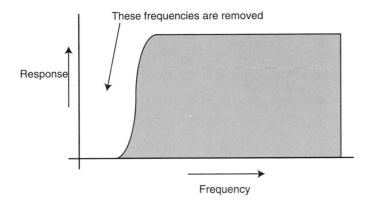

Figure 37-2 High-pass filter response.

frequencies. Add notch filters at harmonics of these frequencies (although the harmonic content will reduce in the higher overtones).

37.4.2 A Rumble in the Jungle

Rumble from turntables is removed with a high-pass filter (Figure 37-2). Be aware that there are useful bass frequencies in music as low as 30 Hz, and you may want to preserve these.

37.4.3 Hissing Fits

Similarly, there are high-frequency components that you want to preserve while removing hiss. Hiss is removed with a low-pass filter (Figure 37-3), but this should be gated so that you don't lose program material. Then the filter can clean the quiet passages and be deactivated when the noise won't be noticed.

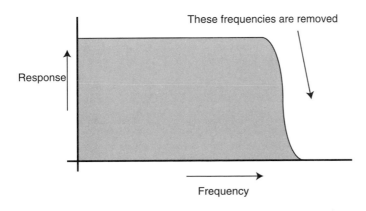

Figure 37-3 Low-pass filter response.

37.4.4 Plug-In Tools

Try to obtain a plug-in for your video-editing software that accomplishes everything you require. The Waves plug-ins offer a variety of modules that compress, limit, de-noise, and perform just about any audio processing you might want to do to a sound track. They work on Mac OS and Windows, so they are available regardless of the platform you are running your workflow on.

37.4.5 Cyclic Noise

There may be other cyclic noises, such as motors or other ambient sounds, that have been picked up inadvertently. These might repeat at very low frequencies and may be hard to remove. But if you have the time and if the sound recording is valuable enough, sampling some silence from the same source as the original recording and trying to establish what the noise floor (Figure 37-4) is like without any audio superimposed on it gives you a reference for designing a more sophisticated de-noiser.

In an ideal situation, the loudest noise source will still be quieter than the quietest program material. If that is the case, then a simple noise gate can be applied. Often the noise level is higher than the quietest passages, so some intelligent level tracking needs to take place.

You can also see that the program-signal levels are much larger in magnitude than the noise. This illustrates the signal-to-noise ratio.

37.4.6 Noise Gating

Applying a noise gate at the input stage is a good idea. This is when the analog signal is first digitized. If the gating is processed in the digital domain, it can be applied far more carefully and selectively. Figure 37-5 shows how this affects a waveform.

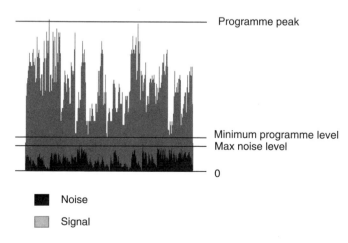

Programme peak

Minimum programme level
Max noise level
0

Figure 37-4 Noise floor.

■ Noise
▢ Signal

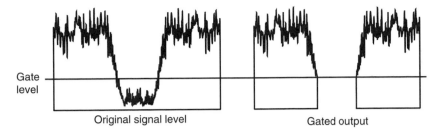

Figure 37-5 labels: Gate level, Original signal level, Gated output

Figure 37-5 Threshold noise gating.

37.5 Operating System Support

Modern operating systems support a lot of audio-processing capabilities, and in the case of Mac OS 10.4, there are sample accurate-audio-processing frameworks that would allow you to construct a sample player that could loop a repeating background noise track and then add an out-of-phase copy to your recording. This would neutralize the noise without damaging the audio you want to keep. Designing software that does this kind of thing is a specialist art, and there are commercially available tools that do it very efficiently.

37.6 Audio Sweetening

Applying some pre-emphasis to the audio may help it make the best of the target platform. Music producers do this with pop songs when they equalize them so they sound great on small speakers. They do this because most of the time, people are listening in the car or on portable radios—with small speakers.

Modern codecs such as AAC+ use a technique called spectral band replication that puts back some information at the decoding end, based on what it finds in the encoded bit stream. The output is therefore not an exact copy of the input material but is a simulacrum of it that the human ear finds pleasing.

Some of these operations increase noise components that were previously masked. To avoid this problem, be careful where you place this pre-emphasis operator in your workflow. It should not affect the audio being routed to every platform. Instead, you should apply this in a platform-specific way in the workflow path that is unique to each target device. Pre-emphasis is not always necessary if the destination playback system has its own equalization (EQ) capability. Also, be aware that pre-emphasizing the bass and outputting it on a high-powered system will cause it to boom and growl somewhat.

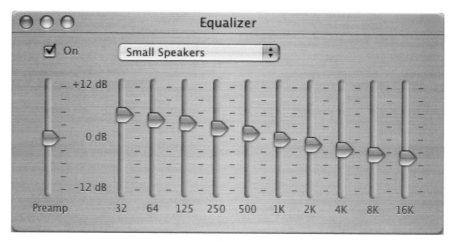

Figure 37-6 Small-speaker EQ setting in iTunes.

37.6.1 Equalization

If you know that the audio is going to be played on a handset with a small loudspeaker, then boosting the bass frequencies may help a little at the receiving end. Figure 37-6 shows the appropriate equalizer settings for small speakers in the iTunes interface.

Encoding audio for use on 3GPP devices benefits from the application of a little compression. This is analog compression, the sort that fattens the bass end of the frequency spectrum.

If you know that the target device has a limited-frequency response, you may be able to reduce the work done by the audio codec if you band-limit the audio before it goes through the codec.

37.6.2 Analog Compression

Compression in the context of analog audio also describes a process where the waveform is altered in a nonlinear way in order to prevent clipping and to add a pleasing richness to the sound. The compressor dynamically alters its behavior according to the loudness of the passage being processed. It is often combined with a noise gate and limiter so that they all work together.

The concept of a compressor revolves around a mapping of the input level to the output level. As the input level increases, the output level has progressively more attenuation, so the relationship is nonlinear. This has the effect of flattening the waveform at the maximum excursion and squashing the waveform more at its extremes. Figure 37-7 shows how a compressor gently flattens the waveform.

The effect is subtle but noticeable, and somewhat pleasing when you hear the audio. A similar effect is attained when you turn on the loudness circuit in your hi-fi.

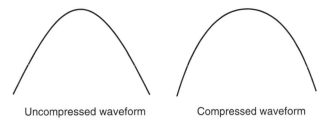

Uncompressed waveform   Compressed waveform   **Figure 37-7** Analog compression.

37.7 Level Adjustment

Find the loudest passage in the audio and then adjust the overall volume of the tracks to make sure that the peak volume does not exceed an acceptable loudness level.

The overall level of the audio should be consistent and not go up and down significantly. In the quiet passages, there is fine detail that must be accentuated. Applying that adjustment across the entire piece makes loud portions too noisy and causes clipping. This is analogous to setting the brightness and contrast of a picture.

Some kind of automatically adjustable compensation must be applied. That includes some gain adjustment and a compressor-limiter to prevent the sound volume from fluctuating. The result will be a more even and consistent track. This ought to have been done as part of the production process if you are encoding commercial material. Your source may be some home-movie footage or something that has been recorded live. Some audio tracks are spliced together from a variety of different sources. It is useful to have the necessary tools already available to cope with audio processing when the need arises.

The optimum level to set is to ensure that the peaks in your audio don't exceed a level that is 3 dB down from the 0 dB reference on the VU or PPM meter on your audio monitor.

Setting the gain so that the loudest passage reaches a level commonly known as 0 dB is too high for some compression software. The recommended value of 3 dB below the reference allows the compression tools some headroom to cope with transients. The 0 dB level will be indicated by a mark of some kind on your audio-level meter, or if you use an LED monitor, it may turn red when this level is reached. Figure 37-8 shows how the audio level is adjusted.

Be careful that you adjust the levels consistently across all of the tracks you are encoding. This is important because otherwise you will inadvertently pan the audio "image" off center and the sound will not be delivered as intended.

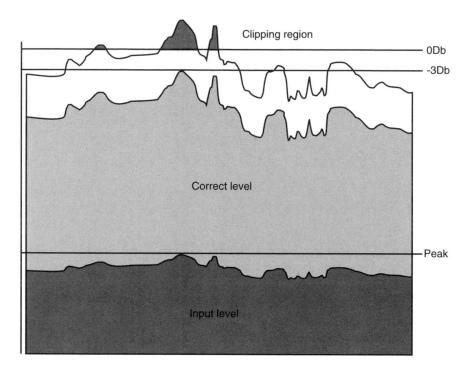

Figure 37-8 Clipping the audio.

This might introduce audible noise that was too quiet to hear previously. Use of special noise-gated gain filters and compressor limiters may yield a sufficiently loud output without bringing up the background noise. It all depends on what has been recorded and the quality of the original source material. The argument applies equally well to video and audio content.

This may become quite complicated when you are processing surround sound with 5 or 6 tracks of audio that must remain mixed to the right level, must not be allowed to go out of sync or out of phase, and may contain sounds of varying volume. That peak-level setting is an aggregate. Don't check just one channel; there may be a louder sound in one of the others.

In the same way that video gets crushed if you set the white level too high, audio squares off the tops of the wave shapes when clipping occurs. The effect of this clipping sounds horrible and can damage the speaker drivers on the system playing the audio.

It is worthwhile to use a specialized tool for normalizing the audio.

37.8 What Is a VU Meter?

You monitor levels using VU meters on your audio console. They may be small mechanical meters or a set of LEDs arranged in a bar. Figure 37-9 shows you what to look for on your audio console.

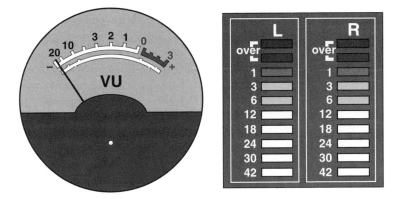

Figure 37-9 VU meters.

The meter on the left is the traditional electro-mechanical design. On the right is an example of the more modern electronic LED bar-graph display.

37.9 Surround-Sound Track Assignments

If everything you have done so far has been carried out carefully, it will not be necessary to remap the surround-sound tracks. But if you arbitrarily ingested them without any automatic track assignment, you should check that the sound is associated with the appropriate channels. Pairs of channels must be grouped so that the encoder deals with several alternative stereo pairs.

Modern coding systems should be aware of the 5- and 6-channel surround-sound systems and ought to do a lot of this automatically for you. Some ingest processes allow for only two channels of audio to be ingested at a time, and it is such systems that often necessitate this fix-up stage.

Mono and stereo audio would be presented as shown in Figure 37-10.

Surround and other multi-speaker systems look more similar to Figure 37-11.

Theater systems have many more surround speakers, although they may not all be driven independently. The highest specification for theaters is the Lucasfilm THX system, which must be calibrated and tested by Lucasfilm engineers before the THX badge can be put up on the wall.

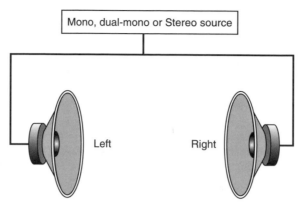

Figure 37-10 Stereo speakers.

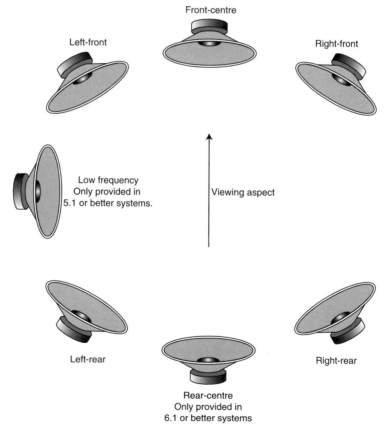

Figure 37-11 Surround speaker arrangement.

37.10   Processing Legacy Formats

If you are ingesting audio from some old legacy formats, the players are sometimes hard to obtain. Vinyl records will give the best frequency response at higher speeds, but old 78-RPM records are made of a brittle material that imparts more noise.

Because we can alter the sample rates and change the playback time of the audio, it might be feasible to sample a 78 RPM at 33 RPM in an emergency. The playback speed can then be increased to the correct value in the digital domain and re-sampled. This also applies to 45-RPM singles.

A sample rate of 48 KHz at 33 RPM is equivalent to sampling the 78-RPM record at 112 KHz. This might offer the chance to remove more noise from the recording than if it had been sampled at 48 KHz and 78 RPM. The shape of the grooves and the amount of movement of a gramophone needle are different for vinyl and 78-RPM disks. You will still need to fit a cartridge and stylus that is suitable for the kind of disk you are playing, even if you are sampling at a slower speed.

37.11   Low Bit Rate Scenarios

The human eye is more forgiving than the ear. Make sure that the audio still sounds intelligible even if the frame rate goes down. More advanced encoding techniques are being developed in research labs, some of which are aimed at the mobile phone market and provide some interesting solutions to lip sync. It may be possible to deploy some of those techniques. For example, regionalizing the area of interest within the frame might allow the encoder to work harder on the facial expression and keep the frame rate up so that lip sync is preserved. It is possible to achieve the same thing by making sure that the presenter stays still and that the background is stationary.

37.12   Time to Encode

That's it! We're ready to encode. All the video is ready and the audio is set up. Just select a codec and kick off the job. In the next chapter we'll tie up the loose ends, talk about batch-job control and how to initiate the encoder, and then we're done.

Encoding—Go for It!

38

38.1 On the Home Stretch

We are nearly at our journey's end. This is where we make the final choice about how our video is going to be compressed and commit to that processing job to create the final output. Everything we've done up to now has been geared toward this part of the process, and yet it seems such a small and insignificant step by itself.

Recall that at the beginning of the book, I said it was all about the context and the preprocessing and that the compression itself was a rather trivial part of the process. Now that will be borne out.

38.2 The Big Compromise

When we started this journey I talked about video compression being a compromise. This is where that compromise takes place.

You may want all of the following:

- High quality
- Low bit rate
- Full frame rate
- Fast encoding
- Low cost

You may be able to accomplish two or perhaps three of these, but only at the expense of the ones you are prepared to sacrifice.

An analog digital video recorder (DVR) that is live-recording the off-air signal cannot drop frames. So it must compromise on quality in order to maintain the throughput. The compromise on bit rate has more to do with the available storage capacity in a PVR. The capacity is measured in hours according to the recording quality you select.

High-performance encoding systems for industrial-strength solutions are not likely to be cheap.

Maintaining high quality at low bit rates requires the encoder to work very hard indeed and this reduces the chances of processing in real time. Therefore, small bit rate and high quality are possible, but not if you want the output delivered quickly. This may be possible if you spend more money on parallelizing the problem across a distributed architecture. Building grids or render walls is not trivial and certainly is not cheap.

Analog recording systems are cheap but suffer from time-base problems that can cause the whole frame to arrive early or late. The capture system can usually compensate for this, but not always. Sometimes the problem is related to the tape, and this is apparent when you experience a syncing problem at the same point in the playback every time.

A more difficult issue to do with time bases is horizontal synchronization. This can cause each line to be displaced slightly left or right of its correct position. Any vertical edges then become ragged. This introduces some high-frequency components in the vertical axis, and these are hard to encode. Fixing this problem is very difficult and complex, so you will often put up with it in order to save sinking a lot of cash into your equipment—hat is, unless quality becomes a dominant factor and you then are able to justify deploying some heavyweight solution.

38.3 Now Set Up Your Codec

Codecs represent the video as a series of macroblocks. Making the encoding lossy at the macroblock level reduces the bit rate. The encoder expends a lot of effort on the motion estimation/compensation logic. This reduces the number of macroblocks to be included in the output stream but it is computationally very expensive.

The H.264 codec is especially compute intensive in this area but is amazingly efficient compared with all the other codecs once the video has been compressed.

 Always purchase the professional versions of the encoding tools. They will generate better-quality results than the limited-edition or basic versions.

If you have the time, set the encoder to do the most thorough job on the compression. It will take longer, but provided you have not over-promised to your customers, that compression should not take longer than you would have predicted (given some experience, of course). Switch on 2-pass encoding, variable bit rate, and any additional tools that the encoder deploys to do a better job.

38.3.1 First Choose the Codec if Necessary

Choose the codec you want to use if the choice hasn't already been forced on you by circumstances beyond your control. Decide how the encoder is going to process the content. The trade-off is whether to encode quickly and sacrifice coding quality or to take some extra time and produce a more compact file.

38.3.2 Set the Bit Rate for the Video

Set the limit in kilobits per second (Kbps) for the video track. In Popwire Compression Master, when encoding with MPEG-4, the optimal range is from16 Kbps to 2000 Kbps. Check the specifications for the codec you are using to find the optimal setting.

Table 38-1 shows some example bit rates/file sizes for encoding video. These are just ballpark guidelines, and your service offering will dictate exactly what values you should be using.

A small picture size implies a lower frame rate, typically 15 fps. The medium-sized picture is about a quarter the area of a full-sized TV and can probably cope with a normal frame rate. The full-size service is all the pixels and all the frames.

 Rapidly moving content may increase the bit rate required or may reduce the quality to remain within the same bit rate target.

Audio bit rates depend mainly on the number of channels. This is not as simple as it sounds. A 6-channel surround-sound service can be delivered as 6 discretely coded audio streams. In the new and emerging coding systems, it is coded with a mono mix with differential signals added at lower bit rates for the additional streams. These need to be decoded and cascaded to reveal the additional tracks.

 Speech will code more economically than music.

The AAC codecs deliver very good audio at 64 Kbps and excellent audio at 128 Kbps. Usable multi-channel audio is possible at bit rates in the 500 to 750 Kbps range and premium quality surround is possible at 1.5 Mbps or better. This will improve as codecs evolve.

Table 38-1 Guideline Bit Rates for Video

Media	QCIF	CIF	Full size
Ordinary streamed content	70-bps stream	250-Kbps stream	500-Kbps stream
Premium streamed content	150-Kbps stream	440-Kbps stream	880-Kbps stream
Downloadable content	500-KB file	1.5-MB file	5-MB file
Downloadable movies	1-MB file	25-MB file	3.5-GB file
TV quality—SDTV MPEG-2	n/a	n/a	4-Mbps stream
TV quality—SDTV H.264	n/a	n/a	2.3-Mbps stream
TV quality—DDTV H.264	n/a	n/a	7-Mbps stream

38.3.3 Complexity and Motion Estimation

High complexity is sometimes presented as a parameter you can define. It is sometimes preset and it may be called other things. Look for settings in the encoder that talk about motion estimation or motion compensation.

Selecting a high-complexity setting in Popwire Compression Master automatically invokes a more advanced motion-estimation algorithm, which slows down the encoding but improves the quality of the picture. This should be especially helpful at low bit rates.

38.3.4 Controlling Complexity in the Decoding Process

If it is possible, we need to compress the video in such a way that it is easy for the media player to decode. Increasing the complexity of the decoding process reduces the target audience because more computing power is needed to run the decoder. If we can maintain a low decode complexity coefficient, then more people with older and less powerful systems can continue to enjoy our content.

You may need to trade off compression ratio against decoding complexity to achieve the desired balance. You would do this perhaps by limiting the use of some of the more sophisticated compression tools that the encoder offers.

Determining which of these tools to avoid using comes down to a diligent profiling of your target audience to establish what they are capable of decoding. Of course, this should have happened some time before you pressed the 'OK' button on the encoder start-up screen.

38.3.5 Buffer Sizing

Define the size of the buffer for the video frame if necessary. If you have access to this parameter, it probably has different ranges of values in each encoder. Setting the encoder to run with a small buffer might force the clip to be encoded as a constant bit rate (CBR) file. Allowing a larger buffer may automatically flip an internal switch so the content is encoded as a variable bit rate (VBR) file. You would probably prefer to explicitly control this, but unless you are running a broadcast installation, it's probably not worth worrying about.

38.3.6 *Traffic Shaping*

Provided you have access to this level of control, the variable buffer verifier (VBV) dynamically controls the buffer size for the video frame. This is also related to VBR and CBR settings.

 When deciding the setting for GOP structures, remember that 15 frames is the maximum for PAL and 18 is the maximum for NTSC if you are encoding with MPEG-2 for DVD publication.

Use VBR when streaming content on your *intranet* and on the Internet. Buffers can be set to store between 5 seconds and a minute of video for Internet and high-bandwidth networks.

Use CBR bit rate settings when you are streaming to networks with a low bandwidth, such as mobile-phone networks running GPRS protocols. For these low-bandwidth networks, a CBR setting with a small buffer that is under 5 seconds is optimal.

In circumstances where the bit rate changes and you get peaks due to the content containing scene dissolves or periods of high motion, bit starving is provided by 2-pass compression. This is no use for video conferencing, which must have 1-pass compression and zero latency.

38.3.7 *Automatic Frame Dropping*

Popwire Compression Master and Popwire's other encoding tools provide a feature called Frame Skip Probability. This comes into play if the bit rate cannot be sustained. The value you define in this parameter sets the priority for frames that can be skipped during coding in order to maintain the desired bit rate. When you are coding footage for use on platforms such as GPRS or 3G mobiles, this is helpful because of the extreme bandwidth limitations. It is also beneficial for content that is streamed via a dialup modem connection.

Popwire encoding software allows key frames to be set in four different modes:

- Natural Key Frames Only: The codec decides when to insert a key frame. This mode would be used when a scene change is detected, for example.
- Natural Key Frames With Distance: This works similarly to the Natural Key Frames selection but forces a key frame periodically whether a scene change is detected or

not. This is useful on lossy connections because if a sync error happens, the player can reconstruct its image again when the next key frame arrives. You can determine the maximum distance according to the service level you want to provide.

- Key Frame (Every): Key frames are inserted only at predicted times.
- All Key Frames: When very high bit rates are used, you can discard P- and B-frames and just encode I-frames for transmission. This results in very good presentation quality but is less efficient in terms of compression factors.

38.4 Define Any Postprocessing That Is Required

Not a great deal of additional processing is necessary on the final output other than packaging it into the correct kind of file container. You might also set up the destination for the output-compressed file at this stage.

You could do some hinting on the file if you intend to stream it. This is mandatory for files that are going to be streamed via the RTSP protocol. Ignore this step if you don't intend to stream the files.

Another possible postprocess is the embedding of any text tracks, URL tracks, or other metadata. This must be done after compression. It is better to deliver caption texts as a separate text stream rather than a burned-in image, as it leads to a cleaner presentation with no compression artifacts. It is also much more efficient in terms of bit-rate usage.

There is postprocessing that takes place at the client end but this is in the decoder and happens after the bit stream has been converted back into a pixmap.

38.5 Setting Up a Batch-Encode Server

If you are only going to run the occasional encode job, it is not worth the effort of setting up a batch-encoding process. On the other hand, if you are running a service delivering encoded video, you want to be able to throw encoding jobs at a farm of encoders without too much manual effort. In a more extreme situation such as running a major news Web site where you are creating upwards of 200 five-minute clips every day for a variety of platforms, a workflow process driving a batch-oriented encoder farm is the only way to solve the problem.

Products such as the Popwire Compression Engine offer an industrial-strength, server-based solution. Other possibilities at the high end are solutions by Telestream, which has a highly engineered batch-transcoding product called Flip Factory. At the lower

Run the compression jobs on the fastest computers you can find. This will result in encoding with smoother motion, more detail, and better sound and will allow you to access the higher data rate setting more easily. It will also get the job done more quickly!

end of the scale and under the "roll your own" heading is an AppleScript-driven workflow built around an application that uses QuickTime. Even the humble movie player running on an installation that has been blessed with a QuickTime Pro license becomes a very powerful tool with the addition of some AppleScript support.

For batch-based workflows, use Telestream Flip Factory, Sorenson Squeeze, Discreet Cleaner, Popwire Compression Master, or Apple Compressor.

Most of the compression tools implement batch processing in one way or another. Many use a watch folder approach. This is a folder that they monitor for the arrival of new files and then process them as soon as they are noticed.

38.6 Quality-Assurance Processes

There are various places in the end-to-end process where quality assurance should monitor the performance of your systems. The incoming picture quality must be checked. This is normally a subjective analysis and one person may not notice any artifacts whereas another may be totally horrified by what he or she perceives as terrible quality.

Quality costs money. Cheap tools are of poor quality, so always buy the best you can afford.

This is a very difficult thing to mechanize since the measurement of picture quality is such a human-oriented task. Mechanical principles might be applied by running decoders and differencing the compressed copy against the original. This is going to at least triple the time taken to process the video because of the unpacking and comparison processes requiring a similar compute power and additional storage to be made available.

The comparison process needs to be somewhat "fuzzy." because there is some difficulty in defining what exactly is a good enough quality level. A completely non-trained person who has never seen very high quality displays in the laboratories might be satisfied with a quality level that is approximately the same as a VHS recording. Someone who has worked as a TV diagnostic or research engineer and has seen the very-high-definition TV displays at the NAB or IBC conferences will find that same VHS-quality level very unsatisfactory.

It is difficult to do this kind of measurement and comparison automatically, even when some artificial intelligence is used. There is no substitute for human intervention when running quality assurance on your compression farm.

Then there is the technical side of the process. You may have mandated certain bit-rate requirements, and you must verify that the video is compressed to comply with them. For example, if you cap the bit rate of a video channel in a multiplex or transponder, you cannot afford for the video to burst at a greater bit rate unless a saving is made elsewhere in the multiplex. If the transport stream running within the multiplex exceeds the bit-rate capacity available, the multiplex will break and you end up with an interrupted transmission. The receiver will resynchronize but your viewers will be displeased.

38.7 Summary: How to Achieve Good Quality Every Time

There are aspects of video processing that have a material effect on the quality of our compressed-video output. Having some insights into them will help as we move toward the goal of compressing some footage. We should also bear them in mind as we plan how to build a system to do this compression work.

These last few chapters are what it is all about. Everything in the book up to this point prepared you for that journey, step by step through the encoding process. You might not have thought some of the earlier stuff was relevant, but now you understand why video compression works the way that it does. Recall my earlier assertion, at the beginning of Chapter 5, about going back in time to reinvent some of those technologies so that they would compress more easily.

By now you can appreciate 1) why compression has become so complex and 2) that that is because of technology choices made in the early days of the television evolutionary process. Those decisions were perfectly reasonable at the time, but we are paying a high price in terms of processing power and throughput in our compression systems. With the advent of worldwide adoption of HDTV systems, which are progressively scanned and operate at similar display formats everywhere, we may be able to eliminate some of this complexity over the next 10 to 20 years.

In the last chapter we will look at the future—where digital video might be going over the next few years and the implications for video compression.

Where Shall We Go Next?

39.1 Back Home Again

If you have read this far, you will have realized that there is a lot of fine detail to understand when compressing video. You need to know about many things other than the compression process because the bulk of your work happens before you compress a single frame.

If you take each individual piece of knowledge separately, none of the steps involved is very complex. It's just that there are rather a lot of them and if you compress your video and leave out some of the preprocessing tricks or do them in the wrong order, it degrades the quality of your output.

This concluding chapter looks beyond compression to examine some topics that crop up in advanced work. It also ties up a few loose ends and looks at some speculative ideas and new technologies that are not yet implemented but could be interesting avenues of research.

The emerging high-performance computing systems built with massively parallel clusters offer huge performance benefits and this leads to new ways to approach the compression process with distributed algorithms. An example of a massively parallel cluster is the one built by Virginia Tech. That system is a cluster of 1100 dual-processor Macintosh G5 computers connected together with a very fast switched network and running some software in addition to the underlying operating system so that work can be shared across as many nodes as necessary. The Virginia Tech system was, for a short time, the 3rd fastest computer on the planet.

Software developers are already considering how the video-compression task should be divided and distributed in such a clustered system. Taken to its extreme, we might imagine that a 1000-node cluster would compress video 1000 times as fast as a single node. There is the problem of splitting, distributing, and then gathering the results together, but even if this slows the process somewhat, the gains are still likely to be profound. Breaking the video into sequences based on the number of frames in a closed GOP might be a way forward. It simplifies the distribution process as well as the re-aggregation of the coded output.

39.2   The Future Is Digital

Analog TV is essentially dead. Plans are being drawn up for the eventual switch-off and replacement with digital TV services. In fact this needs to happen, otherwise the bandwidth won't be available for the high-definition TV services that are being planned for deployment.

The city of Berlin has already turned off all the analog transmissions, and small communities elsewhere in the world are already well on the way to migrating to an all-digital delivery.

39.3   Which Codec Will Win?

H.264 is clearly the future as far as video coding is concerned, at least for the next 10 to 15 years and possibly beyond that. The VC-1 codec may become relevant if the standards-ratification process moves forward rapidly enough. This is running into some difficulties and is taking far longer than first expected.

MPEG-4 as a family of standards is extremely important. It brings together many diverse areas of work under one umbrella and standardizes the whole multimedia-authoring environment. Using that MPEG-4 framework with MPEG-7 and MPEG-21 will also be important as we describe content with metadata and attempt to rights control its deployment in an interoperable way.

Most of what we need to make MPEG-4 content is already available. It's just that we create multimedia in a variety of different ways on different devices. The changes required to support MPEG-4 are largely incremental across the portfolio of digital-media authoring tools. It simply requires some incentive to encourage people to manufacture the plug-ins or minor upgrades.

The encoding process for any codec that expects to be dominant and long lived must be capable of implementation at a price the industry is willing to pay. This requires that the complexity of compression not become a burden on the CPU, in order to keep compression times low.

The dominant codec must also provide the best available compression ratio. This is the factor by which the output is smaller than the input data.

It is also vitally important that the decoding workload be capable of implementation in very inexpensive hardware. Some HD tests have demonstrated that HDTV coded with H.264 is borderline on some very powerful desktop systems when played back. The situation for VC-1 is even worse because it suffers from a higher decoder complexity. This is not going to help its chances of being adopted.

Special hardware decoder chips will solve this, and it's not expected to cause any great delay to the rollout of HDTV services delivered with H.264 coding.

Analog switch-off in the United Kingdom:

http://www.bbc.co.uk/info/policies/pdf/digital_switchover_report.pdf

39.3.1 *Maybe the Future Is H.264*

Encoding with the H.264 standard is quite independent of the MPEG-4 frameworks. It stands alone as a codec in its own right. MPEG-4 is only one of a variety of contexts in which it can be applied. Depending on whether you are broadcasting a TV bit stream or an IP-based broadband service, you may embed the encoded video in an MPEG-2 transport mechanism or an RTSP stream of some kind.

Codec plug-ins for H.264 will almost certainly be available for all platforms and frameworks in which video coding is currently used and some that we haven't yet thought about.

The European Broadcasting Union (EBU) is developing a strategy for high-definition TV in Europe. Although the exact format and presentation are not 100% clear, it looks very likely that the H.264 codec will be adopted for this. It remains yet to be clarified whether the raster size will be set at 720 or 1080 lines but it will probably be progressively scanned and run at a frame rate of 50 Hz. Bit rates of around 8 Mbps are being proposed, which would allow 2 channels to be delivered within a single *DTT* multiplex. A DSat transponder could carry 5 or 6 channels of high density at this bit rate depending on how the multiplexing is accomplished.

H.264 is certainly becoming very popular in the digital TV industry. Several satellite TV operators have indicated that it is their codec of choice for next-generation TV services.

39.3.2 *Or Perhaps the Future Is VC-1*

Everything we might say about the potential of H.264 is also largely true of the SMPTE VC-1 standard. Both are being proposed as possible coding schemes for HDTV broadcasts and next-generation DVD players.

The VC-1 standard is independent of Microsoft because it is going to be licensed through SMPTE or its agents. WM-9 will continue to be available as an alternative under quite different licensing rules. VC-1 might be widely available and deployed on all operating systems. WM-9 will be available on Windows and whatever other platforms Microsoft deems beneficial to its marketing.

Codec plug-ins for VC-1 will probably be available for most platforms and frameworks in which video coding is used. At this stage it seems it will not be as dominant as H.264 but it is very early in the life cycle for both codecs and hard to see beyond the short-term future for both of them.

The biggest uncertainty about VC-1 is the current progress of the standardization process. This appears to have become bogged down in a series of discussions and is not moving forward as rapidly as was first anticipated. Originally, Microsoft promised a standard within 6 to 12 months of the commencement of the process. A year later, no clear date has emerged for the release of the final document, probably because the amount of work that was required was underestimated. It is likely that there will eventually be a VC-1 standards document but the question now is whether it will be in time to gain any market share that has not already been won by H.264.

The chances of VC-1's achieving any kind of dominance seem to be receding as H.264 gains acceptance. There are predictions that any deployments of VC-1 will be short lived and likely replaced by H.264, as the open standard is more attractive. Some satellite TV services have already declared that VC-1 is not under consideration. We will have to wait and see how this plays out.

39.4 W3C Baseline Formats

The W3C baseline formats describe the variety of media types that are used within a SMIL container. This accomplishes many things that Flash and MPEG-4 might do with interactive presentations but lacks the capability of packaging the entire presentation into a single container.

There appears to still be much work to do on this W3C standard but it is certainly worth watching. SMIL provides some rapid-previewing mechanisms and for simple presentations, it is remarkably easy to publish using existing frameworks and workflow systems that are already deployed for publishing dynamically generated web sites, XML, and RSS feeds.

39.5 Multimedia with MPEG-4

An important distinction of MPEG-4 is that it addresses topics well outside the boundaries of video compression. Modeling in 2D or 3D come into play and there is much in MPEG-4 that is designed to be of use for interactive- and multimedia-content developers.

Multimedia authoring tools will use compressed video as an asset object to be aggregated with other assets in a composite application that is played back on a suitable target device.

Much more information about MPEG-4 and the other related standards such as MPEG-7 and -21 is available at the MPEG Industry Forum web site.

39.5.1 Why Is MPEG-4 Different from the Other Video Formats?

Because MPEG-4 is so much more than a video standard, it is differentiated somewhat from the previous MPEG standards. Advances in video compression that correspond to MPEG-1 and MPEG-2 form only a small part of the MPEG-4 specification. The other parts describe structured audio, 3D scenes, meshes, and all manner of object-based constructions.

39.5.2 MPEG-4 Systems-Layer Framework

The MPEG-4 systems layer provides a much more sophisticated scene-construction environment, allowing for structured audio and video and even 3-dimensional scenes.

W3C baseline formats: http://www.w3.org/TR/2000/WD-smil-boston-20000622/baseline_formats.html

MPEG-4 Net: http://www.mpeg4.net/resources/

MPEGIF: http://www.mpegif.org/

Interactivity and scripting support and active code written in Java and JavaScript are all possible.

39.5.3   MPEG-4 FlexMux Timeline

The *FlexMux* provides a way to interleave data from separate elementary streams into one serial bit stream. MPEG-2 was able to do this, but it lacked some significant capabilities for ensuring that timeliness could be synchronized with external events.

The MPEG-4 design is scoped to manage a very large number of simultaneous streams and solve interactivity and trigger synchronization problems that are very hard to deal with when deploying MPEG-2 on digital video broadcast (DVB) systems, for example.

39.5.4   Object-Based Hierarchical Model

The MPEG-4 framework is an open-standards approach to storing video in an object-based form. This is very much like the way that content is stored in a QuickTime movie, and promotional statements from Apple state that "both MPEG-4 and QuickTime are from the same DNA."

This bodes very well for the availability of tools for authoring MPEG-4 content, as it wouldn't be very hard to convert the export mechanisms that currently write QuickTime files so that they make MP4 object container (BIFS) files instead.

39.5.5   Scene Descriptions

MPEG-4 places all the video objects into a scene description. That scene may actually just describe a surface that is completely covered by a video object, so you would see no significant difference from the way that an MPEG-2 video player works.

Significant benefits are available because this scenic environment is a true 3D space. Very interesting presentations that look like a digital video effects (DVE) unit was used are possible. The scenes are described in a language called BIFS, which is short for Binary Format for Scenes. BIFS evolved from the VRML standard, which was in use in the late 1990s but was not widely deployed at that time.

39.5.6   Scene Construction

MPEG-4 BIFS provides some very sophisticated techniques for deconstructing a scene into component objects. The foreground and background are transmitted separately and then composited into a single image in the playback system. The background might be a still image while the foreground is a presenter. Weather forecasts are often made this way with a computer-generated graphic keyed into the background behind a presenter.

MPEG-4 lets you deliver the images separately and with the coding efficiency taken into account, you might reduce the bit rate to 20% or less compared with coding full-frame video in MPEG-2.

The MPEG-4 wired content is only demonstrated in prototype form at present although it was being heavily touted as a new technology in 2001. The iVAST (now known as DG2L) and Envivio companies both had tools available as early as 2002.

Tools for developing the systems-layer interactive components (the BIFS stuff) are beginning to appear. There are online resources such as the MPEG Industry Forum (MPEGIF) mentioned above, with links to supplier Web sites where you can download open-source kits and demonstrations of proprietary tools.

39.5.7 Multi-Plane Display Model

The BIFS scene allows a multi-plane presentation to be created, such as floating objects in front of one another and changing their transparency. All of these effects are available with coding systems prior to MPEG-4 but special code would have to be built into the application to manage the effects. Now, with MPEG-4, it is an integral capability of the player. This saves you a great deal of time as a developer of playback applications because this player will inevitably be built in as an operating system component—but not yet. When it is, the intelligence will be carried in the content rather than having to delegate decision-making control to the application.

39.5.8 Nesting

Because a BIFS scene is constructed by inserting a video object, you may be able to accomplish the effect you are aiming for by deconstructing your scene into a series of nested BIFS packages. MPEG-4 allows you to embed another MPEG-4 package within the scene you are working on. This goes beyond the permitted complexity of the profile and level that you are working to. You should check that your player supports this but provided the aggregation is compliant with the standard, it should work. It has been proven to be practical with the EnvivioTV plug-in.

39.5.9 Structured Audio

If you recall, Chapter 7 was concerned with the compression of linear audio that has been ingested along with the video. MPEG-4 supports a variety of different audio objects.

The MPEG-4 standard describes a lot more than just the AAC-format audio compression that is becoming more popular. It also provides for some structured audio that allows speech and music samples to be delivered with instructions on how to re-synthesize the output at the receiver/player. This offers a way to deliver extremely low bit-rate, high-quality audio, but requires that the player has a complexity equal to that of a MIDI sequencer and software synthesizer. That is currently beyond what MPEG-4 players are capable of outside of a few laboratories, but it is an interesting direction for future development, especially when combined with the BIFS scene description to allow sound sources to be placed into a 3D environment.

These structured audio components would very likely be authored in other tools such as MIDI editors or text-to-speech renderers—tools that are already widely available. MPEG-4 support merely needs to be added incrementally.

39.5.10   *Texture-Coded Video*

The MPEG-4 standard sees the video as a texture that is painted onto the surface of an object. Other than that, the video is coded in a similar way to the MPEG-2 coding process using DCT algorithms.

Simple shapes such as a rectangle are straightforward and already supported. It is only necessary to indicate the size of the rectangle required. There is a minor limitation that the size of the textured rectangle must be an integer multiple of the size of a macroblock.

The shape of the object that the video is being painted onto may change the visual appearance. This is not the same as alpha shape-coded video. Rather, it is analogous to projecting a film image onto the side of a building. Any overlap will spill over the sides but it is nevertheless still being projected.

39.5.11   *Sprites*

Sprites are used as static background objects, and they may be much larger than the viewing rectangle. The sprite image is delivered early on in the stream and then it can be panned and scanned as necessary to use it as a background image. Some animation systems treat sprites as cell-animated character overlays but this is not how sprites appear to be used in MPEG-4. That kind of animation is dealt with separately.

Certain efficiency techniques are available to deliver only those parts of the sprite that are needed, when they are needed. Several of the tools provide a bandwidth-analysis feature to help with this. Envivio 4Mation (originally known as Broadcast Studio Author) has this built in. LiveStage Pro has a tool called Deliverator to do the same sort of thing although that only operates on QuickTime wired movies at present.

39.5.12   *Mesh Models*

Video content can be texture mapped onto a moving mesh. Several common examples exist where a moving fish is modeled as a mesh. This mesh is spatially distorted while playing back a video picture on the tiled surface.

39.5.13   *Face and Body Animation*

Face and body animation (FBA) is designed to support avatars and other similar models and is a special case of the mesh-based texture-mapping technique. Using the facial animation specified by MPEG-4 would allow video conferencing to take place at bit rates of 1 Kbps or better.

Version 2 of MPEG-4 provides the body-animation support, and significant data reduction is possible by using these structured techniques to recreate the desired scene.

This is well outside the territory of simple compressed video and more in the domain of computer-animated special effects. Display systems don't often have the necessary computational capability to support photorealistic modeling of this structured animation. But that will come in due course.

This technology is designed to be deployed in mobile situations. When the mobile camera is able to reliably "read" the human face and reduce the expression to some mathematical description, very low bit rates will be possible.

39.5.14 Profiles and Levels

The complexity issues have been simplified somewhat by the work done by the Internet Streaming Media Alliance (ISMA), which has developed a series of profiles and levels that bound the problem. The player determines what the profile is, to ascertain what functionality it will need to invoke. The level tells it the scope and size of the data that it must deal with.

The profiles and levels available to implementers of the MPEG-4 standard are summarized in detail in Appendix G. You must be careful to code your video to a profile and level that matches the player that you are targeting. If you don't, then the player should display an error alert and complain that the format is unsupported. That is a best-case scenario. Less compliant players may attempt to decode the stream assuming it is okay, and they will soon run into serious difficulties.

A particularly well-implemented player might be smart enough to ignore the more complex aspects of the video that it cannot decode. The playback would be compromised but a usable moving image would be displayed even though it not at the highest quality.

Such players are still some way off as the MPEG-4 standard is still very new and the licensing requirements are such that they discourage many people from taking it up at present.

39.5.15 MPEG-4 Risk Analysis

Some risks are involved if you plan to go with MPEG-4 as part of your strategy. There are in fact only a small number of companies that provide MPEG-4 authoring tools and these are listed in the appendices. There are potentially many more but they need to upgrade their existing tools to cope with the MPEG-4 content in addition to what they already work with.

The support for BIFS will grow in due course when there are appetites for adding identical cross-platform interactive content to the World Wide Web, DVDs, PVRs, and broadcast TV. MPEG-4 has the potential to deliver that genuine "author once, deploy everywhere" model.

There is a risk at present that you will be locking into a minority codec/player. The video aspects are portable and playable across a wide variety of platforms. But the BIFS support is still quite restricted and authoring tools for it are rare.

While there are risks associated with adopting MPEG-4, there are also risks associated with ignoring it. You may get left behind. The licensing situation is substantially resolved and as the terms become more attractive, the take-up may well be rapid and widespread. If you choose what looks to be an attractive alternative today and lock into that, you may regret that decision within just 12 to 18 months. Electing to keep your options open at this stage is a good strategy.

There are still some unresolved issues regarding the multiple and separate licenses required for audio, video, BIFS, and the MPEG-4 systems layer. At present there is no incentive to address this because there are no players and no one is making content on a commercial basis. I am convinced that this will get dealt with appropriately when the time is right.

Of course, there are many possible benefits to be enjoyed. The MPEG-4 standard has the potential to completely revolutionize the delivery of linear video and rich-media services. The interactive capabilities go far beyond what is possible and what has been accomplished so far with digital TV, interactivity on TV, and DVD products.

39.5.16 *Summary of Where MPEG-4 Is Useful*

Expect to see the video aspects of MPEG-4 (H.264) being deployed in mobile devices. PDAs stand to make great use of multimedia if a compact and lightweight player could be developed with a small enough computational footprint.

All manner of devices are being implemented in the consumer marketplace, such as phone units with built-in address books and fax facilities; videophones as opposed to mobile video-enabled devices will not be far behind.

Grocery shopping from a fridge-mounted console doing e-commerce with your grocery supplier is an almost trivial thing to implement.

Electronic program guides equivalent in depth of content to a paper-based TV listings magazine are possible. These could be embedded within your DVR and linked to remote data services.

39.6 Cross-Platform Portable Interactivity

Experimental work with the Envivio Broadcast Studio Authoring Tool (now called 4Mation) has proven that it is remarkably portable. Envivio has produced a plug-in component (EnvivioTV) that enhances the capabilities of QuickTime, RealNetworks, and Windows Media player sufficiently to understand the BIFS scene descriptions.

It also works on Mac OS X and Windows, delivering a "play back anywhere" experience that only needs to be authored once. This is something that multimedia and Web-based AV service providers have been anticipating for some time.

The BBC News Interactive TV team produced a prototype interactive program using the Envivio tools and demonstrated this at the NAB 2003 conference in Las Vegas. The work was also presented as a paper at the Brighton Euro-iTV conference in March 2004. Refer to the Euro-iTV conference proceedings for further details.

The BBC Newsnight demonstration runs on any of the three players identically regardless of the kind of desktop in use. Figure 39-1 shows a screenshot as an example.

Brighton Euro-iTV conference: http://www.brighton.ac.uk/interactive/euroitv/index.htm

Figure 39-1 Newsnight demo picture.

Envivio is to be commended for its work on the interactive aspects of the MPEG-4 standard. Envivio and the Fraunhofer Institute are members of a very select community of researchers that are driving this forward.

You should consult Envivio for details of its authoring tools. The Envivio plug-in will be required until Apple, RealNetworks, and Microsoft implement BIFS support natively in their players. If you are requesting the Envivio plug-in, it is rather bad manners to be obtaining it so as to play content you created with its competitor's products. The honorable thing is to talk to Envivio staff about doing some business with them if you are planning to exploit their generosity in providing a player plug-in.

39.7 Compliance Recording of Interactivity

The same rules on compliance recording apply to interactive and multimedia content. This is quite a tough nut to crack. Recording the interactive material requires that you look at the recording process in a completely different way.

Compliance recording of video is based on replacing an analog system with something that simply digitizes the analog content. To preserve the interactive data that was transmitted, it is necessary to extract the relevant parts of the data stream and record them. This allows the digital video be extracted and stored as well. A wholly digital approach reduces the amount of hardware required and the implementation can be built in a more distributed fashion.

There are issues with time stamping and the relevance of playing back stored interactive content, especially if it links to a networked connection. Any remote services that were being accessed when the video was broadcast may not be available later when the compliance-research request is made. These issues are also relevant for DVR-based systems that store multimedia for time-shifted playback.

Quite a lot of research still needs to be done in order to make recorded multimedia a viable proposition.

39.8   Shape-Coded Embedding

Work is in progress to adapt the MPEG-4 Part 2 alpha-channel shape-coded video-compositing support so that it is also adopted by Part 10. This implies changes to the file structure with new atom types being introduced. The ordering of the macroblocks in the file according to their decoding sequence will then need to encompass the alpha-masking block decoding. Implementing a moving matte (see Figure 39-2) to composite one moving image over another is then possible with the more compact H.264-coded video.

Using the shape-coded video and the still images as a background opens up the possibilities for providing some interactive controls to view the images as a slide show with very little bit-rate overhead. Since the assets are already being delivered, the only additional coding overhead is a small button graphic and some script code.

39.9   Hidden Data Within the Video

Since the mid-1970s, broadcasters have been inserting more hidden information into the video stream. Because of the bandwidth of the transmission system, there are limits to the capacity of this hidden data. The text services use this to deliver their data in the lines that are normally outside the visible picture area. Theoretically, there could be data embedded in any of the lines that are not used for picture information. In practice only a few of them are used.

Your video input circuits at the point of ingest may or may not allow this information to be preserved. Some may blank out any lines that don't contain genuine picture data. In that case you will not be able to use these data lines to assist your workflow. If the data lines are preserved intact, then with the addition of some extra supporting code, your workflow may exploit this data.

39.9.1   *Teletext Signals*

The most prolific data source outside the picture is the Teletext data feed. In the United Kingdom and other countries, this provides a lot of useful data. For example, there is a complete program listing looking ahead about 24 hours. There is "now and next"

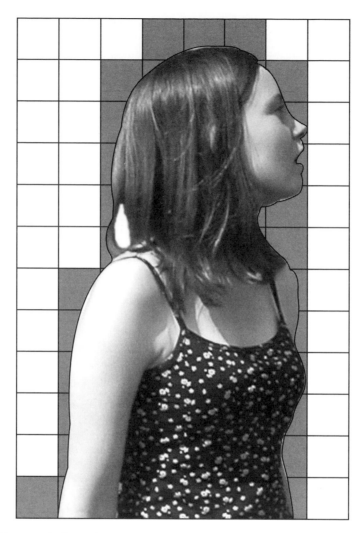

Figure 39-2 Shape-coded moving matte.

information, weather data, traffic, and news. Probably one of the most popular features of this service is the live sports-results reporting. These are updated very rapidly as the results come in.

Of course, much of this data is only useful during the broadcast and it is only guaranteed to be present at all in direct off-air signals. Video recorders do preserve some of the data but the recording does not preserve all the available lines. The lack of sufficient bandwidth seriously compromises the data and it may not contain any usable information at all.

The standards for transmitting Teletext data are widely known and available publicly on the Internet. It is not complex, and a simple data slicer that works like a 50%

threshold coupled with a framing analyzer should be able to extract the information without any difficulty if the lines are accessible in the digital domain.

39.9.2 Subtitles and Closed Captioning

The Teletext service in the United Kingdom (and elsewhere) carries an open-captioning service on Page 888. If you can detect the Teletext data, you may be able to pull off the caption texts and insert them into a text stream within your video-storage file as the video is ingested. Preserving the lines so they have to be cropped later allows this data extraction to be done offline as a separate process.

The wide-screen signaling (WSS) data in a PAL transmission also serves to indicate the kind of subtitling that is provided. For example, it indicates whether the subtitles exist within the Teletext data.

39.9.3 Aspect-Ratio Signaling

It is certainly useful to know whether the content was intended for viewing in normal-aspect ratio or wide screen. You may be able to detect these signals when ingesting some off-air content. Extracting this from an analog service will be the same as Teletext-data extraction.

On the NTSC service, the signaling is placed on lines 20 and 283 but in the PAL system the signaling is only present on line 20. The format of the signaling is different, too. There are quite a few additional service-oriented data values in the WSS data on the PAL system.

If you use the S-VHS connection format, the wide-screen signaling is provided by a DC offset voltage that does not affect the transmission of the picture information and can be sensed easily at the receiving end.

This signaling is also implemented in the digital TV services but of course it is done in a completely different way. It is possible to signal the aspect ratio in the MPEG header but if the signal is delivered within the stream, it must appear on a GOP (Group of Pictures) boundary. The header supports a 4-bit aspect-ratio field that can be set to indicate square samples, 4:3 or 16:9. There are other values but they are not meaningful. Another 4-bit field in the header describes the video frame rate. Again, not all the values are used. These values are coded into the header of the video sequence. It is beyond the scope of this book to get into "bits and bytes" but some coverage of the bit-stream organization and structure was presented in Chapter 14.

When processing recordings off air, you might be able to use the wide-screen signaling to identify where the advertising breaks are. In the United Kingdom at least, ads are broadcast in wide screen even on the breaks during 4:3 aspect-ratio broadcasts.

39.10 D-Cinema and Subtitles

Now that films can be delivered digitally, the subtitles can also be added without requiring an additional print to be created. The textual data is stored in a track that runs alongside the picture and this is the same data that would have gone out to air on a TV system.

The DTS company that develops surround-sound systems has found a way to super-impose subtitles at the time of projection. Because the company is well versed in synchronizing multi-channel sound tracks to film and video, it becomes very easy to synchronize a subtitle track.

The DTS system delivers the audio on a separate CD-ROM disk and that allows the picture to be delivered on a single generic print of the movie that is the same all over the world. The different language sound tracks are accomplished just by swapping the disk.

The subtitle data is synchronized and presented with an auxiliary projector, which renders the overlay and projects it in addition to the normal picture. This is such a simple idea, it is incredible no one thought of doing it years ago.

This approach is beneficial from the encoding point of view because text does not encode very well and these subtitles would be in a different motion plane, which would void the use of motion compensation in the area they occupy.

39.11 DVR Systems

The convergence of TV and information technology will continue with TV-Anytime and other technologies, which add value to the viewing proposition.

The broadcast-TV industry is facing a scenario where appointment viewing is replaced by cached playback systems modeled after the TiVo devices. This has major implications for interactivity and ensuring that programs are broadcast at scheduled times.

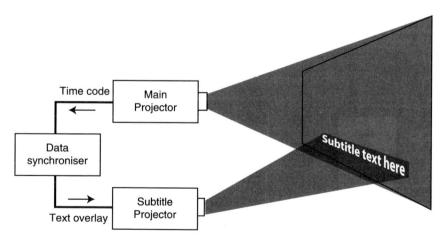

Figure 39-3 DTS subtitle-overlay projection.

DTS Cinema Subtitling: http://www.dtsonline.com/
PDC description: http://625.uk.com/pdc/

Going back to watching TV the old way is unthinkable after use of a TiVo for any length of time. This will easily become the dominant way to watch TV. There is speculation that TiVo has some very good ideas being prepared for rollout in the future. So far, they have already innovated some very interesting product enhancements.

39.11.1 *Program Delivery Control*

Program Delivery Control (PDC) was introduced in order to tell a video recorder when to start and stop recording a program. It is available in the United Kingdom and on some European broadcast services.

Not all broadcasters have deployed the necessary equipment to support this and some are not always reliable regarding the timely nature that is required for this to be useful. Nevertheless, PDC does provide a useful mechanism for triggering an encode process if the information can be captured at ingest time. The PDC code is broadcast approximately once every second during the program and contains a program identification code, which the VCR looks for.

39.11.2 *TV-Anytime*

TV-Anytime is a standard that has been developed by manufacturers and broadcasters in order to describe a subset of the metadata associated with a TV program. This subset is one that would be useful in creating an Electronic Program Guide (EPG) and embodies what is required to produce a satisfactory PVR or DVR experience for the end user.

The core of the standard revolves around the description of a CRID (Content Referencing Identifier), which uniquely identifies an item of content. That item might be a program, series of programs or even a segment of a program. Using publicly available metadata sources, your PVR would enquire through a search engine for CRIDs that match a particular query. That might be a program name or other descriptive information about genre or mood. Having obtained a CRID (or possibly several CRIDs), the PVR resolves them to discover the location of the program. That location might be an URL on the Internet or it might be a date, time, and channel number on a broadcast service. The PVR makes the necessary arrangements to obtain the program when it is available.

39.12 Metadata

Metadata preparation is becoming increasingly important as part of the workflow process. This will let customers find your content with publicly available metadata that is served from index repositories placed around the edge of the Internet.

TV-Anytime Forum: http://www.tv-anytime.org/

Digital Television Group (DTG): http://www.dtg.org.uk/

Digital Terrestrial Action Group (DigiTAG): http://www.digitag.org.uk/

This is where a hybrid platform that combines broadcasting with a network connection comes into its own. It is the model that TiVo has been using since they originally launched their service. The networked connection (in the case of TiVo and dialup modems) is used to collect schedule data. This is then aggregated and filtered using the preferences defined by the viewer and the appropriate recordings are triggered.

39.12.1 MPEG-7

The MPEG-7 standard is designed to augment the other MPEG standards and provides a Multimedia Content Description Interface. As such it doesn't describe the multimedia assets or interactive experience itself. That is done by MPEG-4. Instead, MPEG-7 deals with information about the multimedia that will assist in the management and filing. This "information about data" is called metadata. So MPEG-7 standardizes the metadata that describes the purpose and meaning of the multimedia while MPEG-4 describes the essence data.

This abstraction is quite important. If you have a video clip, the playable file is described by MPEG-4 but a textual description of it would be stored as an MPEG-7 object.

39.12.2 MPEG-21

This standard builds on the earlier work done with MPEG-1, 2 ,4, and 7, which describe the multimedia content and provides the abstraction between essence and metadata. The MPEG-21 work, which is currently in progress, addresses the movement of the multimedia around a network and the consumption of it by users on various platforms. This also addresses the issue of digital rights management. Like the earlier standards, the MPEG-21 documents are divided into several parts. Profiles will be developed in order to reduce the complexity so that interoperable products can be manufactured.

39.13 Historical Milestones and Looking into the Crystal Ball

To put the current work into context and look a little further ahead to new standards work in progress, Table 39-1 enumerates some important milestones in the world of video and audio compression so far. We also look a little bit into the future based on announcements and project launches that have been made public so far. There are some intriguing developments on the horizon. It remains to be seen whether these predictions come true, of course.

39.14 Concluding Notes—Planning Another Trip?

Our journey through the workings of video compression is now completed. If I have not bored you to death by now, you should have a solid grounding in how video compression works, enough at least to start doing some compression yourself. If you want to study further, you should now find the books written by master compressionists and experts in the subject far less daunting.

Table 39-1 Compression-Related Technology Timeline

Year	Milestone
1982	Compact disks (CDs) introduced, which deliver 44.1 KHz samples at a bit rate of 705 Kbps per channel.
1990	The date is approximate but H.261 shows up around here somewhere.
1991	QuickTime 1.0 introduced.
1992	MPEG-1 delivers video on the PC, Internet, and CD format disks. QuickTime released for Windows.
1993	MPEG-1 Audio layer 3 (MP3) standard. Usable quality attainable at 80 Kbps per channel. During this year the ITU started work on H.26P. That later became H.263. They also initiated work on H.26L. That evolved into H.264. MPEG support in QuickTime demonstrated. Experimental work and field trials in the United Kingdom by Apple, Oracle, and British Telecom on computer-based set-top boxes and the distribution of TV via cable networks.
1994	QuickTime 2.0 and QTVR introduced for Mac OS and Windows. H.262 and MPEG-2 appear.
1995	H.263 developed for videoconferencing applications.
1997	MPEG-2 Advanced Audio Coding (AAC). Typically operates at about 64 Kbps per channel. The ITU formed the Video Content Experts Group (VCEG) this year. QuickTime 3.0 introduces many new features. QuickTime 4.0 introduces an interactive architecture that is later exploited by LiveStage.
1998	The ITU issues a call for proposals for technology to be included in H.26L.
1999	MPEG-4 Part 2 video being discussed.
2001	MPEG calls for proposals to incorporate compression technologies in MPEG-4 video. ITU responds. Everyone realizes it would be silly to carry on independently and the Joint Video Team (JVT) is established. This is a profound example of what other groups working on a variety of standards should look at and consider doing.
2002	AAC+ demonstrated with Spectral Band Replication and usable quality within 56K modem bit rate. Meanwhile, the JVT group freezes the technical specification for H.264 late this year. Envivio and iVAST show prototype encoders and MPEG-4 systems-layer products.

Continued

Table 39-1 Compression-Related Technology Timeline (Continued)

Year	Milestone
2003	MPEG-4 High Efficiency AAC (HE-AAC). This operates at about 24 Kbps delivering stereo at 48 Kbps. H.264 final draft released and the licensing issues come to the fore. BBC News Interactive TV group demonstrates MPEG-4 Part 2 video embedded in a BIFS package built using Envivio tools. The Popwire Technology company showed their Compression Master product encoding in H.264 format at IBC. Microsoft WM9 very prominently displayed at IBC. In Japan, 3.15 million HDTV sets are sold.
2004	H.264 is very predominant at NAB and many companies are showing related products. Also at NAB, Apple demonstrates QuickTime playing back H.264 video at full HD (1080p) resolution. Envivio demonstrate complex EPG and VOD systems and very good compression ratios via their H.264 hardware encoders. DVB-H introduced. DVB approves H.264/AVC and HE-AAC for inclusion in the standard for delivery systems in Europe. This paves the way for HDTV with surround sound. VOOM launches with an H.264-based multi-channel TV service with a mix of SD and HD content. IBM and others launch the open Digital Media Framework. Astra trials Euro 1080 HDTV broadcasts.
2005	Standards working groups are looking at MPEG-4 Lossless Audio Coding (ALS) that is expected to be delivered during this year. This would be equivalent to CD audio but at a reduced bit rate of 325 Kbps per channel. H.264 begins to look like the dominant new codec and a worthy successor to MPEG-2. Improvements in H.264 during and after its rollout indicate a potential for a 10 fold increase in channels within the available spectrum. Support for VC-1 begins to wane. There is speculation that HD display capabilities might be provided in gaming consoles as early as this. Regular transmission of DVB-H services is expected to begin. Moore's law breaks down and computer manufacturers seek alternative ways to improve systems performance by modifying computer architectures now that it becomes more difficult to reduce transistor sizes further. Some comfort is derived from performance improvements demonstrated by the IBM Power 5 architecture and the Cell processor developed for the Sony Play Station Portable (PSP). These performance gains are the result of smarter design rather than further miniaturisation.

Table 39-1 Compression-Related Technology Timeline (Continued)

Year	Milestone
	Mobile video in handheld devices increases in popularity.
	Home media centres start to become important. All manner of computer/video hybrid consumer devices interoperate to build distributed media solutions for the home. Some call this the Digital Living Room. Alternative solutions that compete with and potentially improve on the TiVo model appear.
	Consumer video editing systems now capable of editing HD content (iMovie for example).
	Holographic storage devices from Optware and InPhase technologies become available. Potential for 30 GBytes on a postage stamp sized card. Even bigger capacities in the pipeline up to 1.6 TBytes per device.
	Projected delivery of 30-Mbps Internet connection to domestic users has been suggested by digital TV cable providers in France.
2006	The MPEG-4 Spatial Audio Coding (ASC) specification is expected to be completed during this year. This is planned to deliver 5.1 surround sound at 21 Kbps per channel within a total of 128 Kbps.
	DTT-based HDTV services should start to be rolled out in Europe.
	BSkyB is expected to launch HD services on satellite in the United Kingdom.
	Ultrawideband wireless devices will start to be sold to consumers. Ultrawideband is aiming to deliver 100 Mbps although Intel is pushing for 500 Mbps. It is known as World Wide Spectrum Efficiency (WWiSE) and IEEE 802.11n.
	U.S. broadcasters are expected to begin giving up parts of the analog spectrum if things go according to plan with the transition to digital TV.
2007	Marketing projections are expecting to see 100 million DVB-H-compatible handsets in use.
	TV operators are expected to start handing their analog TV spectrum back to the US Federal Government.
2008	It is predicted that 1.4 million European homes will have deployed HDTV in time for the Beijing Olympics.
	Some predictions are as high as 24 million HD-ready consumers.
	DTT HDTV services should increase as capacity is freed up by analog switch-off.
	Providers of D-cable services should start to roll out European HDTV by this time.
	Consumer-oriented VDSL carriage of IPTV services start to become more widely available and profitable.
2009	The DVB-H standards are expected to be deployed to 300 million mobile users by now.
	Current speculation suggests that analog TV is completely turned off in the United States by now. That may be too optimistic.
	European viewers are predicted to have access to 500 HDTV channels at this point.

Continued

Table 39-1 Compression-Related Technology Timeline (Continued)

Year	Milestone
	Somewhere around this time, we might hope that achievable delivery bit rates will have reduced to 50% of what they are now as a result of the H.264 encoder evolution.
2010	There is a potential for HDTV to become a mass-market phenomenon in Europe as early as this. The 1080p50 bit rates and decoding become feasible given hardware improvements. Early adopters will have been using HDTV for a while; now a lot more high-end users will start to buy equipment. TV-Anytime predict that $100 will purchase sufficient disk space to store 14 thousand hours of video.
2012	Current speculation is that HDTV goes mainstream in Europe by now and is available to all consumers at affordable prices. The Office of Communications defines the end of 2012 as the complete closedown of analog TV in the United Kingdom.
2013	Predictions of 130 million pay TV homes.

Getting the best out of compression systems is not just a question of flipping a couple of switches. There is far more to it than that. Even with the most sophisticated coding tools it is still important to keep a human being in the loop.

The H.264 codec is going to exercise our developers as they create better encoders for it and that is not the end of the story. In 2003, commentators were reluctant to take H.264 seriously. In 2004, it became a proven codec and started to become widely adopted but few products shipped. In 2005, the market for H.264 software is set to explode with many companies offering coding and playback support right across the board.

MPEG-7 and MPEG-21 work is underway; scalable video coding and H.265 are being talked about if not yet started as works in progress. There is much still to do and more journeys yet to undertake.

A

Problem Solver

A.1 Solving Problems with Your Compression

This appendix lists some common problems when compressing video and provides some advice about how to solve them. The information is presented in a Q & A style.

The Picture Keeps Jumping

Check the quality of your input video source. If you are using VHS, try connecting via an S-VHS connector or add a time-base corrector between the VCR and the digital sampler.

My Compressed Output Has Noise All over It, Even on Still Pictures

If your source has background noise because it is of low quality, switch on a grain-removal filter if you have one.

The Picture Looks Dull

Turn on the gamma correction and increase it a little. If that does not provide enough correction, look at modifying the brightness and contrast as well.

There Is Noise on the Black Background of the Credits Sequence

Set the black level with a calibration tool. Make sure you check the preview window to see both raw and processed examples of the footage.

The Text in the Credits Sequence Is Unreadable

You will probably have to retype the titles and create some compression-friendly video as still frames. Avoid scrolling text in credits. Perhaps the credits are good enough that appropriate still frames from them can be selected and reworked in your nonlinear editor or FX power tools.

Compression Bit Rate Is Not as Good as I Had Hoped

Work through all the steps listed in Chapters 31 to 38. If you still get poor quality at the bit rate you attempted, try reducing the image size and frame rate.

Moving Objects Are Doubled and Very Fuzzy

Apply some de-interlacing to your footage before compressing it. Adaptive is best.

I Want a Bigger Image—Should I Scale It Up?

No. Let the player do it. There is no point in wasting bit rate by scaling the video and then compressing it. The player interpolates up once it decodes the video.

My Input Video Is Unstable

If this is due to camera movement from a handheld shot, from gate weave, or from the camera or telecine, then run it through After Effects and use the motion tracking to stabilize it. Don't forget that other tools may offer the same capability.

There Is Some Movement in the Background That I Don't Like

Use Final Cut Pro FX script, or After Effects, Combustion, or Commotion, to fix up the offending items. These tools copy undamaged pixels from previous or following frames to remove unwanted objects.

The Colors Are Too Dark and It All Looks Underexposed

Load the video into a nonlinear editor (NLE) like Final Cut Pro and apply the 3-point color corrector.

The Bottom of the Raster Is Very Untidy and Badly Synced

Use cropping to remove it. Analog input tends to have some instability when it is taken from consumer video formats like VHS.

The Bit Rate Goes Very High on Scene Changes

Make sure you eliminate complex effects on transitions such as dissolves.

My Source Tape Has Been Cut Down From a Longer Master and Looks Horrible

Go back to the source tape and ingest from that. Then do the cutting in an NLE. Dubbing from one analog format to another just causes degenerative damage. This is called generational loss.

I've Mixed NTSC and PAL Footage and It Looks Jittery

Choose your target format and then use After Effects to change the time base for any video that is not in the correct format. Then edit it together. Don't throw stuff at your compressor that looks horrible to start with. Fix it up first if you can.

How Can I Save Lots of Bit Rate for Mobile Phone Output?

Apply some or all of these corrections:

- Reduce the length.
- Re-render any edits to remove transition effects.
- Stabilize any moving video.
- Crop in to the action-safe or text-safe area.
- Reduce the frame rate.
- Choose still frames and make it into a slide show.
- Blur the detail in the chroma channel to reduce the high frequencies.
- Turn it into grayscale and discard the color.
- Mix down the audio from stereo to mono.

Must I Scale the Video When I Move It from One Format to Another?

Not always. A 625-line video can scale down to 525 but a crop might work just as well. A 525-line video might introduce artifacts when scaled up to 625 so adding a margin around the edges and retaining the same-sized video could be a better solution. Run some tests and preview the results.

Captions and Subtitles Look Horrible When Compressed

Crop them out and focus on the area of interest.

What Is the Best Interpolation Algorithm to Use?

Bi-cubic interpolation is better than bi-linear. Both are better than nearest neighbor.

Should I Sharpen the Image?

Sharpening should be avoided whenever possible. It is the opposite of de-noising and introduces more grain noise. Over-sharpening makes the edges too harsh and leads to overshoot artifacts.

Which Is Best, CBR or VBR?

Constant bit rate (CBR) is good when you know that your footage must fit within a budgeted bit rate. Variable bit rate (VBR) delivers better quality when the content is "bursty" and requires an occasional peak in the bit rate. If you want VBR but also some of the benefits of CBR, apply traffic shaping and video buffer verification (VBV) techniques to modify the buffer contents.

The Video Drops Out When the Color Is Bright

You might be generating some illegal colors that your video input cannot cope with. Insert a color legalizer or desaturate the color a little.

The Video Jumps up and Down Very Rapidly

This might be the twittering effect you get when the field dominance is set incorrectly. This is caused during compression by switching the field order in the parameters. Some compression tools support this but not all. You may be able to fix it if you change the field dominance as you process. Investigate, test, and preview to see if it works.

My Compression Session Seems to Take a Very Long Time

Apart from the obvious question about whether your computer is up to the task, you might have set the compression parameters well outside the optimum range of values and turned on every single compression tool available to you. Some compressors are designed around web-based output and have problems creating HD or SD output at TV bit rates.

I Want to Apply Cropping to Only a Small Section

Import the video into After Effects or an NLE/FX tool that supports key-frame scaling and apply the scaling and cropping only to the sections that you want.

The Motion Doesn't Look Quite Right

Check that you have applied pulldown correction if it is required. If the footage contains anything shot on film, it is highly likely that you will have to remove the pulldown. Further processing with video effects and editors may have masked the pulldown.

When Should I Remove Dust and Scratches From Film Input?

As early as possible. After cropping if you like but before scaling. Well before de-noising and grain removal. The rule of thumb is to remove dust before any blurring operation.

How Do I Set the Right Audio Level?

Look for the loudest passage, find the peak waveform in that section, and adjust the gain to ensure this peak only reaches 3 dB below the reference level.

What Are the Best Bit Rates to Aim For?

For broadband, choose 350–500 Kbps and for modem, 28–56 Kbaud should support a pay-load of 20 to 40 Kbps. Mobile phones are capable of 64 Kbps. Table A-1 summarizes typical bit rates across a variety of different transport types:

A-1 Bit Rates for Different Transport Types

Format	Bit rate
Broadband	350–500 Kbps
Modem	28–56 Kbaud
Broadcast TV	3–5 Mbps
SDTV video with MPEG-2	4.5 Mbps
SDTV video with H.264	2 Mbps
HDTV video with H.264	5–6 Mbps
Uncompressed SDTV video	25 Mbps
Edit-quality DV video	25–50 Mbps

What Are the Best Formats for Different Devices?

Table A-2 lists a selection of settings that are appropriate for some standard ways that the encoded output must be deployed.

A-2 Example Compression Settings

Format	Settings
Low bit-rate mobile format	64 Kbps, *QCIF* or smaller image, and 15 fps frame rate.
PDA format	160 × 160 pixels, 65K colors, and compressed using Kinoma.
Streaming format	320 × 240, 18 fps, and compressed with Real, Windows Media, or H.264.
Modem-quality video	56 Kbps, low frame rate, small picture size, mono audio sampled at 22 KHz.
Broadband video	Whatever you can squeeze in at 500 Kbps. With H.264, this could be near TV sized.
Broadcast format	720 × 579 or 480, coded with MPEG-2 at 4 Mbps or H.264 at 2 Mbps.
Store and forward format	TV resolution, full frame rate, high-quality H.264 at 3 Mbps.

Hardware Suppliers

B.1 About This Appendix

This appendix is compiled from research done at several IBC and NAB conferences. The information here is not exhaustive, of course and supplements the coverage in chapter 29. A few companies whose products are particularly interesting are discussed in some detail. They are arranged in alphabetical order so as not to imply any special preference.

There is no need for me to describe the more well-known companies:

- Sony
- Panasonic
- Hitachi
- JVC
- Mitsubishi
- Sanyo
- RCA

B.2 ADC

The benefits of purchasing your networking and signal connectivity solutions from ADC is that it offers products that will integrate well with one another. These days, a video system is a combination of audio, telephony, video, and Ethernet. Added to this are fiberoptics and the media are connected together in both analogue and digital formats. This can be difficult to manage coherently if you purchase supplies from different manufacturers.

You will still need to purchase your routing products from specialist manufacturers but your structured cabling should be much easier to manage and more economic to install if you can purchase in bulk from one place.

B.3 AJA

AJA Video Systems makes video cards that have some similarity to Blackmagic Design's products. Blackmagic Design develops some drivers for the AJA video cards as well as their own cards. AJA also makes a useful range of podule adapters and rack-mount convertors, as well as the Io range of FireWire interfaces.

B.4 Belkin

Belkin makes all those useful little add-on gadgets and PCI card plug-ins that sort out problems. If you blow up a FireWire interface on a Macintosh computer, plug in a Belkin PCI FireWire card and save yourself the cost of an expensive logic board repair. The company makes a range of products for iPods as well.

B.5 Blackmagic Design

This company was founded by Grant Petty, who used to be involved with Digital Voodoo. Blackmagic has introduced video cards at prices that the industry is totally stunned by. It is possible to OEM these cards into systems and build broadcast-quality infrastructure for costs that are several orders of magnitude less than they would have been several years ago.

Blackmagic Design has begun to diversify into workgroup video products for switching and routing. This company will be well worth watching at future IBC and NAB exhibitions.

B.6 Envivio

There is a lot to like about Envivio as a company. Its products are innovative and right at the leading edge. The company has been involved in MPEG-4 standards-based compression systems since the standards were published, and probably before that. Envivio has some hardware- and software-based solutions to MPEG-4 coding. It is also one of very few companies with competence and products that support the MPEG-4 Part 1 systems layer. This positions Envivio very well to take advantage of all that the MPEG-4 standard has to offer. If you go with a standards-based approach, you should examine this company's product offerings to see if they provide what you need.

Be sure to check out the following Envivio products:

B-1 Particularly Interesting Envivio Products

Product	Description
4Caster	Broadcast that encodes MPEG-4 ASP and AVC (H.264) in real time for media transport and IPTV. An enterprise version is also available and a mobile version supports encoding for 3GPP mobile phones.
4Coder	A non-real-time encoder for IPTV and enterprise applications.
4View	An MPEG-4 decoder for PAL and NTSC video.
4Sight	MPEG-4 and H.264 streaming server for broadcast and broadband applications.

B-1 Particularly Interesting Envivio Products (Continued)

Product	Description
4Front	A platform for deploying MPEG-4 BIFS packages via an integral EG and service-management portal.
4Mation	MPEG-4 BIFS editing tools for authoring interactive MPEG-4 content.
4Manager	Software-driven, real-time control server for managing multiple encoder and streaming-server systems at an IPTV head-end.

B.7 Hamlet

Hamlet makes a variety of useful monitoring tools. The most intriguing is a palm-top waveform monitor that is small enough to carry around in your toolkit for diagnosing problems in the field.

B.8 Leivio Technologies

Leivio is an example of how the compression industry is attracting both small and large companies. Make sure to look at the smaller companies' offerings. Sometimes they have some innovative features that may be useful, and they are often very cost-effective. Leivio is just such a company that builds a no-frills product that simply does what it says on the box.

B.9 Optibase

The Optibase Moviemaker 200S is a plug-in card that works with Power Mac G5 systems running Mac OS. It is designed to encode MPEG-1 and MPEG-2 for DVD, SVCD, and VCD products. The encoding is good up to 10 Mbps with remote control of the source VTR and Dolby Digital audio pass-through. This card also supports variable bit-rate encoding and scene detection.

The MovieMaker 400 is an alternative, higher-spec unit for encoding MPEG-4 content and currently only works with the Windows operating system.

B.10 Skymicro

This manufacturer produces the Merlin05 plug-in PCI card that handles hardware compression. Currently it encodes and decodes MPEG-2 and DV and is supported on Windows, Linux, Irix, Solaris, and Mac OS X.

B.11 Snell & Wilcox

The Snell & Wilcox group supplies a wide range of hardware for broadcast and professional use. Of particular interest is its new range of standards-conversion and restoration hardware based on its Alchemist and Archangel Ph.C architecture. Demonstrations of this system showed some remarkable ability to restore old footage. Very badly damaged material was rendered usable again with the following artifacts being dealt with very effectively:

- Grain
- Scratches
- Flicker
- Gate weave
- Dropouts

The reasonable cost of the system as well as the processing speed mean that footage that would not previously have merited restoration can be processed and presented in a form that is possibly better even than when it was shot.

This system is designed to cope with 525- and 625-line originated content and is relevant to organizations with a large amount of archived material to process.

B.12   Tektronix

The range and scope of products available from Tektronix have always been very large. Test signal generation, monitoring, and processing systems are all available. Tektronix also provides a lot of useful white papers covering the technical aspects of digital TV systems.

B.13   Thomson

The Grass Valley ViBE encoder will create MPEG-4 output and is designed to offer reliable bandwidth management.. This targets it at the broadcast end of the business where it might be installed as part of a head-end feeding a digital TV service.

B.14   VBrick Systems

VBrick Systems has been developing encoder products for some time. The company supplies MPEG-2 and MPEG-4 encoders that operate at a variety of standards and resolutions.

B.15   ViewCast (Osprey and Niagra)

The ViewCast Osprey video cards have been used with Windows-based video systems for some years now. RealNetworks endorses them and provides a sales outlet to use them as part of the RealVideo encoding systems. The Osprey 100 is a low-cost PCI card that works with most Windows operating system variants. For more professional systems, the Osprey 500 may be more suitable.

Viewcast also make the SCX software and the Niagra encoder hardware systems. These provide encoder management and storage for the encoded video.

B.16 Supplier Contact Details

Table B-2 summarizes the contact details for a selection of suppliers you might find helpful.

B-2 Hardware Encoder Suppliers

Company	*URL*
ADC Telecommunications:	http://www.adc.com/
AJA:	http://www.aja.com/
Belkin:	http://world.belkin.com/
Blackmagic Design:	http://www.blackmagic-design.com/
Digital Rapids:	http://www.digital-rapids.com/
Envivio:	http://www.envivio.com/
Hamlet:	http://www.hamlet.co.uk/
Hitachi High-Technologies America:	http://www.hitachi-hta.com/
Hitachi:	http://www.hitachi.com/
JVC:	http://www.jvc.com/
Leivio:	http://www.leivio.com/
Mitsubishi TV:	http://www.mitsubishi-tv.com/
Optibase:	http://www.optibase.com/
Panasonic:	http://www.panasonic.com/
Pixelmetrix:	http://www.pixelmetrix.com/index.shtml
RCA:	http://www.rca.com/
Sanyo:	http://www.sanyo.com/
Skymicro:	http://www.skymicro.com/
Snell & Wilcox:	http://www.snellwilcox.com/
Sony Professional:	http://bssc.sel.sony.com/Professional/ startpage.html
Tandberg:	http://www.tandbergtv.com/
Tektronix:	http://www.Tektronix.com/video
Thomson/Grass Valley:	http://www.thomsongrassvalley.com/
VBrick:	http://www.vbrick.com/
ViewCast Niagra:	http://www.viewcast.com/
Viewcast Osprey Video:	http://www.viewcast.com/products/ osprey.html

C

Software Suppliers

C.1 Software Encoder Suppliers

This list is compiled from research done at several IBC and NAB conferences as well as news of product updates and releases. The listings are not exhaustive, of course. (A few companies whose products are particularly interesting are discussed in some detail in Chapter 30.) They are arranged in alphabetical order here so as not to imply any special preference. There is no need to describe the well-known companies, but here is a list of most well known, followed by more detailed descriptions of the other software suppliers.

- AVID
- Fast
- Apple QuickTime
- Microsoft
- Real Networks
- Discreet
- Sorenson
- Popwire Technology
- Telestream

C.2 For Linux Users

Much of what goes on with video on the Linux operating system is the result of a community of hard-working enthusiasts pooling their efforts for everyone's mutual benefit. We are starting to see some interest from manufacturers, with a few products being delivered on the Linux platform in addition to Windows and Mac OS.

Many of these tools work from the command line, and this provides a way to build automated workflows since you can easily wrap command-line functionality in shell scripts.

If you want to build a Linux-based system, then check out the following:

- Karl Beckers' xvidcap application.
- The gui driven version of xvidcap is gvidcap.

- The ffmpeg toolkit, which is available for all platforms you are likely to need it on.
- Arne Schirmacher's Kino application for Firewire DV input and editing.
- The dvgrab command line tool for Firewire DV input.

There are many other useful links and resources available at Arne Schirmacher's Linux DV web site. See the list of URLs at the end of this appendix for details.

C.3 Adobe

You will very likely purchase and install some Adobe software. The company's products are all good, reliable, and robust. These days some items are not as widely supported as they used to be, but this shouldn't cause you any problems because, for example, on a Mac OS system you will probably be using Final Cut (Pro or Express) instead of Premier anyway. That's probably why Adobe discontinued support for Premier on the Mac. On Windows, you have a large variety of alternatives to choose from.

Table C-1 Adobe Software Products

Product	Description	Platforms
After Effects	Useful as a power tool for special effects and key frame-based restoration jobs	Mac OS and Windows
Photoshop	Image touch-up and title generation	Mac OS and Windows
Encore	DVD authoring.	Windows only
Illustrator	Title generation, diagram and information-page creation	Mac OS and Windows
Premier	Video editing	Windows only

C.4 Canopus (ProCoder)

This is a compression framework application much like Squeeze or Cleaner. ProCoder is only available on Windows but is a competent alternative and functionally similar. The application implements watch folders and supports a variety of popular input and output formats.

The Canopus company has been supplying encoding software for some years. During 2004, the ProCoder Station software was launched; this adds batch coding and workflow control. This is not a cheap solution by any means, but it is designed to fit into a networked architecture and be shared by many users.

The transcoding capabilities are similar to those provided by the Telestream Flip Factory product. ProCoder Station is aimed at the professional and the medium- to large-sized organization.

Although the ProCoder software and ProCoder Station only work on Windows, because the workflow mechanisms are also able to receive input files via FTP, they can be integrated with workflows that are built on Mac OS X and use Final Cut Pro.

C.5 Dicas

Dicas offers a range of plug-ins and encoders that work on the Windows platform. The company focuses on H.264 presentation and has products that work with Direct Show APIs. The DS Suite offers support for MPEG-4, 3GPP, and AVC (H.264). Interestingly, you can buy just those modules that you need, which can help you save on cost.

C.6 HipFlics

The manufacturers of the LiveStage application for manipulating wired QuickTime movies develop this. HipFlics is designed to be simple to use and to exploit the coding capabilities built into QuickTime.

C.7 Nero Digital

The Nero Digital encoder supports the MPEG-4 Part 2 video encoder and also supports H.264. The audio is processed using High-Efficiency AAC. This encoder can be installed on a PC operating system or embedded into an encoder/decoder chipset.

C.8 ViewCast

ViewCast manufactures the Niagra SCX software, which is useful for controlling a suite of Osprey-based streaming-video encoders in a RealNetworks video-encoder farm. This software is bundled with the Niagra encoder hardware system.

C.9 Vitec

Vitec Multimedia manufactures MPEG encoding and decoding solutions as well as other ancillary tools.

C.10 Supplier Contact Details

Table C-2 summarizes the contact details for a selection of suppliers and software applications that you may find helpful.

Table C-2 Software and Suppliers

Company	URL
3ivX:	http://www.3ivx.com/
AcuLearn:	http://www.aculearn.com/
Adobe:	http://www.adobe.com/
ADS Technologies:	http://www.adstech.com/
AIST:	http://www.aist.com/
Akamai:	http://www.akamai.com/
Anystream, Inc:	http://www.anystream.com/
Apple:	http://www.apple.com/
Asf Tools:	http://www.geocities.com/myasftools/
Atrium Communications Ltd:	http://www.atriumcom.com/dotnet/atrium/netscape/welcome.htm
AVI Joiner:	http://www.hitsquad.com/smm/programs/AVIJoiner/
Avid:	http://www.avid.com/
BIAS:	http://www.bias-inc.com/
Bitvice:	http://www.innobits.se/
Boris fx:	http://www.borisfx.com/
Canopus (Pro Coder):	http://www.canopus-uk.com/
Dicas:	http://www.mpegable.com/
Discreet (Cleaner):	http://www.discreet.com/
DivX:	http://www.divx.com/
DropDV:	http://www.dropdv.com/
dvgrab:	http://kino.schirmacher.de/article/view/78/1/7/
FFmpeg:	http://ffmpeg.sourceforge.net/index.php
Forbidden Technologies:	http://www.forbidden.co.uk/
Fraunhofer H.264 reference software:	http://iphome.hhi.de/suehring/tml/download/
gvidcap:	http://rpmfind.net/linux/rpm2html/search.php?query=gvidcap
Harmonic Inc:	http://www.harmonicinc.com/
HipFlics:	http://www.totallyhip.com/hipflics.asp
Huelix Solutions Pte. Ltd Ltd ScreenPlay:	http://screenplay.huelix.com/
ImageMind Software:	http://www.imagemind.com/
Inlet Technologies, Inc:	http://inlethd.com/

Table C-2 Software and Suppliers (Continued)

Company	*URL*
InterMedia Solutions:	http://www.intermedia-solutions.net/
IPS Ltd:	http://www.iplockdown.net/
iStablize:	http://www.istabilize.de/
iVCD:	http://www.mireth.com/pub/ivme.html
iVideo:	http://www.waterfallsw.com/ivideo/
Kasenna:	http://www.kasenna.com/
Kino:	http://kino.schirmacher.de/
LiveChannel Pro:	http://www.channelstorm.com/
Microsoft:	http://www.ltimate.com/windows/windowsmedia/
Nero Digital:	http://www.nero.com/
OPTX International:	http://www.screenwatch.com/
Pegasys TMPGEnc:	http://www.pegasys-inc.com/en/product/
Pinnacle Systems:	http://www.pinnaclesys.com/
Popwire Technology:	http://www.popwire.com/
Re:Vision Effects:	http://www.revisionfx.com/
Real Networks:	http://www.real.com/
Red Giant:	http://www.redgiantsoftware.com/
Scientific-Atlanta:	http://www.sciatl.com/
Scopus:	http://www.webcamsoft.com/en/en-index.html
Sorenson (Squeeze):	http://www.ltimate.com/
Tandberg TV:	http://www.tandbergtv.com/
TechSmith Corporation:	http://www.techsmith.com/
Telestream:	http://www.telestream.net/
Ulead:	http://www.ulead.com/
Ultimatte:	http://www.ltimate.com/
VideoLAN (VLC):	http://www.videolan.org/
Virage, Inc:	http://beta-www.virage.com/index.html
Vitec:	http://www.vitecmm.com/
Vqual:	http://www.vqual.biz/
Webcam Corp:	http://www.webcamsoft.com/en/en-index.html
Winnov:	http://www.winnov.com/
Wirecast:	http:///varasoftware.com/
xvidcap:	http://xvidcap.sourceforge.net/

Film Stock Sizes

D.1 Summary of Nominal Characteristics

Table D-1 is a summary of the nominal characteristics of some popular film formats.

Table D-1 Properties of Popular Film Sizes

Format	Width	Height	Aspect ratio	Pix-W	Pix-H	Mbytes per frame	Mbytes per sec	Gbytes per hour
IMAX	69.6mm	48.5mm	1.43:1	8004	5578	127.72	3065.34	10777
IMAX Dome	69.6mm	50.3mm	1.38:1	8004	5785	132.46	3179.11	11177
Todd AO	52.6mm	23.0mm	2.2:1	6049	2645	45.78	1098.61	3862
Std 70mm	48.5mm	22.1mm	2.2:1	5578	2542	40.56	973.33	3422
VistaVision	37.7mm	25.2mm	1.5:1	4336	2898	35.95	862.72	3033
Cinerama	3×27.6mm	25.0mm	2.72:1	3174	2875	26.11	626.58	2203
CinemaScope (wide)	23.2mm	18.2mm	2.55:1	2668	2093	15.98	383.43	1348
CinemaScope	22.8mm	18.2mm	2.35:1	2622	2093	15.70	376.82	1325
Panavision	21.3mm	18.2mm	2.35:1	2450	2093	14.67	352.03	1238
Std 35mm	21.0mm	15.2mm	1.38:1	2415	1748	12.08	289.86	1019
Std 16mm	9.65mm	7.21mm	1.34:1	1110	829	2.63	63.18	222
Pathé 9.5mm	8.5mm	6.4mm	1.33:1	978	736	0.72	12.36	44
Super 8mm	5.5mm	4.0mm	1.36:1	633	460	0.83	19.98	70
Std 8mm	4.6mm	3.4mm	1.36:1	529	391	0.59	14.20	50

Note:

- The width and height in the table above are quoted in pixels.
- Cinerama simultaneously projects three pictures that must be carefully synchronized. Stitching these together digitally will yield a better result than scanning an optically combined sub-master. The optical combination process results in two lighter bands down the screen where the segments join.
- Normal TV aspect ratio of 4:3 can be represented as 1.33:1 to compare it with the above film formats.
- Wide-screen TV aspect ratio of 16:9 can be represented as 1.78:1 to compare it with the above film formats.
- Maximum practical scanning resolution is assumed to be 115 pixels per mm based on published details of an 8K scanning system for IMAX format. This equates to 2921 pixels per inch. Scanning resolutions actually vary widely according to film size, grain size, and the age of the stock being scanned. Film scanners typically operate at 2K, 4K, and 6K nominal resolution across the frame, with the vertical resolution depending on the aspect ratio.
- Although the computations for bit rate are based on 24 frames per second (fps), consumer film is also used at 18 fps to conserve footage and increase running times.
- The bit rate per second and per hour is for uncompressed data scanned at the highest practical resolution.
- The bit rates for Pathé 9.5 are based on calculations for monochrome pictures. Very little color stock (if any) was available when this format was popular in the first half of the 20th century.
- Authoritative figures for the sound synchronization offset and the audio bandwidth are not available at this time.
- More information is available at the Film Center web site.

Film Center: http://www.film-center.com/formats.html

Video Raster Sizes

E.1 Summary of Nominal Characteristics

Table E-1 is a summary of the nominal characteristics of some popular video formats. A few of these are included for historical reasons and others are in the process of being introduced.

Some estimates of pixel resolution are offered, and these are based on best possible quality. Your resolvable detail could be lower than some of these values. Define a baseline around your own system and your observed quality in order to compute the exact storage capacities. It is OK to overestimate the storage required, and these figures should be accurate enough for most capacity-planning needs.

Note:

- Although PAL is noted as having 576 lines, some documents state that it has 574. You should inspect your source material to establish which it is. If necessary, add or crop pairs of lines at the top and bottom to adjust to your requirements.
- Interlaced services have a half line at the bottom of each field in order to reposition the next scan in between the lines of the previous one. That may explain the missing 2 lines, since 576-line rasters could be constructed from 574 full lines plus 2 half lines.
- The 405-line service was only monochrome, so there is no color information to code in the output. That is why it requires far less bit rate than expected.
- The values used for pixel resolution are non-square for visible and nominal equivalents for the physical raster value. Sampling frequency and therefore resolution in the horizontal axis may vary considerably from one application to another. The noted values are commonly used, but you may use other values for different pixel aspect ratios if there are parameter settings available for them in your compression system.

Film specifications: http://www.camerasunderwater.co.uk/web—site/info—/Technical.html

Interlace: http://broadcastengineering.com/ar/broadcasting_understanding_interlace/

Table E-1 Video Raster Sizes

System	Vis W	Vis H	Aspect ratio	Raster W	Raster H	Scanning	Fps	Mbytes/ frame	Mbytes/ sec	Gbytes/ hr
405i25	400	380	4:3	500	405	Interlaced	25	0.14	3.62	12.74
525i30	720	480	4:3	780	525	Interlaced	29.97	0.99	29.63	104.18
625i25	720	576	4:3	864	625	Interlaced	25	1.19	29.66	104.28
625i25 Wide	720	576	16:9	864	625	Interlaced	25	1.19	29.66	104.28
720p60	1280	720	16:9	1650	750	Progressive	60	2.64	158.20	556.18
1035i30	1920	1035	17:9	2200	1125	Interlaced	30	5.69	170.56	599.63
1080i30	1920	1080	16:9	2200	1125	Interlaced	30	5.93	177.98	625.71
1080p60	1920	1080	16:9	2200	1125	Progressive	60	5.93	355.96	1251.41
1080p30	1920	1080	16:9	2200	1125	Progressive	30	5.93	177.98	625.71
1080i25	1920	1080	16:9	2640	1125	Interlaced	25	5.93	148.32	521.42
1080p25	1920	1080	16:9	2640	1125	Progressive	25	5.93	148.32	521.42
1080p24	1920	1080	16:9	2750	1125	Progressive	24	5.93	142.38	500.56

MPEG-2 Profiles and Levels

F.1 MPEG-2 Complexity

MPEG-2 is simplified by defining a set of profiles and levels that help to constrain the tools that encode and decode MPEG-2 content. This helps decoder manufacturers build products that handle a defined level of functionality. The encoder manufacturers then have a clear target and some bounded limits within which their bit-stream creation can be engineered.

F.2 MPEG-2 Profiles

Table F-1 lists the profiles that are defined for MPEG-2:

F-1 MPEG-2 Profiles

Profile	Description
Simple (SP)	A very simple profile that does not support B-frames, thereby allowing decoders to be stripped down to the bare essentials for implementation in low-cost hardware.
Main (MP)	Most of the consumer-oriented work is done with this profile.
4:2:2 (422P)	This is being standardized by SMPTE for use in studio situations.
SNR	Separate base and enhancement layers provide a moderate-quality base signal and a low noise output when both are combined. Transmitters modulate the two signals at different power levels to gain a further reach for the base signal. Fringe reception areas will see the base signal but may not be able to pick up the enhancement layer because the signal level will be too weak.
Spatial (SPT)	Spatial transformations deliver base and enhancement layers at two resolutions.
High (HP)	Spatial transformations deliver base and enhancement layers at two resolutions but at higher bandwidths.
Multi-view (MVP)	A special coding mechanism for stereoscopic film; it has two separate streams, one for each eye.

F.3 MPEG-2 Levels

Table F-2 lists the level that are defined for MPEG-2:

F-2 MPEG-2 Levels

Level	Size
Low (LL)	352 × 288 pixels
Main (ML)	720 × 576 pixels (approx)
High 1440 (H14)	1440 × 1152 pixels (normal aspect ratio)
High (HL)	1920 × 1152 pixels (wide aspect ratio)

Note:

- The SNR, Spatial, High, and Multi-view profiles are not relevant to video production and therefore you will not encounter them very often when compressing video.
- MPEG-2 is not very useful for Internet delivery.
- Within these profiles, the levels define raster sizes.

F.4 Profiles and Levels Combined

A shorthand notation is used to describe these combinations. The abbreviated names for profile and level are separated by an @ character. Of the 24 possible combinations, only the following ones are defined as ueable at present:

F-3 Profiles and Levels

Level	Simple	Main	SNR	Spatial	High	4:2:2
Low		MP@LL	SNR@LL			
Main	SP@ML	MP@ML	SNR@ML		HP@ML	422P@ML
High 1440		MP@H14		SPT@H14	HP@H14	
High		MP@HL			HP@HL	422P@HL

Mapping these together we get raster sizes and bit rates, as described in Table F-4.

F-4 Profile and Level Properties

Profile	Level	Abbreviation	Width	Height	Color	Bit rate	Fps
Simple	Main	SP@ML	720	576	4:2:0	15 Mbps	60i/30p
Main	Low	MP@LL	352	288	4:2:0	4 Mbps	60i/30p
Main	Main	MP@ML	720	576	4:2:0	15 Mbps	60i/30p
Main	High 1440	MP@H14	1440	1152	4:2:0	60 Mbps	60p
Main	High	MP@HL	1920	1152	4:2:0	90 Mbps	60p
SNR	Low	SNR@LL	352	288	4:2:0	4 Mbps	60i/30p
SNR	Main	SNR@ML	720	576	4:2:0	15 Mbps	60i/30p
Spatial	High 1440 (base layer)	SPT@H14	720	576	4:2:0	8 Mbps	60i/30p
Spatial	High 1440 (enhance-ment layer)	SPT@H14	1440	1152	4:2:0	60 Mbps	60p
High	Main (base layer)	HP@ML	352	288	4:2:0 or 4:2:2	2 Mbps	60i/30p
High	High 1440 (base layer)	HP@H14	720	576	4:2:0 or 4:2:2	10 Mbps	60i/30p
High	High (base layer)	HP@HL	960	576	4:2:0 or 4:2:2	13 Mbps	60i/30p
High	Main (enhance-ment layer)	HP@ML	720	576	4:2:0 or 4:2:2	20 Mbps	60i/30p
High	High 1440 (enhance-ment layer)	HP@H14	1440	1152	4:2:0 or 4:2:2	80 Mbps	60p
High	High (enhance-ment layer)	HP@HL	1920	1152	4:2:0 or 4:2:2	100 Mbps	60p
4:2:2	Main (1)	422P@ML	720	576	4:2:2	50 Mbps	60i/30p
4:2:2	Main (2)	422P@ML	720	608	4:2:2	55 Mbps	60i/30p
4:2:2	High	422P@HL	1920	1152	4:2:2	400 Mbps	60p

Note:

- SP@ML does not support B-frames.
- The 4:2:2 profile @ High level (422P@HL) is standardized by SMPTE and not by MPEG.
- The Main Profile at Main Level (MP@ML) is relevant for SDTV distribution and DVD disks at bit rates between 2 Mbps and 6 Mbps.
- The Main Profile at High Level (MP@HL) is relevant to HDTV distribution at 20 Mbps.
- The other profiles are not relevant to TV but may be useful for other application projects.
- Profile/level combinations other than MP@ML and MP@HL are likely to be superseded very soon by the H.264 codec.

F.5   MPEG-1 Constrained-Parameters Bit Stream

This is sometimes tabulated with profiles as MPEG-1 (CPB). It represents an MPEG-1 constrained-parameters bit stream, which must also be supported by MPEG-2 decoders. When it is also combined with level definitions, it describes a raster size of 768×576 at 30 Hz delivered at a bit rate of 1.856 Mbps.

G

MPEG-4 Profiles and Levels

G.1 MPEG-4 Complexity

MPEG-4 is far more complex than earlier video codecs. Indeed, the video coding is expressed only in Parts 2 and 10 of the standard, and these describe two completely separate codecs. First, let's summarize the component parts in MPEG-4. After that, we will examine the profiles and levels defined for MPEG-4 Part 2. These are many and complex. The H.264 standards group defines a rather smaller set and hence the MPEG-4 Part 10 coding is also simpler. Those will be described separately from MPEG-4 Part 2.

Profiles are intended to define a set of tools that are available, and levels define the range of appropriate values for the properties associated with them.

G.2 MPEG-4 Parts 1 to 21 with Amendments

Table G-1 is an outline of the different component parts and amendments of the MPEG-4 standard. New items are occasionally added to this list and it has grown somewhat during the time this book was being prepared. The amendments are included as child items of each part. Some amendments have been omitted since they are not listed on the ISO web site and therefore are not available at this time. There are also corrigenda to the standards, which have been omitted.

Table G-1 MPEG-4 Parts and Amendments

Part	Amendment	Description
1		Systems layer that defines scene descriptions, multiplexing, synchronization, buffering, and intellectual property protection.
	1	Extended BIFS.
	3	Intellectual Property Management and Protection (IPMP) extensions.
	4	SL extensions and AFX streams.
	7	Use of AVC (Advanced Video Coding) in MPEG-4 systems.

Continued

Table G-1 MPEG-4 Parts and Amendments (Continued)

Part	Amendment	Description
	8	New Object Type Indication code points.
2		Description of natural and synthetic visual components. This is the successor to MPEG-2.
	1	Error-resilient, simple scalable profile.
3		Description of natural and synthetic audio components.
	1	Bandwidth extension.
	2	Parametric coding for high-quality audio.
	3	MP3 on MP4.
4		Conformance testing for bit streams and devices.
	1	Conformance testing for MPEG-4.
	2	MPEG-4 conformance extensions for XMT and media nodes.
	3	Visual—new levels and tools.
	4	IPMPX conformance extensions.
	5	Conformance extensions for error-resilient, simple scalable profile.
	6	Advanced Video Coding conformance.
	7	AFX conformance extensions.
5		Reference software examples.
	1	Reference software for MPEG-4.
	2	MPEG-4 reference software extensions for XMT and media nodes.
	3	Visual—new levels and tools.
	4	IPMPX reference software extensions.
	5	Reference software extensions for error-resilient, simple scalable profile.
	6	Advanced Video Coding and audio SBR reference software.
	7	AFX reference software extensions.
6		The Delivery Multimedia Integration Framework (DMIF), which describes a session protocol for carriage of components over generic interfaces.
7		Optimized visual reference software.
8		Carriage of MPEG-4 components over IP networks.
9		Reference hardware specifications.
10		Advanced Video Coding (H.264).
	1	AVC professional extensions to add transparency.
11		Scene description and application engine (breaking BIFS out of Part 1).

Table G-1 MPEG-4 Parts and Amendments (Continued)

Part	Amendment	Description
	2	Advanced text and 2D graphics.
	3	Audio BIFS extensions.
	4	XMT and MPEG-J extensions.
12		ISO base media-file format.
	1	File format extensions and guidelines.
13		Intellectual Property Management and Protection (IPMP) extensions.
14		MP4 file format.
15		Advanced Video Coding (AVC) file format.
16		Animation Framework eXtension (AFX).
17		Streaming text format.
18		Font compression and streaming.
19		Synthesized texture stream.
20		Lightweight Application Scene Representation
21		MPEG-J Extension for rendering

Many implementers are only considering a few parts and not all the available capabilities that the standard defines. To implement the entire standard would be a major challenge for any company.

G.3 MPEG-4 Part 2 Profiles and Levels

Note that we are only discussing the visual profiles. MPEG-4 also supports other profiles for audio, graphics, and scene graphs. These are beyond the scope of our discussions on video compression. They will be of interest to content producers who are aggregating compressed video with other asset types to create interactive multimedia presentations.

G.3.1 Natural Visual Profiles

These profiles describe video that has been filmed or is based on what we normally think of as a frame-based video session.

Table G-2 MPEG-4 Part 2 Natural Visual Profiles

Profile	Description
Simple	Straightforward encoding of rectangular content at low bit rates for use on mobile systems.
Simple Scalable	Provides additional support for multiple quality streams being delivered simultaneously and allows for spatial and temporal scaling.
Advanced Simple (v2a)	An additional simple profile with extra features for 2D support.
Fine Granularity Scalable (v2a)	An enhanced scalable profile with support for 2D structures.
Advanced Real-Time Simple (v2)	Provides additional coding supported by messages received from the player so as to code in real time for videophone applications.
Core	Adds arbitrarily shaped video objects to the Simple profile and is aimed at more interactive scenarios.
Core Scalable (v2)	Allows regions of the object to be scaled spatially, temporally, and with the SNR scaling described in MPEG-2.
Main	Interlaced video support, sprites, and transparency of objects are added to the Core profile.
N-Bit	Where the video may have unusually low or high bit depths, this profile adds 4 to 12-bit video support to the Core profile.
Advanced Coding Efficiency (v2)	Very efficient coding support for acquisition devices such as cameras, scanners, and video digitizers.
Simple Studio	Designed for use in studio environments.
Core Studio	Designed for higher-quality production use.

G.3.2 Synthetic Visual Profiles

The synthetic video profiles support more structured descriptions of the moving images. These will be useful in the future but are not considered in the discussions on encoding normal linear video.

Table G-3 MPEG-4 Part 2 Synthetic Visual Profiles

Profile	Description
Simple Facial Animation	Provides all the information that is needed to construct a simple facial model, perhaps to implement an avatar.
Simple Face and Body Animation (v2)	Facial animation plus additional support for bodies.

Table G-3 MPEG-4 Part 2 Synthetic Visual Profiles (Continued)

Profile	Description
Scalable Texture	Supports the mapping of static image textures onto surfaces.
Basic Animated 2D Texture	Provides scalability for Spatial and SNR coding and mesh-based animation of still images texture-mapped onto object surfaces. Basic facial animation is also supported.
Advanced Scalable Texture (v2)	Very efficient still-image compression. Also adds tiled objects, wavelet coding, arbitrary shapes, and scalability.
Advanced Core (v2)	A combination of Core Visual and Advanced Scalable Texture Synthetic Visual profiles. Very appropriate for network-connected interactivity and multimedia.
Hybrid	Designed to support rich-media applications as well as arbitrary shapes, temporal scaling of video objects, and some synthetic-object support.

G.3.3 Levels

The profile and level descriptions have been simplified somewhat for MPEG-4, just to describe the video attributes that are important to us when encoding footage for use in a target profile and level. There are almost 20 columns of information defined against each level for each profile but much of that is only of interest to the codec implementer or when constructing multiple video-object scenarios.

Table G-4 MPEG-4 Part 2 Levels and Profiles

Profile	Level	Width	Height	Color	Max bit rate	Fps
Simple	L0	176	144		64 Kbps	15p
Simple	L1	176	144		64 Kbps	15p
Simple	L2	352	288		128 Kbps	15p
Simple	L3	352	288		384 Kbps	30p
Simple Scalable	L1	352	288		128 Kbps	15p
Simple Scalable	L2	352	288		256 Kbps	30p
Advanced Simple	L0	176	144		128 Kbps	60p
Advanced Simple	L1	176	144		128 Kbps	60p
Advanced Simple	L2	352	288		384 Kbps	40p
Advanced Simple	L3	352	288		768 Kbps	60p
Advanced Simple	L3b	352	288		768 Kbps	60p
Advanced Simple	L4	352	576		3000 Kbps	60i/30p

Continued

Table G-4 MPEG-4 Part 2 Levels and Profiles (Continued)

Profile	Level	Width	Height	Color	Max bit rate	Fps
Advanced Simple	L5	720	576		8000 Kbps	60i/30p
Fine Granularity Scalability	L0	176	144		128 Kbps	60p
Fine Granularity Scalability	L1	176	144		128 Kbps	60p
Fine Granularity Scalability	L2	352	288		384 Kbps	40p
Fine Granularity Scalability	L3	352	288		768 Kbps	60p
Fine Granularity Scalability	L4	352	576		3000 Kbps	60i/30p
Fine Granularity Scalability	L5	720	576		8000 Kbps	60i/30p
Advanced Real-Time Simple	L1	176	144		64 Kbps	15p
Advanced Real-Time Simple	L2	352	288		128 Kbps	15p
Advanced Real-Time Simple	L3	352	288		384 Kbps	30p
Advanced Real-Time Simple Natural	L4	352	288		2000 Kbps	30p
Core	L1	176	144		384 Kbps	60p
Core	L2	352	288		2000 Kbps	60p
Core Scalable	L1	352	288		768 Kbps	30p
Core Scalable	L2	352	288		1500 Kbps	60p
Core Scalable	L3	720	576		4000 Kbps	60i/30p
Main	L2	352	288		2000 Kbps	60p
Main	L3	720	576		15000 Kbps	60i/30p
Main	L4	1920	1088		38400 Kbps	60p
N-Bit	L2	352	288		2000 Kbps	60p
Advanced Coding Efficiency	L1	352	288		384 Kbps	30p
Advanced Coding Efficiency	L2	352	288		2000 Kbps	60p
Advanced Coding Efficiency	L3	720	576		15000 Kbps	60p
Advanced Coding Efficiency	L4	1920	1088		38400 Kbps	60p
Simple Studio	L1	720	576	YUV + alpha	180 Mbps	60i/30p
Simple Studio	L1	720	576	RGB	180 Mbps	60i/30p
Simple Studio	L2	720	576	YUV	600 Mbps	60i/30p
Simple Studio	L2	720	576	RGB + 3 alpha	600 Mbps	60i/30p
Simple Studio	L3	720	576	RGB	900 Mbps	60i/30p

Table G-4 MPEG-4 Part 2 Levels and Profiles (Continued)

Profile	Level	Width	Height	Color	Max bit rate	Fps
Simple Studio	L3	720	576	YUV + alpha	900 Mbps	60i/30p
Simple Studio	L4	720	576	RGB	1800 Mbps	60i/30p
Simple Studio	L4	720	576	RGB + 3 alpha	1800 Mbps	60i/30p
Simple Studio	L4	2000	2000	RGB	1800 Mbps	30p
Core Studio	L1	720	576	YUV + alpha	90 Mbps	60i/30p
Core Studio	L1	720	576	RGB	90 Mbps	60i/30p
Core Studio	L2	720	576	YUV	300 Mbps	60i/30p
Core Studio	L2	720	576	RGB + 3 alpha	300 Mbps	60i/30p
Core Studio	L3	720	576	RGB	450 Mbps	60i/30p
Core Studio	L3	720	576	YUV + alpha	450 Mbps	60i/30p
Core Studio	L4	720	576	RGB	900 Mbps	60i/30p
Core Studio	L4	720	576	RGB + 3 alpha	900 Mbps	60i/30p
Core Studio	L4	2000	2000	RGB	900 Mbps	30p

Note:

- Note that not all levels from L0 to L5 are supported in every profile.
- Level descriptions for profiles are omitted where they are inappropriate for compressed-video content. These are mainly the synthetic video profiles that support still images texture-mapped onto a mesh. These are not encoding video in the same way but describe render parameters so that a moving image can be reconstructed as an animation.
- The frame sizes, color models, and fps ratings should be taken as general guidelines and not descriptions of specific minimum or maximum values.
- The size of the video is determined by a limit on the number of macroblocks that can be used at a particular level.
- Color information is described only where relevant as a limiting parameter for the source content.
- Advanced Simple Natural Visual Profile and Fine Granularity Scalability Natural Visual Profile were introduced at the version 2 amendment for 2D support.

- Advanced Coding Efficiency, Core Scalable, and Advanced Real-Time Simple Natural Visual Profiles were introduced at version 2.
- Level 3b is introduced by a late-breaking amendment.

G.3.4 Levels and Macroblocks

The MPEG-4 specification does not dictate frame sizes in pixels. Because the video can be arbitrarily shaped, the limit is defined in terms of 16-× 16-pixel macroblocks, which can be presented in non-rectangular arrangements. Table G-5 summarizes these values for some profiles and levels.

Table G-5 Levels Versus Macroblocks

Profile	Level	Max macroblocks	Shape coding
Simple	0	99	
Simple	1	99	
Simple	2	396	
Simple	3	396	
Advanced Real-Time Simple	1	99	
Advanced Real-Time Simple	2	396	
Advanced Real-Time Simple	3	396	
Advanced Real-Time Simple	4	396	
Simple Scalable	1	495	
Simple Scalable	2	792	
Core	1	198	√
Core	2	792	√
Advanced Core	1	198	
Advanced Core	2	792	
Core Scalable	1	792	√
Core Scalable	2	990	√
Core Scalable	3	4032	√
Main	2	1188	√
Main	3	3240	√
Main	4	16320	√
Advanced Coding Efficiency	1	792	√
Advanced Coding Efficiency	2	1188	√

Table G-5 Levels Versus Macroblocks (Continued)

Profile	Level	Max macroblocks	Shape coding
Advanced Coding Efficiency	3	3240	√
Advanced Coding Efficiency	4	16320	√
N-Bit	2	792	√

Note:

- Level-0 video must not exceed 176 horizontal or 144 vertical.
- These values are important because they must fit within buffer sizes agreed on by the standards working group participants.
- Players' compliance with the standard requires that they have buffers of a particular size available.

G.4   MPEG-4 Audio Object Types

The MPEG-4 audio specifications describe a range of different algorithms that can be used to code the audio in the most appropriate and effective way. These are identified by short mnemonic names and ID-values that are embedded in the content stream. The decoder recognizes the algorithm that has been used to encode the audio and selects the correct decoder for it.

Table G.6 lists a selection of the Audio Object Types (AOTs) that are currently defined. Some of these are still under development and may not have been standardized yet.

Table G-6 Audio Object Types in MPEG-4

AOT	Description	ER
AAC main	The main Advanced Audio Coding algorithm.	
AAC LC	Low complexity.	√
AAC SSR	Scalable Sampling Rate.	
AAC LTP	Long-Term Predictor.	√
AAC SBR	Spectral Brand Replication. Used in HE-AAC (AAC+).	
AAC Scalable	Scalable coding.	√
TwinVQ	Transform-Domain Weighted Interleave Vector Quantization.	√
CELP	Code-Excited Linear Prediction. Used for speech coding. Also available in an error-resilient form.	√

Continued

Table G-6 Audio Object Types in MPEG-4 (Continued)

AOT	Description	ER
HVXC	Harmonic Vector XCitation.	√
HILN	Harmonics, individual lines, and noise. A parametric encoder.	
BSAC	Bit-Sliced Arithmetic Coding.	√
AAC LD	Low-Delay coding.	√
ULD	Ultra-Low Delay. This algorithm introduces only 6 milliseconds of delay. This makes it ideal for telecoms use or live production with wireless microphones.	

Most of these algorithms can be augmented with error-resilient support, in which case they would be prefaced with the letters ER and would be identified with a different ID value. These rows are flagged in the ER column of the table.

Some work on describing the complexity of the encoded data in a numeric way has been done. Processor Complexity Units have been defined for each of these object types in order to help plan the computing capacity required. You can find out more about this from the MPEG Industry Forum.

G.5   H.264 Profiles and Levels

By comparison with MPEG-4 Part 2, the H.264 codec has very few profiles. That does not mean it has fewer tools, just that there are fewer definitions of how they are made available in encoding applications. Table G-7 summarizes the profiles.

The support for levels includes 5 main levels and 10 other sub-levels. The 15 levels in total are available across all of the profiles.

Table G-7 H.264 (JVT) profiles

Profile	Description
Baseline	Low-latency applications such as videoconferencing.
Main	Designed for broadcasting use.
Extended	Previously known as Profile-X. This is designed for streaming applications.

G.5.1   Baseline Profile

This profile is designed to encode quickly, and as a consequence, no B-slices are permitted. Therefore, pictures can be transmitted in the same order as they are encoded and no delay is introduced. The following capabilities are supported:

- I-slices
- P-slices
- De-blocking filter on decode
- No field coding for interlacing
- No adaptive frame/field coding
- Quarter-pixel motion vectors
- Macroblock segmentation for temporal prediction
- Variable-length coding (CAVLC)
- CABAC not supported
- Arbitrary slice ordering
- Flexible macroblock ordering
- Redundant slices

G.5.2 Main Profile

This profile is designed to support broadcast-TV applications. Most of the baseline profile is supported, but a few items are omitted and a few new features are added. The main profile capabilities are the following:

- I-slices
- P-slices
- B-slices
- De-blocking filter on decode
- Field coding for interlacing
- Adaptive frame/field coding
- Weighted prediction to support bit-rate bursting on transitions
- Quarter-pixel motion vectors
- Macroblock segmentation for temporal prediction
- Variable-length coding (CAVLC)
- CABAC

G.5.3 Extended Profile

The extended profile is available for use when building streaming-video systems. It is a superset of the baseline profile with some additional features. It also includes most of the main profile capabilities. Here is a summary of what it supports:

- I-slices
- P-slices
- B-slices
- De-blocking filter on decode
- Field coding for interlacing
- Adaptive frame/field coding
- Weighted prediction to support bit-rate bursting on transitions

- Quarter-pixel motion vectors
- Macroblock segmentation for temporal prediction
- Variable-length coding (CAVLC)
- CABAC not supported
- Arbitrary slice ordering
- Flexible Macroblock ordering
- Redundant slices

ISMA Profiles

H.1 The Standards

The specifications are available on request from the ISMA web site. They comprise the following:

H.2 ISMA Version 2.0

The Internet Streaming Media Alliance has released the second generation of its specification. This integrates the latest streaming-media technologies. The version 2.0 specification improves on the existing ISMA version 1.0. It adds support for new codecs for mobile devices and high-definition TV (HDTV).

The new ISMA 2.0 specification supports the following features:

- Advanced Video Coding (H.264/AVC)
- High-Efficiency Advanced Audio Coding (HE-AAC)

H-1 ISMA Standards Documents

Document	Version	Date
ISMA Implementation Specification	version 1.0	August 2001
ISMA—Corrigenda to Implementation Specification	version 0.10	May 2004
ISMA Implementation Specification plus Corrigenda	version 1.0.1	June 2004
ISMA Encryption and Authentication Specification	version 1.0	February 2004
ISMA Implementation Specification revised draft	version 2.0	December 2004

ISMA organization: http://www.isma.tv/

ISMA organization alternate: http://www.ism-alliance.org/

Internet Engineering Task Force: http://www.ietf.org/

Motion Picture Experts Group: http://www.cselt.it/mpeg/

- IP Transport of audio and video using SDP and RTP/RTSP
- Storage in MPEG-4 file format (.mp4)

The ISMA 2.0 specification begins to look at open standards-based multimedia in the enterprise with these work items:

- Rich-media object synchronization
- Closed captioning
- Enterprise DRM
- Live server failover specification

H.3   ISMA 1.0 Profiles 0 and 1

The Internet Streaming Media Alliance (ISMA) was formed by a group of interested companies who wished to simplify the development of streaming services, servers, and players by defining some constraints on performance and bit-rate requirements. These address the optimal service levels for modem-delivered video, broadband-delivered video, and higher-bit-rate services on fast networks. The two profiles that have been published to date are compared in Table H-2.

The parameters specified by these profiles are carefully chosen to be practical, given the current technological capabilities. They are developed in consultation with other standards bodies. Note that the 3GPP mobile profile is substantially the same as ISMA profile 0 but is designed for mobile devices.

H-2 ISMA Version 1.0 Profiles

Attribute	Profile 0	Profile 1
Target	Narrowband and wireless applications.	Broadband. This is a superset of Profile 0 and allows a richer browsing experience.
Codec	MPEG-4 Part 2 video, Simple Profile, Level 1	MPEG-4 Part 2 video, Simple Profile, or Advanced Simple Profile, Level 3
Raster size	176 × 144 (QCIF)	352 × 288 (CIF)
Frame rate	15 fps	30 fps (assumed to mean 25 in Europe)
Audio	High-Quality Audio Profile at Level 2. CELP and low-complexity AAC.	High-Quality Audio Profile at Level 2. CELP and low-complexity AAC.
Sample rate	Up to 48 KHz	Up to 48 KHz
Max bit rate	64 Kbps	1.5 Mbps

For descriptions of what these profiles mean in detailed terms, you should consult the ISMA specifications.

H.4   ISMA 2.0 Profiles 2,3, and 4

The new version 2.0 ISMA standard adds three more profiles, which are summarized in table H-3.

H-3 ISMA Version2.0 Profiles

Attribute	Profile 2	Profile 3	Profile 4
Target	Low resolution video or audio only services.	Broadband. SDTV resolution video services.	Fast local area network, HDTV applications.
Codec	MPEG-4 Part 10 video, Baseline Profile, Level 2	MPEG-4 Part 10 video, Main Profile, Level 3	MPEG-4 Part 10 video, Main Profile, Level 3
Raster size	352×288 (CIF)	720×576 (D1-PAL)	1280×720 up to $2k \times 1k$
Frame rate	30 FPS	30 FPS (assumed to mean 25 in Europe)	30 FPS or 60 FPS ...at smaller picture sizes.
Audio	HE-AAC Audio Profile at Level 2.	AAC Audio Profile at Level 3.	AAC Audio Profile at Level 4.
Sample rate	Up to 48 KHz	Up to 48 KHz	Up to 48 KHz
Max bit rate	1.2 Mbps	3.7 Mbps	15 Mbps

File Types

I.1   File Types

Most operating systems distinguish between one file type and another by using a three- or four-letter file extension. Mac OS Classic used a four-letter code for type and creator properties, which were stored in the file metadata information. Both mechanisms are supported in Mac OS X. Windows uses file extensions to associate the file with an application, while Linux- and UNIX-based systems delegate the file-type recognition to the application-level software.

These file-mapping mechanisms are used by the operating system to run the appropriate application when the file is opened, although it is the shell or finder/explorer application that arbitrates this.

Table I-1 summarizes file extensions and the owner, codec, or service that they are associated with.

Table I-1 Video- and Audio-Related File Extensions

Extension	Description
.3g2	3GPP2 mobile phone video/audio
.3gp	3GPP mobile phone video/audio
.3gp2	3GPP2 mobile phone video/audio
.3gpp	3GPP mobile phone video/audio
.aaf	Advanced Authoring Format (used by MXF)
.aif	QuickTime Audio Interchange File Format
.aic	QuickTime Audio Interchange File Format (compressed)
.aifc	QuickTime Audio Interchange File Format (compressed)
.aiff	QuickTime Audio Interchange File Format
.amc	AMC Media File
.amr	AMR Audio File
.asf	Windows Media Advanced Systems Format file

Continued

Table I-1 Video- and Audio-Related File Extensions (Continued)

Extension	Description
.asx	Windows Media Advanced Stream Redirector metafile
.au	Sun and NeXT UNIX audio
.avi	Windows video format (Audio Visual Interleave)
.bwf	Windows WAVE audio format
.cda	CD Audio Track
.cdda	CD Audio Track
.cpk	Film format (as indicated by M-Player)
.dcr	Shockwave movie
.dir	Shockwave movie
.dvr-ms	Microsoft Media Center off-air TV Digital Video Recording file.
.dxr	Shockwave movie
.ev2	Emblaze video
.flc	AutoDesk Animator movie
.fli	AutoDesk Animator movie
.flv	Flash video file
.gsm	GSM Audio file
.hcm	Huffman compressed FSSD files
.hcom	Huffman compressed FSSD files
.iff	Amiga 8-bit audio files similar to .wav
.ivf	*Indeo* Video Technology
.jpg	JPEG image
.kar	MIDI music (Karaoke)
.m15	MPEG-1 media file
.m1a	MPEG-1 audio
.m1s	MPEG-1 audio
.m1v	MPEG-1 video
.m3u	MPEG media queue file often used as an Audio MP3 play list
.m4a	MPEG-4 audio (AAC)
.m4b	MPEG-4 iTunes audio (AAC audio book)
.m4p	MPEG-4 audio (AAC rights protected)
.m4v	MPEG-4 video (rights protected)
.m75	MPEG-1 media file

Table I-1 Video- and Audio-Related File Extensions (Continued)

Extension	Description
`.mid`	MIDI music
`.midi`	MIDI music
`.mii`	MIDI music
`.mod`	Amiga multi-channel audio file
`.mov`	QuickTime movie
`.mp1`	MPEG-1 Audio
`.mp2`	MPEG-1 Audio layer 2
`.mp3`	MPEG-1 Audio layer 3 (MP3 audio)
`.mp4`	MPEG-4 audio, video, and multimedia
`.mpa`	MPEG-1 Audio layer 2
`.mpe`	Moving Pictures Experts Group (MPEG)
`.mpeg`	MPEG-1 video or audio
`.mpg`	MPEG-1 video or audio
`.mpg4`	MPEG-4 audio, video, and multimedia
`.mpm`	MPEG-1 audio
`.mpv`	MPEG-2 video
`.mpv2`	MPEG-2 video
`.mxf`	Material exchange Format
`.png`	PNG image
`.prx`	Windows Media profile
`.qcp`	QUALCOMM PureVoice
`.qt`	QuickTime Version 1 & 2 file (deprecated)
`.qti`	QuickTime Image
`.qtif`	QuickTime Image
`.qtl`	YUV SECAM or PAL image
`.qtvr`	QuickTime VR panorama
`.ra`	Real Audio
`.raf`	Early Real Audio Format files
`.ram`	Real Audio Redirector metafile
`.raw`	Raw audio file (but might contain graphics instead)
`.rax`	Real Audio
`.rf`	Real Flash clip

Continued

Table I-1 Video- and Audio-Related File Extensions (Continued)

Extension	Description
.rif	Similar to .wav files (8 and 16-bit)
.riff	Similar to .wav files (8 and 16-bit)
.rm	Real Media
.rmd	Real Media
.rmi	Windows Media (MIDI)
.rmj	Real Media
.rmm	Real Media Redirector metafile
.rms	Real Media
.rmvb	Real Media
.rmx	Real Media
.rp	Real Pix streamed images
.rpm	Real Plug-in Redirector metafile
.rt	Real Text streamed captions
.rtsp	RTSP stream descriptor file
.rv	Real Video
.rvx	Real Video
.sami	Windows Media text format for captioning
.sb	Raw audio data
.sdp	SDP stream descriptor file
.sdv	SD video
.sf	IRCAM Sound file
.smf	MIDI music
.smi	Windows Media SMIL format for multimedia
.smil	SMIL multimedia
.smp	Turtle Creek Sample Vision file
.snd	Sun & NeXT UNIX audio
.sng	Legacy audio format
.spl	FutureSplash player
.ssw	Flash sealed media file
.sswf	Flash sealed media file
.sw	Signed word raw audio file
.swa	MPEG-1 Audio layer 3 (MP3 audio)
.swf	Shockwave Flash player

Table I-1 Video- and Audio-Related File Extensions (Continued)

Extension	Description
.ub	Unsigned byte raw audio file
.ul	Sun & NeXT UNIX μ-Law audio
.ulw	Sun & NeXT UNIX μ-Law audio
.vfw	Windows video format (Audio Visual Interleave)
.voc	SoundBlaster Creative Voice audio file
.wav	Windows WAVE audio format
.wave	Windows WAVE audio format
.wax	Windows Media Audio Redirector metafile
.weu	Windows Media Encoding configuration
.wm	Windows Media Video
.wma	Windows Media Audio
.wmd	Windows Media Download Package
.wme	Windows Media encoder session
.wmp	Windows Media
.wms	Windows Media Player skin
.wmv	Windows Media Video
.wmx	Windows Media Redirector metafile
.wmz	Windows Media Player skin
.wpl	Windows Media Playlist metafile
.wvx	Windows Media Video Redirector metafile

To find out more about file-type extensions, check out the file extensions web site.

I.2 MIME Types

The MIME-type values are used by the web server to instruct the web browser about the kind of media being downloaded. The web browser is then able to invoke the necessary helper application or plug-in to handle that kind of media.

Table I-2 summarizes the popular MIME types for AV content.

File extensions: http://filext.com/index.php

Table I-2 MIME Types for Popular Audio and Video Formats

Player	*Helper*	*File type*	*MIME type*
3GPP2 audio	Player	.3g2	audio/3gpp2
3GPP2 video	Player	.3g2	video/3gpp2
3GPP audio	Player	.3gp	audio/3gpp
3GPP video	Player	.3gp	video/3gpp
3GPP2 audio	Player	.3gp2	audio/3gpp2
3GPP2 video	Player	.3gp2	video/3gpp2
3GPP audio	Player	.3gpp	audio/3gpp
3GPP video	Player	.3gpp	video/3gpp
AIFF CD quality audio	Player	.aif	audio/aiff
AIFF audio	Browser	.aif	audio/x-aiff
AIFF audio	Player	.aifc	audio/aiff
AIFF audio	Browser	.aifc	audio/x-aiff
AIFF CD-quality audio	Player	.aiff	audio/aiff
AIFF audio	Browser	.aiff	audio/x-aiff
AMC media	Player	.amc	application/x-mpeg
AMR audio	Player	.amr	audio/amr
Windows Media	Browser	.asf	video/x-ms-asf
Windows Media	Browser	.asx	video/x-ms-asf
μ-Law/AU audio	Player	.au	audio/basic
Video for Windows (AVI)	Browser	.avi	video/avi
Video for Windows (AVI)	Browser	.avi	video/msvideo
Windows Video	Browser	.avi	video/x-msvideo
Video for Windows (AVI)	Browser	.avi	video/x-msvideo
WAVE audio	Browser	.bwf	audio/wav
WAVE audio	Browser	.bwf	audio/x-wav
AIFF audio	Player	.cdda	audio/aiff
AIFF audio	Browser	.cdda	audio/x-aiff
AutoDesk Animator (FLC)	Browser	.flc	video/flc
AutoDesk Animator (FLC)	Browser	.fli	video/flc
GSM audio	Browser	.gsm	audio/x-gsm
MIDI music	Browser	.kar	audio/mid
MIDI music	Browser	.kar	audio/midi

Table I-2 MIME Types for Popular Audio and Video Formats (Continued)

Player	Helper	File type	MIME type
MIDI music	Browser	.kar	audio/x-midi
MPEG media	Browser	.m15	video/mpeg
MPEG media	Browser	.m15	video/x-mpeg
MPEG audio	Browser	.m1a	audio/mpeg
MPEG audio	Browser	.m1a	audio/x-mpeg
MPEG media	Browser	.m1a	video/mpeg
MPEG media	Browser	.m1a	video/x-mpeg
MPEG audio	Browser	.m1s	audio/mpeg
MPEG audio	Browser	.m1s	audio/x-mpeg
MPEG media	Browser	.m1s	video/mpeg
MPEG media	Browser	.m1s	video/x-mpeg
MPEG media	Browser	.m1v	video/mpeg
MPEG media	Browser	.m1v	video/x-mpeg
AAC audio	Browser	.m4a	audio/x-m4a
AAC audio book	Browser	.m4b	audio/x-m4b
AAC audio (protected)	Browser	.m4p	audio/x-m4p
Video (protected)	Browser	.m4v	video/x-m4v
MPEG media	Browser	.m75	video/mpeg
MPEG media	Browser	.m75	video/x-mpeg
MIDI music	Browser	.mid	audio/mid
MIDI music	Browser	.mid	audio/midi
MIDI music	Browser	.mid	audio/x-midi
MIDI music	Browser	.midi	audio/mid
MIDI music	Browser	.midi	audio/midi
MIDI music	Browser	.midi	audio/x-midi
QuickTime Movie	Plug-in.	.mov	video/quicktime
MPEG audio	Browser	.mp2	audio/mpeg
MPEG audio	Browser	.mp2	audio/x-mpeg
MPEG video	Browser	.mp2	video/mpeg
MPEG media	Browser	.mp2	video/x-mpeg
MP3 audio	Player	.mp3	application/octet-stream
MP3 audio	Browser	.mp3	audio/mp3

Continued

Table I-2 MIME Types for Popular Audio and Video Formats (Continued)

Player	Helper	File type	MIME type
MPEG audio	Browser	.mp3	audio/mpeg
MP3 audio	Browser	.mp3	audio/mpeg3
MP3 audio	Browser	.mp3	audio/x-mp3
MPEG audio	Browser	.mp3	audio/x-mpeg
MP3 audio	Browser	.mp3	audio/x-mpeg3
MPEG-4 media	Browser	.mp4	audio/mp4
MPEG-4 media	Browser	.mp4	video/mp4
MPEG audio	Browser	.mpa	audio/mpeg
MPEG audio	Browser	.mpa	audio/x-mpeg
MPEG media	Browser	.mpa	video/mpeg
MPEG media	Browser	.mpa	video/x-mpeg
MPEG video	Browser	.mpe	video/mpeg
MPEG audio	Browser	.mpeg	audio/mpeg
MPEG audio	Browser	.mpeg	audio/x-mpeg
MPEG video	Browser	.mpeg	video/mpeg
MPEG media	Browser	.mpeg	video/x-mpeg
MPEG audio	Browser	.mpg	audio/mpeg
MPEG audio	Browser	.mpg	audio/x-mpeg
MPEG video	Browser	.mpg	video/mpeg
MPEG media	Browser	.mpg	video/x-mpeg
MPEG-4 media	Browser	.mpg4	audio/mp4
MPEG-4 media	Browser	.mpg4	video/mp4
MPEG audio	Browser	.mpm	audio/mpeg
MPEG audio	Browser	.mpm	audio/x-mpeg
MPEG media	Browser	.mpm	video/mpeg
MPEG media	Browser	.mpm	video/x-mpeg
MPEG media	Browser	.mpv	video/mpeg
MPEG media	Browser	.mpv	video/x-mpeg
QUALCOMM PureVoice audio	Browser	.qcp	audio/vnd.qcelp
QuickTime Movie	Plug-in.	.qt	video/quicktime
QuickTime	Player	.qtl	application/x-quicktimeplayer

Table I-2 MIME Types for Popular Audio and Video Formats (Continued)

Player	*Helper*	*File type*	*MIME type*
RealAudio	Browser	`.ra`	`audio/x-pn-realaudio`
Real Audio	Player	`.ra`	`audio/x-realaudio`
RealAudio	Player	`.ram`	`audio/vnd.rn-realaudio`
RealAudio	Browser	`.ram`	`audio/x-pn-realaudio`
Real Flash	Player	`.rf`	`image/vnd.rn-realflash`
Real Player	Player	`.rm`	`application/vnd.rn-realmedia`
RealAudio	Browser	`.rm`	`audio/x-pn-realaudio`
RealAudio	Browser	`.rpm`	`audio/x-pn-realaudio`
Real Plug-in	Plug-in.	`.rpm`	`audio/x-pn-realaudio-plugin`
RTSP stream descriptor	Player	`.rts`	`application/x-rtsp`
RTSP stream descriptor	Player	`.rtsp`	`application/x-rtsp`
RealVideo	Player	`.rv`	`video/vnd.rn-realvideo`
SDP stream descriptor	Player	`.sdp`	`application/sdp`
SDP stream descriptor	Player	`.sdp`	`application/x-sdp`
SD video	Browser	`.sdv`	`video/sd-video`
MIDI music	Browser	`.smf`	`audio/mid`
MIDI music	Browser	`.smf`	`audio/midi`
MIDI music	Browser	`.smf`	`audio/x-midi`
μ-Law/AU audio	Player	`.snd`	`audio/basic`
FutureSplash Player	Player	`.spl`	`application/futuresplash`
MP3 audio	Browser	`.swa`	`audio/mp3`
MPEG audio	Browser	`.swa`	`audio/mpeg`
MP3 audio	Browser	`.swa`	`audio/mpeg3`
MP3 audio	Browser	`.swa`	`audio/x-mp3`
MPEG audio	Browser	`.swa`	`audio/x-mpeg`
MP3 audio	Browser	`.swa`	`audio/x-mpeg3`
Macromedia Shockwave Flash	Player	`.swf`	`application/x-shockwave-flash`
μ-Law/AU audio	Player	`.ulw`	`audio/basic`
Video for Windows (AVI)	Browser	`.vfw`	`video/avi`

Continued

Table I-2 MIME Types for Popular Audio and Video Formats (Continued)

Player	Helper	File type	MIME type
Video for Windows (AVI)	Browser	`.vfw`	`video/msvideo`
Video for Windows (AVI)	Browser	`.vfw`	`video/x-msvideo`
WAVE audio	Browser	`.wav`	`audio/wav`
WAVE audio	Browser	`.wav`	`audio/x-wav`
Windows Media	Browser	`.wax`	`audio/x-ms-wax`
Windows Media	Browser	`.wax`	`audio/x-ms-wma`
Windows Media	Browser	`.wm`	`video/x-ms-wm`
Windows Media	Browser	`.wma`	`audio/x-ms-wma`
Windows Media	Player	`.wmd`	`application/x-ms-wmd`
Windows Media	Browser	`.wmv`	`video/x-ms-wmv`
Windows Media	Browser	`.wmx`	`video/x-ms-wmx`
Windows Media	Player	`.wmz`	`application/x-ms-wmz`
Windows Media	Browser	`.wvx`	`video/x-ms-wmv`
Windows Media	Browser	`.wvx`	`video/x-ms-wvx`
Digital Rights Management	Plugin	Undefined	`application/x-drm`

Notes (caveats and health warnings about these values):

- You should check that the players you are targeting are compatible with the MIME types you define in your server.
- This list is not authoritative but merely a collated snapshot of values seen "in the wild."
- There may be meaningful MIME type and file extension combinations that are not listed here.
- This information is collated from a variety of sources on the Internet and also from some working server config files.
- The Helper column indicates common default behavior.
- Users can override these settings in their browsers if they want to.
- When configuring servers, a comma-separated list of file types is associated with a single entry for each MIME type.

I.3   File Sizes

For a system you are building to handle compression, you will need provide enough space to store the source movie (in whatever format it is provided to you) and the output files from the compression tool. The calculation comes down to storing a certain number of hours of content. Table I-3 summarizes the storage capacity for a 5-minute clip in a variety of formats. This was tested fairly unscientifically and is only intended to give a basic idea of file sizes to assist with your capacity planning.

Table I-3 File Sizes Versus Formats

Format	File size
3GPP 64 Kbps (H.263)	2.867 MB
3GPP 64 Kbps (MPEG-4)	2.867 MB
ISMA Profile 0 (MPEG-4)	6.9 MB
ISMA Profile 1 (MPEG-4)	13.9 MB
QuickTime Sorenson Video 2	73.9 MB
QuickTime Video	96.4 MB
QuickTime Sorenson Video 3.1	90.9 MB
QuickTime MPEG-4 Part 2	99.9 MB
MPEG-2 multiplexed stream	150.0 MB
QuickTime Motion JPEG B	154.1 MB
QuickTime Motion JPEG A	154,9 MB
QuickTime JPEG 2000	160.5 MB
QuickTime uncompressed 8-bit 4:2:2	165.7 MB
MPEG-2 broadcast compatible (Audio and video split into 2 files, total size given)	198.9 MB
QuickTime H.263 codec at best quality	209.7 MB
QuickTime uncompressed 10-bit 4:2:2	271.4 MB
QuickTime Pixlet codec	310.5 MB
DV25 (estimated)	937.5 MB
PAL DV converted from muxed MPEG-2 with DropDV	1.01 GB
PAL DV shot on a handycam (***)	1.01 GB
QuickTime Component video	1.5 GB
DV50 (estimated)	1,875 GB
525i30 NTSC raw	2.575 GB
625i25 PAL raw	3.106 GB
YUV420 converted from muxed MPEG-2 with Compression Master	4.43 GB
SDI format A—Composite NTSC (143 Mbps)	5.362 GB
D-cinema, 24 fps 1920 × 1080 delivered on HDCAM	5.96 GB

Continued

Table I-3 File Sizes Versus Formats (Continued)

Format	*File size*
SDI format B—Composite PAL (177 Mbps)	6.637 GB
30 FPS HDTV 1920 × 1080 HDCAM compressed (7:1)	7.449 GB
SDI format C—4:2:2 component (270 Mbps)	10.125 GB
SDI format D—4:2:2 component (16:9) (360 Mbps)	13.5 GB
25 FPS 1080 × 720 commercial definition—raw	16.294 GB
30 FPS HDTV 1920 × 1080 4:2:2	34.761 GB
D-cinema, 24 fps 1920 × 1080 raw	41.713 GB
30-fps HDTV 1920 × 1080 raw	52.142 GB

Notes:

- Some of the default settings create small movies that are fine when viewed at those sizes.
- The small movies don't scale up very well.
- The QuickTime graphics codec introduced some interesting artifacts that might be useful as special effects if you over-compress the movie and then scale it back up again.

In addition to the uncompressed source footage, it is necessary to provide sufficient space to store the resulting compressed-video output. The target compression ratio will determine how much space that will require. One way to calculate that is to take your target bit rate and multiply that by the duration of the video. That tells you how many bytes the finished program will require. An easier calculation is to just double the number you first came up with for uncompressed footage. Any extra disk space will be helpful as your needs increase–and they will.

Source-Video Formats

J.1 Video Formats

Table J-1 summarizes source-video formats with some descriptive commentary about them. This list is representative but not exhaustive and you may have content presented to you in other formats.

J-1 Source-Video Formats

Format	Characteristics
Betacam	A Sony format for storing studio-quality analog video.
Betacam SP	Another Sony studio format.
Betamax	A defunct consumer-video format marketed unsuccessfully by Sony against the VHS format from JVC. VHS won the marketing battle, but there is some archival material still extant in the Betamax format. The tape cassettes were used as the basis for the Sony professional line of Betacam recording systems.
Digital 8	A consumer digital-video replacement for Video 8 and Hi8. Digital 8 is compressed but only contains I-frames. The compression ratio is 5:1 and the codec is a special DVC-format DCT. The throughput is 25 Mbps video-data rate.
DV	Often delivered via FireWire interfaces. DV is compressed but only contains I-frames. The compression ratio is 5:1 and the codec is a special DVC-format DCT. The throughput is 25 Mbps video data rate
DVCAM	The professional variant of the DV format marketed by Sony and Ikegami. DVCAM is compressed but only contains I-frames. The compression ratio is 5:1 and the codec is a special DVC-format DCT. The throughput is 25 Mbps video-data rate.

Continued

J-1 Source-Video Formats (Continued)

Format	Characteristics
DVCPro	The professional variant of the DV format marketed by Panasonic, Philips, Ikegami, and Hitachi. DVCPro is compressed but only contains I-frames. The compression ratio is 5:1 and the codec is a special DVC-format DCT. The throughput is 25 Mbps video-data rate.
DVCPro HD	A high-definition variant of the DVCPro format.
HDCAM	A Sony format that has a 7:1 compression ratio and stores high-definition TV on Betacam tapes.
Motion JPEG	An I-frame based codec with individual frames coded using JPEG.
Pixlet	An I-frame codec developed by Apple and Pixar with the individual frames coded using wavelets.
S-VHS	An improved version of VHS, which yields usable video for compression.
U-Matic	An ancient analog format, no longer used but there may be significant amounts of archived material in this form.
VHS	A domestic format of average to low quality. Tapes can be recorded in SP and LP modes. These tapes are not a good source of video for compression.

K

Source-Audio Formats

K.1 Relevant Audio Formats

A selection of formats that you might encounter when processing and encoding audio is enumerated in Table K-1.

K-1 A Variety of Audio Formats

Format	Description
μ-Law	This is an old legacy codec for use in telephony applications. The μ-Law codec is widely available on UNIX-based systems. It may be worth being able to decode this, but it has few applications for an encoder nowadays.
a-Law	A variant on the μ-Law codec also used for telephony. The a-Law codec is of little use now that we have better codecs available. Being able to decode it may gain access to some legacy audio files.
AAC format	Part of the MPEG-4 standard but has been superseded by AAC+. This was originally developed as part of the MPEG-2 standard. The MPEG-4 implementations are somewhat extended. At the same bit rate as MP3, the quality is far superior. At the same subjective quality, AAC files are much smaller than MP3 files. Because it is another open standard it is already well supported and will be more widely supported in the future. Currently available via Apple iTunes and RealNetworks Rhapsody, and used in 3G cell phones.
AAC+ format	Also known as HE-AAC. This is an improved version of the AAC format, likely to become a dominant format in the future. This variant adds Spectral Band Replication. Running this at 128 bps delivers a stereo output that is claimed to be indistinguishable from the original. AAC plus is being deployed on XM Satellite Radio and used in 3G cell phones.

Continued

K-1 A Variety of Audio Formats (Continued)

Format	Description
AC-3	A surround-sound format developed by Dolby Laboratories.
AIFF	CD audio ingested into a Mac OS system is stored in AIFF files. The data rate is around 172 Kbps.
ALS	A lossless audio codec being developed as part of the MPEG-4 standard.
Apple Lossless	This is a codec that is only available in iTunes and QuickTime on version 6.5.1 and above. This codec is very good at compressing audio for archival purposes or when you want guaranteed lossless encoding. It will reduce an audio file to about 50% of the original size, but it is not designed as a deployment codec. The Apple Lossless codec could be useful for embedding audio into applications or games.
ASPEC	A DCT-based audio-encoding standard.
ATRAC	The audio codec used for MiniDisc players.
ATRAC3 plus	A more advanced version of the proprietary Sony ATRACS format. Used in MiniDisc players. Reputed by some experts to be superior to MP3.
HE-AAC	High-Efficiency AAC. Another name for AAC plus.
IMA 4:1	This codec is good enough quality to retain 5.1 surround-sound encoding and output it intact. IMA compresses to about 25% of the original size and it is not variable. It is supported in QuickTime and Microsoft video for Windows. This could be good for storing content on a home media server where you very definitely want the surround sound to come back out properly.
MACE	Macintosh Audio Compression and Expansion is a very old codec from when 8-bit computers were used. It is useful to have a MACE playback mechanism for it but no new content should be converted to MACE.
MP3 format	MPEG-1 layer 3 audio files have been used to exchange audio for some time. They are somewhat lossy, but having tools to extract raw audio from them may get you out of trouble occasionally. The quality of MP3 content is generally considered good enough for consumption. Bit rates lower than 128 Kbps may not deliver sufficient quality. There are a lot of tools for creating MP3 files and many playback applications and portable products. MP3 is likely to be superseded by AAC in the future. The main attribute is total ubiquity—MP3 audio is available virtually everywhere.

K-1 A Variety of Audio Formats (Continued)

Format	*Description*
MPEG-1 audio—layer 1	A simplified variant of MUSICAM.
MPEG-1 audio—layer 2	This is identical to the MUSICAM standard.
MPEG-1 audio—layer 3	Also known as MP3, it is based on the ASPEC audio-compression system.
MUSICAM	Masking pattern adapted Universal Sub-Band Integrated Coding and Multiplexing. This is designed to be used in Digital Audio Broadcasting (DAB Radio).
QDesign Music	This is considered to be a legacy codec, which was quite complicated to operate. A newer version is available in QuickTime but this will likely be superseded as the AAC codec increases in popularity. The version 2 codec is about the same as MP3 in terms of quality but stores the information in a more compact form, resulting in smaller file sizes. MP3 beats it on popularity but in terms of quality versus size it is somewhere between MP3 and AAC.
Qualcomm PureVoice	A telephony codec that is good for speech but not much else. It is useful for extracting voice from recordings with other ambient noise since it ignores everything but speech. This codec is not great at high signal levels so you may want to adjust levels before encoding. Compression ratio is very good when it is used for speech-only audio tracks.
RealAudio	A family of codecs for different applications from low-quality voice to high-quality stereo music and surround sound.
SC	Surround sound 5.1 format. Also being proposed for delivering satellite radio to moving vehicles.
Windows Media Audio	These are otherwise known as WMA. There are several alternative codecs but they are not all available on every platform. Naturally, they are all well supported on Windows.

K.2 Audio Supplied with Source-Video Formats

Table K-2 summarizes source-video formats with some descriptive commentary about the audio most often delivered with them.

K-2 Source-Audio Formats

Format	Characteristics
Betacam	A Sony format for storing studio-quality analog video and audio.
Betacam SP	Another Sony studio format. Analog audio.
Betamax	A defunct consumer-video format with analog audio.
Digital 8	A consumer digital-video format very similar to DV but that existed for some time before DV was popularized. Same audio support as DV.
DV	Audio is delivered along with the video when it is ingested via Firewire. Accepts 44.1 KHz, 48 KHz, and 32 KHz sample rates. Often there are analog inputs on the recorders as well.
DVCAM	The professional variant of the DV format. Same audio support. This is the Sony version.
DVCPro	The professional variant of the DV format. Same audio support. This is the Panasonic version.
DVCPro HD	A high-definition variant of the DVCPro format. Same audio support.
HDCAM	Analog or AES digital audio.
Motion JPEG	No particular audio format associated with this codec.
Pixlet	No particular audio format associated with this codec.
S-VHS	An improved version of VHS with analog audio.
U-Matic	An ancient analog format, no longer used. Audio will be analog as well as the video.
VHS	A domestic format of average to low quality. Analog audio.

Formats Versus Players

L.1 What Plays What

Although the support for different formats changes from time to time, the players generally continue to support a format once they have adopted it. An exception to this is the Microsoft Windows Media player, which used to play Real Media files but no longer supports them.

L.2 Real Networks

The latest versions of the Real Networks player support the following audio and video file types:

- All file formats for Real Networks, RealSystems, RealONE, and so forth.
- HTML web pages
- JavaScript script content
- ActiveX controls (but only on Windows platforms)
- SMIL multimedia files
- Flash animations
- QuickTime movie files
- Windows AVI files
- MPEG MP3 audio files
- MPEG 1, 2, and 4 audio/video files
- AAC audio files

L.3 Windows Media

The most recent version of Windows Media Player Series 10 Beta supports the following audio and video file formats:

- All Windows and Microsoft proprietary media file formats
- CD audio tracks (.cda)

- MPEG-1 (`.mpeg`, `.mpg`, `.m1v`)
- MPEG-1 Audio Layer 3 (`.mp3`)
- MPEG-1 Audio Layer 2 (`.mp2`, `.mpa`)
- M3U (`.m3u`)
- Musical Instrument Digital Interface (`.mid`, `.midi`, `.rmi`)
- Audio Interchange File Format (`.aif`, `.aifc`, `.aiff}`)
- Sun Microsystems and NeXT (`.au`, `.snd`)
- Indeo Video Technology (`.ivf`)
- Some pre-version 3.0 QuickTime content (`.mov`, `.qt`)

The following are specifically not supported:

- Real Networks content (`.ra`, `.rm`, `.ram`). All Real Networks formats are supported if you install the RealONE player for Windows.
- Post-version 2.0 QuickTime content (`.avi`, `.mov`, `.qt`). All QuickTime formats are supported if you install QuickTime for Windows.
- MPEG-4 (.mp4). The MP4 format is supported if you install the Ligos LSX-MPEG Player or the Envivio TV plug-in. For more information about the Ligos LSX-MPEG Player, visit the Ligos player web page. For more information about Envivio TV, visit the Envivio TV plug-in web page.

L.4 QuickTime

The following is a selection of the formats supported by the QuickTime player:

- 3GPP
- 3GPP2
- AIFF
- AU
- Audio CD Data (Mac OS 9)
- AVI
- FLC
- Karaoke
- Macromedia Flash 5
- MIDI
- MPEG-1
- MP3 (MPEG-1, Layer 3)
- M3U (MP3 Playlist files)
- MPEG-2[**]

Ligos player: http://www.ligos.com/lsx_mpeg_player.htm

Envivio TV player: http://www.envivio.com/products/etv/download.jsp

- M4A, M4B, M4P (iTunes 4 audio)
- QCP
- QuickTime Movie
- SD2 (SoundDesigner 2)
- SDP
- SDV
- SF2 (SoundFont 2)
- SMIL
- System 7 Sound (Mac OS 9)
- VDU (Sony Video Disk Unit)

The following additional video codecs are supported:

- Animation
- Apple BMP
- Apple Pixlet (added at QuickTime 6.4)
- Apple Video
- Cinepak
- Component video
- DV and DVC Pro NTSC
- DV PAL
- DVC Pro PAL
- Graphics
- H.261
- H.263
- H.264 (added at QuickTime 7)
- JPEG 2000 (Mac OS X)
- Microsoft OLE (decode only)
- Microsoft Video 1 (decode only)
- Motion JPEG A
- Motion JPEG B
- MPEG-4
- Photo JPEG
- Planar RGB
- PNG
- Sorenson Video 2
- Sorenson Video 3
- TGA
- TIFF

Note:

- Pixlet is only supported on Mac OS X.

The following audio codecs are supported:

- 24-bit integer
- 32-bit floating point
- 32-bit integer
- 64-bit floating point
- AAC (MPEG-4 Audio)
- a-Law 2:1
- AMR Narrowband
- Apple Lossless Encoder
- IMA 4:1
- MACE 3:1
- MACE 6:1
- MS ADPCM (decode only)
- QDesign Music 2
- Qualcomm PureVoice (QCELP)
- μ-Law 2:1

The following video formats require the installation of a downloadable component or additional plug-ins available from Apple:

- On2 VP3
- ZyGoVideo
- Streambox
- Microcosm
- MPEG-2

Connectors

M.1 Connections

This appendix describes the physical connections that you might have to make. It is provided to help those who may be unfamiliar recognize what the connectors are. I have purposely left off the pin assignments and signal descriptions because it is better to use store-bought cables than to make them up yourself—that is, unless you are building studios on a large scale.

Most of the connection diagrams are shown looking directly into the pins of the connector. Where it is helpful, a side view is also shown.

M.2 Signals Being Connected

Table M-1 summarizes the kinds of signals you can expect to encounter.

M-1 Signal Types

Type	Description	Connector
SDI	A serial digital interface, which is a digitized version of the analog component signals. Virtually all video connections within a studio environment will take place with SDI signals. That means the luma and chroma difference signals are carried in an interleaved format as separate bit	75-Ohm coaxial cable connected with BNC plugs/sockets. Some equipment allows tee splitters to be inserted while other equipment may be extremely sensitive to a drop in the signal level. This connection is good for about 100 feet of co-axial cable. Fiber-optic transducers can be used to connect racks that are further away with only a local signal being carried via coax.

Continued

M-1 Signal Types (Continued)

Type	Description	Connector
	streams. Most commonly you will find this being driven at 25 Mbps (DV25) or 50 Mbps (DV50). Beware of the specifics, because there are differences between the American and European bit structures and the hardware may support one or more of a variety of SDI-based protocols.	
Composite	Although there are digital versions of this kind of signal, this is most often an analog signal. This is predominantly a consumer format although some offline studio and desktop equipment for monitoring may use this, too.	A single-screened cable and connector using an RCA jack (a.k.a phono plug).
S-Video	Designed as a superior connector, which delivers the luma and chroma signals down separate wires.	A 4-way cable with special mini-plugs at each end. In an emergency, an Apple ADB keyboard cable will serve as an S-Video connector. This signal may also be delivered via a SCART (Peritel) connector.
Consumer audio	Line-level signals compatible with hi-fi separates.	RCA jacks, otherwise known as phono plugs. Sometimes the audio is supplied on quarter-inch jacks and also mini-jacks (3.5mm diameter).
Balanced analog audio	Studio and professional-style audio connectivity.	XLR jacks with latching connectors.
AES digital audio	Often embedded into a video signal.	A variety of connection options from hardwired, Krone frames, quarter-inch jacks, and bantam jacks.

M-1 Signal Types *(Continued)*

Type	Description	Connector
SPDIF	Consumer and semi-professional digital audio connected using optical fiber.	Special SPDIF connectors on the equipment or lately provided through a special 3.5mm jack-compatible connector in Apple iMac G5 systems.
FireWire	Also known as IEEE 1394 and iLink.	A 6-pin connection can supply bus power and a smaller 4-pin connection will not.
USB	Common variants known as USB 1.0 and USB 2.0. Used for connecting keyboards, mice, low-capacity storage devices, and outboard audio/MIDI interfaces.	A flat, 4-pin connector available in several form factors.

M.3   Icons and Symbols

FireWire equipment should carry the proper icon adjacent to the FireWire connectors. The panel with the connector may or may not have the word FireWire (Figure M-1) there as well; it might have the number 1394 nearby, too.

Equipment manufactured and licensed by Sony will carry the iLink logo rather than the FireWire logo (Figure M-2).

USB equipment has several logos. The important icon that is placed on cables and connectors is shown in Figure M-3.

Figure M-1   FireWire logo.

Figure M-2 Sony iLink logo.

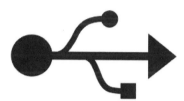

Figure M-3 USB connector logo.

M.4 Video Connectors

Table M-2 summarizes the different kinds of video connector in normal use. There are some variants that are subtly different from one another.

M-2 Video Connectors

Description	Picture
75 ohm coax BNC	
RCA phono jack	
SCART (Peritel)	

M-2 Video Connectors (Continued)

Description	Picture
MUSA patch bay U-Link	
S-VHS	
RF antenna connector	

Notes:

- Gather together a collection of adapters and couplers. This will sometimes get you out of difficulty when connecting a new piece of equipment.
- Cables with BNC connectors are usually good for very long distances. Fifty feet should be fine for most situations where a good signal level is injected at the input. Don't be silly and run five miles of cable. It won't work without repeaters.
- Having some long cables that you can loop back is useful for testing circuits.
- Very long cables can be used as attenuators in an emergency. Obviously they aren't calibrated but you can rely on the signal loss to reduce a 'hot' output. It might introduce some noise though.
- Buy some attenuators.
- Make sure you connect like with like. Don't connect component signals to composite inputs. It looks like it works sometimes but you lose the colour information.
- Avoid connecting video equipment using RF (antenna cables). Its OK for monitoring purposes but not much else. On the other hand, old TV receivers make cheap monitors but may only have RF connectors. You won't want to do this if you are a broadcaster, but the amateur videographer and compressionist can economize in many ways like this.

M.5 Computer Display Connectors

Table M-3 summarizes connectors used to send video from your computer to the display. These are not usually a source of compressible video unless you use a scan converter and down-sample the output to a video resolution. These days, you would do the recording entirely inside the computer in a digital form.

M-3 Computer Display Connectors

Description	Picture
DVI	
EVC	
VGA/D-Sub	
Macintosh video port	
Digital flat-panel display	

Notes:

- The DVI cables come in different varieties. The DVI connector carries digital and analog signals on different pins. Some cables omit the analog connections that you might need for certain displays. The DVI-D cable is digital only. The DVI-I cable carries both analog and digital signals.
- Cable lengths may be an issue at very high resolutions. You may need to purchase shorter cables if you are not getting the expected video quality.
- Fitting ferrite cores to the cable can help. This increases the induction and cancels out capacitive effects that can be problems at very high frequencies.
- Having DVI to VGA and any other adapters you can find is a useful thing for your toolbox.

- Some types of equipment (laptops for example) use a mini DVI connector format. You must use an adaptor for this in order to connect the equipment to any other devices.

M.6 FireWire and USB

These are summarized together because they can be used to transfer either video or audio or both. They can also be used to connect other peripherals. Table M-4 shows a variety of connectors.

M-4 FireWire and USB Connectors

Description	Picture
FireWire—400 6-way	
FireWire—400 4-way	
FireWire—800	
USB 1 Type B	
USB 1—Type A	
USB 1—Type A (special Apple-keyed variant)	
USB 2 miniature—5 pin	
USB 2 small—4 pin	
USB 2 large—4 pin	
Nikon mini USB	

Notes:

- Don't lose your camera cables. They are very expensive to replace, because you can only get them from the camera manufacturer and they or the dealer will over-charge for them (because they have to be ordered as a special item).
- If it doesn't fit, don't force it. It is possible to jam some connectors in the wrong way round if you push them hard enough. They should be a snug fit and feel 'right' when you plug them in. Forcing cables in the wrong way can supply high voltages where they shouldn't go or reverse the polarity of something. Putting power supply voltages down signal lines probably permanently damages the equipment and the damage happens so quickly that your reflexes won't be quick enough to unplug it in time.
- Very short FireWire patch cables are very hard to come by. Half a meter is usually the shortest you can buy in shops. Patch cables that are just a few inches long are handy for keeping the rear of your computer system neat and tidy. Likewise with all the other cables. Keep them as short as you can.

M.7 Audio Connectors

The plugs and sockets shown in Table M-5 are predominantly analog audio connections.

M-5 Audio Connectors

Description	Picture
Quarter-inch standard jack	
Bantam jack	
Mini jack (3.5mm)	
XLR	
Combined quarter-inch jack and XLR	

Continued

M-5 Audio Connectors (Continued)

Description	Picture
Neutrik speaker connectors	

Notes:

- Be careful when mixing balanced and unbalanced audio. Use a Balun transformer if you can.
- Gender switching adapters for XLR connectors can be a life saver. Get some for your toolkit.
- The standard jack sometimes isn't. While the plug fits into the throat of the socket, it may be a little too long or short to engage properly with the sprung connector inside the socket. Having several different manufacturers' jack plugs on your cables means you can try another cable to see if it is any better.
- Pulling the jack out by a distance of 0.5 mm sometimes engages the connector more reliably. Having some fibre or plastic washers that fit over the jack plug shaft might help you do this without having to hold the plug yourself. A rubber band might do the trick too.
- Some cables sold for musicians to connect guitars to their laptop audio inputs might be useful for solving a connection problem between your audio equipment and the computer.
- Cheap audio-to-USB adapters are becoming more widely available. These are sold in music shops for connecting analog instruments directly to the USB bus.
- Refer to the AES web site for downloadable specifications on audio connectors.

M.8 Communications and Networking Connectors

These connectors are used for telecoms, MIDI, and networking.

Audio Engineering Society (AES): http://www.aes.org/

M-6 Communications and Networking Connectors

Description	Picture
MIDI (DIN5 way)	
Modem connector RJ 11	
Ethernet connector RJ-45	
BT plug (UK)	
RS 232/485 DB9	
RS 232 DB25	

Notes:

- There are other DIN plug formats.
- DIN plugs with 2 pins are usually a loudspeaker connections. Don't connect them to a line input.
- Some 5-pin DIN connectors carry balanced or unbalanced audio, especially on older consumer audio equipment made for the European market.
- Sometimes you will find a 7-pin DN connector on a piece of equipment.

- Beware that some DN connectors are also used for control inputs and might carry higher-than-expected DC voltages.
- Carrying some DIN breakout cables might be a good idea. These have a DIN connector on one end and phono (RCA jack) connectors on tails at the other end with a box of back-to-back couplers. They let you make up a variety of connections between different plug and socket configurations.

M.9 Optical-Fiber Connectors

The costs of optical-fiber connections are becoming low enough that they are being more widely deployed.

M-7 Optical-Fiber Connectors

Description	Picture
Apple hybrid 3.5 mini jack with optical coupler	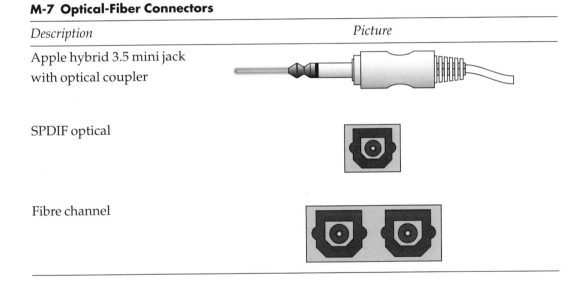
SPDIF optical	
Fibre channel	

Notes:

- Avoid bending or flexing optical fiber cables. They are made of glass and can crack internally.
- Optical fiber cables should not be bent round a tight corner.

M.10 Power Connectors

While the mains socket on the wall will be different, the connector on the back of your equipment will be the same all over the world.

M-8 Power Connectors

Description	Picture
IEC (Kettle lead)	
Figure 8	
DC transformer input	

Notes:

- Check the voltages and polarity of DC supplies.
- Preferably, use the one supplied with the equipment.
- Make sure that fuses are replaced with the correct values.
- Check that the equipment operates at the voltage you expect. Modern equipment operates at 110 volts and 220/240 volts. Older equipment has selector switches that must be set correctly before you power up the equipment.

M.11   Useful URLs

Here are some useful URLs where you can find out more information about cables and connectors and their pin-outs.

M-9 Connector Web Site URLs

Description	URL
My cable shop:	http://www.mycableshop.com/techguide.html
Network Technologies:	http://www.networktechinc.com/technote.html
How Stuff Works:	http://www.howstuffworks.com/
Tom's Hardware:	http://www.tomshardware.com/
RJ Jack Glossary:	http://www.arcelect.com/RJ_Jack_Glossary.htm
ADSL guide:	http://www.adslguide.org.uk/guide/connections.asp
Webopedia:	http://www.webopedia.com/

Important Standards and Professional Associations

Table N-1 Important Standards

Standard	Name or Number
AAF	AAF Object Specification v1.1
	AAF Stored Format Specification v1.0.1
	AAF Low-Level Container Specification v1.0.1
	AAF Edit Protocol
AES/EBU Audio	AES-1992
AES/EBU Audio	ANSI S.40-1992
AES/EBU Audio	IEC-958
DVB Handheld digital video (DVB-H)	ETSI—EN 302 304
DVB HDTV on Satellite (DVB-S2)	ETSI—EN 302 307
DVB Satellite digital TV (DVB-S)	ETSI—EN 300 421
	ETSI—TR 101 198
DVB Terrestrial digital video (DVB-T)	ETSI—EN 300 744
	ETSI—TR 101 190
H.264	ITU H.264 (05/03)
ISO MPEG-1	ISO 11172
ISO MPEG-2	ISO 13818
ISO MPEG-21	ISO 21000
ISO MPEG-4	ISO 14496
ISO MPEG-7	ISO 15938
SMPTE VC-1	To be published
TV-Anytime Phase-1	ETSI – TS 102 822
AACS	Advanced Access Content System

Table N-2 Professional Associations and Standards Bodies

Abbreviation	Full name
AAFA	Advanced Authoring Format Association
ACM	Association for Computing Machinery
ACM SIGGRAPH	ACM Special Interest in Graphics Group
AES	Audio Engineering Society
ANSI	American National Standards Institute
ATSC	Advanced Television Standards Committee
AVCA	AVC Alliance
BCDF	Broadband Content Developer Forum
BKSTS	British Kinematograph Sound and Television Society
BSI	British Standards Institute
CCITT	Consultative Committee for International Telephony and Telegraphy (see ITU)
DTAG	Digital Terrestrial Action Group
DVB	Digital Video Broadcast
DVPA	Digital Video Producers Association
EBU	European Broadcasting Union
ECMA	European Computer Manufacturers Association
ETSI	European Telecommunications Standards Institute
IEE	Institute for Electrical Engineers
IEEE	Institute for Electrical and Electronic Engineers
IETF	Internet Engineering Task Force
ISMA	Internet Streaming Media Alliance
ISO	International Organization for Standardization
ITU	International Telecommunications Union
JPEG	Joint Photographic Experts Group
M4IF	MPEG 4 Industry Forum (see MPEGIF)
MPEG	Motion Picture Experts Group
MPEGIF	MPEG Industry Forum
NAB	National Association of Broadcasters
Pro-MPEG	Pro-MPEG consortium
RTS	Royal Television Society
SMPTE	Society of Motion Picture and Television Experts
TV-AF	TV Anytime Forum
W3C	World Wide Web Consortium

Glossary

Topic	Description
1394	Sometimes used as an abbreviation that describes FireWire interfaces. This is derived from the IEEE 1394 standard number.
16mm	A semi-professional and professional film format. Low-budget features, TV programs, and news-gathering all used 16mm.
14×9	A compromised aspect ratio midway between 16×9 and 4×3 (12×9) that fits reasonably well on TV displays of either type.
16×9	Widescreen TV formats use an aspect ratio of 16 units wide by 9 units high.
24p	A common abbreviation used to describe film formats that are digitized at 24 frames per second (fps) on a progressively scanned raster.
2.5G phone	An intermediate mobile phone format based on 2G equipment with some basic 3G features introduced ahead of the full 3G launch.
3:2 pulldown	A technique used to convert 24-fps movie film to 30-fps video. Extra fields are inserted periodically in sequences based on repeating the same frame of film 3 times and then 2 times. Two cycles of this pattern yields a synchronized framing of the film with the video. The 3232 sequence is called the cadence.
35mm	Hollywood movie and cinema format for feature films. High-quality TV material might have been shot in this format.
3G phone	Modern mobile telephone handsets are known as 3G because they are based on a third-generation technology. 1G was analog, and 2G was basic digital services but included WAP and SMS. 3G introduces video and multimedia and other data services.
3GPP	Based on the H.264/MPEG-4 codecs. This is the abbreviated name for the Third-Generation Partnership Project. It was formed in order to facilitate the development of globally interoperable mobile phones.

Continued

Topic	Description
3ivX	Widely available encoder based on MPEG-4. Stands alone but offers very good performance and a quality product. It compares favorably with other Windows- and QuickTime-based MPEG-4 encoders. The compression efficiency is good. This codec is available for a variety of platforms including Windows, Mac, and Linux. In fact, it is supported on several variants of Linux and some TV set-top boxes as well.
4:4:4	Luma and chroma sampled at full resolution.
4:2:2	Luma sampled at four times the sub-carrier frequency. Chroma sampled at half the resolution on the horizontal axis and down-sampled in the vertical axis.
4:1:1	Double-sized aperture cell to allow higher compression ratio for chroma. 8:2:2 is a more functional description of the sampling.
4:2:0	Only one chroma sample for the whole *block* of luma samples.
4 × 3	Normal aspect ratio for TV. This is gradually being replaced by widescreen TV. This is sometimes called 12 × 9.
70mm	Top-end cinematic film-presentation format. The stock is used vertically for 70mm film and horizontally for VistaVision and IMAX presentations.
8mm	A popular format for home movie production that was made obsolete by the introduction of home video cameras. Film comes in standard and Super 8mm formats. Sony adopted 8mm tape as a video format.
9.5mm	An early home movie format that was popular before the development of the more compact 8mm systems.
AAC	Advanced Audio Coding is a format for compressing audio that was introduced with the MPEG-4 standard. An enhanced variant is known as AAC+.
AAC+ (AAC Plus)	A more advanced form of audio coding based on the existing AAC coding plus Spectral Band Replication. Also known as High Efficiency Advanced Audio Coding (HE-AAC).
AAFA	Advanced Authoring Format (AAF) Association.
AC Coefficient	The first coefficient of a DCT transform is the DC component. This is a constant average value across the whole macroblock. All of the other coefficients are variable according to the level of detail in the block. The frequency of the detail increases from left to right and top to bottom. So this is the part of the DCT output that describes the image detail in frequency terms and is non-zero if the image in the block is not a solid area of the same color. The values of the coefficients get smaller towards the right bottom corner as the level of detail falls off.

Topic	*Description*
ACM	Association for Computing Machinery.
ACM Siggraph	ACM Special Interest in Graphics Group.
Active picture area	This is the part of the picture that we are most interested in when compressing video. Outside of this are synchronization signals and blank lines, some of which carry data and subtitling information.
Adaptive Quantizing	A means of controlling the quantization of the audio or video according to the instantaneous demands of the compression bit-stream output.
ADC	Analog-to-Digital Converter.
ADSL	Asymmetric Digital Subscriber Line. Domestic high-speed broadband interface using the existing telephone network. The upload and download speeds are not the same.
AES	Audio Engineering Society.
AES/EBU	A standardized format for digital audio that is much used in the broadcasting environment. High-end equipment will have an AES digital input or output.
Aliasing	An artifact on the video that shows a disjoint that is most noticeable when objects in the scene are moving horizontally.
Anamorphic	A means of squashing the picture when written to the storage medium (video or film) and then expanding it on playback. Isomorphic stretching is a zoom. Anamorphic stretching happens in just one axis, so it is used to make widescreen images when the delivery mechanism is a standard aspect ratio.
Animation	This is a special QuickTime codec developed for use with animated content. At the best-quality setting it is lossless. The color space is the highest possible resolution and samples at 4:4:4. The performance is optimal for large, flat areas of the same color and text. This is useful for working on credit sequences and is also used as a transfer codec by animators and effects artists. It is available wherever QuickTime is installed.
ANSI	American National Standards Institute.
Antialiasing	A method for smoothing the jagged edges (stair steps) often seen in graphics or video. The method reduces the jagged edges by placing intermediate shades of color or gray around the steps.
API	Applications Programming Interface.
ASF	Active Streaming Format. A Microsoft file format for digital video playback over the Internet or on a standalone computer. Kind of a wrapper around any of a number of compression types, including MPEG. Part of Netshow, a proprietary

Continued

Topic	*Description*
ASF (Continued)	streaming media solution from Microsoft. Biggest competitor is Real Networks. While this 'wrapper' supports many standard formats, ASF files are themselves proprietary. This file format is sometimes called the Advanced Systems Format.
ASIC	Application-Specific Integrated Circuits.
Aspect Ratio	The relationship between the height and the width of a picture. Standard aspect ratio is 4×3 and wide screen is 16×9.
Asymmetry	We can allow encoding to take longer than playback unless we are encoding live content. Even then it can be buffered unless it's a video-conferencing application. Decoding must take place in real time in order to maintain the playback speed.
Atom	A small component object within a structured movie file. It is called an atom because it is generally indivisible to a smaller component without special tools and techniques.
ATSC	Advanced Television Standards Committee.
AVC	Advanced Video Coding describes a format for compressing video that was jointly developed by ISO MPEG and the ITU. It is also known as MPEG-4 Part 10 and H.264.
AVI	Audio Video Interleaved. A Microsoft format for digital audio and video playback from Windows 3.1. Somewhat cross-platform, but mostly a Windows format. Has been replaced by the ASF format but is still used by some multimedia developers.
Backward-motion vector	A motion-compensation vector used when the video is playing in reverse.
Bandwidth	A term borrowed from radio and TV broadcasting to describe the capacity required to transport information from one place to another. Broadcasting engineers used the term to describe the frequencies on either side of the carrier that were used as a consequence of modulating an audio or video signal by that carrier frequency. Computing specialists adopted the terminology to loosely describe bit rate.
Baseband	A means of transmitting using a single carrier frequency shared by all nodes. All nodes must be aware of each other's traffic to avoid collisions. Ethernet is such a network.
BCDF	Broadband Content Developer Forum. Now called the Broadband Services Forum.
Beating	When two signals of similar frequency are mixed, they alternately enhance and cancel one another at a cyclic rate equivalent to the difference between them. For example,

Topic	Description
	one motor spinning at 1500 RPM with another bolted to the same chassis that is spinning at 1200 RPM will generate a 300 Hz of rattling noise. A computer monitor set to scan at 60 Hz with a florescent lamp shining on it that is running at 50 Hz (European mains frequency) will exhibit a 10-Hz flicker.
Betacam	A family of video recorders used for professional work and made by Sony. The latest models use IMX format. The Betacam family includes Digital Betacam, which is often refered to as Digibeta or d-Beta.
Bézier	Named after a French mathematician, this is a kind of curve that is generated mathematically. Sometimes called Spline curves, they are much used in interpolation software. Useful for spatial, temporal, and color interpolation.
B-frame	A bi-directional difference frame.
BIFS	Binary Format for Scenes. Derived from VRML but represented in a binary form as the scene description within MPEG-4.
Bit	Binary digit. The smallest representable quantity inside a computer system.
Bit rate	The number of bits that can be transported per second is described as a bit rate. Some common speeds are 56K (for dial-up modems), 384K (for most video-conferencing), and 10 Mbps (for a low-speed Ethernet). Faster Ethernet circuits run at 100 and 1000 Mbps.
Bit stream	The output of a video-compression coder.
Bitmap	A description of an area of picture elements or pixels. This would more accurately be called a pixmap.
BKSTS	British Kinematograph Sound and Television Society.
Block	Usually taken to mean a macroblock.
BPS	Bits per second.
Broadband	A telecommunications connection, usually to the home or small office, that provides transfer data rates of between 500 Kbps and 2 bps. Speeds in excess of 8 Mbps and even as high as 25 Mbps are speculated about for the future.
BSI	British Standards Institute.
Byte	A collection of 8 bits gathered together and manipulated as a single unit.

Continued

Topic	Description
Cascade	Several processing steps connected together in a series, one after the other. Not recommended for compression logarithms.
CCD	Charge-coupled devices are used in digital video cameras as imaging sensors.
CCITT	Consultative Committee for International Telephony and Telegraphy. See ITU.
CD	Compact Disk is a format developed by Phillips for delivering digital audio.
CD-ROM	Compact Disk-Read Only Memory is a derivative of CD audio that allows data to be stored on the disk for use by computer systems.
Chunk	A fragment of data in an object-structured video file that is larger than an atom but smaller than a track. The process of breaking down the video into pieces is sometimes informally called chunking. A chunk most likely corresponds to a GOP (Group Of Pictures).
CIF	Common Intermediate Format, Common Interchange Format, or Common Image Format, depending on the source you consult. It describes an image size that is 352×288 or 352×240 pixels depending on whether the source is 625 or 525 lines. The ITU H.261 standard originally specified this image size.
Cinepak	This is a very old legacy codec from the early days of QuickTime.
Cinepak mobile	This is a mobile variant of the Cinepak codec.
CMYK	Cyan, magenta, yellow, black. The primary colors used to print images on paper.
Codec	A software or hardware device to encode and decode video, audio or other media. The encoder and decoder for a particular compression format. The word is contracted from Coder-Decoder. The codec refers to both ends of the process of squeezing video down and expanding it on playback. Compatible coders and decoders must be used and so they tend to be paired up when they are delivered.
Coefficients	The output of the DCT algorithm yields one DC coefficient, which is the average value for the 8×8 macroblock, plus 63 AC coefficients, which describe the frequency distribution of image-intensity changes across the macroblock.
Complexity	Complexity in video compression describes how the compression process is carried out. This translates to how easy it is to decode. If the decoding process is too complex, the hardware needs to be more powerful. Complexity can be

Topic	*Description*
	controlled by limiting the variety and type of compression tools that are used during the encoding process.
Concatenate	The process of joining several items together in series is concatenation. This is different from summation, which is an arithmetic process. In a concatenated result, the original items are usually still visible and can often be separated again if there is sufficient delimiting information. Sometimes the word concatenate is used to describe cascaded process components.
Contention	The number of clients contending for a limited number of service connections describes the contention ratio. Broadband services might potentially deliver 500 Kbps, but if two such users connect to a service that can only deliver 500 Kbps, their resulting throughput will be about half what they expect. This is a contention ratio of 2:1. Contention sometimes describes bit-rate sharing and sometimes the number of connections available.
Contrast Ratio	The ratio of difference between the black and white values of a picture. A larger ratio is preferable in order to show more detailed and subtle detail.
DAC	Digital-to-analog converter.
DC Coefficient	The coefficient at the start of the DCT output for a macroblock where there is no frequency component. This is essentially the average value for the macroblock pixels.
DCable	Digital TV services delivered, usually according to a DVB standard, along a cable-connected infrastructure between the head-end and the consumer.
DCT	Discrete Cosine Transform algorithms are used in MPEG encoders to compress the video.
Dirac	A codec developed by the BBC Research and Development department. Dirac is an attractive alternative because it is open source and patent free. More important, it has been designed in such a way that it does not infringe on any patents and therefore is not subject to any license fees. It uses a new coding technique that is not DCT based. It is an experimental prototype but the source code is available for you to build yourself.
Dithering	Creates the illusion of a new color that isn't actually supported by the medium. It creates intermediate shades by combining dots of primary color in various patterns.This is a way of achieving gray-scales and is commonly used in newspapers.

Continued

Topic	Description
DivX	A popular standard for compressing video to a reasonably good quality at low bit rates. A 2-hour movie compresses to a size that comfortably fits on a CD-ROM. This is derived from the MPEG-4 standard with some additional enhancements that make it noncompliant in some minor respects.
DOM	Document Object Models are used to describe the content structure of a Web page, for example.
DPI	Dots per inch
DRM	Digital Rights Management seeks to control access to content so that commercial models can be built.
DSat	Digital TV broadcast using DVB standards from the head-end, up to a satellite, and back down to a consumer's receiving dish aerial.
DSP	Digital Signal Processors. These are programmable microprocessors that are optimized for processing audio and video.
DTAG	Digital Terrestrial Action Group.
DTT	Digital TV broadcasting using DVB standards via the terrestrial broadcast infrastructure that was originally installed to distribute analog TV services.
DV	DV is a standard digital video format used in DVCAM and DVCPro equipment. This is a transfer codec with various derivative and related siblings and is often used with FireWire. DV is used at the low end in TV production but at the high end of semi-pro and amateur cameras. There are variants for higher-performance professional use. All DV-based codecs yield good-quality video. The DV codec is very portable across professional and amateur systems and virtually all desktop-editing systems support it. You should avoid recompressing it until you are ready to convert it to a delivery format.
DV25	Digital video compressed to transfer at 25 Mbps is called DV25. The compression is slightly lossy but undetectable to the human eye. This format is used in distribution systems.
DV50	Digital Video transferred at a bit rate of 50 Mbps with such slight compression as to be almost undetectable with measuring equipment. This format is used in production systems.
DVB	Digital Video Broadcasting. Part of the EBU that standardizes digital TV systems.

Topic	Description
DVCAM	A popular professional format of video recording and storage that is a slight compromise on quality in order to reduce the cost but is good enough for news-gathering footage for broadcast TV. It is likely to become popular as a high-end consumer format.
DVCPro50	The NTSC and PAL variants of this correspond to the lower spec DVCPro formats. Because of the higher bit rate, the compression is reduced to 3.3:1 instead of 5:1. DVCPro50 also supports the 4:2:2 color sampling but results in larger files. Recompression should be avoided unless going to a target delivery format. This is a production format.
DVCPro—HD	This is the HDTV format and operates at several raster sizes from 1080i60 to 720p60. It supports higher data rates and color sampling is improved over other DV formats; uses a 4:2:2 sampling format. Designed for broadcast or D-cinema use. This format delivers excellent quality for all uses but is also quite bulky and not intended for amateur use. DVCPro supports variable compression ratios. The files created in this format are huge and while there is some light compression, it still requires large systems to cope. You only need this codec to work in high definition for broadcasting purposes.
DVCPro—NTSC	This is the North American standard version that runs at 30 fps with 525 lines, Y'UV color space, and operates at a compression ratio of 5:1.
DVCPro—PAL	This is the European standard version that runs at 25 FPS with 625 lines, Y'UV color space and operates at a compression ratio of 5:1.
DVD	Digital Versatile Disk is a format that was developed for the delivery of movies and other data sets that are too bulky for transfer on a CD format.
DVD-ROM	The computer equivalent of a DVD, designed for similar applications as CD-ROM but providing much greater capacity.
DVPA	The Digital Video Producers Association is a group of like-minded professionals who collaborate and provide mutual support and training. Their seminars are particularly informative.
DVR	A Digital Video Recorder describes what was previously called a Personal Video Recorder. A PVR typically has analog I/O, while a DVR interacts directly with a digital TV service. The distinction is somewhat blurred and there isn't any hard and fast rule for which term is the most appropriate.

Continued

Topic	*Description*
DWT	Discrete Wavelet Transform.
EBU	The European Broadcasting Union governs the standardization of TV in European markets.
ECMA	European Computer Manufacturers Association.
Elementary Stream	The video and audio is compressed by the codec to form an elementary stream that just contains one kind of media. These are then multiplexed together to form a program stream.
Emblaze	An early Java-based codec that was interesting but never became widely used.
Ensharpen	The TechSmith Ensharpen codec is designed for screen-capture applications. It is quite efficient for that use but has limited availability across platforms.
Entropy coding	The coding of the string of DCT coefficients that are created by the DCT encode of a macroblock.
Ethernet	A networking system for connecting computers together.
Extranet	The networking outside of your own internal network or intranet is called an extranet.
FCIF	Full Common Intermediate Format. An alternative to CIF that qualifies the size in contexts where QCIF might be mentioned as well.
FEC	Forward Error Correction.
Field Dominance	The order in which the odd or even fields of an interlaced raster are presented.
FireWire	An interface designed to support hard disks and fast video transfers. Originally developed by Apple Computer, it has become ubiquitous as an interface for downloading material from portable DV cameras.
FlexMux	Flexible Timeline Multiplexor introduced with the MPEG-4 systems layer. This allows some very sophisticated interactive and multimedia services to be constructed and also solves one major problem with MPEG-2 where timelines in program streams are difficult to splice and trigger interactive events from.
Forbidden Technologies	This is an interesting codec that uses edge-based coding. Interestingly, as the compression ratio increases and the quality decreases, the image begins to resemble a cell-animated cartoon but the edge detail remains until the very last.
Forward motion vector	A motion-compensation vector used when the video is playing forward in the normal way.

Topic	Description
Frame	A single picture within a video sequence.
G.711	An audio codec supporting 3.4-KHz speech at 56 and 64 Kbps.
G.722	An audio codec supporting 7-KHz speech at 48, 56, and 64 Kbps.
G.728	An audio codec supporting 3.4-KHz speech at 16 Kbps.
Genlock	Generator locking describes the technique of synchronizing the film shutter in a camera with an external electronic source. This generator locking is also used to sync any two arbitrary video systems together. Studio and production environments typically provide genlock signals via a distribution amplifier so that all the equipment can be synchronized to the same timing.
Global motion compensation	A spatial transform applied to the whole picture in order to reduce the residual motion vectors required in each macroblock.
H.221	A standard that describes the transmission frame structure. This is based on frame multiplexing for a 64- to 1920-Kbps ISDN channel.
H.231	Describes a Multipoint Control Unit (MCU) for video-conferencing systems with more than 2 end-points.
H.243	A system for establishing communication between three or more terminals with circuits that have a capacity of up to 2 Mbps. This is sometimes called multi-point conferencing.
H.261	An ITU standard codec for video-conferencing video streams. H.261 uses the Discrete Cosine Transform (DCT) algorithm to compress video so it can be accommodated within a bandwidth of 64 Kbps to 2 Mbps. This standard also defines the CIF and QCIF image formats. This is a legacy codec.
H.263	Another ITU video-conferencing standard codec; offers better compression than H.261. This is particularly well suited to compression down to the low bit rate available through dial-up modems. Probably not an optimal choice these days. Used to be a good codec for use on low-powered playback hardware.
H.264	The newest and most advanced codec. This is the one codec to rule them all. It is a modern codec developed for consumer applications at much better bit rate/performance trade-offs than MPEG-2. Although not technically a video-conferencing standard, some telecommunications companies are looking at deploying this for delivery of video content to mobile phones.
H.26L	Early trials of the H.264 standard were tested under the H.26L nomenclature.

Continued

Topic	*Description*
H.281	A standard that defines local and remote camera control for video-conferencing systems.
H.320	A higher bit-rate ITU standard for video-conferencing via ISDN or through a reserved portion of the bandwidth available on a T1 connection.
H.323	This is an ITU standard for video-conferencing that takes place over networks that don't guarantee an available bandwidth. The Internet is such a network; the traffic may be transferred in bursts and must be interleaved with traffic following completely different point-to-point connections. Compliant implementations must also support H.261 video content. Suited to use on TCP/IP networking over LAN and WAN connections and via the Internet.
H.324	An ITU standard that describes video conferencing taking place over standard telephone lines.
HDCAM	A Sony tape format for recording high-definition TV.
HD-Mac	High-Definition Multiplexed Analog Component. A standard for HD that was being developed for analog systems in Europe. It fell by the wayside and was such an unsatisfactory and expensive experience that it has discouraged companies from taking up HD in Europe until now.
Helix	An open-source project initiated by RealNetworks to make video-streaming servers and production systems more widely available.
Hi8	The Sony 8mm tape format designed for consumer use. Hi8 is an analog format.
Home Media Server	A domestic server for storing large bulk quantities of audio, video, and other media for consumption in the home.
Home Theater System	A system for presenting movies in a cinema-like fashion at home. This might be a stand-alone system or a client on a network built around a home media center.
HSL	Hue Saturation Lightness. A way of describing color as an alternative to using red, green, and blue values.
HTTP:	Hyper-Text Transfer protocol. The means by which Web browsers request content from Web servers. This is a protocol that describes how to request some data and how it will be delivered back by the responder.
IEE	Institute for Electrical Engineers.

Topic	Description
IEEE	Institute for Electrical and Electronics Engineers.
IEEE 1394	Otherwise known as FireWire. The standard was developed originally by Apple Computer and then ratified by the IEEE.
IETF	Internet Engineering Task Force. This is a group that develops and publishes new standards for use on the Internet.
I-frame	An Intra frame is another name for a key frame in a video sequence.
iLink	The FireWire interface on Sony equipment is referred to by this brand name.
Indeo Video	This is a video format developed by Intel. It was well supported on Mac OS 9 but a codec has not been made available for Mac OS X. Availability on Windows is more common.
Interlaced scanning	A means of doubling the perceived resolution by scanning only the alternate lines on each pass down the screen. There are two fields, one each for the odd and even lines being displayed.
Intra coding	Macroblock coding that only refers to other blocks within the same frame.
Intranet	Your own private network system, which may or may not be accessible via the Internet.
IP address	The unique numerical network identity for a computer within a particular sub-network. These values may be duplicated on other networks.
ISDN	Integrated Services Digital Network
ISMA	Internet Streaming Media Alliance.
ISO	International Standards Organization.
ITU	International Telecommunications Union.
JMF	Java Media Framework. A useful portable framework for developing cross-platform and cross-format solutions.
JPEG	Joint Photographic Experts Group.
JVT	Joint Video Team. Formed by combining members of the ISO/IEC/MPEG working group with the ITU-T/VCEG working group to develop the H.264 standard. Sometimes used as another name for H.264 due to the codec being developed by a Joint Video Team.
Kbps	Kilobits per second.
Kinoma	A codec developed for use with mobile PDA devices.
LAB	Lightness plus color components A and B.

Continued

Topic	*Description*
LAN	Local Area Network. Usually Ethernet running at 10 Megabits or 100 Megabits. Sometimes 1000 Mbits are deployed and referred to as Gigabit Ethernet.
LCD	Liquid Crystal Display. A special form of crystal that changes the amount of light propagated through it when an electrical charge is placed on either side of it. Polarizing filters are used to display a light or dark segment of a display. Originally used in calculators, it can now be used in TV displays.
LED	Light-Emitting Diode. A self-illuminating display used to make flat-screen TV sets.
LNB	Low Noise Block in a satellite receiving dish.
M4IF	MPEG 4 Industry Forum. See MPEGIF.
Mac address	The genuinely unique network hardware address for your Ethernet interface. This is supposed to be guaranteed to be unique worldwide but some manufacturers of Ethernet interface cards have used the same number multiple times. Be careful of this when adding networking capability to machines on the same sub-network with multiple cards from one manufacturer.
Macroblock	Video pictures are degenerated to blocks of 16×16 or 8×8 pixels so that similarities can be found.
Macromedia Flash	Useful for embedding into multimedia presentations but has some limitations due to its proprietary nature. It is ubiquitous.
Mbps	Megabits per second. Digital video transmitted via satellite using MPEG-2 compression typically uses 3.5 to 4.5 Mb/s to carry the content stream.
Media center	A centralized system that contains media for sharing among several or more client systems.
Mesh (1)	A set of connected polygons that describe a surface onto which a texture can be mapped. Used in MPEG-4 as part of the structured video coding and display mechanism.
Mesh (2)	A networking strategy where broadband connections through a community can be organized using a mesh of connected nodes. Sometimes called a community mesh or peer-to-peer network.
Microcosm	The Digital Anarchy Microcosm codec is a 64-bit lossless implementation. It delivers excellent quality but has limited availability. Digital Anarchy has a variety of alternative codecs available.

Topic	Description
Modem	The modem equipment at each end of a telephone line is used to create a data connection between two systems. The word is contracted from modulator–demodulator. Modulator–demodulators are used to transfer digital signals over analog telephone lines.
Motion compensation	The use of motion vectors to improve the compression of macroblocks by recycling previously decoded blocks and applying a move to them before adding residual data.
Motion estimation	The process of generating motion-compensating vectors during the encoding process. Technically, this is the most difficult part of the algorithm to understand.
Motion JPEG	A means of creating moving-image files by storing a series of still images that are individually coded with the JPEG standard protocol. This is a key frame-only format but now that the JPEG standard has been revised to the wavelet-based JPEG 2000 version, this is a somewhat dated codec. Motion JPEG is still widely used since it is embedded in a lot of studio-quality video servers but it is a legacy format when choosing codecs for new projects.
Motion vector	This is used to compensate for motion when constructing one macroblock from another. These vectors can be forward- or backward-referencing and are specified in two dimensions.
MP3	MPEG-1 Audio Layer 3.
MPEG	Motion Picture Experts Group. A working group within the ISO/IEC standards body. This group is concerned with the standardization of moving-picture representations in the digital environment.
MPEG-1	The original MPEG video standard designed for CD-ROM applications and other similar levels of compression. This is a legacy format. Still useful for some solutions but new projects should use a later codec.
MPEG-2	Widely used for digital TV and DVD products. A much-improved codec that supersedes MPEG-1 in many respects. It has been popularized by DVD content encoding and DVB transmission.
MPEG-3	This was cancelled because the proposed work was included in MPEG-2 with a small enhancement.
MPEG-4	A huge leap forward in the description of multimedia content. MPEG-4 is the essence container.

Continued

Topic	Description
MPEG-4 Part 2	The original video standard for MPEG-4 was referred to as MPEG-4 visual. While the compression is not as efficient as Part 10 of the MPEG-4 standard, there are some interesting features that Part 2 offers for multimedia applications. These additional features may be added to a later version of the MPEG-4 Part 10 standard. This codec is not recommended for use in new projects.
MPEG-4 part 10	A codec that has been developed jointly by the ISO/MPEG and ITU-T/VCEG working groups. Currently equivalent to H.264.
MPEG-7	The metadata standard. This describes the content that is stored in MPEG-4 essence packages.
MPEG-21	The rights-control systems of the future will be built around MPEG-21 standards. These describe how MPEG-4 content is allowed to be accessed and will use MPEG-7 metadata as part of the process.
MPEGIF	MPEG Industry Forum. This was previously known as the MPEG-4 Industry Forum.
Multiplex	On digital terrestrial TV (DTT) and digital audio broadcasting (DAB), the transport streams are delivered in a multiplex that corresponds to one tunable channel on the broadcasting medium. The receiver can then extract a transport stream (another name for a multiplex) and dismantle it to retrieve the individual channels.
NAB	National Association of Broadcasters.
Narrow-band	Another way of describing modem-based dialup connections as opposed to ADSL broadband connections.
Node (1)	One item within a tree-structured collection of objects either in a file or in memory.
Node (2)	A single computer on a network.
NTSC	National Television Standards Committee.
Nyquist	Harry Nyquist postulated the rule that sampling must take place at twice the maximum frequency that you require to be recorded. Subsequent research suggests that higher sample rates are necessary to fully recover the shape of the wave form at that frequency, since the Nyquist rule only recovers a square wave at the maximum frequency. Many ideas that we take for granted in telecoms and digital media stem from work that Harry Nyquist did in the early 20th century, long before TV was invented.

Topic	*Description*
Object	A fragment of data that is self-contained within a package. The object has properties that can be examined or changed and methods that can be executed procedurally.
Object oriented	A technique of encapsulating data with descriptions of the functional behavior so that systems can be constructed with a set of component parts. The internal implementation of an object is private and hidden. Only the published API is visible. This leads to significant reuse of the same coding.
Ogg-Vorbis	An open-source alternative to the other codecs for audio compression.
OLED	Organic Light-Emitting Diodes. A new technology for creating displays that can be "printed" onto a plastic substrate. This allows very flexible and cheap displays to be manufactured.
Overcranked	Moving pictures that were shot at a slower speed than that used to project or view them.
Package	A container for multimedia. Commonly stored as a file.
Packet	A fragment of data that is transmitted on a network. The packet transfer is acknowledged or requested again in resilient systems. The process of creating packets is informally called packetizing.
PAL	Phase Alternate Line. This is the format used in the UK and elsewhere in place of the NTSC transmission format used in the USA. The name describes the way that the color information is coded with a phase reversal of the information on each alternate line. For compression purposes we wouldn't be concerned with that phase reversal, as the capture card would have used it to decode the color information. However, we do need to ensure that we correctly choose PAL or NTSC according to the material being captured, as the two systems are incompatible.
PDA	Personal digital assistants are small, handheld devices that have a touch-sensitive display for interacting with.
P-frame	A predictive frame.
Pixel	A single picture element. This describes the color and transparency at a single unique Cartesian coordinate within an image plane.
Pixlet	This is a special codec developed by Apple for Pixar. Pixlet is specifically designed to deliver high-quality, frame-accurate video around a corporate network. Each frame is compressed as a single block, thus eliminating artifacts caused by macroblock-based compression algorithms. The picture is coded with a

Continued

Topic	Description
	wavelet-based compressor. The codec name is contracted from Pixar wavelet. It has a pretty good compression ratio and the specifications quote an example of reducing a 6-GB file down to 250 MB. It is only available on the Macintosh platform and requires a G5 processor. The animation codec is a viable alternative unless you need high performance. Then you would probably justify deploying G5 machines wherever you need them. One of the important features is that it is a key frame-only codec.
Pixmap	An area of pixels.
Port	One of many thousands of connections that can be made to an IP-addressed system. Ports are blocked by firewalls and must be accessible in order to join a session between any two systems.
Porting	The process of re-engineering a product so it works on another platform. We do a lot of this with content, too.
Program stream	Program streams are created by multiplexing the elementary streams containing the media. These program streams are then multiplexed in groups to create a transport stream. The transport stream has other supporting data added and is then fed to the broadcasting medium. That is sometimes called a multiplex or a transponder.
Progressive scanning	Scanning from the top of the screen to the bottom in one pass. Computer displays typically use progressive scanning and TV receivers typically use interlaced scanning.
Pro-MPEG	Pro-MPEG consortium. Start here when looking for MXF information.
PVR	Personal video recorders were first successfully launched by TiVo but early work on the concept was done by MIT many years before. The MIT work used multiple analog video recorders with computer-controlled serial interfaces—certainly primitive but functionally recognizable. The future of these devices will be dependent on standards such as TV-Anytime.
QCIF	Quarter Common Intermediate Format. Commonly defined as 176×144 or 176×120 depending on whether a 625- or 525-line source is used.
Quantization	The process of reducing the variability of data so that it uses one of a set of predefined values. Snapping to a grid is another way of understanding quantization. The quantization process is applied to the DCT output to reduce the data in that block.

Topic	*Description*
QuickTime	A platform for developing and playing rich multimedia, video, and interactive content. It is not a codec but a platform. It has some unique codecs that are not available anywhere else but you should be using open-standard codecs rather than these. When it is referring to a video format, it is talking about a codec jointly developed by Apple and Sorenson. It gets improved from time to time as successive versions of QuickTime are released. This is a popular name for the Sorenson codecs.
Raster	The technical name for the collection of scan lines that make up a TV picture.
Real Networks video	Originally shipped in 1996 as a derivative of the Real Networks audio system. It has undergone a more or less annual revision. As of 2004, it is broadly comparable to H.264 in terms of its compression efficiency and quality. A longtime favorite and versatile video playback format. It is proven and reliable. The server and player technology should live on to play the newer open-standard codecs even if the Real Networks video format itself becomes less popular. These are the guys that started it all.
REC 601	A standard recommendation for the coding of 4:2:2 sampled images. It is the primary standard for studio-based and professional systems.
RGB	Red–green–blue. The triad of colors used in CRT displays.
RTP:	Real-Time Protocol.
RTS	Royal Television Society.
RTSP:	Real-Time Streaming Protocol.
SBR	Spectral Band Replication. A technique for encoding high-quality audio more efficiently.
SCTP:	Stream Control Transmission Protocol. This is designed for telephony and video-conferencing applications. Its major benefit is that it has the low transport latency of UDP and supports many connections at each end. This allows the transmitting end to be supported by multiple hosts so it can fail over and allow the receiving end to be one or more clients.
SDI	Serial Digital Interface. Used commonly in studio environments.
SECAM	The TV standard used in France, which corresponds to PAL and NTSC. It stands for "Systeme Electronique Couleur Avec Memoire."

Continued

Topic	Description
SheerVideo	This is a lossless codec with a low compression ratio of about 2:1. It has limited availability and is only supported on Mac OS X. For any portability that is required, the animation codec is probably better suited.
SIF	Source Image Format. Usually describes a TV standard that an image was originally derived from.
Slice	A sequential run of macroblocks in a frame of video. This is a group of horizontally ordered blocks and never more than an entire row with modern codecs.
SMPTE	Society of Motion Picture and Television Engineers.
Sorenson 3	A codec originally shipped within Apple QuickTime. The codec is now available independently and is also still available within the QuickTime architecture. Sorenson version 3 is a codec that produces good quality even when the bit rate is wound down quite low. Artifacts are minimal at low data rates. File size and bit rate gets large at high-quality settings. The bit rate sometimes spikes when presented with video that is difficult to encode. Sorenson 3 is a good general-purpose codec but H.264 will likely replace it in due course. Versions of Sorenson prior to version 3 are legacy codecs.
Sorenson Spark	This is the video codec used in Flash.
Betamax	A tape format introduced for consumer use by Sony Corporation. It delivered a good performance compared with the rival JVC VHS system that dominated the market. Sony evolved the cartridge format into a range of professional formats known as Betacam and its derivatives.
Stream	A single component, which can be received and then unpacked. Streams may contain other streams multiplexed inside them.
Streaming server	A server for delivering the packets that make a stream. They must be delivered reliably and continuously at a rate that averages out to be real time.
Sub-sampling	Sampling an analog signal at larger intervals in order to reduce the amount of data recorded. Unfortunately, the higher-frequency information is lost at the source.
Systems layer	The part of an MPEG standard that describes the containment of the video and audio streams and the control of their playback.
T1	A very fast network link for connecting enterprises to the Internet.

Topic	Description
T.120	A standard that describes data conferencing. It includes references to T.121, T.122, T.123, T.124, T.126, and T.127.
TCP/IP	Transmission Control Protocol/Internetworking Protocol describes the message format and connection mechanisms that make the Internet possible. It is built on top of UDP. It contains ack/nak (acknowledge/negative acknowledge) protocols to ensure that all packets have arrived It does this at the expense of timeliness.
Theora	The open-source video-compression counterpart to the Ogg Vorbis encoder.
TiVo	A company that developed the first widely available PVR product. Their name is becoming synonymous with PVR products in the same way that the word Xerox is often used to describe any copy machine. Strictly speaking, you should not describe something as a TiVo unless it is a TiVo-manufactured PVR, and describing products by other manufacturers as 'TiVo like' is also considered detrimental. These PVR devices are also sometimes known as DVR devices, since they operate with digitized video even when their I/O is analogue.
Transponder	On a Digital Satellite system (DSat), the transport stream is delivered one per transponder. Each transponder is quite separate from the others.
Transport stream	A stream that carries one or more video programs from the broadcaster to the client.
Trigger	Data messages embedded in streams can carry event-based information to cause things to happen in the client device.
Triple play	Video, telephony, and broadband services delivered via a single cable. Also used in other contexts to describe TV receivers that play VHS cassettes and DVDs.
Truespeech	Truespeech is a codec used for low-bandwidth encoding of speech (not music). It was created by the DSP Group.
TV-AF	TV-Anytime Forum.
TV-Anytime	A standard that describes the metadata required to make a distributed PVR service work.
UDP	Universal Datagram Protocol. This is a lower-level protocol under TCP/IP that guarantees immediate transfer of data but may lose some packets.
VC-1	The SMPTE standards work that is preparing Windows Media Series 9 for ratification is known as VC-1.

Continued

Topic	*Description*
VC-9	A former potential name for the SMPTE VC-1 codec. Another name that identifies Windows Media Series 9 video coding.
VCEG	Video Coding Experts Group. A working group within the ITU who participated in the development of the H.264 codec.
VHS	Video Home System. Developed by JVC and made popular in the 1970s and 80s.
VideoLAN	An open-source media-player developer.
VistaVision	A very wide-screen, high-resolution film format. Discontinued in theaters but famous for having been used as an originating format for the Star Wars movie special effects.
VivoActive	A media player.
VLC	A popular open-source media player.
VOP	Another name for a frame of video as described in MPEG-4.
Vorbis	See Ogg-Vorbis.
VP3	An open-source video codec.
VR	Virtual reality.
W3C	World Wide Web Consortium.
WAN	Wide Area Network.
Wavelet	A more sophisticated compression algorithm that replaces DCT.
Windows Media Series 9	A codec developed by Microsoft as an alternative to QuickTime or Real Networks. This is a proprietary codec that is best deployed on Microsoft Windows-based systems. The version 9 codec allegedly uses wavelets and is comparable to H.264. At the point when H.264 was ratified as a standard, Microsoft offered Windows Media Series 9 to SMPTE as a competing standard. It remains to be seen whether this becomes a truly open standard and opinions are divided on what the outcome will be. Microsoft came to the game quite late but played a very strong hand. They still are not dominant in the video world but their offerings are competent and reliable when used on the Windows platform.
WM9	An abbreviation that refers to Windows Media Series 9 codecs.
Word	Commonly, 16 bits collected together into a single unit and manipulated together. Sometimes used to describe units larger than 16 bits.
XviD	An open-source video codec.

Topic	Description
ZygoVideo	This is a very efficient codec at low data rates. Reckoned to be about the best there is at those very low bit rates. However, some testers report that the quality is not as good as with Sorenson Video 3 or MPEG-4. The results depend very much on the way you define parameter settings and the nature of the video you are compressing. The availability of this codec may be limited, and it must be downloaded as a QuickTime component.

Bibliography

Austerberry, D. *The technology of video and audio streaming.* Boston: Focal Press, 2002.

Born, G. *The file formats handbook.* New York: International Thomson Computer Press, 1995.

Follansbee, J. G. *Get streaming!* Boston: Focal Press, 2004.

Gilmer, B. (Ed.) *File interchange handbook.* Boston: Focal Press, 2004.

Moeritz, S., and Diepold, K. *Understanding MPEG-4.* Boston: Focal Press, 2004.

Ohm, J.-R., van der Schaar, M., and Woods, J. W. "Interframe wavelet coding—Motion picture representation for universal scalability." *Signal Processing, Image Communication* (Volume 19, Issue 9, 2004): 877–908.

Pereira, F., and Ebrahimi, T. (Eds.). *The MPEG-4 book.* Upper Saddle River, NJ: Prentice Hall, 2002.

Poynton, C. *Digital video and HDTV algorithms and interfaces.* San Francisco: Morgan Kaufmann, 2003.

Puri, A., and Chen, T. (Eds.). *Multimedia systems, standards, and networks.* New York: Marcel Dekker, 2000.

Waggoner, B. *Compression for great digital video: Power tips, techniques, & common sense.* Lawrence, KS: CMP Books, 2002.

Watkinson, J. *The MPEG handbook.* Oxford: Focal Press, 2001.

Webliography

The Standards Makers

Description	URL
1394 Trade Organization	http://www.1394ta.org/index.html
AACS Licensing Authority	http://www.aacsla.com/
AAF Association	http://www.aafassociation.org/
American National Standards Institute (ANSI)	http://www.ansi.org/
ASF specification	http://www.microsoft.com/windows/windowsmedia/format/asfspec.aspx
Audio Engineering Society (AES)	http://www.aes.org/
AVC Alliance	http://www.avc-alliance.org/
British Standards Institute (BSI)	http://www.bsi-global.com/
Digital Video Broadcasting Organization (DVB)	http://www.dvb.org/
DVD Forum	http://www.dvdforum.org/
ETSI	http://www.etsi.org/
European Broadcasting Union (EBU)	http://www.ebu.ch/
European Computer Manufacturers Association (ECMA)	http://www.ecma-international.org/
Institute for Electrical and Electronics Engineers (IEEE)	http://www.ieee.org/
Institution for Electrical Engineers (IEE)	http://www.iee.org/
International Organization for Standardization (ISO)	http://www.iso.org/
International Telecommunications Union (ITU)	http://www.itu.int/
International Webcasters Association (IWA)	http://www.webcasters.org/
Internet Engineering Task Force (IETF)	http://www.ietf.org/
Internet Streaming Media Alliance (ISMA)	http://www.isma.tv/

Continued

The Standards Makers (Continued)

Description	URL
Joint Photographic Experts Group (JPEG)	http://www.jpeg.org/
JPEG 2000	http://www.jpeg.org/FCD15444-1.htm
MPEG-4 Industry Forum (M4IF)	http://www.m4if.org/
MHP Organization	http://www.mhp.org/
MPEG Industry Forum (MPEGIF)	http://www.mpegif.org/
Motion Picture Experts Group (MPEG)	http://www.cselt.it/mpeg/
Pro-MPEG	http://www.pro-mpeg.org/
RFC Archive	http://www.rfc-archive.org/
Society of Motion Picture and Television Experts (SMPTE)	http://www.smpte.org/
TV Anytime Forum (TV-AF)	http://www.tv-anytime.org/
Video Coding Expert Group (VCEG)	http://ftp3.itu.int/av-arch/
World Wide Web Consortium (W3C)	http://www.w3.org/

Conventions and Trade Shows

Convention	URL
National Association of Broadcasters (NAB)	http://www.nab.org/
Audio Engineering Society (AES)	http://www.aes.org/
Broadband Services Forum (BSF)	http://www.broadbandservicesforum.org/
IBC—The World of Content Creation, Management, and Delivery	http://www.ibc.org/
Video Forum	http://www.videoforum.co.uk/
The Production Show	http://www.productionshow.com/
Apple Worldwide Developers Conference (WWDC)	http://developer.apple.com/
Professional Lighting and Sound Association (PLASA)	http://www.plasa.org/
MIPCOM—The International Marketplace for Entertainment Content	http://www.mipcom.com/
MITEL Conference	http://www.bemltd.com/
SMPTE Technical Conference	http://www.smpte.org/
Cable-Tec Expo	http://expo.scte.org/
Euro-iTV conference 2004	http://www.brighton.ac.uk/interactive/euroitv/index.htm

Specialized Trade and Professional Journals and Magazines

Title	URL
DV Magazine	http://www.dv.com/
Computer Video Editing	http://www.computervideo.net/
Televisual	http://www.televisual.co.uk/
IEEE Transactions on Broadcast Systems	http://www.ieee.org/organizations/society/bt/
Internet Video Magazine	http://www.internetvideomag.com/
Film & Video Magazine	http://www.filmandvideomagazine.com/
AV Video Multimedia Producer	http://www.avvideo.com/
Sound & Vision	http://www.soundandvisionmag.com/
Digital Video Editing	http://www.digitalvideoediting.com/
DV & FireWire central	http://www.dvcentral.org/

The Rest of the Links

Description	URL
2d3 Steadymove	http://www.2d3.com/
3ivX	http://www.3ivx.com/
A comparison of Internet audio compression formats	http://www.sericyb.com.au/sc/audio.html
A discussion of the merits of DV vs. Betacam	http://www.dvcentral.org/DV-Beta.html
Accordent	http://www.accordant.com/
ACM Special Interest in Graphics Group (ACM SIGGRAPH)	http://www.siggraph.org/
Act, Inc.	http://www.act.org/
AcuLe@rn	http://www.aculearn.com/
ADC Telecommunications	http://www.adc.com/
Adobe GoLive	http://www.adobe.com/golive/
Adobe	http://www.adobe.com/
ADS Technologies	http://www.adstech.com/
ADSL Guide	http://www.adslguide.org.uk/guide/connections.asp
Advanced Access Content System	http://www.aacsla.com/

Continued

The Rest of the Links (Continued)

Description	URL
Advanced Television Standards Committee (ATSC)	http://www.atsc.org/
After Dawn Glossary	http://www.afterdawn.com/glossary/
AIST	http://www.aist.com/
AJA Video	http://www.aja.com/
Akamai	http://www.akamai.com/
Alchemy TV	http://www.miglia.com/
altShiiva	http://hetima.com/psp/altshiiva.php
American Museum of Photography	http://www.photographymuseum.com/guide.html
American Widescreen Museum	http://www.widescreenmuseum.com/
Analog Devices Inc.	http://www.analog.com/
Analogue switch-off in the UK	http://www.bbc.co.uk/info/policies/pdf/digital_switchover_report.pdf
Androme	http://www.androme.be/
Anystream, Inc.	http://www.anystream.com/
AOL Time Warner Inc.	http://www.aoltw.com/
Apple Computer, Inc.	http://www.apple.com/
Apple Developer Connection	http://developer.apple.com/
Apple QuickTime developer information	http://developer.apple.com/quicktime/
Apple QuickTime movie trailers	http://www.apple.com/trailers/
Apple QuickTime utilities	http://developer.apple.com/quicktime/quicktimeintro/tools/
Apple QuickTime	http://www.apple.com/quicktime/
Apple XSAN	http://www.apple.com/xsan/
Archivers.8m.com	http://archivers.8m.com/
Ardour	http://ardour.org/
Arri	http://www.arri.com/
Art Of Lossless Data Compression, The	http://compression.ru/artest/index_e.html
AsfTools:	http://www.geocities.com/myasftools/
Association for Computing Machinery (ACM)	http://www.acm.org/

The Rest of the Links (Continued)

Description	URL
Atemc	http://www.adt-inc.com/products/ateme/ateme_prod_ov.htm
Atrium Communications Ltd.	http://www.atriumcom.com/dotnet/atrium/netscape/welcome.htm
Audacity	http://audacity.sourceforge.net/
Avid	http://www.avid.com/
AVIJoiner	http://www.hitsquad.com/smm/programs/AVIJoiner/
Bayer dithering (open-source code)	http://www.cs.rit.edu/usr/local/pub/pga/Graphics/GIF/gr/dither.c
BBC Colledia (a.k.a. Jupiter)	http://www.bbctechnology.com/
BBC News Online	http://www.bbc.co.uk/news/
BBC Ventures Group	http://www.bbcventuresgroup.com/
Belkin	http://world.belkin.com/
Ben Waggoner	http://www.benwaggoner.com/
Betacam information	http://betacam.palsite.com/home.html
BIAS	http://www.bias-inc.com/
Big Camera, The	http://www.thebigcamera.com.au/
Bijective compression before encryption	http://bijective.dogma.net/index.htm
BitBand Technologies Ltd.	http://www.bitband.com/
Bitvice	http://www.innobits.se/
Blackmagic Design	http://www.blackmagic-design.com/
Bluebell Communications	http://www.bluebell.tv/
BMCO—Berlin	http://www.bmco-berlin.com/
British Kinematograph Sound and Television Society (BKSTS)	http://www.bksts.com/
Broadband Content Developer Forum (BCDF)	http://www.bcdforum.org/home/
Bryant Broadcast Supplies	http://www.bryant-broadcast.co.uk/
Cable-Tec Expo	http://expo.scte.org/
California Museum of Photography	http://www.cmp.ucr.edu/
California State University, Fresno	http://www.csufresno.edu/
Cameras Underwater Glossary	http://www.camerasunderwater.co.uk/
Canford Audio	http://www.canford.co.uk/
Canopus (Pro Coder)	http://www.canopus-uk.com/

Continued

The Rest of the Links (Continued)

Description	URL
Case Western Reserve University	http://www.cwru.edu/
Charles Poynton's gamma FAQ	http://www.poynton.com/PDFs/GammaFAQ.pdf
Cineca	http://www.cineca.it/
Cinecitta Studios	http://wwwcinecittastudios.it/
Cinegy Cinelyzer	http://www.cinegy.com/
Cinema Eye	http://www.cinemaeye.com/
Cinemas Online	http://www.cinemas-online.co.uk/index.phtml
Cinepak	http://www.cinepak.com/
Cintel International Ltd.	http://www.cintel.com/
Cisco Systems	http://www.cisco.com/
Codeweavers	http://www.codeweavers.com/site/products/
Coding Technologies	http://www.codingtechnologies.com/
Communicast	http://www.communicast.com/
Communications and Signal Processing Lab	http://www.isr.umd.edu/Labs/CSPL/cspl.html
Compression FAQ	http://www.faqs.org/faqs/compression-faq/
Computer Video Magazine	http://www.computervideo.net/
Consumer Electronics Org	http://www.ce.org/
Content Acceleration	http://www.ehyperspace.com/
ContentGuard	http://www.contentguard.com/
Creative Commons	http://creativecommons.org/
Creative Mac safe areas	http://www.creativemac.com/2002/11_nov/features/download8021122.htm
Crystal Vision	http://www.crystalvision.tv/
CTM Debrie Cinematography	http://www.ctmsolutions.com/
Dalsa Digital Cinema	http://www.dalsa.com/dc
Darwin home page	http://developer.apple.com/darwin/
Data Compression Lab	http://rcs.ee.washington.edu/COMPRESSION/homepage.html
Data Compression Resource Center	http://www.rasip.fer.hr-research-compress-center.html

The Rest of the Links (Continued)

Description	URL
Data-Compression.com	http://www.data-compression.com/
Definition of public domain	http://www.fact-index.com/p/pu/public_domain.html
DekTec StreamXpert	http://www.dektec.com/
Demon Internet	http://www.demon.net/
DeShaker	http://home.bip.net/gunnart/video/Deshaker.zip
Dicas	http://www.dicas.de/
Digital Broadcasting Experts Group	http://www.dibeg.org/
Digital Display Working Group	http://www.ddwg.org/
Digital FAQ	http://www.digitalfaq.com/
Digital Film Tools	http://www.digitalfilmtools.com/index.htm
Digital halftones by dot diffusion	http://portal.acm.org/citation.cfm?id=35039.35040
Digital Living Network Alliance	http://www.dlna.org/home
Digital Rapids	http://www.digital-rapids.com/
Digital Television Group (DTG)	http://www.dtg.org.uk/
Digital Terrestrial Action Group (DigiTAG)	http://www.digitag.org/
Digital Video Information	http://www.digvid.info/
Digital Video Producers Association (DVPA)	http://www.dvpa.com/
Digi-Vue	http://digi-vue.com/about.html
Dirac	http://www.bbc.co.uk/rd/projects/dirac/overview.shtml
DirecTV	http://www.directv.com/
Discreet (Cleaner)	http://www.discreet.com/
DivX Digest	http://www.divx-digest.com/
DivX	http://www.divx.com/
DMB Monitoring systems by onTimetek	http://www.ontimetek.com/
DMD Secure	http://www.dmdsecure.com/
Document Image Compression and Analysis	http://www.cfar.umd.edu/~kia/Publications/Thesis/Thesis-HTML.html
Dolby Laboratories Inc.	http://www.dolby.com/

Continued

The Rest of the Links (Continued)

Description	URL
Dolby Laboratories screen size document	http://www.dolby.com/movies/m.in.0009.screensize.html
DropDV	http://www.dropdv.com/
DTS Cinema Subtitling	http://www.dtsonline.com/
DTS:	http://www.dtsonline.com/
DV Forge	http://www.dvforge.com/index.shtml
DV Magazine	http://www.dv.com/
DV resources	http://www.dvcentral.org/index.html
dvgrab	http://kino.schirmacher.de/article/view/78/1/7/
DVB-H information	http://www.dvb.org/index.php?id=278
DVD HQ bit rate calculator	http://dvd-hq.info/Calculator.html
DVP Technology	http://www.dvp.co.il/
Dynapel SteadyHand	http://www.dynapel.com/
EBU standards web site	http://www.ebu.ch/en/index.php
Ecasound	http://www.eca.cx/
EDN DSP companies listing	http://www.ednasia.com/dsp2003.htm
ElGato	http://www.elgato.com/
Electronics Weekly DSP special issue	http://www.electronicsweekly.com/Issue200.htm
Emblaze	http://www.emblaze.com/
Envivio TV player	http://www.envivio.com/products/etv/download.jsp
Envivio	http://www.envivio.com/
Equator Technologies	http://www.equator.com/
Eyeheight LegalEyesHD	http://www.eyeheight.com/
FFmpeg	http://ffmpeg.sourceforge.net/
File extensions	http://filext.com/index.php
Film Center Formats Glossary	http://www.film-center.com/formats.html
Film format info	http://en.wikipedia.org/wiki/Film_formats
Film specifications	http://www.camerasunderwater.co.uk/web_site/info_/Technical.html

The Rest of the Links (Continued)

Description	URL
Filmlight Ltd.	http://www.filmlight.ltd.uk/
Final Cut Planet	http://www.dvcreators.net/finalcutproplanet/
Firepad	http://www.firepad.com/catalog/index.php?productID=2
Floyd-Steinberg derived algorithms	http://www.wellesley.edu/CS/pmetaxas/ei99.pdf
Forbidden Technologies	http://www.forbidden.co.uk/
Four CC codec resources	http://www.fourcc.org/
Fraunhofer Institute for Integrated Circuits	http://www.iis.fhg.de/
Fraunhofer H.264 reference software	http://iphome.hhi.de/suehring/tml/download/
FSSG	http://www.cini.ve.cnr.it/
Fuji TV Network	http://www.fujitv.co.jp/en/
Fujitsu	http://www.fujitsu.com/
George Eastman House	http://www.eastmanhouse.org/
GNU Copyleft initiative	http://www.gnu.org/copyleft/copyleft.html
Go Movie Trailers	http://www.gomovietrailers.com/
Guide to Digital Television, The	http://www.digitaltelevision.com/dtvbook/toc.shtml
Guide to DSP—Data Compression	http://www.dspguide.com/datacomp.htm
gvidcap	http://rpmfind.net/linux/rpm2html/search.php?query=gvidcap
Hamlet waveform monitors	http://www.hamlet.co.uk/
Harmonic Inc.	http://www.harmonicinc.com/
Hauppage	http://www.hauppage.com/
HDR camera	http://www.spheron.com/products/SpheroCamHDR/hdri.html
HDTV.com resources	http://www.hdtv.com/
Helix server	https://helixcommunity.org/
HipFlics	http://www.totallyhip.com/hipflics.asp
Hitachi High-Technologies America	http://www. Itachi-hta.com/

Continued

The Rest of the Links (Continued)

Description	URL
Hitachi Semiconductor	http://www.hitachisemiconductor.com/
Hitachi	http://www.hitachi.com
HmaxF Ultimate Recursive Lossless Compression Research	http://www.geocities.com/hmaxf_urlcr/
How Stuff Works	http://www.howstuffworks.com/
HTTP Compression Proxy	http://www.vigos.com/
Huelix Solutions Pte. Ltd.	http://screenplay.huelix.com/
Huffman codes and Fibonacci numbers	http://mathforum.org/epigone/sci.math/twalgixskay/
IBC	http://www.ibc.org/
IBM Research MARVEL MPEG-7 Video Search Engine	http://mp7.watson.ibm.com/marvel/
IBM	http://www.ibm.com/
IEEE Transactions on Broadcast Systems	http://www.ieee.org/organizations/society/bt/authorinfo.htm
ILM OpenEXR	http://www.openexr.org/
Image Compression resource 1	http://www.dogma.net/DataCompression/ImageCompression.shtml
Image Compression resource 2	http://www.acm.org/crossroads/xrds6-3/sahaimgcoding.html
ImageMind Software	http://www.imagemind.com/
IMAX 15/70 information	http://www.1570films.com/
Informations about MPEG-1 Audio Layer 3	http://www.e.kth.se/~e92_sze/mpg.html
Inka Entworks	http://www.inka.co.kr/
Inlet Technologies, Inc.	http://inlethd.com/
Interactive Advertising Bureau (IAB)	http://www.iab.com/standards/index.asp
Interlace documentation	http://broadcastengineering.com/ar/broadcasting_understanding_interlace/
InterMedia Solutions	http://www.intermedia-solutions.net/
International Centre of Photography	http://www.icp.org/

The Rest of the Links (Continued)

Description	URL
International Color Consortium	http://www.color.org/
International Multimedia Telecommunications Consortium	http://www.imtc.org/
Internet Archive	http://www.archive.org/
Internet FAQ Archive	http://www.faqs.org/
Internet Movie Database (IMDB)	http://www.imdb.com/
Intervox Communications	http://www.intervox.com/
IPDC Forum	http://www.ipdc-forum.org/
IPS Ltd.	http://www.iplockdown.net/
ISMA organization	http://www.ism-alliance.org/
iStabilize	http://www.iStabilize.de/
iVCD	http://www.mireth.com/pub/ivme.html
iVideo	http://www.waterfallsw.com/ivideo/
Jo Blo's movie trailer index	http://www.joblo.com/movietrailers2A.htm
jp2Tools	http://www.jp2tools.de/English/
JPEG FAQ	http://www.faqs.org/faqs/jpeg-faq/
JVC	http://www.jvc.com/
Kasenna	http://www.kasenna.com/
KDDI R&D Laboratories	http://www.kddilabs.jp/eng/index.html
Kino	http://kino.schirmacher.de/
Kinoma codec	http://www.kinoma.com/products.html
Kramer Electronics	http://www.kramerelectronics.com/
LEAD Video Codec	http://www.leadtools.com/video-codec.htm
Lecture on Vector Quantization	http://www-it.et.tudelft.nl/itcolleges/et10-38/hc/hc6/index.htm
Leivio	http://www.leivio.com/
Ligos Indeo	http://www.ligos.com/
Ligos player	http://www.ligos.com/lsx_mpeg_player.htm

Continued

The Rest of the Links (Continued)

Description	URL
Limelight Networks	http://www.llnw.com/
Linux Flash 7 player	http://macromedia.mplug.org/
Linux TV	http://www.linuxtv.org/
Live Channel streaming service	http://www.channelstorm.com/
Lossless Compression of Audio	http://www.firstpr.com.au/audiocomp/lossless/
LUC	http://www.luc.ac.be/
Lysis	http://www.lysis.com/
M99 Data compression	http://www.michaelmaniscalco.homepage.com/
Macromedia	http://www.macromedia.com/
Macrovision	http://www.macrovision.com/
Manga trailers	http://www.manga.com/trailers/
Massachusetts Institute of Technology Sagrada movie (1996)	http://cat2.mit.edu/sagrada/
Matrix trailer	http://whatisthematrix.warnerbros.com/
Media Publisher, Inc. (MPI)	http://www.media-publisher.com/
Microsoft DV-AVI spec	http://www.microsoft.com/whdc/archive/dvavi.mspx
Microsoft TechNet	http://www.microsoft.com/technet/security/bulletin/MS01-056.mspx
Microsoft Windows Media home	http://www.microsoft.com/windows/windowsmedia/default.aspx
Microsoft Windows Media Licensing	http://www.microsoft.com/windows/windowsmedia/licensing/
Microsoft Windows Media series 10 DRM	http://www.microsoft.com/windows/windowsmedia/drm/default.aspx
Microsoft Windows media servers	http://www.microsoft.com/windows/windowsmedia/9series/server.aspx
Microsoft Windows Media	http://www.microsoft.com/windows/windowsmedia/
Microsoft Windows XP SP 2	http://www.microsoft.com/technet/prodtechnol/winxppro/maintain/
Microtek Glossary	http://www.microtek.nl/Community.php?Community=Glossary

The Rest of the Links (Continued)

Description	URL
MIPCOM	http://www.mipcom.com/
Miranda Technologies	http://www.Miranda.com/
Mireth MacSVCD	http://www.mireth.com/pub/mac-svcd-bdl.html
MITEL	http://www.bemltd.com/
Mitsubishi TV	http://www.mitsubishi-tv.com/
Modified Floyd-Steinberg algorithm	http://www.cs.indiana.edu/pub/techreports/TR458.pdf
Mohamed Qasem's Vector Quantization Page	http://www.geocities.com/mohamedqasem/vectorquantization/vq.html
Motion wavelets compressor	http://www.aware.com/products/compression/motionwavelets.htm
MP3 (Audio)	http://www.iis.fraunhofer.de/
MP3 FAQ	http://www.2look4.com/faq.html
MPEG FAQ	http://www.crs4.it/~luigi/MPEG/mpegfaq.html
MPEG info	http://www.tnt.uni-hannover.de/project/mpeg/audio/
MPEG Video Wizard	http://www.womble.com/mvw-text.htm
MPEG	http://www.chiariglione.org/mpeg/
MPEG-1 FAQ	http://bmrc.berkeley.edu/frame/research/mpeg/mpegfaq.html
MPEG-2 FAQ	http://bmrc.Berkeley.edu/frame/research/mpeg/mpeg2faq.html
MPEG-21	http://www.chiariglione.org/mpeg/standards/mpeg-21/mpeg-21.htm
MPEG2Works	http://www.mpeg2works.2ya.com/
MPEG-4 Net	http://www.mpeg4.net/resources/
MPEG-4	http://www.chiariglione.org/mpeg/standards/mpeg-4/mpeg-4.htm
MPEG-7	http://www.chiariglione.org/mpeg/standards/mpeg-7/mpeg-7.htm
MPEGable	http://www.mpegable.com/

Continued

The Rest of the Links (Continued)

Description	URL
MPEG-LA	http://www.mpegla.com/
MPEG-VCR:	http://www.womble.com/vcr-text.htm
M-Player homepage	http://www.mplayerhq.hu/
MXF	http://mxf.info/
My ASF tools	http://www.geocities.com/myasftools/
My Cable Shop	http://www.mycableshop.com/techguide.html
NagraVision	http://www.nagravision.com/
n-ary Huffman Template Algorithm	http://alexvn.freeservers.com/s1/huffman_template_algorithm.html
National Association of Broadcasters (NAB):	http://www.nab.org/
National Museum of Film & Photography	http://www.nmpft.org.uk/
NEC Corporation	http://www.nec.com/
Nero Digital	http://www.nero.com/
Net & TV	http://www.netntv.co.kr/
Network Technologies Inc.	http://www.networktechinc.com/technote.html
Neutrik Connectors	http://www.neutrik.com/
NHK 4000 line display	http://www.nhk.or.jp/strl/publica/dayori-new/en/rd-0210e.html
Nokia	http://www.nokia.com/
NVidia	http://www.nvidia.com/page/home
Official FAQ for alt.binaries.sounds.mp3, The	http://www.top.net/taenus/
Ogg Vorbis	http://www.vorbis.com/
Oki Electric Industry Co. Ltd.	http://www.oki.com/
Olympus SH880	http://www.Olympus.co.jp/en/news/2004a/nr040414sh880e.cfm
OmniTek digital video monitoring	http://www.omnitek.tv/
Open Mobile Alliance (OMA)	http://www.openmobilealliance,org/
Optibase Ltd.	http://www.optibase.com/
OPTX International	http://www.screenwatch.com/
Oratrix	http://www.oratrix.com/
Pace Micro Technology	http://www.pacemicro.com/
PAGEot	http://www.qtbridge.com/pageot/pageot.html

The Rest of the Links (Continued)

Description	URL
Panasonic	http://www.panasonic.com/
Pandora International	http://pogle.Pandora-int.com/
PDC description	http://625.uk.com/pdc/
Pegasys TMPEnc	http://www.pegasys-inc.com/en/product/
Philips Electronics	http://www.philips.com/
Pinnacle Systems	http://www.pinnaclesys.com/
Pioneer DVD specifications	http://www.pioneer.co.jp/crdl/tech/dvd/4-3-e.html
Pixelmetrix preventive monitoring	http://www.pixelmetrix.com/
PLASA	http://www.plasa.org/
Popwire Technology (Compression Master etc)	http://www.popwire.com/
Principles of Compression Techniques	http://www.cdt.luth.se/~johnny/courses/smd074_1999_2/CodingCompression/
Production Show, The	http://www.productionshow.com/
Programming.Source.Data Compression	http://www.dc.ee/Files/Programm.Packing
Qtilities	http://www.qtilities.com/
QuickTime Streaming Server	http://www.apple.com/quicktime/products/qtss/
RACINE-S	http://www.racine.eu.com/
RCA	http://www.rca.com/
RE:Vision Effects	http://www.revisionfx.com/
Real Export Plug-in	http://www.realnetworks.com/products/realexport/index.html
Real Networks developer resources	http://www.realnetworks.com/resources/index.html
Real Networks tools and plug-ins	http://www.realnetworks.com/resources/toolsplugins/
Real Networks video embedding	http://www.realnetworks.com/resources/samples/embedded.html
Real Networks	http://www.real.com/
Real Networks	http://www.realnetworks.com/
RealOne player	http://www.realnetworks.com/resources/samples/realone.html

Continued

The Rest of the Links (Continued)

Description	URL
Red Giant	http://www.redgiantsoftware.com/
Reference List on Image Compression	http://www.icv.ac.il/DataBases/ biblio/bibliography/ image-proc80.html
Retro Film Media International	http://www.retrofilm.com/index2.html
RJ Jack Glossary	http://www.arcelect.com/ RJ_Jack_Glossary.htm
Rorke Data	http://www.rorke.com/
Royal Television Society (RTS)	http://www.rts.org.uk/
RTSP org	http://www.rtsp.org/
RTT	http://www.rtt.tv/
Samsung DMB chips	http://www.Samsung.com/
Sanyo	http://www.sanyo.com/
Scientific-Atlanta	http://www.sciatl.com/
Sci-Fi movie page	http://www.scifimoviepage.com/
Scopus	http://www.scopus.net/
Siemens Business Services UK	http://www.sbs.siemens.co.uk/
Serious Magic	http://www.seriousmagic.com/
Shockwave file format specification	http://www.openswf.org/
Signal Processing and Multimedia Information Infrastructure	http://www-isl.Stanford.edu/ ~gray/iii.html
Skymicro	http://www.skymicro.com/
SMILGen	http://www.smilgen.org/
Snell & Wilcox	http://www.snellwilcox.com/
SofTV.net	http://www.softv.net/
Sonic Foundry	http://www.sonicfoundry.com/
Sony Professional	http://bssc.sel.sony.com/ Professional/startpage.html
SonyStyle online store	http://www.sonystyle.com/
Sorenson Spark Pro Codec	http://www.sorenson.com/ solutions/prod/mx_win.php
Sorenson	http://www.sorenson.com/
Source Coding/Data Compression resources	http://www.hn.is.uec.ac.jp/~arimura/ compression_links.html

The Rest of the Links (Continued)

Description	URL
Standby Program	http://www.standby.org/
Storage Tek	http://www.storagetek.com/
Streamcrest Associates	http://www.streamcrest.com/
Streaming Media Bible	http://streamingmediabible.com/
Sun Java API referenc:	http://java.sun.com/reference/api/index.html
Sun Java Media	http://java.sun.com/products/java-media/jmf/2.1.1/formats.html
Sun Microsystems	http://www.sun.com/
Synthetic Aperture test gear plug-in for Adobe After Effects	http://www.synthetic-ap.com/
Tandberg TV	http://www.tandbergtv.com/
Techsmith Camtasia	http://www.techsmith.com/
Tektronix	http://www.Tektronix.com/video
Telecom Italia Lab	http://www.telecomitalialab.com/
Telestream Windows Media Plug-In for QuickTime	http://www.flip4mac.com/
Telestream	http://www.telestream.net/
Televisual Magazine	http://www.televisual.com/
Texas Instruments DSP	http://www.dspvillage.com/
Texas Instruments Semiconductors	http://support.ti.com/
Texas Instruments	http://www.ti.com/
Thales H.264 analyser	http://www.thales-bm.com/
Thesaurus.com	http://thesaurus.reference.com/
Third Generation Partnership Project (3GPP)	http://www.3gpp.org/
Third Generation Partnership Project 2 (3GPP2)	http://www.3gpp2.org/
Thomson – Grass Valley	http://www.thomsongrassvalley.com/
Thomson	http://www.thomson.net/
Time For DVD	http://timefordvd.com/tutorial/SurroundSound.shtml
TiVo desktop software	http://www.tivo.com/4.9.4.1.asp
TiVo kernel patches	http://www.tivo.com/linux/linux.asp
TiVo	http://www.tivo.com/

Continued

The Rest of the Links (Continued)

Description	URL
Tom's Hardware	http://www.tomshardware.com/
Twin VQ	http://sound.splab.ecl.ntt.co.jp/twinvq-e/
Ulead	http://www.ulead.com/
Ultimatte	http://www.ultimatte.com/
Unibrain (FireWire products)	http://www.unibrain.com/home/
University of Glasgow	http://www.gla.ac.uk/
University of Washington	http://www.washington.edu/
Vara Wirecast	http://www.varasoftware.com/
Vbrick Systems, Inc.	http://www.vbrick.com/
Vector Quantization Compression Algorithms	http://www.msdmag.com/frameindex.htm?98/9802art2.htm
Vector Quantization of Image Sub-bands	http://citeseer.nj.nec.com/cosman96vector.html
Via licensing org	http://www.vialicensing.com/
Video and Audio Compression Page	http://www.cs.cf.ac.uk/Dave/Multimedia/node196.html
Video Forum	http://www.videoforum.co.uk/
Video on Palm devices	http://www.manifest-tech.com/media_pda/palm_video.htm
Video Quality Experts Group (VQEG)	http://www.its.bldrdoc.gov/vqeg/
VideoHelp	http://www.videohelp.com/
VideoLAN (VLC player)	http://www.videolan.org/
VideoReDo	http://www.drdsystems.com/VideoReDo/?src=dvdrHelp1
Viewcast Niagra	http://www.viewcast.com/
Viewcast/Osprey Video	http://www.viewcast.com/products/osprey.html
Viewsonic	http://www.viewsoniceurope.com/
Virage, Inc.	http://beta-www.virage.com/index.html
Vistek Electronics Ltd.	http://www.vistek.tv/
VISUALmpeg	http://www.mpeg-analyzer.com/
Vitec	http://www.vitecmm.com/
Vqual:	http://www.vqual.biz/

The Rest of the Links (Continued)

Description	URL
W3C Baseline Formats	http://www.w3.org/TR/2000/ WD-smil-boston-20000622/ baseline_formats.html
Wanadoo Broadband	http://www.wanadoo.co.uk/
Wavelet Transform and Vector Quantization paper	http://graphics.stanford.edu/ ~liyiwei/project/ee372/report.html
Waves sound processing plug-ins	http://www.waves.com/
Webcam Corp	http://www.webcamsoft.com/en/ en-index.html
Webopedia	http://www.webopedia.com/
Which is the best audio compression algorithm?	http://www.math.auth.gr/~axonis/ studies/audio.htm
Wikipedia	http://en.wikipedia.org/wiki/ Main_Page
Windows Movie Maker	http://www.microsoft.com/ windowsxp/using/moviemaker/ default.mspx
Winnov	http://www.winnov.com/
Win TV	http://www.hauppage.com/
Wirecast	http://varasoftware.com/
Wireless Multimedia Forum	http://www.wmmforum.com/
WIS Technologies Inc.	http://www.wischip.com/
Womble Multimedia	http://www.womble.com/ products.htm
Worldwide TV standards	http://www.ee.surrey.ac.uk/ Contrib/WorldTV/
xvidcap:	http://xvidcap.sourceforge.net/

Index